# LEADERSHIP IN RECREATION AND LEISURE SERVICE ORGANIZATIONS

# LEADERSHIP IN RECREATION AND LEISURE SERVICE ORGANIZATIONS

## CHRISTOPHER R. EDGINTON
*UNIVERSITY OF OREGON*

## PHYLLIS M. FORD
*UNIVERSITY OF OREGON*

*WITH*
KARL W. CLONINGER
*OKLAHOMA STATE UNIVERSITY*

KATHLEEN J. HALBERG
*UNIVERSITY OF OREGON*

SUSAN R. EDGINTON

**JOHN WILEY & SONS**
NEW YORK   CHICHESTER   BRISBANE   TORONTO   SINGAPORE

*Library of Congress Cataloging in Publication Data:*

Edginton, Christopher, R.
    Leadership in recreation and leisure service
organizations.

    Includes index.
    1. Recreation leadership.    I. Ford, Phyllis M.
II. Title.
GV181.4.E34   1985        790'.023        84-10459
ISBN 0-471-86864-7

Printed in the United States of America

10  9  8  7  6  5  4  3  2  1

This book is dedicated to John G. Williams, Director of Parks and Recreation, Sunnyvale, California. John is an individual with great strength of character, who has a commitment to high ideals and values and to the development of others. It was John who supported my initial interest in writing and who continues to inspire my efforts.

**C.R.E.**

This book is also dedicated to Janet R. Mac Lean, professor emerita, Department of Recreation and Park Administration, Indiana University, who personifies the definition of a leader as "One who has a compass in the head and a magnet in the heart." It is she who, by example, enthusiasm, and excellence in leading, sparked my initial interest in writing about leadership in leisure services.

**P.M.F.**

# PREFACE

Leadership is the single most important factor in the success of any recreation and leisure service organization. The satisfaction of participants and fellow professionals, as well as the stature of a recreation and leisure service organization within a community, is directly tied to the type and quality of leadership evidenced within an agency. Leadership is pervasive at all levels of organization. It is required of individuals in managerial, supervisory, and direct face-to-face positions. Although leadership is important at all levels, it is the direct face-to-face leadership level where the critical participant-leader exchange occurs. With this in mind, this book focuses on leadership at this level.

Recognizing that the responsibilities of an individual providing leadership at the direct face-to-face level in recreation and leisure service organizations are many and varied, this book provides the reader with a basic introduction to the competencies needed to succeed at this level. This book is divided into two sections and presents a blend of conceptual, theoretical, and practical content. The conceptual and theoretical information presented can be applied to leadership at all levels, including managerial and supervisory levels. The practical or "hands on" content of the book is directed toward providing the reader with the information necessary to serve effectively as a face-to-face leader.

Part One of the book presents an overview of the conceptual and theoretical components that are central to the leadership process. Included are discussions of leadership styles, models and processes, group dynamics, communication, and participant motivation. Furthermore, a chapter discussing leadership roles and principles applicable to the direct face-to-face leader is also included. The assumption in presenting this initial material is that the reader should have an understanding of the underlying principles, theories, concepts, and values of the profession and of leadership in order to apply them in a practical sense.

The second section of the book, Part Two, contains chapters that describe practical application of various leadership methods and procedures in a cross section of recreation and leisure service settings. The material is presented in a "hands on" practical manner. This information can be applied in a number of settings, and can be used to organize, promote, and lead successfully given recreation and leisure activities and programs.

We enjoyed writing this book! The authors share a strong belief in the value of hands-on, direct, face-to-face leadership. Although all the authors have served in administrative or supervisory positions, our exuberance and excitement are for the role that the direct face-to-face leader plays. When conceptualizing this book, we authors discovered that not only had we all been face-to-face leaders in the past, but that we all *currently* are involved in direct, face-to-face leadership roles in our extracurricular activities. Chris Edginton is a scoutmaster; and Phyllis Ford serves as an interpretive naturalist, leading community groups on weekend tours; We continue to enjoy the direct face-to-face leadership role and pursue opportunities to engage in it.

Chapters 1 to 5 of this book, dealing with leadership in recreation settings, leadership theories, group dynamics, participant motivation, and communication were prepared by Christopher Edginton. The author of Chapter 6 was Phyllis Ford. Phyllis Ford also wrote chapters dealing with risk management, social recreation, tournaments, arts and crafts, songs, leading in the out-of-doors and games and contests. Susan Edginton wrote the chapter dealing with value development. Kathleen Halberg wrote two chapters: "Leading Older People" and "Working with People with Disabilities." Karl Cloninger contributed to the chapters dealing with tour and travel programs, officiating, dramatic activities, aquatic activities, organizing and leading clubs, coaching youth sports, volunteers, festivals and pageants, meetings, and working with community groups. Chris Edginton also prepared the chapter on the leader as an instructor and contributed to chapters dealing with leadership roles and principles, organizing and leading meetings, coaching youth sports, officiating, leading community groups, leading volunteers, festivals and special events, leading dramatic activities, aquatic activities, clubs, and travel and tour programs. The chapter dealing with leading self-directed activities was coauthored by Ford and Edginton.

## ACKNOWLEDGMENTS

We are grateful for the support and influence of a number of individuals. At the University of Oregon, Effie Fairchild has served as a major source of inspiration, influencing and shaping our values and attitudes relative to the importance of the topic of leadership. She personifies the energetic, enthusiastic, and personable face-to-face leader. In addition, we are grateful for the managerial leadership provided by Celeste Ulrich, dean of the College of Human Development and Performance at the University of Oregon. Dean Ulrich has provided us with the motivation to engage in this venture and also has provided the support network necessary to complete it. Our support network has included Dawne J. Dougherty, Eugen K. Beugler, and Mary Grannon, who attended to the typing and retyping of this manuscript. Their efforts were greatly appreciated, and without their assistance, we would not have been able to meet our deadlines.

We are also indebted to those individuals who have had a direct influence on our development as professionals. A number of these people, as a result of their teaching and scholarly works, as well as of their personal concern for our development, have contributed to our ideals, values, and skills as leaders. Some of the individuals within the academic environment whom we would like to thank include Mae Stadler, Lou Charlotte, Sandy Little, Ken Kim, Reynold Carlson, and Ardith Frost. Some of the individuals serving as practitioners in the field who have contributed to our development include Jack Robinson, Gary Walker, Cleve Williams, Del Thorpe, Betty Wieseman, and Dan Plaza.

**Christopher R. Edginton**
**Phyllis M. Ford**

# CONTENTS

## PART I

### CHAPTER ONE
### LEADERSHIP IN RECREATION AND LEISURE SERVICE SETTINGS

Recreation and Leisure in North
  American Society                       4
Leaders and Leadership                   6
Recreation and Leisure Service
  Leadership                            12
Summary                                 20
Discussion Questions                    21

### CHAPTER TWO
### LEADERSHIP THEORIES, STUDIES, STYLES, AND MODELS

Theories of Leadership                  22
Leadership Studies, Styles, and
  Models                                27
A Comprehensive Approach to
  Leadership                            43
Summary                                 47
Discussion Questions                    48

### CHAPTER THREE
### GROUP DYNAMICS

What Is a Group?                        52
Group Roles                             63
Techniques Useful to the Leader         66
Summary                                 71
Discussion Questions                    72

### CHAPTER FOUR
### PARTICIPANT MOTIVATION

The Motivation Process                  74
Participant Motivation:
  The Role of the Leader                83
Participation Benefits                  91
Summary                                 97
Discussion Questions                    98

### CHAPTER FIVE
### COMMUNICATIONS

Defining Communication                 100
Types of Communication                 101
Functions of Communication             103
The Process of Communication           104
Perception and Communication           106
Styles of Communication                112
Active Listening                       115
Techniques of Communication            117
Barriers to Effective
  Communication                        121
Summary                                123
Discussion Questions                   124

### CHAPTER SIX
### FACE-TO-FACE LEADERSHIP

Types of Direct, Face-to-Face
  Leadership                           125
Guidelines for Direct, Face-to-Face
  Leadership                           138
Planning and Implementing
  Activities                           144
Participant Safety                     151
Public Relations                       152

Summary   155
Discussion Questions   156

## PART II

## CHAPTER SEVEN
## RISK MANAGEMENT

Standard of Care   161
Risk Management Plans   164
Summary   175
Discussion Questions   175

## CHAPTER EIGHT
## THE ROLE OF THE LEADER IN VALUES DEVELOPMENT

Leadership Roles in Values
   Education   179
Values Clarification   181
Summary   188
Discussion Questions   188

## CHAPTER NINE
## THE LEADER AS INSTRUCTOR

Learning and Instruction   191
Organizing the Instructional Effort   193
Summary   201
Discussion Questions   201

## CHAPTER TEN
## THE SELF-DIRECTED PROGRAM

Demographic Changes   202
Pedagogy and Andragogy—
   The Differences   204
Leading Adults: Some Ideas   210
Summary   212
Discussion Questions   212

## CHAPTER ELEVEN
## ORGANIZING AND LEADING MEETINGS

Types of Meetings   213
The Planning Process   214
Implementation of the Meeting   232

Evaluation and Follow-up   233
Summary   234
Discussion Questions   235

## CHAPTER TWELVE
## COACHING YOUTH SPORTS PROGRAMS

The Coaching Function   237
Individual Team Organization   240
Summary   247
Discussion Questions   247

## CHAPTER THIRTEEN
## OFFICIATING

Officiating Philosophy   248
Officiating Roles Assumed in
   Selected Sports   249
Characteristics of a Good Official   250
Officiating Duties   251
Summary   255
Discussion Questions   255

## CHAPTER FOURTEEN
## LEADING COMMUNITY GROUPS

The Role of the Leader   256
Objectives of Community Groups:
   What Are They?   257
Types of Community Groups   257
How Does the Leader Enable
   Community Groups to Act?   259
Summary   269
Discussion Questions   269

## CHAPTER FIFTEEN
## LEADING VOLUNTEERS

The Volunteer   271
Planning the Volunteer Effort   272
Recruitment, Selection, Placement,
   Orientation, and Supervision of
   Volunteers   274
Evaluation and Recognition   279
Summary   279
Discussion Questions   279

**CHAPTER SIXTEEN**
LEADING OLDER PEOPLE

Benefits of Participation in
Recreation and Leisure Programs
and Activities                                281
Some Leadership Objectives                    282
Who Are Older Persons?                        282
The Role of Attitudes and
Stereotypes                                   283
Settings in Which the Leader Works
with Older Persons                            284
Summary                                       288
Discussion Questions                          288

**CHAPTER SEVENTEEN**
WORKING WITH PEOPLE
WITH DISABILITIES

The Right of the Individual with
Disabilities                                  290
The Leader and Mainstreaming
Integration                                   290
Orientation to Disabling Conditions           294
Roles and Techniques                          297
Adapting Activities                           300
Summary                                       303
Discussion Questions                          304

**CHAPTER EIGHTEEN**
ORGANIZING FESTIVALS
AND PAGEANTS

What Are Festivals and Pageants?              306
Types of Festivals and Pageants               307
Role of the Leader in Festivals
and Pageants                                  309
Choosing a Theme                              310
Organizing Festivals and Pageants            310
Summary                                       315
Discussion Questions                          316

**CHAPTER NINETEEN**
SOCIAL RECREATION

Purposes and Values of Social
Events                                        318
The Social Activities Pattern                 319

Summary                                       328
Discussion Questions                          328

**CHAPTER TWENTY**
LEADERSHIP OF ARTS
AND CRAFTS

Arts versus Crafts                            331
Crafts                                        332
Arts                                          336
The Cultural Arts                             339
Community Arts                                340
Summary                                       343
Discussion Questions                          343

**CHAPTER TWENTY-ONE**
ORGANIZING AND LEADING
DRAMATIC ACTIVITIES

Objectives of the Dramatics
Program                                       344
The Role of the Dramatic Activities
Leader                                        344
Types of Dramatic Activities                  345
Summary                                       360
Discussion Questions                          360

**CHAPTER TWENTY-TWO**
LEADING SONGS

The Settings for Singing                      362
Leading Songs                                 362
Leading and Control                           363
Teaching Songs                                364
Summary                                       365
Discussion Questions                          366

**CHAPTER TWENTY-THREE**
LEADERSHIP IN THE
OUTDOORS

Outdoor Leaders' Roles and
Settings                                      368
Outdoor Leadership Techniques                 369
Human Needs and the Outdoors                  371
Care of the Environment                       373
Summary                                       373
Discussion Questions                          374

**CHAPTER TWENTY-FOUR**
LEADING AQUATIC ACTIVITIES

Leadership Roles                            375
Techniques for Leading Aquatic
  Activities                                380
Aquatic Safety                              383
Types of Aquatic Activities                 384
Summary                                     388
Discussion Questions                        389

**CHAPTER TWENTY-FIVE**
ORGANIZING AND LEADING
CLUBS

Types of Clubs                              391
How to Organize a Club                      395
Summary                                     397
Discussion Questions                        398

**CHAPTER TWENTY-SIX**
ORGANIZING AND LEADING
TOUR AND TRAVEL
PROGRAMS

Why Do People Travel?                       399
Types of Tours                              400

The Role of the Leader                      401
Summary                                     406
Discussion Questions                        406

**CHAPTER TWENTY-SEVEN**
GAMES AND CONTESTS

Types of Games                              407
Types of Contests                           413
Leading Games and Contests                  416
Summary                                     422
Discussion Questions                        422

**CHAPTER TWENTY-EIGHT**
TOURNAMENT
ORGANIZATION

Self-perpetuating Tournaments               424
Round Robin Tournaments                     428
Elimination Tournaments                     430
Miscellaneous Tournaments                   434
Summary                                     439
Discussion Questions                        439

Index                                       441

# PART ONE

Part One of this book contains six chapters and presents a conceptual and theoretical overview of the topics of leadership, group dynamics, communications, and motivation. Why present and discuss theories and conceptual ideas? A theory or conceptual idea helps us to organize our knowledge and facts regarding phenomena into meaningful and useful information that enables us to explain, describe, and predict behaviors and events. Furthermore, theories and conceptual ideas are generalizable; that is, they can be applied to many different settings, situations, and individuals. Once general conceptual and theoretical knowledge has been learned, it can be adapted to specific situations.

Our goal in this portion of the book is to set forth concepts and theories that can be related to the recreation and leisure profession and that can be widely applied to many different settings within the field. An understanding of the conceptual and theoretical ideas presented should increase the reader's awareness of the impact that the leader can have on the recreation and leisure environment and those within it. An effective leader is able to provide dynamic recreation and leisure services that meet the needs, wants, and interests of participants. The pathway to successful leadership is based on a strong conceptual and theoretical foundation. An individual with this base of knowledge has the tools to become a leader who is confident, competent, and committed and whose efforts are recognized, appreciated, respected, and enjoyed.

# 1

# LEADERSHIP IN RECREATION AND LEISURE SERVICE SETTINGS

Having fun at Family Vacation College, University of Oregon. This leader enjoys her role and is appreciated for her efforts.

As the amount of leisure available to individuals has increased, there has been a corresponding growth in the organization and provision of recreation and leisure activities in the form of programs and services by public, private, and commercial agencies. These types of organizations require the involvement of professionally trained individuals to provide leadership for the host of functions that take place within them. Leadership is found at all levels of organization within agencies providing recreation and leisure services. It is required of individuals serving in management, supervisory, and direct, face-to-face roles.

The responsibilities of individuals providing leadership are varied and diverse. For the individual working as a counselor in a camp setting, leadership may involve teaching and leading songs; for the playground leader, it may require coaching skills; for the aerobics dance instructor, it may demand knowledge of motivation techniques; for the supervisor, it may focus on his or her ability to resolve conflict; and for the manager, it may be reflected in his or her skills to promote and interpret effectively the program of the agency to the community as a whole. In any case, a knowledge of leadership, leadership styles, communications, group dynamics, and motivational techniques and processes are essential general skills or concepts that should be mastered by the leader. Furthermore, the leader should have a knowledge of the specific technical skills that can be used in select recreation and leisure service settings. For example, the step-by-step processes involved in organizing a campfire program, leading an organized game or song, organizing a tournament, or planning a retreat are specific technical skills that may be acquired and applied by the leader.

## RECREATION AND LEISURE IN NORTH AMERICAN SOCIETY

Opportunities for recreation and leisure experiences are pervasive within North American society. Increased affluence, expansion of technology, and changing attitudes toward work and play have dramatically affected the life-styles of North Americans. Economically, expenditures for the consumption of recreation and leisure products and services exceed hundreds of billions of dollars per year.[1] This dramatic outlay of money for recreation and leisure services may be directly tied to the changing concept of the nature of work and leisure. Today individuals use recreation and leisure in order to seek self-fulfillment, satisfaction, and self-expression. More and more, individuals are defining themselves and their roles through their leisure. This is a dramatic reversal from a time when individuals identified themselves solely by their occupations or professions. Individuals often identify themselves today according to what they do or experience during their leisure. "The answer to the old question, 'What do you do?' is not as interesting as asking, 'How do you play?' "[2]

*Leisure: What Is It?*    There is no universally accepted concept of leisure. It has been defined as a block of time, as a state of mind,

and as an activity. When defining leisure as a *block of time*, we think of it as a time when individuals are free to pursue those things that are of interest to them. Within this block of time, individuals choose what they want to do; they may be active or passive. When leisure is viewed as time, it has been suggested that one's life routine can be divided into three parts: existence, subsistence, and leisure or discretionary time. The second approach to defining leisure is to view it as a *state of mind*. This approach is advocated by many contemporary philosophers and researchers. Viewing leisure as a state of mind suggests that the individual's perception of what constitutes a leisure experience is the central determinant of whether or not a leisure experience has occurred. In other words, if individuals feel or think that they are experiencing leisure, then, in fact, they are. This opens up the possibility for leisure to occur at various times and places and in a variety of circumstances. The last approach to defining leisure is dependent upon an analysis of the types of *activities* in which individuals engage. Leisure is described or defined in terms of such *activities* as arts, sports, games, volunteering, traveling, reading, swimming, and so on.

If we view leisure as a state of mind or something that one experiences, there are criteria that can be used in order to measure and define it. Commonly, these are considered to be precursors to the leisure experience. Three specific criteria have been identified by social psychologists studying this topic: perceived freedom, intrinsic motivation, and perceived competence.

*Perceived freedom* refers to the notion that individuals must feel that they have independence and latitude in order for the leisure experience to occur. An individual who does not feel forced or constrained to participate has a higher degree of perceived freedom than one who is compelled to participate. Also, the individual who does not feel inhibited or limited by the environment has a higher degree of

[1] "Recreation: A $244 Billion Market," *U.S. News & World Report*, August 10, 1981, p. 61.

[2] Landon Y. Jones, *Great Expectations: America and the Baby Boom Generation* (New York: Ballantine Books, 1980), p. 336.

perceived freedom. Individuals who perceive that they have control over their own behavior, as opposed to those who attribute events in their lives to chance, fate, or luck, also have a higher degree of perceived freedom.

When individuals are motivated from within, they are said to be *intrinsically motivated*. Intrinsically motivated individuals are able to reward themselves and are not dependent upon external rewards. The intrinsically motivated individual has a greater sense of perceived freedom, hence, a greater opportunity to experience leisure. Individuals who are intrinsically motivated achieve feelings of satisfaction, enjoyment and gratification that are inwardly defined and controlled.

Finally, the perception an individual has of his or her competence while engaging in an activity will affect the leisure experience. Individuals must have a *perception of competence* in order to attain a leisure "state of mind." This is not to say that they must *be* competent, but only that they must perceive themselves as such. Knowledge of these three precursors to leisure (perceived freedom, intrinsic motivation, and perceived competence) can be used by the leader to provide a motivating environment that enables individuals to achieve positive leisure experiences.

*Recreation: What Is It?*    A common definition of recreation suggests that it is an activity that is engaged in voluntarily that is satisfying to the individual. Many definitions of recreation also suggest that it must have some socially redeeming qualities. The term *wholesomeness* is often used to describe or define this dimension of recreation. Recreation is also frequently viewed as a way of restoring or refreshing oneself for work or as a balance to work activities.

Although the terms *recreation* and *leisure* are thought to be redundant by many, the authors have employed both of these terms in the title of the book and throughout their discussion because it was felt that they capture the breadth and diversity of the field. Furthermore, the lay person or "person on the street" may relate better to either one of these terms, depending on his or her previous experience, background, or knowledge of the field. Until the philosophers of our field clarify the points of distinction between these two terms more precisely and until the perceptions of the public are more clearly focused on one term or the other, the authors feel that the use of both terms interchangeably is appropriate.

## ORGANIZATIONS PROVIDING RECREATION AND LEISURE SERVICES

There are many organizations that create and distribute recreation and leisure services. They range from nonprofit, governmental agencies to profit-oriented commercial ones. Such organizations may be involved in travel and tourism, entertainment services, food and hospitality services, and the provision of areas and facilities. Some organizations target their services toward one particular age group whereas others have a broader focus. Organizations may be very specialized in nature, providing a few specific activities and programs, or they may attempt to cater to a broader segment of the population. All organizations depend upon efficient and effective leadership in order to serve those individuals at whom their services are targeted.

Sessoms, Meyer, and Brightbill have suggested that there are three general types of organizations involved in the creation and delivery of recreation and leisure services: public, private, and commercial.[3] Public agencies are funded primarily by taxes and provide recreation and leisure services at the local, county, state, and federal levels of government. Private agencies, also referred to as voluntary agencies, are nonprofit organizations that receive their support from donations, fund-rais-

[3]H. Douglas Sessoms, Harold D. Meyer, and Charles K. Brightbill, *Leisure Services: The Organized Recreation and Park System* (Englewood Cliffs, N.J.: Prentice-Hall, 1975), pp. 13–15.

ing activities, and membership fees. Agencies in this category include the Boy Scouts, Girl Scouts, Camp Fire, Boys and Girls Clubs, YMCAs, YWCAs and others. The last category—commercial organizations—includes those agencies that have profit as their primary motive. This category may include amusement and theme parks, resorts, fitness and tennis centers, racquetball centers, travel agencies, movie theaters, and so on. Professional leadership is found in all these types of agencies and at all levels of organization.

## LEADERS AND LEADERSHIP

There are many different types of leaders in our profession. Consider the playground leader, coach, leisure counselor, activity instructor, Boy Scout leader, outreach worker, guide, interpretive naturalist, lifeguard, and others. In organized recreation and leisure services, the leader plays the key role in assisting individuals to achieve the leisure experience. Leaders serve as facilitators, teachers, moderators, encouragers, and motivators, providing direction to individuals and groups.

### WHAT IS A LEADER?

*A leader can be thought of as an individual who guides, directs, and influences the attitudes and behavior of others.* A leader guides participants toward goals that are intended to meet their individual needs, wants, and interests while, at the same time, achieving the goals of the recreation and leisure service organization. Providing guidance to individuals may involve presenting, directly or indirectly, the path that the participant should follow in order to achieve desired ends. For example, a leader might suggest that *"leisure in one's life provides balance."* This is a form of guidance. The leader may also guide an individual by suggesting various activities in which the individual can become involved to meet his or her leisure needs. In this sense, the leader *guides* the participant.

As the participant becomes involved in a program or activity, the leader may also provide *direction*. Direction can be thought of as, or is often equated with, giving commands to others. The leader will give direction to others in the form of instructions and orders and by example. For example, the lifeguard provides direction to individuals by ordering them not to run on the swimming pool deck. The activity instructor provides direction to class members by assigning and explaining tasks. Direction need not be viewed negatively, but rather can be viewed positively depending upon the perceptions of the participant and his or her willingness to take direction. We also equate directing with the idea that the leader "shows the way." In other words, the leader provides direction by helping individuals determine "what to do, how to do it, and where to do it" in order to accomplish individual and group goals.

Lastly, the leader *influences* the behavior of others. In fact, many authors have written that "leadership is influence." Influence is the power to affect the behavior of others without force. For example, a leader may use his or her influence to persuade individuals to engage in a certain activity. Often influence is based upon the use of motivational principles. In most recreation and leisure settings, the leader must lead by the influence of his or her personality, knowledge, or attractiveness to others rather than by the authority of his or her position within the organization.

Specifically, what do leaders do? There are a number of functions and responsibilities that leaders carry out.[4] Some of these include the following.

1. *Building Comradery and Cohesiveness.* Leaders help individuals within the group to feel a part of the group and help the group as a whole to feel like a unit.

[4]Adapted from H. Douglas Sessoms and Jack L. Stevenson, *Leadership and Group Dynamics in Recreation Services* (Boston: Allyn & Bacon, 1981), pp. 6, 7.

2. *Identifying and Defining Goals.* Leaders help individuals and groups identify, define, and clarify their goals and objectives. This involves helping individuals understand what they are trying to achieve (their aims) as well as their needs, interests, and wants.

3. *Developing Methods and Procedures to Achieve Goals.* Often the leader will work with individuals and groups to identify and clarify the methods and procedures that can be used to achieve their goals. Frequently individuals know where they want to go, but not how to get there.

4. *Organizing the Work of Others.* An important responsibility of the leader is the process of organizing. It involves the establishment and creation of roles, a group or organizational structure, as well as a reward system. Organizing also often involves the establishment of a network of communication.

5. *Motivating Others.* The leader is often the energizing or motivating force within the group. In this role, the leader encourages individuals to participate, act, and demonstrate other behavior conducive to the attainment of group goals.

6. *Evaluating the Work of Others.* The leader is often the individual who determines whether or not goals and objectives have been met. He or she does this by measuring the discrepancy between actual performance and the standards initially established by the group. In the event that there is a discrepancy, the leader would suggest or take corrective action.

7. *Representing the Group.* The leader may be the individual that represents the group to others, speaking on the behalf of group members. The leader may represent the group's needs, interests, and wants to other organizations or to groups within the community.

8. *Developing Group Members.* A key responsibility of the leader is the development of others. In recreation and leisure service organizations, the development of the leadership capabilities, skills, knowledge, and attitudes of others is consistent with the philosophy of the profession. In this role, the leader encourages self-help, self direction, and voluntary involvement.

9. *Establishing the Group Atmosphere.* The leader is responsible for establishing the climate of the group. Individuals may sometimes find that their relationships within a group are pleasant and productive whereas in other situations they may find the reverse to occur. The leader plays a key role in establishing a *positive* group climate.

10. *Promoting the Ideals of the Profession.* Recreation and leisure service leaders are often in a position to promote the ideals of the profession. Such ideals as protection of the environment, for example, may be promoted by the leader within the context of his or her role.

As one can see, there are numerous functions and responsibilities that are carried out by the leader. Many are carried out simultaneously, adding to the complexity of the leader's role. A group cannot function effectively or meet goals without a leader. A leader facilitates the achievement of goals by guiding, directing, and influencing the actions and behavior of others.

### ASSUMING THE LEADERSHIP ROLE

A question that may be asked is, "How does the leader assume this role?" Shivers has suggested that there are four possible ways in which a leader assumes his or her position: by appointment, by election, by emergence, or as a result of charisma.[5] The following list discusses each of these avenues for assumption of the leadership role.

[5]Jay S. Shivers, *Recreational Leadership: Group Dynamics and Interpersonal Behavior* (Princeton, N.J.: Princeton Book Co., 1980), pp. 103–113.

*Appointment.* Often, individuals will be appointed to positions of leadership. They are usually appointed on the basis of the knowledge they hold or the skills that they possess. For example, instructors might be appointed to assume the roles of leaders in instructional classes because of their knowledge of the topic presented. The same could be said for playground directors or lifeguards. Appointed leaders are usually concerned with the maintenance of organizational policy and usually have the sanction and authority of the agency as their primary means of influence. The amount of influence that an individual may possess as an appointed leader can be directly related to the type and level of the appointed position held.

*Election.* Individuals also occupy leadership roles with considerable influence because they have been elected by others to fulfill these roles. For example, in the recreation and leisure setting, sports groups often elect a member to serve as the captain of the team. This individual would serve to represent the interests of the group in various ways, of which some are prescribed by the rules of the game and others emerge situationally. Individuals are elected to serve in leadership roles for a variety of reasons. Some individuals are elected because they are well thought of or are popular with group members. Others are elected as a result of their past performance and leadership capabilities. Still others may be elected because of their expertise or knowledge. Election of an individual to a leadership role does not necessarily predict his or her success as a leader.

*Emergence.* The emergent leader is one who, because of certain conditions, assumes the leadership role. We often think of this as a spontaneous event in which existing conditions result in the creation of an opportunity for an individual to lead. To illustrate,

picture a group of individuals dropping into a gymnasium on a Saturday afternoon. As they begin to interact, someone may emerge from the group to suggest that they organize to engage in a more structured form of the activity. This emergent leader may suggest a process of dividing group members up, help establish the rules, and help create the social climate. Emergent leaders may have varying perceptions of their roles because they are usually untrained. The emergent leader is more likely to assume a leadership role when his or her skills, abilities, knowledge and interests complement the needs of the existing situation.

*Charisma.* The charismatic leader is one who occupies the leadership role as a result of the power of his or her personality. Some individuals are highly attractive to others because of those intangible qualities that have been termed charisma. Charismatic leaders are able to assume the leadership position, not so much by what they say, but rather because of their personal demeanor and behavior that imbues their message with a special quality. In the recreation and leisure setting, ''charisma may be observed among children's groups, where a counselor, coach, or beloved teacher is the recipient of an adoration almost bordering on love.''[6]

In recreation and leisure settings, all these different avenues for the assumption of the leadership role are found. Appointed leaders are selected to organize and deliver programs and services and activities. They may either be paid or serve on a volunteer basis. Elected leaders are formally elected as board members or commissioners or informally elected as team captains, group leaders, and group representatives. Emergent leaders are found wherever groups of individuals form. They

[6]Ibid., p. 114.

are especially prevalent in drop-in recreation and leisure service programs, clubs, citizen task force groups, or advisory groups. The charismatic leader, like the emerging leader, is found wherever groups of individuals form. Because of their personal demeanor and behavior, leaders of this type can have great influence upon those around them. It should be noted that individuals may also assume leadership roles as a result of a combination of factors. A charismatic leader, for example, might simultaneously be an appointed, elected, or emergent leader.

**WHAT IS LEADERSHIP?**

*Leadership is the process employed by the leader to assist individuals and groups in identifying and achieving their goals.* Leadership may involve listening, persuading, suggesting, doing, and otherwise exerting influence on others. We often think of leadership as the act of influencing others to do ''what *you* want them to do because *they* want to do it.'' A key factor in the process of leadership is the leader's style. Leadership style often defines the way in which the leader will interact with the group. Some leaders have a very task-oriented style whereas others focus on facilitating interaction between individuals.

How does a leader determine whether or not his or her leadership is successful? There are guidelines that may be used by the leader as a measure of his or her effectiveness. A leader may assume that his or her efforts are successful if the participants being led can be influenced to do the following.

1. Choose the leader's interpretation of the processes to be employed in achieving individual and group goals over opposing views.
2. Follow the leader's processes or methods for achieving individual and group goals.
3. Perceive that their individual goals can best be achieved by accepting the guid-

ance, direction, and influence of the leader.
4. Perceive that the leader is open-minded toward their views and willing to change or modify processes and ends in order to meet their individual needs, wants, and interests.
5. Perceive that the leader is consistent in his or her behavior, as well as rational in choosing methods and processes for the achievement of goals.
6. Perceive that the interpretation of the leader concerning the methods and processes for the achievement of goals is consistent with their social norms and customs.[7]

From a functional standpoint, these guidelines represent a method for measuring the effectiveness of the leader. It should be pointed out that each situation encountered by the leader will result in a new and different challenge. The method or methods used by a leader to help one group achieve its goals may not be appropriate within another group. However, the issue is not only the types of methods chosen to accomplish goals, but also whether or not individuals choose to *follow* the leader's direction or guidance. In other words, a leader may employ different methods and still reach intended goals by virtue of his or her leadership ability. Conversely, two leaders may employ the same methods, yet only one may reach intended goals because the other leader does not possess sufficient leadership skills.

In using the preceding guidelines to assess one's effectiveness as a leader, the reader should be reminded that they represent behaviors that are characteristic of a group over the long term when leadership is successful. Not in every situation will the group choose the goals and methods presented by the leader

[7]Adapted from Clayton Reeser, *Management: Functions and Modern Concepts* (Glenview, Ill.: Scott, Foresman, 1973), p. 270.

or perceive the leader as open-minded and consistent. Nor would this necessarily be desirable. Furthermore, although leaders in many recreation and leisure settings will encourage the group to make its own decisions, that is, to identify and choose its own goals and methods, use of the democratic procedure by the leader does not guarantee the success of the group. If the leader presented democratic decision making as an alternative and the group wanted authoritarian decision making, then one would say that the leader was not successful (in reality, a group usually chooses a democratic decision-making process).

### LEADERSHIP AND POWER

There is a direct and close relationship between power and leadership. The recreation and leisure service leader who understands this relationship and can use it to meet individual and group goals will be more likely to achieve success. Often individuals view the use of power negatively; however, it is through the exercise of power that the leader influences the behavior of others.

Power can emanate from several sources. Franch and Raven have identified five sources of power: formal or legitimate power, reward power, coercive power, expert power, and referent power.[8] These authors suggest that each of these sources of power is interrelated. An individual may use situationally one type of power or a combination of types of power. A discussion of these five types of power, as related to recreation and leisure service leaders, follows.

*Legitimate or Formal Power.*   We often think of legitimate or formal power as the influence that the recreation and leisure service leader has as a result of his or her position within an organization. In other words, the leader's authority to influence individuals is inherent in the position that he or she occupies. The swimming pool lifeguard, for example, holds power by occupying the position. Individuals choosing to use the swimming pool facilities have an obligation to accept the influence of the lifeguard's position. Formal or legitimate power is created through the establishment of hierarchical structures where superior-subordinate positions are established.

*Reward Power.*   Reward power can be thought of as the leader's ability to provide positive reinforcement to individuals. As such, the leader influences others by offering rewards to those who comply with or follow the leader's direction. As will be stressed later in the chapter on motivation, the leader can provide many different types of reinforcement, both tangible and intangible. The leader can provide praise, recognition, status, money, special privileges, and other incentives that positively influence behavior. The playground leader can, for example, use reward power to influence and shape the behavior of children in the program. This can be accomplished by praising a child for returning equipment, providing ribbons and certificates for attendance, or allowing certain children to assume leadership roles for exemplary behavior or a combination of these.

*Coercive Power.*   When individuals do not follow the direction of the leader, the leader may use the threat of punishment to influence behavior. Coercive power is used in both direct, overt ways and indirect, covert ways. Suggesting to an individual that he or she will lose privileges as a result of inappropriate behavior or withholding praise or recognition are common examples of the use of coercive power. We often use coercive power when individuals are threatening the safety and well-being of others. For example, if a child on a playground is throwing rocks at other children, the leader may threaten banishment

[8]John R. P. French, Jr., and Bertram Raven, "The Basis of Social Power," in D. Cartwright (ed.), *Studies in Social Power* (Ann Arbor, Mich.: Institute for Social Research, 1959).

from the playground. Caution should be exercised by the leader when employing coercive power. Constant threats of punishment can result in feelings of hostility, frustration, and rage on the part of participants. The authors suggest that the use of coercive power should be employed only when other forms of power have been exhausted or hazardous conditions are involved or both.

*Referent Power.* Often individuals will gain power because they have the ability to attract other individuals by virtue of their personalities. Certainly, this is an important source of power for recreation and leisure service leaders. We can all visualize the dynamic, enthusiastic, energetic, and personable recreation and leisure service leader. We often talk about the charismatic qualities of this type of person. Participants may become involved and stay involved in activities solely because of their attraction to a particular leader. It is interesting to note that individuals with a strong attraction to a particular leader will identify and stay involved with that particular person regardless of the types of rewards and punishments provided.

*Expert Power.* Another source of power is that of expert power. When an individual leader has a particular skill, level of knowledge, or type of expertise, he or she is able to influence others by virtue of this special knowledge. We can all visualize the leader who is not personable, but who can captivate and influence others because of his or her thorough knowledge of and expertise in a given subject. For example, the recreation and leisure service leader interpreting nature may be able to instill an excitement and enthusiasm for this subject in spite of a lack of charismatic qualities.

Although little research has been conducted relative to the impact of various sources of power, one might speculate as to the effectiveness of each of these five types of power within recreation and leisure service organizations. First, it is likely that the effectiveness of different types of power will be situationally determined. For example, in a situation in which there are rules and regulations that result in narrowly defined role expectations for participants, the use of legitimate or formal power may be the most appropriate and effective means of influence. In another situation that is more informal and is based on voluntary participation, a combination of reward and referent power may be the most effective means of influence. Second, the use of punishment may have unexpected and undesirable results. Coercive power may result in and produce greater resistance on the part of participants. Often resistance to threats of punishment results in hostile acts by participants that are more disruptive than their original negative behavior. Third, referent and expert power are perhaps the two most influential sources of power in recreation and leisure settings where the leader works on a face-to-face basis with a small group of individuals.

The way in which the recreation and leisure service leader uses power and the type of power he or she employs will affect the ability of participants to engage in satisfying leisure experiences. Power is the means whereby the leader assists individuals and groups in forming and achieving goals. It is not something to be avoided by the recreation and leisure service leader, but rather a tool to be used in a positive way. Leaders who become power hungry, using their influence to increase their own self-importance or their dominance over others, are using their influence inappropriately. There is often a thin line between the leader who uses power for his or her own ends and one who uses power to help others achieve individual or group goals. Power should be understood and used in appropriate and positive ways by the recreation and leisure service leader.

## LEADERS AND FOLLOWERS

Where there are no followers, there are no leaders. Surprisingly, leaders often forget this axiom. They don't realize that their base of support is centered in their followers. The leader who does recognize the importance of followers will in all likelihood be a more successful leader than one who does not. Perhaps the best training for being a leader is actually being a follower. In fact, we have all been involved in the role of follower, and many of our perceptions of what it takes to make a good leader are based upon our own previous experiences and observations. We have all observed individuals who were able to fulfill successfully the leadership role, and many of us have attempted to model our own leadership styles after such individuals.

Why do individuals follow others? Sessoms and Stevenson have suggested that there are three explanations for this behavior, related to the concepts of efficiency, satisfaction, and experience. These are detailed in the following discussion.

*Efficiency.* One of the possible reasons that individuals follow leaders is that they don't want to become involved themselves in the leadership function. As Sessoms and Stevenson indicate, people follow because "it is easier to let someone else do it for you."[9] Often individuals view the delegation of their power to a leader as being the most efficient and practical method for achieving group goals.

*Satisfaction.* Followers who are satisfied with the status quo or the projected plans will tend to follow willingly. In other words, if things are moving along smoothly and followers are content with the way that events are arranged, there is a tendency to follow the current leader or leaders. It is interesting to note that in unstable economic times more people file to run for elected offices than in stable times.

*Experience.* One's previous experience will also influence whether or not he or she assumes the role of a follower or leader. Individuals who have not occupied leadership roles in the past are not as likely to occupy them in the future. Individuals who have had successful experiences as followers—or as leaders—often seek out those same roles. For example, it is often heard that an individual is "more *comfortable* as a follower."

Individuals become followers in certain situations because their needs are being met, whether because of their past experiences or the satisfaction they derive as a group member. It is interesting to note that in times of crisis people tend to rally to a leader, almost as if they acknowledge their need to be followers and to be led through the event. The leader should recognize the importance of the motivation of the follower. This will provide the leader with insight that may be useful in dealing effectively with his or her followers and that may aid in the choice of a type of leadership style and the choice of processes and methods to be used.

## RECREATION AND LEISURE SERVICE LEADERSHIP

Leaders in recreation and leisure service organizations play a key role in the provision of activities, programs, and services. These types of organizations are value laden, and the role of the leader is one of directing, guiding, and influencing individuals so that the goals and values of the organization are promoted while at the same time the needs of individual participants are met. The goals of most recreation and leisure service organizations focus on assisting individuals to grow and to develop their capabilities; promoting wise use of leisure time; providing areas and facilities to meet leisure needs; and promoting citizenship, mental health, physical fitness, social development, creativity, self expression, intellectual growth, and spiritual development.

[9]Sessoms and Stevenson, op cit., p. 81.

*Recreation and leisure service leadership can be defined, therefore, as the process of assisting individuals and groups in identifying and achieving their needs, while at the same time meeting the goals of the organization.* This process involves the acquisition and allotment of organizational resources—human, fiscal, and physical—in such a way that these goals can be achieved. It further involves the development of programs, activities, and services that translate these resources into leisure experiences for participants.

## LEVELS OF LEADERSHIP IN RECREATION AND LEISURE SERVICE ORGANIZATIONS

Leadership is found at all levels within recreation and leisure service organizations. Not only is it essential in the actual delivery of services where the trained professional interacts with participants on a face-to-face basis, but it also exists in a broader context where the recreation and leisure service professional provides leadership to the community as a whole. It exists within organizations as professionals lead their subordinates and peers assisting them in the planning, organizing, and implementation of their assigned tasks. Leadership in recreation and leisure service organizations is not exclusively practiced by the professional, but is also exercised by volunteers, lay persons, and other individuals interested in supporting and encouraging the development of the activities, programs, and services of an agency. Generally speaking, we can identify four distinct types of leadership found in recreation and leisure service organizations. They are direct or face-to-face leadership, supervisory leadership, managerial leadership, and civic or community leadership. Following is a discussion of each.

*Direct or Face-to-Face Leadership.* Direct, face-to-face leadership can be thought of as that leadership that takes place in the relationship between the participant and the leader. This type of leadership can involve instructing, coaching, counseling, refereeing, moderating, and facilitating group interaction. It is characterized by direct, face-to-face contact between the leader and the participant on a one-to-one basis or leader to group. Individuals occupying roles as playground leaders, recreation specialists, coaches, officials, attendants, and lifeguards are engaged in face-to-face leadership. Such leaders are employed for their technical knowledge and skill as well as their ability to relate to and interact with individuals in a positive fashion. Direct, face-to-face leadership is the backbone of structured activities provided by recreation and leisure service organizations.

*Supervisory Leadership.* Supervisors or middle managers within recreation and leisure service organizations are also leaders. Supervisors provide direction to individuals helping them to carry out their tasks and to resolve both personal and job-related problems. Supervisory leadership involves overseeing the work of others in such a way that they are helped to accomplish the goals of the recreation and leisure service organization. Supervisors are employed for their technical knowledge as well as their human relations skills. They must have the ability to encourage, stimulate, motivate, and evaluate their subordinates. They often lead by example and are the individuals primarily responsible for assisting the direct, face-to-face leader in the accomplishment of his or her assigned tasks.

*Managerial Leadership.* Managerial leadership is that leadership which is provided by the organization's top administrators or executives. These individuals provide overall direction to the organization, establishing broad goals, providing motivation, engaging in long-range planning, establishing and administering reward systems, and overseeing those individuals who are directly accountable to them. Managerial leadership is also evidenced in the efforts of administrators or executives to interpret the organization's services, programs, and activities to its target population. In this sense, the manager guides a community's efforts in establishing and providing recreation and leisure services. Managerial leadership tends to be broader, more expansive, and conceptual in nature than face-to-face or supervisory leadership.

***Civic or Community Leadership.*** Public recreation and leisure service agencies promote and encourage involvement of citizens and lay persons in the governance and operation of their programs, services, and activities. This is evidenced by the large number of volunteers serving as board members, commissioners, advisory group members, and individuals serving as volunteers in programs dealing with youth sports, older persons, cultural arts, and so on. Individuals engaged in this type of leadership may act as policymakers, representing citizens interests. They may provide leadership by interpreting needs, providing input regarding the distribution of organizational resources, and actively promoting the work of the agency to the community as a whole. The degree of support and leadership provided by individuals assisting recreation and leisure service agencies as volunteers in the capacities mentioned earlier can often determine the success or failure of the organization's efforts.

In Part One of this book, the reader is to be exposed to a number of theories and concepts regarding leadership, group dynamics, communication, and motivation. All the concepts discussed in this part of the book are applicable, in a general sense, to the four types of leadership found in recreation and leisure service organizations. For example, motivation principles can be applied by the *manager* to motivate individuals occupying supervisory positions and by the *face-to-face leader* to motivate and deal effectively with participants. The same can be said regarding the use of other concepts presented in the first part of this book, such as choice of an appropriate leadership style, the establishment of an active listening posture in communicating with others, and selection of small-group techniques and procedures in order to work effectively with various types of groups.

## LEADERSHIP AND THE LEISURE EXPERIENCE

Leisure experiences by definition require voluntary involvement, a sense of freedom, and they are often spontaneous in nature. As a result, individuals must be attracted to programs, activities, and services and must perceive them to be desirable, beneficial, and meaningful in order to participate in them. The recreation and leisure service leader must appeal to the needs, wants, and interests of potential participants in order to involve them in services and activities. For example, it has been determined that a participant, in order to have a leisure experience, must feel a sense of freedom and perceived competence and must also be intrinsically motivated. The role of the leader, therefore, is to create an environment in which these needs can be met. This will be discussed more fully in Chapter 4, which deals with the subject of participant motivation.

Although the leader must initially attract individuals to participate voluntarily in activities and services, once individuals do become involved, the intensity of the experience is in great part due to the voluntary commitment of participants. The leader has a special responsibility to use the power or bond that emerges within the leisure experience in ways that are beneficial to the participant. The enthusiasm, energy, sense of humor, wit, empathy, and warmth of the leader may determine whether or not participants enjoy a successful leisure experience, once attracted to it. In other words, the degree to which the face-to-face leader communicates effectively with each participant and the way that the participant perceives the leader may well determine the success of the participant's experience.

Some of the desirable relationships that can be established between the face-to-face leader and the participant that are useful in facilitating the leisure experience are these.

*Shared Expectations.* The participant comes to the leisure setting with certain expectations, and the leader likewise has his or her own expectations. If the expectations of both parties are not congruent or complementary, the possibility that the participant will experience succcessful leisure will be diminished. The feeling of perceived competence, necessary for the achievement of a successful leisure experience, is related to the concept of shared expectations. The participant's expectations for his or her performance should be related to the leader's expectations, expressed in terms of the skill level that has been established.

*Trust.* Trust occurs between individuals when they have a mutual confidence in the capabilities and intentions of one another. Without a trust relationship, the extent to which the leader can influence the participant and vice versa in order to produce a satisfying leisure experience is limited.

*Effective Communication.* Two-way communication between the leader and the participant is essential. Providing opportunities for feedback, as well as use of active listening skills, is necessary to facilitate effective two-way communication. Effective communication helps the leader and the participant mold the leisure experience to meet their respective needs.

*Shared Decision Making.* One of the key elements of a successful leisure experience is perceived freedom. Shared decision making helps to create the feeling of participants that they have control and freedom within the leisure experience.

*Cooperation.* There must be a willingness to engage in a give-and-take exchange on the part of the participant and the leader. For example, the participant must be willing to take direction from the leader in exchange for the opportunity for a particular leisure experience.

*Sense of Risk and Spontaneity.* Spontaneity helps to create the illusion of freedom, which is necessary to the leisure experi-

ence. Spontaneity is often associated with a sense of risk or the unpredictability of a situation.

*Positive Reinforcement.* Leaders must be encouragers of others. They do this by encouraging others to give their best, have fun, express their feelings, and relax. We often view enthusiastic and energetic leadership as a way of positively reinforcing individuals. In turn, when participants positively reinforce the leader, they encourage the leader to do his or her best. Positive reinforcement can contribute to the climate of the leisure environment—building comradery and cohesiveness.

*Social and Emotional Bond.* The leader's interest in each participant and the way that that interest is expressed in terms of warmth, humor, and empathy can create a special bond between the participant and the leader that contributes to the leisure experience.

In most cases, it is the responsibility of the leader to initiate the preceding types of relationships. The leader, for example, may ask participants to share their expectations and offer his or her own expectations. The leader will often initiate the action that reinforces others and establishes a social and emotional bond. The responsiveness of participants or their willingness to become involved in these relationships will, in turn, support the leader and contribute to the power or potency of the leisure experience.

### GOAL DIRECTED BEHAVIOR AND LEADERSHIP

If the recreation and leisure service leader guides, directs, and influences the participant, a logical question that can be asked is, "Toward what end?" In other words, "What ends, values, or behavior does the leader promote?" The reader should understand that most behavior is *goal directed*. This means that people participate in activities because they have a need, want, or interest that can be met by the activity. The role of the leader, therefore, becomes one of directing, guiding, or influencing individuals to take action in order to satisfy their needs, wants, and interests. Thus, recreation and leisure service leadership is goal directed.

Not only are recreation and leisure service organizations interested in meeting participants' needs, wants, and interests, but they also have their own goals and objectives that they must attempt to meet. For example, most recreation and leisure service organizations are concerned with the promotion of leisure experiences that will have a long-term effect upon the participant. These types of agencies are concerned not only with the immediate benefits of the leisure experience to the participant, but in a broader sense also with the eventual impact on the community and society as a whole of the individual influenced and shaped by leisure experiences. Thus, the leader in any recreation and leisure service organization will want to have both a perspective of the needs of participants and an understanding of the broader goals of the organization.

One of the basic questions that the leader may want to encourage participants to ask is whether or not their participation in a given activity is "worthwhile." As Godbey has indicated, "In choosing leisure activity, I believe that the first question is not 'What is pleasurable?' but rather, 'What is worth doing?' "[10] Godbey indicates that the search for pleasure should not be the primary focus of participation—not that pleasure is unimportant, but rather that the individual should seek experiences that provide opportunities for learning and growth. In the light of this concept, then, the role of the leader is also to guide, direct, and influence the behavior of participants in such a way that their leisure experiences become worthwhile.

Some of the goals[11] of recreation and leisure service organizations that relate to shaping the behavior of the participant are listed as follows.

*Exploration.* Exploration involves a testing of new ideas, involvement in new environments, and a sampling of experiences that have not been previously encountered. The leader can foster a sense of exploration by creating new and different leisure opportunities.

*Self-discovery.* As the word *self-discovery* implies, opportunities for it center on helping the participant explore his or her own feelings, values, and ideas. There are many ways that the leader can arrange opportunities for self-discovery from retreats to writing to photography classes. Self-discovery is a by product of most recreation and leisure activities.

*Creativity.* Creativity occurs when an individual has an opportunity to make an original or unique contribution. It is the act of being inventive and constructing something that can be appreciated from an aesthetic standpoint. We think of the creative writer, artist, dancer, and so on. All these types of activities can be fostered and promoted by the recreation and leisure service leader.

*Mental Health.* Many recreation and leisure service activities foster relaxation, a sense of well-being, a feeling of being refreshed mentally, and a feeling of stress reduction. These, in turn, may contribute to a positive outlook on life or, in other words, a healthy mental attitude. The leader can play an important role in contributing to the positive mental health of participants.

*Social Relations.* Interaction with other individuals has historically been a primary goal

[10]Geoffrey Godbey, *Leisure in Your Life: An Exploration* (Philadelphia, Pa.: Saunders College Publishing, 1981), p. 11.

[11]This list was drawn from a study conducted in the United States and Canada to determine the goals of municipal park and recreation departments.

of recreation and leisure service organizations. Recreation leaders can provide opportunities that allow individuals to interact with others and develop their social skills. Social isolation can contribute to mental instability.

*Intellectual Growth.* Creating opportunities for the participant to learn new skills and acquire new knowledge is a major part of the work of the recreation and leisure service leader. Not only does the participant acquire cognitive knowledge during some leisure activities, but also may ''learn'' attitudes, values and opinions.

*Physical Fitness.* Physical development is an activity that is fostered by the recreation and leisure service leader. We see many physical activities and programs led by leaders, including individual, dual, and team sports; New Games; and so on.

*A Sense of Self-determination and Independence.* Many recreation and leisure activities are designed specifically to promote a sense of self-determination and independence on the part of participants. Such activities as hiking, camping, backpacking, canoeing, field trips for children, and scuba diving usually require some independence of thought and judgment and freedom of action.

*Wise Use of Leisure.* By participating in activities and programs offered by recreation and leisure service organizations, participants are likely to develop an appreciation for the wise and full use of leisure. Values are promoted within the context of activities and programs that teach participants about worthy, productive, and socially accepted ways for using one's leisure.

*Promoting Family Unity.* Many recreation and leisure organizations have, as their primary function, the development of family unity. The leader works to strengthen families by encouraging family participation in

A family enjoying leisure together at Marriott's Great America, Santa Clara, California.

activities and the reinforcement of existing family ties. Even though a family may not participate in a structured activity together, often families will congregate to watch one or more family members engage in activities or sports, contributing to a feeling of support and togetherness within the family. The family in the above picture is enjoying a day of recreation at Marriott's Great America.

*Enjoyment of Life.* By taking part in recreation and leisure service activities, participants will probably enhance their enjoyment of life. Encouraging participants to value, appreciate, and become sensitized to life experiences can help them enjoy life more fully.

*Concern for the Environment.* Encouraging participants to understand, value, and appreciate our ecological system is an important goal that is often pursued by recreation and leisure service organizations and leaders. Two themes have emerged, one focusing on preservation and one on conservation of the environment. In either case, the participant who gains an appreciation of his or her environment is more in touch with it.

*Promoting Cooperation.* Recreation and leisure service organizations foster cooperation by providing opportunities for individuals to work and play together noncompetitively. New Games serve as an example of the promotion of this ideal. Leaders also can encourage cooperation by sharing decision making and teaching respect for others.

*Learning About Others and Other Cultures.* Leaders can help individuals understand other individuals and their cultures by offering recreation and leisure settings and activities that are based upon these other cultures. An appreciation of other cultures can broaden an individual's horizon and perspective.

*Citizenship.* The leader can help develop citizenship among participants by promoting an understanding of our country, government, and social customs, norms, and mores. Learning how to be a "good citizen" might involve learning and understanding how democracy works, how the rights and privileges of others are protected, and so on. Encouragement of citizenship was a prime goal in the development of many early playgrounds and continues to be so in many youth-serving organizations.

These, then, are the goals or ends toward which most recreation and leisure service organizations work. They provide the justification or basis for influencing the behavior of participants.

**To Lead or Not to Lead?**  To what extent do recreation and leisure service leaders direct individual participants? To what extent do

leaders guide participants? Do leaders use their skills, knowledge, and expertise to move participants toward predetermined goals? Or do leaders use their skills to help individuals make their own decisions and come to their own conclusions? Jean Mundy, a noted expert in leisure education, provided the following insight while speaking to students and faculty at the University of Oregon.

There is one course that I would like to go somewhere and teach: that is how *not* to lead. . . . [As students] . . . you all know the right things to do. You know, for example, all the mechanical moves . . . how to get people in a circle, in two lines . . . etc. [When] . . . some kid comes up to you on the playground and says . . . "Johnnie took the box hockey stick," you can walk over with the discipline that you've learned and say in your best first grade voice, "Johnnie, give him back the box hockey stick."

You have learned how to discipline, control and to get kids to do what you want them to do by intimidation. However, those two kids do not know any more about resolving conflict. They do not know any more about other ways to share, or alternative types of decision making [because of your intervention]. We exercise our leadership abilities, but the kids are not that much better off in terms of their own skills or knowledge. I think if we are going to help people in leisure we have got to begin developing facilitators . . . helping people to learn how to govern, make their own decisions and be self-determining.[12]

As one can see, the type of leadership Mundy is referring to requires that the leader focus on the development of individuals, especially their ability to think for themselves, make independent decisions, and exercise self-control and self-discipline. The type of leadership that Mundy is suggesting requires that the leader take risks: risks in allowing in-

[12]Jean Mundy, "Leisure Manifestations of Human Problems," a speech given at the Department of Recreation and Park Management, University of Oregon, February 25, 1982.

dividuals to explore their own feelings and values, risks in establishing meaningful relationships with people, and risks in allowing the participant to interact with the environment in new and different ways. In order for significant growth to occur, some individuals may need an opportunity for self-testing and freedom independent of a control-oriented leader.

As a means of facilitating independent decision making and self-control, an open responsive dialogue can be established. For example, leaders can enable participants to develop an internal locus of control by allowing them to draw their own conclusions about their behavior and the environment. In other words, the leader, rather than "telling" the participant what to do or what to think, can ask probing questions that allow the participant to formulate intelligent and accurate conclusions. Such questions as these—"What do you think you should do about this?" "What do you think I should do as the leader and why?" "How can you help this to be a better experience for you and the others?"—can help participants develop perceptions and conclusions that will aid them in dealing with current problems or successes, as well as with future situations that are similar.

The authors suggest that, in order to be successful, the leader must not only develop skills, knowledge, and expertise of a technical nature, but must also establish a philosophy or set of assumptions that can guide their use. Each situation that the leader will be faced with will require a unique blend of knowledge and skills. Research in the area of leadership has supported the idea of situational relevance of methods. However, although the methods employed should be varied to meet each given situation, the philosophical assumption of the leader should remain constant. For example, the leader serving as a coach may employ different coaching methods in working with various age groups or skill levels; however, the leader's underlying philosophical assumption—emphasizing skill development and fun rather than "winning at all costs"—should remain constant with all groups.

***The Leader as a Standard Seeker.*** There are diverging philosophies concerning recreation and leisure. One contemporary philosophy of leisure suggests that pleasure should be pursued as an end in itself with no thought of purpose or of whether or not it is "worthwhile." Another philosophy suggests that individuals should pursue leisure in order to fulfill their potentials, the term *potential* being undefined. Still another philosophy would suggest that individuals' use of leisure should be measured by the establishment of standards or norms. In terms of the first philosophy, is it not a waste of our human resources to focus only on the importance of the leisure experience for pleasure rather than considering the many outcomes in *addition* to pleasure that can be derived from such participation? As Paul Haun wrote over two decades ago in *Recreation: A Medical Viewpoint*, "Fun is the steadfast goal of recreation, yet not its purpose."[13] The second philosophy mentioned often frustrates participants, for they have no way of determining whether or not they *have* achieved their potentials. In addition, use of this philosophy can result in a tendency of the individual to focus inward, concentrating only on his or her *own* potential. The third philosophy can be challenged in terms of how and by whom standards for successful leisure experiences are set. Poor standards might result in an inaccurate perception of one's leisure experiences.

It is the authors' opinion that recreation and leisure service leaders are, in fact, standard seekers and setters as suggested by the third philosophy. We do establish levels of expectations and norms of behavior for individuals engaged in leisure. Therefore it is extremely important that leaders understand

[13]Paul Haun, *Recreation: A Medical Viewpoint*, ed. Elliot M. Avedon and Francis B. Arje (New York: Bureau of Publications, Teachers College, Columbia University, 1965), p. 18.

and appreciate their roles as standard seekers and setters. They must be cognizant of the fact that the standards that are set by leaders will have a profound effect on the leisure experience of participants and may even overlap into other areas of their lives. A coach of a youth sports team, for example, exerts tremendous influence on the lives of the children he or she supervises. The standards that are set by the coach, as well as the coach's behavior as a model, will directly influence the children's formulation of values concerning their participation in this type of activity. If the coach is very competitively oriented, de-emphasizing honesty in favor of winning ("cheat to win"), this value may be transmitted to the children and even may be carried over by them into other sports and other life activities.

The prevailing philosophy in the recreation and leisure field is one of helping individuals develop themselves to their potentials, promoting individual growth and development. The authors see this goal as a desirable one. Often, the terms *enabling* or *facilitating* are associated with this philosophy. We see the role of the leader using this philosophy as one of assisting individuals to *identify*, *define*, and *achieve* their potentials. This may involve helping individuals establish goals and identify the means by which goals can be achieved. In helping individuals establish goals, the leader may also work to help them enlarge or broaden their perspectives. The leader may also help individuals establish standards that serve to measure their progress toward their goals. Thus, even using the prevailing philosophy, emphasizing the development of individual potential, the leader may find himself or herself acting as a standard setter.

The authors feel that recreation and leisure service leaders have a special responsibility as standard setters. The leader should operate in a moral and ethical manner, establishing high ideals to guide his or her own behavior and serve as a model for participants. The leader should also establish high standards that challenge individuals to do their very best personally. Furthermore, the leader should establish ideals that foster an appreciation of the social, cultural, and physical environment.

## SUMMARY

Leadership is found at all levels within recreation and leisure service organizations. The leader is an individual who leads others by guiding, directing, and influencing their behavior. Among the major responsibilities of leaders are building comradery and cohesiveness, identifying and defining goals, developing methods to achieve goals, organizing the work of others, motivating others, evaluating the work of others, representing others, developing others, establishing a group atmosphere, and promoting the ideals of the profession. A leader can be appointed or elected or can assume his or her position by emerging spontaneously to meet group needs or because of charismatic qualities.

Leadership is a process in which the leader assists individuals and groups to identify and achieve their goals. Successful leaders are often able to influence the interpretation of group goals and processes. They are usually perceived by their followers as open-minded, rational, consistent, and nonmanipulative.

Individuals may follow a leader because they do not want to become involved in the leadership task themselves, they are satisfied with the leader's work, or they do not have the appropriate experience to lead or because of a combination of these factors. It is important for the leader to remember that where there are no followers, there are no leaders.

Recreation and leisure service leadership can be thought of as a process that helps individuals and groups meet their needs while at the same time meeting the goals of the recreation and leisure service organization. Leadership is found and practiced at four levels within recreation and leisure service organizations. These are direct or face-to-face, supervision, managerial and civic or community levels. Effective leadership helps participants meet their leisure needs, wants, and interests. When working with participants to facilitate the leisure experience, the leader should attempt to share expectations, build trust, communicate effectively, share decision making, foster a sense of cooperation, create a sense of risk or spontaneity, provide positive reinforcement, and establish a social and emotional bond with the participant.

The work of the recreation and leisure service leader is value laden, directed toward promoting a number of professional goals. Among these goals are the fostering of a sense of exploration, self-discovery, and creativity. Other goals are promotion of mental health, social interaction, intellectual growth, physical fitness, a sense of self-determination and independence, and a wise use of leisure. Still other goals are promotion of family unity, enjoyment of life, concern for the environment, citizenship, cooperation, and assisting individuals to understand others. The authors view leaders as standard setters, establishing levels of expectations and norms of behavior for individuals engaged in leisure.

## DISCUSSION QUESTIONS

1. What is a leader? What is leadership?
2. Identify ten functions and responsibilities of leaders.
3. Identify and discuss four ways that leaders assume their roles.
4. What guidelines can be used to measure the effectiveness of a leader? Identify six specific guidelines.
5. What is the relationship between power and leadership?
6. Identify and define five sources of power.
7. What is the relationship between leaders and followers?
8. Identify four distinct types of leadership within recreation and leisure service organizations. What is the difference between each of these types of leadership?
9. Identify eight factors that contribute to a positive relationship between the leader and the participant. What are some of the goals of recreation and leisure service organizations?
10. How can the leader's philosophy influence his or her relationship with participants? What is meant by the statement "The leader is a standard setter"?

# 2

# LEADERSHIP THEORIES, STUDIES, STYLES, AND MODELS

Recreation and leisure service leadership styles vary. This leader appears to be using a democratic style of leadership to interact with his group.

When leadership is mentioned, everyone has a view as to what constitutes a successful or unsuccessful leader. There have been literally thousands of books and articles directed toward this topic. It is a particularly exciting and interesting topic to explore because of our fascination with people in leadership roles and the part that power plays in the leadership process.

In this chapter, we will explore leadership in terms of three major areas of concern. The first of these is the theoretical or conceptual orientations from which our ideas of leader-

ship have emerged. Second, we will explore various leadership studies, styles, and models. Particular emphasis, in this section, will be placed on the progression of knowledge in this area. Finally, we will present and discuss a model that provides a comprehensive approach for determining one's leadership style.

## THEORIES OF LEADERSHIP

Several theoretical bases for explaining and understanding leadership have emerged. These theories have focused on such variables as the traits of the leader, the conditions that exist within groups, and other situational or environmental variables. In this portion of the book four theoretical approaches to studying leadership will be described: the great man theory, the trait theory, the group theory, and the situational theory.

### GREAT MAN THEORY

The *"great man" theory of leadership* is based on the notion that leaders are a product of their times; that is, individuals become leaders because of certain historical events that lead to or provide a platform for their leadership. Certainly, we can point to many such individuals in the past who have assumed leadership roles, changing or altering the course of history, such as Abraham Lincoln, Martin Luther King, Jr., Henry Ford, and others. In the recreation and leisure service field, those individuals whom we credit with great influence upon the course of history relative to our profession include such individuals as Jane Addams, Frederick Law Olmsted, Luther Gulick, Joseph Lee, Stephen Mather, and John Muir.

Drawing on the work of Eugene E. Jennings, the individual who coined the term great man theory, Sessoms and Stephenson have described different categories of "great men." We have adapted these as follows."[1]

*Princes.* Individuals who have a great drive for power fall into this particular category. This individual uses power to develop his or her base of influence or stature. Certainly history has a number of individuals who have sought power for their own self-aggrandizement. For example, think of Hitler.

*Heroes.* Often there are individuals in history who distinguish themselves because of their insight and sincerity and "are followed, admired and obeyed almost to a point of worship."[2] Modern heroes in American culture include such individuals as John Glenn, former astronaut and a U.S. Senator. These individuals have "the right stuff."

*Democratic Hero.* The democratic hero is the individual who through the democratic process emerges as the leader of a nation or state. The leader in this role would be affirmed by the voting members of society and draw his or her power from the endorsement received through this process.

*Great Average Person.* The great average person is like the hero, although solely the product of a democratic culture on the premise that a democracy breeds a "special" kind of person. This person is an individual who actively participates in the affairs of his or her and others' lives and as a result occupies a leadership role.

*Receptive Person.* According to this classification, leadership is often a product of the interaction of the individual and the situation. A person distinguishes himself or herself as a leader when he or she is "in the right place at the right time" and takes advantage of opportunity presented and has the skills needed at that time and place in history. A great example of this type of leadership was shown in Eugene McCarthy's candidacy for president, based on an anti-Vietnam War platform.

*Eventful Person.* The eventful person exerts leadership and changes history as a result of the "type" of person he or she is, for example, an individual of character acting in a way that he or she sees as right. As a result of this type of leadership, history continues on a course different from the one it would have taken had it not been for this leader's intervention. A good example of this type of leader is Anwar Sadat.

*Nietzsche's Superman.* An individual who is self-directed, using power to seek freedom of action and thought, is characteristic of the superman leader. This is an individual who possesses the ability to overcome the constraints imposed by society's institutions. Nietzsche believed that this type of individual would be able to develop to the utmost of his or her capabilities.

*The Superior Person.* The superior person model suggests that leadership is based on a sense of self-worth and self-respect. The superior person bases his or her accomplishments purely on the force of will. The superior person model also suggests that leaders must not be too different from followers, as at times they must be pre-

[1]H. Douglas Sessoms and Jack L. Stevenson, *Leadership and Group Dynamics in Recreation Services* (Boston: Allyn & Bacon, 1981), pp. 23–26.
[2]Ibid., p. 24.

pared to assume the role of the follower as well as of leadership.

The great man theory of leadership is an interesting approach, although its validity can be questioned. There is a strong interest in the personalities of individuals and their leadership successes. How did John D. Rockefeller create a corporate giant from a few oil wells? How did General George Patton defeat the Germans in North Africa? How was Martin Luther King, Jr., able to rally Americans, black and white, to the cause of civil rights? There is no denying that many individuals as leaders have been responsible for dramatic changes in society. However, there is no way of determining whether or not these changes can be solely attributed to these individuals. The great man theory is based on the assumption that certain individuals are born with certain traits that would allow them to occupy leadership roles at any time in history. This may not be the case, however.

## THE TRAIT THEORY

The *trait theory of leadership* is based on the assumption that there are certain unique personality characteristics or individual traits that make an individual a leader. The great man theory of leadership provided the stimulus for this theory. Because the great man theory suggested that individual leaders were born and not made, a great deal of time and energy has been spent trying to identify and isolate those traits that are possessed by leaders. Numerous research studies have been done concluding that leaders are more intelligent, self-confident, and so on. However, there is no sustaining research evidence to suggest that certain traits—or a group of traits—will presuppose effective leadership.

The usefulness of the trait approach to leadership is its focus on traits that, although they may not presuppose successful leadership, may well point the way. Some of the traits that appear to be related to effective leadership are the following.

*Intelligence.* A leader's ability to think analytically, creatively, and with reason is a reflection of intellectual prowess and, often, of leadership ability.

*Desire for Achievement.* Effective leaders have a desire for achievement. This means that they pursue success and have a strong motivational drive to reach goals.

*Decisiveness.* The ability to make decisions appears to be a trait of effective leaders. Decisiveness is related to the ability to solve group problems in a competent and creative manner.

*Maturity.* Effective leaders tend to be individuals who are responsible and dependable and who have the ability to act in independent ways. They also usually have a long-term time perspective. In addition, mature individuals often have broad interests and a sense of self-awareness and control.

*Confidence.* Effective leaders usually possess a large degree of confidence in their ability to work with others to achieve goals. The more effective leaders demonstrate a "quiet" confidence.

*The Ability to Work with Others.* The ability to relate to and work with other individuals and group members is an important trait of effective leaders. This is because the leader who wants to accomplish goals must have the cooperation and support of others. The more effective leader is also able to inspire others.

*Initiative.* Effective leaders have the ability to act independently. We often refer to this as the leader's ability to act as a self-starter.

*Flexibility.* The ability to adapt to different individuals or different situations or both is another important trait of effective leadership.

Although the trait theory of leadership provides a number of interesting concepts for consideration, there is no substantial research evidence that determines whether one trait or a combination of traits is responsible for successful leadership.

## GROUP THEORY

Another approach to leadership is known as the *group theory*. This approach draws its impetus from the idea that there is an interaction between group members and their leader that affects the leadership role. Basically, the leader is seen as an individual who fulfills a role expectation and assists the group in achieving its goals. Because of this reciprocal arrangement, the leader is provided with certain status and rewards while the group develops a sense of satisfaction from achieving its desired ends. The group theory of leadership suggests that the process between a leader and group members is a two-way process of influence.

The group theory of leadership is built primarily on the work of Homans's exchange theory.[3] His theory suggests that there are rewards and costs associated with the interaction between the leader and the group. In order for a leader to be identified as such by a group or before the leader assumes the responsibility of leadership or both, the rewards to both parties must be greater than the cost. Rewards that result from the exchange process must satisfy the needs of both the leader and the group.

Homans suggests that there are three factors that are directly related to one another in the establishment of the exchange process.[4] They are these.

*Activities.* Activities can be thought of as common tasks in which people participate. Leaders and group members share in the achievement of tasks.

*Interactions.* Interaction is communication that takes place within a group. Interaction can be thought of as a process whereby individuals reach goals, resolve conflicts, and coordinate the work of the group.

*Sentiments.* The level of attraction of individuals for one another—how they "feel" about each other or the emotional bonding between individuals or both—can be thought of as sentiments.

These three elements are interrelated. The more that individuals share activities, the more likely they are to interact. In addition, the more interaction there is, the greater is the social or emotional bonding between individuals. The same can be said with respect to interaction: the greater the interaction, the greater is the likelihood of shared activities and emotional bonding. Lastly, the same can be said for sentiments: The greater the level of social and emotional attraction between individuals, the greater the likelihood that they will share activities and interact with one another. This explanation is used to define group formulation. Usually groups that are involved in all three of these activities are strong viable units.

Although this approach to viewing leadership—the exchange process—provides a rationale for the emergence of leaders within groups, it does not take into account the importance of other factors that affect the emergence of a leader such as traits or the needs of the situation. Nonetheless, it does support the idea that group satisfaction may be related to group effectiveness and may be tied to the support of the group to a leader.

## SITUATIONAL THEORIES

The *situational theory of leadership* is based on the premise that situational variables determine the use of a particular style of leadership. According to this theory, the successful leader will make an evaluation of various situational variables such as the goals of the group members, the methods used to achieve goals, the capabilities of group members, and perhaps other forces such as the economic, political, social, and cultural milieus when selecting a

---

[3]George C. Homans, *The Human Group* (New York: Harcourt, Brace and World, 1950), pp. 43–44.
[4]Ibid.

leadership style. Again, the situational theorist would suggest that there is no "one best" leadership style that should be employed in all situations. In certain situations, an autocratic leadership style might be useful whereas, in other situations, a democratic style might be more effective.

The situational approach to leadership can be used in applying leadership styles to the product life cycle concept. The product life cycle concept suggests that products and services have a life just like humans. The same might be said of groups and organizations.

The life cycle stages are initiation, development, growth, maturity, and decline. The role of the leader can change dramatically as a group or organization moves through different stages in the life cycle. The situational approach to leadership would then be particularly appropriate as the group or organization moves through the various stages of the life cycle. For example, in the initiation stage, the leader would be more of an originator-inventor. Table 2.1 presents the relationship of various stages in the life cycle with basic leadership skills.

**TABLE 2.1**    Relationship of Basic Leadership Skill and Capability to the Stages of the Life Cycle

| Life Cycle Stage | Leadership Roles | Leadership Qualities | Basic Skill Requirement |
|---|---|---|---|
| 1. Initiation | Originator-inventor | Innovation<br>Independence<br>Self-confidence<br>Risk-taking<br>Vision | Perceptual and conceptual |
| 2. Development | Planner-organizer | Investigation<br>Planning<br>Evaluation<br>Judging<br>Organizing<br>Negotiation<br>Decision making | Analytical,<br>external-behavioral<br>interpersonal relations |
| 3. Growth | Developer-implementer | Delegation<br>Motivation<br>Supervision<br>Achievement<br>Decision making | Budgeting, scheduling,<br>controlling, intergroup<br>relations |
| 4. Maturity | Administrator-operator | Maintenance<br>Coordinating<br>Efficiency seeker | Internal intergroup<br>relations |
| 5. Decline | Successor-reorganizer | Type A<br>Innovative<br>Change agent<br>Risk-taking vision<br>Strategic<br>Planner | Perceptual and<br>conceptual, external<br>interpersonal relations |
| | | Type B<br>Efficiency<br>Seeking<br>Change agent | Budgeting, controlling,<br>internal intergroup<br>relations |

*Source:*   Carroll V. Kroeger, "Managerial Development in the Small Firm." © 1974 by the Regents of the University of California. Reprinted from *California Management Review*, Vol. XVII, No. 1, p. 43, by permission.

# LEADERSHIP STUDIES, STYLES, AND MODELS

Research in the area of leadership can be traced to the now classical study reported by Lewin, Lippitt, and White in 1939 in the *Journal of Social Psychology*. Since this study, there have been numerous attempts to investigate leadership. In this section of the chapter, the authors have identified eleven different studies or style models related to leadership. Discussed are the Lewin, Lippitt, and White studies; the Ohio State studies; the managerial grid; the University of Michigan studies; Likert's system of management; Tannenbaum and Schmidt's leadership continuum; situational models of leadership; Fiedler's contingency model of leadership effectiveness; the path-goal theory of leadership; Reddin's 3-D theory of management effectiveness; and the tri-dimensional leader effectiveness model. Each of these studies or models presents a unique conceptualization. Some have built on the work of others, but all are significant.

## THE LEWIN, LIPPITT, AND WHITE STUDIES

The Lewin, Lippitt, and White studies are especially important and interesting to the recreation and leisure service profession because they dealt with recreation leaders who worked with boys' hobby clubs.[5] Basically, Lewin, Lippitt, and White engaged in a number of experiments to determine the impact of various leadership styles on the behavior of ten-year-old children. Their first experiment viewed various leadership styles over a three-month period of time with a group involved in the activity of theatrical mask making. Their second set of experiments, which were considerably more extensive than their first, also viewed various leadership styles in clubs organized on a voluntary basis with a broader se-

[5]Kurt Lewin, Ronald Lippitt, and Ralph K. White, "Patterns of Aggressive Behavior in Experimentally Created Social Climates," *Journal of Social Psychology*, May 1939, pp. 271–276.

lection of activities, including mask making, mural painting, soap carving, and model airplane construction.

A key element in the Lewin, Lippitt, and White studies was the designation of different classifications of leader behavior. In the first study, two leadership styles, *democratic* and *authoritarian*, were identified and studied. In the second set of studies, a third leadership style—*laissez-faire*—was added. These leadership styles can be defined as follows.

*Democratic Leadership Style.* A democratic leadership style implies that individual group members are consulted in the decision-making process by the leader. The role of the leader is to suggest alternatives and establish a work path that the group can follow and to assist and encourage individuals. Objectivity and fair-mindedness in providing praise as well as criticism of the efforts of group members is essential. The democratic leadership style does not force group members to work with other individuals within the group whom they don't want to work with.

*Authoritarian Leadership Style.* Activities of the group are tightly controlled by the leader using an authoritarian leadership style. All policies and interpretation of policies are spelled out by the leader. This might include the specific work path a group may follow as well as the techniques that may be employed. The leader may dictate which group members will work together. Often the authoritarian leader will remain aloof from active participation, establishing an impersonal demeanor as opposed to a friendly or hostile one. The leader in the picture on the following page is being specific in the directions that are being given to these young athletes. He appears to be employing an authoritarian leadership style.

*Laissez-faire Leadership Style.* The laissez-faire leadership style is characterized by a lack of control or structure. In other words,

This leader is ''spelling out'' to participants what must be done, exemplifying an authoritarian style of leadership.

the leader gives the group complete freedom in decision making. The leader might supply various materials to the group or offer to supply additional information; however, no attempt is made to influence the behavior of the group directly. Nor is there an attempt to affect selection of projects or the methods of work used by the group to complete activities. Furthermore, only limited attempts are made to comment on the progress of the group.

In the first study conducted by Lewin, Lippitt, and White, one group of children under autocratic leadership was compared with a group under democratic leadership. The second study compared four groups of boys who successively experienced all three types of leadership—democratic, autocratic, and laissez-faire. In the first study there was a higher amount of hostility when autocratic leadership was present than when democratic leadership was present. The same was the case with aggression between boys. In the second study, the same aggressiveness pattern was found with one group; however, other groups directed by autocratic leaders showed an apathetic pattern of behavior. In the study, boys reported liking their democratic leader when compared with their autocratic leader. They also reported liking their laissez-faire leader.

The major contribution of the Lewin, Lippitt, and White studies was the description of leadership styles. These have served as a basis for the teaching and training of recreation and leisure service leaders and, as well, have served as a basis for other research projects and studies. They represent a useful conceptualization that pioneered research in the leadership area.

## THE OHIO STATE STUDIES

The next important set of studies on leadership was initiated in 1945 by the Bureau of Business Research at Ohio State University.[6] These individuals established a number of in-depth research studies focusing on leader behavior. A group of researchers from such disciplines as psychology, sociology, and economics created and developed an instrument that could be used to analyze leadership behavior in a variety of situations and settings. The testing instrument was known as the Leader Behavior Description Questionnaire (LBDQ). This questionnaire was designed to help the researchers determine how leaders in diverse settings carry out their work. The researchers studied armed forces personnel, civil servants, educators, students, individ-

[6]Ralph M. Stogdill and Alvin E. Coons, *Leader Behavior: Its Description and Measurement* (Columbus, Ohio: Bureau of Business Research, Ohio State University, 1957).

uals involved in the manufacturing process, and others.

Two key facets of leadership behavior were identified by the Ohio State studies as *initiating structure* and *consideration*. These two important dimensions of leadership behavior can be defined as follows.

*Initiating Structure.* Initiating structure refers to the way in which the leader establishes and defines group goals as well as the resulting group structure and role expectations. The initiating structure might include such factors as the organizational structure, channels of communication, and methods used to carry out various tasks undertaken by the group. We often think of initiating structure as the task or production orientation of the leader.

*Consideration.* Consideration can be thought of as the relationship that develops between the leader and his or her subordinates with regard to the latter's ideas and feelings. For example, strong consideration would be evident in groups where leaders and subordinates had a high degree of mutual trust, respect, friendliness, and fellowship. We often think of the consideration factor as the "people orientation" of the leader.

Both initiating structure and consideration were viewed by the researchers in this project as separate facets of leadership behavior; however, they suggested that by combining consideration and initiating structure, one could account for the total common-factor variance contributing to an individual's leadership behavior. For example, Halpin and Weiner, Ohio State researchers, found in one of the first studies conducted that 83.2 percent of the common-factor variance contributing to these individuals' leadership behavior could be explained by the two factors of consideration and initiating structure.[7] Consideration accounted for 49.6 percent of the common-factor variance; and initiating structure, for 33.6 percent of the common-factor variance.

The value of the Ohio State studies was the discovery that the two elements of leadership behavior—consideration and initiating structure—could be combined. Prior to these studies, an individual's leadership style was viewed in only one dimension or direction. It was thought that an individual was either task oriented—and perhaps authoritarian—or people oriented—and perhaps democratic. These studies demonstrated that the combination of these two variables was important in certain leadership situations. The findings of the Ohio State studies have influenced the development of leadership and management style theories and models.

Figure 2.1 presents a leadership style model that portrays the two dimensions identified in the Ohio State studies. In this model, *consideration* has been defined as one's human relations orientation, and *initiating structure* has been defined as one's task orientation. By presenting the various options, ranging from low to high, along a continuum and placing one orientation vertically and the other horizontally, we have four (4) possible combinations of leadership styles. A leader could use one of the four styles presented. A high task orientation and a high human relations orientation would suggest that the leader is concerned with both the needs of the participant and the accomplishment of group goals or the completion of procedures and methods associated with these goals. An individual focusing only on the task to be completed within the group would have a high task orientation and a low human relations orientation. On the other hand, a leader who was primarily concerned with the interaction of himself or herself with group members and not the goals of the group would have a high human relations orientation and a low task orientation. Finally, leaders who were somewhat passive and uninvolved might be viewed as having a low human relations and low task orientation.

[7]Ibid., pp. 39–51.

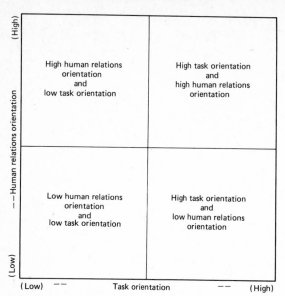

**FIGURE 2.1**   A leadership style model portraying the Ohio State studies' dimensions.

The Ohio State studies did not suggest which of these styles were most appropriate, only that differing conditions and environments produced a different mix of the two dimensions of leadership.

***The New Managerial Grid.***®   A widely recognized leadership style model was developed and perfected in the 1950s by Robert R. Blake and Jane S. Mouton. Their model, called "The New Managerial Grid," includes two dimensions: concern for production and concern for people.[8] Concern for production, according to these individuals, involves an orientation toward the production of products or services and focuses on quantitative measures such as the volume of a sales, and so on. Concern for people involves the establishment of trust relationships, friendship, and concern for the well-being and worth of other individuals.

As indicated in Figure 2.2, The New Managerial Grid places the two variables—con-

cern for people and concern for production— along two axes. A concern for production is represented by the horizontal axis, and the concern for people is represented by the vertical axis. A nine-point scale is used to characterize the level of intensity of commitment of either of the two variables. The number 9 would represent a high concern whereas the number 1 would represent a low concern. Using this method, Blake and Mouton have identified five different managerial leadership styles.[9]

*1,1 Impoverished Management.*   The impoverished managerial leadership style is characterized by low concern for production and a low concern for people. The leader using this particular managerial leadership style would have little influence over other individuals. Furthermore, the leader would probably be operating as a functionary, passing off responsibility to others for decision making and task completion. This person would be primarily interested in maintaining a low profile of noninvolvement.

*1,9 Country Club Management.*   A high concern for people and a low concern for production is the general orientation of the 1,9 managerial leadership style. This leader is concerned with other individuals and the establishment of a friendly, comfortable work environment. The needs of people come first in this particular style. The leader would act more as an encourager than as an enforcer and would be more concerned with maintaining a harmonious environment than with meeting task assignments.

*9,1 Authority-Obedience.*   The 9,1 orientation to managerial leadership style finds the leader with a high concern for production and a low concern for people. A leader using this managerial style is often viewed as a task master. In other words, this type of

[8]Robert R. Blake and Jane S. Mouton, *The New Managerial Grid* (Houston: Gulf Publishing Co., 1978), p. 11.

[9]Ibid.

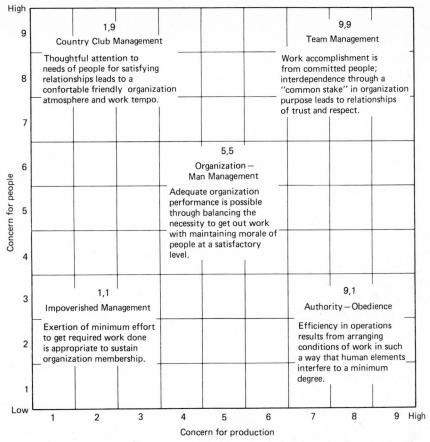

High

9 — 1,9

Country Club Management

Thoughtful attention to
needs of people for satisfying
relationships leads to a
confortable friendly organization
atmosphere and work tempo.

9,9

Team Management

Work accomplishment is
from committed people;
interdependence through a
"common stake" in organization
purpose leads to relationships
of trust and respect.

5,5

Organization—
Man Management

Adequate organization
performance is possible
through balancing the
necessity to get out work
with maintaining morale of
people at a satisfactory
level.

1,1

Impoverished Management

Exertion of minimum effort
to get required work done
is appropriate to sustain
organization membership.

9,1

Authority—Obedience

Efficiency in operations
results from arranging
conditions of work in such
a way that human elements
interfere to a minimum
degree.

Concern for people

Low

Concern for production

**FIGURE 2.2**    Black and Mouton's management grid. (*Source*: The Managerial Grid
Figure from *The New Managerial Grid*, by Robert R. Blake and Jane Srygley Mouton
[Houston: Gulf Publishing Company, Copyright © 1978], p. 11. Reproduced by
permission.)

leader is primarily concerned with achieving the goals of the organization or completing a task. In order to accomplish this, this leader may overlook or minimize employee needs and concerns. Often the leader's authority, based on his or her position in the organization's hierarchical structure, is used to control individuals in order to accomplish group or organizational goals.

*5,5 Organization-Man Management* .This is a middle-of-the-road style of managerial leadership. The leader tries to balance the needs of the organization with the needs of individuals. Basically, the leader in this sit-

uation compromises both the goals of the organization and the goals of employees.

*9,9 Team Management.* Team management is accomplished by creating relationships of trust, openness, and respect for one another through a mutual commitment to the goals of the organization and to one another. As Blake and Mouton suggest in Figure 2.2, this is facilitated by creating a sense of interdependence and a common stake in the work of the group.

Blake and Mouton suggest that the first four managerial leadership styles just described do not represent effective approaches. They feel that effective managerial leadership occurs when an individual is using the 9,9 team management style. They argue that a leader should have high standards and should seek a high level of performance from subordinates. They feel that when subordinates have an opportunity to be involved in the planning and decision-making activities within a group or organization or have developed a high level of trust and confidence between each other, they are most productive. Thus, the effective leader is one who is equally concerned with the needs of people and the work of the organization or group.

### THE UNIVERSITY OF MICHIGAN STUDIES

In 1947, the University of Michigan Survey Research Center also began to investigate leadership behavior.[10] Funded by the Office of Naval Research, this research group was interested in determining the factors that contribute to the productivity of the group and to the satisfaction that is derived by group members participating in group activities. Attempting to overcome some of the methodological difficulties that were encountered in other research efforts, the Michigan group established systematic measures of the perceptions of the individuals studied. This was extremely important, for they were looking at such factors as morale, supervision, and productivity.

The Michigan study team postulated that leadership behavior could be plotted on a continuum. At one end of the continuum would be the leader whose behavior is participant centered. This leader would be interested in the feelings, ideas, opinions, and values of individual group members. Following this line of thinking, the leader would have primarily a "people-oriented" leadership style at this end

of the continuum. At the other end of the continuum would be the leader whose behavior is production oriented. The individual possessing this style would be task oriented and concerned primarily with achieving the goals of the group as a whole. This type of leader would be more concerned with arranging conditions, methods, and procedures used by the group in order to accomplish group goals.

Two findings emerged from the Michigan studies. First, it was found that individual satisfaction in a work situation was contingent upon the presence of a participant or employee-centered leader. The study also suggested that satisfaction was not related to productivity. These studies provide another perception of leadership behavior. They are often used to support the use of a people-oriented leadership style.

***Rensis Likert's System of Management.*** The Michigan studies provided the basis for the development of Rensis Likert's four basic styles of leadership behavior in his "systems of management."[11] Likert has suggested that leadership styles exist on a continuum ranging from autocratic to participative. Four basic styles that appear on this continuum, according to Likert, are exploitive autocratic, benevolent autocratic, consultative, and participative team. Although these were designed for use in the management of organizations, they can be adopted for use by recreation and leisure service leaders in group situations.

*Exploitive Autocratic.* The recreation and leisure service leader using this style of leadership makes all the decisions for the group. In other words, the leader decides what is to be accomplished by the group and also when, where, and how it is to be accomplished. There is a low degree of trust and mutual confidence between the leader and the members of the group when

[10]Daniel Katz, Nathanial Maccoby, and Nancy C. Morse, *Productivity, Supervision, and Morale in an Office Situation* (Ann Arbor, Mich.: Survey Research Center, University of Michigan, 1950).

[11]Rensis Likert, *The Human Organization* (New York: McGraw-Hill, 1967).

this system is employed. Basically, the leader feels that his or her way of doing things is most appropriate and does not trust others to participate in the planning and decision-making process.

*Benevolent Autocrat.* The leader using the benevolent autocrat approach to leadership behavior, still makes all the decisions for the group, but allows some variances in the performance of group tasks, as long as individuals abide by established policies and procedures. This is a paternalistic approach to leadership and results in a relatively low level of trust and confidence between leaders and group members.

*Consultative.* The consultative approach to leadership finds the leader seeking input from group members and allowing them to assist in the decision-making process. However, the leader maintains control over the final decision-making prerogatives. In situations where this type of leadership style is employed, individuals feel free to offer their ideas, suggestions, and opinions concerning both the goals of the group and the methods used to achieve them. This style creates opportunities for increased trust and confidence for the leader and his or her subordinates.

*Participative Team.* This is a democratic approach to leading groups. It suggests that there is a need for the full involvement of group members in the planning and decision-making process. Individuals feel free to offer their ideas and suggestions, and there is a high degree of confidence and trust between the leader and group members. The leader functions as a facilitator, linking the group with other groups and environmental components.

Likert suggests that the participative team approach to leadership is the most effective. Although Likert's systems approach to leadership behavior has not been investigated within a recreation and leisure service setting, it is obvious that the voluntary nature of the involvement of individuals in recreation and leisure-oriented groups would tend to be complemented by the participative group style of leadership behavior. Likert's systems concept can be criticized from the standpoint that not all leadership situations may require a high degree of confidence, trust, and shared decision making in order to achieve intended goals.

*Tannenbaum and Schmidt's Leadership Continuum.* Another leadership model that dichotomizes leadership style along a continuum in terms of its orientation is the Tannenbaum and Schmidt leadership continuum.[12] As indicated in Figure 2.3, the leader has a number of options regarding decision making and the way in which individuals are allowed to work within a group situation. At one end of the continuum, the leader is authoritarian and task oriented. Great emphasis is placed upon use of authority. The leader at this end of the continuum would make decisions by himself or herself and announce these decisions to the group. At the other end of the continuum, the leader is democratic and human-relations oriented. This type of leader would allow individuals in the group environment to have a great deal of freedom in carrying out their roles and assignments. This leader would also permit individuals to operate freely within certain limits established by the leader and the group.

Along the Tannenbaum and Schmidt leadership continuum, there are also other options available to the leader. These options consist of different combinations of freedom for group members and use of authority by the leader. For example, at the midpoint of the continuum, the leader presents tentative decisions that are subject to change once the

[12]Robert Tannenbaum and Warren H. Schmidt, ''How to Choose a Leadership Pattern,'' *Harvard Business Review*, May-June 1973, p. 166.

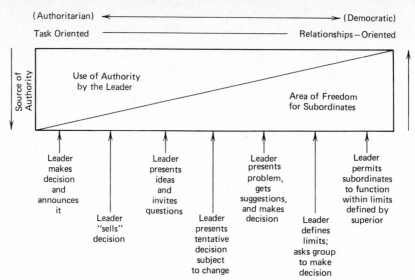

**FIGURE 2.3**    Tannenbaum and Schmidt continuum of leadership behavior. (*Source*: Reprinted by permission of the Harvard Business Review. An exhibit from ''How to Choose a Leadership Pattern'' by Robert Tannenbaum and Warren H. Schmidt [March/April, 1958]. Copyright © 1958 by the President and Fellows of Harvard College; all rights reserved.)

group has reviewed the issue or situation. Tannenbaum and Schmidt suggest that a leader should carefully select an appropriate style. Such factors as the leader's skills, knowledge, and experience should be taken into consideration, as well as the skills, knowledge, and experience of group members. Furthermore, they point out that each situation will be different. In certain situations, the time constraints may require rapid decision making whereas in other situations a more consultative, participative style of leadership may be engaged. Certainly the nature of the task to be performed by the group would also have an impact on the appropriateness of different leadership styles.

Tannenbaum and Schmidt suggest that an open, subordinate-centered leadership style that emphasizes group participation can be employed when certain conditions are present. They suggest, for example, that when individuals have the skills, knowledge, and background to engage in the decision-making process, they should be allowed to do so. Also they suggest that a participative style of leadership can be employed effectively when working with individuals seeking freedom, autonomy, and independence of action within the group situation. Tannenbaum and Schmidt point out, however, that a more open participative style of leadership functions well only when individuals are committed to and understand the goals of the group.

These authors do not suggest that the leadership style at one end of the continuum is more appropriate than the leadership style at the opposite end. They stress the importance of situational leadership, basing the choice of a style of leadership from the various points along the continuum upon the needs of each situation. If, as indicated in the preceding paragraph, individuals are highly committed to a group and are seeking involvement and perhaps independence in decision making, the leader might want to choose the more democratic style of leadership. On the other hand, if it appears that there is a need for greater control, the leader might want to choose a more autocratic style of leadership. There is no "one best" style of leadership according to Tannenbaum and Schmidt. They recommend that the leader remain flexible and open to the use of different styles in different situations.

## SITUATIONAL MODELS OF LEADERSHIP

Although previous research investigation provided insight into the leadership of individuals, many of the theories did not provide an adequate explanation for the situational factors influencing leadership. Such variables as the expectations of those being led, the external factors influencing the work of a group, the opportunities for interaction between the leader and group members, and the type of task undertaken by a group, focus attention on the need for a situational model to explain leadership behavior. A little over a decade ago Fred Fiedler presented a model for leadership effectiveness that took into consideration a variety of situational factors. He called this paradigm a *"contingency" model of leadership effectiveness.*[13]

***Fiedler's Contingency Model of Leadership Effectiveness.*** Fiedler's model purports that there is no "one best" leadership style. Like the Tannenbaum and Schmidt continuum, this model suggests that a particular individual's leadership style must be situationally determined. This means that in order to be effective, a leader must use a leadership style that complements the needs of a given situation. The heart of the contingency model has to do with the degree of favorableness of the situation to the leader. Favorableness is determined by three basic factors.

*Leader-Member Relations.* This factor influencing favorableness toward the leader can be thought of as the extent to which the

[13]Fred Fiedler, *A Theory of Leadership Effectiveness* (New York: McGraw-Hill, 1967).

leader feels that he or she is accepted by group members. Leader-member relations is the most important variable in the determination of favorableness of a situation to the leader. The potential relationships between the leader and group members may be dichotomized to illustrate this point. For example, the relationship may be characterized by hostility or congeniality, openness or withdrawal, trust or suspicion.

*Task Structure.* Task structure can be thought of as the extent to which role expectations are clearly defined within the group. In certain situations, the roles that individuals occupy are highly structured and well defined with clarity and precision. In other situations, tasks are not so clearly defined and, as such, create role ambiguity and uncertainty as to the way in which activities within the group are to be carried out. Task structure not only refers to the role expectations of the group, but also—and perhaps more importantly—to its goals.

*Position Power.* Position power refers to the degree of influence that a leader has. As previously indicated, the leader's power can be drawn from a number of sources, including the authority he or she is granted as a result of official sanction. Other sources of power are the influence of the leader upon the group through the use of rewards and punishments, through his or her attractiveness to the group, and through his or her expertise and knowledge.

According to Fiedler, the concept of favorableness can be viewed as existing on a continuum. At one end of the continuum are situations highly favorable to the leader. At the other end of the continuum are situations highly unfavorable to the leader. Situations that are characterized by good leader-member relations and a well-defined structure and task and where the position of power of the leader is well established or high—these situations are characterized by Fiedler as being highly favorable to the leader. On the other hand, situations at the other end of the continuum, characterized by poor leader-member relations and lack of a well-defined structured task and where the position power of the leader was not established—these situations are characterized by Fiedler as being highly unfavorable to the leader. Along the continuum, there could be varying degrees of favorableness, including an intermediate degree of favorableness of a given situation to the leader. This concept is illustrated in Figure 2.4.

Fiedler was interested in determining which leadership styles would be most effective at various points on his continuum. In order to measure leadership style, he developed an operational procedure to calculate how individuals were perceived in the group environment by their leader. The first part of this procedure attempted to determine the leader's perception of his or her least preferred co-

worker (LPC) and most preferred co-worker (MPC). Measurement of how leaders perceive co-workers was based on the assumption that this perception would affect their relationship with others and, hence, their effectiveness. The second procedure was a measurement Fiedler called "the assumed similarity between opposites (ASO) score." This was determined by calculating the difference between LPC and MPC scores. These two procedures were related to two leadership styles identified by Fiedler. They are these.

*Human Relations or "Lenient" Style.* The leader using the human relations leadership style tends to be permissive. Leaders who do not perceive a large degree of difference between the most preferred co-worker and the least preferred co-worker are likely to fall within this category of leadership style.

*Task-Directed or "Hard-Nosed" Style.* The leader using the task-directed style of leadership is task oriented and controlling.

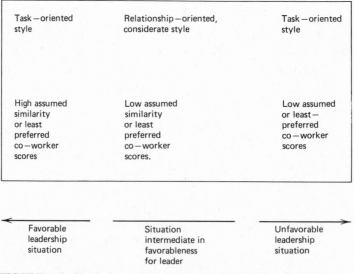

**FIGURE 2.4**   Fiedler's contingency model of leadership. (*Source*: From Fred E. Fiedler, *A Theory of Leadership Effectiveness* [New York: McGraw-Hill Co., 1967, p. 14].)

Leaders who perceive a large degree of difference between the most preferred co-worker and the least preferred co-worker are likely to fall within the task-directed category of leadership style.

Empirically based research evidence that was collected by Fiedler indicates that the task-directed or "hard-nosed" style of leadership is more successful in situations that are very favorable and very unfavorable to the leader. In other words, in situations where the leader has control over all the alternatives and has established good relationships with group members, a task-directed style is most effective. In addition, in situations where the leader "needs to be in control of the situation" because the task to be accomplished is poorly defined or the leader-member relations are poor or both, a task-directed style is more effective. Finally, Fiedler suggests that in situations of intermediate or moderate favorableness or unfavorableness, the human relations or lenient style of leadership is most successful.

Interestingly, Fieldler also maintains that it may be better to structure a situation to fit a leader's style than use the traditional approach of training the leader to adapt to his or her environment. This idea has implications for recreation and leisure service leadership in that certain individuals may be better suited to lead in certain situations. It is apparent that not every recreation leader may be good at instructing, lecturing, coaching, counseling, and leading games and activities. Therefore, it may be more appropriate to match the leader with the situation for which he or she is best qualified. Although this may seem obvious, it is surprising how seldom this occurs.

**Path-Goal Theory of Leadership.**    The path-goal approach to leadership attempts to combine various elements of motivation with leadership. Basically the path-goal theory of leadership is concerned with the assessment of the satisfaction, motivation, and performance of group members and the relationship of these elements to leadership style.[14] This theory suggests that a leader's behavior may be tied to group members' immediate or long-term satisfaction. In turn, group members are motivated when their satisfaction triggers performance. There are a variety of things that a leader can do to affect the satisfaction of group members. For example, the leader can clarify expectations, organize a reward system, provide recogniton, give praise, eliminate barriers, and, in general, assist individuals in meeting their own needs while at the same time satisfying group goals.

The path-goal theory of leadership suggests that different leadership styles should be used in different situations. The role of the leader is to be aware of and use the various styles appropriately to affect employee motivation, satisfaction, and productivity. A leader may use one or more of the styles presented in this theory, depending upon the situation. These styles can be summarized as follows.

*Directive Leadership.* This approach to leadership is one that is very authoritarian and task oriented. No attempt is made to involve individuals in the decision-making process. Essentially, the leader tells group members what to do and how to do it. This style of leadership is dependent on role clarity as well as on an acceptance of the expectations of the leader by group members.

*Supportive Leadership.* Supportive leadership relates to the needs, interests, and desires of group members. The leader using this style of leadership is concerned with establishing a positive, supportive relationship with group members. The leader is open and responsive to suggestions made by group members.

[14]Robert J. House and Terence R. Mitchell, "Path-Goal Theory of Leadership," *Journal of Contemporary Business*, Autumn 1974, pp. 81–97.

*Participative Leadership.* This style of leadership is an open one, wherein the leader is responsive to opinions, ideas, and suggestions of group members. The leader, however, retains the final authority to make decisions. This type of open style allows for individuals to air their concerns while at the same time providing for the maintenance of a control structure.

*Achievement-Oriented Leadership.* In this style of leadership, the role of the leader is to challenge group members. This might involve the establishment of high standards or the expectation of high output. The leader, once standards and expectations have been formed, encourages group members to attain the goals. Instilling confidence in group members is an important function of the leader using this leadership style.

The role of the leader using the path-goal theory of leadership can be thought of simply as employing the appropriate style to "clear the path" for group members to achieve their own goals as well as the goals of the group or organization. Thus, this leadership style is used to remove barriers, resulting in improvement of satisfaction, in turn resulting in greater motivation and performance.

There are a number of research findings that support this model.[15] It has been found, for example, that a directive leadership style results in a higher level of satisfaction when group members are engaged in tasks that are poorly defined. Conversely, a directive leadership style does not produce a great deal of satisfaction in situations where tasks are clear and well defined. Supportive leadership creates the greatest amount of satisfaction when individuals are dealing with tasks that produce a sense of frustration. In the recreation and leisure service field, for example, supportive leadership is often extremely es-

sential when an individual is learning a new skill that is frustrating and requires time and energy to master. Support given to this individual by the recreation and leisure service leader is necessary to ensure a satisfying leisure experience. Participatory leadership is viewed as producing a higher level of satisfaction among individuals who are involved in "nonrepetitive ego-involving" tasks.[16] Many leisure experiences are nonrepetitive and do involve ego involvement on the part of the participant. Therefore, the participatory leadership style is well suited to the recreation and leisure service environment. Finally, achievement-oriented leadership has been found to produce a greater sense of satisfaction in situations where individuals are performing ambiguous, nonrepetitive tasks.[17]

***Reddin's 3-D Theory of Management Effectiveness.*** Reddin's theory of leadership also suggests that the dictates of a given situation will affect the type of style that can be employed effectively by the leader. William Reddin, professor at the University of New Brunswick, maintains that the major determinant of a leader's leadership style should be the results that are achieved with it and not the type of personality of the leader. Reddin's model is built on the premise that the two essential components of a leadership style are relationship and task orientation. His view of these variables is similar to that depicted in the model presented in Figure 2.1; that is, he believes that an individual's leadership style can be a combination of both the task and relationship orientations. He defines the four cells in Figure 2.1 as follows: Separated (low task-low relationship orientation); Dedicated (high task-low relationship orientation); Related (low task-high relationship orientation); and Integrated (high task-high relationship orientation).

According to the Reddin model, each of

[15]Fred Luthans, *Organizational Behavior*, 2d ed. (New York: McGraw-Hill, 1977), p. 447.

[16]Ibid.
[17]Ibid.

these four styles can be either appropriately or inappropriately applied. Thus, the four basic cells give way to eight different leadership styles. These are defined in the following list.

*Executive.* A leader who is using a high task orientation and a high relationship orientation in a situation where such behavior is appropriate and who is, therefore, more effective; perceived as being a good motivating force who sets high standards, treats everyone somewhat differently, and prefers team management.

*Compromiser.* A leader who is using a high task orientation and a high relations orientation in a situation that requires a high orientation to one or neither and who is, therefore, less effective; perceived as being a poor decision maker, as one who allows various pressures in a situation to influence him or her too much and who is avoiding or minimizing pressures and problems rather than maximizing long-term production.

*Benevolent Autocrat.* A leader who is using a high task orientation and a low relationship orientation in a situation where such behavior is appropriate and who is, therefore, more effective; perceived as knowing what he or she wants and knowing how to get it without creating much resentment.

*Autocrat.* A leader who is using a high task orientation and a low relationship orientation in a situation where such behavior is inappropriate and is, therefore, less effective; perceived as having no confidence in others, as unpleasant, and as interested only in the immediate task.

*Developer.* A leader who is using a high relations orientation and a low task orientation in a situation where such behavior is appropriate and who is, therefore, more effective; perceived as having implicit trust in people and as being primarily concerned with developing them as individuals.

*Missionary.* A leader who is using a high relationship orientation and a low task orientation in a situation where such behavior is inappropriate and who is, therefore, less effective; perceived as being primarily interested in harmony.

*Bureaucrat.* A leader who is using a low task orientation and a low relationship orientation in a situation where such behavior is appropriate and who is, therefore, more effective; perceived as being primarily interested in rules and procedures for their own sake and as wanting to control the situation by their use and as conscientious.

*Deserter.* A leader who is using a low task orientation and a low relationship orientation in a situation where such behavior is inappropriate and who is, therefore, less effective; perceived as uninvolved and passive or negative.[18]

Reddin suggests that a leader must have the ability to "flex" his or her style in order to be effective. Style flex can be thought of as the ability to change one's leadership style according to the needs of a given situation. Reddin suggests that a leader who uses one basic style has a low degree of flexibility and a leader who used multiple approaches has a high degree of style flexibility. He warns that an individual may inappropriately change his or her style. This is called "style drift." Style drift may occur as a well-thought-out act or as a result of inattention to the needs of the situation.

Research in the recreation and leisure service field has been conducted by Edginton, using a diagnostic instrument developed by Reddin, to determine the leadership styles of professionals in the province of Ontario, Canada.[19] The findings regarding the leadership

[18]William J. Reddin, *Managerial Effectiveness* (New York: McGraw-Hill, 1970), pp. 41–43.

[19]Christopher R. Edginton, "A Study of the Relationships Between Management Style and Propensity for Risk Taking Among Leisure Service Personnel," doctoral dissertation, University of Iowa, 1975, p. 77.

style profiles of these professionals are illustrated in Figure 2.5. As can be seen, the distribution of the scores of the 124 respondents resulted in a relatively flat profile, without the emergence of a dominant or supportive leadership style. The highest score recorded, however, was that for the category of "Developer," where the mean score was 9.8. Other scores were as follows: Deserter, 6.1; Missionary, 9.3; Autocrat, 7.5; Compromiser, 8.2.; Bureaucrat, 7.5; Benevolent Autocrat, 8.6; and Executive, 7.4.

With regard to these findings, Reddin has noted that a flat distribution cannot be interpreted with any large degree of certainty. He suggests that leaders with a flat profile are not using a dominant leadership style because a particular type of occupation may not require a particular type of style. On the other hand, he has suggested that leaders with a flat distribution be highly flexible or drifting from one style to another. Nonetheless, the profile

that did emerge would suggest that positions in the recreation and leisure service field require a high degree of relationship orientation.

Interestingly, Reddin has developed a list of 20 indicators for his basic styles of leadership.[20] These indicators help define the role of the leader of a group as related to various leadership styles. The list follows (with Reddin's description of each indicator).

*Separated Leadership Style (Low Task Orientation-Low Relations Orientation)*

- To examine—systematic analysis of materials and documents.
- To measure—measurement or evaluation.
- To administer—following rules and procedures in a deliberate manner.
- To control—overseeing operations, personnel, fiscal resources.
- To maintain—keeping records.

[20]Reddin, op. cit., pp. 94–95.

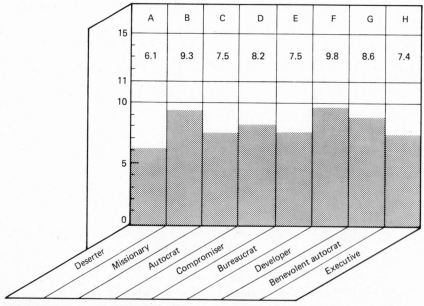

**FIGURE 2.5** Leadership styles of park and recreation professionals. (*Source*: Christopher R. Edginton, "A Study of the Relationships Between Management Style and Propensity for Risk Taking Among Leisure Services Personnel," doctoral dissertation, University of Iowa, 1975, p. 96.)

*Dedicated Leadership Style (High Task Orientation-Low Relationship Orientation)*

- To organize—planning the work of a group; assigning tasks.
- To initiate—starting activities and tasks independently.
- To direct—supervising the work of others; giving commands.
- To complete—to get the task at hand done.
- To evaluate—both individual and group performance.

*Related Leadership Style (Low Task Orientation-High Relationship Orientation)*

- To trust—open and candid communications; confidence in one another.
- To listen—attentive, active listening.
- To accept—genuine acceptance of other ideas, opinions.
- To advise—to provide friendly input.
- To encourage—to support.

*Integrated Leadership Style (High Task Orientation-High Relationship Orientation)*

- To participate—to be involved with others in the decision-making process.
- To interact—to provide interpersonal communication.
- To motivate—to create an environment that stimulates action.
- To integrate—to fuse individual needs and group goals.
- To innovate—to create an open forum for the free expression of ideas and opinions.

This list of indicators provides a synopsis of the different types of behaviors that a leader might exhibit in different situations. In one situation, the recreation leader may be called to provide encouragement in the form of support to individuals. In another situation, the leader may serve to evaluate the performance of participants against a standard. In still another situation, the leader may be involved in the organization of an activity that may require extensive planning, including the assignment of tasks to various group members.

The leader will do more than one of these simultaneously.

***Tri-Dimensional Leader Effectiveness Model.*** Hersey and Blanchard have developed a situational leadership theory called the *tri-dimensional leadership effectiveness model*. This model is represented in Figure 2.6 and uses the elements of the Ohio State studies (human relations orientation and task orientation) as well as the "effectiveness" dimension delineated by Reddin. Hersey and Blanchard suggest that one's leadership style will vary according to two variables. The first variable is the level of maturity of group members. The second variable is the demands of the situation. Basically, they argue that the leader should diagnose both the demands of the situation and the level of maturity of group members in order to determine what leadership style would be most appropriate.

Hersey and Blanchard also suggest that maturity can be viewed as existing on a continuum. Specifically, they suggest that a mature individual has ". . . the capacity to set high but attainable goals, willingness and ability to take responsibility, and education and/or experience . . ."[21] relevant to a given task to be performed. They point out that the concept of maturity should not be viewed in a total sense, but rather should be considered only in relation to the undertaking of a specific activity. Thus, it follows that in certain cases some groups will have a higher degree of maturity than others. The leader's style, according to this model, should then complement the level of maturity of the group.

Figure 2.7 details the way in which leadership styles vary depending on the maturity level of an individual or group. Four classifications of styles emerge: telling (S1), selling (S2), participating (S3), and delegating (S4).

[21]Paul Hersey and Keith Blanchard, *Management of Organizational Behavior: Utilizing Human Resources*, 3d ed. (Englewood Cliffs, N.J.: Prentice-Hall, 1977), p. 101.

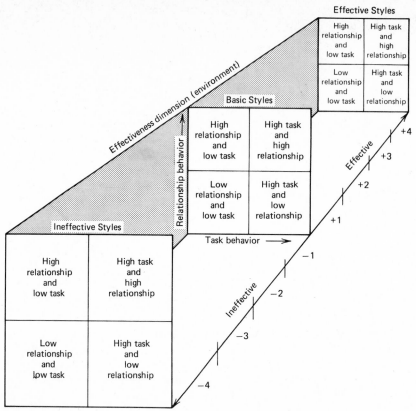

**FIGURE 2.6**   Tri-dimensional leader effectiveness model. (*Source*: P. Hersey/K. H. Blanchard, *Management of Organizational Behavior: Utilizing Human Resources*, 3d ed., © 1977, p. 106. Reprinted by permission of Prentice-Hall, Inc., Englewood Cliffs, N.J.)

Telling finds the leader with a high task and low relationship orientation. Selling is characterized by a high task and high relationship orientation. Participating has a high relationship and low task orientation. Delegating has a low relationship and low task orientation. As the "task relevant" maturity level of group members increases, Hersey and Blanchard maintain that the leader should modify his or her leadership style. For example, in situations where individuals possess a high degree of task maturity, a leader would use the S4 style (low task orientation-low relationship orientation). Think of a group of individuals whose knowledge and skills are well developed and who are extremely well motivated and self directed. The leader's role in this sit-

uation would be one of providing direction and defining roles and clarifying role expectations. Hersey and Blanchard suggest that there may be a progression in leader behavior as a group's task relevant maturity increases. A leader may change his or her style from S1 to S2 to S3 to S4 progressively as the group matures.

To illustrate this latter point, think of a group of children who have signed up for an archery instruction program and are attending their first class. As a whole, the group's knowledge and skills, as related to the use of archery equipment, may be very limited. Because safety is important in this particular activity, the leader might use a very directive task-oriented approach initially. The leader

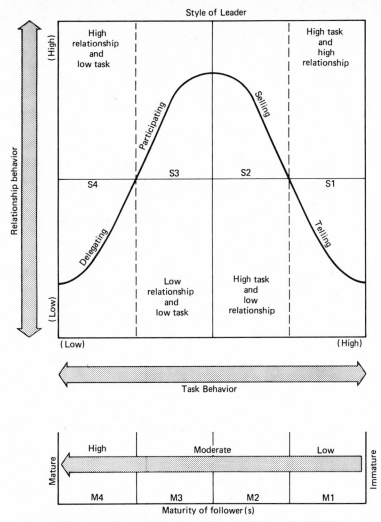

**FIGURE 2.7**    Situational leadership. (*Source*: P. Hersey/K. H. Blanchard, *Management of Organizational Behavior: Utilizing Human Resources*, 3d ed., © 1977, p. 170. Reprinted by permission of Prentice-Hall, Inc., Englewood Cliffs, N.J.)

would point out, specifically, what behaviors were acceptable or desirable. As the group's understanding of the conditions affecting the use of archery equipment was internalized and practiced, the leadership style employed by the leader could change. Ultimately, the leader would want to decrease his or her influence as the participants gained in their skills and knowledge and were able to assume a more responsible posture.

## A COMPREHENSIVE APPROACH TO LEADERSHIP

For a leader to be effective, he or she should consider all the relevant variables influencing the selection of a particular leadership style. Figure 2.8 presents a model that outlines the variables that should be taken into consideration in developing one's leadership style. This model incorporates three important factors: the leader, the group members, and the situation. Careful consideration should be given to all these dimensions, for they are interrelated with and influence one another. The leader influences group members and the situation, group members influence the situation and the leader, and the situation influences the leader and the group. In reviewing a *situation*, a leader must evaluate the effects of external forces, group goals, methods and procedures used to achieve group goals, and the type of environment. The members of the *group* also must be evaluated in order to determine the most appropriate leadership style. The leader should analyze the knowledge, skills and abilities of group members, their need disposition, previous experience, and task-relevant maturity. Finally, the *leader* should be aware of and assess his or her own knowledge, skills and ability, need disposition, experience, style flexibility, and source of power.

It is important to remember that the purpose of leadership is to influence others to achieve their own or the group goals. In selecting an appropriate leadership style, the leader may have no control or limited control over the *situation*. For example, external political, economic, and social forces may not be influenced by the leader in an immediate and direct fashion. Even though the purpose of leadership is to influence the individuals or group being led, the probability of changing the *group members'* knowledge, need disposition, or even maturity is difficult. Therefore, the key element in the process of selecting an appropriate leadership style is the ability of the *leader* to change his or her own behavior.

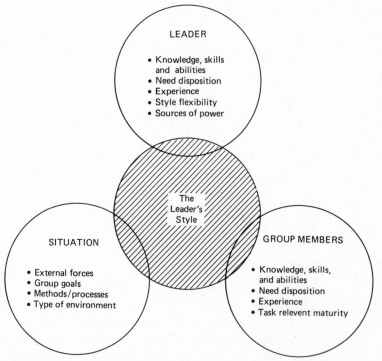

**FIGURE 2.8**   A Comprehensive approach to leadership. (*Source*: From R. W. Mondy, R. E. Holmer, and E. B. Flippo, *Management Concepts and Practices*, Copyright © 1980, Allyn & Bacon, Inc., p. 323. Reprinted with permission.)

The leader must do this while being conscious of the other forces and factors that affect the achievement of group and individual goals. For example, the leader may not necessarily be able to change the maturity level of group members, but he or she can employ a leadership style that fits this particular factor as it influences the achievement of group goals. Following is a brief analysis of each of the components of the comprehensive approach to leadership.

## SITUATION

When we use the term *situation*, we are referring to what the group is trying to accomplish and the methods and procedures that are to be employed to achieve it. Furthermore, we are referring to external and internal forces that may affect the work of the leader and the group. In analyzing the situation, the leader must be sensitive to both the obvious and the sub rosa factors that exist in the environment.

*External Forces*. External forces refer to those factors in the environment that affect the organization and are beyond the direct control of the leader and the group. For example, if the leader is organizing a picnic in the park and it rains, the leader must respond to this factor. The leader will have no control over this external variable. Knowledge of such influences as the political structure of a community, social norms and customs, cultural preferences, and the prevailing economic conditions can be essential in achieving group goals and suggesting a relevant leadership style.

*Group Goals*. Goals can be thought of as the ends or aims of an organization. The leader should not assume that groups really have a clear understanding of what their goals are. Some groups seemingly have well-stated goals, but in reality they pursue other ends. Group goals provide a framework for decision making within groups. The formulation of group goals also helps the leader determine the methods and procedures that will be necessary to achieve them.

*Methods and Processes*. There are numerous methods and processes that can be used in achieving group goals. A leader may have to use a process or procedure that is already in place. Other times, the leader will be able to use his or her discretion in choosing methods or processes. Each situation will be unique in terms of the particular processes that can be adapted to the local conditions of the group. A coach, for example, may be required to adapt a drill that may have been used for another type of team.

*Type of Environment*. When viewing the environment, the leader must consider two dimensions. The first is the relative stability or instability of the environment. Some environments are very stable, encouraging a more task-oriented leadership style. The second dimension to be considered by the leader is the unique conditions found in the environment. There may be specific norms, roles, and social conditions that the leader must respond to in choosing a leadership style.

## GROUP MEMBERS

Consideration of each group member as well as the characteristics of the group as a whole is essential in establishing an appropriate leadership style. Perhaps the leader should be most sensitive to the needs, desires, and expectations of group members, for it is these individuals whom the leader wishes to influence. Good listening skills are essential in this process. Four factors related to group members that should be considered by the leader follow.

*Knowledge, Skills, and Abilities*. Each individual within a group possesses different knowledge, skills, and abilities. It is incumbent upon the leader to gain an awareness of the capabilities of each individual group member. In a sense, the leader must take stock of the resources of the group as reflected by the abilities of each member. Assessment of the knowledge, skills, and abilities of group members can be useful in the organization of group tasks. Obviously, the leader wants to maximize the group's resources.

*Need Disposition.* The needs, wants, and interests of individual group members is another essential component in the process of determining one's leadership style. Individuals affiliate with or join groups for a variety of reasons. Some individuals are motivated because of the opportunities for social relationships; others, because of the opportunities for achievement and increased self-esteem. Still others become involved in groups in order to learn and grow.

*Experience.* The level and type of experience of group members should also be considered by the leader in determining his or her style. Prior successful experience of group members may allow the leader to be less directive and authoritarian in nature. On the other hand, a lack of experience on the part of group members may prompt the leader to assume the reverse role.

*Task-relevant Maturity.* As previously indicated, task-relevant maturity refers to whether or not an individual has the capacity to set and attain high goals and a willingness to take responsibility. Viewing maturity on a continuum, the leader will want to vary his or her style according to the level of maturity of group members. It is important to reemphasize that the concept of maturity should only be applied to the task at hand.

## THE LEADER

The leader can be the key to meeting individual and group needs. Because of the influence of the leader, the group as a whole is moved to action. When this action is directed toward meeting the goals of the group, the group succeeds. Some of the factors that are important in the development of a successful leadership style are detailed in the following list.

*Knowledge, Skills, and Abilities.* Like group members, leaders bring their own knowledge, skills, and abilities to the group. The leader's awareness of his or her strengths and weaknesses can be important in the selection of a leadership style.

*Need Disposition.* The expectations of the leader, as well as his or her own needs, wants, and interests, also influence the type of leadership style that will be employed. Achievement-oriented leaders, for example, have a different motivation from those who are not so oriented. One leader's behavior may be characterized by a high degree of risk taking and entrepreneurial type of behavior whereas another leader may exhibit a low degree of risk taking.

*Experience.* The leader who has developed successful patterns of interaction with individuals in a group situation will obviously draw on these in the future. Thus, the previous experience of an individual will greatly influence the leadership style that he or she adopts.

*Style Flexibility.* Style flexibility can be thought of as a behavioral attribute of the leader. Some leaders have the ability to change to meet varying conditions. Other leaders may be rigid and may lack the ability to adapt their basic leadership style to differing situations.

*Source of Power.* As indicated in Chapter 1, there are five different sources of power: legitimate or formal, reward, coercive, referent, and expert. If a leader's only source of power is, for example, legitimate or formal, the leader may be forced to use a more task-oriented, authoritarian style of leadership. On the other hand, if the leader has a strong basis of attraction with group members, another style of leadership may emerge.

The ability of a leader to evaluate accurately each of the three components—the situation, group members, and the leader—will influence his or her success as a leader. The misinterpretation of these factors can lead to the adoption of an inappropriate leadership style.

## SUMMARY

In this chapter the authors have presented and discussed a number of leadership theories, studies, styles, and models. From a theoretical standpoint, leadership has been studied from four perspectives. First, the great man theory is built on the notion that leaders are born and not made, emerging throughout history to occupy positions of leadership. Second, the trait theory is based on the idea that there are certain personality characteristics or traits that are possessed by successful leaders. The next approach, the group theory, suggests that leaders emerge within groups when there is a reciprocal relationship of rewards between the leader and the group. Finally, situational theories suggest that there is not "one best" leadership style, but that the leader must be flexible in his or her leadership style to meet the demands of a given situation.

Eleven different leadership studies, styles, and models were presented by the authors as contributing significantly to our understanding of leadership. The Lewin, Lippitt, and White Studies investigated three different leadership styles: democratic, authoritarian, and laissez-faire. Two dimensions of leader behavior—initiating structure and consideration—were identified in the Ohio State research study concerning leadership. The managerial grid by Blake and Mouton is a model that aligns concern for production and concern for people along two axes. They were able to identify five different managerial leadership styles. The University of Michigan studies viewed the two variables—concern for people and concern for production—as existing on a continuum. Rensis Likert perfected this concept and offered a number of styles that could exist on such a continuum, including exploitative, autocratic, benevolent autocrat, consultative, and participative group. Tannenbaum and Schmidt also used the continuum concept to present different combinations of freedom and use of authority.

Recently, situational models of leadership have come to the forefront of discussion in the leadership area. Fiedler's contingency model of leadership effectiveness suggests that the favorableness of the situation can influence the type of leadership style used by the leader. Such factors as leader-member relations, task structure, and the position power of the leader influence the favorableness of the situation. The path-goal theory of leadership suggests that different styles should be used by the leader to remove barriers that affect employee motivation, satisfaction, and productivity. Reddin's 3-D theory of management effectiveness suggests that a leader must be flexible in adapting his or her style to the dictates of a given situation. The tri-dimensional leader effectiveness model, developed by Hersey and Blanchard, suggests that the task-relevant maturity level of group members is a critical variable influencing the adoption of a leadership style.

In order to determine what leadership style to employ, the authors have suggested the use of a three-dimensional model. The leader must be aware of the situation, the group members, and his or her own behavior or demeanor. The authors suggest that a key process in deciding upon a leadership style is the ability of the leader to understand his or her behavior consciously and change it to meet the needs of group members and the dictates of the situation.

## DISCUSSION QUESTIONS

1. What is the great man theory of leadership? Trait theory? Group theory? Situational theory?
2. Identify traits that are related to effective leadership from your own experience.
3. What are the characteristics of democratic, authoritarian, and laissez-faire leadership styles?
4. What are the characteristics of a task-oriented leader? A relationship-oriented leader?
5. Some leadership studies and style models present task-relationship orientations on a continuum; others present them on a grid. What are the implications of these ways of viewing the dimensions of leadership behavior?
6. What does it mean to say that there is no ''one best'' leadership style?
7. How can one's leadership style assist group members in removing barriers?
8. What does the term *task-relevant maturity* mean? What implications does this have for one's leadership style?
9. What variables does an individual have to consider when selecting a particular leadership style?
10. Pick any three leadership studies or style models, and compare and contrast their various dimensions.

# 3

# Group Dynamics

Many recreation and leisure activities require group participation and cooperation. This activity is taking place at Family Vacation College, University of Oregon.

In North American society, participation in groups consumes a large portion of our time. Individuals belong to groups for varied reasons. Some individuals establish membership in a group for the purpose of socialization and comradery whereas others join groups in an effort to contribute their skills to enhance or better the community in which they live. Membership in some groups is short-term in nature whereas membership in other groups is long-term, or perhaps lifelong.

The study of groups and group dynamics is especially important in the recreation and leisure service profession. Group activities offered by recreation and leisure service organizations and led by trained professionals are one of the most important services provided by these types of agencies. Participation in such group activities offers many recreation and leisure opportunities for individuals.

## DEFINING GROUP DYNAMICS

When individuals interact in groups, there are patterns of action that occur that influence their behavior. We can think of group dynamics as the study of the interaction that takes place between individuals within a group setting. Group dynamics not only are concerned with the factors that influence communication and interaction between individuals, but are also concerned with other forces in the physical, social, and cultural environment that influence these patterns of interaction. We study group dynamics in order to understand group behavior, with the goal of improving the kind and quality of interaction that take place within the group process.

Group dynamics are not only concerned with the way that people interact and behave in a group situation, but also with the techniques that can be used to improve group effectiveness. The techniques employed by recreation and leisure service leaders can vary from goal setting to organization of small-group discussions. The more familiar the leader is with available techniques and their relationship to successful group performance, the more effective the leader will be. The ability to use the appropriate technique at the appropriate time to facilitate positive group interaction distinguishes a good leader from a poor one.

Thus, we can define group dynamics as *the study of groups, including patterns of interaction within the group, external forces that influence the group, and techniques and processes that can affect group behavior.* An analysis of these variables allows us to understand why groups behave as they do. Patterns of interaction within the group can also be referred to as *internal group dynamics.* Internal group dynamics are involved with group communication as well as other factors that influence interaction such as

group goals, size, atmosphere, leadership patterns, and participation. *External forces* that affect group activities include such factors as organizational and institutional values and expectations, physical structures, community values and expectations, and other group affiliations. *Techniques and processes* used to influence group behavior can be thought of as the tools that the leader can use to assist the group in achieving its goals. For example, the leader can serve as a facilitator, resource person, or enabler or a combination of these, acting on his or her knowledge of such techniques as leadership style, communications styles, role playing, brainstorming, small-group discussion, and problem solving.

### GROUP DYNAMICS AND THE RECREATION AND LEISURE SERVICE LEADER

There are a variety of situations in which the recreation and leisure service leader can benefit from a knowledge of group dynamics. Consider the leader who works with classes, clubs, teams, activity groups (i.e., camp groups), and neighborhood groups. All these formats for recreation and leisure activities require knowledge of group dynamics. In addition, the leader also works with professional peers and lay persons interested in the provision of recreation and leisure services. Thus, knowledge of group dynamics is useful in conducting professional relationships, including working with staff members (in a formal organizational structure), advisory and policy-making boards, and volunteer associations and also with colleagues in professional societies and associations. The use of group dynamics within some of these types of groups is discussed as follows.

*Instructional Groups.* An important component of many recreation and leisure service organizations is the provision of opportunities for development of skills, knowledge, and attitudes, through instructional groups. Most instructional programs are operated as classes in a group setting or situation. The leader in

Here, a leader teaches children to dance. This group can be classified as instructional. Willamalane Park and Recreation District, Springfield, Oregon.

this setting should have knowledge of such variables as group atmosphere, group learning principles, communication styles, and group interaction. It is interesting to note that recreation and leisure service organizations operate these types of programs for individuals who *choose* to participate rather than for individuals who are required to participate. Therefore the motivation of participants is strong. Leisure counseling and education groups fall within the category of instructional groups because they focus on attitude and skill development.

*Social Groups.*    Often individuals attend recreation and leisure service programs in order to interact with others. In fact, individuals often enroll in instructional groups with the dual purposes of not only learning something, but also socializing with others. The leader of social groups should be familiar with ways that he or she can assist individuals to meet, mix, and interact with others within a positive and supportive environment. The leader in this setting should have knowledge regarding how to establish and work with clubs, manipulate large and small groups, and implement counseling techniques.

*Volunteer Groups.*    Many recreation and leisure service organizations use volunteers. The

development, organization, and operation of a volunteer network may involve the establishment of standards for behavior and the creation of a sense of membership within the organization. Volunteers become involved in organizations for many reasons. One reason may be the need for a sense of group affiliation. Another may be a need for social interaction, and still another may be a need to serve others. In any case, the leader should be aware of those forces that influence the volunteers who work in the group environment.

*Competitive Groups.*    Competitive groups are comprised of those individuals who are members of teams and who play in leagues, tournaments, and contests provided by recreation and leisure service organizations. Knowledge of group dynamics can be essential in dealing successfully with these types of groups. Knowledge of recognition mechanisms, reward structures, and methods for the establishment of group norms should be possessed by the leader working with competitive groups. It is also important that the leader have the ability to build group morale or a sense of esprit de corps. Considerable status is associated with winning and being a part of a winning team in our society. A knowledge of group dynamics may also be used to transfer

Sports teams are among the most common types of competitive groups. This team is participating in the Eugene Sports Program, Eugene, Oregon.

the focus of competitive groups away from the competitive aspect of the recreation experience and toward the value of participation as an end in itself.

***Boards, Citizen Advisory Groups, and Neighborhood Associations.***   The involvement of citizens or lay persons in the policy and decision-making processes of the recreation and leisure service organization is a well-established tradition within our field. These individuals are paid or volunteer their services to assist the organization in developing its programs and services. Specific knowledge related to the conducting of formal meetings and the formulation of goals can assist the leader in working effectively with boards, citizen advisory groups, and neighborhood associations. The leader should be able to help such groups establish meeting agendas; seek out, acquire, and process information; make decisions; and interact with other groups.

***Professional Colleagues.***   The recreation and leisure service leader often works within a formal organization. This is the case within public park and recreation departments, voluntary youth serving agencies, or commercial recreation enterprises. In all these formal organizations, the most common work unit is the group. The ability of the leader to have an impact on a large organization may very well be a direct result of his or her ability to work successfully in small groups. The leader's knowledge of group dynamics can be useful in establishing rapport with others, building group morale, problem solving, identifying goals, and communicating effectively with others.

***Professional Societies and Associations.***   Most leaders in the recreation and leisure service field belong to one or more professional societies or organizations. They engage in these types of activities in order to promote the work of the profession as well as their own professional interests. Most work in these types of organizations occurs in smaller groups that are task oriented. The individual's knowledge of group dynamics can be useful in this type of setting, in terms of committee organization, management of conferences, workshops and training institutes, and communication and interaction. Professional organizations also confer status on individuals through the process of certification or registration. Knowledge of why and how groups confer status could be useful to the leader in establishing a successful program of this type.

## WHAT IS A GROUP?

There are a number of definitions for the term *group*. Some individuals have suggested that a group can be thought of as a highly unified collection of individuals. Others have suggested that groups work toward goals. Still others have maintained that individuals within a group must be dependent upon one another. To categorize "a collection of individuals" as a group is not sufficient. In order to be termed a group, a collection of individuals must have ties to one another that result in a sense of interdependence or interrelatedness or both. Interdependence or interrelatedness is the extent to which individuals are tied together in their actions and behavior. Therefore, we can define a group as "*a collection of individuals who interact with one another in such a way that they are interdependent to some degree.*"[1] In fact, interdependence-interrelatedness is the variable common to all groups.

The use of a gymnasium by individuals can provide an example of the concept of "the group" as it is suggested in the preceding definition. On any given night, a number of individuals may be present at a gym, shooting baskets, exercising, running, and so on. This collection of individuals does not constitute a "group." Why? Because each of the individ-

[1]D. Cartwright and A. Zander, *Group Dynamics* (New York: Harper & Row, 1968), p. 46.

uals has his or her own goals and is not tied to the others present in the gym. On the other hand, the same collection of individuals could come to a gym to participate with others as a basketball team, and they *would* be categorized as a "group." They would be classified as a group because they would possess the same or similar goals and would engage in interaction and cooperation and, as such, would be interrelated and interdependent.

## PRIMARY AND SECONDARY GROUPS

Individuals join different groups for different reasons. We affiliate with different professional societies and associations to enhance our careers. We join religious groups to affirm our spiritual values. Social and fraternal groups provide us with an opportunity to interact with others, develop friendships, and use our leisure. We join community-oriented associations and groups in order to contribute to the development and well-being of our cities and towns. We are involved in numerous informal groups based on a variety of factors, including our neighborhoods, children, recreation interests, and so on. Membership in one's family constitutes a group affiliation as well. All these different types of groups can be categorized according to their presence in two major categories: primary groups and secondary groups.

*Primary Groups.*   The term *primary group* refers to a setting in which intimate, face-to-face interaction and cooperation occurs. This type of group offers opportunities for individual interaction and self-expression. In situations where individuals live, work, or play together, intimate, face-to-face interaction occurs; hence, primary groups are formed. Perhaps the most easily identified example of a primary group is the family. Although the size of a group can affect its degree of intimacy, large groups as well as small groups can be primary.

*Secondary Groups.*   Secondary groups involve human interaction that is transferable, readily redirected to other individuals, and defined in specific standardized terms. Whereas a relationship within a primary group assumes holistic acceptance of the individual and deep and extensive communication, secondary groups' transactions are narrow and limited to the transaction itself. For example, when an individual purchases a ticket to the theater, the interaction between the ticket seller and the participant is stereotyped to conform to the "normal" routinized behavior that occurs between other clerks and clients. Were the ticket seller to be replaced, the individual could readily redirect the process of interaction to the new ticket seller.

The activities, programs, and services provided by recreation and leisure service organizations can be viewed as involving secondary groups; that is, the interaction that takes place between the leader and the participant is transferable from one person to another. Interestingly, however, the leisure *experience* occurs as a result of primary group interactions. It is a highly personal, individually defined experience and requires satisfaction on the part of the participant. Although the relationship that develops between the leader and the participant is often formal, emphasizing the characteristics of secondary group interaction, the result for the individual may be more consistent with primary group interaction. Murphy and others have suggested that there is a need to view individuals in a more holistic sense in order to facilitate deeper and more extensive communication as a desirable aid to the leisure experience.

On the other hand, this is not to suggest that the establishment of a primary relationship between the leader and the participant is necessary or even desirable. Individuals may be engaged in recreation and leisure pursuits for a host of reasons, including recognition, achievement, and self-worth as well as other motives that have social value. In certain situations, it may be desirable to maintain a more formal relationship, especially where there is a need to maintain objectivity. An individual may, for example, value the recognition provided by the leader. A leader who is biased by his or her personal relationship with a participant may not have the ability to make objective judgments about the participant's performance.

## THE INFLUENCE OF GROUPS IN OUR LIVES

Membership in groups can directly influence our lives, can shape and mold our behavior, and can influence our perceptions. Groups provide individuals with information and role models and may influence individuals through peer pressure. Zimbardo and Ruch have suggested that there are at least four sources of group influence. These are shared participation, public commitment, social support, and normative standards.[2] There follows a description of each of these sources of group influence.

*Shared Participation.* Shared participation refers to the involvement of individuals in the decision-making process. When an individual becomes personally involved in decision-making processes, he or she becomes an active part of the change process. When this occurs, the individual is more likely to undergo changes in his or her behavior as it is related to group activities.

*Public Commitment.* When an individual makes a commitment in a group publicly, the individual is more likely to follow through on the commitment than if the commitment were made in private. Because individual behavior is influenced by the approval of others, the behavior of an individual is shaped by the expectations formed when an individual makes a public

commitment. In order to receive group approval, the individual must follow through on his or her commitment.

*Social Support.* Involvement in a group reinforces individual decisions to act. When an individual has the support of a group, his or her confidence is increased that decisions made are appropriate. Group support, in other words, reinforces individual decision making and increases the individual's confidence in the viability of his or her decisions.

*Normative Standards.* Groups also provide expectations of the way that group members are supposed to behave. We can think of these expectations or standards as social norms. Social norms are the stated or implied rules that govern the way that individuals are to respond in a given situation. They provide a bench mark from which individuals can compare their behavior with the established standards for group behavior.

The influence of group participation upon individuals in recreation and leisure settings is evident within many activities and programs. Basketball team members, for example, will be influenced as a result of association with their group. Individual team members may be provided with social support through teammates' encouragement of their decisions made while playing, leading to increased confidence. Individuals often become involved in group decision making in the form of game strategy (formally or informally), leading to a commitment to the decisions made and to a greater commitment to the group as a whole. Individual team members may also begin to assume behavior indicative of group norms. For example, we have all seen the "athletic strut" that is practiced by many. Team members may also wear certain clothing to practice or distinctive clothing that is adopted into their street wear (jackets, shoes, wristbands). In addition, they may adopt roles for them-

[2]Philip G. Zimbardo and Floyd L. Ruch, *Psychology and Life*, 9th ed. (Glenview, Ill.: Scott, Foresman, 1976), pp. 401–402.

selves. One member may formally adopt the leadership role; another, the mediator role; and still another, the role of hard worker. These roles may or may not be carried over into other areas of life. Status may also be conferred upon team members, depending upon the situation. There would be a great deal of status, for example, attached to membership on the senior high first-string team because there are relatively few individuals that can attain such a position. Less status would be attached to membership on the seventh grade third-string team because membership is not as exclusive and does not involve the acquisition of unusual skills. Within the group itself, status may be accorded to various members of the team, for example, the highest scorer, the best defensive player, the player getting the most rebounds, and so on.

*Groups Promote Psychological Stability.* The existence of groups in our lives also plays an important role in maintaining individual psychological stability. Groups provide opportunities for direct, face-to-face interaction with other individuals. Without this opportunity, relationships become less intimate and fragile, leading to a state called *anomie*. This term coined by the sociologist Durkheim suggests that the more highly specialized and complex society becomes, the more likely it is that some individuals within society will find themselves without adequately defined roles or rules regulating behavior. Groups formed as a result of programs and services offered by recreation and leisure service organizations and led by the recreation and leisure service leader do provide opportunities to counter the adverse effects of anomie. Participation in group recreation activities can provide opportunities for intimate social relationships and norms or rules to regulate behavior and can confer status on group members. All these benefits can contribute to the psychological well-being of the individuals participating.

## GROUP PROPERTIES

As the reader will recall, a group can be thought of as a collection of individuals who interact with one another and, as a result, develop a degree of interdependence. Group interdependence can also be thought of as the cohesiveness or unity that exists between group members. However, some groups show a higher degree of interdependence than others. Thus, it can be suggested that the degree of interdependence of a group can be viewed as existing on a continuum. At one end of the continuum there is a high degree of unity among group members, and at the other end of the continuum there is a lack of cohesiveness or unity among group members. Groups at the latter end of the continuum are often characterized by feelings of anomie.

Wilson has suggested that there are six properties that influence the degree of interdependence necessary to solidify a collection of individuals. They are interaction, norms, status structure, goals, cohesiveness, and a common perception of membership.[3] The extent which group interdependence exists will be affected by each of these six properties. The more highly developed a group is in terms of one or more of the properties, the greater the degree of interdependence within the group. The following is a description of these six properties.

*Interaction.* Interaction refers to the communication that takes place between individuals within a group. A high degree of interrelatedness within a group exists when there is high frequency of communication and an equal distribution of communication between individual group members. Furthermore, the tone or nature of the interaction will influence the degree of interrelatedness. Friendly interaction characterizes highly interrelated

[3]Stephen Wilson, *Informal Groups: An Introduction* (Englewood Cliffs, N.J.: Prentice-Hall, 1978), pp. 26–49.

groups whereas antagonistic interaction produces the reverse effect.

*Norms*. Norms can be thought of as the behaviors expected of group members. Norms represent the view of the majority of group members as to what individuals "should do, ought to do, and are expected to do."[4] Groups that have a high degree of interrelatedness have developed a great number of norms to guide behavior, and, more important, among group members there is a high degree of consensus concerning these norms. Conversely, groups with a low degree of interrelatedness have few norms and a low degree of consensus. In groups that have a high degree of interrelatedness, individuals who deviate from norms are negatively sanctioned (e.g., scolded, embarrassed, or censured).

*Status Structure.* Status structure can be thought of as the roles of individual group members. Whereas norms involve similar behavior for members of the group, the status structure within the group results in diverse roles for individual members. Roles are expectations that are defined or developed for each group member. When group members have a high degree of consensus regarding their roles, there is correspondingly a high degree of interrelatedness within the group. Furthermore, a high degree of interrelatedness can also be said to exist when there are few challenges to the status or role structure within the group. As is the case with group norms, in highly interrelated groups, an individual who deviates from the role expected of him or her (the status structure) is negatively sanctioned.

*Goals.* Group goals can be differentiated from personal goals in that group goals require group members to cooperate with one another to achieve them. Group goals, in fact, are characterized by their cooperative nature. Regardless of the individual or individuals

[4]Ibid., p. 29.

who contribute the most toward achievement of the goal, or goals, it is the entire group that attains the goal or goals. Groups that have a high degree of interrelatedness have many defined goals and a high degree of consensus among members as to which goal to pursue. Moreover, groups with a high degree of interrelatedness cooperatively pursue goals for group-oriented motives rather than personally oriented motives. Conversely, groups that have a low degree of interrelatedness have few defined goals and a high degree of disagreement as to which goals to pursue.

*Cohesiveness*. Cohesiveness refers to the degree to which individuals are attracted to their group. The satisfaction or pleasure that group members derive from group participation is a major determinant of cohesiveness as is the interpersonal attraction between individuals. The stronger the attraction between individuals and the stronger the satisfaction derived, the higher the degree of interrelatedness. Cohesiveness is often determined by using sociometric techniques, which will be discussed later in this chapter. When individuals are not isolated and there is an absence of cliques within groups, cohesiveness also is increased. On the other hand, when there are a low degree of interpersonal attraction, a high degree of isolation, and a large number of cliques, the degree of interrelatedness declines significantly.

*Awareness of Membership*. Awareness of membership refers to the extent to which individuals perceive themselves as a part of the group. Often this is measured by simply asking individuals whether or not they feel they are part of the group. Awareness of membership can also be thought of as the individual's sense of belonging to a group. Another factor contributing to awareness of membership is the morale of the group. Morale can also be thought of as esprit de corps. Groups that have a high degree of awareness and high morale are said to have a greater degree of interrelatedness. Those groups with a low degree of awareness of membership and a low sense of morale have a low degree of interrelatedness.

Knowledge of these six properties can be useful to the recreation and leisure service leader in establishing groups that contribute to the psychological well-being of its members. If the leader understands that factors such as positive interaction, role consensus, even distribution of communication, or the lack of cliques within a group can influence its degree of interrelatedness, he or she can work to create a group environment in which desirable elements *are* present. In working with existing groups, the leader can attempt to strengthen those weak areas that will adversely affect group functioning. For example, the leader could clarify the status structure in such a way that roles would be more explicit, providing group members with a clearer understanding of what to expect from one another. It is interesting to note that recreation and leisure activities are often used within groups to build morale or esprit de corps.

*Sociometry.* A technique that can be used to view interpersonal attraction in groups has been developed by J. L. Moreno.[5] Moreno terms this procedure *sociometry*. Sociometry can be thought of as a procedure for identifying patterns of interaction among group members. Within a group the patterns of interaction that emerge will vary from group to group. Within groups some individuals will be sought out by others whereas other individuals will be isolated even though within the group. By understanding these patterns of interaction, the leader can reshape the group patterns to increase opportunities for interac-

tion and, hence, satisfaction between and among group members.

In order to interpret and analyze the patterns of interaction that take place within a group, Moreno set forth a method for visually interpreting this information. He termed this visual interpretation a "sociogram." A sociogram portrays the structure of the group, including subgroup patterns, friendship patterns, and patterns of interaction between individuals within the group. Figure 3.1 serves as an example of a sociogram. This figure represents the patterns of interaction for a group of Cub Scouts.

In the preceding example, a leader was asked to have each of the cubs "name their three best friends within the group." Characteristics other than friendship could have been explored, such as intelligence, athletic ability, citizenship, and so on; however, this particular exercise investigated friendship for the purpose of dividing boys into two dens according to this variable. In the investigation of a basic area, it is important to avoid ambiguity and ensure that group members understand clearly what information is being sought. In the diagram presented, the boys' choices of best friends within the group are represented by arrows. The arrows that are directed only one way represent the choice of one boy by another. Arrows that are directed both ways represent choices by two boys of one another. The concentric circles represent the number of times the boys were chosen by the other boys. Boys were thus chosen five or more times—or as few as once—and placed accordingly within the circle. In the sociogram, *Bobby* can be identified as being relatively isolated. He was chosen only once by the seven other boys. On the other hand, *Vince* is viewed positively by the boys as he was a choice of six of the eight other boys. There seems to be an interactive relationship between *Eric, Chuck, Vince, Scott,* and *Mark.* All these boys are choosing one another as friends. The relationship between *Bobby* and

[5]J. L. Mereno, *Who Shall Survive?* (Washington, D.C.: Nervous and Mental Disease Publishing Company, 1934).

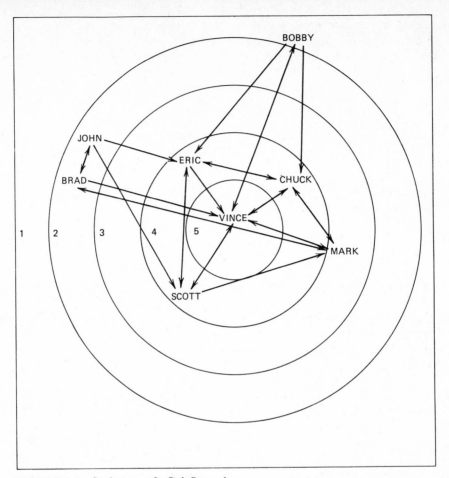

**FIGURE 3.1**   Sociogram of a Cub Scout den.

*Vince* keeps *Bobby* involved in the group. The relationship between *John* and *Scott* and *Brad* and *Mark* keep them involved in the group.

In this case, the sociogram was used to identify friendships in order to place the boys in two dens. However, it pointed out the importance of finding ways to integrate boys who are isolated into the main group. We, for example, did not want to separate *Bobby* and *Vince* because of their relationship and *Bobby's* isolation. We also wanted to maintain the relationship with *John* and *Brad* and ultimately place them in a group with *Mark* and *Scott*. Use of the sociogram in this case offers a satisfactory way of dividing the boys and helping

them maintain their friendships. Without this tool, the leaders of the group would have made the separation based on their "best guess," possibly resulting in unhappiness on the part of some of the boys.

The sociogram should be looked at as a mechanism that can be used by the recreation and leisure service leader to provide an indication of the cohesiveness of a group. It allows the leader to determine personal attraction of individuals to one another based on some criteria. This technique could be especially useful in a therapeutic recreation setting, where the leader is attempting to promote interaction and friendship. By using various techniques, the leader might promote new relationships that result in increased contact and interaction between individuals.

## GROUP LEADERSHIP

As the status structure of a group emerges, certain individuals occupy roles that we call leadership roles. The status structure allows for the identification of role expectations for group members. The higher the status conferred upon an individual, the more likely he or she is to be referred to as a leader. Conversely, the lower the status of an individual the lower the probability that he or she will occupy a leadership role. One's status within a group may change, however, depending upon the tasks to be accomplished or the processes to be employed. Thus, depending upon the circumstances, leadership roles can change hands.

Generally speaking, there are three variables that influence whether or not an individual occupies a role of leadership within a group. The first of these is the amount of *influence* that an individual has within the group. The amount of influence that one possesses is based on the authority associated with one's role within the group. Authority may be conferred as a result of a formal position that one holds or by virtue of one's knowledge or ability to persuade others. A second variable that can be indicative of leadership has to do with the process of communication or *interaction* within a group. Individuals who hold leadership roles are often at the center or focal point of group interaction. The individual may serve to generate, organize, or distribute information to group members or effect a combination of these actions. The person occupying this role is often viewed as a leader. The third variable associated with leadership is *sociometric popularity*. Sociometric popularity is based upon one's ability to solve instrumental and socioemotional problems associated with group functioning. Sociometric popularity, more specifically, is based on the perception of a group that an individual has the ability to lead them to their goals successfully.

Leaders in groups perform various functions. For example, they enforce the norms of the group, thereby increasing group interrelatedness. This is done via a system of rewards and punishments that the leader is able to use by virtue of his or her status within the group. Furthermore, the leader serves as a role model. Group members usually place higher expectations on the leader than other group members. They expect the leader to exemplify the highest ideals and exhibit the highest level of performance.

With regard to recreation and leisure service organizations, Shivers has suggested that there are clearly defined functions that the leader can play within the group. These include the following:

*Guidance and Coordination.* Guidance of group activities toward desirable goals, coordination of interpersonal relations, and elimination of conflicts to conserve group structure are three of the most significant functions.[6]

*Group Morale.* Support and encouragement from the leader and the assistance he or she gives each individual in assuming responsibilities as a participant result in personal gratification.[7] This support and encouragement increases group morale.

*Stimulating Achievement and Productivity.* The leader by virtue of his or her personality and organizational skills spurs others in the group to action.

It is important to recognize that leadership can emerge as a function of the group process, or it may be assigned. For example, within a recreation and leisure service activity, there may be a person who emerges from within the

[6]J. S. Shivers, *Recreational Leadership: Group Dynamics and Interpersonal Behavior* (Princeton, N.J.: Princeton Book Company, 1980), p. 128.
[7]Ibid., p. 129.

group to assume an informal leadership role. At the same time, there may be a leader formally assigned by the recreation and leisure service organization to instruct, lead, coach, or otherwise supervise the activity of the group. In the latter case, the individual's influence as a leader comes primarily through the formal authority assigned by the agency. In the former case, the leader's authority may be a result of knowledge, personality, and so on. In other words, the recreation and leisure service leader is characterized by a formal sanction of leadership, some formal training, and stability as a leader. The informal leader is characterized by group support due to some form of inherent leadership ability.

In either case, it is important to remember that the leader is a vital member of the group. The leader serves to stimulate others and facilitate achievement of group goals. The leader is often an individual who can provide insight into group problems and initiate action to solve them. The wise formal leader should try to identify the informal leader or leaders within the group and seek their assistance. The informal leader or leaders can provide support for the formal leader or conversely can undermine the effort of the formal leader, depending upon the working relationship that is developed between them.

## COMMUNICATION IN GROUPS

Groups, especially small ones, provide the basis for intimate interpersonal interaction. Therefore, it is extremely important that the recreation and leisure service leader have an understanding of the communication process as it applies to small groups. Skill in communications is tied to the quality of behavior within small groups. Although we will discuss the process of communication more thoroughly in Chapter 5, it may be useful to identify the types of interaction that potentially can occur in small groups. Success in recognizing and encouraging appropriate forms of communicative interaction within small

groups can directly affect the achievement of group goals. The use of inappropriate or ill-conceived patterns of interactions can be detrimental not only to the achievement of group goals, but also to personal success of the individuals within the group.

Small-group communication demands a more intimate, direct process of interaction, than that employed with large groups. Individuals involved in small groups do not, for example, expect to be addressed as if they were a part of a formal audience. Individuals expect to be able to interact with the leader and others within the group freely and to participate in an exchange of information rather than receive only one-way communication from the leader. The small-group communication process should be one of give-and-take. Individuals within small groups are only willing to listen if their responses are also heard and acknowledged. Individuals involved in the process of communication within small groups often communicate their personal needs and goals while at the same time contributing to the group problem-solving process in order to achieve group goals. The more sensible and coherent the process of communication is within a small group, the more likely it is that the group will achieve its goals.

Avedon has identified five types of communication that can occur within a small group. These include interindividual, unilateral, multilateral, intragroup, and intergroup communication.[8] The communication process within the small group implies an exchange of information between parties. In other words, there are expectations within the small group that the group members will be responsive to one another; that they will take into account the feedback received from others in formulating further responses. A description of each

[8]Elliott H. Avedon, *Therapeutic Recreation Service: An Applied Behavioral Science Approach* (Englewood Cliffs, N.J.: Prentice-Hall, 1974), pp. 166–170.

of the five types of communication Avedon cites as being used within small groups follows.

*Interindividual.* Communication of this type involves interaction of one individual with another. This type of group is referred to as a dyad, meaning that it involves two people. The direct interpersonal transaction that takes place within a dyad can result in several outcomes. It can create greater commitment on the part of both individuals to achieve goals that have been mutually agreed to, or it can result in hostility, competition, aggressiveness, or other behavior that prevents goal attainment.

*Unilateral.* Unilateral communication involves interaction between an individual and two or more persons. In other words, there are a number of interindividual interactions taking place simultaneously. The unilateral relationship is usually a competitive one, where the focus of the group's attention is toward one individual, who tends to be an antagonist.

*Multilateral.* Multilateral interaction or communication involves three or more individuals. Multilateral communication is often competitive with individuals interacting with one another laterally. However, no one individual is an antagonist as in the unilateral communication described earlier.

*Intragroup.* Intragroup communication focuses on the achievement of a goal that is mutually subscribed to by all members of the group. Requiring two or more individuals, this form of communication is cooperative rather than competitive. Groups that have achieved intragroup communication have a higher degree of interrelatedness than those that do not. Interaction tends to be give-and-take in nature, with individuals willing to compromise their positions taking into account the ideas, feelings, and values of others.

*Intergroup.* Intergroup communication occurs between groups and is focused on the achievement of a goal that is sought by both groups. This form of communication often operates with the mutual understanding of rules and regulations as well as standards of behavior.

The recreation and leisure service leader, depending upon the goals of the group or the expectations of participants, will want to encourage different types of communication. For example, in competitive game situations, unilateral or multilateral communication, contributing to the group structure, may be appropriate. However, if the purpose of the group is to solve problems or to encourage cooperative group behavior, intragroup and intergroup communication may be more effective.

**Group Size.** The size of a group will influence its operation. Small groups may offer, for example, more opportunities for communication with others within the group. Small groups also offer group members more opportunity for the development of social relationships. Although small groups may have less "talent" to be used in problem solving, they are also characterized by a greater willingness of group members to participate in problem-solving and decision-making processes, for small groups are perceived as being less threatening than large groups. In addition, the small-group member has greater access to the leader than the large group member. The role of the leader is more difficult when in charge of a large group because he or she may not have the time to interact meaningfully with each group member.

Group size may play an important role in the selection of leadership techniques. For example, the leader will want to use communication techniques that are suited to the size of the group. A lecture type format may be appropriate for a large group, but a group discussion might be more appropriate for a small group. However, the leader can create a small-group atmosphere within a larger group by clustering individuals into smaller groups for discussion or problem solving. By doing this, the leader can take advantage of the larger number of individuals in terms of their expertise, knowledge, and information and still make them feel more comfortable and willing to share by placing them within the small group atmosphere.

## GROUP CONFLICT

Within all groups there is a potential for conflict. Group conflict is not necessarily something that one should fear or attempt to avoid. In fact, many individuals would suggest that conflict, which is inevitable in many group situations, is necessary to facilitate positive group change. Therefore, the recreation and leisure service leader should be aware of the causes of conflict as well as the ways in which it can be used to assist group behavior in a positive fashion. Conflict within groups can be due to three factors: incompatible goals, status incongruities, and differences in perceptions.

*Incompatible Goals.* Often individuals come together in a group situation with divergent opinions and values concerning the goals of the group. This incompatibility of goals can lead to conflict. An example of this in the recreation field can be found when differences in coaching goals exist on sports teams. One coach on a team may see his role as one of winning games whereas another coach on the same team may view his role as helping to develop skills. Team members or parents of team members or both may also have goals of their own or may be aligned with one of the two coaches.

*Status Incongruities.* Status incongruities are frequently a source of conflict within groups, especially where there is no formal authority structure established and accepted by the group members. Basically, status incongruities refer to the differences in opinion that arise regarding the status accorded to roles within the group. Conflict can occur when an individual perceives his or her status in a different light from other group members.

*Differences in Perceptions.* The differences in perceptions that group members have of goals, processes, roles, and other factors can all be sources of conflict. Each person receives information and screens it according to such variables as their past experience, beliefs, values, interests, and knowledge. Differences in perceptions due to the influence of these variables can lead to conflict. The process of perception will be discussed fully in Chapter 5, dealing with perception and the communication process.

There are a number of strategies that can be used to overcome conflict within groups. First, the leader can attempt to create a *buffer* between group members involved in conflict. The leader using this approach would try to have each of the parties avoid each other in order to minimize the friction that would ordinarily occur. Another strategy that can be employed by the leader is to help group members to *understand* how they impact on one another. The leader using this strategy does not attempt to help group members avoid conflict, but rather attempts to help them understand their own behavior and its influence on others. Often an individual will not be aware of the effect of personality quirks, methods of giving direction, attentiveness, and responsiveness. The leader can attempt to provide group members with insight and strategies for changing their behavior in order to facilitate positive group interaction. Lastly, the leader can *rearrange* the group structure in order to reduce conflict. This might involve changing the roles and expectations of individuals.

The leader's and group members' perceptions of conflict can have a great deal of influence on whether such conflict has a negative or positive impact on individual or group behavior or both. If the leader and group members view conflict as a way to bring about change and encourage innovation, the conflict will be seen as natural and useful to the group. If, on the other hand, conflict is viewed as something to be ignored or as being unnecessarily disruptive to the group, a negative attitude to conflict will develop. The leader should work toward developing a positive orientation toward conflict, one that can be of assistance in achieving group goals.

## GROUP ROLES

There are various roles that individuals can assume within a group situation. Some roles contribute to the effective functioning of the group as an interpersonal unit whereas other roles contribute to the effective functioning of the group as it relates to the tasks at hand. Still other roles played within groups have nothing to do with the solving of problems or the maintenance of group activities, but rather focus on the individual needs of one or more group members at the expense of others within the group. These types of roles are often viewed as being detrimental to overall group behavior. Individuals can play more than one role within a group. For example, an individual may volunteer information in one situation within the group whereas in another situation within the same group he or she may seek to clarify the opinions of others. Basically, we can think of group roles as existing in three categories: *general task roles, group building and maintenance roles*, and *individual antigroup roles*.[9]

[9]George M. Beal, Joe M. Bohlen, and J. Neil Raudabaugh, *Leadership and Dynamic Group Action* (Ames, Iowa: Iowa State University Press, 1967), pp. 103–110.

## GENERAL TASK ROLES

Individuals engage in general task roles in order to contribute to the work of the group. Often they will become involved in identifying, defining, and suggesting solutions to problems affecting the group. Some of the specific ways that an individual can act out general task roles include the following.

*Initiator-Contributor.* The individual who contributes his or her ideas is characteristic of the initiator-contributor. Often this role involves making suggestions or proposing solutions to problems.

*Information Seeker.* The individual within this role attempts to clarify information presented by others. This individual seeks additional relevant facts or seeks to validate the accuracy of information presented or both.

*Opinion Seeker.* The opinion seeker attempts to clarify values rather than facts. This individual would ask for assessment of the moral implications of actions proposed.

*Information Giver.* The individual within this role offers information to others that is based on facts and experience. The information given is "authoritative" in nature and can help to enhance understanding of the task at hand.

*Opinion Giver.* The opinion giver offers his or her values or beliefs regarding the task at hand. This individual does not offer factual information, but rather offers personal values, beliefs, and opinions.

*Elaborator.* The elaborator attempts to give depth to the discussion by giving examples and rationales and by attempting to discover what would happen if a certain course of action were adopted. The elaborator expands the discussion to enable the group to develop a more comprehensive understanding of a particular concern.

*Summarizer.* The individual who pulls facts, opinions, and values together is the summarizer. The person in this role tries to assist the group in determining where it was, where it is, and where it wants to go.

*Coordinator-Integrator.* The role of coordinator-integrator involves selection of various ideas, opinions, values, beliefs, and facts and their organization into an integrated concept. The coordinator-integrator tends to work with ideas and concepts and attempts to determine the relationships that exist between these.

*Orienter.* The orienter keeps the group on task. This is often done by reminding the group of the task to be accomplished or the goals to be achieved.

*Disagreer.* The person who disagrees looks at the other side of the issue. This may involve taking an opposite point of view and arguing accordingly. This person questions the facts, opinions, and values of others.

*Evaluator-Critic.* The evaluator-critic uses standards to elevate the progress of the group. The individual in this role measures the group's procedures, facts, and other factors relevant to the group's progress against standards of excellence.

*Energizer.* The energizer can be thought of as a motivator. The individual in this role attempts to rouse the group toward action or increase the productivity of the group in terms of quality or quantity.

*Procedural Technician.* The procedural technician assists group procedure by handling the distribution of materials and objects, as well as by dealing with seating arrangements and notifying group members of meetings.

*Recorder.* The recorder is involved in the writing down of concepts or ideas. Often a recorder will work at a blackboard or with an overhead projector, setting down information presented by group members. The recorder is important to the group process as many ideas can be lost in a verbal exchange.

## GROUP BUILDING AND MAINTENANCE ROLES

Group building and maintenance roles focus on encouraging and building cooperation among group members. These are extremely important to successful group functioning. There is often a need to assist individuals positively by suggesting ideas, clarifying positions, and presenting facts. Group building and maintenance roles can be thought of as the social-emotional support activities that group members provide one another in the group setting. Often the leader who is using a democratic leadership style will focus on these types of roles. Some of the group building and maintenance roles in which individuals can engage include these.

*Encourager.* The encourager is like the cheerleader. He or she provides praise, encouragement, and support to others. This is done by actively supporting other individuals without necessarily agreeing with their points of view.

*Harmonizer.* Often within groups there are disagreements and conflicts. The harmonizer works to help individuals overcome their disagreements and attempts to help relieve tension within the group. Timing is important in the harmonizer role, for the right comment or intervention at the right time can serve to head off conflict or break tension.

*Compromiser.* The compromiser role also deals with the mediation of conflict. The compromiser provides alternatives to points of view or yields in his or her point of view or both in order to maintain group harmony.

*Gatekeeper.* Often channels of communication will become clogged in group interaction. The role of the gatekeeper is to keep communication channels open and ideas and facts flowing.

*Standard Setter.* The individual in this role attempts to establish standards for the group in terms of its output and internal processes. The group can use these standards to engage in evaluation of its progress or effectiveness.

*Group Observer-Commentator.* The individual involved in this role provides information in the form of ''feedback'' to group members concerning the processes used by the group. This might involve informing the group of the extent to which communications are open, appropriate procedures are being employed, and so on.

*Follower.* There are certain situations in which the follower role is extremely important. By listening and being attentive to the ideas of others, one can facilitate the group process. This is especially true when others in the group are extremely excited or have a strong commitment to their ideas and values.

## INDIVIDUAL ANTIGROUP ROLES

We term individual behavior that adversely affects group performance as ''individual antigroup roles.'' The incidence of such roles can provide an enormous problem for the leader as well as other group members. In a recreation and leisure setting, one must be careful to balance the desires of individuals with the needs of the group. When individual behavior is clearly detrimental to group functioning, the leader must act to resolve the problem in order to protect the quality and integrity of the group experience. Some of the individual antigroup roles are these.

*Aggressor.* As the term aggressor implies, the individual in the aggressor role is involved in the attack of others within the group in terms of their ideas, values, or feelings. The aggressor will often attack the personality of the other individual rather than the

issue at hand. Attack by the aggressor may involve personal disapproval, questioning the status or value of another, and so on.

*Blocker.* The blocker disagrees with everything presented. This role involves an extremely negative orientation wherein the individual opposes others without a rational justification. Such behavior is a serious problem in group and interpersonal communication.

*Recognition Seeker.* Often an individual will try to be the focus of group attention. As a result, the recognition seeker will engage in such behavior as clowning, boisterous behavior, bragging, and so on.

*Self Confessor.* The individual who is a self-confessor uses the opportunity presented by the group setting to present personal ideas, feelings, and values that he or she feels are important. The self-confessor, for example, may attempt to increase the ''cosmic awareness'' of the group at the expense of the tasks at hand.

*Playboy.* Often an individual will come into a group with a nonchalant or cynical attitude. As a result, he or she will make a mockery of the group process by horsing around, making loud asides, restless behavior, and so on.

*Dominator.* An individual within the dominator role will try to dominate the work of the group. The dominator monopolizes conversation or uses threats of his or her position of authority or superior knowledge to limit discussion and interaction. This is usually reflected in an authoritarian leadership style of behavior.

*Help Seeker.* The individual engaged in the role of help seeker pleads for the assistance of others because he or she feels unqualified, confused, or not able to grasp the ideas and concepts being presented. The expectation is that the other group members will shoulder the work and responsibilities of this ''weaker'' group member.

*Special Interest Pleader.* The special interest pleader is the cause-oriented individual who uses the group forum to promote *personal* interests although using such catch phrases as "the environment," "grass roots," "the poor," and "the participant" to justify his or her ideas, values or beliefs.

The role or roles that are assumed within a group can have a direct influence on its success or failure because some roles (group task roles or group building-maintenance roles) are conducive to effective group performance whereas others (individual antigroup roles) are characteristic of groups that perform poorly. The leader, with a knowledge of group roles, may be able to change his or her own role or the roles of others within the group to facilitate a more positive group atmosphere or to facilitate completion of a task. Consider the youngster in a Little League program who is not satisfied with *anything*. This type of child may not like the rules, the position played, the coach, the field, and so on. In other words, the child's enactment of this role (the blocker) is interfering with the group process; the needs of one individual are interfering with the needs of the group for cohesiveness and cooperativeness. The leader may be able to transform the blocker role into a positive one with a knowledge of group roles so that the child is able to achieve recognition in a positive way. For example, the leader may allow the child to lead the exercise program, serve as a base coach, or serve as scorekeeper.

## TECHNIQUES USEFUL TO THE LEADER

There are a number of specific techniques that can be useful to the recreation and leisure service leader working with large and small groups. For example, there are specific techniques that can be used in the organization of such large groups as clinics, workshops, conferences, and retreats. There are also specific techniques that can be used for the organization of pageants, festivals, and other special events. Techniques that can be used with such large groups are covered in Part Two.

## SMALL-GROUP TECHNIQUES

Most work in organizations is done in small groups. Therefore, it is appropriate to have knowledge of some of the techniques that can be useful in assisting small groups achieve their goals. In this section, a brief overview of some of the generalizable techniques that can be useful to the small-group leader will be presented. In Part Two of the book, we will focus more specifically on detailed techniques that can be used by the leader in a number of different settings.

The most important variable influencing the choice of techniques to be employed by the leader is group size. As the term *small group* implies, it is being assumed that the number of individuals with whom the leader is working is between three (3) and twenty (20) individuals. It is not appropriate to identify a specific number of people as constituting an optimal group size, for other variables, such as the task to be performed, the willingness of the participants to contribute, and the need for a large or small input of information, may affect this factor. However, whatever small-group techniques are employed, they should provide an opportunity for all group members to give and receive information. In larger groups, because of sheer size, there is a possibility that exchange will be limited or that it will be confined to a one-way interaction. Small-group techniques, on the other hand, are characterized by the opportunity for individuals to exchange ideas, opinions, and values in an open and free manner. Two small groups techniques to be discussed are the small group discussion and committee meetings.

*Small-Group Discussion.*    When individuals meet within a group structure to present and discuss ideas, opinions, and beliefs, we call it a *small-group discussion.* Small-group discussions can be thought of as informal meetings of group members directed toward the establishment of the goals of the group and the process or processes to be used to accomplish these goals. Small-group discussion is used when group members are willing to engage in open communication, are relatively skilled in terms of human relations, and are willing to contribute to the solving of problems and the creation of new ideas. The small-group discussion method might be chosen for one or more of the following reasons.

• To identify and explore mutual concerns, issues, or problems.
• To increase awareness, appreciation, and understanding of mutual concerns, issues, or problems.
• To generate interest in ideas, issues, and problems.
• To supply and diffuse information and knowledge.
• To motivate a group to action.
• To involve members in the problem-solving process.
• To get members to crystallize their own thinking.
• To form group opinions or consensus.
• To assist members to express their ideas in a group.
• To create an awareness of issues and problems.
• To encourage and stimulate members to learn more about problems and ideas.
• To develop a core group of people for leadership purposes.
• To develop an informal and permissive group atmosphere.[10]

In leading small-group discussion, the leader should have a clear understanding of the goals of the group as well as the problem or issue to be reviewed. The leader should work to ensure that each group member has an equal and adequate opportunity to present his or her ideas in a supportive environment. The leader should help clarify viewpoints while at the same time stimulating group members to offer alternative viewpoints. Often the leader will want to insert humor or other comments to break the tension that may develop in this type of discussion.

Some of the specific techniques that can be used to aid small-group discussions are the following.

*Circular Discussion Method.* The leader using the circular discussion method arranges group members in a circle and allows them to present their viewpoints, in order, around the circle. This is done after a brief initial presentation of the topic. This method is designed primarily for discussion of controversial issues.

*Brainstorming.* Brainstorming is a problem-solving process. It focuses on obtaining input from group members about a problem at hand. The critical step in the brainstorming process is the generation of ideas, and it is the *quantity* of ideas, not the quality, that is important. No critical judgment is made of ideas, and all are welcome.

*Buzz Group.* The buzz group technique involves the subdivision of a group into smaller units so that they are encouraged to interact. This method is often used with larger groups although it can be useful in smaller groups when there is a need for more intimate, face-to-face interaction. It encourages group members to express their ideas and opinions, more so than any other form of small-group discussion.

*The Huddle Method.* The leader using the huddle method breaks a large group into small groups and limits discussion to a very short period of time (usually under 10 min-

[10]Ibid., p. 182.

utes). This method has the same advantages of the buzz group although the timed discussion encourages the presentation of ideas quickly.

*Case Study.* A case study is a written portrayal of a real life or lifelike situation. With this technique, individuals are asked to read a case study prior to discussion and offer solutions to the problem in the ''case.'' Group members also try to identify factors that would affect various solutions. The case study may have implications for a similar situation that has been, is, or will be confronted by the group. Or the case study method may be seen as a way for group members to hone their problem-solving and decision-making abilities.

*Role Playing.* Role playing is another technique that can be used to aid small-group discussion. The idea behind role playing is to have individuals within the group act out various scenarios. The role-playing dialogue is allowed to unfold spontaneously to a predetermined situation. This exercise allows group members to assume roles they normally wouldn't assume and react to situations within those roles. Thus, group members can gain insight that they might not otherwise attain. Once the role has been played, group members engage in a discussion of the responses that have taken place.

*Experiential Exercises.* Experiential exercises are structured learning exercises that focus on the group members' feelings or values toward a particular topic or subject. Group members are given a written hypothetical situation and asked to imagine themselves within that situation and solve the problem involved. Usually, progression through these types of exercises teaches group members a larger lesson or ''truth.'' These types of exercises allow group members to personalize concepts to be used as a basis for discussion. Structured experiential ex-

ercises are often useful ways of channeling or shaping a group's thinking so that it is focused on the topic at hand.

Although many small-group discussions are spontaneous, a large number of small-group discussions require some preplanning. For example, the leader should determine the most appropriate time for the meeting and should also consider the location, materials, and supplies needed, and so on. Will the group need an overhead projector? Blackboard? Is one day better for most of the members than another? The seating formation of group members may also be planned ahead to facilitate the type of discussion desired. For example, the leader should attempt to ensure that group members are able to have eye contact with one another. Figure 3.2 presents different types of seating arrangements that can be used in small-group discussions.

***Committee Meeting.*** Committees are found in all organizations, including recreation and leisure service organizations. In most cases they operate on a more formal, structured basis than the small-group discussion. Committees usually specify roles and tasks to individuals, hence conferring status. Some committees are appointed on a permanent basis whereas others are ad hoc in nature. Ad hoc committees are usually organized for a short period of time in order to investigate or solve a specific problem or issue or both. Basically, a committee can be thought of as a group of individuals who have been designated, as a group, to accomplish a specific set of goals and objectives.

A committee may perform a number of different functions. Some committees are advisory in nature whereas others have final decision-making authority. In addition, some committees have as their primary function or task the coordination of various activities within an organization. Two other functions that may be assumed by committees include provision of information and implementation

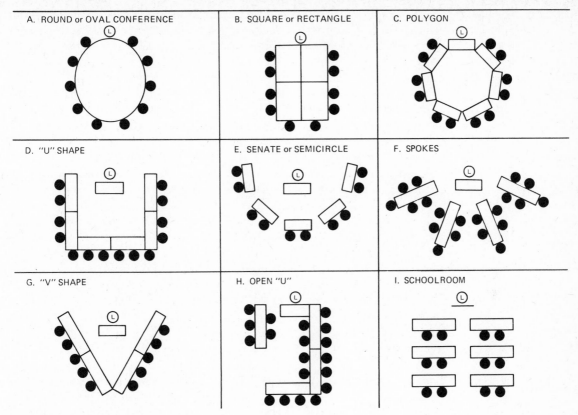

**FIGURE 3.2**    Possible seating arrangements for meetings.

of services. In the recreation and leisure service field, there are committees such as the municipal park and recreation board that can be either a decision-making body or an advisory body depending on the type of enabling legislation of the state. Committees can be elected or appointed. Again, in the case of the municipal park and recreation board, members may be elected or appointed to various committees, such as finance, planning, and personnel.

Committees are not always viewed in a positive light. Many individuals disdain committee work. They feel that it is laborious, time-consuming, and tedious. Luthans writes of some of the ridicule that is directed toward committees. He offers the following platitudes.

A camel is a horse designed by a committee.

The best committee is a five-person committee with four members absent.

In a committee, minutes are taken but hours are wasted.

A committee is a collection of the unfit appointed by the unwilling to perform the unnecessary.[11]

Obviously, there are some problems with committees. One of the largest disadvantages of a committee is that it is time-consuming and can be costly. Furthermore, individuals often question consensus or group decision

[11]Fred Luthans, *Organizational Behavior*, 2d ed. (New York: McGraw-Hill, 1977), p. 370.

making. The criticism is that individuals water down their positions in order to accommodate the needs of others. Some individuals would also suggest that committee members can stand behind group decisions, thereby avoiding the responsibility for errors. It is difficult to hold a committee member responsible for the actions of the entire group.

On the other hand, committees can help promote cooperation and collaboration among individuals. The pooling of ideas, knowledge, and other resources often enables the formulation of creative and expansive solutions to problems. Committees also provide an opportunity for individuals to receive recognition and status as a result of their committee membership. This often serves to motivate individuals to become involved when ordinarily they would not. Committees can also serve as training grounds for individuals. As new members are circulated into the committee, older members can serve as role models and offer information. Thus, a committee can be an excellent opportunity for individuals to learn and grow.

Committees usually follow a formal agenda format; that is, they plan, in advance, the items or topics to be discussed at a meeting. A typical agenda format follows.

1. Call to order.
2. Role call.
3. Reading of the minutes.
4. Committee reports.
5. Old business.
6. New business.
7. Announcements.

Agendas are useful because they provide information to committee members as well as presenting the order of events as they are to occur at the meeting. They tell the committee members what topics will be covered in the meeting and when. If there are special reports for committee members to make or hear, they will know at what point this is to occur.

An important role in a committee is that of the chairperson. The chairperson can be thought of as the official leader of the committee. He or she is responsible for leading the meeting, including moderating and controlling the discussion. The chairperson will want to be conscious of the time involved in the meeting itself. Ensuring that the committee meeting follows an appropriate tempo and pace is an important function of the chairperson. The committee chairperson must not only be a good listener, but also must be supportive of other individuals. He or she should have the ability to cut to the heart of issues and concerns. The chairperson is also responsible for establishing and following the rules of procedure that the committee is to follow. The most common format used in committees is that of *Robert's Rules of Order*. These rules aid in the processing of information in the committee meeting. They are often referred to as parliamentary procedures.

Another important task undertaken in committees is the recording of transactions. We refer to this as keeping the minutes of the committee. Minutes of meetings usually record who attended the meeting, when and where it was held, and what decisions were made. Minutes often include summaries of discussions, debates, or other items that were useful in formulating committee strategy. Taking minutes can be a demanding task. The individual who acts as the recorder must be able to understand the issue at hand and record with accuracy the substance of the committee's discussions and decisions.

The interaction of committee members with one another and the chairperson is essential to group effectiveness. The cohesion or tension that develops between committee members may directly influence the success or failure of the group. Committee members should be willing to share their ideas and should be open to the suggestions and comments of others. They must be willing to compromise their opinions in order to work toward broader group goals. Committee members, like the chairperson, must be sensitive to group dynamics. The timing of their statements and their ability to listen actively to other committee members are vital.

## SUMMARY

In this chapter we have focused on the topic of group dynamics. Group dynamics can be thought of as the study of groups, dealing with patterns of interaction within groups, external forces that influence groups, and the techniques and procedures that can be used to affect group behavior. There are a number of situations in which the recreation and leisure service leader can apply his or her knowledge of groups, including instructional groups, social groups, volunteer groups, competitive groups, citizen groups, and professional societies and associations.

A group can be thought of as a collection of individuals who are interrelated and interdependent. There are two types of groups: primary and secondary. Primary groups involve face-to-face intimate interaction and cooperation among individuals. Secondary groups involve human transactions in which the communication is transferrable from one person to another. There are a number of factors or properties that determine the degree of interrelatedness or interdependence within given groups. Six of these properties are interaction, norms, status structure, goals, cohesiveness, and awareness of membership. A tool that can be used to measure one or more of these properties is known as sociometry. Sociometry can be thought of as a procedure for identifying patterns of interaction among group members.

As the status structure of a group emerges, so do leadership roles. The extent to which an individual occupies a leadership role is dependent upon three variables: influence, communi-cation, and sociometric popularity. Influence is related to power and can be conferred as a result of formal position or by virtue of one's knowledge or ability to persuade others. Individuals who are the center or focal point of group interaction assume leadership roles because of their integral involvement in the communication process. Knowledge of sociometric popularity can help the leader to guide the group toward the achievement of group goals.

There are a number of roles within the group that group members can assume. These roles can be divided into three categories: general task roles, group building and maintenance roles, and individual antigroup roles. Some of the behaviors that are associated with general task roles include serving as an initiator-contributor, information seeker, opinion seeker, information giver, opinion giver, elaborator, summarizer, coordinator-integrator, orienter, disagreer, evaluator-critic, energizer, procedural technician, and recorder. Behavior associated with group building and maintenance roles include acting as an encourager, harmonizer, compromiser, gatekeeper, standard setter, observer-commentator, and follower. Individual antigroup roles that have an adverse or negative effect on the group include acting as an aggressor, blocker, recognition seeker, self-confessor, playboy, dominator, help seeker, and special interest pleader.

Knowledge of techniques involved in working with small groups and committees can be useful to the recreation and leisure service leader because most work in organizations is handled by small groups. A key to working with small groups is understanding the processes that are involved in small-group discussion. These types of discussions allow group members to present their ideas, opinions, and beliefs. Some of the techniques that can facilitate small-group discussions are the circular discussion method, brainstorming, buzz groups, huddle method, case study, role playing, and experiential exercise. Committees are engaged in a number of functions, including providing advice, coordinating, providing information, implementing services, and serving as a final decision-making body.

## DISCUSSION QUESTIONS

1. Define group dynamics. What three components are involved in group dynamics?
2. Identify and discuss various groups with which the recreation and leisure service leader may work.
3. Define the term *group*. What does it mean that individuals must be interrelated and interdependent upon one another in order to be a group?
4. What is the difference between primary and secondary groups? In terms of the leisure experience, what is the role of primary and secondary groups? Explain.
5. Identify and define six properties of groups.
6. What is sociometry? How can this be used in the recreation and service field?
7. What variables affect the ability of an individual to assume a leadership role?
8. What are four causes of group conflict? What can the leader do to overcome conflict within groups?
9. List behaviors that can be exhibited in general task roles, group building and maintenance roles, and individual roles.
10. Identify techniques that can be used by the leader to facilitate a small-group discussion. What are some problems in working with committees?

# 4

# PARTICIPANT MOTIVATION

Motivating the participant often involves giving positive reinforcement and encouragement, as this coach is doing.

Why does an individual participate in one leisure activity and not in another? Why do some individuals thrive on competition whereas others avoid it at all costs? How can

children be encouraged to play with each other harmoniously? How can the leader encourage participants to get involved in new activities? How can a recreation and leisure service organization make people "want" their services? The answers to these questions are complex and focus attention on the role of motivation in our lives. When we ask what makes us behave as we do, we must refer to the motivation process.

Individual behavior is based upon principles of motivation. Therefore, it is important for the recreation and leisure service leader to have a basic knowledge of these principles. Understanding the process of motivation helps us understand causes of human behavior, including leisure behavior. Motivation is not something we can "see," but rather involves assumptions about physiological and psychological operations (internal variables) that are *inferred* from observations.

Internal variables affecting behavior can be described using various terms. "The words we use to label the inner states behind this variable all share some implication of causal determination: purpose, intention, goal-directed, need, want, drive, desire, motive."[1] However, different psychologists may use

[1]Philip G. Zimbardo and Floyd L. Ruch, *Psychology and Life* (Glenview, Ill.: Scott, Foresman, 1976), pp. 197.

these terms in various ways when describing the motivation process. Some psychologists use the phrase "drive" when discussing motivation that is primarily biological and the terms "motive" and "need" when discussing motivation that is primarily psychological and social. Some use the term "drive" when discussing biological motivation, with "need" being a precurser to a biological drive. Still others prefer the use of the term "need" to describe biological drives whether or not they result in behavior. And finally, others use the term "need" when discussing motivation that is physiological, psychological *or* social, or a combination of these.

In this chapter, we will use this latter categorization and will use the term "need" to discuss motivation that is physiological, psychological and social. The term "drive" will be used to describe a state that often follows the existence of a need or needs and that is characterized by the activation and direction of behavior.

The recreation and leisure service leader who understands the motivation process is able to influence the behavior of participants. The leader can use a knowledge of motivation to predict its influence on behavior and perhaps ultimately to help participants shape their behavior in such a way that their leisure needs are met. An understanding of motivation also allows the leader to account for differences in behavior among participants. In short, a leader with such knowledge is able to gain insight into the causes of certain participant behaviors and to predict and assess the influence of leader behavior upon participants.

## THE MOTIVATION PROCESS

Figure 4.1 illustrates the motivation process. The motivation process is characterized by five steps, including: (1) the existence of needs; (2) the initiation of drives; (3) selective attention to relevant stimuli; (4) initiation of

goal-directed activity; (5) attainment of a reward or goal; and (6) the reduction of the drive. There follows a discussion of each of these variables.

### NEEDS

The term often associated with need is that of *deficiency*. When an individual has an imbalance—physically, psychologically, or socially—he or she has a need. Physiological needs are those deficiencies associated with biological drives, such as the need for food,

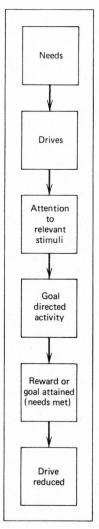

**FIGURE 4.1** The motivation process.

water, sex, and sleep. Physiological needs reflect the desire of individuals to maintain an internal equilibrium. This is known as homeostasis. Psychological and social needs are more difficult to assess, but equally important. The need for companionship, social interaction, safety, love, self-esteem, self-worth, self-actualization, recognition, power, and achievement are all examples of psychological and social needs.

How does the recreation and leisure service leader gauge needs? What sources of information are available to measure this factor? Mercer[2] has suggested that recreational need can be conceptualized from four different perspectives, and Godbey[3] has added a fifth component to this model. These conceptualizations are the following.

*Expressed Needs.* Expressed needs can be thought of as those activities, programs, and services in which an individual currently participates. Expressed needs can be simply determined by asking an individual, ''What recreation and leisure activities do you engage in?''

*Felt Needs.* Felt needs are those needs that an individual feels he or she would like to participate in in the future. They are based on the individual's wishes and desire to fulfill interests and wants. Felt needs can be determined by asking the individual, ''What recreation and leisure activities would you like to engage in in the future that you have not engaged in in the past?''

*Normative Needs.* Normative needs are established by expert groups suggesting minimum standards for services. Establishment of standards implies that certain baseline services are necessary to meet individuals' physiological, psychological, and social needs. For example, standards related to spatial arrangements (i.e., accessibility of open space) are based on the assumption that individuals require the option of access to such areas as parks, playgrounds, and wilderness areas. Lack of adequate open space creates a ''need,'' therefore.

*Comparative Needs.* When an individual compares himself or herself with another in terms of needs, interests, and wants, he or she may identify comparative needs. Comparative needs are often associated with peer group values. In other words, individuals compare their leisure life-styles with others, and then when they perceive a difference, often they develop needs, wants, and interests based on these perceived differences.

*Created Needs.* Created needs are developed when individuals are taught to value a particular leisure experience and, as a result, are inclined to want to continue to participate in it. Created needs or wants are learned behaviors. Often the recreation and leisure service organization will teach individuals to value an activity. As Godbey indicates, individuals don't often know what they want to do during their leisure and consequently respond well to guidance.[4]

A classic conceptualization of needs is offered by Abraham Maslow. Maslow suggests that needs can be hierarchically arranged from lower order needs to higher order needs. His arrangement of needs is predicated on the assumption that needs are arranged according to priority and that lower order needs must be satisfied before the next higher order of needs can be met, and so on up the hierarchy. At the bottom of Maslow's hierarchy are *physiological needs*. These include the need of the individual for food, drink, and sex. These needs are followed by the need for safety, the need

---

[2]David Mercer, ''The Concept of Recreation Need,'' *Journal of Leisure Research*, Winter 1973, p. 39.

[3]Geoffery Godbey, *Leisure in Your Life: An Exploration* (Philadelphia: Saunders College, 1981), pp. 275.

[4]Ibid.

for belongingness-love, the need for self-esteem, and the need for self-actualization. According to Maslow, the lower order needs are of top priority as long as they are unsatisfied. Once they are satisfied, however, the individual is free to pursue the higher needs. Maslow notes, however, that it is possible for one to achieve higher level needs without lower level needs being met. Consider the starving artist, for example.

When we consider the role of the recreation and leisure service leader, relative to Maslow's hierarchy, it can be seen that certain restrictions occur when individuals are operating at the lower levels of the hierarchy. At these lower levels (e.g., physiological and safety), there is little that would involve the recreation and leisure service leader. However, as the individual moves up the hierarchy, the leader can gauge his or her leisure offerings to correspond with the stages or steps to which the participant progresses. For example, certain activities might be more appropriate for participants who want to satisfy the needs associated with esteem whereas other (more creative) activities might be more appropriate for participants who have progressed to the need for self-actualization.

The recreation and leisure service leader attempting to help participants meet their needs should also be aware of Erikson's stages of psychosocial development. These stages of development have a profound effect on the types of needs that individuals must attempt to meet. Erikson specifically postulates eight stages from infancy to old age, described in the following list. Each stage is characterized by a conflict that must be resolved for the individual to be able to cope with conflict at other stages. These conflicts and their resolutions relate to the motivation process and the needs that the individual experiences at each stage.

*Trust vs. Mistrust.* (First year of life.) Depending on the quality of the care received, the infant learns to trust the environment; to perceive it as orderly and predictable; or to be suspicious, fearful, and mistrusting of its chaos and unpredictability.

*Autonomy vs. Doubt.* (Second and third years of life.) From the development of motor and mental abilities and the opportunity to explore and manipulate emerges a sense of autonomy, adequacy, and self-control. Excessive criticism or limiting the exercise of the child's exploration and other behaviors leads to a sense of shame and doubt over his or her adequacy.

*Initiative vs. Guilt.* (Fourth to fifth year of life.) The way parents respond to the child's self-initiated activities, intellectual as well as motor, creates either a sense of freedom and initiative at one extreme or, at the other, a sense of guilt and a feeling of being an inept intruder in an adult world.

*Industry vs. Inferiority.* (Sixth to eleventh year.) The child's concern for how things work and how they ought to operate leads to a sense of industry in formulating rules, organizing, ordering, being industrious. However, a sense of inferiority may be promoted in a child when these efforts are rebuffed as silly, mischievous, or troublesome. It is during this stage that influences outside the home begin to exert a greater influence on the child's development—at least for middle-class American children.

*Identity vs. Role Confusion.* (Adolescence from 12 to 18 years of age.) During this period, the adolescent begins to develop multiple ways of perceiving things, can see things from another person's point of view, behaves differently in different situations according to what is deemed appropriate. In playing these varied roles, the person must develop an integrated sense of his or her own identity as distinct from all others, but coherent and personally acceptable. Where such a "centered" identity is not developed, the alternatives are to be confused about who one really is or to settle on a "negative identity"—a socially unacceptable role, such as that of a "speed freak" or the "class clown."

*Intimacy vs. Isolation.* (Young adulthood.) The consequences of the adult's attempts at reaching out to make contact with others may result in intimacy (a commitment to other people) or else in isolation from close personal relationships.

*Generativity vs. Self-Absorbtion.* (Middle age.) Here one's life experiences may extend the focus of concern beyond one's self or family, society, or future generations. This future orientation may not develop, and instead, like Scrooge in *A Christmas Carol*, a person may become concerned with only material possessions and physical well-being.

*Integrity vs. Despair.* (Old age.) In this last stage of life, one looks back on what it has been all about and ahead to the unknown of death. As a consequence of the solutions developed at each of the preceding stages, one can enjoy the fulfillment of life with a sense of integrity. But despair is what faces the person who finds that life has been unsatisfying and misdirected. Too late, either to look back in anger or ahead with hope, the life cycle of such a person ends with a whimper of despair.[5]

These stages offer the leader a profound insight into the human being at various stages in his life. This insight should help the recreation and leisure service leader plan more effectively for individuals at each of these stages.

**DRIVES**

The step in the motivation process that follows the existence of needs, is the initiation of drives. We use the term drive as meaning an

[5]Erik Erikson, *Childhood and Society* (New York: Norton, 1950), as cited in Zimbardo and Ruch, op. cit., pp. 254–255.

activator and director of behavior. A drive is the energizing process that results in movement toward the fulfillment of a need. Different needs will result in the activation of different drives. Also, the stronger the drive (i.e., greater thirst), the more the activity. Specifically, a drive is a result of internal conditions within the individual that direct that person toward a specific goal. For example, a drive to socialize might result from a need for companionship.

Drives cannot be "seen," only inferred. In other words, by considering available information regarding *stimulus conditions* and *behavior that is observable* one can make assumptions regarding the internal variable "affecting" behavior. For example, *if* one observes that children at a birthday party (1) have not had anything to drink for several hours, (2) that they have been active and running, and (3) that they have been eating salty peanuts (stimulus conditions) *and* that the children (1) ask for something to drink, (2) consume several cups of punch, and (3) request water if punch is unavailable (behavior that is observable), *then* one might assume that "thirst" is an intervening variable in this situation. In other words, it is possible to observe individual behavior and, as a result of such observation, infer that certain internal physiological or psychological processes were likely involved. Drives are often linked with the concept of energy arousal. This concept implies that the individual becomes active in order to meet a need. Drives are directed by needs. They enable individuals to focus or channel their energies in such a way that their behavior results in the fulfillment of a need or alleviation of a deficiency.

It is important to recognize that drives can vary from culture to culture. Moreover, drives can vary among individuals within a given culture. In certain cultures, the motivation to engage in leisure behavior may be stronger than it is in the United States or Canada. In other cultures, the motivation to work may actually be stronger as a result of a greater likelihood that individuals will experience deficiencies of food, shelter, and security without the expending of considerable work effort. Although there is no clear-cut agreement as to how drives should be classified, most psychologists suggest that there are primary and secondary drives. Primary drives are related to such factors as hunger, thirst, sex, sleep, and avoidance of pain. Although primary drives are important to a comprehensive understanding of the motivation process, secondary drives are more relevant to our discussion. An important distinction to be made between secondary and other drives is that secondary drives must be learned. They are not biologically innate, but rather are initiated and satisfied by social and psychological factors. Although the inability to attain social and psychological goals may not be life threatening, as are biological deficiencies, it can result in emotional deprivation and limitation of life satisfaction. The following motives or drives[6] have been categorized as secondary.

*Competence.* Competence refers to the ability of individuals to interact successfully with their environment. This suggests that individuals are motivated to master their leisure environment. Perceived competence is an important component of the leisure experience.

*Novelty or Curiosity.* Individuals desire to explore or manipulate their environment or both. Psychologists have suggested that individuals, when placed in novel situations, have a natural curiosity to search out or explore them. Certainly, this can be seen when viewing the behavior of children.

*Activity.* Individuals have a desire for activity. This is supported by studies that have found that children will seek out opportunities for physical activity. Activity allows individuals to interact with their environment.

*Affection.* Human love or affection, as a drive, is focused on the individual's desire for nurturing, emotional support, and comfort. Although affection is an unlearned drive and, therefore, classified as a primary drive by some psychologists, its inclusion in this category seems appropriate in light of its relevance to the leisure experience.

*Achievement.* The desire to achieve or excel is a strong motivator in today's society. The need for achievement is characterized by goal-seeking behavior, an emphasis on personal responsibility, risk-taking behavior, and a desire for performance evaluation.

*Power.* The desire for power can be thought of as the desire to control or influence others. The drive for power is not thought to be inborn, but rather is thought to stem from feelings of childhood powerlessness and insecurity. Evidence of the search for power is prevalent in North American society today. This has obvious implications for organizational leadership.

*Affiliation.* The drive to interact, create associations, and create and maintain friendships are all factors associated with the desire for affiliation. Individuals who have a strong desire for affiliation are viewed as being likely to participate in parties and social events, as well as in groups and organizations.

*Freedom of Choice.* Individuals desire to retain their freedom of choice. This is related to the concept of reactance. Reactance can be thought of as the actions of the individual to resist decisions that are "made *for*

---

[6]This list of motives was drawn from the following sources: Fred Luthans, *Organizational Behavior*, 2d ed. (New York: McGraw-Hill, 1977), pp. 317–332; David C. McClelland et al. *The Achievement Motive* (New York: Appleton-Century-Crofts, 1953); and Zimbardo and Ruch, op. cit., pp. 380–388.

them.'' In other words, individuals will refuse to be pressured into actions that restrict their freedom.

*Social Approval.* As individuals, we are involved in many activities in order that others will ''notice, appreciate, honor, help, or love and cherish us.''[7] The desire to gain approval from others is extremely strong, and individuals will go to considerable lengths to accomplish this.

*Altruism.* Altruism can be thought of as helping others without expectation of external rewards. This is important to the recreation and leisure service field, for altruism encourages individuals to volunteer as coaches, leaders, and so on. Donations of land, funds, and equipment may also be related to altruism. Altruism is thought to be related to feelings of empathy by some theorists.

*Consistency.* Individuals have a desire for balance and consistency in their lives. Leisure is often viewed as a counterbalance to work. Individuals will work to correct inconsistencies, particularly when they receive pieces of information that are inconsistent with one another (termed *cognitive dissonance*).

*Security.* Individuals have a desire to be secure. They will avoid situations that are dangerous or threaten their security. In addition, they may actively attempt to prevent breaches of security by taking preventative measures.

*Status.* Many individuals have a desire to possess and maintain material symbols of status in our society, such as expensive homes, expensive clothes and so on. There are many leisure-related status symbols— boats, travel, as well as the use of equipment and apparel with the ''right'' labels.

[7]Zimbardo and Ruch, op. cit., pp. 385.

## ATTENTION TO RELEVANT STIMULI

Once an individual's needs have resulted in drives, the next step in the motivation process occurs. The individual at this point becomes engaged in attention to relevant stimuli. Relevant stimuli can be defined as information that relates to the individual's current state of need. This information may be in the form of words and phrases or may involve other information processed through the five senses. For example, an individual motivated by a desire for safety will attend to such relevant stimuli as stop lights, traffic signs, or sirens. With the knowledge gained from such cues or information, the individual may accomplish one or more of the following: to predict the likelihood of future events, actually to control events, or to alter his or her behavior to make it more appropriate and effective in terms of the events forecasted or a combination of these. In short, the individual receives information (or cues) that are psychological, social, or physical in nature signaling the imminent occurrence of such varied events as danger, pleasure, or relief.

How does this concept (attention to relevant stimuli) relate to participant-leader interaction? The participant attending a recreation and leisure activity is immediately subjected to many cues and bits of information. The participant will look around and perhaps see smiles, friendly faces, special equipment, brightly colored posters, and individuals in casual clothing suggesting activity and will listen to verbal cues such as ''fun,'' ''good time,'' ''glad you are here.'' From these cues, the participant will be able to predict the likely occurrence of a pleasurable and possibly exciting and creative experience. In other words, the participant is able to form expectations, based on the verbal and visual cues that are received. As the participant begins actually to engage in the activity, he or she will continue to receive cues possibly such as laughter, movement, and jumping up and down and to receive verbal cues such as "great catch," "this team played great," "boy, are you fast." As the participant receives initial cues and these later cues, he or she is able to shape his or her behavior to correspond to the opportunities that are currently being offered. In this way, the participant's behavior is more effective in terms of the opportunities offered and the likelihood that his or her needs will be met.

How does the participant know that certain cues, such as smiling, positive verbal phrases, and play equipment signal the likelihood of certain outcomes? In order for the participant to predict an outcome, he or she must have had prior experience with the stimulus. Specifically, the stimulus must have been paired, sometime in the past, with a certain type of outcome. Smiling, for example, has been paired many times with positive outcomes. Consequently, the participant would have learned that smiling is a very reliable predictor of "fun." In the same vein, play equipment would likely have been paired many times with fun. However, had it *not* been paired with "fun," but had it been paired with misfortune instead, it might signal "danger" to the participant and act as a predictor of the likelihood of a fear-laden experience. The signals that cues impart, then, may vary with the individual participant. What is a positive signal to one individual may be a negative signal to another participant. The topic of "cues" will be covered in more depth later in this chapter.

### GOAL-DIRECTED ACTIVITY

The step in the motivation process that follows attendance to relevant stimuli is actual behavior or goal-directed activity. Goal-directed behavior is the detectable manifestation of drives such as desire for power, affection, approval, and so on. It can be defined as behavior that results in the reduction of a

Marriott's Great America theme park offers many "cues" that signal fun and excitement to participants, such as smiles, bright colored rides and costumes, and festive music.

need or drive. In simple terms, this means that goal-directed activity should be viewed as an indication of the individual's inner state. It should not, however, be viewed as a total picture of the individual's needs. Observing behavior provides us with an opportunity to learn about the individual by associating stimulus conditions and observable behavioral outcomes with the motives that are likely to cause that type of behavior.

When motivation acts as a catalyst for behavior, that behavior is said to be "goal directed" or "purposeful." Goal-directed activity is engaged in to meet the needs of the individual. For example, the need for companionship may result in a drive for affiliation with others. As the reader will recall, the drive for affiliation involves the desire to interact with others and to produce friendships. The goal-directed activity associated with this drive might find the individual joining a club, attending group social activities, or becoming a member of an athletic team. In other words, goal-directed behavior works to alleviate the needs and drives of the individual. When an individual is hungry, the goal-directed activity becomes the search for food. Obviously, the more complex secondary motives, such as the desire for power, altruism, status, and achievement, often result in complex patterns of goal-directed behavior.

Goal-directed activity can be "assisted" by attention to relevant stimuli. Input from the leader, for example, can nudge participants toward the type of goal-directed activity that will best meet their goals. For example, the participant engaged in creative activity might assimilate such information as "praise is given for extensive use of color," "praise is given for individuality," and "praise is given for using several types of mediums" and use these to give direction to his or her behavior in order to fulfill needs related to recognition, achievement, competence, status, and social approval.

Leisure behavior can be a result of many and varied drives. All the drives listed in prior pages serve as motivators for leisure. Some drives may be stronger for one person than for another. Certain drives seem to be more evident today than in past years. For example, more individuals today are involved in high adventure, risk-oriented programs, suggesting an increased need for novelty, risk, and adventure. The great interest in travel provides another example of the increased need for novelty, adventure, and change. Leisure is also often used as a vehicle for social approval and status, as evidenced by participation in cultural activities; "in" sports such as tennis, sailing, and raquetball; and the installation of expensive home entertainment centers.

## ATTAINMENT OF REWARD OR GOAL

The next component of the motivation process, goal attainment, is dependent on the previous component, goal-directed activity. Goal-directed activity often results in the individual's goal attainment. The point at which this occurs and the individual's needs are met is a subjective measure that can only be determined by the individual himself or herself. One individual involved in a sport may have to hit only one base run to meet needs for recognition, achievement, and social approval. Another individual involved in the same sport may have to hit several home runs to meet the same need. In a social situation, one individual may need to make only one friend to achieve goals related to affiliation whereas another individual may need to be "the center of attention" in order to meet this same need.

When the individual's goal is met, a reinforcement process occurs. Since the behavior that the individual has engaged in has, indeed, brought about the realization of the intended goal, the individual forms an expectancy that similar behavior in the future will again bring about similar results. The individual, for example, who has participated in a summer playground program may, as a result of the activity and effort expended in this program, have had such needs fulfilled as recognition, novelty, achievement, pleasure, and social approval. This individual will expect, as a result of this experience and the consequent fulfillment of needs and meeting of goals, that similar future experiences will meet these same needs. In other words, he or she will be more likely to participate in next year's summer program and may even generalize his or her experience to include an expectancy that all recreation and leisure service organization activities are likely to provide opportunities for goal fulfillment.

As mentioned, goal attainment and goal-directed activity are interrelated. Not only does goal-directed activity have an influence on goal attainment, but goal attainment and the *way* that the goal is attained will have an influence on future behavior related to the same goal. How strongly or how quickly the goal is achieved will affect the likelihood that the individual will engage in behavior to reproduce the experience. On the other hand, if the goal is delayed, the individual may not pursue it as strongly in the future. We don't like to ''wait'' for things. For example, a youngster involved in making ice cream on the playground may be rewarded with the fulfillment of needs for pleasure and achievement, but the delay of the goal may disincline the youth from participating in this same activity in the future. On the other hand, youngsters involved in relay races, with an immediate goal fulfillment of prizes (related to pleasure, achievement, and approval) at the end of the race, may be motivated to engage in similar future activities if offered.

## NEED AND DRIVE REDUCTION

The final step in the motivation process is the reduction of needs and drives. When needs and drives are reduced, the individual, as an obvious consequence, will not actively attempt to engage in behavior associated with meeting the need, even though the habit may be a strong one. For example, an individual who loves to play tennis, but has not been able to play all winter will be strongly motivated to take action that will enable him or her to play tennis in the spring and early summer. However, by late fall the same individual may have had enough tennis playing and, as a result, may decline an invitation to play even if it is offered. Therefore, the degree to which an individual's need has been met will influence behavior usually associated with meeting the need. It is important that the recreation and leisure service leader be aware of this phase of the motivation process, since it can have a considerable affect on the motivation of participants. For example, it may be relatively easy to interest children in a summer playground program at the beginning of the summer but by midsummer or the end of the summer, when the children have been involved in the program for some time, their drive to participate actively may not be as strong. The leader may have to put forth some extra effort in order to maintain interest in the program.

***The Role of the Environment in the Motivation Process.*** The motivation process just presented is based on the stimulus-response theory of motivation. This motivation model suggests that individual behavior occurs in response to primary biological needs and learned secondary needs. Recently, it has been suggested that this need reduction model to explain motivation, especially as it relates to leisure, fails to take into account the influence of the individual on the environment. Discussing the influence of the individual on the environment, Kusyszyn has written thus.

1.  There is a strong basic human motive: to have an effect on our environment . . .
2.  We need to have an effect on our environment in order to confirm our existence. . . . We confirm our existence when we have an effect on our environment by becoming aroused . . .
3.  Having an effect on our environment can . . . give us a sense of self-worth. . . . When we consciously and purposefully set out to have a specific effect on our environment and we succeed producing that effect, we feel good about the whole event . . .
4.  By having an effect on our environment and by becoming aroused through feedback we get from producing the effect, we put ourselves into an altered state of consciousness.[8]

[8]Igor Kusyszyn, *A Theory of New Motivation*, in Joseph Levy, ''Motivation for Leisure: An Interactionist Approach,'' a chapter in Hilmi Ibrahim and Rick Crandall, *Leisure: A Psychological Approach* (Los Alamitos, Calif.: Hwong Publishing Co., 1979), p. 167.

The altered state of consciousness produced by an individual's arousal, as a result of being able to affect the environment, is often associated with a leisure or play experience. Various terms have been used to describe this state, including *peak, arousal,* and *flow.* The term *peak experience* was coined by Maslow[9]; *arousal,* as it relates to leisure, by Ellis[10]; and *flow,* by Csikszentmihalyi.[11] Each of these individuals has developed models to explain his respective concepts.

Ellis's "arousal-seeking" theory of play suggests that play occurs when individuals seek arousal by interacting with the environment in ways that are above and beyond those needed for survival.[12] While engaged in this arousal-seeking activity, the individual "learns." As a result of this learning, future play behavior is shaped, and, with the continuance of arousal, play behavior becomes more complex. Developmental stages reflect this progression to more and more complex levels of play. In short, this model suggests that the environment and the individual interact, resulting in learning, which, in turn, influences future behavior.

Csikszentmihalyi's concept of flow is a compelling construct explaining the interaction of the individual with the environment.[13] It provides a basis for understanding boredom and anxiety. He suggests that the leisure experience is influenced by the individual's skill level as it relates to the challenge present within the environment. When the challenge presented in the environment is greater than the individual's skill level or knowledge, the individual experiences anxiety. Conversely, when the challenge presented in the environment is less than the individual's skill level or

knowledge, boredom results. When the two factors—challenge of the environment and skill level of the individual—are matched, the individual enters into a state of flow or, as Csikszentmihalyi indicates, the "autotelic" experience. The environment (challenge) and individual (with skills) interaction described in this model provides a basis for explaining outcomes of the leisure experience. This may account for the fact that some individuals are motivated to participate in certain activities whereas others are not.

## PARTICIPANT MOTIVATION: THE ROLE OF THE LEADER

What is the role of the recreation and leisure service leader in motivating participants? What does a face-to-face leader do that motivates participants to participate in activities and derive expected as well as unanticipated benefits from their involvement? These are complex questions, primarily because of the individual nature of the leisure experience, variables in individual dispositions and perceptions, and, last, the unpredictability of the interaction between the leader and participants.

In a review of the process of motivation, it is important to establish some assumptions. First it can be assumed that individuals seek out *experiences*, not products, activities, services, facilities, and so on. In other words, the individual who buys ski equipment is really purchasing a "ski experience." A second assumption is that individuals participate in activities because of the expectation of some gain or benefit. More specifically, individuals participate in activities in order to meet needs. The third assumption is that the leader will play a key role in shaping, molding, or providing experiences that meet leisure needs. In the case of the face-to-face recreation and leisure service leader, this key role is one of structuring the environment in order to motivate individuals in such a way that they

[9]Abraham H. Maslow, *Toward a Psychology of Being* (New York: Van Nostrand Reinhold, 1968).

[10]Michael G. Ellis, *Why People Play* (Englewood Cliffs, N.J.: Prentice-Hall, 1973), p. 118.

[11]Mihalyi Csikszentmihalyi, *Beyond Boredom and Anxiety* (Washington, D.C.: Jossey-Bass, 1975).

[12]Ellis, op. cit.

[13]Csikszentmihalyi, op.cit.

experience leisure successfully. The leader's knowledge of appropriate communication, group dynamics, and leadership techniques enables this to occur.

Structuring of the environment primarily involves the creation of cues that signal to the participant that a certain type of experience is available. For example, participants often seek out experiences that are exciting. By shaping the environment, the leader can produce conditions that indicate the likelihood of an exciting experience. The leader, for example, might use a communication style and pattern that have a high degree of energy and enthusiasm and that reflect a keen interest and excitement about the impending experience. This type of cue provides a signal to the participant that his or her need for excitement can be met. Even though it is trite, we often say that enthusiasm is contagious. This is an example of that maxim.

The leader can mold the environment in such a way that participants are unaware that their expectations are being shaped. Consider, for example, the leader who wants to plan and implement a dance for teenagers. The experience that the teenagers desire is one full of excitement, social interaction, euphoria, and fun. What can the leader do to set the stage for this type of experience? In advance, through various promotional mechanisms, the leader may advertise the activity in such a way that its potential for excitement and fun is emphasized. This advertisement of the dance will present cues that create expectations. Expectations, in turn, will motivate the participant to go to the dance. Once the leader has advertised the dance, he or she might engage in preparations that will provide further cues that meet participants' anticipation of excitement. These preparations might include dramatic lighting, festive decorations, the selection of exciting and loud music. All these preparations by the leader may not be consciously acknowledged by participants; however, the environment will be shaped in such a way that their expectations for excitement will be met, and they will have a good time.

At the dance itself, the leader may interact one on one with participants in such a way that further cues as to the nature of the experience are given that enable the participant to be self-motivated and meet his or her needs for excitement and fun. For example, the leader might interact with participants in an effusive, enthusiastic manner, might attempt to insert some element of unpredictability into the evening's activities to heighten the excitement further, and might dance with some of the participants that are not yet dancing. *This type of interaction with participants, one on one or leader-group, is the crux of face-to-face activity leadership. The dynamics of interaction that takes place between the leader and the participant or participants is the heart of recreation and leisure service leadership. The success or failure of this interaction is often directly tied to the extent to which a participant achieves the desired ends of a leisure experience.*

Another situation that serves to illustrate the importance of leader-participant interaction in the motivation process is the relationship that is developed between a coach and team members collectively and individually. Team members come into this leisure experience with different desires, interests, expectations, and needs. One team member, for example, may have a desire for increased capability in the sport to be played. Another member may have a desire to achieve greater recognition through participation in the sport. Still another team member may have a need for social interaction that can be fulfilled by a team experience. Or team members may have several needs that can be met by participation in the sport. The coach, as the leader of the group, can interact with team members to provide encouragement, instruction, and direction. The coach may praise an individual team member for an outstanding play, thereby providing the team member with a sense of achievement and increased capability. The coach may also attempt to develop a sense of comradeship and cooperation that will facilitate social interaction within the group and thereby fulfill the need of some team members for this type of reinforcement. The coach might use cues in order to shape the situation so that it meets *individual* needs for a leisure experience. For example, the coach may give a team member a slap on the behind to signal approval of achievement or may talk in a conspirational, intimate manner to promote a "team" esprit de corps. These cues set the stage for self-motivation to occur on the part of team members. For example, the team member who receives the slap on the behind will continue to feel "reinforced" when engaging in the rewarded behavior.

Figure 4.2 presents a model demonstrating the process of participant-leader interaction. In this process of interaction, the leader usually is aware of the participant's needs either from the participant himself or herself or via the leader's perceptions. In order to create an environment in which these needs can be met and individuals can become self-motivated, the leader must become aware of the participants' expectations. For some participants, fantasy might be the major reason for pursu-

ing leisure. For another participant, escape might be the desired outcome of the leisure experience. The leader can structure the environment by providing cues to either influence expectations or reinforce behavior. In the former case, cues attempt to shape the preliminary attitudes, interests, and emotions of the participant to "fit" the experience at hand. In the latter case, cues reinforce or reward the participant for behavior that occurs during the leisure experience in order to help the participant meet needs.

There are three basic types of cues that the recreation and leisure service leader can provide to the participant by structuring or arranging the physical, social or psychological environments or a combination of them. By structuring or arranging the environment we mean that the leader organizes it consciously or unconsciously and in such a way that it evokes or reinforces desired leisure behavior.

### CUES IN THE PHYSICAL ENVIRONMENT

The way in which the physical environment is arranged has a great deal of influence on participant behavior. In simplistic terms, the recreation and leisure service leader can manipulate the physical environment by changing

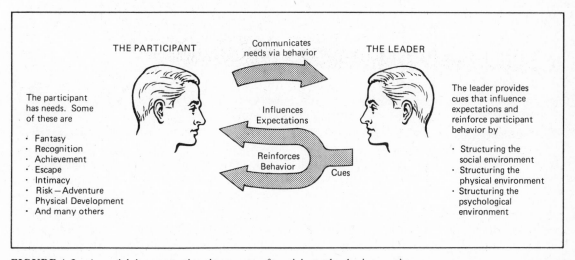

**FIGURE 4.2**   A model demonstrating the process of participant-leader interaction.

such things as lighting, spatial arrangements, color, decorations, and other factors. For example, the seating arrangement of individuals for a group discussion can be set up in such a way that all individuals are facing each other in a circle. This arrangement of the physical environment may promote group interaction and discussion. In another situation, the leader may want to arrange the chairs so that the participants focus toward the individual at the front of the room. Leaders often try to create a mood with lighting, for example, by lowering the lighting in order to allow participants to feel less inhibited and thus create a more dramatic effect in a dance situation. Decorations may also be put up to give a festive, light, colorful, and cheery feeling. Again, this is a manipulation of the physical environment.

Spatial arrangements can be manipulated to create feelings of intimacy or perhaps freedom from restrictions. For example, it would be inappropriate to hold a knitting class in a gymnasium. The leader would want to conduct this type of class in a more intimate, smaller area. Individuals also feel more intimate in environments with more objects—for example, couches, chairs, tables—than they do in rooms that are relatively bare. If a leader wanted to create a mood of intimacy and belonging in a teenage center, for example, he or she might want to manipulate the environment so that it would be "comfortably cluttered."

In terms of larger spatial arrangements, theme parks serve as a good example of how the manipulation of the physical environment is used to evoke certain participant responses. The location of the soda pop stand will follow directly after that of a popcorn stand, thus manipulating the environment to serve the participant best.

The color of the environment can also have an influence on the participant's behavior and feelings. Green and blue, for example, are soothing and restful colors and might be in-

corporated into areas of discussion and introspection. Red and orange are exciting, stimulating colors that might be used effectively in areas to be used for high-energy leisure experiences. The manipulation of color, like the other manipulations of the physical environment (light, spatial effects, and so on) provide cues to the participant as to the type of experience that is available. It contributes to the anticipation and expectations of the participant in a channeled or focused manner.

## CUES IN THE SOCIAL ENVIRONMENT

Organization or manipulation of the *social environment* can also influence participant behavior. When we speak of the manipulation of the social environment, we are referring to the leader's ability to create opportunities for friendship, interaction, love, companionship, membership, recognition, and so on. Because of the nature of face-to-face leadership, social manipulation is often directly dependent on, and related to, the individual leader's personality, demeanor, and behavior. When the recreation and leisure service leader is open, effusive, energetic, enthusiastic, and interested in others, this can be viewed as behavior that affects the social environment. This type of behavior is natural with many leaders and occurs without conscious awareness of its impact on the behavior of participants. This type of behavior evokes responses from participants; it is a motivator of people. In the right situation and circumstance, it is a very powerful factor, directly related to the success or failure of participants to anticipate and achieve leisure experiences.

In contrast to the affective behavior of the leader, there are actual structural manipulations of the social environment that the leader can initiate to influence participant behavior. As discussed in Chapter 3, the types of groups and group sizes, for example, can affect the likelihood that friendships, companionship, interaction, and so on will occur. If a group is divided into threes for discussion or activities, these triads may be more subject to dissention, argument, and hostility. By dividing the group by twos for activities, one can minimize these problems and achieve greater harmony among and between participants.

There are also very direct ways that the leader can intervene or provide cues that will result in the participant's feeling recognition, hence being motivated. Leaders often use rewards such as ribbons, trophies, medals, certificates, verbal recognition, and praise to manipulate the social environment and provide cues that stimulate participant involvement and interest. There are tangible and intangible forms of recognition. Tangible forms of recognition take the form of ribbons, trophies, and so on, as mentioned. Intangible recognition is awarded by giving verbal praise or a pat on the back or allowing special privileges, and so on. These two types of cues can be used by the leader in conjunction with one another; intangible recognition can be reinforced with tangible rewards and vice versa. The leader can motivate participants without the use of tangible cues or forms of recognition; however, it is difficult, if not impossible, to motivate participants without intangible forms of recognition, such as verbal praise.

## CUES IN THE PSYCHOLOGICAL ENVIRONMENT

The manipulation of the *psychological environment* can also influence participant behavior. When we speak of the psychological environment, we are referring to the participant's need for self-knowledge, novelty, aesthetic satisfactions, self-worth, self-identification, achievement, power, mastery, and transcendence.[14] The manipulation of the psychological environment may be more difficult than manipulation of the social or physical environments. There are many things that the

leader can do, however, to influence the perceptions of the participant, which may, in turn, influence whether or not he or she is motivated. For example, it has been suggested that individuals must have an illusion of competence and freedom in order to enter into the leisure experience successfully. It is possible for the leader to create freedom within the environment by allowing the participant to choose among alternatives. Although those alternatives may be carefully structured, the individual can be led to feel a sense of freedom. The leader can give the illusion of competence by creating challenges equal to individual skill levels. Or the leader may group participants according to level of skill (e.g., slow break versus fast break basketball). Participants may develop feelings of self-worth and identification by being part of a team and perhaps by being delegated a leadership role. A leadership role may also provide a participant with a sense of power and prestige. In fact, the leader may want to provide opportunities for all group members to become involved in a leadership role in some way.

It is important for the leader to allow the participant to evaluate his or her *own* performance and benefits from leisure participation. The leader can help participants develop self-knowledge and a sense of self-worth by offering appropriate dialogue or cues that allow participants to formulate their own opinions regarding their leisure experiences. For example, the leader should mirror the participant's feelings and observations rather than offering his or her own observations, allowing the *participant* to develop the conclusions. Rather than telling a child, ''You did a good job,'' the leader should say, ''You look as if you feel pretty good about your performance today,'' prompting the child's internal response, ''I am pretty pleased!'' This type of psychological cue allows the participant to assess himself or herself and develop conclusions that are more conducive to feelings of self-

[14]Lloyd A. Heywood, *Recreation For Older Adults: A Program Manual* (Toronto: Ministry of Culture and Recreation, 1979), p. 12

worth. When we are told that we "did a good job," often our response is to think, "I could have done better," or "I really didn't." If we draw our own conclusions, this is avoided.

## LEADER–PARTICIPANT INTERACTION

Figure 4.3 depicts a model that links the process of leader-participant interaction with the more comprehensive model of motivation. The reader will recall the model of motivation presented earlier in the chapter. Our discussion now will focus on the role of cues by the recreation and leisure service leader in the motivation process. Cues facilitate the motivation process. As individual needs are perceived by the leader, the leader can begin to form cues that will respond to these needs. Cues can also be presented as the participant moves to the second stage of the motivation process, that of attention to relevant stimuli.

It is at this stage that the participant is likely to interpret the leader's cues and form his or her expectations-anticipation. Following the formulation of participant expectations, the participant will exhibit behavior; this behavior can be directed by cues toward certain ends. As cues shape the participant's behavior, it becomes more goal directed. The leader at this time also receives information from the participant that is useful in determining the effectiveness of the cues being given and is useful in determining whether or not cues should be changed or modified. These efforts by the leader and the participant are continued until the need or needs of the participant are fulfilled.

In discussing the motivation process, Edginton and Williams have suggested that the recreation and leisure service professional can directly influence four important variables.[15] They indicate that a leader can assist an individual to meet his or her leisure needs through the processes of expectancy, availability, abil-

[15]Christopher R. Edginton and John G. Williams, *Productive Management of Leisure Service Organizations: A Behavioral Approach* (New York: Wiley, 1978), pp. 104–108.

ity and satisfaction. Each one of these will be discussed in relation to the motivation process. Following is a description of each of these processes that can be used by the leader.

*Expectancy.*  According to the theory of expectancy, whether or not an individual will participate in a given activity is dependent on past experience. Those individuals who have had their needs satisfied in the past through participation in an activity are more likely to participate in similar types of activities to meet similar needs in the future. The leader's knowledge of those activities that have previously resulted in the meeting of an individual's expectations of benefits can aid him or her in planning future activities and services that will meet these same needs. Often cues that are related to the individual's past experiences will motivate him or her to participate in current or future experiences or both. Very simply, the leader can remind the participant of the "great time" he or she had "before" to motivate him or her to participate in a future activity.

*Availability.*  Availability is related to the individual's perception of his or her environment. Individuals may or may not perceive that a situation can meet their needs. One individual may perceive a situation to be a great opportunity to meet a need whereas another individual may view the same situation as being devoid of such opportunities. In the case of the first individual, motivation to become involved will occur because it is perceived that goals can be achieved and needs satisfied. In the case of the second individual, involvement is not likely to occur because benefits and rewards are not perceived as being available. The leader can influence participants' perceptions by making the goals appear more accessible. For example, the leader can structure an activity so that a lower skill level is needed to be successful.

*Ability.*  The recreation and leisure service leader can work with individuals to help them

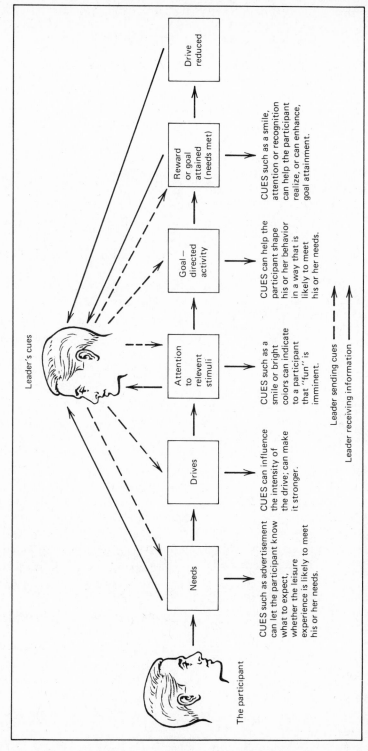

**FIGURE 4.3**  A model relating the effects of participant-leader interaction on motivation.

to improve their ability, which, in turn, will influence their perceived competence. The participant must have a perception of ability in an area of activity in order to seek out an opportunity for participation in it. A focus of recreation and leisure service organizations is the development of leisure skills and abilities. Instructional programs provided by organizations are directed toward helping individuals attain not only exposure to activities, but also minimum competence in them. Individuals who become frustrated and lose their motivation because of a lack of ability will not only be more likely to drop out of the activity, but may avoid it in the future (because of expectancy).

*Satisfaction.* The leader can greatly influence the amount of satisfaction an individual derives from an activity. Satisfaction is influenced by the willingness of the leader to provide praise or recognition. In Chapter 1 the authors stressed the importance of providing positive encouragement to individuals and cited it as a key to successful leadership. The ability to provide praise in such a way that participants are positively reinforced is an important leadership skill. It has major influence on the motivation process and is appropriate with any age group and at any skill level. Meaningful feedback is crucial to the participant's development of feelings of self-worth, self-esteem, and satisfaction.

Knowledge of the processes of motivation enables the recreation and leisure service leader to detect and meet the needs of participants successfully. The more the leader is aware of this process and the more proficient he or she becomes at sending cues that help shape expectations and behavior, the more likely the leader is to succeed in assisting individuals to meet their leisure needs.

### REMOVING BARRIERS

Perhaps another way of viewing the role of the recreation and leisure service leader in the motivation process is as an individual responsible for assisting in barrier removal. There are many barriers that can occur and that prevent individuals from achieving desired goals. These barriers sometimes are within the influence of the participant, whereas at other times they are within the leader's sphere of influence. The inability to overcome barriers to the leisure experience often results in frustration, anxiety, and aggression and negatively influences the psychological and social development of individuals. For example, individuals often act defensively when confronted with new opportunities for participation because they may feel that they lack the skills to participate effectively.

Some of the barriers that can prevent individuals from achieving a satisfying leisure experience have been identified by Edginton et al.[16] They are the following.

*Attitudinal.* A person's attitude toward leisure may influence his or her ability to participate successfully in a recreation activity, program, or service. Since attitudes are learned, the leader can help the individual develop new and more positive attitudes.

*Communicative.* The way in which information is transmitted to individuals can contribute to the formation of barriers, especially if it is transmitted at the wrong time, using the wrong channel of communication, and without sufficient opportunity for feedback.

*Consumptive.* The consumptive type of barrier relates to the influence of commercial organizations on leisure behavior. Commercial organizations exert considerable effort and expense in order to encourage consumption of products that may not meet individual needs.

*Temporal.* Not all leisure experiences are linked to mechanical, linear clock time. The bondage of the clock often affects lei-

---

[16]Christopher R. Edginton, David H. Compton, and Carole J. Hanson, *Recreation and Leisure Programming: A Guide for the Professional* (Philadelphia: Saunders College Publishing, 1980), pp. 214–217.

sure fulfillment. Too much time, as well as a lack of time, can create barriers.

*Social-Cultural and Economic.* Often an individual's social, cultural, and economic status will determine his or her leisure preferences. Lack of money obviously can be a barrier. The leader can attempt to equalize opportunity that might be affected by these variables.

*Health.* An individual may have physical or emotional factors that may act as barriers. The leader can attempt to structure activities in such a way that they circumvent these barriers to participation.

*Experiential.* Previous adverse experiences or the simple lack of previous involvement can act as barriers. The leader can attempt to help the individual overcome adverse feelings regarding participation or develop skills and knowledge that will facilitate a successful leisure experience or both.

All these barriers can adversely affect leisure motivation and participation. Recreation and leisure service leaders should work with individuals to help them identify and formulate solutions to overcome them. There are some recreation leaders who create more barriers than they remove. The leader should establish a positive atmosphere in which his or her primary consideration is the *removal* of barriers. By doing so, the leader can contribute positively to the motivation process rather than negatively.

## PARTICIPATION BENEFITS

A chapter on motivation is incomplete without addressing the benefits that are derived by the participant. It is the anticipation of benefits (the fulfillment of psychological, social, and physical needs) that motivates the individual to become involved in leisure experiences. As indicated, individuals seek *benefits or the expectation of benefits* rather than activities or products. In other words, individuals are looking for experiences that will meet their needs in a way that is beneficial to them. The recreation and leisure service leader should view activities, programs, and other services as vehicles that enable individuals to satisfy their expectations and achieve desired benefits. In this sense, programs are not the ends but the means to an end. They are a way of organizing and distributing agency resources to meet participant needs.

A number of authors have identified the potential benefits of the leisure experience. Heywood, for example, suggests that potential participant benefits can be categorized into four classifications: psychological-emotional well-being, social well-being, physical well-being and spiritual well-being.[17] His categorization of benefits is further subdivided into specific experiences that may occur within these categories. For example, group belonging, communication, problem solving, and fun-enjoyment are listed as benefits that can occur in certain activities within the "social well-being" category.

Table 4.1 presents Heywood's conceptualization. This table depicts potential participant benefits along one axis and program areas on the other. This particular chart was developed for use with older adults. The subcategories within each of the four general classifications could be expanded for other age groups. The same could apply when developing specific activities for other groups. For example, a twelve-year-old may not be interested in a death and dying class or retirement counseling program, but many of the activities depicted would cut across all age groupings. And certainly the format is a useful conceptualization that offers a comprehensive approach to relating potential benefits to specific activities.

Murphy et al. have suggested that recreation and leisure service agencies provide opportunities for a variety of behaviors. They suggest that "the basic method used by agen-

[17]Heywood, op. cit., pp. 74–75.

**TABLE 4.1**   Potential Participation Benefits

| Category | Activity | Blood Pressure | Resting Pulse | Pulse Recovery | Lung/Breathing Capacity | Endurance | Muscle Tone | Muscle Strength | Coordination/Flexibility | Posture | Weight Loss | Control Weight | Tolerance to Stress | Tension Release | Relieve Strain/Fatigue | Relaxation | Healthy Appearance | Personal Enrichment | Communion with Self | Communion with Nature | Communion with Others | Catharsis | Service to Others |
|---|---|---|---|---|---|---|---|---|---|---|---|---|---|---|---|---|---|---|---|---|---|---|---|
| | | **PHYSICAL FITNESS** | | | | | | | | | | | | | | | | **SPIRITUAL WELL-BEING** | | | | | |
| **PHYSICAL ACTIVITY** | Aquabics | • | • | | • | • | • | • | • | • | • | • | • | • | • | • | • | • | | | | • | |
| | Bike Exerciser | • | • | | • | • | • | • | • | • | • | • | • | • | • | • | • | • | • | | | • | |
| | Biking Club | • | • | | • | • | • | • | • | • | • | • | • | • | • | • | • | • | | • | | • | |
| | Fitness Exercises | • | • | | • | • | • | • | • | • | • | • | • | • | • | • | • | • | | | | • | |
| | Jogging/Running | • | • | | • | • | • | • | • | • | • | • | • | • | • | • | • | • | | | | • | |
| | Walking Club | • | • | | • | • | • | • | • | • | • | • | • | • | • | • | • | • | | • | | • | |
| | Golf Instruction | • | | | | | • | | • | • | | | | • | | | | • | | | | • | |
| | Shuffleboard | • | | | | | • | | • | | | | | • | • | | | • | | | | • | |
| | Angling/Casting | | | | | | • | | • | • | | | | • | • | | | • | | | | • | |
| **ARTS/CRAFTS HOBBIES** | Horticultural | | | | | | • | | • | • | | | | • | • | • | | • | • | • | • | • | • |
| | Leatherwork | | | | | | • | | • | • | | | | • | • | • | | • | | | | • | |
| | Fabric/Yarn/Metal | | | | | | • | | • | • | | | | • | • | • | | • | | | | • | |
| | Sewing/Needlecraft | | | | | | • | | • | • | | | | • | • | • | | • | | | | • | |
| | Gardening (Apt.) | • | • | • | | | • | | • | • | | • | • | • | • | • | | • | | | | • | • |
| | Gourmet Cooking | | | | | | | | • | | | | | • | • | • | | • | | | | • | • |
| | Photography | | | | | | | | | | | | | • | • | • | | • | | | | • | |
| **CULTURAL EDUCATIONAL** | Tax Return Workshop | | | | | | | | | | | | | • | • | • | | • | | | | | |
| | Concerts | | | | | | | | | | | | | • | • | • | | • | | | | | |
| | Instructional Dance | • | • | • | • | • | • | • | • | • | • | • | • | • | • | • | • | • | | | • | • | |
| | Nature Walks | • | • | | • | • | • | | • | • | • | • | • | • | • | • | | • | | • | | • | |
| | Home Repair | | | | | | | | • | | | | | • | • | • | | • | | | | | |
| | Radio Broadcasting | | | | | | | | | | | | | • | • | • | | • | | | | | • |
| | French Classes | | | | | | | | | | | | | • | • | • | | • | | | | | |
| | Cultures/World | | | | | | | | | | | | | • | • | • | | • | • | | • | | • |
| | Retirement Counsel | | | | | | | | | | | | | • | • | • | | • | • | • | | | |
| | Drama Clubs | | | | | | | | | | | | | • | | • | | • | | | | • | • |
| | Death and Dying | | | | | | | | | | | | | • | • | • | | | | | • | • | • |
| **SOCIAL RECREATION** | Swim Party | • | • | • | | • | | | | | | • | | • | • | • | | | | | | • | |
| | Phone Reassurance | | | | | | | | | | | | | • | • | • | | • | • | | • | • | • |
| | Friendship Circle | | | | | | | | | | | | | • | • | • | | • | • | | • | • | • |
| | Nostalgia | | | | | | | | | | | | | • | • | • | | | | | | • | |
| | Play Day | • | | | | • | | | | | | • | | • | • | • | | | | | | • | |
| | Dancing Party | • | • | • | | • | | | | | | • | | • | • | • | | | | | • | • | |
| **TRAVEL** | Fishing Trips | | | | | | • | | | | | | | • | • | • | | • | | • | | • | |
| | Winter Weekend Frolic | | | | | | | | | | | | | • | • | • | | • | | • | | • | |
| | Camping | | | | | | • | | | | | • | | • | • | • | | • | | • | | • | |
| | Media Travel | | | | | | | | | | | | | • | • | • | | • | | | | | |
| | Vacation Camping | | | | | | • | | | | | | | • | • | • | | • | | • | | • | |
| | Travel Clubs | | | | | | | | | | | | | • | • | • | | • | | • | • | • | |
| | Arts Appreciation | | | | | | | | | | | | | • | • | • | | • | | | | • | |

TABLE 4.1 (Continued)

| | | SOCIAL WELL-BEING | | | | | | | | PSYCHOLOGICAL/EMOTIONAL WELL-BEING | | | | | | | | | | | | | |
|---|---|---|---|---|---|---|---|---|---|---|---|---|---|---|---|---|---|---|---|---|---|---|---|
| | | Increase Social Contacts | Group Belonging | Communication | Leadership Opportunities | Problem-Solving | Social Interaction | Fun/Enjoyment | Community Awareness | Involvement | Friendships | Cooperation | Recognition/Prestige | Competitiveness | Sense of Accomplishment | Positive Reinforcement | Knowledge/Skill Develop | Peace of Mind | Personal Growth | Avoid Routine | Develop New Interests | Creativity | Relieve Worries |
| **PHYSICAL ACTIVITY** | Aquabics | • | • | • | | | • | • | | • | • | | • | | • | • | • | | | • | • | • | | • |
| | Bike Exerciser | • | • | • | | | • | • | | • | • | | • | • | • | • | | | | • | • | | | • |
| | Biking Club | • | • | • | • | • | • | • | • | • | • | • | • | | • | • | | | | • | • | | | • |
| | Fitness Exercises | • | • | • | | | • | • | | • | • | | • | | • | • | • | | | • | • | | | • |
| | Jogging/Running | • | • | • | | | • | • | | • | • | • | • | • | • | • | | | | • | • | | | • |
| | Walking Club | • | • | • | • | • | • | • | | • | • | • | • | | • | • | • | | | • | • | | | • |
| | Golf Instruction | • | • | • | | | • | • | | • | • | | • | • | • | • | • | | | • | • | | | • |
| | Shuffleboard | • | • | • | | | • | • | | • | • | | • | • | • | • | | | | • | • | | | • |
| | Angling/Casting | • | • | • | | | | • | | • | • | | • | • | • | • | • | | | • | • | | | • |
| **ARTS/CRAFTS HOBBIES** | Horticultural | • | • | • | | • | • | • | | • | • | | • | | • | • | • | | | • | • | | | • |
| | Leatherwork | • | • | • | | | • | • | | • | • | • | • | | • | • | • | | | • | • | • | • | • |
| | Fabric/Yarn/Metal | • | • | • | | | • | • | | • | • | • | • | | • | • | • | | | • | • | | | • |
| | Sewing/Needlecraft | • | • | • | | | • | • | | • | • | | • | | • | • | • | | | • | • | | | • |
| | Gardening (Apt.) | • | • | • | • | • | • | • | | • | • | • | • | | • | • | • | | | • | • | | | • |
| | Gourmet Cooking | • | • | • | • | • | • | • | | • | • | • | • | | • | • | • | | | • | • | • | | • |
| | Photography | • | • | • | • | • | • | • | • | • | • | • | | | • | • | • | | | • | • | • | • | • |
| **CULTURAL EDUCATIONAL** | Tax Return Workshop | • | • | • | | | • | | | • | • | | | | | | • | • | • | • | • | | | • |
| | Concerts | • | • | • | • | • | • | • | • | • | • | • | | | | • | | | • | • | • | • | | • |
| | Instructional Dance | • | • | • | • | | • | • | | • | • | • | • | | | • | • | | | • | • | | | • |
| | Nature Walks | • | • | • | • | | • | • | • | • | • | • | | | | • | • | • | • | • | • | | | • |
| | Home Repair | • | • | • | • | • | • | • | | • | • | | | | • | • | • | • | • | • | • | | | • |
| | Radio Broadcasting | • | • | • | • | • | • | • | • | • | • | | | | • | • | • | | | • | • | | | • |
| | French Classes | • | • | • | | | • | • | | • | • | | • | | • | • | • | | | • | • | | | • |
| | Cultures/World | • | • | • | • | | • | • | | • | • | • | | | • | • | • | | | • | • | | | • |
| | Retirement Counsel | • | • | • | | • | • | • | • | • | • | | | | • | • | • | • | • | • | • | | | • |
| | Drama Clubs | • | • | • | • | • | • | • | • | • | • | • | • | | • | • | • | | | • | • | • | • | • |
| | Death and Dying | • | • | • | | | • | | | • | • | | | | • | • | • | • | • | • | | | | • |
| **SOCIAL RECREATION** | Swim Party | • | • | • | • | • | • | • | | • | • | • | • | | | | | | | • | | | | • |
| | Phone Reassurance | • | • | • | | | • | • | | • | • | | | | | | | • | | • | | | | • |
| | Friendship Circle | • | • | • | • | • | • | • | | • | • | • | | | | | | • | | • | | | | • |
| | Nostalgia | • | • | • | • | • | • | • | | • | • | • | | | | | | | | • | | • | • | • |
| | Play Day | • | • | • | • | • | • | • | | • | • | • | • | • | | | | | | • | | | | • |
| | Dancing Party | • | • | • | • | • | • | • | | • | • | • | • | | | | | | | • | | | | • |
| **TRAVEL** | Fishing Trips | • | • | • | • | • | | • | | • | • | • | • | | • | • | • | | | • | | | | • |
| | Winter Weekend Frolic | • | • | • | • | • | • | • | | • | • | • | | | • | | • | | | • | • | | | • |
| | Camping | • | • | • | • | • | • | • | | • | • | • | | | • | • | • | | | • | • | | | • |
| | Media Travel | • | • | • | | • | • | | | • | • | • | | | | | • | | | • | • | • | • | • |
| | Vacation Camping | • | • | • | • | • | • | • | | • | • | • | | | | • | • | | | • | • | | | • |
| | Travel Clubs | • | • | • | | | • | • | | • | • | • | | | | • | • | • | • | • | • | | | • |
| | Arts Appreciation | • | • | • | • | • | • | • | | • | • | • | | | | • | | | • | • | • | • | | • |

*Source:* Lloyd A. Heywood, *Recreation for Older Adults: A Program Manual* (Toronto: Ministry of Culture and Recreation, 1979), pp. 74–75.

cies to structure opportunities that encourage different kinds of recreation behavior is the creation and/or manipulation of physical and human environments.''[18] Murphy et al. add that the human environment may be manipulated or influenced through communication techniques, leadership styles, and other instructional activities as well as by the creation of a positive interpersonal climate. Some of the behaviors that these authors suggest that recreation and leisure service agencies can provide opportunities for are these.

*Socializing Behavior.* These types of experiences provide opportunities for individuals to interact with one another.

*Associative Behavior.* Often individuals seek opportunities to gather together around a common interest. This is indicative of associative behavior.

*Acquisitive Behavior.* Acquisitive behavior involves the desire of the individuals to collect and gather together items of interest. Often individuals will then form clubs or groups to display and discuss their collections.

*Competitive Behavior.* The desire to test one's skills, strategies, and endurance against others results in competitive behavior.

*Testing Behavior.* Testing oneself against a standard is characteristic of testing behavior.

*Risk-taking Behavior.* Often individuals seek out experiences that are novel, unpredictable, and dangerous. This is an example of risk-taking behavior.

*Vicarious Experiencing.* Individuals may derive satisfaction from viewing or reading about the experiences of others, in other words, experiencing the activity vicariously.

*Explorative Behavior.* Seeking out environments new to the individual, through travel, reading, or even scientific investigation is characteristic of explorative behavior.

*Sensory Stimulation.* The stimulation of the individual's senses can provide pleasure and is sought by individuals as a benefit of the leisure experience.

*Physical Expression.* The opportunity to experience movement, both fine and gross motor movement, is an experience often sought by individuals.

*Creative Behavior.* The ability to express oneself in new and meaningful ways is an experience that individuals often seek. There are many avenues for this type of behavior.

*Appreciative Behavior.* The appreciation of the efforts of others can be a satisfying experience sought by individuals.

*Variety-seeking Behavior.* Individuals seek opportunities that will enable them to have experiences that are not in their daily routine. Leisure is often an alternative to the routine of work, for example.

*Anticipatory and Recollective Behavior.* The anticipation that occurs before involvement in an activity often produces a sense of excitement and euphoria. Furthermore, the recollection of previous leisure involvement produces similar feelings.

Murphy and Howard have also proposed a conceptualization of the different experiences available through leisure. These authors suggest that individuals can be influenced and motivated by their desire to seek out various types of experiences. Furthermore, they note that individual needs may be influenced by the individual's ''particular socio-economic, cultural, ethnic, environmental and personality'' variables.[19] Murphy and Howard suggest

[18]James E. Murphy, John G. Williams, E. William Niepoth, and Paul D. Brown, *Leisure Service Delivery System: A Modern Perspective* (Philadelphia: Lea and Febiger, 1973), pp. 73–76.

[19]James F. Murphy and Dennis R. Howard, *Delivery of Community Leisure Services: A Holistic Approach* (Philadelphia: Lea and Febiger, 1977), p. 116.

that recreation and leisure experiences can be classified in five categories, including physical, intellectual-educational, psychological, spiritual, and social categories. Although they suggest that this list is not inclusive, it does provide a basis from which to view the potential for individual expression in various leisure activities, programs and services. Table 4.2 presents the major headings and specific benefits or outcomes that can be derived from participation in these activities.

Still another conceptualization related to the benefits of the leisure experience is that presented by Howard and Crompton.[20] They suggest that certain benefits are sought by individuals and that knowledge of these can serve to aid the recreation and leisure service organization in its programming efforts. One of the interesting points that they make is that individuals may participate in the same activity, but for different reasons and with different expectations. This raises the interesting point that in a given program, activity, or service, individuals can derive many different benefits depending on their interpretations and needs. Conversely, individuals may derive the same benefits from different programs or activities. Benefits, according to Howard and Crompton, may include the following.

- Desire for social interaction with others.
- A gain in prestige. The mastery of a particular skill may be regarded as a form of "conspicuous consumption," which brings forth peer group recognition.
- Excitement.
- Ego satisfaction of achievement; a desire to be successful.
- A desire for security; to be a part of a group that gives connectedness to others; and a sense of affection.

- A feeling of being important and having responsibility; growth of self-worth.
- Fantasy, illusion, offering a temporary escape from everyday activities.
- Relaxation. Mental relaxation that may be obtained from hard or no physical effort.
- Acquisition of knowledge or satisfying curiosity.
- Happiness.[21]

Last and perhaps the most interesting conceptualization tied to the benefits of the recreation and leisure experience is that reported by Grey in *Parks and Recreation*.[22] Reviewing the essays of 75 college students regarding their most significant and memorable recreation experiences, Grey has complied a list of potential benefits of leisure participation. Although he cautions the reader that he makes no claim of scientific validity, he suggests that our current conceptualization of benefits is far too limiting. Grey suggests that the following benefits are associated with the recreation and leisure experience.

- Heightened or reduced sensitivity to sensory data such as temperature, color, and odor.
- Time distortion.
- Anticipation and expectation.
- Reflection and a pleasant memory.
- Escape.
- Novelty.
- Relaxation.
- Self-testing, challenge, and achievement.
- Improved self-image.
- Feeling a part of nature, beauty and awe.
- Self-discovery.
- Positive feedback and applause.
- Culmination, a turning point, a reward for extended participation, and a watershed life event.

---

[20]Dennis R. Howard and John L. Crompton, *Financing, Managing and Marketing Recreation and Park Resources* (Dubuque, Iowa: Brown, 1980), p. 311.

[21]Ibid.
[22]David F. Grey, "What Is This Thing Called Recreation?" *Parks and Recreation*, Vol. 15, No. 3, March 1980, pp. 632–664, 694.

**TABLE 4.2**   Benefits from the Leisure Experience

| Physical | Intellectual-Educational | Psychological | Spiritual | Social |
|---|---|---|---|---|
| relief of tension | mastery | anticipation | ecstasy | interpersonal relationships |
| relaxation | discovery | reflection | mind expansion | friendships |
| exercise | learning | challenge | transcendence | trust |
| motor skill | insight | accomplishment | revelation | companionship |
| development | intensified skills | excitement | release | involvement |
| rehabilitation | new experience | achievement | contemplation | fellowship |
| fitness | develop avocations | aesthetic appreciation | meditation | communication |
| coordination | cultural awareness | self-image | wonderment | group and family unity |
| physical | learning about one's self | introspection | | develop sense of |
| growth | evaluation | security | | community |
| muscle tone | synthesis | pleasure | | compatibility |
| rejuvenation | problem-solving | self-confidence | | appreciation |
| testing of body | | self-actualization | | cultural sharing |
| capabilities | | enjoyment | | concern for others |
| | | exhilaration | | belonging |
| | | self-expression | | interaction |

*Source:*   James F. Murphy and Dennis R. Howard, *Delivery of Community Leisure Services: A Holistic Approach* (Philadelphia: Lea and Febiger, 1977), p. 116.

- Heightened insight, perspective, clarity, and illuminating experience.
- Order, regularity, clear and precise limits, and rules.
- Introspection, sorting out of life experience, release from sensory overload, contemplation, and communication with one's self.
- Communion, love, friendship, and identification with a group.
- Personal development, learning, and an extension of ability.
- Refreshment, personal renewal, and recovery of powers.
- Common experience, shared hardships, and teamwork.
- Risk, apprehension, and fear.
- Unity of mind and body, grace, and coordination.
- Feelings of excitement, freedom, control, power, creativity, inner peace, harmony, reward, and competence.[23]

[23]Ibid.

As can be seen from viewing these authors' conceptualizations regarding the benefits of leisure, some descriptions are more quantitative whereas others are more qualitative. For example, Haywood's chart suggests that lowering of blood pressure can be a benefit of leisure participation. This is a quantitative measure in that blood pressure can be measured and compared against a standard. On the other hand, Grey suggests that "feeling a part of nature, beauty and awe" is also a benefit of leisure participation. Grey's description involves subjective, rather than objective, observation.

In an attempt to understand the benefits of the leisure experience, it appears, therefore, that these benefits can be either subjective or objective. It is often difficult to measure the leisure experience, for it may consist of feelings, experiences, and thoughts that are not easily observable. Often the leisure experience must be inferred by observing the relationship between behavior prior to and after actual participation. Thus, the anticipation and recollection stages of the leisure experience become valuable cues that the leader can use to determine the nature of the leisure experience and the motives that may have been involved. If it is not possible to measure objectively the benefits of leisure participation as they relate to the fulfillment of leisure needs (and hence motivate individuals to participate in them), some subjective appraisal must occur. The leader might want to be sensitive to expressions that correspond to the likelihood of a leisure experience having occurred. For example, Grey has suggested that time distortion, a speeding up or slowing down of a sense of time, is experienced by individuals involved in leisure. Individuals experiencing time distortion might make such comments as "time stood still" or "an hour seemed like a minute."[24] Coupled with expressions of satisfaction, such comments can provide a leader with clues that would indicate that the participant had had a leisure experience.

The *benefits* that participants expect to derive should shape the leader's choice of activities, methods of promotion, and the format or way in which the program is packaged and presented to the individual. These factors will influence individuals' perceptions of whether or not they think the program will provide them with the benefits they expect and will meet their expectations. The manipulation of these variables in business organizations and private organizations is characterized by the tendency to sell "an idea" rather than a product or service. The "Life Be In It" public awareness program adopted by the National Recreation and Park Association from the State of Victoria, Australia, provides a good example of this concept. The "Life Be In It" slogan stresses the benefits that can be derived from participation in "life" rather than directing individuals to participate in specific activities offered by agencies. The

creative use of leisure is the "idea" that is being promulgated.

## SUMMARY

The behavior of individuals is largely a result of motivation. The motivation process consists of five steps, including (1) the existence of needs; (2) the initiation of drives; (3) attention to relevant stimuli; (4) initiation of goal-directed activity; (5) reward or goal attainment; and (6) reduction of needs and drives.

Needs are often viewed as a deficiency. Drives or motives are activators of behavior. Primary drives can be thought of as involving such factors as hunger, thirst, sleep, avoidance of pain, and maternal care. Secondary drives, which are of concern to the recreation and leisure service leader, can be related to such factors as novelty, affection, achievement, power, affiliation, freedom of choice, social approval, altruism, consistency, security, and status. Individuals attend to relevant stimuli in order to pick up cues that will help them shape their behavior to suit the current situation. This helps them to meet their needs. Behavior, which is goal directed, enables individuals to fulfill their needs. Influencing the motivation process is the environment. The interaction between the individual and the environment affects the process of motivation and results in learning. This learning, in turn, influences future behavior.

The role of the recreation leader in motivating participants is one of providing cues to assist the individual in shaping behavior. There are three environments that the leader can affect, including the social, physical, and psychological environments. Cues in the physical environment involve manipulations of such things as lighting, spatial arrangements, color, and decorations. The cues in the social environment are related to facilitating interaction between two or more people. Grouping of individuals, provision of extrin-

[24]Ibid., p. 633.

sic and intrinsic rewards, forms of recognition, and one's leadership style are the major tools of the leader in this area. Psychological cues refer to those cues that assist the individual in developing a sense of self-worth, self-identity, power, and so on. Basically, the leader works to influence the perception of the individual. Another important role in the motivation process is removing barriers that affect the leisure experience. Some of the barriers to leisure fulfillment are attitudinal, communicative, consumptive, temporal, social, cultural and economic, health, and experiential.

One of the major factors in the motivation process is the realization that individuals seek benefits or expectations of benefits rather than the activity or service itself. There are many, many benefits that can be achieved through leisure participation. A short list of benefits includes happiness, relaxation, fantasy, fun, illusion, social interaction, and excitement.

## DISCUSSION QUESTIONS

1. Why is understanding the motivation process important to the recreation and leisure service leader?

2. What is the process of motivation?

3. What are some ways used in the recreation and leisure service field to identify needs? Identify and discuss at least five different ways.

4. What is the difference between primary and secondary drives?

5. Identify ten secondary motives, and discuss how activities could be organized to relate to these drives.

6. What do the terms *peak experience, arousal,* and *flow* have in common? What influence does the environment play regarding these terms?

7. List ten (10) cues that the leader can give an individual in each of the social, psychological, and physical areas.

8. What barriers can the leader remove in order to assist the individual in achieving leisure?

9. What does the statement ''individuals seek benefits or the expectation of benefits rather than activities or products'' mean?

10. Identify twenty (20) possible benefits of the leisure experience.

# 5

# COMMUNICATIONS

Effective communication involves listening, responding to nonverbal cues, giving feedback, as well as sending information.

We live in a society in which our ability to communicate with one another determines, to a large extent, whether we will succeed in our work and leisure. Communication is a process that binds together human activity. In the recreation and leisure setting, communication is essential in understanding and interpreting the rules of games, providing instruction, giving directions, and conveying feelings and emotions. The recreation and leisure service leader who communicates effectively can better meet the needs of those he or she serves.

In this chapter, the authors will explore the various dimensions of the communication process. Specifically, communication will be defined, the various components of communication will be described, and a model of the communication process will be presented. This chapter will also present information concerning types of communication, functions of communication, perception and communication, styles of communication, techniques of communication, and barriers to effective communication. In addition, the importance of active listening will be discussed.

# DEFINING COMMUNICATION

The term *communication* is widely used in contemporary society although it may have different meanings to different people. Most definitions of communication suggest that concepts, ideas, and thoughts must be transformed into a set of symbols and then transmitted to another party for communication to occur. However, other theorists have also suggested that human communication is a process that is interpersonal in nature and can be said to have occurred only if changes in the behavior of the receiver take place. In other words, for communication to exist between individuals, those communicating must attach some value or meaning to the symbols and process of exchange, and act on the information received.

We can think of communication, then, as a process of exchange that is directed toward conveying meaning and achieving understanding between individuals that leads to changes in the behavior of the receiver or receivers. It is an exchange that occurs between two or more persons through words, tone of voice, gestures, facial expressions, posture, and other means. This exchange can also be facilitated via visual representation and electronic-technological processes. Communication may be defined as a dynamic human transaction that results in the transmission of feelings and thoughts to another.

For communication to be effective, the ideas, concepts, and thoughts being transmitted must not only be clearly sent, but they also must be understood by the receiver. As just mentioned, many believe that successful communication occurs only when the behavior of the receiver has been altered by the

communication. In other words, in effective communication the receiver understands and accepts the message being transmitted in such a way that it affects his or her behavior. As you will recall, an important goal of the recreation and leisure service leader is to facilitate human happiness. For this to occur, the leader must encourage behavioral change. This is done almost exclusively through the process of communication.

## INTERPERSONAL AND ORGANIZATIONAL COMMUNICATION

The recreation and leisure service leader is concerned with two types of communication: interpersonal and organizational. *Interpersonal communication* is the process of transferring information and influencing the behavior of people on a one-to-one basis. It is essential for effective interaction between the leader and the participant and, thus, is central to the achievement of the recreation and leisure experience. The ability of the leader to establish effective communication with individual participants will directly influence their acquisition of skills and knowledge and their formulation of attitudes. It is also via the communication process that the leader generates enthusiasm, builds interest, conveys excitement, provides recognition and a sense of achievement, and creates a relationship of trust. Any or all of these variables may contribute directly to the building of a successful and rewarding leisure experience.

*Organizational communication* is the second type of communication that is of concern to the recreation and leisure leader. Organizational communication can be thought of as the way in which an agency transmits information to its staff and participants concerning its goals. It involves the establishment of channels of communication within a hierarchical organizational structure in order to transmit reports, complaints, requests, orders, inquiries, and information both within and outside of the organization. Within the organization, a formal program of organizational communications establishes the methods of exchange that can occur between and among various levels within an organization, both horizontally and vertically. It provides a method for orderly transmission of financial, program, and human resource information. For example, many recreation and leisure service organizations establish formal internal procedures for communicating information. These procedures can range from the way in which incoming telephone messages are recorded and distributed to the way in which parties are informed of the status of financial accounts under their direction.

Organizational communication is also concerned with the information that is transmitted to an agency's constituents. This is often thought of as the official communication that the recreation and leisure service organization provides to its public or publics. This type of external communication should be closely monitored or managed by the organization. Not only should the organization monitor such obvious techniques of communication as news releases, but also—and perhaps more important—it should monitor or manage the contact that takes place between the public and members of the recreation and leisure service organization. The status, well-being, and success of an organization may hinge on its ability to cultivate positive feelings of goodwill toward itself. This is done primarily by understanding that patterns of exchange, whether they be via the written media or simply between individuals, should be managed and controlled. For example, many municipal park and recreation departments operating summer playground programs, conduct orientation and training programs for their summer seasonal staff prior to the start of the program. Often an important part of such orientation and training programs is to impart to the new staff an understanding of the organization's goals and policies related to communication with the public.

### TRANSACTIONAL COMMUNICATION

Communication, as indicated, is a dynamic process. It is a process that involves a transaction between one individual and another or between one individual and a group of individuals. The term *transaction* suggests that communication, to be effective, must involve more than *telling* or talking *at* another individual. Transactional communication implies that communication is two-way interaction rather than one-way and, therefore, can affect the sender as well as the receiver. In other words, an individual sending a message will receive feedback that may affect his or her initial perceptions, values, or ideas. Transactional communication is interaction *with* people rather than communication *to* people. In the recreation and leisure service field, transactional communication is essential in that the basis of the profession is the meeting of individual needs and interests. A two-way exchange facilitates this goal.

A transactional relationship suggests that people are both sending and receiving messages. When we discuss communication, we often think only of sending messages and not of the other responsibilities inherent in a two-way exchange. The need to get and give feedback is as important as sending information. The leader who develops listening and observing skills will be able to engage more successfully in transactional communication. Most communication in organizations is decidedly directive and one-way. Therefore, there is a need to encourage two-way transactional communication within recreation and leisure service agencies.

## TYPES OF COMMUNICATION

There are numerous types of communication that the recreation and leisure service leader will use or be exposed to. Of primary concern are verbal and nonverbal types of communication, for they are involved in the leader's face-to-face interaction with participants.

Other types of communication include that which is written (visual symbols) and that which is transmitted via technological or electronic processes or both. A brief discussion of these various types of communication follows.

*Verbal.*   Verbal communication is the form of communication most often used by the recreation and leisure service leader. It can either be a one-way or two-way form of interaction; however, the former is seldom effective. The ability of the leader to give direction, listen, provide empathy, and generate enthusiasm is accomplished primarily through verbal interaction with others. The ability to communicate effectively with individuals and groups often will spell the difference between success or failure in the implementation of activities. In the structured recreation and leisure service activity, face-to-face interaction with the participant is the vehicle that is used to assist the participant in achieving leisure experiences. Often this interaction is the essence of the experience. This is especially the case in activities that emphasize social interaction. Through verbal interaction the leader can create a sense of excitement, euphoria, adventure, and heightened expectation.

*Nonverbal.*   Nonverbal communication refers to communication that takes place via physical cues other than speech. For example nonverbal communication may occur as a result of an individual's apparel, facial expression, posture, body rhythms, and body movement. We often refer to nonverbal communication as "body language."[1] By "reading" body language, the leader can gain clues as to the intentions, level of interest, and motivation of participants. There may be inconsistencies between what is communicated verbally by individuals and what they com-

municate nonverbally. The use of sarcasm is an example of how nonverbal communication might vary from verbal communication. An individual might say, for example "Nice day," accompanied by a grimace or a frown, meaning that it really is not. The leader not only should attempt to read the body language of others, but should be mindful of his or her own body language and the effect that it may have on the communication process.

*Written.*   Written communication involves the use of printed or handwritten language for the purpose of transmitting information or knowledge. This could include reports, brochures, fliers, advertisements, books, pamphlets, magazines, letters, memoranda, phone messages, and so on. The rapid growth and expansion of knowledge can probably be attributed, in this century, to the growth of written communications. The number of books published each year increases as does the volume of correspondence that is carried out between individuals and organizations. It is important for the leader to recognize that written communication represents not only the *individual* writing the communication, but the organization as well. Thus, it is important to word and review written communication carefully that is to go out from the organization in order to ensure that it is accurate, complete, and grammatically correct and carries the meaning intended.

*Electronic-Technological.*   Electronic-technological communication is involved with all forms of technological-electronic processing, including the computer, television, radio, telephone and motion pictures. Although electronic-technological communication may overlap into some of the categories mentioned earlier in that it can be a vehicle for verbal, nonverbal, and written communication, the authors feel that it is also a unique entity. It is often said of television and motion pictures that the "medium is the message."

[1]Lawrence Rosenfeld, "Nonverbal Communication in the Small Group," in Robert S. Cathcart and Larry A. Samovar, *Small Group Communication: A Reader*, 2d ed. (Dubuque, Iowa: Brown, 1974), p. 270.

*Visual Symbols.* Visual symbols are used extensively in contemporary society. They are representations of a more complex idea that provides the individual with a quick visual clue or reference point. Logos are perhaps the most obvious example of this type of communication. When we see the "golden arches" of McDonalds, we see it as a representation of hamburgers. Other uses of visual symbols include the use of signs to control routine behavior (e.g., stop signs) or the use of symbols to advocate a political ideology, for example, the use of the donkey to represent the Democratic party. The leader can use visual symbols to enhance communication with others.

The recreation and leisure service leader should carefully consider the various types of communication in order to to select the communication process that will be most effective in various situations. Although the leader is primarily concerned with verbal and nonverbal face-to-face interaction, he or she should recognize the importance of other types of communication in instruction, activity leadership, and other areas of leadership. Computer-based instruction, for example, may effectively assist lecture-type presentations made by the leader. Visual symbols can be used to create a mood or to elicit a certain type of response from participants. It should also be noted that some individuals are more visually oriented, whereas other individuals are more verbally oriented. Communication that can respond to both of these orientations will be the most successful.

## FUNCTIONS OF COMMUNICATION

Communication serves a number of functions. It provides a vehicle for individuals to interact with others in four primary ways: (1) persuasion and influence, (2) information, (3) social and expressive relations, and (4) conflict resolution. A discussion of each of these functions of communication follows.

### PERSUASION AND INFLUENCE

One of the primary functions of communication is the persuasion of others. *Persuasion* suggests that one will change or modify the behavior of another individual via the communication process. We persuade others by appealing to their emotion, reason, intelligence, logic, and vanity. Generally speaking, persuasion is a process of gradually securing the cooperation of others. Closely related to the notion of persuasion is that of *influence*. Influence can be thought of as the power of one individual to affect the behavior of another. Persuasion and influence are keys in the communication process. Communication intended to influence carries values and is intended to: (1) impress and stimulate, (2) change beliefs or convince and (3) move an individual to action.

### INFORMATION

Another function of communication is to pass on information that informs or reminds, or teaches. The individual involved in this type of communication provides or receives information that is useful, interesting, or necessary. The information that is communicated may be facts, figures, processes, and so on. Generally speaking, information is transmitted by using a didactic format; that is, the sender relays the information via lectures, films, tape recordings, books, periodicals, and so on. The purpose of the didactic method is to explain and expound upon a particular subject. The recreation and leisure service leader is often involved in the transmission of information, especially as it is related to the teaching of skills and informing the public of leisure opportunities.

### SOCIAL AND EXPRESSIVE RELATIONS

A third function of communication is that of encouraging social interaction and expressive behavior. *Social* communication is essential to human well-being. Social communication enables individuals to develop self-image, maintain contact with others, develop sensual acuity, and develop intellectually. Our common everyday communication such as hugs, handshakes, small talk, banter, and other expressions of interest provide a vehicle for social interactions with others. *Expressive* communications convey our emotional reactions to situations. They are based on feelings that are associated with both verbal and nonverbal communication. A prime function of communication is to provide us with the tools to express love, joy, pleasure, enthusiasm, interest, frustration, anger, happiness, and grief.

## CONFLICT RESOLUTION

Conflict resolution is another primary function of communication. Through communication, individuals are able to resolve conflicts resulting from differences in values, beliefs, and attitudes. Conflict is pervasive in our North American society. It exists between individuals, groups, organizations, and nations. It ranges from deviant thought to overt physical force and occurs almost wherever individuals interact with one another. Conflict need not necessarily be viewed in negative terms as it may serve a productive function in some cases if it promotes effective communication.

The individual communicating can be engaged in more than one communicative function. For example, an individual may give a speech that presents information and, at the same time, attempt to persuade and influence the listener. Although knowledge of all these functions of communication is important to the leader, the area of social and expressive communication may be the most important to those in the recreation and leisure service profession. As a profession, we attempt to enable participants to express their emotions and feelings and to interact with other individuals. More specifically, we attempt to provide opportunities that enable individuals to express their excitement, enthusiasm, pleasure, and joy as well as vent their frustrations, anger,

and disappointment in a socially acceptable positive manner.

## THE PROCESS OF COMMUNICATION

A model of the process of communication is presented in Figure 5.1. This model, initially developed by Berlo in 1960, suggests that communication is a process consisting of a number of interrelated components. The model represents the communication process as consisting of separate and distinct components; however, in reality the communication process operates in a simultaneous fashion.[2] Furthermore, it is important to recognize that an individual may be a sender and receiver of information at the same time. For example, in face-to-face communication with another, an individual might send a message while at the same time receiving verbal or nonverbal clues or both from the receiver.

The components that make up the communication process are the sender-encoder, message, channel, and decoder-receiver. The following paragraphs explain each of these components.

### SENDER-ENCODER

The sender-encoder can be thought of as the individual or electronic technological device that originates the communication. For communication to occur, one must first prepare the message for transmission. We usually think of the encoding process as a way of preparing ideas, thoughts, and concepts for transmission to another individual or other individuals. Basically, it involves the conversion of complex intellectual information into a set of symbols. Language is the most common set of symbols used for transmission of ideas. Language can be thought of as a type of code in which a set of symbols represents an idea, thought, or concept. When technological channels of communication, such as the com-

[2]David K. Berlo, *The Process of Communication* (New York: Holt, 1960).

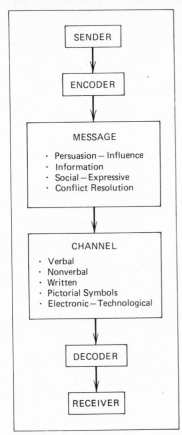

**FIGURE 5.1**    The process of communication: The Berlo model.

puter, are used, the same process occurs. Ideas are coded in the language of the computer.

For effective communication to occur, symbols used in the communication process must be mutually understood and accepted by both parties. When individuals inappropriately encode or decode information transmitted, inaccurate communication may result that leads to misunderstanding. For example, words often have different meanings for different people. Consequently, the message may be encoded; however, the receiver may not decode the message accurately. Nonverbal messages may also be encoded or decoded inappropriately. The recreation and leisure

service leader should be aware of the need for accurate encoding of information for transmission. He or she should not, for example, use an adult vocabulary when attempting to communicate with children.

## THE MESSAGE

We can think of the message that is being communicated as the cognitive or effective information that is transmitted or both; that is, it is the idea, thought, or concept that the sender is attempting to communicate to another individual. As previously indicated, communication has four functions: persuasion, information, social-expressive relations, and conflict resolution. The message being communicated to another individual will usually fall into one of these four categories.

Often a message transmitted from one individual to another may carry more than one meaning. Multiple meanings in messages create uncertainty as to whether or not the message will be transmitted accurately or as intended. Thus, the way in which messages are communicated or the channel of communication selected can be a critical element in effective communication, adding needed meaning. The sender, then, should not only be aware of the need for accurate encoding, but also should be aware of the importance of choosing an appropriate channel for the transmission of the message. For example, some messages are most effectively transmitted by picture rather than by the written word. It should also be remembered that every message is viewed from two different perspectives. The same message may be seen differently by the sender-encoder and the receiver-decoder. Later in this chapter, the authors will discuss the effects of perception on communication. A knowledge of differences in perceptions can help an individual avoid or correct encoding that might be misinterpreted owing to differences in perceptions.

## THE CHANNEL

The channel of communication is the medium that couples the sender to the receiver. Previously, the authors defined five channels of communication: verbal, nonverbal, written, electronic-technological and visual symbols. These channels, in turn, can be broken into a number of subcategories. The selection of an appropriate channel of communication is essential to the communication process although it may not be a *conscious* choice on the part of the sender.

Numerous problems are associated with the selection of an inappropriate channel for communication. For example, a recreation and leisure service leader who attempts to orient his or her summer staff verbally, without written instruction in support, may find that a lack of communication results. A group of individuals are not likely to remember extensive organizational policy, dress codes, rules of conduct, schedules, and so on without use of a written channel of communication.

## RECEIVER-DECODER

Decoding can be thought of as the translation of a message by a receiver. The decoding process is concerned with the acquisition of the intended meaning of the message transmitted by the sender, leading to behavioral change. In other words, decoding, like encoding, attempts to ensure that messages received are an *accurate* reflection of the message sent. The receiver should not only understand the message but should also exhibit the change in behavior that the message was intended to cause for communication to be effective. Usually, the decoder has two primary resources with which to decode messages: his or her senses and mental processes. Individuals receive information through their senses—hearing, seeing, tasting, touching, and smelling. Mental processes, that is, complex intellectual thought processes, also assist in the decoding process. These mental processes, however, are value laden and, therefore, may interfere

in the decoding process. The recreation and leisure service leader should be aware that the message he or she sends may not be accurately decoded owing to differences in perceptions or the use of inappropriate symbols (e.g., the use of professional jargon). In order to communicate effectively, therefore, the recreation and leisure service leader may want to check with the participant or participants to make sure that the intended message has indeed been received accurately.

## PERCEPTION AND COMMUNICATION

Perception is a major factor influencing the process of communication. The way that one selects, organizes, and interprets information will affect directly how effectively he or she communicates with others. Perception can be thought of as a psychological process. It is dependent on the use of one's physical senses (the ability to see, hear, touch, smell and taste); however, it is a complicated cognitive process that involves the processing and categorization of information received through the senses. One might say that our senses provide us with raw data (information) from which decisions can be made that will ultimately influence how an individual reacts to, or interacts with, his or her environment.

Why is it important that the recreation and leisure service leader understand perception? In a general sense, the role of the recreation and leisure service leader is to create conditions that allow the participant to *perceive* that he or she is at leisure. Social psychologists often suggest that a number of conditions must precede the leisure experience. Among these are the need for an individual to experience perceived freedom and perceived competence. Perceived freedom is characterized by a feeling on the part of the participant that he or she has control. Therefore, the leader, in order to be effective, must understand the conditions that must be created for the participant to feel that he or she is in control. Such conditions can be produced by involving the participant in the decision-making process, not forcing participation, allowing the participant to pace himself or herself through an activity, and so on. Perceived competence is characterized by a feeling on the part of the participant that he or she has achieved a degree of mastery over an activity. The issue is not the actual skill level of the individual as it relates to an external standard, but rather the individual's own perception of his or her ability (subjective appraisal rather than objective appraisal based on standards). The University of Chicago sociologist Csikszentmihalyi has suggested that the individual's perception of his or her skill level as it relates to the challenge offered by a given activity will influence the success with which participation is likely to take place.[3] An individual who perceives that his or her skill level is higher than the challenge of the activity, according to Csikszentmihalyi, will experience boredom. Conversely, an individual who perceives that his or her skill level is lower than the challenge of the activity will experience anxiety. The role of the leader, in dealing with these perceptions, is to structure the environment so that it is likely that perceived skill level will correspond to the challenges offered by the activity. The leader can accomplish this in three ways. First, he or she can attempt to change the individual's perception of his or her skill level through encouragement, support, positive feedback, and so on. Second, the leader can actually help the individual develop a higher level of skill through an educational process. Third, the leader can present the individual with activities and tasks that correspond to the individual's current skill level.

In its broadest sense, understanding perception also enables the leader to understand participants' attitudes, values, motives, and,

hence, behavior. It is interesting to note, for example, that research studies have shown that individuals who are physically attractive are perceived by others to be more intelligent, personable, and kind than their less attractive cohorts. It has also been shown that individuals have a tendency to seek out and relate to individuals with beliefs and values similar to their own. They are also more likely to believe others when they espouse values and beliefs that correspond to their own. These examples demonstrate the pitfalls that the leader should be aware of when attempting to deal with the perceptions of individuals, for such perceptions may not be totally accurate. In the first instance just given, the perception that physical attributes and intelligence correspond to one another is obviously not true. In the latter case, perceptions are likely to be biased and based upon "what a person wants to hear." The point is that perceptions will greatly influence people although such perceptions may be inaccurate when compared with empirically verified scientific investigation.

Consider the recreation and leisure leader whose job it is to program for individuals with physical disabilities. If indeed physical beauty is commonly perceived to be associated with desirable attributes (intelligence, kindness, and so on), the leader might perceive individuals with physical disabilities as lacking these qualities or even being more likely to exhibit negative qualities such as poor temperament, mental lassitude, and so on. These perceptions will affect the leader's expectations and the way that the leader communicates with these individuals. However, the leader who has an understanding of perception will be in a position to communicate more effectively and plan effectively for those whom he or she serves.

An entire generation can establish a certain framework or set of perceptions that are carried throughout their life span. The political scientist Newman has suggested that generations can be identified by their "common ex-

[3]M. Csikszentimihalyi, *Beyond Boredom and Anxiety* (San Francisco: Jossey-Bass, 1975).

periences, the same decisive influence, and similar historical problems.'' He suggests that a generation's perceptions are influenced by those events that occur and by the social, cultural, and political climate that exists when the generation is 17. One of the authors of this book was born in 1946, turning 17 in 1963. The most marked event that occurred in 1963 was the assassination of John F. Kennedy. This event was shared by all the members of this cohort. It is burned into our memories, even to the extent that events, people, and places that were part of the experience remain etched in the minds of those involved. With this in mind, this author recently asked a group of first-year students majoring in park and recreation management to raise their hands if they were old enough to recall this historical event. Two students out of 35 raised their hands. This generation, then, has a different base of shared experiences. Therefore, the way that they perceive the environment and ultimately shape their ideas and communicate with others will vary from that of other generations.

Bearing in mind the differences in shared experiences that affect the perceptions of each new generation, we can see that communication between generations may be affected. Many individuals who shared the experiences of the 1930s with shortages in jobs and necessities have different perceptions of material possessions, work and leisure than those who shared the experiences and perceptions of the 1960s, characterized by affluence, freedom, and mass education. Many 1930s individuals cannot understand why others aren't consumed by a desire for products and are not willing to defer gratification in order to achieve them. They are not able to understand why others do not place a high degree of importance on job security. Many 1960s individuals, on the other hand, really cannot understand how others can tie themselves to a single job for years at the expense of freedom of movement, freedom of thought, and freedom to pursue alternative life-styles. When these two groups attempt to communicate, they often perceive the environment in two distinctly different ways and, therefore, have great difficulty relating to one another's needs.

Another example of the way that one's generation influences perceptions is related to the perceptions of various age groups toward leisure. Our grandparents often viewed play, recreation, and leisure as frivolous unless work related (e.g., barn raising, quilting bees). Our parents' generation often viewed recreation, leisure, and play as a way of restoring or refreshing oneself for work. The result was recreation as an activity that was conducted during discretionary time in order to help them work more productively. Finally, the current generation ''works to play.'' In other words, the focus of life tends to be upon recreation and leisure, and work serves as a vehicle that can be shaped, altered, and modified to facilitate play. Because the values of each of the generations are different, the relative importance attached to recreation and leisure will vary.

## PERCEPTUAL SELECTIVITY

There are numerous factors or variables in the environment that affect the perceptual process. Our senses do not attend to all the stimuli that exist, but rather select the stimuli that are relevant to our current situation and needs. Right now, the reader may be in an environment in which the radio is playing, cars are going by, people are talking, the dishwasher is running, and so on; however, many of these sounds are not ''heard'' or perceived. The individual's perceptive process determines the stimuli that are to be selected for attention at any given moment. Some of the environmental variables that influence perception, according to Luthans, are ''intensity, size, contrast, repetition, motion, and novelty and familiarity.''[4] A discussion of these six variables follows.

[4]Fred Luthans, *Organizational Behavior*, 2d ed. (New York: McGraw-Hill, 1977), pp. 259–261.

*Intensity.* The intensity with which a stimulus is presented will affect the likelihood that it will be attended to. The louder, brighter, more pungent, more textural stimuli are, the more attention they will receive. The recreation and leisure service leader who desires to receive a great deal of attention by participants might consider wearing bright clothes, using a whistle, talking loudly, and so on.

*Size.* The larger an object is, the more likely it is that it will be perceived. In promoting a program, a large brochure is more likely to be attended to than a small one.

*Contrast.* Individuals are more likely to perceive things that stand out from their surrounding environment. For example, a sign painted green and placed in a park to warn the public of danger will not be perceived as well as one painted bright yellow or red. The leader who wants to conduct an activity that requires close attention on the part of the participants might want to choose a quiet classroom setting (which would offer a contrast with his or her directions) as opposed to conducting the same activity in a gym or playground, in which the noisy surroundings would compete for the participants' attention.

*Repetition.* The more often a stimulus is repeated, the more likely it is that it will be attended to by the individual. The recreation and leisure service leader who repeats his or her directions more than once will be "heard" by the participants and heard more accurately than the leader who states things only once. It should be pointed out, however, that excessive repetition in communications can result in the participants' "tuning out."

*Motion.* Individuals will pay more attention to things that move than they will to stationary things. According to Luthans, "advertisers capitalize on this principle by creating signs which incorporate moving parts. Las Vegas is an example of advertisement in motion."[5] An application of this principle in the recreation and leisure service field would be the use of demonstrations in instruction.

*Novelty and Familiarity.* The individual is more likely to notice a novel stimulus in a familiar setting *or* a familiar stimulus in a novel or new setting. The recreation and leisure service leader conducting a six-week activity course who notices a decrease in the interest of participants may want to use novel stimuli to rebuild interest in the program. For example, a leader conducting a summer playground program may want to bring in a local sports figure one week.

It is important to remember that all these variables are related; that is, events may be characterized by more than one of these variables and correspondingly may receive more attention from the individual as a result. The recreation and leisure service leader, in establishing comunications with participants, needs to keep in mind how each of these variables can relate to the way that individuals perceive the leader, the activity, and the experience as a whole.

## CANNON'S MODEL FOR PROCESSING INFORMATION USING APPERCEPTIVE MASS[6]

In its simplest terms, Cannon's model can be thought of as a mechanism for determining our perceptions and as an aid to decision making as we process information. The term apperception suggests that an individual has the ability to develop a perception by the means of a mass of ideas in his or her mind. In other words, apperceptive mass can be thought of as a complex intellectual concep-

[5]Ibid., p. 261.
[6]"A Model for Processing Information Using Apperceptive Mass" was developed by Edward C. Cannon, Jr. Cannon, assistant professor, Humboldt State University, conceptualized this model in 1981 and assisted the authors in preparing the draft to explain its various aspects. He is also responsible for drawing the figures presented in this portion of the text. The model is used with his permission and is copyrighted. Permission to use the model must be obtained directly from him.

tualization that assists an individual to perceive reality, process information, make life decisions and ultimately communicate to others.

Figure 5.2, Cannon's model for processing information using apperceptive mass, presents a step-by-step process whereby an individual uses various cognitive and experiential sources of information in perceiving a given situation. The complex intellectual conceptualization that occurs within the mind of the individual, as presented in the figure, consists of processing information about one's environment, personal goals, values, past experiences, personal evaluation of hearsay, and social relationships. A brief definition of each of these variables follows.

*Environment.* The physical environment or geographical location of the participant or both are major factors influencing his or her perception of a given situation. For example, an individual living in New York City, used to dense spatial relationships, will have a different perception of land use, social interaction, and physical accessibility from an individual residing in Kanosh, Utah, with a population of 350. An individual living in a dense urban population may have a different perception of time use related to travel. To commute 30 miles or more to a cultural event may be commonplace to the New Yorker whereas the rural dweller might consider this excessive travel for the reward.

*Personal Goals.* The aspirations, level of achievement, and desires of an individual will greatly influence his or her perception of information being transmitted. An individual who is a high achiever concerned with his or her level of status might, for example, place a higher value on messages that communicate information regarding material possessions, finances, and so on. If an individual's goal in life is to acquire a million dollars, this will in turn affect the way that he or she perceives incoming information and ultimately makes life decisions relating to that goal. On the other hand, if his or her personal goals are altruistic, this will also influence his or her perception of the world.

*Values.* Societal norms and customs, religious beliefs and personal values also influence the process of perception. In Eastern cultures, for example, marriages between individuals are still often arranged by their families or societies. In Western cultures, this is not the case. On the contrary, our societal customs and norms suggest that this is unacceptable. Obviously, these two different cultural values influence perceptions of the entire dating and courting process. Thus, our personal values influence greatly the process of perception in a very personal way.

*Past Experiences.* An individual's past experiences will influence how he or she perceives a given situation. For example, an individual who has a previous leisure experience that has resulted in a sense of enjoyment, satisfaction, and fun will tend to view similar opportunities favorably in the future. In other words, if an individual has had a positive or negative past experience, this will color or affect his or her current or future perceptions of leisure opportunities. Consider, for example, an individual who has never been able to drive a golf ball successfully. When an opportunity to play, read about, or watch golf presents itself, the individual may engage in avoidance behavior owing to past experience.

*Personal Evaluation of Hearsay.* Often the comments that are made by other individuals about a situation, leisure activity, or even another person will affect an individual's perception. For example, a film critic's judgment of a popular movie may influence an individual's decision to attend or not to attend it. The greater value that one places on the judgment of the other individual or individuals transmitting the information, the greater the likelihood that it will influence one's perception of a given situation.

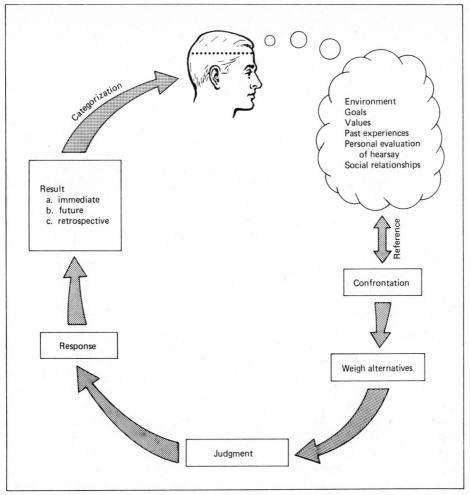

**FIGURE 5.2**    A model for processing information utilizing apperceptive mass. ©
Edward C. Cannon, 1981.

*Social Relationships.*    The individuals that we commonly associate with in our lives, such as our parents, siblings, work associates, and friends, have a direct influence on our perceptive processes. The shared values common to a family unit, for example, will influence an individual's ability to process information and make decisions. Although individuals often have values parallel to those of their immediate family and peer group, there also is a potential for conflict based on differences between family members regarding personal goals, personal values, and perhaps experiences. One's social relationships serve as a reference point for decision making.

According to Cannon, the first step in processing information using apperceptive mass is confrontation. An individual who is faced with a decision must draw upon his or her reference points within the apperceptive mass in order to respond appropriately. Basically, an individual draws on the apperceptive mass in an integrated fashion; that is, he or she draws from those variables that relate to the situation at hand, combining information that will aid in the perception, decision-making, and communication processes.

The next step in the process involves the weighing of various alternatives. The weighing of various alternatives is based on the information currently stored in an individual's apperceptive mass. Once the alternatives have been weighed or considered, the individual will make a judgment as to what would be an appropriate response or behavior. For example, a recreation and leisure service leader responding to a request for information concerning types of children's activities would review his or her apperceptive mass for knowledge regarding games. The leader might recall activities that he or she has led in the past that were successful or unsuccessful, games that were suggested by others, or activities that fit a particular value orientation, for example, noncompetitive new games. With that information in mind, the leader would form a response and communicate it to the individual requesting information.

The result of this communicative interaction is important, as it provides additional information for future judgments and communication. Again, if we review Figure 5.2, the results of the information communicated to another individual can be categorized in terms of immediate results, future results, and retrospective results. Immediate results, using the example given earlier, might be the feedback the leader receives in the form of endorsement and support of the ideas being presented. The future results might be later influenced by the response of children to the games and activities once they have actually been implemented. For example, the recreation leader might seek feedback concerning the success or failure of the games and activities suggested. Finally, retrospective results involve the recategorization of the results obtained in future or immediate categories or both as a result of conflicting feedback. In other words, an individual, in the example

given earlier, might receive positive immediate feedback, but, after implementation of the activities, might receive conflicting information. In "retrospect," the individual, then, would file or categorize this information for future reference, adjusting previous input.

Cannon's model for processing information and understanding apperceptive mass is useful because communication essentially involves decision making. A recreation and leisure service leader must draw on his or her apperceptive mass to respond to various stimuli. It is important to recognize that one's apperceptive mass will directly influence not only what is communicated, but more importantly how effectively communication takes place. When responding to the comment "John is slow," an individual develops a judgment based on his or her apperceptive mass. Figure 5.3 presents one possible representation of an individual's conceptualization of the idea "John is slow." The picture in Figure 5.4, presents another possible representation of an individuals conceptualization of this phrase based on values, past experience, environment, and so on. In this case, the idea communicated is one of John as a slow runner. On the other hand, the conceptualization presented in Figure 5.4 symbolizes a different idea; that John is not too bright. It is important for the reader to note that such differences are the basis for almost all communicative problems. If one can bridge the differences in perceptions that occur between individuals, communication will be enhanced.

## STYLES OF COMMUNICATION

There are a number of styles of communication that can be employed by the recreation and leisure service leader. Depending on the situation, the leader may want to consider using one style of communication versus another. For example, if the purpose of the communication is to share ideas with another individual, the style of communication used

**FIGURE 5.3**    © Edward C. Cannon, 1981.
One view of "John is slow."

**FIGURE 5.4**    © Edward C. Cannon, 1981.
Another view of "John is slow."

will be different from what it would be if the purpose of the communication were to persuade another individual. One style of communication might be more direct and forceful whereas the other style might be more subtle and indirect. Often, when resolving conflict, the leader will want to draw out the ideas of others.

Figure 5.5 presents a model that depicts the various styles of communication that can be used by the recreation and leisure service leader. There are four basic styles of communication: developmental, relinquishing, controlling, and defensive. Each of these approaches, in turn, can be subdivided into two categories. As an individual moves from the top to the bottom of the model, counterclockwise, his or her style of communication becomes increasingly aggressive. Moving clockwise from the top of the model, an individual becomes more submissive as he or she moves toward the bottom of the circle.

*Developmental Approach.*    The developmental style of communication is based on sharing of information and exploring the ideas of oth-

ers. It involves a willingness to listen and offers an opportunity to present ideas. No attempt is made to win others to one's point of view. *Informing* involves the contribution of ideas, stimulation of discussion, and the sharing of information. The other portion of the developmental approach, *exploring*, involves a willingness to listen to the opinions of others. It may also entail probing; that is, asking individuals questions that help them expand on their ideas and thoughts and giving support in the form of verbal and nonverbal feedback. The developmental approach is best employed when there is a need for individuals to share information or build joint commitment or both.

*Controlling Approach.*    The controlling approach to communication is one of trying to influence, persuade or dominate others. The sender tries to influence other individuals to act in a manner consistent with the sender's interests or desires. Often we see the controlling approach to communication in the enforcement of rules and regulations in sporting

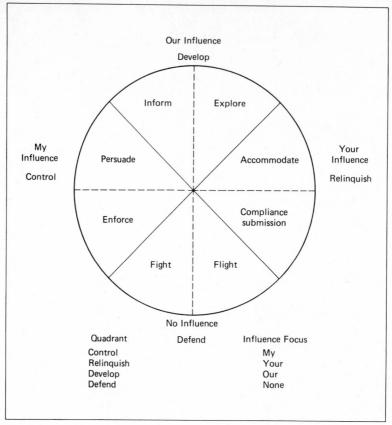

**FIGURE 5.5** A model showing the influence of communication. (*Source: Building Team Effectiveness* [Westport, Conn.: Educational Systems and Designs, Inc., 1970], p. 39.)

activities. The official uses the power of his or her position to ensure that a game is conducted according to the rules. *Persuasion* involves directly selling one's ideas to another individual or individuals. When one is using the *enforcing* style of communication, authority, superior knowledge, or the threat of undesirable action or a combination is often employed.

***Relinquishing Approach.*** There are situations where an individual will defer to another's point of view or knowledge of a situation or both. This approach to communication is known as the relinquishing approach. Often, when the recreation and leisure service

leader is dealing with an issue that is very important to another individual, he or she may defer to the other's wishes. This does not mean that the leader necessarily relinquishes his or her own values or opinions, but rather that emotional issues may be better handled using this approach, at least temporarily. Certainly there are many situations in the recreation and leisure service profession when an individual becomes highly emotional or "charged up." Rather than trying to alter the behavior of the other individual, one may find it more effective to allow the emotional individual to express himself or herself. Two patterns—*accommodate* and *compliance-submission*—find the individual deferring to another's viewpoint in various degrees. In the former case, the individual attempts to maintain his or her point of view or integrate it with the other's point of view. In the latter case, the individual completely defers to the other's point of view, interests or suggestions.

*Defensive Approach.*    There are situations in which an individual will either withdraw from the communication process or strike out in anger. For example, an individual may become so frustrated in discussing an issue that he or she may begin to focus away from the issue and engage in character assassination and "dumping." This style of communication is known as the defensive approach. It usually is viewed as an inappropriate communication style except when there are ethical, legal, or moral implications that force the individual to withdraw. As the individual reaches the bottom of the model, two options are available: *flight* or *fight*. Flight involves complete withdrawal from the communication process. Fight occurs when an individual strikes out and attacks the other individual, verbally or physically.

## ACTIVE LISTENING

A major responsibility of the successful communicator is listening to others. The ability to listen carefully to others is a skill that can be developed. We use the term *active listening* as a way of stressing the importance of learning how to listen to others. This type of listening implies active participation on the part of the listener rather than merely passive absorption of comments made by others. In other words, the communicator actively seeks to understand what another individual is trying to communicate.

Active listening is a process that directly affirms or acknowledges an individual's emotional and intellectual needs, interests, and desires. It requires that one give understanding to an individual without necessarily agreeing. It simply offers support for another's point of view. Often, because of poor listening skills, we shut off an individual prior to discovering the basis for his or her point of view. This essentially closes the door to communication as it ignores or rejects the other's thoughts, feelings and, in a sense, his or her very being. In rejecting other individuals by failing to listen appropriately, we create feelings of mistrust, disloyalty, and lack of confidence.

Active listening allows the communicator to become more sensitive to what he or she hears and, as a result, to become more sensitive to those communicated with. The active listener often becomes less argumentative and more willing to incorporate the views of others. In addition, active listening enables those individuals communicated with to feel as if their ideas, suggestions, and comments are worthwhile. As such, it increases the flow of information that can be used in problem solving.

### WHAT SHOULD THE LEADER AVOID?

Often, when listening to an individual, one is more concerned with one's own needs than the needs of the other. We may want the other individual to see things from our viewpoint. In order to achieve this end, we may threaten, cajole, plead, or show contempt for the other's point of view. In short, the listener often tries to change the other's point of view rather than attempting to listen with understanding to the ideas, comments, feelings, and information transmitted by others. Usually, poor listening is characterized by behavior such as constant interrupting, avoidance of eye contact, hurrying the speaker, use of automatic responses (e.g., "uh huh," "OK," "yeah"), failure to ask the sender to expand on his or her ideas, a tendency to "put down" the sender's ideas, and a tendency to ignore the feelings or body language of the sender. Several comments are presented as follows that reflect both poor responses and active listening.

| Sender's question | Poor response | Active listening |
|---|---|---|
| "The fees for this program are too high! I'm not getting my money's worth." | "Well, I don't set them. Don't bother me about it!" | "It seems to you that the fees should be lower, I take it?" |
| "This basketball league is a disgrace. It's poorly organized." | "It has always been organized this way. We aren't changing it!" | "You think we need to talk about the league's organization?" |
| "Don't you think I've improved my baseball skills—hitting and fielding?" | "Yeah, but you still have a lot that you do wrong, like holding your bat on your shoulder." | "Sounds as if you feel that you've really improved your baseball skills!" |

In each of these situations, the individual responding in the poor response category closed off further communications. Furthermore, telling individuals, "Don't bother me," or "You still do a lot wrong," sends a negative message to the individual about his or her worth. It reduces the possibility of additional positive communication and creates barriers between individuals. By failing to deal with the comments and feelings of others in a way that provides understanding without necessarily agreeing with the individual, active support is denied. On the other hand, the active listener does not necessarily agree with the sender, but the way is left open for additional communication. This enables further discussion of the situation, provides an opportunity for the sender to expand his or her feelings or comments, and provides an opportunity for positive interaction.

Interestingly, because the leisure experience is highly personal and individually defined, there must be a rapport between the leader and the participant that enables the participant to reach conclusions about his or her own behavior. The open-ended supportive responses that characterize active listening are conducive to this. In the example given earlier, the active listener responding to the individual commenting on the improvement in baseball skills says, "Sounds as if you feel that you've really improved your baseball skills," requiring a conclusion to be drawn by the *participant* rather than by the leader. With this approach, it is up to the participant, rather than the leader, to define and evaluate the success of his or her performance.

## DEVELOPING ACTIVE LISTENING SKILLS

There are a number of active listening skills that can be acquired and developed. Following are some of the skills that are conducive to active listening.

*Learn to Listen to Yourself.* The active listener should be in touch with his or her own feelings, prejudices, values, and needs in order to listen effectively. We all have biases that can influence or even block our ability to listen accurately and effectively. An awareness of these can help the listener overcome them when attempting to communicate.

*Learn to Listen Accurately and Completely.* The active listener lets an individual complete his thoughts and express his thoughts completely before responding. He or she should try to understand what the speaker is trying to convey in his or her message without interrupting or otherwise detracting from the speaker's message.

*Learn to Read Body Language.* The message that an individual conveys will often be more accurately represented by his or her gestures or other body language. The feeling or intensity with which a person presents his concern, interest, or idea is often more valuable to the listener as an indication of the intent of the message. Reading body language should help increase the listener's sensitivity to others.

*Learn to Listen Courteously.* Often individuals fail to demonstrate basic courtesy in listening to others. Their own verbal and non-verbal responses may demonstrate disrespect for the speaker. Being abrupt, curt, or disinterested should be avoided by the active listener. Individuals can learn to be tactful in their responses to others. The rule here is treat others as you would expect to be treated. Making eye contact is essential here.

*Learn to Give and Gather Feedback.* The way that the listener reacts to the speaker's message will communicate a concern or lack of concern for the views of the speaker. The way that the active listener "listens" to the message being presented can convey support, interest, and empathy. It is important to learn how to give feedback that allows for openness and continued positive communication. Often this will involve learning how to mirror, reflect, or clarify the speaker's queries. In order to clarify the communication that takes place, one can use such phrases as "Now you feel, then, that X is the case?" "Let me make sure that I understand you correctly. Please tell me if I'm right." Such feedback increases the accurateness and effectiveness of the communication.

*Learning to Accept Different Viewpoints.* The active listener should learn to respond courteously to the ideas of others even though they may be different from his or her own. In other words, the listener must be willing to accept the ideas of others without necessarily being defensive. Further, the listener should avoid setting up barriers to communication based on personality.

Active listening involves a commitment to other individuals. It implies that the leader is willing to understand and give support to others. This may involve personal risk on the part of the leader as it requires him or her to be open and willing to be exposed to different views. When open to the views of others, the leader may be forced to reexamine his or her *own* views, concerns, and ideas.

## TECHNIQUES OF COMMUNICATION

The recreation and leisure service leader should be familiar with various techniques of communication. Some of the specific techniques of communication that may be used by the leader are face-to-face, small-group, public speaking, and mass communication. These are detailed as follows.

### FACE-TO-FACE COMMUNICATION

Face-to-face or interpersonal communication is a primary technique of communication used by recreation and leisure service leaders. Face-to-face communication suggests a direct one-to-one interaction between a leader and another individual. This type of communication can involve giving or receiving information or both in the form of coaching, lecturing, listening, demonstrating, role playing, and activity involvement. In this latter case, activity involvement, the leader plays with the participant. Interpersonal or face-to-face communication can also involve the sharing of emotional expressions, such as love, joy, grief, sorrow, or excitement. Emotional expressions are subjective in nature, but should be recognized as an essential component of the leisure experience.

Face-to-face communication is profoundly affected by the personality characteristics of the leader. The leader who has a tendency to demonstrate actively a caring attitude toward others will be more successful in face-to-face communication than one who does not. We refer to this as empathy. The leader who is comfortable with other people and who enjoys interacting with others on a one-to-one basis will likely be more effective within the face-to-face leadership role. The ability of the leader to express his or her own feelings and emotions and listen and respond to the feelings of others is also conducive to effective face-to-face communication. The effective face-to-face leader can be characterized as genuine, responsive, and having respect for the needs of others.

In order to increase the quality of face-to-face communication, the leader may disclose his or her feelings, thoughts, beliefs and values, and ideas as they relate to the existing situation. This is a dynamic process that serves to increase the intimacy between individuals and, as a result, facilitates the communication process. It is known as ''immediacy,'' and it is one of the most important factors influencing interpersonal communication. Using this approach to communicate, the leader might express his or her own personal feelings or encourage the participant to do the same in order to create a meaningful dialogue. For example, the leader might state, ''I am uneasy. I'm asking myself if I am paying enough attention to you.'' ''I feel as if we are having fun, but I don't know if I am expressing it well.'' Such statements open the door for a mutual exchange between the two parties—the leader and the participant.

Face-to-face communications can also involve confrontation between individuals. The idea of confrontation often conjures up negative feelings. We have all been the subject of irresponsible interpersonal attacks and perhaps attempt to avoid such situations in the future. However, confrontation, when handled appropriately, is a useful form of interpersonal communication that can facilitate the communication process. By confrontation we mean that individuals are provided an opportunity to examine their own behavior. By having to account for feelings and ideas and examine these in relation to others, an individual is allowed by the process of confrontation to modify or change his or her ideas or behavior or both.

## SMALL-GROUP COMMUNICATIONS

Much of the work of the recreation leader is carried out in small groups. Whether coaching a girls' basketball team, teaching a knitting class, leading New Games, or discussing contemporary events with friends, one is engaged in small-group communications. For the recreation and leisure service leader to be successful in leading small groups, he or she must be able to use communications skills within a group setting. Regarding the leader's role within groups, Wofford, Gerloff, and Cummins have written this.

> We are members of many more groups today than at any other time. These groups tend to be less permanent, stable, and enduring in nature. Consequently, communication skill becomes increasingly more important; one must be able to interact quickly and to relate effectively on a limited time basis. The successful . . . [leader] . . . today must become adept at establishing close, open relationships. One who remains guarded and defensive in the group context will be unable to succeed in a wide range of situations.[7]

Thus, the ability to communicate effectively in small groups is extremely important. Whether one is planning or implementing a program, communicating effectively with other individuals is essential to the successful operation of the organization. It can influence the identity of a group, its social structure, and the extent to which it achieves its goals. Communication within small groups also builds cohesiveness and is a primary vehicle for establishing behavioral norms and patterns.

As indicated in Chapter 3, communication within groups often focuses on three areas: process, task, and relationship. Communication activities focusing on the *process orientation* of a group are concerned with the vehicles

[7]Jerry C. Wofford, Edwin A. Gerloff, and Robert C. Cummins, *Organizational Communication: The Keystone to Managerial Effectiveness* (New York: McGraw-Hill, 1977), p. 251.

used to transmit and receive information. Information is processed by talking, listening, and acting out or demonstrating. Use of the most appropriate of these vehicles to process information will facilitate communication. The process orientation of a group also refers to the assignment of responsibilities or the establishment of channels of communication or both. When a group picks a leader, that individual assumes a certain role that, in turn, defines how communication with the group will occur.

*Task orientation* refers to the content communicated within the group. This might involve an introduction of information, a debate, analysis, or decision making or a combination of these. For example, a leader involved in small-group communication within a basketball team might lecture or demonstrate (*process orientation*) to teach zone defense (*task orientation*).

Small-group communications also are concerned with the *relationship orientation* between members of the group. Often within a group there will be tensions due to differing expectations that can influence the flow of communication. In the basketball example given earlier, the team's *relationship orientation* might center on the building of a "teamwork" philosophy, building esprit de corps and attempting to avoid tensions related to individual performances.

Does group communication vary from individual, one-to-one communication? The processes used in individual communication are basically the same as those employed in group communication; however, predictably, group communications are more complex. The dynamics of interaction that take place in a group usually are more formal or structured than interaction in face-to-face communication. Face-to-face interaction is more amenable to spontaneous changes in both the type of communication and the style of communication. If the leader communicating individually desires to change from written to verbal to nonverbal communication as the situation

demands, he or she may do so and consequently is able to respond to the communication needs of the individual more readily. On the other hand, when group consensus must be achieved as to the most appropriate type of communication in a given situation, the flexibility with which the leader can change types or styles of communication may be limited.

## PUBLIC SPEAKING

Good public speakers are in demand. The recreation and leisure service leader who can express himself or herself effectively is an asset to his or her organization. Public speaking can be thought of as the art of moving an audience to belief and action.[8] Gordon offers the following description of public speaking and some of its purposes.

> A speech may, of course, serve either individual or organizational purposes, be motivated by profit or charity, and be by invitation or self-initiated. The subject matter may be broadly classified as educational, economic, political, spiritual or recreational. When a speaker addresses an audience he seeks to draw an audience closer to certain ideas, feelings or actions. . . . speeches may reinforce established loyalties or promote new ones; they may entertain, inform, impress, convince, or any combination of these that serves the purpose of the speaker to influence the audience.[9]

The development of a speech involves several steps or procedures. The first step in the development of a speech is to *identify the audience* or intended receivers of the speech. The leader should know the type of audience he or she will be speaking to and its purpose for listening to the presentation. Some audiences represent a casual collection of individuals whereas others may assemble in order to pursue mutual interests. In giving a speech, the leader should ask two basic questions: (1) What do I know about the audience? (2)

[8]William I. Gordon, *Communication: Personal and Public*, (Sherman Oaks, Calif.: Alfred Publishing Co., 1978), p. 365.
[9]Ibid., pp. 206–207.

What does the audience know about me and my topic? These questions are asked primarily to gauge how information should be presented and how it is likely to be perceived.

The second step in the development of a speech is to *state specific goals* of the speech. What knowledge or action does the speaker want the audience to exhibit at the conclusion of the speech? In other words, what is the purpose of the speech? Is it to entertain people? Is it to inform people? Is it to encourage people to join an organization? Is it to influence people to give money to a cause? Is it to encourage people to participate in a recreation and leisure service activity? The leader should be specific in describing his or her goals, stating precisely "*what* behavior you want to happen, *who* you want to perform it and *when*."[10] Once these first two steps have been taken—identification of the audience and the goals of the speech—the speech may be organized.

Organization of the speech usually follows the same format as a term paper, with inclusion of an introduction, body, and summary or conclusion. As a rule of thumb, the speaker wants to inform, entertain, and enlighten the audience. This involves designing a speech that will create interest, provide information, and move individuals to action. Forms of support of a speaker's point of view or topic, that can be used in a speech are explanations, illustrations, and evidence. *Explanations* help the speaker clarify the relationships between ideas, thoughts, and concepts. An idea within a speech can be highlighted by using a story, analogy, metaphor, or simile. *Illustrations* are often included in a speech to help bring to life an idea, concept, or thought. Both from real life and imagined, illustrations often intensify the interest of the audience and promote the speaker's point of view. *Evidence* in the form of observable or statistical data is also useful in the support of a person's idea. Also, the use of inductive and deductive reasoning can help sharpen the speaker's point of view.

[10]Ibid., p. 217.

**Mass Communications.**  Mass communications can be thought of as the information that is transmitted in an organized fashion by an agency or institution. We think of mass communications as those involved in reporting the news and information via television, newspapers, telecommunications, radio, magazines, books, and so on. In today's society, mass communications have made possible an instantaneous transmission of pictures of people, places, and events and ideas. It is estimated that television sets are viewed an average of six hours and eight minutes per day in American homes. Over one billion individuals attended movies in 1980, and expenditures for magazines, newspapers, and books are millions of dollars per year.

In the foreseeable future, several trends would seem to be forthcoming. First, the establishment of home entertainment via cable television or personal computers or both is just beginning to occur. Personal computers, although currently not meeting market projections, will provide individuals with opportunities for new and instantaneous forms of communication. This type of technology is providing new forms of communication that are directly affecting the leisure experience and the way in which individuals interact with one another. For example, a semipro football team recently developed an interactive relationship with their fans via cable television. A system was established whereby those watching the game on television could vote, from a list of alternative plays, for a particular play to be run. Thus, this vehicle of communication gave these fans direct control over the game. The possibilities for transactional (two-way) communication using these techniques are growing.

Recreation and leisure service organizations use mass communications to promote and report on activities and services. Certainly, many recreation and leisure service organizations are involved in newsworthy activities that are reported in the newspapers and on television and radio. In addition, mass communications are used to advertise and publicize services. This is done through the preparation of commercial radio and TV spots (or in the case of public recreation and leisure service agencies, the preparation of public service announcements), news releases, magazine and newspaper advertisements, interviews, photographs, and other media opportunities. In the transmission of information, basically the leader is communicating information concerning "who, what, when, where, and how." When one is developing copy for radio or television, it is important to recognize that they are personal and direct channels of communication. The communications flow should be more conversational, informal, and casual. On the other hand, when one is writing for newspapers or magazines, communication occurs usually in inverse pyramid style; that is, the body of the story may be reported first and the details follow it. The "headline" is used first to attract reader interest. In either case, the information communicated to the reader must be streamlined to fit the time or space available.

The recreation and leisure service leader should provide accurate, complete information to the public served by mass communications. The misrepresentation of a product or service or inaccuracies due to lack of preparation or poor preparation can adversely affect the credibility of an organization. Knowledge of the various types of mass communication as well as how they can be used is essential to the leader wishing to promote the activities and programs of his or her organization effectively.

## BARRIERS TO EFFECTIVE COMMUNICATION

Leaders may become frustrated or discouraged when they fail to communicate effectively. Understanding the barriers to communication can help the leader increase the likelihood that communication will be effective. Barriers can be thought of as impedi-

ments that prevent the recreation and leisure service leader from transmitting information or prevent the participant from understanding the information. As indicated previously, it is important to recognize that communication is a two-way process. The lack of effective communication can occur as a result of such variables as breakdown, misunderstanding, and lack of empathy between the sender and the receiver. In some cases, failure can be attributed to the sender; in others, it may be the fault of the receiver, or it may be the fault of both parties.

When poor communication occurs, what is the responsibility of the leader? Basically, the recreation and leisure service leader should attempt to identify and define barriers. Initially, the leader should analyze his or her own behavior or pattern of communication. The leader should ask himself or herself, "How am I projecting myself?" "Do people understand the meaning of the terms and phrases that I am conveying?" The second step in the identification of barriers is the analyzation of the receiver's behavior and its effect on the communication process. The leader cannot initially change the communicative behavior of the participant. The leader can, however, alter his or her own behavior in order to communicate better with the receiver (on the "receiver's terms"). Once communication has been achieved, the leader can facilitate behavioral changes in the participant, including communicative changes, allowing for an easier and more effective two-way exchange. For example, a recreation and leisure service leader coaching a children's baseball team may need to communicate initially with the children in very simplistic and "nontechnical" terms in order to guide the children effectively into a knowledge of the sport. Later, however, once the leader has taught the children the rules and technical terms, parallel communication can occur based upon a shared "language."

Mondy, Holmes, and Flippo have classified communication barriers in three categories: technical, semantic, and psychological. Technical barriers can be thought of as variables in the environment that can influence communication. They include such factors as timing, communications overload, cultural differences, and short-circuiting. Semantic barriers are problems resulting from language and the interpretations applied to various words within one's language. Finally, psychological barriers mainly arise from an individual's perceptions of situations or his or her interpersonal relationships with other people or both.[11] A brief discussion of some of the barriers in the communication process as classified by these authors follows.

*Timing.* The leader must recognize the importance of timing of the information that is to be transmitted to the participant. The receptiveness of the individual to a particular idea, concept, or thought may depend on timing of the message. In teaching, instructors often refer to the "teachable moment. This occurs when the readiness of the students as well as the information being transmitted are interrelated and appropriate to one another.

*Communications Overload.* Basically, when an individual tries to transmit too much information too fast, a potential problem or barrier is communications overload. Individuals may become bogged down and disinterested and "tune out" when they are presented with more information than they can handle at one time. This problem is rampant in contemporary society where individuals are constantly bombarded with information from the media as well as other sources.

*Short-circuiting.* Often individuals do not allow the sender to complete his or her message. Rather the sender may be interrupted, or the receiver may form a mental response to a communication before it is even complete.

[11]R. Wayne Mondy, Robert E. Holmes, and Edwin B. Flippo, *Management: Concepts and Practices.* (Boston: Allyn & Bacon, 1980), pp. 383–387.

The intended message is "short-circuited" and may be misinterpreted or missed entirely. The lack of active listening creates ill will and may lead to mistrust and suspicion.

*Cultural Differences.* Customs and norms may vary from culture to culture, affecting the communication process. One culture may communicate more aggressively and effusively, whereas another culture may communicate in a more reticent and formal manner. Failure to recognize these differences and adjust to them may hinder communication between individuals from two such cultures. Or one culture may be interested in fast communication and quick results whereas another culture may tend toward lengthy communication and careful deliberation. Again, adjustment on the part of both parties would be necessary to facilitate effective and accurate communication.

*Language.* The level of the vocabulary and knowledge base of the sender and the receiver must be matched for effective communication to take place. Esoteric, problematic, theoretical, and conceptual information transmitted to an individual incapable of dealing in such terms will not be appropriately received. In this case, practical, concrete, and direct communication may produce greater understanding. Use of a vocabulary that consists of many terms that are sophisticated and beyond the grasp of the receiver is a barrier to communication.

*Meanings Associated with Words, Jargon, and Professional Nomenclature.* Different meanings can be attached to words by a select group within society and can affect the communication process. The term *hip* has an anatomical meaning as well as implications for social awareness. The differences in the meanings of words can create barriers. Excessive use of professional jargon when communicating with those unaccustomed to it will also create a barrier to communication. The terms *delivery system, planning horizons, proxy goals*, and *target markets* have little meaning to the lay person.

***Knowledge of What You Say.***    Individuals often speak without thinking. As a result, the sender may have an incomplete picture of what he or she is trying to transmit. It is more difficult for the receiver to piece together a complete message if the sender is offering his or her message in a fragmented way. The sender should have an organized mental picture of what he or she is trying to transmit and should avoid such phrases as "you know," "the thing," and so on.

***Filtering.***    Related to the way in which individuals perceive the world, filtering can often become an overt and direct way of manipulating information. Individuals may color information so that it conforms to their desires and wishes, thereby altering the communication that has occurred. This can result in misinformation in the communication process.

***Trust and Openness.***    If individuals feel that others are not honest or have a hidden agenda, communication can be affected. The need for trust and openness in communications is essential to the process. If the receiver lacks confidence in the honesty of the sender, the message may be ignored, devalued, or distorted. In addition, it is difficult to talk about problems or personal experiences when the trust factor is low.

***Perception Sets.***    As previously indicated, the perceptual set of an individual greatly influences the communication process. This type of barrier to communication may be influenced by one's age, sex, political views, social status, and family orientation, as well as by other life experiences that have molded or shaped an individual's perceptions.

***We Hear What We Want to Hear.***    One of the most common barriers to communication is the tendency to hear or see what one wants to. An individual has a tendency to evaluate information based on predetermined conceptions. For example, an individual may have a negative orientation toward life and no matter how careful, positive, and joyful the information is that is presented, the individual will "find something wrong with it."

## SUMMARY

Communication is a process that helps individuals share their thoughts with one another. It is the way in which human feelings and ideas are transmitted. Communication attempts to convey meaning and to assist in understanding between individuals.

The communication process consists of a number of interrelated components: the sender-encoder, message, channel, and receiver-decoder. Basically, the sender conceptualizes an idea, thought, or feeling. This, in turn, is encoded by using symbols that can be understood and accepted by both the sender and the receiver. The message being transmitted usually attempts to inform, persuade, convey social or expressive behavior, or resolve conflict. The channel of communication can be thought of as the type of communication employed. Verbal, nonverbal, written, electronic-technological, and visual symbols are different types of channels of communication. The last step in the communication process is the receiving-decoding function, wherein the message is received and evaluated by the individual.

The recreation and leisure service leader is concerned with two-way or transactional communication. This is a process of interacting *with* individuals rather than *to* individuals. Transactional communication attempts to ensure that there is adequate feedback to individuals, including the use of listening and observational skills. Listening or active listening is a process in which the sender and receiver seek to understand what the other is attempting to communicate. It involves giving active affirmation or acknowledgment to another's ideas, feelings, or values. As not all communication is verbal or written, the use of observational skills to "read" nonverbal cues is also important.

Influencing the communication process is the way that individuals perceive information that they have received. Perception is a psychological process that assists an individual in selecting, organizing, and interpreting information. It is dependent on both physical senses and complex cognitive processes. There are various factors or variables that influence the way that an individual will perceive a given piece of information or situation. These include his or her environment, personal goals, values, past experiences, personal evaluation of hearsay, and social relations.

Often the communication process will fail. It is important for the recreation and leisure service leader to understand the barriers to effective communication that might cause this to occur. Some of the barriers in the communication process are poor timing, communications overload, short circuit, cultural differences, and language. Others include the filtering process, lack of trust and openness, and one's perceptual set.

## DISCUSSION QUESTIONS

1. Define communications. What is the difference between interpersonal and organizational communications?

2. What is transactional communication? What implications for the leader in recreation and leisure service settings does this concept have?

3. Identify and define five different types of communication. Give two examples of each.

4. Identify and define four functions of communication.

5. What is the process of communication? What is encoding and decoding?

6. How does one's perceptual set affect the process of communication? What variables influence an individual's perceptions? What environmental variables influence the perceptual process? How?

7. What is active listening? How does one build active support for another individual through the listening process?

8. Identify four techniques of communication and provide examples of the ways that they are used within recreation and leisure service organizations.

9. Identify ten barriers to effective communications. Suggest solutions to the problems created by these barriers.

10. Discuss how communications influence the recreation and leisure experience.

# 6

# FACE-TO-FACE
# LEADERSHIP

Pat Foster-Turley, Marine World/Africa USA, gives "Behind the Scenes" tours of the Redwood City wildlife park. Here, she points out the "rookery" of sea lions present in Marine World's Seal Cove area.

The foregoing five chapters of this book relate to theories of leadership, communication, motivation, group dynamics, and leadership in leisure service settings. Although it is incumbent on all leaders to follow general leadership principles, there are additional principles that can be applied in various identifiable and specific leadership situations. This chapter contains a discussion of six types of direct face-to-face leaders and some techniques that can be applied within these roles.

## TYPES OF DIRECT, FACE-TO-FACE LEADERSHIP

The face-to-face leader works directly with people. There are many situations that demand an obvious, direct, and influential leader. Examples include leaders of games, songs, initiative tasks, dance, drama, special events, tours, tournaments, conferences, social events, arts and crafts, playgrounds, and countless other activities. Most of the chapters in Part Two of this text relate to direct, face-to-face leadership of specific activities. Though there are many types of face-to-face leaders, examples of six general, yet diverse, direct face-to-face leadership roles are: direct program leadership, team leadership, instructional leadership, counselor, outreach worker, and host-guide.

## DIRECT PROGRAM LEADERSHIP

Kraus describes group leaders involved in direct program leadership as being either *work oriented* or *program oriented* and differentiates between the two in his text *Recreation Today*.

> *Work-oriented Groups.* In groups that are concerned with carrying out professional responsibilities, there are frequently times when co-workers must share the process of exploring problems, making decisions, formulating plans, or agreeing on recommendations. At these times, the leader is instrumental in helping members of the group define their objectives, maintain a strong group structure, develop plans for attaining their goals, carry out a course of action, and maintain a high level of cohesion and group satisfaction. In order to accomplish these purposes, the group leader may carry out the following functions or may share them with the members of the group.

> - Initiating: keeping the group action moving or getting it under way (examples: suggesting steps to be taken, pointing out goals).
> - Regulating: influencing the direction and tempo of the group's work (examples: summarizing, pointing out time limits, restating goals).
> - Informing: bringing information or opinion to the group.
> - Supporting: creating an emotional climate that holds the group together and harmonizes difficulties.
> - Evaluating: helping group to evaluate its decisions, goals, or procedures (examples: testing for consensus, noting group processes).

> Throughout, in any such task-oriented process, the leader should attempt to do the following: (1) help the group members define the limits of the problem they face and decide which aspect of it they intend to attack; (2) encourage and make it possible for all group members to express their ideas; (3) maintain an atmosphere in which cooperation is stressed and tensions or fears eliminated; (4) keep the discussion or other efforts of the group focused on the work to be accomplished, moving steadily from theoretical considerations to practical results and steps.

> *Program-oriented Groups.* When the leader is in charge of a group of recreation participants engaged in some type of activity, the task at the outset may appear to be rather narrow. It may seem as if all that is expected is to coach a sport, teach crafts, or lead dances. One is likely to find out that, even in such an assignment, there are problems involving interpersonal relationships, scheduling, special events, programs or exhibitions, irregular attendance, and morale. Thus, even in an activity-centered group, group dynamics represent an important concern.

> Beyond this, when the leader is working with a social group in which the dynamics of interpersonal relationships are more important than the particular activity the group happens to be carrying on, a number of the roles must be assumed. In such a situation, the leader may need to assume—or to help group members assume—any of the following roles.

> - *Policymaker.* Helping the group make decisions about relating to goals, membership, meeting time and place, dues, and similar matters.

Here a program leader takes a group of children fishing.

- *Planner.* Helping the group develop specific plans for activities, programs, trips, special events, and other projects.
- *Organizer.* Helping the group evolve ways of structuring themselves, of making concrete plans for action.
- *Resource Person.* Acting as a source of information, knowledge, skills, and contacts.
- *Stimulator.* Inspiring the group and helping to get things going; acting as a source of ideas, suggestions, and motivation.
- *Referee.* Helping the group resolve conflicts and disagreements.
- *Disciplinarian.* In a constructive sense, helping the group members develop rules and other forms of control and impose them of their own volition; exerting controls himself when necessary.
- *Group Symbol.* Acting as an adult image, or model, whom group members admire and respect and whose values and behavior they emulate.
- *Spokesperson.* Acting as a spokesperson for the members of the group, either in the sponsoring agency or in the community at large.

When these functions of the program-oriented leader are examined, it is apparent that the leader is in a position to make a major contribution to the successful operation of the group. In many situations there are choices that must be made, and leadership behavior must be based on sound judgment and assessment of the probable results of several courses of action.[1]

Kraus goes on to describe the duties of the typical direct program-oriented leader (such as playground leader, community center director, or leader of older persons). He lists 12 functions.

- *Plan, Organize, and Conduct Programs.* The leader is responsible, under the general direction of the district supervisor or department head, for planning, organizing, and carrying out a full range of activities and enjoyable activities designed to achieve the key goals of the sponsoring agency and also to promote both the learning of useful leisure skills and the development of the constructive social values of sportsmanship and good citizenship.
- *Lead and Direct Activities.* In addition to the overall program responsibilities, a leader is normally expected to teach, lead, direct, coach, or officiate in a variety of program activity areas, including arts and crafts, storytelling, dance, drama, sports, trips, and nature activities.
- *Guide and Direct Participants.* The leader must work with individuals or groups of participants to promote positive and socially constructive forms of behavior. This includes guiding them in cooperative group relationships, effective group planning and decision making, and respect for public property and community social values.
- *Maintain Control and Discipline.* The leader must obviously maintain order and discipline on the playground or in the center, preventing vandalism, fighting, or other antisocial behavior. In addition, departmental regulations devoted to smoking, gambling, drinking, the use of undesirable language, or other prohibited acts must be enforced and disciplinary measures must be applied when required.
- *Provide a Desirable Model.* Leaders are expected to provide desirable adult models for children and youth in their own behavior and personal habits and to represent the department positively in all contacts with the public or other municipal employees. This involves strict adherence to departmental regulations and seizing every opportunity to present a favorable image of the department and of recreation itself as an important form of community service.
- *Accident Prevention and First Aid.* An essential leadership function is to maintain an effective safety and accident prevention program. This includes vigilant attention to all possible safety hazards, such as defective equipment, and immediate follow-up on

[1]Richard G. Kraus, *Recreation Today: Program, Planning and Leadership*, 2d ed. (Santa Monica, Calif.: Goodyear Publishing Co., 1977), pp. 290–292.

having them repaired, as well as constant teaching and enforcement of desirable safety attitudes and practices in all areas of playground or center activities.

- *Facilities, Equipment, and Supplies.* As indicated, the leader is responsible for regular inspection and supervision of facilities and for reporting problems of cleanliness or maintenance, as well as safety hazards. He or she is also responsible for maintaining an up-to-date inventory of equipment and supplies, for supervising their use, and for requisitioning new materials when necessary. In some departments, leaders also are in charge of scheduling recreation facilities (such as ball fields) for use by other community groups.
- *Supervise Volunteers.* An important function of recreation leaders or center directors is to recruit or enlist volunteers from the community, to train and assign them, and generally to supervise them in program service. When volunteers are intelligently selected, guided, and rewarded—with recognition and appreciation—they make a significant contribution to many recreation programs.
- *Public and Community Relations.* Recreation leaders are normally expected to publicize their programs thoroughly through announcements, fliers, bulletin boards, releases to newspapers and TV stations, and similar methods. In addition, they must maintain cordial and cooperative relationships with neighborhood residents, business people, and community organizations in order to meet neighborhood recreation needs better and to be able to call upon community resources for various forms of help. In larger departments, such efforts are often coordinated through a central office of public and community relations.
- *Reports, Forms, and Evaluations.* The recreation leader is required to keep accurate records of general playground or center attendance, as well as participation in special events or trips. Reports must also be made

out and submitted for other administrative reasons, such as accidents or other special incidents, collection of fees, or disciplinary infractions. The leader is expected to fill out and submit such reports accurately and promptly according to department guidelines and to carry out program evaluations as required.

- *Adhere to Department Regulations.* All recreation and park departments have a code of personnel practices and regulations. Some of these simply describe departmental procedures in areas such as pay, leave or vacation, probation and promotion, and retirement and other ''fringe'' benefits. Others are in the form of regulations governing leaders' responsibilities and behavior in a variety of areas. Leaders must be thoroughly familiar with such procedures and regulations and must adhere to them carefully.
- *Overall Departmental Role.* Finally, playground or center leaders and directors are expected to play a significant role in the department as a whole. This may involve accepting alternative assignments, serving on special committees or task forces, assisting other individuals as requested, making suggestions to improve programs or joining in problem-solving groups, representing the department in community meetings, and generally maintaining favorable relationships with other employees. Leaders are also expected to take part in in-service training programs sponsored by their departments. Beyond these general functions, many recreation leaders may also be called upon to carry out more specialized tasks, involving either advanced responsibility in a particular program area or work with special populations in the community.[2]

The responsibilities just described are carried out to meet the needs of participants while at the same time meeting the goals of the spon-

[2]Ibid., pp. 304–306.

soring organization. Figure 6.1 is an example of a job description for a direct program leadership position.

## TEAM LEADERSHIP

A second type of face-to-face leadership is team leadership. The word *team* usually brings to mind a competition of two groups vying against each other for higher scores.

Certainly, football, basketball, baseball, volleyball, soccer, and all other team sports need leaders either as coaches, instructors, or captains to guide the members toward a cooperative effort that can ultimately lead to winning. A team leader may also direct a group involved in fund raising or lead any other group with a common predetermined goal that can be reached only through successful group co-

---

## CENTER DIRECTOR

### DESCRIPTION

The center director is directly responsible to the recreation supervisor and assists in the administration of recreation programs at his (or her) assigned location.

### EXPLANATION OF DUTIES

- The center director is designated in charge of the park, including all facilities and programs therein.
- Works with individuals and groups as a leader of program activities.
- Plans the programs at the center in the interest of the participants and according to agency policies and objectives.
- Organizes and/or conducts new clubs, classes, activities, or informal education and recreational activities.
- Recommends his or her staff and cooperates with his or her supervisor in conducting training sessions, supervising the activities, and maintaining good working relations among all staff members.
- Recruits and supervises volunteer or part-time leaders and works with them in developing leadership skills.
- Devotes special attention to the needs of the park in making it more attractive and helping to promote recreation programs in the building and in the district.
- Works with groups using the park facilities in scheduling dates and times and in providing guidance and assistance whenever desired.
- Responsible for accurate inventory of equipment and supplies at his (or her) center. Requisitions, issues, receives, and oversees the use of equipment and materials; cares for and maintains equipment and recommends the disposal of equipment and materials for the recreation programs.
- Constantly evaluates the services under his or her direction to ensure a well-balanced program for the community.
- Works cooperatively with neighborhood groups, PTAs and other associations to inform residents of all programs fully.
- Performs other duties as required.

### QUALIFICATIONS

Two years of education or training in the field of recreation. Ability to work with individuals and groups as evidenced by successful experience as a counselor, leader, or volunteer in a previous setting.

---

**FIGURE 6.1**    A job description for a direct program leadership position. (*Source:* Summer Staff Guide, Arlington Heights Park District, Arlington Heights, Ill., p. 4.)

operative efforts. The team leader must perpetuate a group spirit, which means that individual success can be accomplished only through the cooperative efforts of everyone working together and each contributing according to specific assigned roles (e.g., catcher, neighborhood coordinator, and so on).

A team leader must be able to arouse enthusiasm, direct specific actions, demand discipline, arouse positive goal-oriented emotions, resolve personality differences, and teach skills. In recreation and leisure services, the team leader should possess the philosophy that what happens to the individual and to the group may be much more important than winning. There are some municipalities with regulations that each sports competition team is limited to $X$ members, each of whom (regardless of skill) must play a designated minimum number of minutes each game. The leader of such a team is a true team leader, not a coach or game leader.

The team leader may be autocratic at times (obeying rules, accounting for money raised, delegating assignments), democratic at times (consensus on new projects or uniforms, brain-storming for new ideas, discussion of alternative recruiting strategies), but can never display an attitude of laissez-faire without

---

## BASIC FUNCTION

Eugene Sports Program (ESP) coaches must possess attitudes that are in the best interests of the program and the children in general. An ESP coach must be willing to promote the program, maintain a positive attitude toward fund-raising projects, respect rules and regulations, set a good example as a role model for children, and, above all else, keep the best interests of the children in mind at all times.

## APPOINTMENT AND AUTHORITY OF COACHING STAFF

The ESP program directors shall assign all head coaching positions. The head coach has the privilege of selecting his or her assistant coaches and all others who participate in the activities of his or her team, subject to the approval of the ESP staff. When the ESP staff assigns head coaching positions, the following priorities shall be used: (1) A person who has served as a head coach the previous year shall be given first consideration when filling the position for the same team the following year, and (2) second consideration shall be given to those persons who served the team in question as assistant coaches the previous year.

## ACCOUNTABILITY

All volunteer coaches will be directly responsible to the ESP administrative staff for their coaching performance and actions during ESP activities.

## COACHING DUTIES AND RESPONSIBILITIES

The basic role and responsibility of each coach is to prepare the children under his or her supervision for team play in accordance with the ESP rules, regulations, and philosophy. Coaches must comply with the spirit and intent of ESP policies, regulations, and playing rules. Other than team preparation, each coaching staff must complete the following duties.

- Prepare and be present at all practice sessions and games.
- Attend coaches' meetings and clinics.
- Arrange practice times and reserve school facilities with principal.
- Notify students of first player turnout (day, time, and place).

weakening the function of the position. A sample job description for a team leader in the Eugene (Oregon) Sports Program is seen in Figure 6.2.

## INSTRUCTIONAL LEADERSHIP

Whenever the success of an activity depends upon the ability of the participant to execute specific skills, the leader of that activity should be an instructor. Instructional leadership is a third type of face-to-face or direct leadership. Programs in which participants learn to play musical instruments, learn new songs, execute sports skills, perform dances, play new games, follow directions, learn to dive or climb, or perform a myriad of other skills should have instructors. The instructional leader may, in some circumstances, be more effective if an authoritarian leadership style is used. Certainly, activities involving risk or danger need tighter control and more precise skill development than activities that entail creative arts. This does not mean that the leader should be a dictator or use harsh commands, but it does mean that the leader, as an authority on the topic, will set up certain prerequisites (safety policies and order of action) in order to ensure safety and the optimal development of the skill.

It is assumed that the instructional leader

---

- Establish employment with ESP equipment manager to draw equipment and uniforms.
- Complete ESP roster form and check player eligibility.
- Conduct parent orientation meetings.
- Notify team sponsor that he or she has been assigned to your team.
- Take team to photo-taking session.
- Report all game scores when your team wins.
- Complete and file with ESP a coach's registration form.
- If ESP conducts a fund-raising project during the season, make sure that your team is involved 100 percent.
- Return all equipment and uniforms.
- Maintain the highest standards of good contact and sportsmanship at all times.
- Maintain personal conduct that is a credit to ESP.
- Show respect and accept decisions of game officials.
- Teach players to respect game officials properly at all times.
- Maintain complete control over team members.
- Refrain from any action that may arouse players, parents, or spectators to display unsportsmanlike behavior.

### QUALIFICATIONS

To serve as a coach in the Eugene Sports Program, a person must meet the following qualifications.

- Be at least 18 years of age. Assistant coaches may be younger; however, they may never be in charge of a team unless it is supervised by an adult 18 years or older.
- Be of unquestionable moral character. Each volunteer coach assigned to a team will be screened by local law enforcement agencies. Individuals found to have a felony record or misdemeanor involving moral turpitude will not be considered.
- Must be available to conduct practice sessions at least one and a half hours and a minimum of two days a week.
- Must have a good driving record in order to transport players. Individuals with a poor driving record will be allowed to coach, however.

**FIGURE 6.2**  A coach's job description adapted from policies of the Eugene, Oregon Sports Program. Used by Permission.

will attempt to teach the participants to perform in an exemplary manner. Whether it be serving a tennis ball, singing a duet, writing invitations by calligraphy, square dancing, or cooking over charcoal, the leader must have the expectation that the learner will acquire well-developed skills that will enable successful execution of the activity. It is incumbent on the instructional leader to teach the skills correctly and safely and still maintain interest and enthusiasm. A good instructor knows how to balance the work of learning with the play of performing and is able to help learners persist through the arduousness of practice sessions for the reward of successful performances to come.

There are times when precise skill instruction may be modified. If a participant, because of some disability, cannot perform as the skill is described, the leader must be able to modify. A tennis player with one functionally limited arm may not be able to toss the ball for the serve as described in the books on teaching tennis. The ball may be placed, however, on the racquet face and tossed into the air by the serving arm, which can then execute the serve. This is not the regulation serve, but necessary for the player's success. It is in these types of situations that instructors must be innovative and flexible.

## COUNSELOR

The counselor is a fourth type of face-to-face or direct leader. The term *counselor* is used in several diverse recreation and leisure settings to designate one who advises an individual or group concerning behaviors, activities, values, decisions, and the like. For example, a *camp counselor* who is assigned care of approximately eight children is tantamount to in loco parentis for day-to-day living situations (rest, bathing, eating, cleanliness, deportment, and so on) plus the teaching of one or more skills related to the program of a camp program. It might be said that, of all face-to-face leaders, the camp counselor is expected to be the most

versatile (acting as parent, teacher, friend, and confidant) of all leaders. Interestingly, this leader usually is the youngest and least experienced of all face-to-face or activity leaders. The camp counselor is on duty many hours of the day, on call at night, has 24 hours off each week, and a job that lasts two to ten weeks. The sample job description in Figure 6.3 illustrates the diversity of the camp counselor's responsibilities.

The *leisure counselor*, on the other hand, may be one of the most educated and experienced of leaders. These people focus on helping clients understand their leisure potentials and on finding ways to add some meaning to their lives through the leisure experience. Leisure counselors generally work with one client at a time and must be trained and knowledgeable in counseling methods, leisure opportunities, the scope of leisure, leisure activities, and leisure values.

## OUTREACH WORKER

In communities where there is deemed a need for someone to help the residents of economically deprived neighborhoods achieve successful recreation and leisure and social experiences, outreach workers are employed. Outreach workers are face-to-face leaders. These leaders, often called roving leaders or sometimes youth counselors, street club workers, or street gang leaders, have been employed in cities such as New York, Philadelphia, Los Angeles, Washington, D.C., and Richmond, Virginia, since the 1950s. The Roving Recreation Leader Training Guide, published by the Superintendent of Documents, Washington, D.C. offers the following information regarding the roving leader program.

> Although America has been described by Harrington as a Nation of joiners and participants, his description more accurately applied to middle-class Americans. The inhabitants of the "other America," the impoverished and hard-to-reach, rarely seek out or know of organized

---

# TORONTO YMCA
# JOB DESCRIPTION—DAY CAMP COUNSELOR

## BASIC FUNCTION

The counselor's basic responsibility is the personal growth of each camper in his or her group. The counselor utilizes a group setting, together with the natural environment and leadership that constantly demonstrate care and concern for other people, to assist this growth. The counselor utilizes program activities to provide adventure and enjoyment, develop new skills and interests, and satisfy a need for achievement and recognition in the campers.

## AUTHORITY

The counselor has the authority to take necessary action to carry out responsibilities assigned to him or her within the framework of policies and objectives established by the Toronto YMCA.

## ACCOUNTABILITY

The counselor is directly responsible to his or her section director and to program specialists when operating in their area or under their jurisdiction.

## SPECIFIC RESPONSIBILITIES

- Planning, cooperating, and conducting programs with his or her camper group.
- Supervising camp activities, including participation with other groups.
- Planning and supervision of campers during camp special events, such as overnights, parents' nights, and so on.
- Responsible for the health and safety of each camper.
- Participating in staff meetings and training events as scheduled.
- Cooperating with other staff in the organizing and conducting of the camp.
- Maintaining the campsite and camp equipment and supplies.
- Maintaining personal behavior of a responsible, exemplary nature.
- Maintaining neat and clean appearance.
- Following camp administrative procedures regarding buses, attendance and camper reports, emergency procedures, and so on.

## QUALIFICATIONS

- Minimum age 19.
- Experience in day or residence camping or significant related experience.
- Experience in working with children.
- At least one program skill suitable for camp leadership.
- Emotional maturity.
- Good health and vitality.
- Ability to work cooperatively with campers and staff.
- Joy and satisfaction in working with children.
- Enjoyment of outdoor living.
- Willingness to learn.

**FIGURE 6.3** Sample job description for a day camp counselor.

forms of recreation, such as basketball leagues, pool tournaments, talent shows, arts and crafts classes, and other special interest programs. Their recreation usually involves random movements from one place to another, with long stretches of boredom.

Several metropolitan areas are seriously considering the Roving Leader concept and its effectiveness for realistically serving hard-to-reach youth. It has been shown in Washington, D.C., by its Recreation Department; in San Francisco by Youth for Service, in Chicago by the YMCA; and in Buffalo, N.Y., by the Youth Board that a Roving Leader can provide face-to-face leadership different from that normally given by a recreation worker.

When the Giddings Elementary School on the fringe of Hough (Cleveland, Ohio) burned in April 1967, there were rumors that a Maoist group had caused the fire. Eventually, six youth were arrested and sentenced to reform school:

> They had done it for kicks. They had nothing to do and no place to do it. That was what they told the judge, and the Fire Department's arson investigators, the police and the probation officers all agreed that the kids were bored and not political-racist plotters. . . . At the same time, lack of money forced the Police Athletic League to cut back its activities for teenagers from the slums. "We don't have organizations to belong to; we have gangs," explained a ninth grader, at a recent ghetto students' meeting at the Cleveland Board of Education.

There is a dearth of experience in developing programs that [low income and] minority youth can respond to, but there is little experience in developing and refining methods of reaching out to involve them. More important, the recreation programs designed to reach and serve low-income, hard-to-reach youth must be concerned with the "how" of reaching them, as well as the "what" of serving them.

The Roving Leader Program represents a somewhat new dimension in providing leadership for hard-to-reach, delinquent-prone youth that has proved to be highly successful. The Roving Leader usually spends weeks, some-

times months, establishing rapport with individuals and groups. He must start at the level of the group. This is not a short-term undertaking. He works with the youth for a long time—sometimes several years. The final test of the Roving Leader's success is when he is no longer needed.

A Roving Leader is a worker generally assigned to a specific area of the inner city for the purpose of strengthening, extending and stimulating the participation of hard-to-reach youth in wholesome recreation programs and assisting them in utilizing, to the fullest, community resources in the educational, health, employment, and related social service areas.

*Outreach* defines the function of a social service agency when it reaches out and assists, through face-to-face leadership, persons who were unreceptive or previously excluded from the agency's assistance or who were unaware of the available service. [An] *indigenous paraprofessional* is a resident of the neighborhood, often a member of a minority group, and a peer of the participant sharing a common background, language, ethnic origin, style, and interests. Because of his or her ability to work comfortably with the community, the worker is viewed as a community advocate interpreting its needs, interests, and concerns.[3]

A sample job description for a roving leader is shown in Figure 6.4.

### HOST-GUIDE

The last type of face-to-face leader is the guide or host. Many recreation and leisure services necessitate the provision of a guide or host for the participant. For example, many of the visitors to national parks and U.S. Forest Service visitor information sites expect to be guided on tours or trails, to hear lectures, to attend campfire programs, to see slide talks, and to watch demonstrations. A typical list of qualifications for such public information leaders, adapted from Grant Sharpe, follows.

- Appropriate and professional appearance

---

[3]*The Roving Recreation Leader Training Guide* (Washington, D.C.: Superintendent of Documents, 1972), p. 5.

- Pleasant personality
- Politeness
- Knowledge of the organization's functions
- Ability to meet the public and to communicate articulately
- Ability to perform minimal clerical functions
- Ability to organize and to make good use of time
- Ability to control emotion and to exhibit patience
- General knowledge, poise, and maturity
- Loyalty and trustworthiness
- Self-confidence and assurance
- An ability to work closely with other people
- An ability to work alone under loose supervision[4]

Sharpe further defines the duties of information specialists or leaders and some of their functions.

## THE DUTIES

Visitors expect every employee of a public recreation area to be able to answer questions. Therefore, all employees must be instructed in how to handle these contacts, even if all they can do is direct the visitors to the proper source for answers. Some employees may view these questions as interruptions in their work and may be curt, yet a smile and a pleasant reply are most important to the agency's image.

Information duty differs from typical interpretive activities in several ways. One is that it is not quite the same as speaking before a group. Information duty is the information giver and the visitor conversing on a one-to-one basis. Another difference is that the questions asked frequently do not pertain to natural or human history. Finally, the information duty person may or may not be a member of the interpretive staff. Interpreters are sometimes involved, however, and for this reason information duty is considered here.

[4]Adapted from Grant W. Sharpe, *Interpreting the Environment* (New York: Wiley, 1982), pp. 170–171. Used with permission.

The person handling this activity must be genuinely pleasant, friendly, and enthusiastic. He or she must be able to keep these attributes in evidence for several hours at a time. Although the person who stands information duty must be prepared to answer almost any question, most questions will be somewhat repetitive.

To determine the kind of person needed for information duty one needs an accurate description of the job.

As stated above, the purpose of the position is to greet people and to answer questions. The duty station is usually indoors. The person involved may have other duties such as typing, issuing permits, answering the telephone, or operating a two-way radio. The duty may be for several hours at a time. Maintaining a sales counter may be a part of the task as may be assisting other staff members during slack hours. In some instances the person at the desk may be responsible for the entire building, including the maintenance of rest room facilities, overseeing of exhibits, and even running the first aid room. Information duty may require the services and skills of a very special kind of individual. On the other hand, this duty is in some circumstances monotonous, and the variety of tasks assigned information personnel creates some special communication problems.

## THE LOCATION

Information duty usually takes place at one of the following sites.

*Entrance Station.* The usual purposes of the entrance station is to provide a place for the collection of entrance fees. Unfortunately, the press of traffic seldom allows time for conversation. Visitors, however, seeing a person in uniform, expect to have their questions answered. This problem is commonly solved by a general information handout and a map issued by the person at the entrance station. Since this station is typically small, visitor access is not encouraged. If further information services are available in another place, this fact should be communicated to the visitor.

*Name of position:* roving leader.

*Supervisory control:* The services of the roving leader should be supervised by the director of the program or a designated staff member; that is, field supervisor.

*General description of duties:* The function of a roving leader usually assigned to a specific geographic area within a community is that of strengthening, extending, and stimulating participation of hard-to-reach, disadvantaged inner-city youth, who were unreceptive to or excluded from receiving the agency's assistance or who were unaware of the availability of the service. The leader combines awareness with creativity of approach that enables him or her to provide a caliber and type of service related to that of a counselor, adviser, consultant, coach, and friend.

*Specific description of duties:* The duties assigned to roving leaders will vary among different agencies or groups of agencies depending on the nature of their services and the target youth being served, but essentially the roving leader's duties are as follows.

- Provides face-to-face leadership to hard-to-reach youth that is distinctive from that provided by normal playground or agency staff.
- Identifies youth with problems and works with them toward effecting changes in attitudes, actions, and outlook through various programs and activities providing opportunity for relationship, reeducation, and redirection.
- Familiarizes himself or herself with the resources of the community that provide services that his or her agency does not supply.
- Visits target neighborhoods and attempts to spend time with families in the area in order to get to know their problems.
- Locates candidates for specific recruitment projects as they are needed.
- Performs outreach for follow-up purposes on individual youth, getting information from them or bringing them back to the service center if that is required.
- Develops and maintains communication with civil agencies, civic organizations, and related services.
- Prepares necessary records and reports on the youth's status with regard to

*Visitor Center.* One of the main functions of a visitor center is to provide an opportunity for visitors to have their questions answered. This is usually handled by a person on duty in the lobby at a desk easily seen by visitors when they enter the building. Aids to assist the person on duty include a bulletin board, mounted maps, and a nearby relief model.

*Campground Offices.* Some outdoor recreation areas maintain an office in the larger campgrounds, and although its primary function is to assist visitors with campsite assignments, it also serves as an information outlet. The size of the building usually determines whether or not visitors are welcomed inside or greeted through an information window.

*Movable Information Booth.* When conditions warrant, a movable booth should be considered. This could be a structure of poles and canvas, a wooden building built on skids, or a small trailer or caravan on wheels. These are used only during peak visitor seasons.

*Point Duty.* During peaks of the visitor season, such as holidays and weekends, it may be appropriate to station a person at a point of known concentration. Such sites could be scenic overlooks, waterfalls, or other areas, usually with parking facilities. In these circumstances, it becomes a matter of taking the information station to where the people are. A booth may not be necessary unless the weather is often inclement. The duty hours should coincide with heavy-use periods of

*Family* (size, number of children, ages of family members, how many living at home, and so on).

*Occupational status* (work situation in terms of job, relative underemployment, unemployment, and so on).

*Health* (physical, emotional, and mental condition of each member of family).

*Income* (sources and amount of income).

*General qualifications for roving leader:* A candidate for the position of roving leader should possess a significant knowledge of the neighborhood or community in which he or she desires employment. He or she should be able to meet and deal with people, particularly youth from a disadvantaged or delinquent background or both. He or she should possess a high degree of sensitivity and be able to observe an individual and evaluate where the person "is." The roving leader must be a person capable of acting as liaison between all the diverse segments of the community or neighborhood.

*Specific qualifications for roving leader:*

- College training is desirable but not required; work experience should demonstrate a capacity to work with youth.
- High school education or equivalent with on-the-job training in youth work or a related area.
- Completion of a special training institute for roving leaders that includes academic instruction as well as supervised on-the-job training.
- Ability to communicate in the vernacular of the street.

*Suggested selection criteria:*

- Brief written statement (two paragraphs) on why roving leaders in the neighborhood are important to disadvantaged youth.
- An oral interview to determine interest, motivation, ability to meet and deal with hard-to-reach youth, and ability to take oral directions.
- Evaluation of education, work experience, and community involvement.

**FIGURE 6.4**     Sample job description for a roving leader.

the day, which vary from place to place and season to season.

The presence of the information duty person in uniform is all that is necessary to attract visitors. Most questions, as one would expect, will be related to what is in sight; maps, models, and other aids are usually not necessary. A spotting scope or telescope is often provided. The duty person should be well acquainted with the area, for here is a station in the middle of the the natural environment where interpretation as well as general information can be disseminated.

*Roving Duty.* This type of duty is similar to point duty except that the duty person moves about, either on a bicycle, on horseback, or on a motor vehicle, looking for concentra-

tions of people. Rangers on horseback are particularly attractive to visitors. Although use of horses requires special skills, more use of horses by interpreters and information rangers should be considered. Both point and roving duties are an effective means of reaching large numbers of people. The questions during these duties are related heavily to the nearby scene. Of course, if the site is located on a major road, there could be questions related to distances and available services.

Roving duty also provides the opportunity to reach visitors with current information about hazards such as avalanches, high water, and fire danger.

This type of duty is popular with interpretive employees as it provides variety and the opportunity to exercise initiative and creativity.[5]

In all of the preceding cases, the leader must be able to answer countless and sometimes seemingly inane questions repeatedly and always pleasantly. The leader should be able to communicate factually, using correct grammer and a vocabulary of the level of the listeners. Information should be given in a manner respectful to all. Complaints should be handled as if they were compliments. Directions should be given succinctly, accurately, and pleasantly—even if there are clearly written signs in front of the questioner. The size of the group on any hosted or guided trip will vary. In each case, the leader should be very much in evidence, sometimes even in uniform. It is the leader's responsibility to help the group meet its goals and needs in a safe, successful, enjoyable manner while also serving the purposes of the sponsoring agency.

## GUIDELINES FOR DIRECT, FACE-TO-FACE LEADERSHIP

Why do some recreation and leisure service organizations and their leaders succeed whereas others fail? The key factor influencing the success of an organization is the relationship that it develops with its participants or those whom it serves. Although most organizations claim that they are close to their participants and understand their needs, excellent agencies are, in fact, *very close* to their participants. This relationship is often reflected in an attitude developed within an organization that weds the leader to the participant. A people-oriented organization will outperform its counterpart that is less involved with its participants.

It is interesting to note that organizations that are people oriented develop a deep-seated agency philosophy that places a high degree of value on ensuring participant loyalty. In or-

[5]Ibid., pp. 150–154.

der to ensure that participants remain loyal to the organization, the programs, activities, and services provided must be of the highest quality, they must be relevant, and they also must compare favorably with similar programs provided by other agencies. This is exemplified by many private recreation and leisure service agencies, which are very concerned with the needs of participants. As a result, such organizations often attract and maintain the loyalty of participants in spite of competing public programs and services that are offered at a lower cost and may be in closer proximity.

A direct people-oriented attitude is one that permeates all levels of the organization, but perhaps it is no more evident than in the work of the leader with the participant. The recreation and leisure service leader must be eager to serve. This does not necessitate gushy,

Although the chief executive officer of the Willamalane Park and Recreation District, serving over 40,000 people, Dan Plaza seeks opportunities to engage in direct face-to-face leadership. He is a "hands-on" administrator who knows the value of maintaining contact with those served by his organization.

overexuberant, patronizing behavior, but rather warmth, good nature, interest, enthusiasm, and honest concern for the welfare of participants. Peters and Waterman have suggested that direct people-oriented organizations build strategies focused on the elements of *service*, *quality*, and *reliability* in order to maintain participant loyalty.[6] These strategies are discussed in detail in the following paragraphs.

*Service Orientation.* A service orientation suggests that regardless of the activity or product provided by an organization, it is *service through people* that is the key to success. As Peters and Waterman note, in discussing Disneyland and Disney World, "There is no such thing as a worker. . . . Employees are cast members . . . and whenever you are working with the public you are on stage. . . . Participants are treated as Guests—not the lower case "c" customers, but upper case "G" Guests."[7]

*Quality Orientation.* Providing quality services involves striving for excellence. Leaders that require of themselves a high commitment to providing the very best possible recreation and leisure environments produce quality services. Quality orientation can be defined as striving for excellence in every participant-leader interaction that takes place within a recreation and leisure service organization. The leader must make a concerted effort to prepare effectively in order to ensure high quality of services.

*Reliability.* Closely related to the concept of quality orientation is reliability. Reliability infers that the participant can expect quality services when returning to participate in an activity again or when participating in

other activities offered by the organization. For example, in preparing for activities, the leader should realize that although he or she may not find a program novel or stimulating the fifteenth time around, quality must be maintained no matter how many times the game activity has been led.

These then are the strategies with which leaders and their organizations succeed. In addition to these guidelines, there are a number of other leadership techniques that can be used in various recreation and leisure settings. The leader should be able to recognize, evaluate, select, modify, and utilize these techniques of face-to-face leadership.

The material that follows in this section is generalized to apply to most direct, face-to-face leadership situations and may need to be modified or complemented for specific events. More specifically, generalizable leadership techniques regarding the topics of interest and attention, position of the leader, and group formations are discussed as follows.*

## INTEREST AND ATTENTION

Gaining the interest of a group requires the use of a variety of techniques by the leader, as does getting their attention. Gaining interest

*Portions of the following material (pp. 139-151), as well as the sections on Song Leading, Tournaments and Social Recreation, have been adapted from *Informal Recreational Activities—A Leader's Guide* published by the American Camping Association (American Camping Association, Bradford Woods, Martinsville, Indiana 56141). The book was written specifically as a training tool for camp counselors who are often 18 years of age or older and, while they are trained for positions working with youth at summer camps, they are usually people who have not had previous leadership training and whose eventual careers are usually not in the profession of leisure services.

The American Camping Association is the professional membership organization for those involved in providing private, public-, agency-, church- or school-sponsored organized camps. The organization is the national voice of standards for administration and programs in camps. As part of the services of the organization, a publication division provides members and nonmembers the opportunity to purchase books related to games, stories, songs, nature, camping and other activities and leadership techniques.

[6]Thomas J. Peters and Robert H. Waterman, Jr., *In Search of Excellence: Lessons from America's Best Run Companies* (New York: Harper & Row, 1982), p. 157. Used with permission.
[7]Ibid., p. 167.

and getting attention are not synonymous. A group may be enthusiastically interested in an activity, but in order to hear specific directions, they must have their attention gained so they can be quieted and controlled. It is obvious that the first step in prompting interest is leader enthusiasm. It may be that the second qualification for gaining and maintaining interest and attention is voice quality. Every leader needs to make a conscious effort to reach every member of the group vocally. The beginning leader often seems more concerned with what is being *said* than what is being *heard*. Voices must be projected to the furthest members of the group. A leader should talk to the far corners of the room or playing field. Never mind talking directly to those in front; the leader must speak to those in the back rows, and those in front will always hear. Related to voice projection is enunciation. Speaking to groups requires more precise enunciation than does casual conversation.

People want the leader's attention and will return only what they receive. The way the voice is used is an indication of the leader's interest in the endeavors of the group.

Eye contact and facial expressions are also indicators of leader interest and factors that, in turn, prompt interest on the part of participants. A participant likes to be noticed and to receive a smile. Other participants, noticing that the leader looks and smiles at members of the group, seem to appreciate the attention their colleagues receive and stay alert to receive similar attention. The leader should give attention to all people or many people, not just a chosen few, and the attention should be friendly and positive and should include everyone. "In" jokes with specific members of a group serve to divide—not unify—the group.

Any leader who is in charge of a variety of activity programs soon develops a set of steps for leading a group that are followed automatically with consistently successful results. Though there are specific guidelines for lead-

ership of specific programs, the following guideline for leading a group can be applied to most activities.

1. Get the attention of the group.
2. Arouse interest.
3. Direct the group into the formation for the activity.
4. Give directions.

Although these four steps are important, they alone will not guarantee success and need considerable explanation to be fully understood.

*Getting Attention.*    The leader gains the attention of participants by engaging in some action that is distinctive, shortly before the activity commences. Several means of gaining attention are recognized as being effective. Probably the "attention getter" that comes to mind most frequently is the whistle. The whistle is indeed an excellent attention device if used with restraint. The advantage of a whistle is the ease with which it can be heard in a large area such as a playfield or a gymnasium. For this reason, a whistle should not be used in the confines of a small room or with a small group standing in close proximity to the leader. *Overuse* of the whistle soon results in a complete *lack* of attention to it. The leader who blows the whistle for continual random announcements displays a lack of organization.

In small areas or with smaller groups, other noisemakers can suffice to arouse attention. A bell, a horn, a buzzer, the beating of a tom-tom, the clapping of hands, or countless other sounds will attract attention. Preschoolers are often trained to respond to chords played on the piano by stopping their free play and stationing themselves in certain areas in anticipation of a new activity. Most people are familiar with the sound of a knife tapped against a glass as the attention-getting device at a banquet.

Attention also may be gained without the use of noise. In a building, the flashing of the lights can be used. Preschool children can learn that if the leader stands in a specific spot, it means time for a surprise, a story, a new game, or a song. (And what fun it is to catch the leader on "the spot" quite by accident and unprepared for any surprise!)

An attention signal used almost universally in summer camps and among youth-serving agencies is the raised hand. The historical background of the raised hand tells us that when Indians traveled single file through the forest, the leader signaled his followers when to stop and be silent through raising his hand to the height of his head, palm forward. Each person on down the line followed suit; thus, the entire line was stopped without the raising of a mere whisper.

The recreational hand sign for silence is similar. The leader stands silently with raised hand, and each person seeing the hand does the same until the entire room is made up of silent, hand-raised individuals waiting to hear what comes next. It often takes several minutes to quiet a group down in this manner, and on the first few trials it is usually necessary to remind people that the raised hand means quiet. Patience and pleasantness on the part of the leader will soon result in a group conditioned to paying attention to the hand signal. This is an impressive means of getting attention in a dining hall, campfire circle, or meeting room.

Use of the human voice may be good for arousing attention if the voice is well modulated and toned for attention. A *low voice*, with words spoken slowly, is effective where a high, nasal voice is ignored. Many leaders find it necessary to practice projecting their voices so that tones and words are picked up easily by the group members furthest away.

Once attention has been aroused, it must be kept by talking effectively to the entire group at once. Lengthy directions, talking "down" (beneath their maturity and intel-

lect) to any audience, and a voice that is either too soft or too strident will lose the attention of group members as fast as it was gained. Too often leaders talk to groups before getting the attention of everyone. Be sure that everyone in the audience is listening before starting to speak. This takes practice and an awareness of the individuals in the group. Often just waiting patiently and silently will help get the attention of the last few talkers.

*Arousing Interest.*   When directing activities, one hopes that group members will participate with enthusiasm. To encourage enthusiasm, the leader can develop the ability to motivate interest through unique introductions to activities. Simply announcing the name of the next activity is poor methodology for several reasons. It is a dogmatic, authoritarian leader who announces, "Now we are going to play_____." Not only does this antagonize some people, but it also divides the group attention into several foci, some of which may be the following.

1. Good. I like that.
2. Oh, dear. I prefer something else.
3. Too bad. I don't know how to do it.
4. I wonder if he (or she) knows the rules our last leader knew.

In order to maintain attention and to arouse interest and curiosity, one should not announce an activity by title. An activity can be given a buildup according to the season, the weather, the theme of the party, or recent current events. At Christmas, the Calf Roping Relay becomes the Christmas Gift Tying Relay; at Halloween it becomes the Spider's Web. But at no time is it introduced as the String Wrapping Relay.

The purpose of a unique introduction is defeated if one starts with a question such as "How would you like to _____?" for immediately control is lost as the group replies, "Yes," "No," "Goodie," "Yeah,"

"Ugh," "Never," or whatever comes to their minds. Sometimes interest is aroused simply by the leader's manipulating a piece of equipment to be used in the activity, particularly if it is a new activity. The best way to arouse interest in string activities is through forming unique string figures. This serves as an attention getter, interest arouser, and grouping device all in one as curious spectators crowd around to see what is going on.

Granted, it is not easy to think of things to say to introduce activities, but with initiative and practice each leader can develop a personal inimitable style.

## POSITIONS WHEN CONDUCTING ACTIVITIES

A key to gaining and keeping group attention is to stand where you can be seen and heard by all. Because the position of group members may change, the leader must be constantly aware of his or her own position and place himself or herself advantageously as Figure 6.5 indicates. The elevated leader facing the sun is far better off than the leader who forces his or her group to look up at him or her and into the sun. Any speaker working indoors should be careful not to position himself or herself between his or her audience and an

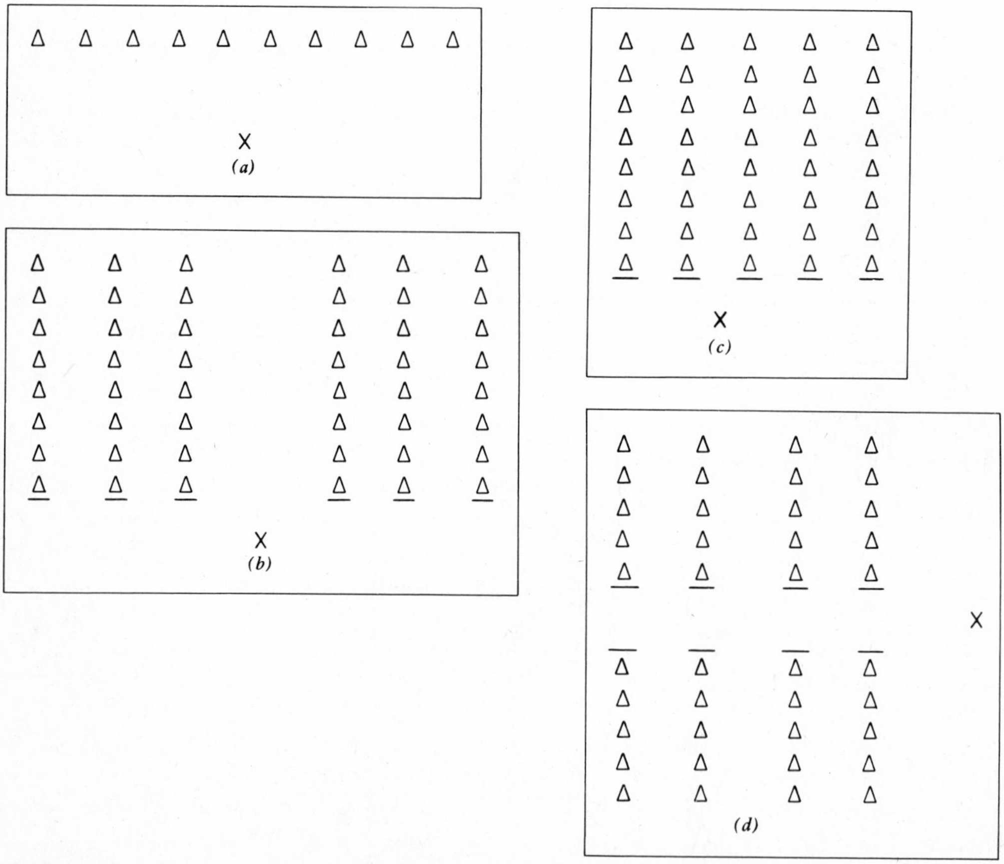

**FIGURE 6.5**  Leader positions for conducting activities. (*a*) Position of leader when working with a single line. *Note.* Leader is positioned equidistant from each end, thus not giving one end less attention than the other. (*b*) Position of leader working with an even number of files. *Note.* Leader is positioned in front of space dividing files in two. Center

undraped window unless he or she wishes to appear as a black silhouette against a brilliant streak of light, thus blinding the group and forcing the focus away from him or her. Both children and adults can understand directions and patterns of movement better if they are positioned where they can visualize them and act them out vicariously as directions are given.

## GROUP FORMATIONS

The leader can use innovative ways to form groups. For example, people can be asked to group together by eye color (blues in one group and browns in another). Those who aren't sure can be used to even up the groups. With a large group of over 50, four groups of approximately equal size can be formed by birthdays. Those in January, February, and March in one group; April, May, and June in another; and so forth. Two groups may be formed simply by dividing the group into two halves by guesswork. The leader can also put numbers on the bottoms of chairs or pass out programs of different colors and have all those sitting on like numbers or all those with like colors group together. To form a group of

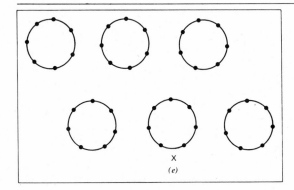

(e)

(f)

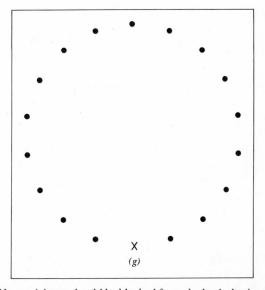

(g)

aisle space is a little larger than space between other lines. No participant should be blocked from the leader's view by another participant. (*c*) Position of leader working with an uneven number of files. *Note.* In this case, leader is *not* centered because standing in front of the center file would obstruct his or her view of all center file participants behind the first one. (*d*) Position of leader working with shuttle relay formation. (*e*) Position of leader working with several circles (or squares). *Note.* Circle members turn to face leader, who explains action, using circle directly in front to demonstrate if necessary. Participants may be seated, or leader elevated, for better control. (*f*) Position of leader working with group in informal or mass formation. *Note.* Leader is elevated. (When one is working with children, they may be seated on the floor or ground, thus elevating the leader.) Caution must be taken out-of-doors to make sure that the sun is *not* behind the leader, thus in the eyes of the group. The leader should face into the sun and wear sunglasses to keep him or her from squinting. (*g*) Position of leader working with circle formation. *Note.* Leader is positioned as an integral part of the circle, preferably between two participants as near to his or her own height as possible. (Standing between two participants towering over him or her dwarfs the leader mercilessly, and standing between two participants greatly shorter accentuates their minuteness if they are adults.)

eight for square dancing, the leader can tell each person to get a partner, and that set of partners can be told to get another set. Then each group of four can join another group of four to make a group of eight. The leader should never count off by twos or threes or fours after the early grades. It is a waste of time and very boring to the participants, who should be more interested in the activity than in hearing "one, two, one, two, one, two" all around the room.

## PLANNING AND IMPLEMENTING ACTIVITIES

The art of leading well appears, on the surface, to be a spontaneous action occurring between the leader and the participants. This apparent ease is rather unfortunate because it induces some people to try to be playground, community center, or camp leaders without the realization that much of the actual work involved in leadership occurs in the preparation. Prior to beginning an activity, the effective leader will consider such factors as the objectives to be sought, the type or types of participation that will be involved, the selection of appropriate activities, the preparation needed (materials and equipment), and the time at which the activity will end. These factors are discussed in detail in the following sections.

### OBJECTIVES

The first step in leading any single activity or series of activities is to understand the fundamental objectives of recreation leadership. We hear much concerning objectives today, often with little understanding of the meaning of the word or of its significance. Simply defined, a set of objectives is really a list of things that we hope to accomplish through a specific activity. Objectives should be attainable; consequently, the things we hope to accomplish should actually be within the sphere of participants' abilities. Regardless of *specific* objectives for each individual activity, the *general* or all-encompassing objectives for recreation and leisure programs are as follows.

- To provide for the enjoyment of the participants.
- To present activities that are both of good quality and safe.
- To teach the skills necessary for successful participation in activities.

It is easy to understand the first objective, for unless an activity is enjoyable or evokes pleasure, it cannot be termed recreation. Sometimes during the learning process an activity may not be pleasurable; however, if enjoyment is eventually forthcoming, the objective has been attained. Since participants differ greatly, the leader is constantly challenged to find a wide variety of activities so that each participant will have a successful leisure experience.

Presenting meaningful and safe activities refers to the selection of activities that are of good quality not only physically, but also socially, psychologically, and emotionally. Leaders must be especially careful that no activity ridicules or embarrasses anyone. All activities should be of a quality that uplifts, and does not downgrade, participants. Indiscriminate selection of activities often results in poor or mediocre quality.

Many leaders feel that the teaching of skills related to activities is of inconsequential importance because recreation is fundamentally concerned with enjoyment and practicing skills is often not enjoyable. This argument is far from sound, and teaching no skills or condoning incorrect skill execution actually does the participant a disservice. The better the skills, the higher the quality of enjoyment.

Beyond these three fundamental, recreation-oriented objectives, each activity is led with additional objectives in mind. Keeping the three fundamental objectives in mind, the leader can move on to planning the program. Figure 6.6 outlines the steps necessary to write objectives.

- It should start with the word *to*, followed by an action verb.
- It should specify a single key result to be accomplished.
- It should specify a target date for its accomplishment.
- It should be as specific and quantitative (or hence measurable and verifiable) as possible.
- It should specify only the ''what'' and ''when''; it should avoid returning into the ''why'' and ''how.''
- It should relate directly to higher level goals of the organization.
- It should be readily understandable by those who will be contributing to its attainment.
- It should be realistic and attainable, but represent a significant challenge.
- It should provide maximum payoff on the required investment in time and resources, as compared with other objectives being considered.
- It should be consistent with the resources available or anticipated.
- It should avoid or minimize dual accountability for achievement when joint effort is required.
- It should be consistent with the basic policies and practices of the organization.
- It should be willingly agreed to by all parties without undue pressure or coercion.

Examples:

To organize and implement an eight-week dance class for *X* female participants, which improves their cardiovascular circulation and is fun and enjoyable.

To produce three special events serving *X* male and female children ages six to ten, focusing on Halloween-related themes, which provide opportunities to interact with other children in a wholesome environment and involve a degree of risk and excitement.

To provide an opportunity for *X* senior citizens to interact with one another in a sports-related activity, which creates opportunities for gross and fine motor movement.

**FIGURE 6.6**    Guidelines for writing objectives. (*Source:* Adapted from George I. Morrisey, *Management by Objectives and Results* [Reading, Mass.: Addison-Wesley, 1970], p. 62.)

## UNDERSTANDING THE PARTICIPANTS

Actual preparation for the recreation program itself is based on knowledge of the facility or area to be used plus an understanding of the needs of the participants. Without a knowledge of the age and sex, and other relevant characteristics of the participants accompanied by an analysis of the proposed activity, no rationale for selecting the recreational program exists. In addition to knowledge of the age and sex of participants, one should keep in mind the group's purpose for attending the event, special factors (such as disabilities, longtime friends, frequency of attendance), and the expectations of the group.

*Encouraging Participation.*    Not everyone wants to participate all the time, and some want to participate but don't know how to join in. A sensitive leader must cultivate an awareness of the latecomers, the standoff ones, the hesitators, the onlookers, and the sour grape types and assume that some of them really do want to participate and need encouragement. One way to get nonparticipants into the act is to ask them to join the group. Maybe they just need the invitation. Some people will respond when assured that the group *needs* them. They may realize they are needed to fill positions, even up the teams, or just be of help by being part of the group.

With the very young, putting out a hand works well as they often reach for the outstretched hand and allow themselves to be led into the action. But beware of this with children over eight, many of whom feel that only babies hold hands. Sometimes people really do not want to participate and should be allowed to watch rather than be forced into an unpleasant situation. Don't assume, however, that they will never want to participate. Give them occasional quiet recognition, and ask again if they would like to join in.

***Correcting Errors.***    No one is perfect, and no matter how carefully instructions are given, participants will make errors. Handling errors tactfully is a skill to be cultivated carefully. Regardless of what kind of error is made, kindness is always the password. There are times when it is advisable to blame errors on your own weakness or poor teaching techniques. Naturally, the best time for this is when the fault really does lie with leadership errors. Children *love* to find a leader who is so human that he or she makes errors. It puts the leader closer to their level. Adults, too, find occasional errors on the part of the leader refreshing. Sometimes, when an activity is complicated, it raises the morale of struggling participants if the leader can pleasantly admit to going too fast or getting too involved. Usually, it is possible to make a quick analysis of the reason for any errors, and, upon analysis, it is often found that errors were made because skills were incorrectly or inadequately taught.

***Let the Participants Lead!***    A few additional but brief comments may help the beginners make their leadership appear experienced. Participate when it is practical, but don't try to play the judge at the same time. Pace the activities so that vigorous ones are interspersed with quiet ones. And, whenever possible, shift the leadership. Let the participants take over. They'll love it!

### SELECTING ACTIVITIES

Each type of recreation program—playground, team, class, trips, party, conference, or other—has its own format that determines the types of activities to be included and the order in which they should be presented. Before actually planning for any one specific program, the leader should be familiar with its objectives, structure, and components.

Activities must be carefully analyzed to determine whether they will be suitable for the group and to ensure a variety of action. Also one must not overlook the equipment needed, the space required, and the time that must be allotted. Many activities otherwise quite acceptable must be eliminated from plans if they are too complicated for the group or too time-consuming, involve unavailable equipment or take up too much space. Whenever an activity is considered desirable but not practical, an effort should be made to adapt it to the situation. Ability to change, modify, and adapt rules, equipment, playing area, and skills is a desirable trait found in far too few leaders.

Each activity proposed should be subject to the following analysis.

- What movement does the activity entail? What skills?
- What form does the activity take?
- What are the psychological attributes of the activity?
- How does this activity differ from other activities in the program?
- How is it similar?
- How can the activity be presented so it is meaningful and safe?
- What are the objectives for presenting this activity? (What should the participant gain from the activity?

Following such an analysis, a leader will be able to answer readily any questions concerning why an activity was included in the program. No activity should be led in order simply to fill time, kill time, or keep busy! Recreation activities can be analyzed in terms of movement and form by use of the following outline.

I. Classification According to Movement
   A. Motor Activity
     1. Fundamental (large muscle) movement
       a. Locomotion
         (1) Moving in a horizontal plane (running, walking,

dancing, crawling, skipping, and so on)
  (2) Moving in a vertical plane (climbing, jumping, and so on)
  (3) Moving through use of a vehicle (sledding, skating, swinging, bicycling, and so on)
  b. Handling Objects (throwing, catching, kicking, hitting, carrying, rolling, and so on)
  2. Accessory (small muscle) movement
    a. Voice (singing, yodeling, cheering)
    b. Fingers (playing guitar, piano, knitting, whittling)
B. Sensory Activity
  1. Sight
  2. Sound
  3. Touch
  4. Feeling
  5. Taste
C. Intellectual Activity
II. Classification According to Form
  A. Noncompetitive Activities
    1. Creative activities
      a. With materials
      b. Without materials
    2. Roving activities
    3. Hunting activities
    4. Imitative activities
    5. Social activities
    6. Acquisitive activities
    7. Aesthetic activities
    8. Vicarious activities
    9. Curiosity
  B. Competitive Activities
    1. Games
      a. Low organization
      b. Team games
      c. Combatants
      d. Dual games
      e. Mental games (table games)
    2. Contests
      a. Relays
      b. Individual
      c. Group

In order to follow this outline, we must make a few explanations. Any recreation and leisure activity is primarily one of three forms of movement: motor, sensory, or intellectual. Although motor, sensory, and intellectual movements are all involved in all recreational activities, each activity utilizes one form of movement to a greater extent than the others.

*Classification by Movement.* Motor activity involves the use of muscles for the success of the activity. *Fundamental muscles* are the large muscles used to move the body or another object; *accessory muscles* are the small muscles that can manipulate objects or produce sounds, but that do not move large objects. Fundamental muscle movement is divided into two parts: *locomotion* or moving the body itself from one place to another and *handling objects* by propelling them or receiving them. There are many forms of locomotion. Some require additional body extensions in the form of skis, skates, bicycles, and so on. Some forms of locomotion are running, jumping, dancing, skipping, dodging, climbing, swimming, canoeing, hopping, leaping, crawling, walking, gliding, and many others. Handling objects through the use of large muscles entails hands and arms, back and legs, and often auxiliary equipment such as bats, racquets, gloves, clubs, cues, and such. Included in the category of handling objects would be throwing, kicking, batting, rolling, catching, hitting.

If an activity involves muscles but does not involve large muscles, it would be classified as an accessory muscle movement. Playing the guitar, knitting, whittling, and so on, involve accessory muscle movement in the form of the small manipulative muscles of the hand. Singing involves the voice and lungs, also accessory muscle movement.

Any activity that is not primarily based on motor action is classified as either a sensory activity or an intellectual activity. Sensory activities are those depending primarily on one or more of the five basic senses: sight, sound, touch, smell, and taste. Intellectual activities are those that place major emphasis upon the thought processes.

Using the preceding definitions, we can classify the movement of all recreational activities. Examples are these.

*Bowling:* Movement: Motor activity, fundamental movement, handling objects, rolling.

*Tag:* Movement: Motor activity, fundamental movement, locomotion, running, and dodging.

*Roller-skating.* Movement: Motor activity, fundamental movement, locomotion, use of auxiliary equipment.

*Knitting:* Movement: Motor activity, accessory movement, fingers.

*Listening to the Symphony:* Movement: Sensory activity, listening.

*Analyzing the Symphony:* Movement: Intellectual.

*Checkers:* Movement: Intellectual. (Here it is the intellect that is important, not the ability to move small objects.)

With activities such as enjoying music, art, or literature, it may be debatable whether appreciation is attained through the senses or the intellect, but it is generally agreed that keen senses are of primary importance and the intellect cannot be used if the senses do not impart the proper messages. Therefore, classification of appreciation is by senses. Analysis of music, however, is an intellectual activity. All leaders need to do in order to classify according to movement is to decide whether the action emphasizes muscles, senses, or the mental process and then define the movement as much as possible.

## CLASSIFICATION BY FORM

Activities can also be classified by form. Classification by form follows the same process as classification by movement. First the classifier needs to determine whether the activity is competitive or noncompetitive. Competitive events entail an opponent or opponents engaged in the same activity. In some activities such as mountain climbing, there may be a competitor present in the form of one's self, and whether this is competitive or not may be a matter of attitude or purpose.

*Noncompetitive Forms.*    If an activity is noncompetitive, it will take one of nine forms. These will be discussed individually.

1.  *Creative play* involves the creative process using materials such as craft work, sculpture, sewing, or woodworking for the final product or using no materials other than the paper on which the creative effort is recorded. Any kind of literary or musical composition is creative.
2.  *Roving activities* include bicycling, exploring, hiking, touring, and sightseeing.
3.  *Hunting activities* refer to hunting, fishing, rock hunting, and the like.
4.  *Imitative activities* are dramatic events, from children's finger plays to charades to dramatic roles.
5.  *Social activities* include the many types of recreation in which people are motivated to participate because of a desire to socialize. Parties, picnics, and banquets are social activities. (See Chapter 19.)
6.  *Acquisitive activities* include collections of material objects such as artwork, stamps, coins, or books.
7.  *Aesthetic activities* are those enjoyed for their form or beauty. They would include art appreciation, nature walks, music appreciation, and so on.
8.  Vicarious activities are those in which the participant experiences events by imagining himself or herself in the role of an-

other. Watching a movie and identifying with the hero is vicarious experience. Listening to a ghost story and becoming frightened is also a vicarious experience.

9. Within the category of *curiosity* are classified activities such as solving a puzzle, reading, and experimenting.

***Competitive Forms.*** Competitive activities are divided into two categories: games and contests. It is important that the recreation and leisure service leader understands the distinctions between these two, for they are different, and both are needed for a well-rounded program.

*Contests* are characterized by competition that has no strategy that outwits the opponent, and that has no interference with the opponent. Archery, golf, and bowling are good examples of true contests, for in none of these does the contestant do anything that interferes with the opponent. There may be strategy in how to pick up a split in bowling, what club to use in golf, or how to allow for the wind in archery. This type of strategy and choice is individual and has nothing to do with interfering with the success of the other players. There is no deception in a contest.

A well-conducted relay is a true contest, for each player is given a specific set of directions to follow. If the directions are not precise and some players discover ways to accomplish the actions faster, the relay becomes a game of strategy. A true relay involves no strategy; the players have no choice as to how to do the activity, and one player should never interfere with another. This is why relay teams should each have their own playing areas and goals and be far enough apart so that no player interferes with other players. Other true contests include simple footraces, most track events, swimming races, jack stones, jump rope contests, competitive art, competitive music, self-testing events, and any other activity where there is no interference with the opponent, no deception, and no strategy.

Games, on the other hand, are characterized by the factors of choice, strategy, and interference with the progress of the opponent. A game is full of unexpected situations, strategy, and deception. In a game the objective is to prevent the opponent from scoring or reaching a goal. In a contest the objective is to reach the goal sooner or with a better score than the opponent but without interference.

Games may be of several types. Low organized games are those with few rules, simple skills, and very little cooperation among players on each team. Examples are tag, hide-and-seek, midnight, crows and cranes. Team games involve many rules, highly developed skill, and great cooperation among members of each team. Examples are baseball, volleyball, basketball, and football. Table games may be low organized games and may involve accessory muscle movement (i.e., pick up sticks), but they are usually mental activities. Table games that involve mental strategy are played on special boards or charts. Checkers, Monopoly, and bridge are some table games.

A combatant activity is an event between two persons that involves strategy and interference. Although they are often referred to as contests, boxing, fencing, and wrestling are true combatant games. Dual-individual games are those in which two people or two pairs of people oppose each other. Tennis and badminton are the activities usually thought of as dual-individual games.

A lead-up game may be a modification of a team game that resembles a game of low organization. Or it may be an improvised simple team game. Specifically, a lead-up game is one that serves to develop the basic skills used in a more complicated game. Keep away, on the most elementary level, is a lead-up game for basketball if the leader is using the game to develop the competitive spirit found between two teams competing for possession of the ball. There are many games that serve as skill-developing lead-ups for basketball, baseball, soccer, and so on.

**TABLE 6.1**   Classification of Competitive Activities

| | | |
|---|---|---|
| Bowling | Movement: | Motor activity, fundamental movement, handling objects, rolling |
| | Form: | Competitive, contest |
| Tag | Movement: | Motor activity, fundamental movement, locomotion, running and dodging |
| | Form: | Competitive, game, low organization |
| Rollerskating | Movement: | Motor activity, fundamental movement, locomotion, use of auxiliary equipment |
| | Form: | Noncompetitive, roving (or, in the case of figure skating, probably imitative) |
| Knitting | Movement: | Motor activity, accessory movement, fingers |
| | Form: | Noncompetitive, creative, with material |
| Symphony | Movement: | Sensory activity, listening |
| Listening | Form: | Noncompetitive, aesthetic |
| Symphony | Movement: | Intellectual |
| Analysis | Form: | Noncompetitive, curiosity |
| Checkers | Movement: | Intellectual |
| | Form: | Competitive, game, table |

Classification of competitive activities listed on page 148 can be seen in Table 6.1.

With a knowledge of types of activities and how they are classified, the leader can readily see that a program consisting of hide-and-seek, crows and cranes, midnight, and steal the bacon lacks variety, for all are low-organized games of fundamental movement involving running, tagging, and dodging. A better selection of activities would be rattlesnake tag, in the pond, crows and cranes, and a few relays.

Because of the interference and deception involved, some people prefer games to contests and vice versa. Because of their natures and interests, some people prefer noncompetitive to competitive activities. And because of individual differences, all people do not feel the same toward physical, mental, or sensory activities. Even if all people as a group did prefer games involving large muscle activity, a recreational program without variety would soon be satiating. The more completely a leader understands the component parts of recreational activities, the better program planner he or she can be.

**PREPARATION AND ENDING**

*After* activities have been selected, the leader should become thoroughly acquainted with them. There is no place for note cards stuck in pockets to be brought forth blatantly or stealthily to find out what goes on next. To run smoothly, a program requires leaders who know their material thoroughly. It may be permissible to make notes on the *sequence* of activities in a program, but to read directions for a skill or words to a song or to look up the roles to an activity says to the participant, "You really were not important enough for me to prepare thoroughly." Furthermore, the participant soon equates leadership with the reading of directions.

While activities are being planned, attention must be paid to details of equipment. Not only must equipment be prepared in advance, but allowance should be made for the unexpected need for extras and for breakage. Plans must also be made for retrieving equipment following an activity. It is amazing how many leaders will go on to a new activity or turn the program over to an associate for a new activity without arranging to complete the previous activity by cleaning up. Certain types of equipment left lying around can be the cause of accidents, and any unused material is unsightly and detracts from the present activity.

A final word of advice in early preparation is to *overplan*. It is far better to plan five extra activities and not use them than to plan five too few and wonder how to fill up the time. Suggestions from the participants may be good in many situations but often are not in keeping with the theme, take too long to explain, require difficult skills or equipment, and, in general, detract from the continuity of a preplanned program.

It is a wise recreation and leisure leader who knows when to stop one activity and lead into another one, and there is no way to predict when is the most expeditious moment. One slogan among many leaders is "Kill it before it dies," which means that one should stop the activity before anyone is tired of it. When this moment may be is an unfathomable question, yet the moment after someone becomes bored with an activity may be easy to see. The leader should try to ensure that everyone has an enjoyable experience, and it is far better to receive groans for stopping an event than groans for continuing an activity in which there is no interest. Still a leader must not stop an activity too soon. There must be ample time to build up an interest, several turns must be taken, and everyone must have a chance for some type of enjoyable participation. A new activity that is fairly complicated may need to be stopped early because it is still new and not a favorite, yet stopping it too soon may prevent participants from having a chance to start an interest in it. "Kill it before it dies" is a wise slogan. Finding the best moment comes only through constant experience, knowledge of the activity, and, above all, a kinship of feeling with and for the participant.

Before one leads any activity, the develop-

ment of a leading plan should be undertaken. An example of a plan flexible enough to fit all occasions is found in Figure 6.7.

## PARTICIPANT SAFETY

Every participant enters a recreation and leisure activity with the expectation of a successful and safe experience. Though safety can never be guaranteed, it is incumbent upon the leader to take all possible precautions to preclude accidents and injuries. Prior to offering any activity, the leader should analyze it for the potential of severity of risk and frequency of risk.

An activity may have a record of severe accidents frequently, severe accidents infrequently, mild accidents frequently, or mild accidents infrequently. One may decide to avoid the risk, reduce the risk, transfer it, or

---

**RECREATION ACTIVITIES LEADING PLAN**

   I. Activity Title
  II. Source
 III. Activity Type
  IV. Participants
   V. Equipment
  VI. Activity Classification
      A. Movement
      B. Form
 VII. Leader's Objectives (What do you wish to accomplish?)
VIII. Behavioral Objectives (What actions will the participants perform that you can actually observe?)
  IX. Steps in Leading (Be CREATIVE here!)
      A. Attention
      B. Interest
      C. Grouping
      D. Etc. (Continue on with as many steps as you can think of.)
   X. Ending

**FIGURE 6.7**  A plan for leading activities.

retain it. Figure 6.8 shows these two concepts in diagram form.

In this figure, Area I represents activities of very frequent but not severe accidents such as blisters from hiking, burns from cooking, or falling while playing dodgeball. Since these activities present little risk of a serious nature, leaders would retain the risk, offer the activities, and reduce the risks through careful planning. Area II represents frequent and severe accidents that would occur in such activities as skydiving, hang gliding, or automobile racing, and the prudent leader or agency will usually avoid these risks by not offering the activity.

Area III represents a low frequency of risk and a low severity of accident. Group singing, discussions, and attending concerts are all examples of activities in Area III. Leaders usually choose to retain risk for all activities in this area as accidents are few and rarely severe. Area IV is of particular importance to a leader as it represents infrequent accidents, but when the rare accident occurs, the result is extremely serious. An example would be a ten-year-old drowning in a rowing lesson on a flat lake or a fall with accompanying concussion while climbing. These activities require a decision. One can move them closer to Area II and avoid them or alter the procedure and transfer the risk. The children can be required to wear Coast Guard-approved life jackets while rowing—even if they are uncomfortable—and the climbers can be required to wear hard hats—even if they are warm. The severity of the risks are thus transferred to less severe risks, and the leader can continue to offer the activity.

The management of risks is discussed in detail in Chapter 7. The purpose of discussing risk here is to alert the activity leader to the necessity of analyzing each activity to predict the potential risk and concomitant severity. Good rules of thumb for all leaders are the following summarized risk assessment guidelines:

- High frequency, high severity—Avoid the activity.
- High frequency, low severity—Reduce the danger.
- Low frequency, high severity—Transfer the risk; modify the activity.
- Low frequency, low severity—Retain the activity, but still be prepared for accidents.

In addition, each leader should learn how to develop risk management plans that will implement means for reducing, controlling, or transferring the risks.

## PUBLIC RELATIONS

All leaders should be concerned with the effect of their actions on the opinions of others toward the sponsoring organization and the recreation and leisure profession. The direct, face-to-face or activity leader is very visible and, consequently, has the potential for influencing public opinion more rapidly, more openly, and more directly than the supervisory or administrative leader. Direct, face-to-face leaders guide, direct, and influence the behavior of participants, in the opinion of many, more immediately and more obviously than leaders who are responsible for committees, volunteer programs, and community groups.

As in any other enterprise, the success of the operation depends largely on how its existence is made evident to the public and the light in which the operation is viewed by others. It is often difficult to interpret leisure services to the public because, unlike the case in other marketable services (i.e., medicine, law, or education), the outcome of leisure services is difficult to define. Nevertheless, the leader must be concerned with developing and maintaining positive public opinions of every program conducted.

### WHAT IS PUBLIC RELATIONS?

As mentioned earlier in this chapter, Kraus lists public and community relations as one of

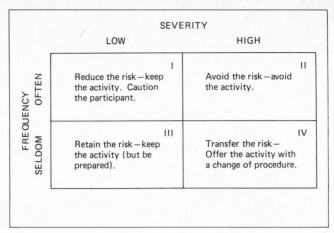

**FIGURE 6.8**   Analysis of possible severity and frequency of accident.

12 functions inherent in the job of a program-oriented face-to-face leader. According to Meyer, Brightbill, and Sessoms, "Public relations, as a function, aims at establishing, preserving, and strengthening the 'goodwill' of the public. ... It is a task that has no end, no boundaries, and no limitations in the forms it takes."[8]

It is difficult to define public relations precisely so that one definition fits all situations relative to the subject, yet most definitions encompass several common elements. Philip Lesly, head of the Philip Lesly Company, a large public relations and counseling firm, defines public relations as all activities and attitudes intended to judge, adjust to, influence, and direct the opinion of any group or groups of persons in the interest of any individual, group, or institution.[9] Clarence Schoenfeld, associate professor of journalism at the University of Wisconsin, states that public relations encompasses those planned policies and practices that an organization employs in order to cultivate a climate of public opinion favorable to the attainment of institutional objectives.[10] Along the same lines, the American Camping Association defines public relations as the planned attempt to interpret an enterprise so that public opinion may be as well informed and as favorable as possible.[11]

Each of the foregoing definitions of public relations encompasses three common elements. Each defines public relations as action oriented, as opposed to passive, and as dynamic as opposed to static. Each states that the action is direction oriented because it is planned or purposeful or has specific intent. And, finally, each defines the goal of public relations as being related to directing opinion in a positive manner.

A less academic definition would suggest that public relations is anything done that affects public opinion. This definition, though lacking depth, carries a certain precautionary tone with it, for it tells us that unplanned actions can also affect public opinion. This

[8]Harold D. Meyer, Charles K. Brightbill and H. Douglas Sessoms, *Community Recreation, A Guide to its Organization* (Englewood Cliffs, N.J.: Prentice-Hall, 1969), p. 416. Used with permission.

[9]Philip Lesly, ed. *Public Relations Handbook* 2nd edition (Englewood Cliffs, N.J.: Prentice-Hall, 1962), p. 861.

[10]Clarence A. Schoenfeld, *Publicity Media and Methods* (New York: Macmillan, 1963), p. 16.

[11]American Camping Association, *Camp Administration Course Outline* (Martinsville, Ind.: American Camping Association, 1961), p. 14.

perhaps should serve as a warning that as long as any aspect of an enterprise is before the public, it is playing an active role in public relations.

**PUBLICS**

For the direct, face-to-face leader attempting to promote positive public relations, there are several different, yet important, publics that may be influenced differently and influenced for different reasons. These publics all perceive different goals for the operation, have different expectations, and maintain different contacts with each program. For simplicity, they may be identified as the participants, the co-workers, the supervisor, the organization, and the general public.

*Participants.* The participants in a program arrive with certain, usually agreed-upon expectations. As a group, they expect to find the leader or leaders prepared and to have all the necessary equipment and facilities arranged. They have hopes for a successful, enjoyable, safe experience of good quality wherein they will be treated fairly and equally. They expect the leader or leaders to be pleasant, clean, and neat. Furthermore, they expect they will be able to hear and understand the leader. All these group expectations are purposefully addressed by the sensitive leader who is meeting the requirements of good public relations.

Besides group expectations, there are individual expectations within the group. One person may expect to learn a new skill whereas another may wish to improve on a skill learned earlier. Some people attend programs for the purpose of socializing and meeting new friends whereas others attend for mental stimulation or physical exercise. The individual needs of each participant must be recognized by the leader or leaders.

*Co-workers.* One's colleagues, working in adjoining sections of the building, preceding and following the leader in one facility, and being members of the same agency, are an-

other ''public.'' Each employee should be able to expect from every other employee respect, cooperation, integrity, and thoughtfulness. Extraneous, avoidable noise from one room in a community center causes a breakdown in positive public relations for the employee in the adjoining room. Gossiping or criticizing co-workers defeats the goal of public relations. Leaving a room or facility disorganized, broken equipment, open windows, unlocked doors, and other thoughtless behaviors cause negative employee relations. Positive colleague relations are fostered through thoughtfulness and consideration.

*The Supervisor.* A leader should act in a professional manner, showing respect for his or her supervisor as well as exhibiting promptness, thoroughness, cooperation, care of equipment, and dependability. How the leader refers to the supervisor when speaking to the participants and how the leader refers to the supervisor himself or herself should be consistent. There is no room for hypocrisy in recreation and leisure services. Use of first names or nicknames may be appropriate in some settings; however, in other situations these may indicate a lack of respect or a familiarity that is not found in most professional circles.

*The Organization.* The organization within which one works is a public that is based on a specific philosophy for serving the leisure needs of the clientele. Leaders are employed with the expectation that they will uphold the standards of the organization and represent it to the best of their abilities. The leader should fulfill his or her job responsibilities in a cooperative manner. He or she should never downgrade or undermine the organization, but rather should work to support the organization in a positive way.

*The General Public.* At all times the leader is a representative of the organization. As such, each leader serves as a representative of that organization at every interface with the general public. The leader may be off duty; however, the public will still associate him or her with the recreation and leisure service organization. In addition, the leader may be perceived as a role model, particularly by children and youth.

Every leader should attempt to be well informed and to be prepared to answer questions about leisure to any member of the community in a friendly, well-articulated manner. Such questions as, Why should I pay taxes for municipal recreation? What is the value of these programs? What is your philosophy of leisure? Why should I spend *my* money to attend *your* resort? What good will I get out of this? and countless other questions should be answered clearly, pleasantly, and completely. It is recommended that every leader consider and formulate answers to questions such as these.

Offensive jokes, language, or appearance reflect negatively on the organization and profession. The leader with the professional approach represents the profession best through appropriate appearance, demeanor, and conversation. It is also incumbent on the leader to refrain from trying to influence participants relative to the leader's own politics, ethics, or religion. One is hired to represent the organization and, unless the organization has a specific dogma to be taught, leaders must separate such personal values from the job. It is a matter of public relations to represent the sponsoring organization, not moral, ethical, religious, or political groups.

### PRINCIPLES OF PUBLIC RELATIONS

In order to elicit favorable opinion effectively, several principles for a public relations program should be developed and followed. A set of guidelines for public relations follows.

- The public relations program is *planned*. It is a conscious effort to influence opinions based on a purpose and a plan.

- Public relations should be continuous. It goes without saying that one cannot plan a public relations program that lasts just a few months. Just as public opinion is formed continuously, so must the public relations program be ever functioning and functional.

- Public relations should be honest. In spite of the fact that a purpose of public relations is to arouse favorable opinions, in no way should the truth be stretched or altered to gain this opinion. Such behavior could result in suits for false advertising. Dishonesty in any form is intolerable.

- Public relations should be all-encompassing and comprehensive. The public should be made aware of the work of the organization in its entirety.

- Public relations must be based on the human element as well as the visual or printed one. Face-to-face contact with all the publics, particularly the general public, must be a primary goal.

## SUMMARY

In this chapter the authors have focused on six distinct face-to-face leadership roles that are common in many recreation and leisure service organizations. These six roles are direct program leadership, team leadership, instructional leadership, counselor, outreach worker, and host-guide. The direct program leadership role can be either work-oriented or program-oriented. Work-oriented leaders are involved in such professional activities as exploring problems, establishing plans, and making recommendations. Program-oriented leaders are directly involved in leading a group of recreation participants in a specific activity. Team leaders are individuals who serve as coaches, captains, or organizers—guiding team members' cooperative efforts. Instructional leaders are involved in teaching, directing, or demonstrating in order to help participants learn new activities, skills, or gain other types of knowledge. The role of the counselor is to serve as an adviser, helping individuals shape values, discover abilities, and acquire skills. Finally, the host-guide assists individuals who are involved in tours, visitations, and so on.

There are a number of general techniques that can be applied in a variety of leadership situations by leaders. These include building interest, gaining attention, knowing where the leader should be positioned when conducting activities, and processes that can be used in establishing group formations. Knowledge of such techniques can help the leader operate effectively. In addition, knowledge of the processes involved in planning and implementing activities is essential to leadership success. The ability to write objectives, understand participants, select appropriate activities to meet participants' needs, and prepare for an event and end it appropriately are all processes with which the leader should be familiar.

Recreation and leisure activities can be classified either by movement or form. Activities classified by movement involve motor, sensory, and intellectual factors. Activities are classified by form usually in terms of whether they are competitive or noncompetitive.

An important dimension in the planning and implementation of recreation and leisure activities is ensuring that participants have a successful and safe experience. Consideration should be given to the potential severity and frequency of any injuries or accidents occurring in recreational activities. The leader is advised to consider eliminating, keeping, controlling, or modifying activities based on potential risk. Participant safety is a primary concern of all leaders.

Another factor in the process of planning recreation and leisure activities is that of establishing leader participant relations. This is often thought of as public relations. Public relations involves the establishment of a sense of goodwill towards participants as well as other ''publics'' influencing the delivery of recreation and leisure services such as the general public, various organizations, institutions and agencies, and co-workers.

## DISCUSSION QUESTIONS

1. What does a direct program leader do? Identify five settings in which recreation and leisure services are delivered where these types of roles exist, and name ten specific job titles reflecting this type of leadership.

2. What does a team leader do? Identify five settings in which recreation and leisure services are delivered where these types of roles exist, and name five specific job titles reflecting this type of leadership.

3. What does an instructional leader do? Identify five settings in which recreation and leisure services are delivered where these types of roles exist, and name five specific job titles reflecting this type of leadership.

4. What does a counselor do? Identify five settings in which recreation and leisure services are delivered where these types of roles exist, and name two specific job titles reflecting this type of leadership.

5. What does a host-guide do? Identify five settings in which recreation and leisure services are delivered where these types of roles exist, and name three specific job titles reflecting this type of leadership.

6. What factors are involved in gaining and maintaining participant interest and attention?

7. What is the process involved in planning and implementing activities?

8. Why is participant safety important in the implementation of recreation and leisure service activities?

9. How do the relationships between the leader and the participant affect the success or failure of a program?

10. What is public relations? What are publics? How does the leader affect an organization's public relations effort?

# PART TWO

The second portion of this book presents a number of specific skills that can be learned by the recreation and leisure service leader and applied in various professional settings. We strongly believe in the "hands-on" approach to leadership, that is, that there are leadership skills that can be identified, taught, and practiced—from leading a song to conducting a community meeting. We also believe in the adage that the best way to learn these skills is to "do it, try it, practice it, and practice it again." With this in mind, Part Two deals with the "nuts and bolts" of selected recreation and leadership skills.

It is interesting to note that most of the effective professionals in the recreation and leisure service field today have had successful experience. Why is this the case? These individuals have, in many cases, served as direct, face-to-face leaders. They know first hand the processes, procedures, and techniques that are involved in the provision of recreation and leisure services, especially in terms of the critical leader-participant interface. They are, in other words, familiar and comfortable with the nuts and bolts of a recreation and leisure service organization's operations and are able to provide strong supervisory or managerial leadership that is based on direct experience.

The chapters that follow focus on a number of leadership processes, procedures, and techniques that can be used by the leader working in different settings, in different program areas, and with different age groups. Specifically discussed are some of the more common leadership roles and techniques that can be used by the leader working in the recreation and leisure service profession. Both traditional leadership topics and more contemporary ones are included. The topic areas presented are not all-inclusive. There are other program areas, settings, and groupings with which the leader may come in contact although the authors have attempted to present and discuss the topics and situations most commonly encountered by the recreation and leisure service leader.

# 7

# RISK MANAGEMENT

Recreation and leisure activities that involve risk must be carefully managed.

The topic of risk management can be approached from a managerial standpoint or from a supervisory standpoint. The manager attempts to manage risks associated with the operation of the recreation and leisure service organization as a whole. For example, the manager decides on the types and amounts of

insurance the agency should carry. The supervisor or leader, on the other hand, has a somewhat more narrow focus. The leader is concerned with the management of risks associated with the specific activities and programs for which he or she is responsible or that are within his or her jurisdiction as a leader. This chapter will focus on the topic of risk management as it relates to the leaders of recreation and leisure service activities and programs.

Risk management is the responsibility of the leader of every program in which there are active participants. Though some activities have more potential for accidents than others and must be planned with extreme caution, there are potential hazards inherent in nearly every program. The injury of a participant in the collapse of a chair during a concert is of no less importance than the injury of a skier who breaks a leg in a fall. As a matter of fact, in the former case, the responsibility was probably entirely that of the sponsoring agency whereas in the case of the skier, it might be claimed that the skier contributed partly to the accident through poor execution of learned skills.

Activities can be generally classified as of high, medium, and low risk. However, these labels may not accurately reflect the risk involved in some activities, for the degree of risk can fluctuate depending on environmental conditions and participant characteristics. A swimming instructor demonstrating a skill in the shallow end of an indoor pool is involving the participant in a low-risk activity compared to a senior citizen attempting the rough mile race in the ocean, yet each is participating in a swimming activity. Finger painting using edible paints for young children is a low-risk craft activity; however, woodworking with power tools may be a high-risk activity. Yet both may be categorized as arts and crafts. Each activity must be examined on its own merit in terms of the characteristics of the participant, the site, and the degree of difficulty of execution of the skill.

The human is a risk-seeking being. Roger Caillois, the French sociologist, has developed four categories of play: *agon, alea, mimicry, and ilinx*, each of which involves some risk. Kraus discusses these as follows.

> *Agon* refers to activities which are competitive and in which the equality of participants' chances is artificially created. Winners are determined through such qualities as speed, endurance, strength, memory, skill, or ingenuity. Agonistic games may be played by individuals or teams; they presuppose sustained attention, training and discipline, perseverance, limits, and rules.
>
> *Alea* includes those games over whose outcomes the contestant has no control; winning is the result of fate rather than the skill of the player. Games of dice, roulette, baccarat, or lotteries are examples of alea. Caillois writes:
>
>> The player is entirely passive; he does not deploy his resources, skill, muscles, or intelligence. All he needs do is wait, in hope and trembling, the cast of the die. In contrast to agon, alea negates work, patience, experience, and qualifications. Professionalization, application, and training are eliminated . . . it supposes on the player's part an attitude exactly opposite to that reflected in *Agon*.[24]
>
> *Mimicry* is based on the acceptance of illusions or imaginary universes; it includes a class of games in which the common element is that the subject makes believe or makes others be-

lieve he is someone other than himself. For children, he writes:

> the aim is to imitate adults. . . . This explains the success of the toy weapons and miniatures which copy the tools, engines, arms, and machines used by adults. The little girl plays her mother's role. . . . The boy makes believe he is a soldier, musketeer, policeman, pirate, cowboy, Martian, etc.

> On the adult level, mimicry is found in theatrical presentations or games involving simulation and role-playing.
>
> *Ilinx* consists of those play activities which are based on the pursuit of vertigo, or dizziness. There are many activities which momentarily weaken the participant's stability of perception. Historically, ilinx was found in primitive religious dances or other rituals which induced trancelike states necessary for worship. Today, it may be seen in children's games that lead to dizziness by whirling rapidly or the use of swings or seesaws; among adults, it may be achieved by certain kinds of dances, amusement park rides such as the whip or loop-the-loop, or the use of alcohol and drugs which destroy the user's equilibrium and self-control.
>
> In Caillois' view the entire universe of play is based on these categories; to some degree they may overlap when activities include elements of more than one type. He also suggests two extremes of style which characterize play and games. The first of these, which he calls paidia, exemplifies exuberance, freedom, uncontrolled and spontaneous gaiety; the second ludus, is characterized by rules and conventions and represents calculated and contrived activity.[1]

[24]Roger Caillois, *Man, Play and Games* (London: Thames and Hudson, 1961), p. 17.

Each of the activity types just detailed entails risk taking. Of the foregoing, *alea* is the one that entails the least need for management of personal physical risk. Since these activities are based on chance, the participant has no control, but merely waits to learn of an

[1]Richard Kraus, *Recreation and Leisure in Modern Society*, Copyright © 1978 by Scott, Foresman and Company. Reprinted by permission. p. 27–28.

outcome. The participant, being passive, invites no personal physical risk although there may be financial, emotional, or psychological risk. In this chapter we are concerned with personal *physical* risk.

It is the three other types of play that may involve varying degrees of physical risk. *Agon*-type activities are competitive and may be very physical in nature. *Mimicry*-types of activities may involve copying the skills of another (i.e., climbing, gymnastics, diving, dancing) and may involve physical risk. *Ilinx*-type activities involving heights, dizziness, and whirling also may entail some physical risk. It is these types of activities that must be controlled by the leader through management for possible accidents.

The management of risks is based on the premise that people should be allowed to participate in selected activities involving risk; however, the likelihood of accidents resulting from such activities should be lessened through control. It should be recognized that the leaders of recreation and leisure services are never ensurers of safety. We cannot guarantee unqualified freedom from accident or injury; it would be impossible to do so. However recreation and leisure service organizations do not want to deny participants the right to participate in an activity of potential yet controlled risk as long as the sponsor has the capability of minimizing the risk. People want to test themselves, to move faster, to climb higher, to perform more difficult figures, to attempt the unattempted. No program should deny the participant the chance to attempt new activities as long as the activity is an integral part of the sponsored event and the participant is prepared for it. Everyone has the right to try and to fail. Inherent in that right is the right to fail without serious physical, mental, or emotional consequences. Also inherent in that right is the right to try again. The goal of the participant is to have a positive experience. There must always be the hope and chance for success; therefore, the goal of the leader must be the control of accidents or injuries so that participants have a chance for success or a chance to fail without serious consequences.

One might argue that there are two purposes in managing risks: the participant-oriented purpose and the agency-oriented purpose. As human, caring leaders, we are morally and ethically bound to manage risks so that few accidents occur and those that do occur are minor. The welfare of participants is our primary concern. We must take care, therefore, that they are unscathed physically and psychologically through our leadership. From a pragmatic point of view, risk management, by preventing or minimizing accidents, can prevent or minimize lawsuits and financial loss. It can be especially effective in preventing lawsuits and financial loss due to negligence. In addition, those programs with low or no accident rates may be eligible for better insurance rates. An agency literally cannot afford *not* to require risk management plans.

## STANDARD OF CARE

Though all leaders are responsible for the safety and care of participants in their programs, there are some whose programs need carefully developed policies for managing potential accidents and injuries. These leaders should develop risk management plans. Risk management plans may be either short or long, depending on the type of activity and the potential risks involved. Regardless of the program or activity, by being involved, either as a volunteer or as a paid employee, one holds oneself out as being *competent*. In the courts of law, this competency is equated with that of a reasonable and prudent *professional* utilizing the best and most current professional practices. This comparison to a reasonable and prudent professional is known as a *standard of care*, and in cases of liability a defendent might be proved negligent if this care were not provided and if the participant were subjected to undue risk. Standard of care is based on three criteria: supervision, conducting the activity, and environmental conditions.

## SUPERVISION

Supervision may be *general* or *specific*. General supervision refers to the three following considerations. First, the leader should have a plan for supervising that includes an adequate number of supervisors and indicates where they are to be located. In hiking trips, 1 leader per 8 hikers plus one extra for emergencies is considered a standard. The ratio of one water safety instructor plus one lifeguard per 25 swimmers plus enough trained guards or watchers to make up a total ratio of 1 per 10 swimmers is a standard recommended for youth camp swimming programs in lakes. The supervisor should know where the other leaders are stationed.

Furthermore, under standard of care, it is expected that all leaders be able to recognize dangerous conditions or signs of trouble and be able to report them correctly. Storms, shivering, fatigue, unsafe practices, and tasks that are too advanced for the participant are but some of the conditions all leaders and leader-helpers are expected to be able to recognize and report.

A third component of general supervision is the ability to perform first aid and emergency care at the current level of practice. To be performing as a reasonable and prudent professional, not only should the leader have current first aid certification, but he or she should be able to react quickly and appropriately to situations unique to the activity. Horseback riding instructors may not remember how to treat victims of drownings immediately; however, they should know how to treat broken bones, concussions, and contusions instantaneously. The leader of a rafting trip should know immediately how to treat for drowning, broken bones, bruises, abrasions, and cuts. A leader doing nothing may be

as negligent as one who acts rapidly but wrongly.

In addition to general supervision, the leader should be involved in *specific supervision* of the participant. The leader must communicate so that the participant can appreciate the risk in terms of his or her ability to perform. A beginner or young child must be made to realize that some skills necessarily precede others and that risk can be overcome only by proper execution of learned skills in order of difficulty. The leader should also be sure that the participant understands safety practices and adheres to them. This may require autocratic techniques, yet it is vital to performing the standard of care. The third practice to consider under specific supervision is the leader's ability to be alert to changing conditions that can cause hazardous conditions. These conditions may be psychological, physical, climatic, or others. For example, such factors as fatigue, cold, or approach of darkness might result in increased hazardous conditions.

## CONDUCTING THE ACTIVITY

Three factors are important in conducting the activity. The first of these is adequacy of instruction and progression. The instructor must know not only how to perform the skill to be taught, but also how to analyze the skill in terms of its components in order to help the participant move from the simple to the complex, from the basic to the advanced, through exercises that are within the capacity and capabilities of the participant. A 10-year-old child may progress rapidly in tumbling skills (perhaps more rapidly than an adult), but there are skill progressions recommended by all expert leaders and writers of tumbling, and every leader should follow these recommended progressions. This applies to almost every activity requiring highly executed skills. Leaders should be familiar with the literature of their field to keep current with the latest thinking on the teaching of special activity skills.

Not only is the leader expected to teach the skills in logical progression, but he or she also must be able to modify plans to meet the age, skill, experience, and maturity of the participant. Children do not use the same judgment as the mature adult. The inexperienced do not perform as the experienced do. The disabled, either physically or mentally, need a longer period of conditioning and training and may need more supervision than other participants. The leader who forgets that the task is to teach people—not activities—is not acting as a reasonable and prudent professional.

The third consideration in the conduct of the activity is that of adequate and proper warning of danger and the accompanying use of protective devices. Wool may be made mandatory clothing for winter outings; hard hats should be compulsory equipment for climbing; spotters and tumbling belts should be required for gymnastics. Again, the leader may need to be autocratic and make no exceptions, even refusing to permit those without proper equipment to participate. In order to perform at an acceptable standard of care, the leader should exclude those without proper equipment from participating in the activity. If the leader were to allow individuals who were not properly attired or equipped to participate in an activity, he or she could be considered to be negligent.

## ENVIRONMENTAL CONDITIONS

A third criterion, on which standard of care is based, is supervision of the activity environment. Again, there are three factors to consider. *Equipment* should be checked, repaired, be in good order, or not used. Use of faulty equipment can be considered an act of negligence if accident or injury results from it. The *conditions* of the building facility or area should be considered for hazards. Such things as dark corridors, loose stairs, slippery floors, and frayed electric cords should be remedied immediately. Sunken logs or sudden drop-offs

in swimming areas, tents pitched in avalanche routes or under dead trees, or hikers caught in lightning storms are all environmental conditions that the leader should attempt to prevent.

The *layout and design* of the facility, trail, route, or building should be known by the leader so that escape routes can be located quickly in case of fire or other disaster. The location of fire extinguishers, emergency help, telephones, and unusual land forms are all part of the environmental conditions of which the leader should be aware.

To reiterate, management of risk entails acting as a reasonable and prudent professional and showing a standard of care according to the following outline.

I. Supervision
  A. General Supervision
    1. Supervisory plan and number and location of supervisors
    2. Awareness of dangerous conditions
    3. First aid knowledge
  B. Specific Supervision
    1. Communicate at level of participant
    2. Participant understands and adheres to safety practices
    3. Alert to changing conditions
II. Conducting the Activity
  A. Adequate Instructions and Progression
  B. Understanding Participants
    1. Age and size
    2. Skill and maturity
    3. Special conditions (mental, physical, etc.)
  C. Warning of Dangers and Required Use of Protective Devices
III. Understanding the Environment
  A. Equipment Checked
  B. Conditions Checked
    1. Man-made structures
    2. Natural hazards
  C. Layout and Design Checked

## RISK MANAGEMENT PLANS

Applicable to any program or activity, a risk management plan is a set of policies, procedures, and regulations for conducting activities that are based on an analysis of participants, equipment, leaders, sites, conditions, and the activities themselves. The details of a risk management plan for high-risk activities such as a canoe trip are much more detailed than for a minimum-risk activity such as a small concert or a committee meeting. A large rock concert or a political rally entails more risk management than does a square dance class or a tour of a museum. Nevertheless, each activity can be planned with the same basic outline and the same elemental considerations. A simple seven-part risk management plan outline is presented in Figure 7.1. The leader can use this plan to develop policies and procedures logically. The form should not be used without instruction, however. The details of each section must be understood so that the policies that are developed are based on complete information. The

```
   I.  Event
  II.  Date(s) and Time(s)
 III.  Location and Facility
         Indoor
         Outdoor
         Conditions
  IV.  Participants
         Number_____ Age(s)_____ Sex_____
         Experience
         Special characteristics
   V.  Leaders
         Name____ Age____   Name____ Age____
         Qualifications      Qualifications
         Certification       Certification
  VI.  Equipment
         Type and number_____
         Condition checked_____
 VII.  Policies
         Attach
VIII.  Emergency Numbers
```

**FIGURE 7.1**  Outline of risk management plan for recreational and leisure activities.

following sections explain the use of the risk management outline.

*I. Event.*   The program or event may be identified as a class, a group meeting, a trip, a social event, a spectator event, a competitive event, a drop-in activity, or a combination of events. The activities themselves may be listed as arts and crafts, dance, drama, music, literary, sports or games, outdoor pursuits, educational, hobby, or service. By designating the program and the activity, the leader starts to form a picture of the types of risks to be managed. A cross-country ski trip implies different risks from a leather craft class, yet each contains potential accidents. A square dance class brings to mind a possible high-energy physical activity under controlled circumstances whereas a rock concert brings to mind a different activity and less obvious control.

*II. Date(s) and Time(s).*   It seems obvious why the dates of the program are stated on the risk management plan; risk management for an activity conducted in the summer might be considerably different from one conducted in the winter. The reasons for stating the times of the activity may be less obvious, however. If an activity takes place in the winter and is an outdoor activity, one needs to think of the time very carefully. The number of hours of daylight in the winter are much less than in the summer. A program that may be held in daylight in the summer between 6:00 A.M. and 9:00 P.M. could not be held in the daylight in the winter when daylight lasts only from 8:00 A.M. to 4:00 P.M. or even for fewer hours if it is cloudy or stormy. A second reason for listing the times during which the activity will take place is in consideration of the working time of the leaders and the possible onset of fatigue. A leader of a field trip to a zoo in a city 100 miles away may be very fatigued if that leader is in charge of driving, guiding, chaperoning, lunch hour, and all other responsibilities with no break in a 12-hour day. More leaders may be required in order to give ample relief time for those in charge.

*III. Location and Facility.* The location of an event and whether it is indoors or outdoors will necessitate control of very different types of potential accidents. The conditions that exist at the location will also affect the potential for risks.

A. *Indoor.* The first thing a leader should do when using an indoor facility is to check automatically for building components that may be needed in case of emergency: light switches, heat controls, electrical outlets, water faucets, drinking water, fire extinguishers, first aid kits, telephones, numbers for police and ambulance, exits, closets for mops and brooms, and wastebaskets for litter. The competent leader knows where each of the foregoing is located and how to use those that may be needed in an emergency.

B. *Outdoor.* The outdoor leader may conduct activities in a city park, a play area, or the vastness of a national forest wilderness area. In the city, broken glass, holes, and dangerous street crossings should be checked each time the site is used. In the outdoors, hazards range from certain poisonous plants and annoying animals to topographical and geographical hazards. In any case, the site should be checked and the possible natural hazards listed.

C. *Conditions.* Conditions under which an activity is conducted refer to weather and climate. A Halloween party on a dark and stormy night, a school picnic on a predicted warm day in May, a field trip in tornado season, a bonfire at a victory celebration in November—each brings to mind conditions that may require the management of specific risks that would not be found under other conditions. Certainly the conditions for snowshoe trips will differ early in, midway through, or at the end of the season. The risk management plan should consider the worst conditions foreseeable at the given time of the event being planned.

*IV. Participants.* The precautions one takes in managing risks will start with an identification of several characteristics of the participants.

A. *Number.* How many will be involved? What is the maximum and minimum number for a safe program? This may depend on external variables. For example, a 36-passenger bus dictates a maximum of 36, including leaders. A financial policy may dictate a minimum number without which the activity will be canceled.

B. *Sex.* The sex of the group members should be noted. It may be approximate in number, but the ratio of males to females is often needed when planning for leaders. For example, when both sexes participate in field trips, it may be necessary to have some male and some female leaders to supervise young children using rest-room facilities.

C. *Specific characteristics.* Characteristics of group members will affect how activities are led. Older persons, sixth graders, high school football players, mentally disabled adults—all require a different set of guidelines for managing risks. Even within these categories one will find differences. Older persons from 65 to 95 vary greatly. Older persons in rest homes are not like those in senior community center dancing groups. In addition, experiences may differ. Events may be held for the beginner, intermediate, or advanced participant. In short, all special characteristics must be recognized and considered in the planning of a safe event. Every possible variable should be considered and every participant should be able to be included with thought and care on the part of the leader.

*V. Leaders.* The policies and procedures for an activity will be based partly on the ability of the leader or leaders to carry them out. When leaders are considered for an activity, attention should be given to their age, number, and qualifications. Age is important only at the lower limits. Various activities require or suggest leaders of maturity, which, though it cannot be a guaranteed corollary of age, is usually affected positively by age. Drivers' licenses are issued at minimum ages set individually by each state; chauffeur licenses generally require older drivers. The American Camping Association recommends the age of 25 for a camp director because it is felt that the experience gained up to that age may make a real difference in the quality of the program offered to children. A 21-year-old leading a field trip to a city museum would be considered more mature and as having potentially better judgment than an 18-year-old.

The number of leaders is likewise a serious consideration. There must be two leaders for most programs and some require ratios of leaders to participants. A swimming program might require one leader for 25 swimmers in a pool whereas on a lake more leaders would be required. A hike for children aged 10 to 12 should have 1 leader per 8 children plus 1 extra for emergencies; a bus trip should have, in addition to the driver, 1 leader for 15 participants if they are children, yet 1 leader is considered adequate for 35 older persons. Older persons require fewer leaders for control but highly trained leaders in terms of first aid and knowledge of the needs of older adults. No standards exist for the ratio of leaders to groups in most activities, but good judgment is always to be assumed in planning for the event.

Leader qualifications are the third consideration in this category. One should assess the training that the leader has had in order to determine whether the leader is qualified for the activity. Certainly, leaders with *current* certification in first aid, water safety instruction, and boating programs are desirable for some activities. Special training through college degree programs, workshops, in-service seminars, and so on, add to the leader's qualifications in most activities. The leader's age,

previous experience, and any other special characteristics that might help make the program safer need to be recorded on the risk management plan.

*VI. Equipment.* Analysis of equipment is usually necessary for proper programming and is mandatory for managing risks. Equipment should be considered in terms of type, number, and condition.

**A.** *Type.* Every risk management program should list the type of equipment to be provided by individuals and by the organization. A sewing class may utilize materials provided by the individual and machines provided by the agency. This is relatively simple. A three-day backpacking trip, however, may list food provided by individuals and stoves by the agency, followed by a long list of equipment that is mandatory and provided by one or the other. For this type of program we would need to know much more information. How much food? What kind? How is it to be prepared? How should it be packaged? What weight? What kind of stoves and fuel will be needed? Of what weight and amount? Some programs will necessitate lists of mandatory and optional equipment duplicated and given to each participant as part of the program itself.

**B.** *Number.* Recording the number of pieces of equipment may be a simple matter. It might be stated, for example, that the agency will provide three sewing machines. Or recording of the number of pieces of equipment might be much more complex. On the backpacking trip, the list might read one tent per two people, one stove per four people, one climbing rope for three people, one first aid kit for the group.

**C.** *Condition.* The condition of all equipment must be checked before, during, and after each event. Any breaks, tears, weaknesses, and so on, should be reported promptly. Any equipment being returned after an event should be returned in excellent and clean condition or be reported and sent for repairs before it is shelved. The recommended risk management plan checklist has a space to record equipment found to be in need of repair and how it was reported.

*VII. Policies.*    The final portion of the risk management plan requires the development of a list of policies and procedures under which risks are managed. These policies are formulated by using the material listed at the beginning of the form. They are dependent on those facts. The event, participants, leaders, and equipment are the prime consider-

ations in developing policies and procedures for managing risks. This list of policies may be the same for many activities, particularly those that are deemed as of "low" or "medium" risk. In these cases, there may be standard procedures for the operation of many similar activities. There may be standard emergency numbers, accident forms to fill in, and procedures for checking equipment. An example of a risk management plan with standard policies is shown in Figure 7.2. This is for an obviously "low" risk activity and can be used as standard practice. An example of a "medium" risk management plan is shown in Figure 7.3.

---

I.   Event  *Song Practice*

II.  Date(s) and Time(s)  *January 30, 1984    4–5 P.M.*

III. Location and Facility
   Indoor  *Multipurpose room   Community Center*
   Outdoor
   Conditions

IV.  Participants
   Number  *50*   Age(s)  *55-up*   Sex  *Men & Women*
   Experience  *N/A*
   Special characteristics  *– Unknown – Hearing? Sight? Health?*

V.   Leaders
   Name  *Jim Singer*   Age _____        Name _____   Age _____
   Qualifications  *Director*              Qualifications
       *New Year Eve Senior Sing*
   Certification                           Certification

VI.  Equipment  *Piano*
   Type and number  *50 folding chair*

   Condition checked  *2 removed as questionable condition*

VII. Policies  *No one stands on a folding chair.*

VIII. Emergency numbers
   *Ambulance*
   *Fire*         *} Posted by Phone*
   *Police*

---

**FIGURE 7.2**  Outline of risk management plan for activities of low risk.

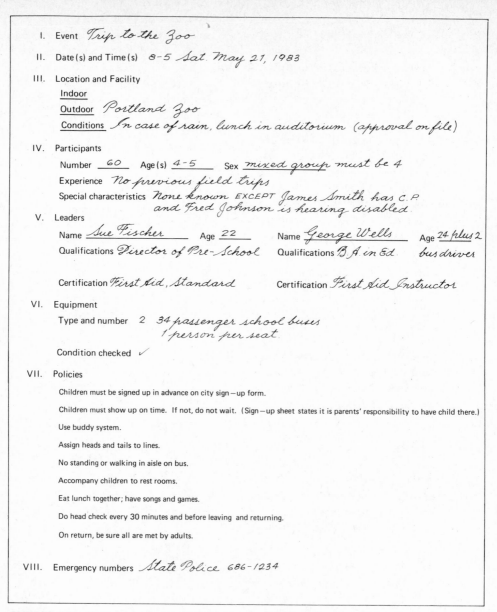

I. Event *Trip to the Zoo*

II. Date(s) and Time(s) *8-5 Sat. May 21, 1983*

III. Location and Facility

    Indoor

    Outdoor *Portland Zoo*

    Conditions *In case of rain, lunch in auditorium (approval on file)*

IV. Participants

    Number *60* Age(s) *4-5* Sex *mixed group must be 4*

    Experience *No previous field trips*

    Special characteristics *None known* EXCEPT *James Smith has C.P. and Fred Johnson is hearing disabled.*

V. Leaders

    Name *Sue Fischer* Age *22* Name *George Wells* Age *24 plus 2*

    Qualifications *Director of Pre-School* Qualifications *B.A. in Ed. bus driver*

    Certification *First Aid, Standard* Certification *First Aid Instructor*

VI. Equipment

    Type and number *2 34 passenger school buses 1 person per seat.*

    Condition checked ✓

VII. Policies

    Children must be signed up in advance on city sign—up form.

    Children must show up on time. If not, do not wait. (Sign—up sheet states it is parents' responsibility to have child there.)

    Use buddy system.

    Assign heads and tails to lines.

    No standing or walking in aisle on bus.

    Accompany children to rest rooms.

    Eat lunch together; have songs and games.

    Do head check every 30 minutes and before leaving and returning.

    On return, be sure all are met by adults.

VIII. Emergency numbers *State Police 686-1234*

**FIGURE 7.3** Outline of risk management plan for activities of medium risk.

Figures 7.4 to 7.9 present a risk management plan developed according to the preceding format but developed in depth for an activity of potential high risk. This activity was a field trip for a group of University of Oregon students in a beginning class in wilderness skills. The group numbered 25 (1 instructor, 7 assistant instructors who were advanced students, and 17 novices who had completed all of a 12-week course except for the final examination and the last field trip).

I. Event: Wilderness Skills I Field Final

II. Date: December 5, 6, and 7

### Friday

6:30 A.M.  Drivers pick up vehicles at State Motor Pool
7:00 A.M.  Students meet at Gerlinger Turnaround—pack vehicles and depart
9:00 A.M.  Arrive at trail heads
2:00 P.M.  Establish minimum impact campsite
             Review map and compass (contours, bearings, triangulations, etc.)
             Planning for Saturday travel (route selection)

### Saturday

6:00 A.M.  Rise and breakfast
SHARP
8:00 A.M.  Cross-country map and compass travel to Upper Island Lake (south shore)
1:00 P.M.  Establish minimum impact campsite
2:30 P.M.  Search-and-rescue techniques, litter construction for evacuation
Evening hike—weather permitting (optional)

### Sunday

6:00 A.M.  Rise and breakfast
SHARP
8:30 A.M.  Search and rescue/evacuation program
11:00 A.M.  Camp cleanup and lunch
12:00 P.M.  Break camp, depart for return x-c map and compass, switch routes
4:00 P.M.  Vehicles rendez-vous at lower trail head
             Stop at Oakridge for dinner
             Trip evaluations
8:00 P.M.  Return to Gerlinger Turnaround

III. Location: Upper Island Lake—Mt. Fuji; Willamette National Forest; Township 22S, Range 5-1/2E; Waldo Lake Quadrangle

Directions: Waldo Lake turnoff from Hwy 58

Trailheads: Island Lake Trail and Mt. Ray Trail

IV. Participants Wilderness Skills Class:

25 over 21 (15 men and 10 women)

See attached sign up sheet.

V. Leaders:

Mike Swiderski, Instructor, 27 years old, First Aid Certificate, Search and Rescue Member, 10 years experience

Merritt Adams
Margaret Buck
Glen Goddard
Marlene Parkhurst                   Students in advanced Leadership class
Scott Parriott
Dave Reuter
Dave Reich

VI. Equipment:
  See attached sheet
VII. Policies:
  A. Goals and Objectives
    1. To develop skills that relate to backpacking, minimum impact backcountry travel and camping.
    2. To build confidence, to provide experiences that will enhance character growth, to increase physical stamina, and to develop self-discipline.
    3. To instill an ethical philosophy toward the wilderness.
    4. To demonstrate competencies in map and compass wilderness travel.
    5. To demonstrate competencies in handling emergency procedure.
    6. To recognize the potential for stressful situations, inclement weather, fatigue, hazards, and cold.
  B. No alcoholic beverages on any part of the trip.
  C. No hallucinogenic drugs on any part of the trip.
  D. Release forms are signed.
  E. All students have met trip prerequisites.
  F. Itinerary will be followed unless leader alters it because of emergency.

**FIGURE 7.4**   Outline of a risk management plan for activities of high risk.

## EMERGENCY CONTACT LIST

| Participant's Name | Emergency Contact Name | Contact Number |
| --- | --- | --- |
| 1. Marlene Parkhurst (L) | Chamilyn Quinn | 683–5806 |
| 2. Margaret Buck (L) | Jerry Winetrout | 687–0563 |
| 3. Glen Goddard (L) | Howard Goddard | (209) 394–8944 |
| 4. David Reich (L) | Betty Smith | 227–5002 |
| 5. Merritt Adams (L) | Brian Knesal | 683–2542 |
| 6. Scott Parriott (L) | Paul Green | 683–8131 |
| 7. Dirk Andersen | Dave Andersen | 485–2442 |
| 8. Frank Palermo | Jackie Guild | 343–6700 |
| 9. Martha A. Price | Kim Colbath | 683–1598 or 683–3247 |
| 10. Liz Paynt | Joe Knab | 683–8396 |
| 11. Lyle Shearer | Rita Ensminger | 345–7449 |
| 12. Mark Wolfe | Connie Smith | 484–3107 |
| 13. Dave Reuter (L) | Camille Wilder | 344–4357 |
| 14. Trudy Reeves | Sue Norton | 683–5265 |
| 15. Suzanne Krippaehne | Dr. Krippaehne | 246–8109 |
| 16. Mark Perry | Vic Sandtslom | 485–9711 |
| 17. Devin Jones | Chuck Crator | 683–4668 |
| 18. Tom Robb | Jim Lynch | 683–1545 |
| 19. Steve Hollenhorst | Mary Jo Zapf | 687–4051 |
| 20. Mike Angell | Evan Kraus | 484–4145 |
| 21. Pat Caddoo | Denny Conn | 746–1163 |
| 22. Mike Swiderski (group leader) | Molly & Denny Reed | 747–0579 |
| 23. Mary Swiderski | Molly & Denny Reed | 747–0579 |
| 24. Alicia Matuson | Wendy Laufer | 726–7769 |
| 25. Jackie Sage | Jackson Soye | 688–0532 |

**FIGURE 7.5**   High risk management plan emergency contact list.

**UNIVERSITY OF OREGON**
**DEPARTMENT OF RECREATION AND PARK MANAGEMENT**

**WILDERNESS SKILLS 1983**

**Suggested Equipment List***

### Items You Could Be Wearing

*wool socks/2 pr.
*wool pants/knickers
*wool shirt
*wool hat
*wool gloves/mittens
*sturdy hiking boots (waterproofed)
*watch
*wool sweater
*rain gear (top and bottom)

### Clothing in Your Pack

*net wool underwear (upper and lower)
long underwear (upper and lower)
*turtleneck
*parka/windshirt
*wind pants
bandanna
*sunglasses/goggles
*gaiters
*windproof overmittens
*vest
*extra wool mittens/gloves
*extra wool socks/2 pr.
*extra wool hat/balaclava
*camp footwear/booties

### Items in Your Pack

*pack/frame (int, ext)
*waterproof pack cover
*lash straps, stuff bags
*knife
*matches/lighter
*map and compass
2 candles
candle lantern
*first aid kit
*food
*water
*warm sleeping bag
ensolite sleeping pad (min. 3/8″)

* = Mandatory

### Items in Your Pack (cont.)

ensolite sitting pad
*cup
*spoon
supergaiters/over booties
*flashlight/batteries and bulb
fire starter/stove primer
notebook, pencil
book/enjoyable reading
nylon cord (30′ × 1/8″)
full parka with hood (insulated)
overpants (insulated)
*toilet kit—tooth brush, paste
lip balm (optional)
avalanche cord
sun cream/block
*plastic trash liners 3 mil (2)
*poncho/ground sheet
whisk broom
space blanket
*whistle
signal mirror
toilet paper

### Equipment to Be Divided

*stove/fuel
extra fuel
*tent, fly, stakes, cord, etc.
pots, lids
*cooking utensils
shovel
cleaning pad for pots
food containers
rope
thermometer (personal, weather)
ski repair kit: binding parts, wire, pliers,
    screwdriver, basket, pole strap, spare
    tip, ski wax, kit-waxes, cork, scraper
pack and stove repair parts
clevis, pins, gaskets
can opener
snowshoes

**FIGURE 7.6**  High risk management plan equipment list.

## HEALTH EXAMINATION FORM

(To be filled in by participant)

NAME_____ BIRTH DATE_____ AGE_____ SEX_____
      last                         first   initial

ADDRESS_____

In case of emergency notify_____ Phone_____

Address_____

## HEALTH HISTORY

I have had the following as checked. Any incurred within the last year are double-checked:

Allergies: Asthma, hay fever,

| | Check | | Check |
|---|---|---|---|
| eczema, others | _____ | Colds | _____ |
| Frequent sore throats | _____ | Discharging ear | _____ |
| Sinus trouble | _____ | Shortness of breath | _____ |
| Headaches | _____ | Convulsive seizures or | |
| Goitre | _____ |    fainting spells | _____ |
| Typhoid | _____ | Night sweats | _____ |
| Tuberculosis | _____ | Frequent diarrhea | _____ |
| Rheumatism | _____ | Other illnesses | _____ |
| Chicken pox | _____ | _____ | |
| Mumps | _____ | | |
| Sleep walking | _____ | Operations_____ | |

I have had the following immunizations as checked:

| | Check | Date | Comment |
|---|---|---|---|
| Tetanus toxoid | _____ | _____ | _____ |
| Typhoid vaccine | _____ | _____ | _____ |
| Diphtheria vaccine | _____ | _____ | _____ |
| Smallpox vaccine | _____ | _____ | _____ |
| Measles vaccine | _____ | _____ | _____ |

Polio vaccine (1st Injection_____) (2nd_____) (3rd_____)
          (Booster_____)

Others_____

Date: _____

_____
                  Signature

**FIGURE 7.7**   High risk management plan health examination form.

# UNIVERSITY OF OREGON
# DEPARTMENT OF RECREATION AND PARK MANAGEMENT

## RESPONSIBILITIES OF STUDENT AND FACULTY IN ACTIVITY COURSES

The Recreation and Park Management courses in which you have elected to participate are either required as part of your major or elected.

Regardless of the case, you must realize that there is a certain assumption of risk which you engender when you participate in active classes such as these. *You must be aware of this assumption.*

Throughout the conduct of each class you will receive competent, progressive, sequential instruction and proper supervision. Every effort will be made to keep all facilities and equipment in good, safe, workable condition.

You will not be asked to do anything which is inconsistent with the activity or is in any way not reasonable and prudent.

However, the entire responsibility is not the instructor's. You, too, have a responsibility. For your own safe participation, and that of your fellow students, you must call to the attention of the instructor any situation which you perceive to be a potential danger to you or your fellow students. This would include, but should not be limited to:

- equipment that has broken or is in need of repair
- when you are not feeling well or are unduly fatigued
- when you have unusual difficulty in performing a skill

Also, you are obligated to follow the rules and regulations set down by the instructor for your safety. This includes the proper dress, such as tennis shoes and protective equipment, e.g., eye glass guards. If you choose not to use such protective equipment provided or requested, you must realize that you are doing so at your own peril and that injury might occur.

We all want a safe environment, but it must be recognized that accidents do occur in active participation. We want vigorous participation, but all of us (instructor, you and fellow students) must use good judgment and work together for safe participation.

Should an injury be incurred during participation in this class, the instructor will make arrangements for transportation to the University Health Center.

The injured party is responsible for all financial obligations incurred in this process and subsequent treatment necessitated by the injury. Because of this, students are encouraged to carry some form of health care insurance. (Student Handbook section of the *Time Schedule*.)

Please discuss with your instructor any known physical problems which may limit your participation in any class. *This should be done by the second class session.* It is important to do this inasmuch as a medical examination is no longer a requirement for admission to the University.

Should you have any questions regarding this statement, please contact your instructor.

**FIGURE 7.8**    High risk management plan guidelines for participation.

---

**ACTIVITY RELEASE AND HEALTH STATEMENT FORM**

This program requires participation in field exercises which are, by their nature, physically demanding. Therefore, all participants must be free of medical or physical conditions which might create undue risk to themselves or others who depend upon them. You should participate in these outings only if you are free of any physical disability. Physical strength is not necessary, although good condition will increase your enjoyment of the outing activities. If there is any doubt about your ability to participate safely in the field activities, you should have a physical examination.

1. What physical disabilities or conditions do you have which might limit your participation in this activity?_____

2. What else might affect your participation?_____

3. What medication are you taking?_____
4. What special dietary restrictions do you have?_____

5. Do you have any allergies?_____ If so, please indicate them below:
   _____Penicillin        _____Horses          _____Dust, hay
   _____Wasps             _____Frostbite        _____Others, List_____
   _____Bees              _____Foods            _____

I have read and understand the nature of the physical demands of this program. I have noted above any medical or physical conditions I have which might affect my activities. I therefore release any and all rights or claims for damages against the University of Oregon and all individuals assisting in instructing and conducting these activities, for any and all injuries, loss or damage suffered by me at, or in any way connected with, these injuries.

Name (PRINT)_____

Signature      _____

Date           _____ Student's Age_____

FIGURE 7.9    High risk management plan health form.

Regarding the formulation of a risk management plan, Ewert has suggested that there are points or stages in a risk management plan at which decisions should be made regarding the direction of the activity or program. The decisions that can be made at these critical junctures are to (1) continue the activity, (2) modify the activity, or (3) terminate the activity. The points or stages that require analysis are centered on evaluation of *participants, leadership, environment, material* (equipment, clothing, and so on), *implementation* (conditions, objectives, group processes), and a *final evaluation* phase (looking at results, outcomes, and worth of the activity).[2] If a weakness occurs at any stage of an activity regarding any of these factors, the activity should be replanned or terminated, as the plan is not stronger than any single link.

Ewert's diagram, on a linear scale, may be easily modified to fit the seven-part risk management plan recommended here. Figure

[2]Alan Ewert, "The Decision Package—A Tool for Risk Management," *Parks and Recreation*, April 1983, pp. 39–41.

7.10 indicates that at any point where a weakness is found, the leader should stop and *replan* the stage until the plan appears to meet criteria of safety or the leader should curtail the

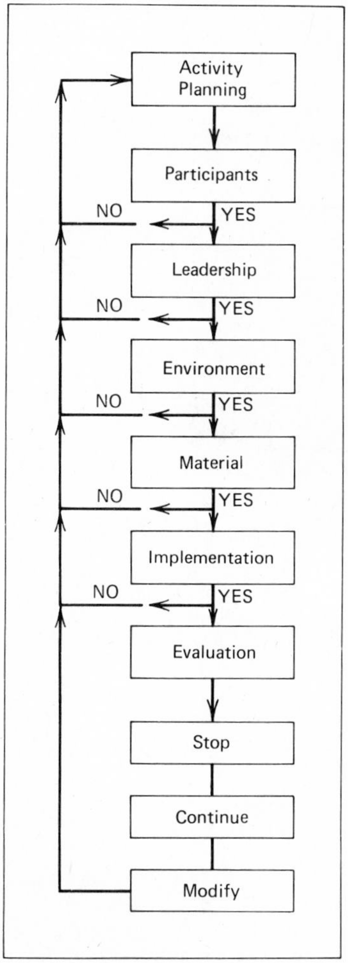

**FIGURE 7.10**  Decision package for risk management (Alan Ewert, ''The Decision-Package: A Tool for Risk Management.'' *Parks and Recreation* [April 1983], pp. 39–41).

event as being unsafe. At no weak point should the leader proceed further.

## SUMMARY

Strong consideration should be given to the development of a program of risk management. This is a responsibility of the leader conducting activities as well as of the agency sponsoring activities. The management of risk is based on the idea that the likelihood of accidents can be lessened if appropriate plans are developed for controlling such risks. Risk management plans usually comprise a set of policies, procedures, and regulations for minimizing risks involved in conducting activities. A variety of factors must be considered, including the type of program offered, the facility used and prevailing conditions, the participants' abilities, and required equipment.

## DISCUSSION QUESTIONS

1. What is meant by standard of care in risk management situations?
2. Discuss the three criteria on which standard of care is based.
3. Differentiate between general and specific supervision.
4. How might a plan for conducting an activity for six-year-olds differ from conducting the same activity for their parents?
5. Develop a checklist for safety conditions of an indoor recreation facility with which you are familiar.
6. What is meant by ''low,'' ''medium,'' and ''high'' risk activities?
7. Develop a risk management plan for a two-day (overnight) trip for 10-year-olds.
8. Using Ewert's ''Discussion Package for Risk Management'' explain where and when a leader replans or curtails an activity.

9. Define a risk management plan, and give two reasons why every leader should develop and follow one for each activity.

10. Develop a risk management program for a recreation activity of your choice.

# 8

# THE ROLE OF THE LEADER IN VALUES DEVELOPMENT

"The Kids on the Block" program helps participants form values regarding the disabled.

All organizations have values, many of which are stated formally as organizational goals. It is inevitable that these values will have an impact on participants. Although a recreation and leisure service organization may deliberately promote values (such as a land ethic), values are also transmitted within the organization's programs unintentionally (as when a leader encourages orderliness and neatness over creativity). Since participants' values will necessarily be shaped and influenced within the context of recreation and leisure service programs and activities, the leaders of such programs should have knowledge and skills in this area.

*Values education*, although commonly employed within the field of education, can be successfully adapted for use by leaders in recreation and leisure service programs and activities. Applied to the recreation and leisure service fields, the values education concept is based on the notion that leaders can help participants develop and define their values through use of selected methods and techniques. It implies that the recreation and leisure service organization should assess its potential impact upon the formation of participants' values and attempt to ensure, through intervention, that this impact occurs in a beneficial and organized way. Also referred to as "moral education," values education can be specifically defined as "direct and indirect intervention (by the leader) which affects . . . both behavior (related to values) and the capacity to think about issues of right and wrong."[1]

There are three major approaches that can be used to facilitate a values education program: the values clarification approach, the cognitive-developmental approach, and the cognitive approach. This chapter will discuss only one of these—the *values clarification* ap-

[1]David Purpel and Kevin Ryan, eds., *Moral Education: It Comes with the Territory* (Berkeley, Calif.: McCutchin Publishing Corp., 1976), p. 5.

proach. Values clarification avoids the promotion of any *one* set of values and typically involves the use of statements and other strategies by the leader to help participants develop and refine *their* values. This approach is especially suited for use within recreation and leisure service programs and activities. This chapter will also attempt to provide the reader with a basic knowledge of the philosophy underlying values education, the roles that the leader might assume within a values education program, and techniques that can be used by the leader to implement values education within recreation and leisure service programs and activities.

### WHAT ARE VALUES?

Values can be thought of as principles or guidelines that an individual regards as being important in life. Very often values that are held will determine the direction of an individual's energy and resources. According to Raths, Harmon, and Simon, values must meet certain criteria in order to be termed "true" values. They state that values should "be chosen freely from alternatives after careful consideration of the consequences, [and they] should be prized, cherished, affirmed and acted upon."[2] Individuals can form values that meet these criteria on their own, or they may be assisted in the formation of values by others. Leaders in the recreation and leisure service field can help participants progress through this "valuing process" to form values by using various methods and techniques.

### VALUES EDUCATION: IS IT VALUE LADEN OR VALUE FREE?

In order for values education within a recreation and leisure service organization to be effective, it should meet three criteria: It should complement the basic values of the community and society, it should support the values of the organization, and it should not *impose* values upon participants. The combination of these three criteria is interesting in that, although a values education program may not attempt to impose values upon participants, it will be somewhat value laden owing to its context within the organization, community, and society and its support of many values associated with these "institutions." Values education should, however, attempt to allow individuals to arrive at their own conclusions or opinions regarding values. Simond, in discussing the values clarification approach to values education, describes a process that

> helps people arrive at an answer. It is not concerned with an ultimate set of values . . . but it does stress a method to help . . . [individuals] . . . determine the content and power of . . . [their] . . . own set of values. It is a self-audit, and an inventory of soul and spirit. A tool to help . . . [people] . . . freely decide between alternatives or among varied choices. It is a methodology to help . . . make a decision, to act, to determine what has value. . . .[3]

Ideally, values education should be as described in this quote: value free. Realistically, however, values may be promoted indirectly. As mentioned earlier, they may be indirectly promoted as a result of the context in which values education occurs. In addition, the use of certain techniques by the leader in the values education process, implies that these techniques have *value*. According to Kirschenbaum,

> If we urge critical thinking, then we value *rationality*. If we support moral reasoning, then we value *justice*. If we advocate divergent thinking, then we value *creativity*. If we uphold free choice, then we value autonomy or *freedom*. If we encourage "no lose" conflict resolution,

---

[2]Ann Colby, "Two Approaches to Moral Education," in *Moral Education: It Comes with the Territory*, David Purpel and Kevin Ryan, eds. (Berkeley, Calif.: McCutchin Publishing Corp., 1976), p. 276.

[3]Sidney B. Simond, *Meeting Yourself Halfway* (Niles, Ill., Argus Communications, 1974), p. xiii.

then we value *equality*. . . . [We] can only say that values clarification is not and never has been "value free."[4]

Values education will not, then, be value free. Although participants may be influenced somewhat in their formation of values by the values of the organization and the values education approach used, the leader can still endeavor to make the values education experience as "value free" as possible.

## LEADERSHIP ROLES IN VALUES EDUCATION

Individuals within recreation and leisure service leadership roles may help participants shape and define their values intentionally or unintentionally. This chapter is concerned with the leader who engages in a deliberate effort to help participants form and act upon meaningful values. Leaders who intentionally engage in values education may assume a direct or indirect role. Furthermore, leaders who assume a direct role may engage in a direct-programmatic role or a direct-integrative role. These leadership roles are all similar in that all of them attempt to avoid imposing a value or set of values upon participants. However, each of these roles finds the leader interacting with participants in a different manner. These three leadership roles, direct-programmatic, direct-integrative, and indirect, are described in the following sections.

### DIRECT-PROGRAMMATIC APPROACH

The leader working in a direct-programmatic values education role designs and organizes program content to relate specifically to the exploration of values by participants. The primary goals and objectives of the activity or program are, in fact, values education. Typi-

cally, the leader in this role uses value-related materials and exercises. Participants involved in values education, whose leader uses this approach, are aware that they are attempting to engage in self-examination and to gain greater self-awareness.

Leisure counseling is an ideal example of the direct-programmatic approach to values education within the recreation and leisure service area. The leader functioning as a leisure counselor uses various methods, materials, and techniques to help participants consider and clarify their values related to leisure and to act upon their values. Some advantages of the direct-programmatic approach are these.

- It provides a more open and honest approach [to values education]
- It is more professional and responsible to be systematic in developing [values education programs]
- Such [an approach] can be more efficient, careful, organized, and focused. Resources and techniques can be better selected and organized when there are specific objectives and goals
- Such an approach can facilitate meaningful evaluation of its effectiveness
- This approach allows [leaders] to specialize . . . which reduces [misinformation][5]

The leader using the direct-programmatic approach to values education in a group situation should be aware of the possible effects of the group on the program. Large group discussions, in particular, may inhibit the values education process. Some of the disadvantages of using a large group discussion format in values education are mentioned here.

- Participants, in the heat of a value discussion, often become defensive of positions they might not even hold.

[4]Howard Kirschenbaum, "Clarifying Values Clarification: Some Theoretical Issues," in *Moral Education: It Comes with the Territory*, David Purpel and Kevin Ryan, eds. (Berkeley, Calif.: McCutchin Publishing Corp., 1976), p. 122.

[5]David Purpel and Kevin Ryan, eds., *Moral Education: It Comes with the Territory* (Berkeley, Calif.: McCutchin Publishing Corp., 1976), pp. 59–60.

- Participants are often motivated by factors irrelevant to the issues being discussed, such as desires to please other students or the leader or both.
- Some members of the group may hesitate to participate.
- Discussion can generate undue pressure on individuals to accept the group consensus.[6]

## DIRECT-INTEGRATIVE APPROACH

A leader may also assume a direct-integrative role within recreation and leisure service programs and activities. In this role, the leaders' input, rather than occurring within a program or activity setting designed specifically for consideration and examination of values, occurs more naturally within the context in which the values in question arise. For example, a baseball coach is a leader who might assume a direct-integrative values education role. In this role, a baseball coach would encourage the consideration and development of values by team members during practice, during games, and at other strategic moments. The opportunities to encourage team members to think about such topics as fairness, sportsmanship, teamwork, honesty, and courage occur naturally in this setting. The direct-integrative approach to values education can be very effective because it occurs in context. Interestingly, John Wooten, the most successful college basketball coach of all time, dealt very directly with the issue of values and involved his players in a plan of value development. Some advantages of the direct-integrative approach are these.

- It provides a natural and functional approach.
- Integration prevents compartmentalization and fragmentation of information.
- It does not require much in the way of special materials and training.

- The framework is a good protection against sloppy thinking.[7]

## INDIRECT APPROACH

The leader assuming an indirect values education role does not attempt to encourage participants to consider and examine specific values. Rather, he or she attempts to provide participants with specific knowledge and skills that they can use to develop values on their own. In other words, the leader within this role attempts to provide participants with the tools necessary to formulate values. For example, in the area of leisure, the leader might help participants attain knowledge related to "the nature of leisure," "important questions related to leisure values," and "decision-making techniques," with the expectation that the participant would take this information and use it to formulate his or her own values. This is a relatively sophisticated approach and may not be applicable in many recreation and leisure service settings.

Values can be assimilated by participants in recreation and leisure settings *without* the intervention of the leader as well. The leader should be aware that this occurs and that values can be transmitted although this is unplanned. The way that participants are treated and accepted by others in the program environment can, for example, have an influence on their values. Participants who see that members of their group are recognized only for success and not for development, improvement, or effort may, as a result, develop values associated with this observation. In addition, the values of participants may be influenced by the values that are promoted by the organization as a whole. Such values as "wise use of leisure is good," "having fun and developing skills is good," and "conservation and protection of the environment is impor-

[6]Adapted from Ann Colby, "Two Approaches to Moral Education," in *Moral Education: It Comes with the Territory*, David Purpel and Kevin Ryan, eds. (Berkeley, Calif.: McCutchin Publishing Corp., 1976), p. 285.

[7]David Purpel and Kevin Ryan, eds., *Moral Education: It Comes with the Territory* (Berkeley, Calif.: McCutchin Publishing Corp., 1976), p. 60.

What values are being transmitted here?

tant'' may be incorporated into the participant's own value system.

## VALUES CLARIFICATION

One of three major approaches to values education, the values clarification approach, is ideally suited for use within recreation and leisure programs and activities. As its name implies, it is a method that can be used by the leader to help participants define and ''clarify'' their values. According to the values clarification approach, a value is defined in terms of seven criteria termed the ''process of valuing'': choosing freely, choosing from among alternatives, choosing after thoughtful consideration of the consequences, prizing and cherishing, affirming, acting upon choices, and repeating.[8] It is the task of the leader using the values clarification approach to help participants progress through this valuing process and acquire meaningful values. This is done primarily through the use of ''value clarifying'' responses by the leader.

The role of the leader in helping participants formulate and clarify their values may vary greatly in terms of its formality or informality. In some instances, the leader may use specific prepared materials and exercises to stimulate thinking about values. However, in other programs and activities, the use of such materials may be impossible or inappropriate, and the leader may want simply to use general guidelines or ''clarifying responses'' or both to promote consideration of values by participants. Some general guidelines that can, and should, be used by the leader using the values clarification approach, regardless of the structure employed or the degree of formality or informality of the leader's role, are listed as follows.

- Encourage individuals to make decisions and make them freely.
- Help them discover and examine available alternatives when faced with choices.
- Help them weigh alternatives thoughtfully, reflecting on the consequences of each.
- Encourage them to consider what they prize and cherish.
- Give them opportunities to make public affirmations of their choices.
- Encourage them to act, behave, and live in accordance with their choices.
- Help them to examine repeated behaviors or patterns in their lives.[9]

There are various techniques that can be employed by the leader to facilitate values clarification. Some of these are more structured and involve the use of prepared materials. Others may simply require that the leader possess and use a repertoire of statements as appropriate. Some of the many values clarification techniques that can be used by a leader are value clarifying responses, value indicators, value strategies, self-contracts, and value sheets. A discussion of each of these follows.

[8]Louis Raths, Merrill Harmin, and Sidney B. Simon, ''Selection from Values and Teaching,'' in *Moral Education: It Comes with the Territory*, David Purpel and Kevin Ryan, eds. (Berkeley, Calif.: McCutchin Publishing Corp., 1976), pp. 76–77.

[9]Adapted from Ann Colby, ''Two Approaches to Moral Education,'' in *Moral Education: It Comes with the Territory*, David Purpel and Kevin Ryan, eds. (Berkeley, Calif.: McCutchin Publishing Corp., 1976), p. 276.

## VALUE-CLARIFYING RESPONSES

Value-clarifying responses are questions that the leader can ask participants in order to encourage them to think about their feelings, attitudes, thought processes, and decisions in an attempt to help them define and "clarify" their values. For example, a leader might ask a participant who has expressed an idea or feeling such questions as, "Is that very important to you?" "Have you felt this way for a long time?" or "How do you know that is right?"[10] Such questions would prompt the participant to reevaluate the accuracy of his or her idea and assess his or her commitment to it. Figure 8.1 presents 30 clarifying responses that can be used by the leader in interactions with participants. The key to using such clarifying responses is to employ a "light touch." They are meant to be mere suggestions and provocations of thought. Several conversations that might occur between a participant and a leader using value-clarifying responses follow.

*Leader.*  Traci, you say you enjoy art?
*Traci.*  Yes, I like it a lot.
*Leader.*  What are some of the things you like most about art?

*Leader.*  David, you say that you think you would like to build model rockets?
*David.*  I think it would be really fun!
*Leader.*  Is there anything you can do about that idea?

*Carole.*  I love running.
*Leader.*  Oh, do you run often?
*Carole.*  Yes, I like to run almost every day.
*Leader.*  Is running important to you?

Each of these conversations is thought provoking, but very brief. It isn't necessary that the participant engaged in these types of conversations arrive at any firm decisions. Nor is it necessary that the conversation even have

[10]Ibid., pp. 91–96.

- Is this something you prize?
- Are you glad about that?
- How did you feel when that happened?
- Did you consider any alternatives?
- Have you felt this way for a long time?
- Was that something you yourself selected or chose?
- Did you have to choose that? Was it a free choice?
- Did you do anything about that idea?
- Can you give me some examples of that idea?
- What do you mean by _____? Can you define that word?
- Where would that idea lead? What would be its consequences?
- Would you really do that, or are you just talking?
- Are you saying that . . . [repeat] . . .?
- Did you say that . . . [repeat in some distorted way] . . .?
- Have you thought much about that idea (or behavior)?
- What are some good things about that notion?
- What do we have to assume for things to work out that way?
- Is what you express consistent with . . . [note something else that the person said or did that may point to an inconsistency] . . .?
- What other possibilities are there?
- Is that a personal preference, or do you think most people should believe that?
- How can I help you do something about your idea? What seems to be the difficulty?
- Is there a purpose back of this activity?
- Is that very important to you?
- Do you do this often?
- Would you like to tell others about your idea?
- Do you have any reasons for [saying or doing] that?
- Would you do the same thing over again?
- How do you know it's right?
- Do you value that?
- Do you think people will always believe that?

**FIGURE 8.1**   Clarifying responses that can be used by the leader. (*Source:* Louis Raths, Merrill Harmin, and Sidney B. Simon, "Selection from Values and Teaching," in David Purpel and Kevin Ryan, eds., *Moral Education: It Comes with the Territory* [Berkeley, Calif.: McCutchin Publishing Corp., 1976], pp. 91–96.)

an "end." The purpose of clarifying responses is served when the participant considers his or her statements in a personal and thoughtful way. Ten specific guidelines for the leader using clarifying responses follow.

- The clarifying response avoids moralizing, criticizing, giving values, or evaluating.
- It puts the responsibility on participants to look at their behavior or their ideas and to think and decide for themselves what they want.
- A clarifying response also entertains the possibility that the participant will *not* look or decide or think.
- It does not try to do big things with its small comments. Each clarifying response is only one of many.
- Clarifying responses are not used for interview purposes. The goal is not to obtain data, but for the participant to clarify his or her ideas and life if he or she wants to do so.
- It is usually not an extended discussion. The idea is just for the participant to think, and he or she usually does that best alone.
- Clarifying responses are often for individuals. A topic in which John may need clarification may be of no immediate interest to Mary. Values are personal things. The leader often responds to one individual although the whole group may be listening.
- The leader doesn't respond to everything everyone says or does in a program or activity setting.
- Clarifying responses operate in situations in which there are not "right" answers, as in situations involving feelings, attitudes, beliefs, or purposes. They are not appropriate for drawing participants toward a predetermined answer. They are not questions to which the leader has the answer already in hand.
- Clarifying responses are not mechanical things that carefully follow a formula. They must be used creatively and with insight, but with their purpose in mind: when a response helps a participant to clarify his or

her thinking or behavior, it is considered effective.[11]

## VALUE INDICATORS

Often participants will make statements that give some insight into the things that they may value. Such statements "point toward" values although they do not necessarily indicate the presence of a value itself. The leader attempting to engage participants in values clarification can be alert for these types of statements, termed "value indicators," in order to respond to them appropriately and productively. Values indicators can be categorized into four types of statements regarding attitudes, purposes, interests, aspirations, and activities. Figure 8.2 offers a list of typical keywords found in each of these four types of statements. The leader can listen for such key words, indicating value-laden topics, in order to respond to them with value-clarifying responses. There follow several examples of statements that would be considered "value indicators" and clarifying responses that could be used by the leader following them.

*David.*   *When I grow up,* I'm going to be a pilot.
*Leader.*   Have you thought about anything else you might be?

*Traci.*   *My hobby is* collecting stamps.
*Leader.*   Did you choose that hobby yourself?

*Carole.*   *I believe* that physical fitness is important.
*Leader.*   What do you mean by physical fitness?

## VALUE-CLARIFYING STRATEGIES

Values clarification strategies are exercises that can be used by the leader to help participants gain insight into their values. The participant engaged in such activities is prompted to examine and evaluate things that are important to him or her in life. The leader

[11]Ibid., pp. 87–88.

**Typical Keywords That Signal the Statement of Attitudes**

| | |
|---|---|
| I'm for . . . | In my opinion . . . |
| I'm against . . . | My choice is . . . |
| I feel that . . . | My way of doing it is . . . |
| I think if . . . | I'm convinced that . . . |
| The way I see it . . . | I believe . . . |
| If you ask me . . . | |

**Typical Keywords That Signal the Statement of Aspirations**

| | |
|---|---|
| In the future . . . | In about ten years I'm . . . |
| When I grow up . . . | If all goes well . . . |
| Someday I'm going to . . . | One of these days . . . |
| My long-range plan is . . . | |

**Typical Keywords That Signal the Statement of Purposes**

We're thinking about doing . . .
On the fifteenth, I'm going . . .
On the way downtown we're . . .
I wrote for the plans . . .
When I get this . . ., I'm going to do that . . .
We're waiting to hear from him . . .
Boy! Will Saturday ever come?
I'd like to . . .

**Typical Keywords That Signal the Statement of Interests**

I love making (or doing) . . .
My hobby is . . .
Yes, I subscribe to . . .
I really enjoy reading about . . .
If I had my choice, I'd take the ticket to . . .
Most weekends I'm over at the . . .
Every night after school, I . . .
Boy, nothing makes me feel better than . . .
I got this catalogue on . . .

**Typical Keywords That Signal a Statement About Activities**

After school, I usually . . .
Last weekend we . . .
On my day off, I went . . .
One of the best things we did Halloween . . .
All yesterday afternoon . . .
We just like to play . . .

**FIGURE 8.2**    Value indicators. (*Source:* Louis Raths, Merrill Harmin, and Sidney B. Simon, ''Selecting from Values and Teaching,'' in David Purpel and Kevin Ryan, eds., *Moral Education: It Comes with the Territory* [Berkeley, Calif.: McCutchin Publishing Corp., 1976], pp. 100–104.)

may use clarifying responses following the use of such exercises to help participants further refine and develop values. Figures 8.3 to 8.7 present five values-clarifying strategies that can be used by the leader. There are no right or wrong answers to the questions posed within these exercises.

Ask participants (the leader does it with them) to number from 1 to 20 on a piece of paper. Then suggest they list, as rapidly as they can, 20 things in life that they really, *really* love to do. Stress that there is no right answer about what people *should* like. No one should be forced to participate. Each has the right to pass.

When everyone has listed his or her 20 items, the process coding responses can be started. Here are some suggested codes that you might ask participants to use.

1. Place the $ sign by any item that costs more than $3 each time you do it.
2. Put an *R* in front of any item that involves some *risk*. The risk might be physical, intellectual, or emotional.
3. Using the code letters *F* and *M*, record which of the items on your list you think your father and mother might have had on their lists if they had been asked to make them at your age.
4. Place either the letter *P* or the letter *A* before each item, the *P* to be used for items that you prefer doing with *people*; the *A*, for items that you prefer doing alone. (Stress again that there is no right answer. It is important to become aware of which are your preferences.)
5. Place a number 5 in front of any item that you think would not be on your list five years from now.
6. Finally, go down through your list, and place near each item the date when you did it last.

**FIGURE 8.3** Strategy no. 1—things I love to do. (*Source:* Adapted from Sidney B. Simon, "Values Clarification vs. Indoctrination," in David Purpel and Kevin Ryan, eds., *Moral Education: It Comes with the Territory* [Berkeley, Calif.: McCutchin Publishing Corp., 1976], p. 129.)

This strategy fits in with Strategy No. 1. After participants have listed and coded their 20 items, the leader might say, "Look at your list as something that tells a lot about you at this time in your life. What did you learn about yourself as you were going through the strategy? Will you please complete one of these sentences and share with us some of the learning you did?"

I learned that I . . .
I relearned that I . . .
I noticed that I . . .
I was surprised to see that I . . .
I was disappointed that I . . .
I was pleased that I . . .
I realized that I . . .

**FIGURE 8.4** Strategy no. 2—I learned that I . . . (*Source:* Adapted from Sidney B. Simon, "Values Clarification vs. Indoctrination," David Purpel and Kevin Ryan, eds., in *Moral Education: It Comes with the Territory* [Berkeley, Calif.: McCutchin Publishing Corp., 1976], p. 130.)

This is a very simple strategy, which teaches us something about our personal priorities. The leader asks each participant to list 13, a baker's dozen, of his or her favorite items around the house that use plugs, that is, that require electricity.

When the participants have made their lists, the leader says, "Now please draw a line through the three that you really could do without if there were suddenly to be a serious power shortage. It's not that you don't like them, but you could, if you had to, live without them. OK. Now circle the three that really mean the most to you and that you would hold onto until the very end.

Again, there is no right answer as to what people should draw lines through and circle. The main thing is for each of us to know what we want and to see it in the perspective of what we like less.

**FIGURE 8.5** Strategy no. 3—baker's dozen. (*Source:* Adapted from Sidney B. Simon, "Values Clarification vs. Indoctrination," David Purpel and Kevin Ryan, eds., in *Moral Education: It Comes with the Territory* [Berkeley, Calif.: McCutchin Publishing Corp., 1976], p. 130–131.)

A Personal Coat of Arms

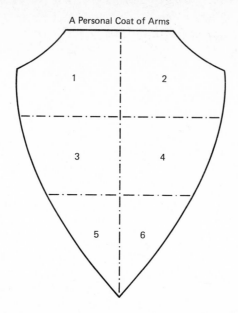

Each participant is asked to draw a shield shape in preparation for making a personal coat of arms. The leader could go into the historical significance of shields and coats of arms, but the purpose of this strategy is to help participants learn the importance of publicly affirming what we believe.

The coat of arms shield is divided into six sections (see figure). The leader makes it clear that words are to be used only in the sixth block. All the others are to contain pictures. He or she stresses that is not an art lesson. Only crude stick figures, and so on, need be used. Then he or she tells what is to go in each of the six sections.

1. Draw two pictures, one to represent something you are very good at and one to show something you *want* to be good at.

2. Make a picture to show one of your values from which you would never budge. This is one about which you have extremely strong feelings and that you might never give up.

3. Draw a picture to show a value by which your family lives. Make it one that everyone in your family would probably agree is one of their most important values.

4. In this block imagine that you could achieve anything you wanted and that whatever you tried to do would be a success. What would you strive to do?

5. Use this block to show one of the values you wished all people would believe and certain one in which you believe very deeply.

6. In the last block, you can use words. Use four words that you would like people to say about you behind your back.

Following the creation of the coats of arms, the leader might want to let participants share them among themselves in small groups.

**FIGURE 8.6**   Strategy no. 4—Personal coat of arms. (*Source:* Adapted from Sidney B. Simon, "Values Clarification vs. Indoctrination," in David Purpel and Kevin Ryan, eds., *Moral Education: It Comes with the Territory* [Berkeley, Calif.: McCutchin Publishing Corp., 1976], p. 132–133.) For information about current Values Realization materials and a schedule of nationwide training workshops, contact Sidney B. Simon, Old Mountain Road, Hadley, MA 01035.)

The leader uses Western Union Telegram blanks or simply has students head a piece of paper with the word *Telegram*. He or she then says, ''Each of you should think of someone in your real life to whom you would send a telegram that begins with these words: I urge you to . . . Then finish the telegram, and we'll hear some of them.''

''I urge'' telegrams help participants discover what they really want. They can also be used several times, and after participants have done five or six, they can be reexamined and ''I learned'' statements made from the pattern of messages carried by the telegrams. In addition, the leader may send the ''I urge'' telegrams of participants that relate to the community to the local newspaper to be considered for the ''Letters to the Editor'' column.

**FIGURE 8.7**    Strategy no. 5—''I urge'' telegrams. (*Source:* Adapted from Sidney B. Simon, ''Values Clarification vs. Indoctrination,'' in David Purpel and Kevin Ryan, eds., *Moral Education: It Comes with the Territory* [Berkeley, Calif.: McCutchin Publishing Corp., 1976], p. 131.)

## VALUES SHEET

A simple, straightforward method that can be used by the leader in values clarification, the value sheet, is simply a list of quotes regarding a value-laden topic that is presented to participants for consideration. Its purpose is to encourage participants to think about and evaluate the different perspectives that can be held regarding a certain value. Figure 8.8 presents a values sheet that offers different perspectives of leisure as a value. After asking participants to read and think about such statements, the leader might then ask them to respond verbally or in writing to such questions as, ''Which statements do you think are true?'' ''Which statements do you think are not true?'' ''Why?'' ''What do you think *your* values are after considering this topic?''

## SELF-CONTRACTS

Self-contracts can be used by the leader to help participants *act* on their values. The leader using this technique asks participants

''Everyone has the right to rest and leisure.''—Universal Declaration of Human Rights

''Leisure not only provides an opportunity to shape values; but it also establishes a setting for expressing them.''—Charles Brightbill

''To be able to fill leisure intelligently is the best product of civilization.''—Bertrand Russell

''The labor system is primarily conceived so that workers produce goods; the leisure system is primarily conceived so that man produces himself.''—Joffre Dumazdier

''The otter is playful,
the beaver is industrious.
Which leads the better life?''—Ti-tzu

''Nations as well as individuals are made or unmade by the way they use their leisure.''—Martin H. Neumayer

''Leisure cannot be equated with idleness. Leisure is a positive attitude, idleness is a negative one.''—Dr. Walter L. Stone

''. . . the pursuits of leisure are great social levelers.''—David Gray and Donald Pelegrino

**FIGURE 8.8**    An example of a values sheet related to the topic of leisure.

to select a value that they hold in high esteem and then to write a contract stating something they can do to demonstrate actively their support for, and commitment to, their value. A participant who states, for example, that he or she values the notion of preservation of the environment might write a contract that he or she will save newspapers at home for one week and deposit them at a recycling station, thereby contributing to the conservation of natural resources. Such self-contracts can be written to encourage some new value-based behavior (such as the saving of newspapers) or to establish commitment to discontinue some old behavior (such as wasting electricity).

All these techniques used in values clarification, of course, lead toward the same goal. Although they involve slightly different approaches, they all attempt to help individuals consider what they value within their lives and what values they feel are personally acceptable and could provide guidance. Typically, these techniques are used in conjunction with one another. For example, the leader might ask participants to engage in exercises that induce them to suggest values toward which they might be inclined, and then follow up with questions or clarifying statements that help participants further define their thoughts and values. In recreation and leisure service programs and activities, however, the use of prepared materials and exercises might not always be appropriate. Depending on the setting, the leader might use such materials or exercises or might use clarifying responses only. In other words, the leader should attempt to use the information provided regarding values education and values clarification creatively and adapt it to the needs of individual program and activity settings.

## SUMMARY

The organization that recognizes its role and the role of its staff in participants' formulation of values can use the values education concept to help participants enrich their lives in a very special way. Often individuals will accept values as their own without having given any real thought to them. Many individuals accept the values of their parents, friends, spouses, or neighbors without consideration of their belief in, or commitment to, such values. Also, individuals often remain "valueless" in certain areas of their lives because they haven't stopped to think about related values.

Any leader of recreation and leisure service programs and activities can help individuals "think" about their values by using values education guidelines and simple values clarification techniques. The benefits to the participant involved in values education can be great. With assistance by the leader, they may be able to clarify and develop values that they will be able to use throughout their lives. They may also develop an awareness of the importance of critical thinking prior to accepting values as their own. Finally, participants may also learn to establish priorities in their lives. They may be able to determine which of their values are most important to them and should be the focus of their attention and energy.

## DISCUSSION QUESTIONS

1. What is values education? How does it apply to recreation and leisure settings?
2. What are values?
3. Is values education either value laden or value free?
4. What roles does the recreation and leisure service leader play in the values education process?
5. What is the direct-programmatic approach to values education? Direct-integrative approach? Indirect approach?
6. What is values clarification?

7. What are some techniques that can be used in the process of values clarification?

8. What values do you think the recreation and leisure service profession promotes?

9. Based on your experience as a recreation leader, give an example of a situation in which you feel that you influenced the values of a participant or participants.

10. Based on what you have learned, reading this chapter, how would you have changed your behavior or interaction with the participant or participants in the above situation?

11. After viewing the five values-clarifying strategies presented in this chapter, can you formulate a values-clarifying strategy of your own?

# 9

# THE LEADER AS INSTRUCTOR

This leader uses the technique of ''demonstration'' in leading this instructional activity.

Recreation and leisure service organizations play an important role in assisting individuals to acquire knowledge and skills related to the use of leisure. Many programs provided by recreation and leisure service organizations find the leader providing instruction to individuals in one or more of a wide variety of leisure activities. We might find a leader providing instruction in knitting, ceramics, bridge, kayaking, basketball, soccer, fishing, fly tying, swimming, skating, gymnastics, oil painting, drama, and many other leisure activities.

Although the recreation leader who provides instruction in a given activity must be competent in the activity area itself, he or she must also, and perhaps more importantly, have an understanding of the learning process in order to instruct effectively. Furthermore, it is important that the leader acknowledge the fact that situational factors will affect the way that the instructional process should be structured. Instructional programs for adults should differ from instructional programs for children, for example. Certification programs that require the mastery of specific competencies may be structured differently from instructional programs that enable the learner to ''take what he or she wants'' from the experience. Participants involved in a beginning level course will have different expectations from individuals involved in an advanced level course.

## LEARNING AND INSTRUCTION

Learning is a natural process. Individuals in their daily lives are continually trying to "figure things out." As a natural process, learning is self-directed, occurring at the discretion of the individual. The process of learning may not only affect the individual cognitively, but may also affect the individual emotionally as well.

The learning process is usually preceded by such feelings within an individual as interest, a desire to be creative, possibly confusion, or a desire to explore or a combination of these. Such feelings may prompt the individual to seek out answers, resolution of conflict, or new insights and experiences. At this point the individual may make discoveries and integrate the new information obtained from his or her experiences with previous perceptions. *Thus, we can think of learning as "a change in an individual's thoughts, emotion or action that results from previous experience."*[1] The process of learning may occur in such a way that we don't know that it has occurred; we may not know that we are learning and changing. On the other hand, learning may represent a very conscious effort on the part of the individual. For example, the child who participates in a recreation program to learn basketball skills has made a conscious effort to learn about this topic. However, the child might also learn values regarding fair play, teamwork, and hard work, unaware that he or she has "learned."

What is the relationship between learning and instruction? *Instruction is the communication of skills knowledge or values.* It is a process that helps the participant learn. Recreation and leisure instruction can be formal or informal,

can occur in a variety of settings, and can be performed by various types of leaders. The host or guide is involved in instruction, as is the coach who teaches athletic skills, the arts and crafts instructor teaching in a traditional classroom setting, and the camp counselor who imparts knowledge related to living skills in the outdoors. All these types of leaders are communicating or imparting knowledge to participants.

Regardless of the type of instructional activity involved, certain elements must be present in the learning environment for the instructional process to be effective. These elements are meaningfulness, supportive social climate, noncoercive participation, and effective communication.

*Meaningfulness.* The learning experience must be personally meaningful to individuals if they are to participate in it actively. If an instructional experience is meaningful to individuals, they will be motivated to learn. This criterion is often initially met within the recreation and leisure instructional setting since participants take part in such activities because they want to, indicating a personal interest, desire, or need. To make experiences meaningful, the instructor must base his or her instruction on the experience, skill level, and perceptions of the participant. Often this means that the participant will help the leader, either directly or indirectly, to structure or shape the content to be explored as well as the processes used to explore the content.

*Supportive Social Climate.* Learning in recreation and leisure service environments requires the existence of a supportive social climate. The instructional leader should actively encourage and support participants and show sincere concern for their development. In the recreation and leisure service profession, we value instructional efforts that are positive in nature and do not resort to ridiculing, belittling, ignoring, or otherwise dealing with participants in a negative manner. A supportive

[1] Ian Robertson, *Sociology* (New York: Worth Publishers, 1977), p. 101.

social climate is one in which affirmation is given to the existence of each person as an individual, recognizing his or her unique qualities. This means treating each participant with respect and dignity and valuing each individual's input, interest, and concerns.

*Noncoercive Participation.*    Unlike the case in formal schooling, participation in instructional programs provided by recreation and leisure service organizations is both voluntary and characterized by a sense of perceived freedom. Participants engage in recreation and leisure instructional activities because they want to be there. If they do not enjoy the experience or find it satisfying, there is no coercive mechanism to keep them in an instructional activity. As such, recreation and leisure service organizations do not share the yoke of coercion that is carried by many formal educational programs and activities.

*Effective Communication.*    Communication in an instructional setting should be a two-way process. Not only should the instructional leader communicate information to the participant, but, if the instructional process is to be effective, participants should feel free to interact with the leader as well and communicate their questions, feelings, and ideas. In addition, the instructional leader must choose instructional methods that will effectively communicate the knowledge, skills, or values that he or she wishes to convey. For example, there are many leisure activities, such as swimming, that must be demonstrated in order to be ''learned'' by participants.

Finally, the instructional leader must communicate with participants in a way that is understandable to them and that acknowledges their level of skill and expertise. For example, the leader instructing elementary school children in beginning archery will use different language and teaching techniques from those that the leader who is instructing adults in a similar program will use.

*Collaboration and Cooperation.*    Collaboration and cooperation suggest that the leader should cooperate with the participant and vice versa. It also suggests that the learning process is a collaborative one, implying a sense of sharing, giving, and interaction rather than a process in which the instructional leader dictates, directs, or controls. The most meaningful instructional experiences are those in which the participant has some input.

All these elements are necessary for an effective instructional experience and can be found within recreation and leisure service settings. Consequently, recreation and leisure service instructional programs are unusually conducive to learning. Meaningful experiences, participated in without coercion and within environments that allow cooperation and collaboration and that affirm the individual dignity of each person, provide a very powerful motivation for learning.

## APPROACHES TO INSTRUCTION

There are two major approaches to the instructional process: the *humanistic* approach and the *systems* approach. The humanistic approach to education focuses on the development and personal growth of *each* individual. Humanistic education is process oriented, suggesting that there is a strong need for the participant and the leader to interact in order to determine appropriate instructional strategies and goals. The systems approach to instruction grew out of the accountability movement of the 1970s. It is based on the notion that there are behaviors or competencies that can be identified, demonstrated, and measured that indicate proficiency in a given skill or knowledge area. Competency statements regarding these behaviors are written as behavioral or performance objectives. These behavioral or performance objectives state the specific behavior that the participant is expected to demonstrate upon conclusion of involvement in a program or sequence of learning activities. With the systems approach, then, an individual's achievement is measured against an external criterion reference standard. As such, it is product oriented, as opposed to being process oriented. The writing of behavioral or performance objectives will be discussed in more detail later in this chapter.

Which approach is better? The humanistic approach or the systems approach? Both have advantages and disadvantages. The humanistic approach, focused on the development of each individual, views the learning process as being open-ended and evolving. This approach may allow for more creativity and flexibility. It encourages individuals to explore beyond any externally placed limits. On the other hand, the systems approach encourages the development of precise objectives that structure the learning process so that the participant exits the learning environment having achieved clearly defined outcomes. Furthermore, the systems approach, being more highly structured than the humanistic approach, is more efficient. A group of participants can be guided through a program of activity, for example, and all can achieve certain competencies whereas, when the humanistic approach is used, the needs of each individual may preclude the ability of the group to move ahead as a whole.

In recreation and leisure service organizations do we use the humanistic approach or the systems approach of instruction? The answer is that we use them both. Many instructional programs are humanistic in nature and concerned with the development and creativity of the individual. As a result they must be open and expansive and must allow a great deal of flexibility. Instructional classes in the arts very often encourage this type of participant behavior. Furthermore, the leisure experience itself is open-ended, free, and expansive and allows the individual to explore his or her potential without external constraints. On the other hand, an instructional class may be designed to help participants attain certain predetermined competencies. A systems approach to instruction might be more appropriate in this situation. For example, in teaching swimming or wilderness survival skills, the instructor is attempting to ensure that participants achieve certain well-defined skills. These skills may be directly related to the safety, survival, or well-being of the individual. The recreation and leisure service leader, then, should choose an instructional approach that is tied to the goals he or she desires to achieve.

## ORGANIZING THE INSTRUCTIONAL EFFORT

The organization of instructional activities in recreation and leisure service organizations is often haphazard at best. Few organizations have a systematic process or plan that guides instructional leaders in the formulation of their roles, learning objectives, goals, or selection of their instructional strategies or procedures. Even if a recreation and leisure service organization does not have criteria to guide the development of instructional programs, the leader should take the initiative and ask himself or herself some basic questions, such as these.

- *What are the goals of instruction*? To have participants achieve certain competencies? To have participants expand their awareness and creativity as individuals? Will the humanistic approach to instruction or the systems approach to instruction better help participants meet the goals?
- *Who are the participants*? What are their ages? Sex? Level of maturity? Motivation? Skill level? Degree of interest?
- *What does the participant want to learn*? What are his or her expectations? What is the participant's purpose for being involved in the program?
- *What do I, the leader, want the participant to learn*? What are my expectations? What do

I want the content of the instructional activity to be? What are the expectations of the organization? Are there expectations of other organizations that I want participants to meet (i.e., Red Cross certification)? What are my motives?

- *What instructional strategy should be used to teach participants?* Should drills be used? Lectures? Experiential education? Discussion groups?

- *How will the instructional content be organized?* Should skills or knowledge to be taught be broken into component parts? Should I teach the parts of the whole first? If so, what would these component parts be?

- *What setting should be used for instruction?* A classroom? A gymnasium? A swimming pool? A tennis court? Indoors or outdoors?

- *What resources are needed for instruction?* Films? Workbooks? Equipment? Other materials or supplies? Human resources—assistants or coleaders?

- *When should the instruction take place?* What season? What time of the day? How long? One hour per week? Every day? Once a month?

- *How will I evaluate whether participants have achieved the goals?* Will I give tests? Will participants be asked to demonstrate a skill? Will participants be asked to show me a final product? Will I need to talk to participants and get input and feedback from them as to whether or not they have achieved the goals?

- *How will I evaluate my own performance as an instructor?* Should I ask participants to evaluate me? Should the organization evaluate my efforts? Does the degree of success of participants reflect my competence as an instructor? Should I get feedback from assistants or co-workers? Should I conduct a self-evaluation based on information from all these sources?

Some of these questions are relatively simple to answer. For example, it might be relatively easy to determine the age and sex of partici-

pants for whom an instructional activity has been designed. On the other hand, it might be more difficult to determine their motivation, expectations, and level of maturity. However, answers to these questions can provide the leader with a basic outline that can be used to guide the development of an instructional activity.

## DEVELOPING INSTRUCTIONAL OBJECTIVES

The leader organizing an instructional activity should first consider the development of instructional objectives. Usually, objectives are written as performance or behavioral objectives; that is, they describe the actual behavior that is expected of participants upon exiting the activity. The use of performance or behavioral objectives is especially important when using the systems approach to instruction; however, it is also recommended that objectives be used for instructional activities based on the humanistic approach. Instructional objectives must be written in terms of behavior that can be observed by the leader. Although other learning may take place, only observable behavior can be measured.

Edginton and Hayes have suggested that there are basically four factors that must be considered in the development of performance objectives. They are the following: (1) What must be known or done by the participant? (2) How is the participant to demonstrate the behavior? (3) What special conditions or circumstances may affect the acquisition of a special behavior? (4) What is the minimum level of achievement of a participant's performance?[2] Figure 6.6 of Chapter 6 describes how to write objectives. It states that the leader should define the desired end results and state these with an action verb. For example, "To throw the ball" is a per-

[2]Christopher R. Edginton and Gene A. Hayes, "Using Performance Objectives in the Delivery of Recreation Services," *Journal of Leisureability,* Vol. 3, No. 4 (October 1976), p. 21.

formance objective that can be demonstrated, observed, and measured.

In the past several decades there have been a number of learning taxonomies that have been developed that can be of help in the writing of performance or behavioral objectives. These learning taxonomies are based on the notion that the learning process is progressive and moves upward from one level to another. Three taxonomies have been developed that deal with *cognitive* behavior, *psychomotor* behavior, and *affective* behavior. Cognitive behaviors refer to those behaviors that are concerned with intellectual processes; psychomotor behaviors refer to those behaviors that are concerned with physical skills; and affective behavior refers to those behaviors that are concerned with attitudes, emotions, or interests. Tables 9.1, 9.2, and 9.3 present the major categories of learning in each of these areas of behavior. These categories are often referred to as "behavioral domains."

How are these taxonomies used? The leader of an instructional activity or program might use this information to structure the learning process so that it is relevant to participants. For example, the leader conducting an activity emphasizing the psychomotor domain could write objectives that would find the participant first observing the activity, then imitating the activity, then practicing the activity through repeated steps and finally adapting the activity to his or her own needs and style. A more specific example of this might be an individual who is learning a tennis stroke. He or she would first observe, then imitate, then practice until the process became routine, and then adapt the skill to his or her own style. Objectives can be written to emphasize one or all of the steps in this process, depending upon the goals of the instructional program.

The instructional process can also be broken down in terms of the component parts of the actual skill or knowledge involved. *It is often easier for participants to learn if the component parts of a skill or area of knowledge are presented one at a time and then merged to form the whole.* For ex-

**TABLE 9.1**    Levels of the Cognitive Domain

| Knowledge | Comprehension | Application | Analysis | Synthesis | Evaluation |
|---|---|---|---|---|---|
| (ability to recall; to bring to mind the appropriate material) | (ability to comprehend what is being communicated and make use of the idea without relating it to other ideas or material or seeing fullest meaning) | (ability to use ideas, principles, theories in new particular and concentrated situations) | (ability to break down a communication into constituent parts in order to make organization of the whole clear) | (ability to put together parts and elements into a unified organization or whole) | (ability to judge the value of ideas, procedures, methods, using appropriate criteria) |
| | | | | | Requires synthesis |
| | | | | Requires analysis | Requires analysis |
| | | | Requires application | Requires application | Requires application |
| | | Requires comprehension | Requires comprehension | Requires comprehension | Requires comprehension |
| | Requires knowledge | Requires knowledge | Requires knowledge | Requires knowledge | Requires knowledge |

*Source:* From *Taxonomy of Educational Objectives: Handbook I: Cognitive Domain* by Benjamin S. Bloom et al. Copyright © 1956 by Longman Inc. Reprinted by permission of Longman, Inc., New York.

**TABLE 9.2**    Levels of the Affective Domain

| Receiving | Responding | Valuing | Organization | Characterization |
|---|---|---|---|---|
| | | | | (generalizes certain values into controlling tendencies; emphasis on internal consistency; later integrates these into a total philosophy of life or world view) |
| | | | (organizes values; determines interrelationships; adapts behavior to value system) | |
| | | (accepts worth of a thing, an idea, or a behavior; prefers it; consistent in responding; develops a commitment to it) | | Requires organization of values |
| (attending; becomes aware of an idea, process, or thing; is willing to notice a particular phenomenon) | (makes response at first with compliance, later willingly and with satisfaction) | | Requires development of values | Requires development of values |
| | | Requires a response | Requires a response | Requires a response |
| | Begins with attending | Begins with attending | Begins with attending | Begins with attending |

*Source:*    From *Taxonomy of Educational Objectives: Handbook II: Affective Domain* by David R. Krathwohl et al. Copyright © 1964 by Longman Inc. Reprinted by permission of Longman, Inc., New York.

**TABLE 9.3**    Levels of the Psychomotor Domain

| Observing | Imitating | Practicing | Adapting |
|---|---|---|---|
| (watches process; pays attention to steps or techniques and to finished product or behavior; may read directions) | (follows directions; carries out steps with conscious awareness of efforts, performs hesitantly) | (repeats steps until some or all aspects of process become **habitual**, requiring little conscious effort, performs smoothly) | (makes individual modifications and adaptations in the process to suit the worker and/or the situation) |
| | | | Requires practice |
| | Requires observation, or reading of directions | Requires imitation | Requires imitation |
| | | Requires observation, or reading of directions | Requires observation, or reading of directions |

*Source:*    From *A Taxonomy of the Psychomotor Domain: A Guide for Developing Behavioral Objectives* by Anita J. Harrow. Copyright © 1972 by Longman Inc. Reprinted with permission of Longman, Inc., New York.

ample, an individual instructing participants in a tennis serve might first teach them how to stand, then how to throw the ball for the serve, then how to hold the racquet prior to the serve swing, then how to swing the racquet in an arc as if to serve, and finally how to merge all these individual components of the serve into an integrated and simultaneous movement that is "a serve."

## INSTRUCTIONAL STRATEGIES

The selection of an appropriate instructional strategy is perhaps one of the most important considerations of the leader. There are numerous instructional strategies that can be employed. The leader should carefully choose one that will complement the goals of the instructional effort, as well as the content to be covered. For example, some skills must be demonstrated whereas other information is best presented in a lecture format or discussion format. Wiles and Bondi have identified 22 instructional strategies that are used in school systems. These can be adapted for use in most instructional programs, however. Their list includes the following.

- *Comparative Analysis.* A thought process, structured by the leader, that employs the description, classification, and analysis of more than one system, group, or the like in order to ascertain and evaluate similarities and differences.
- *Conference.* A one-to-one interaction between leader and participant where the individual's needs and problems can be dealt

One-to-one interaction is occurring between this participant and the leader. This is known as the "conference" approach to instruction.

with. Diagnosis, evaluation, and prescription may all be involved.

- *Demonstration.* An activity in which the leader or another person uses examples, experiments, or other actual performance or a combination of these to illustrate a principle or show others how to do something.
- *Diagnosis.* The continuous determination of the nature of learning difficulties and deficiencies, used in teaching as a basis for the selection, day by day or moment by moment, of appropriate content and methods of instruction.
- *Directed Observation.* Guided observation provided for the purpose of improving the study, understanding, and evaluation of that which is observed.
- *Discussion.* An activity in which participants, under leader or other participant direction or both, exchange points of view concerning a topic, question, or problem to arrive at a decision or conclusion.
- *Drill.* An orderly, repetitive learning activity intended to help develop or fix a specific skill or aspect of knowledge.
- *Experimentation.* An activity involving a planned procedure accompanied by control of conditions or controlled variation of conditions (or both) together with observation of results for the purpose of discovering relationships and evaluating the reasonableness of a specific hypothesis.
- *Field Experience.* Educational work experience, sometimes fully paid, acquired by participants in a practical service situation.
- *Field Trip.* An educational trip to places where participants can study the content of instruction directly in its functional setting, for example, factory, newspaper office, or fire department.
- *Group Work.* A process in which members of the class, working cooperatively rather than individually, formulate and work toward common objectives under the guidance of one or more leaders.

- *Laboratory Experience*. Learning activities carried on by participants in a laboratory designed for individual or group study of a particular subject-matter area, involving the practical application of theory through observation, experimentation, and research or, in the case of foreign language instruction, involving learning through demonstration, drill, and practice. This applies also to the study of art and music although such activity in this instance may be referred to as a studio experience.
- *Lecture*. An activity in which the leader gives an oral presentation of facts or principles, the class frequently being responsible for note-taking. This activity usually involves little or no pupil participation by questioning or discussion.
- *Manipulative and Tactile Activity*. Activity by which participants utilize the movement of various muscles and the sense of touch to develop manipulative or perceptual skills or both.
- *Modeling and Imitation*. An activity frequently used for instruction in speech, in which the participants listen to and observe a model as a basis upon which to practice and improve their performance.
- *Problem Solving*. A thought process structured by the teacher and employed by the participants for clearly defining a problem, forming hypothetical solutions, and possibly testing the hypothesis.
- *Programmed instruction*. Instruction utilizing a workbook or mechanical or electronic device (or a combination) that has been programmed by (a) providing instruction in small steps, (b) asking one or more questions about each step in the instruction and providing instant knowledge of whether each answer is right or wrong, and (c) enabling participants to progress at their own pace.
- *Project*. A significant, practical unit of activity having educational value, aimed at one or more definite goals of understanding

and involving the investigation and solution of problems.
- *Reading*. Gathering information from books, periodicals, encyclopedias, and other printed sources of information, including oral reading and silent reading by individuals.
- *Recitation*. Activities devoted to reporting to a class or other group about information acquired through individual study or group work.
- *Role Play*. An activity in which participants or leaders take on the behavior of a hypothetical or real personality in order to solve a problem and gain insight into a situation.
- *Seminar*. An activity in which a group of pupils, engaged in research or advanced study, meets under the general direction of one or more staff members for a discussion of problems of mutual interest.[3]

In addition to these instructional strategies, the leader will also want to use other instructional materials that complement or enhance the learning process. Materials such as films, tape recordings, slide presentations, computer-assisted instruction, and use of the television are all examples of instructional materials that can aid in the learning process. The leader will want to use a blend of instructional strategies and materials to achieve the goals or objectives toward which he or she is aiming.

## DEVELOPING A LESSON PLAN

Generally speaking, the leader will want to develop not only a statement of objectives, a list of course content, and instructional strategies, but also a lesson plan. A lesson plan should outline the important points to be covered in sequential order during each time that the instructional activity meets. A class-by-class instructional plan helps the leader organize the information to be imparted to participants so that the information to be covered is

[3]John Wiles and Joseph Bondi, *Curriculum Development: A Guide to Practice* (Columbus: Merrill, 1979), pp. 171–172.

in the proper progression and all information is covered within the time allotted. By using a lesson plan, the leader can also determine whether each class has enough content, or too much. This is not to suggest that the leader will not interact with participants spontaneously and in an extemporaneous manner. There are always "teachable moments" that the leader will use to emphasize a point effec-

tively. Some of the items that might be included in a lesson plan for a particular instructional period include objectives; step by step, the content to be covered; important questions to be asked; materials and supplies to be used; and future assignments. Figures 9.1 and 9.2 are examples of general instructional plans used by the River Road (Oregon) Park and Recreation District.

---

Name of class:__*BASIC ITALIC CALLIGRAPHY*__

Your name:__*Louise E. Grunewald*__

Phone #:__*686-9832*__

Complete Address:__*1258 High Street, Suite 2, Eugene, OR 97401*__

Age Group(s) the class is for:__*high school through adult*__

Descriptive Paragraph of your class: (this may be printed in the brochure!)

*This class is an introduction to the Italic alphabet, beginning with monoline and progressing to the broad-edged pen. Emphasis will be on a thorough understanding of the letterforms of this alphabet style and use of the basic materials and tools which are a part of the art of calligraphy. Two sessions will include instruction in layout and design for putting the alphabet to use in creating a finished piece.*

Class Outline:

*8 sessions:*

1. *Monoline lower case*
2. *Monoline upper case*
3. *Broad-edged pen lower case*
4. *Broad-edged pen upper case*
5. *Broad-edged upper and lower/numbers/words/paragraphs*
6. *Layout/design—intro, slides*
7. *Layout/design—in-class project*
8. *Flourishes, etc.*

Time, day, dates available to teach? How many class hours needed daily? Number of classes needed?

*Wednesday evenings 7–9 pm.*
*8 classes*

List and cost of supplies needed for class (if any)?

*collegeruled notebook paper, fine point felt tip pen(s), #2 pencil, 2 ½ mm brause pen nib and holder, white bond paper, ink, book: Italic Calligraphy and Handwriting by Lloyd Reynolds. Total cost about $7. They can bring felt tip pen and ruled notebook paper the first night and I will give them a supply list for next sessions.*

(Continued on next page)

Minimum and maximum number of students?

*10 minimum/20 maximum*

Hourly rate or percentage rate of pay? how much?

*$12.50 or however % can work out to that rate (that is minimum rate)*

Other:

Any questions call Michael or Dale at 688–4052.

Thank you.

River Road Park and Recreation District is an equal opportunity employer.

**FIGURE 9.1**   Instructional Plan: River Road (Oregon) Park and Recreation District

Name of class:   *SCRIMSHAW: THE WHALER'S ART*

Your name:   *NEIL FRYER*

Phone #:   *461–0032*

Complete Address:   *340 Figueroa, Eugene, OR 97402*

Age Group(s) the class is for:   *open*

Descriptive Paragraph of your class: (this may be printed in the brochure!)

*Classically, scrimshaw is etching on ivory. In this class we'll take a look at scrimshaw from past to present. We'll be learning how to "scratch" on micardasynthetic ivory. The student will learn the techniques used in creating black and white and colored scrimshaw.*

Class Outline:

    *I. Scrimshaw: History and overview*
    *II. Preparing the "ivory"*
    *III. Black and white techniques of scrimshaw*
    *IV. Color techniques of scrimshaw*
    *V. Kinds and sources of ivory*

Time, day, dates available to teach? How many class hours needed daily? Number of classes needed?

*7–10 pm on Tues, Wed, or Thur*
*10 weeks*
*(I am also teaching two other classes with you.)*

List and cost of supplies needed for class (if any)?

*"Higgins" ink—black*
*"Pelican" ink—black, red, yellow, blue*

*10 square inches of micarda/student*
*(@.50¢ per sq. inch)*

ONE SET OF INK PER CLASS IS ALL THAT IS NECESSARY

Minimum and maximum number of students?

*13 minimum, maximum to room capacity*

Hourly rate or percentage rate of pay? how much?

*80%*

Other:

*recommend $15/student + lab fee*

Any questions call Michael or Dale at 688–4052.

Thank you.

River Road Park and Recreation District is an equal opportunity employer.

**FIGURE 9.2**   Instructional Plan: River Road (Oregon) Park and Recreation District

## SUMMARY

Learning is a natural process, in which all individuals engage. Instruction is a way of communicating skills, knowledge or values or a combination of these to participants to aid them in the learning process. A number of conditions must be present in recreation and leisure service settings for effective instructional activities to occur. These include meaningful content, supportive social climate, noncoercive participation, effective communication, collaboration, and cooperation. There are two basic instructional approaches that can be used to develop instructional programs and activities: the humanistic approach and the systems approach. The humanistic approach is process oriented whereas the systems approach is product oriented. Both are used in recreation and leisure service settings.

## DISCUSSION QUESTIONS

1. Define learning. What is the relationship between learning and instruction?
2. What elements must be present in the learning environment for the learning process to be effective?
3. Identify and describe the two major approaches to instruction. How are they used in recreation and leisure service settings?
4. What factor should one consider in organizing instructional programs?
5. What learning taxonomies have been developed to assist in the use of performance objectives?
6. Identify, define, and provide examples of ten instructional strategies used in recreation and leisure settings.

# 10

# THE SELF-DIRECTED PROGRAM

These adults, participating in a dance program, might best be served by andragogical approach to programming.

From a historical perspective, much of the training of professionals in the area of recreation leadership has focused on helping them develop skills to lead children. In fact, as a profession we have become highly skilled in organizing and leading playground programs, camps for youth, youth sports programs, and youth clubs and groups such as scouting, YMCAs, and so on. Do the strategies and techniques that we use in leading these programs work effectively with other age groups? Or should leadership training include information regarding techniques and skills that can be used in working with other age groups, such as adults? In this chapter we will explore the process of working with adults as a recreation and leisure service leader.

As a profession, we are witnessing a dramatic shift in our constituency. As a result, we are being asked to alter dramatically not only the types of services we provide, but also the way in which these services are being presented. This change in services has occurred because of massive demographic shifts in the population of North American society from a majority of youth to a majority of adults. As Sessoms has written, ". . . changes in the age composition of the population . . . challenge the park and recreation profession and require a new orientation if the system is to remain vital. We live in an adult oriented society. Recreation and park professionals must come to grips with programming for adults. They constitute the largest segment of the population. They will pay for services vital to their lifestyle, but will not support those systems perceived as nonresponsive or dysfunctional."[1]

## DEMOGRAPHIC CHANGES

Almost all the recreation agencies mentioned in the previous paragraphs started at the turn of the century. Many new agencies, institutions, and organizations emerged as a result of societal concerns for children's labor conditions, immigration problems, the educa-

[1]H. Douglas Sessoms, "Adult Programming," *Leisure Today,* October 1981, p. 24.

tional system, and crowded urban conditions with a lack of play areas. At that time, adults, the majority of whom were in the work force, did not have the concept of leisure during discretionary time that we find today. The work week entailed long hours and extended into Saturday afternoons in many cases. Off-the-job time, by necessity, was devoted to self-maintenance activities. There were no work-saving devices, immediately available markets, and shopping centers or rapid transit systems. The majority of Sundays, for most people, were spent in religious activity. In short, people had to work hard to survive. All in all, society was not concerned with providing opportunities for leisure programs during the non-working time of adults.

According to Thorstein Veblen in *Theory of The Leisure Class* (1899), the wealthy families in the late 1800s demonstrated a conspicuousness in their consumption of leisure activities and in owning leisure-related goods such as horses, kennels, tennis courts, carriages, and separate summer homes. These individuals were independently wealthy and, according to Veblen, produced nothing for society, thus being labeled as "the leisure class." With the leisure class not having a need for leisure or-

ganizations and agencies and with the working class spending their nonwork time in home, self-care, and church-related activities, the need for leisure programs for adults lagged far behind the need for children's programs.

Toward the end of the twentieth century, the shift in population and the relative ease in meeting the needs of day-to-day living amenities have resulted in more opportunities for adults to participate in enjoyable experiences in their off-the-job hours. Table 10.1 presents estimates of the population of the United States, according to age groups, for 1970, 1980, and predictions for 1990. Underhill has suggested that this table presents two significant findings. The first is that the population is growing older. For example, in 1970 the percentage of the population that was 65 and above was 10 percent of our total population. In 1990, it is predicted that 19 percent of the total population will be 65 or older. In actual numbers these figures represent an increase of 30 million in this older age category. The second significant finding is the growth in population of those individuals who were born between 1946 and 1964. This is known as the baby boom generation. As one can see, by re-

**TABLE 10.1**   Total U.S. Population 1970–1980–1990 by Age Group (in millions)

|  | Total | 0–19 | 20–34 | 35–49 | 50–64 | 65 + |
|---|---|---|---|---|---|---|
| 1970 | 209 | 76.8 | 45.6 | 34.8 | 30.7 | 20.9 |
|  | 100% | 37% | 22% | 17% | 14% | 10% |
| 1980 | 240 | 69.5 | 61.2 | 40.2 | 43.8 | 36.3 |
|  | 100% | 29% | 25% | 17% | 13% | 16% |
| 1970–1989 Percent change | + 15% | – 10% | + 34% | + 15% | + 7% | + 73% |
| 1990 | 265 | 64.5 | 62.2 | 51.5 | 35.8 | 51 |
|  | 100% | 24% | 23% | 20% | 14% | 19% |
| 1980–1990 Percent change | + 10% | – 7% | – 1.5% | + 28% | + 9% | + 40% |
| 1970–1990 Percent change | + 27% | – 16% | + 36% | + 48% | + 16% | + 144% |

*Source:*   A. H. Underhill, "Population Dynamics and Demography," *Leisure Today*, October 1981, p. 4. This table is reprinted with permission from the *Journal of Physical Education, Recreation and Dance*, October, 1981, p.34, American Alliance of Health, Physical Education, Recreation and Dance.

viewing this chart, as the baby boom generation passes through its life span, it expands
each age category through which it moves.
(See Table 10.1.)

Discussing the baby boom generation,
Jones has written, "No single generation has
had more impact on us than the baby boom,
and no single person has been untouched.
The baby boom is, and will continue to be,
the decisive generation in our history."[2] This
factor alone is a major motivating force in the
development of this chapter. It stands to reason that the values and attitudes of this generation toward work and leisure have and will
continue to have impact upon society as a
whole. As the baby boom generation moves
from its tempetuous youth in the 1960s to its
adult phase, new leisure behaviors and patterns will emerge. It also stands to reason
that, if existing organizations are to survive,
they will need to adapt their services to meet
the needs of this segment of the population. In
addition, we will undoubtedly see many new
organizations and agencies emerging to respond to this group as it evolves.

## PEDAGOGY AND ANDRAGOGY— THE DIFFERENCES

The leadership techniques for children's leisure activities have been based historically on
educational theory and practice. The art and
science of working with children is labeled
*pedagogy*, from the Greek stem *paid* or "child"
and *agogus* meaning "guiding or leading."
While the word originally referred to children, common use has led to dropping the reference to child, and usually people assume
that the word pedagogy means "teaching"
regardless of age. The word *andragogy* was introduced in Germany in 1883 and brought to
the United States by Malcolm Knowles in the
mid-1960s. The word comes from the Greek

stem *andr* (adult) and the classical group noun
*agoge* (leading). Thus, today *pedagogy refers to
the art and science of teaching children* whereas *andragogy refers to the process of helping adults learn or
facilitating self-directed leisure activities.* In the
broadest sense, when the principles of pedagogy and andragogy are applied, the reference to age is often dropped. Thus, the term
*pedagogy* is often used in situations involving
teaching or leading *others* whereas *andragogy* is
often used in reference to *self-directed* programs.

There are a number of differences between
leader-directed and self-directed learning.
These are shown in Table 10.2 as adapted
from the field of education. It should be understood that this dichotomy is based on a
continuum, not as an either-or situation, and
that in groups, individuals may be at various
points on the continuum. However, on the
whole, children are more likely to be on the
left side of the continuum and adults on the
right side of the continuum. For example,
the two-year-old is not very self-directed compared to the 22-year-old. The less mature the
individual, the more pedagogical the leader's
approach should be; the more mature the individual, the less pedagogical the leader's approach should be. Because of their lack of maturity, limited experiences, interest in the
present, and lack of ability to be self-directing, most children are assumed to exhibit
leader-directed behaviors. Whereas adults
usually exhibit behaviors on the self-directed
side of the continuum. Some adults, however,
may select a leader-directed leisure experience similar to that of a child because of an interest in a specific topic, specific activity, a desire for an extrinsic reward, or a lack of earlier
experience. Teenagers may exhibit both
leader-directed and self-directed behaviors. It
is possible to say, then, that they would likely
fall within a wide area in the middle of the
continuum.

The first set of assumptions in Table 10.2
regarding *perception of the participant* refers to
the fact that the leader-directed participant is

[2]Landon Y. Jones, *Great Expectations: America and the Baby Boom Generation* (New York: Ballantine Books, 1980), p. 1.

**TABLE 10.2**   A Comparison of Assumptions of Leader-Directed Behaviors and Self-Directed Behaviors

| Assumptions about | Leader-directed leisure behaviors (usually associated with the instruction of children) | Self-directed leisure behaviors (usually associated with the instruction of adults) |
|---|---|---|
| Perception of the participant | • Dependent upon others | • Self-motivated individual behaviors |
| Status of participants' experience | • Built on progression of earlier experiences leading to selected outcomes | • Based on own past experiences with chance to grow |
| Readiness for new experiences and new learning | • Varies with maturity | • Based on life problems and life tasks |
| Orientation to learning time perspective | • Topic or activity centered for future use | • Task- or problem-oriented. Solutions based on current need. Focus on NOW |
| Motivation | • Extrinsic award (ribbons, badges, trophies) and intrinsic rewards (praise, winning, peer acceptance) | • Intrinsic incentives (personal growth, self-actualization, self-esteem, belonging, fulfilling curiosity) |

viewed as being dependent upon the leader whereas the self-directed participant is self-motivated and self-directed. For example, a child is viewed as being dependent on others whereas adults are usually viewed by others as being self-motivated.

The second set of assumptions regards the status of the experience of participants. Generally, we see leader-directed participants as being inexperienced and thus develop progressive programs to meet their needs. This progression of learning experiences is directed with an eye toward the fact that these participants need *leader-selected* outcomes. The self-directed participant, on the other hand, is generally viewed as having the ability to participate in activities that draw from past experiences and knowledge with a chance to grow as an individual with individually selected goals. On the other hand, with a child, the leader usually engages in one-way communication (from the leader to the participant) because it is assumed that the experience of the leader is a primary resource for the learning of the child. For example, with adults, the leader usually attempts to engage in transactional communication. In this case, the expe-

rience of all, both the leader and the participants, is valued as a resource for the leisure experience. *A Trainer's Guide to Andragogy* points out the differences between the andragogical and pedagogical approaches to education, as they relate to participant experience.

In the tradition of pedagogy, the tendency has been to regard the experiences of children as being of little worth in the educational process. It is probably for this reason that the method of pedagogy has been up to this point at least, largely oriented toward "one-way communication techniques." Andragogy, on the other hand, abounds with "experiential" two-way and multi-directional techniques. In this way the experiences of all participants can be utilized as resources for learning. When students function as teachers and learners at the same time, utilizing their experiences to facilitate the learning process, this difference between andragogy and pedagogy becomes apparent.[3]

In terms of *readiness for new experience and new learning*, the assumptions are that the readi-

[3]John D. Ingalls, *A Trainer's Guide to Andragogy*, Superintendent of Documents, U.S. Government Printing Office, Washington, D.C., 20402, 1973, pp.6,7.

ness of leader-directed participants varies with their level of maturity whereas self-directed participants are all assumed to have reached a similar level of maturity. For example, children are grouped according to ages, classes, skills, and experiences. Adults, on the other hand, group themselves according to their interests and experiences. The adults are ready to identify their own program needs. Adults, however, will select leader-directed programs when they seek new skills or new experiences.

*Orientation to learning and time perspective* refers to the topics or activities learned and the time frame within which they will be used. For the leader-directed participant, leisure behaviors are usually topic or activity centered, for example, playing a game, singing a song, learning a craft, and so on. From the leader's perspective, the topics and activities are being learned for future application and development. For the self-directed participant, many leisure behaviors have a focus on a total project or problem or task. With the solutions based on current need or needs, the focus is problem centered rather than topic centered. For example, a crafts class for children is usually organized to teach the skill as the primary goal of instruction, with the intention that that skill will be used in adult life. On the other hand, an adult program in decoupage may have multiple objectives. For one adult participant, the primary goal may be to acquire a new skill. For another, the primary goal may be socialization, with a secondary goal of skill development. For still another adult participant, the primary goal may be opportunities for creativity.

These two differences regarding orientation to learning and time perspective were described in terms of opposite ends of the continuum in Table 10.2. A leader of adults may find participants at either end of the continuum in the same leisure activity. For example, an activity titled "creative writing" may be attended by individuals who wish to dis-cuss the creative writing attempts of their fellow class members while also socializing. In this case, they are actually discussing their current ability in creative writing. At the same time, there may be an individual in the class who is interested in a highly structured course that develops creative writing skills, topic by topic, because of personal aspirations to become a creative writer. In this case, the leader will be challenged to employ a variety of strategies along the continuum.

Knowles has added a fifth assumption regarding the difference between leader-directed behavior and self-directed behavior, which he terms *motivation*. To Knowles, the motivation for leader-directed activities comes in the form of extrinsic awards such as ribbons, badges, certificates and trophies, as well as the intrinsic rewards of peer acceptance, winning, ego building. For the self-directed participant motivation is usually entirely intrinsic and takes the form of personal growth, self-actualization, self-esteem, belonging, and fulfillment of curiosity.

## PEDAGOGY AND ANDRAGOGY— THE PROCESSES

Leader-directed (pedogogical) techniques may be utilized in situations involving children, adults, and groups of all ages whereas self-directed (andragogical) leadership is generally practiced in adult leisure settings. The seven stage processes for each of these approaches are compared in Table 10.3, adapted from Malcolm Knowles. In the table, *setting*, refers to the physical, interpersonal, and organizational climates under which the program is conducted. In leader-directed leisure, the setting is formal, as in a classroom, organized with predetermined locations for participants, furniture, equipment and so on. It is often competitive with two well-coached teams vying against each other. The leader and often the organization establishes the format for the setting. There is little interpersonal communication.

**TABLE 10.3**    A Comparison of Processes of Leader-Directed Leisure and Self-Directed Leisure

| Elements: | Leader-directed leisure | Self-directed leisure |
|---|---|---|
| Setting | Formal, organized, competitive leader-oriented, judgmental | Informal, equal status, cooperative, supportive, agreement by consensus. Leader facilitates |
| Organization and planning | Primarily by the leader | Through participant decision-making process |
| Asessing interests, needs, and values | Primarily by the leader | By consensus or agreement |
| Goals, outcomes | Primarily leader-set | By negotiation with consensus |
| Planning the sequence of events and activities | By units, by part vs. whole, logical sequence, building purposefully from past events | By projects (whole vs. part) sequencing in terms of personal desire, individual readiness |
| Implementing leisure activities | Techniques, rules, format, transmitted by leaders. Practice drills, assigned steps and projects for earning awards | Independent activities, group projects, discussions, sharing, experiential |
| Evaluation | Primarily by the leader | By mutual group consent, through self-gathered data, by completion of projects |

Adapted from Malcolm Knowles. *Self-Directed Learning* (Chicago: Associated Press, 1975).

In self-directed leisure, the setting is informal. The participants and the leader share an equal status, wherein the leader is a facilitator rather than a director. The furnishings may be comfortable, informal, and arranged by participants. Time is devoted to getting acquainted, sharing ideas, and socializing. The organization is viewed as being cooperative and supportive in establishing the comfort of the group. The physical arrangement is usually decided by consensus rather than by the leader.

The process of *organization planning* within leader-directed leisure settings is almost always implemented by the leader. It is the leader who plans and organizes the activities. In self-directed leisure, the organization of the program occurs with participant involvement in the decision-making process. Examples of leader-directed leisure programs are an art class, a tournament, a team sport coached by a leader, or any activity where a leader structures the format. In a self-directed leisure program, planning is done mutually by the leader and the participant or participants, with the leader involved as a participant in the group.

*Assessing interests, needs, and values,* in a leader-directed leisure program, is a function attended to primarily by the leader. A birthday party for six-year-olds directed by a leader is usually planned according to the *leader's* perceptions of the interests and needs of the participants and based on the leader's values. If this were not the case, six-year-olds might plan too many overly exciting activities, a mixture of indigestible refreshments, and perhaps even dangerous activities.

Self-directed leisure programs involve the *participants* in the assessment of their own leisure interests, needs, and values, which are established by agreement of the group. Using a similar example, groups may plan social events based on mutually agreed upon interests, needs, and values. Because of the maturity of the participant in self-directed activities, it is assumed that the values will be in keeping with societal mores.

In leader-directed leisure settings, *goals and outcomes* are primarily established by the leader whereas in self-directed leisure programs, goals and outcomes are generally established by group negotiation with consensus. In a leader-directed outdoor program, the leader may establish a twelve-mile hike as a goal, which the participants will meet. In a self-directed program, the participants discuss various lengths for the hike and reach an agreement based on consensus of group members.

In planning the *sequence of events and activities*, the leader of a leader-directed leisure experience will plan purposefully, in a logical sequence, the order in which events are to occur. An example of this is a leading plan. The event may be divided into specific units, part by part, each of which contributes to the integral whole. For example, the skills of throwing, catching, batting, running, fielding, and pitching are often led separately before the game of baseball is played as a whole. The sequence of events is planned so that each one builds purposefully on previously learned skills, knowledges, and attitudes.

In self-directed leisure programs, the sequencing of events and activities is conducted in terms of the desires of the group. It is assumed that the group already has a foundation of basic skills on which to build and can undertake projects by starting at any one of a number of steps needed to reach the goal. As a matter of fact, in self-directed leisure programs, because of the wide variety of individual readiness levels, different events and activities may be conducted by segments or portions of the group rather than having everyone follow through step-by-step each of the components of the project. In a baseball game that is self-directed, the group will probably form a team, play awhile, and then analyze what skills need to be reviewed and discuss the best way to do it.

*Implementing* leisure activities requires two different processes. In leader-directed activi-

ties, techniques, rules, and format are transmitted to the participants by the leader. Leaders may assign practice drills or guidebooks or may designate specific steps and projects to be followed for earning badges or awards. The participant follows the instructions or directions designated by the leader. In self-directed leisure activities, the program is often independent of the leader's goals and wishes. The group may divide the program into a variety of activities that are participated in independently by various portions of the group rather than have everyone doing the same thing. The program is implemented through discussions, sharing, and experiential involvement with the leader acting as a facilitator, rather than a director.

*Evaluation* of leader-directed leisure programs is conducted primarily by the leader. It may be expressed in terms of "You did well" or "You have made a lot of improvement" or "You had the best score" or "You have earned your badge." In a self-directed leisure program, evaluation occurs through mutual group consent, with the members of the group stating, "We did well" or "We succeeded," or by having members of the group gathering data that support group evaluation of individual portions of the project, parts of which may be assessed as being better than others. Evaluation here is not so much on the final result or product as it is on the process the group went through to complete the project. Evaluation here is relative to the group's effort in meeting its goals as much as it is to the goals having been met. No one person loses or fails because of a leader or any other individual making that decision. Any individual or any project that is deemed successful merits praise on the basis of group consensus. Success in the self-directed process is measured in terms of the group or individual expectations, not the expectations of the leader.

In the andragogical process, evaluation is not a dead end, but a process that can be used to move on to the assessment of different needs and to find ways to meet them. Rather than being a single-minded orientation toward a judgment and comparison with past events or scores, it is an orientation toward changing the situation to bring about success in the future. In the andragogical process, each individual is measured in terms of his or her ability, not in comparison with others in the group. As long as an individual makes a contribution to the group goals, in keeping with his or her own unique abilities, his or her achievement could be assessed highly. In this process, the unique characteristics of each individual can contribute to the success of the enterprise.

One can never assume that every program will be run entirely either as a leader-directed program or as a self-directed program. A leader-directed leisure *setting* (formal) may be used in a self-directed leisure activity with the group making the decisions in planning, assessing, and goals. On the other hand, the self-directed group may, through consensus or agreement, plan a very logical and purposeful sequence of events and implement precise techniques, rules, and assignments for completing them. The point being made here is that most recreation and leisure leadership with adults occurs with self-directed groups. Although many of the leadership techniques in this text relate to specifics—for example, arts and crafts, games, songs, tournaments, and so forth—the prudent leader should understand that there may need to be some modifications in the leadership process to meet the goals of the self-directed group. It may be a challenge for a leader to understand that a participant in what may appear to be a leader-directed program with an identifiable progression may require some modification of the leadership process so that it meets that participant's self-directed leisure needs.

Because the concept of self-directed activities is relatively new to both educators and leaders in leisure settings, most leaders apply pedagogical methods, and examples of andra-gogical approaches are not yet abundant. For example, a bus tour for older persons may be planned *for* the group using the pedagogical process whereas a more successful trip could be planned *by* the group of participants. The participants might select the route and go through a "dry run" examining possible rest stop sites, contacting restaurants along the way to sample food, and arranging for accommodations for a busload of visitors. They might develop the interpretive message to explain the points of interest and make policies for the trip. The participants-leaders might require that members of the planning committee serve as tour guides and that each one have a current Red Cross first-aid card and cardiopulmonary resuscitation training. The foregoing example of a self-directed trip for older persons is actually implemented at Celeste Campbell Senior Center in Eugene, Oregon, and came about as the result of participant-voiced criticism of being "left out" of the planning process.

Another example of a pedagogical approach that became an andragogical method is that of the nursing home that requested a group of students majoring in recreation to "put on" a Halloween party followed by a birthday party *for* the residents. At the end of the student-directed (pedagogical) second party, several residents announced they could "do it better ourselves." From that time on, the programs were directed by the residents with occasional facilitation by one staff member.

One of the best examples of the conflict between the leader who may be pedagogical and the group that needs an andragogical approach is that of the host-guide or environmental-historical interpreter. In the case of visitors to a national or state park interpretive program, the *setting* may be formal (e.g., a lecture hall, theater, or campfire site), or it may be informal (e.g., a group gathered informally around an exhibit, a family participating in a nature hike, or friends watching a demonstration of candlemaking). To the visitors, however, the setting is always informal, and they may enter or leave a program at any point, regardless of interruption. The visitors may or may not pay attention to the interpreter; they may whisper, laugh, and jostle each other in spite of the leader's desire to maintain a formal setting. The *organization and planning* of the program probably has been done by the leader so that a logical sequence of progression will occur. The visitor, on the other hand, may have planned to spend only a short time in that setting and may ask questions, the answers to which are out of sequence with the planned program.

In the situation of a park interpreter, the *guide or ranger* may have assessed the *needs* of the group to be related to the natural or historic importance of that park. The *actual needs* of the visitor, on the other hand, may relate to a desire for family socialization. Or the visitor's main interest may be in getting away from a cold breeze, finding a restaurant, or even moving on to another park.

In the case of evaluation, the leader may ask, "Did they learn anything?" or "Did I arouse their interest in the topic?" or "Do they now appreciate what is here?" The visitor's evaluation may include, "It was too cold" or "There were too many people" or "I just met someone from my home town!" or "I've got to tell Aunt Harriet about this. She'll love it!"

In the foregoing example, as with many similar situations, leaders are challenged to adjust their pedagogical process to that of andragogy. In each of the six direct-program leadership roles discussed in Chapter 6 as well as in work-oriented leadership situations, there is opportunity to understand the maturity of the participants; their experiences; their readiness for new experiences; their orientation to the activity; and their motivation, needs, and goals with the purpose of following andragogical processes. In time—probably because of the increase in the number of adults participating in leisure programs—the andragogical processes will become as common as pedagogical approaches.

## LEADING ADULTS: SOME IDEAS

Sessoms has indicated that "adults expect to be treated as adults, who make their own decisions about their leisure behavior." What does this mean? What implications does this have for the work of recreation and leisure leaders? From our standpoint, it is evident that there is a great need to use a self-directed leadership style or approach in dealing with adults.

The main articulator of andragogy in the recreation and leisure service field, Gaylene Carpenter, has suggested that this process can be applied to any situation where adults are capable of learning new knowledges.[4] She suggests that the primary function of the recreation and leisure service leader for adults is that of facilitation. Basically, the recreation leader serves as a facilitator, catalyst, enabler, and resource provider, helping individuals gain knowledge of resources necessary for satisfying leisure learning experiences. Carpenter points out the importance of using a reward structure based on internal incentives and curiosity rather than on external rewards and punishments.[5]

If we assume that most adults operate as mature individuals, then use of a leadership style that allows participants to be self-directed would appear to be most appropriate. Table 10.4 presents the maturity-immaturity continuum as developed by Chris Argyris. This model finds leader-directed behavior more appropriate where the individual is operating in an immature state. An immature state is defined as acting passively, depending on others, capable of behaving in few ways,

[4]Gaylene Carpenter, "A Short Course in Andragogy," *California Parks and Recreation*, Summer, 1983, p. 14.

[5]Ibid.

and so on. However, although individuals may initially be in a dependent, passive state, as they gain knowledge or wisdom that increases their level or depth of experience, they may move to a more mature state characterized by independence. At this level, individuals are capable of making decisions that affect their leisure experience. They are capable of self-directed, independent leisure behavior. In addition, they are not only capable of self-directed independent behavior, but they also *require* some control over, or involvement in, decisions affecting the planning, organization, and implementation of the leisure activity in order to feel that their leisure experience has been a successful one.

The following guidelines are offered for leaders who work with adults.

- Adults expect to be treated with dignity and respect. They expect to feel valued as individuals, and they expect their opinions to be respected and given credence.
- Leaders should recognize the value of the uniqueness of individuals. It is important that the leader remember that each group will have individuals who will bring unique skills, experiences, and knowledge to the group environment.
- The leader should attempt to determine both individual and group goals. Individual goals within groups can vary tremendously. Some attempt should be made by

the leader to identify and respond to the individual desires and expectations expressed by group members.
- Leaders should work to create a supportive social climate. This is important to build a relationship of trust and openness that facilitates positive communication.
- Adults find leisure experiences more personally meaningful if they are actively involved in the decision-making processes.
- Adults respond to personally relevant leisure experiences; that is, leisure experiences that draw upon meaningful past experiences of individuals are often more successful than those that deal in abstractions.
- Adults respond to leaders who are genuinely concerned with their welfare and needs. They respond to leaders who are concerned with their interests and desires.
- In developing relationships in groups of adults, the leader should work to create trust between group members and between the leader and group members.
- The leader should attempt to interact with participants in a parallel fashion rather than in a superior-subordinate way. Respect for the leader should be based on the leader's knowledge and skills and resources rather than solely on his or her position within the organization.
- The leader should be able to adjust the goals of the activity or program, where ap-

**TABLE 10.4** Immaturity–Maturity Continuum

| Immaturity | Maturity |
|---|---|
| Passive | Active |
| Dependence | Independence |
| Behave in a few ways | Capable of behaving in many ways |
| Erratic shallow interests | Deeper and stronger interests |
| Short time perspective | Long time perspective (past and future) |
| Subordinate position | Equal or superordinate position |
| Lack of awareness of self | Awareness and control over self |

*Source:* Paul Hersey, Kenneth H. Blanchard, *Management of Organizational Behavior: Utilizing Human Resources*, 2d ed., copyright © 1972, p. 51. Reprinted by permission of Prentice-Hall, Inc., Englewood Cliffs, N.J.

propriate, to meet the needs of group members. It is not unusual for the goals of the group to be different from the goals of the leader, and some modification of the initial goals may be necessary.

In discussing roles and responsibilities that recreation and park professionals can assume, Sessoms has defined four actions that may be undertaken to program more effectively for adults. He suggests that some of the actions that might be taken are the following: (1) expand informational and educational functions, (2) develop technical assistance capacity, (3) employ a decentralized approach in providing services, and (4) use the high technologies of electronics.[6] The first role described basically involves leisure counseling and leisure education, which is a face-to-face leadership function. The second role, providing technical assistance to individuals and groups, finds recreation professionals as consultants, enablers, and initiators. Again, a face-to-face leadership function. Thus, we might surmise from Sessoms's writings that there will be face-to-face roles in which recreation professionals will engage when working with adults. They will be different from the face-to-face roles in which the profession has engaged in working with children and will provide new and challenging opportunities to individuals interested in working with adult populations.

## SUMMARY

In this chapter, we have focused on the role of the leader working with adults. Demographic shifts in population have occurred, resulting in an increase in the adult population. Historically, recreation and leisure service organizations have focused their services on children within our population. Therefore, one of the greatest challenges today is the restructuring of our leadership methods and procedures to focus also on the adult population.

To point out the difference between approaches used when working with children and working with adults, we have discussed the concepts of pedagogy and andragogy. Both of these terms have emerged from the education field. Pedagogy refers to the process of teaching children. It results in leader-directed behavior. Andragogy, on the other hand, refers to the process of helping adults to learn. It results in self-directed, self-motivated leisure behavior.

## DISCUSSION QUESTIONS

1. How have population dynamics in the United States affected approaches to providing recreation and leisure services?
2. What is pedagogy?
3. What is andragogy?
4. Give five examples of leader-directed behavior.
5. Give five examples of self-directed behavior.
6. Compare and contrast andragogy and pedagogy.
7. Identify 10 guidelines for working with adults.

[6]H. Douglas Sessoms, ''Adult Programming,'' *Leisure Today,* October 1981, p. 24.

# 11

# ORGANIZING AND LEADING MEETINGS

This leader is using the lecture method in order to deliver information to an audience of volunteers.

We live in a society in which thousands of meetings occur every day. These types of gatherings may assume many forms, and their purposes may be diverse. They may pertain to work, leisure, school, or may be related to other situations in which there is a need to group people together to exchange ideas, solve problems, and think in a cooperative fashion. The planning of meetings, whether the form is the conference, seminar, learning laboratory, workshop, clinic, retreat, or institute, can be delineated in a few basic steps. The purpose of this chapter is to acquaint the recreation and leisure service leader with the steps necessary to plan and implement gatherings of this type.

## TYPES OF MEETINGS

Meetings may vary in terms of their distinguishing characteristics. They may vary in purpose, scope, location and duration. Definitions of the most common types of meetings are highlighted as follows.

*Conference.* A conference is a large gathering of individuals who come together to exchange ideas and attain information. Usually lasting from one to five days, a conference will have a variety of speakers on various topics of interest, educational and commercial displays, and decision-making sessions.

*Workshop or Clinic.* A workshop or clinic is a meeting, usually of short duration, the purpose of which is practical instruction in a given subject or topic. Typically, a *work-*

*shop* will focus on the development of participants in terms of their acquisition of knowledge or skills. Often topics are covered that relate to new products, new methods of service delivery, or other technological innovations. A *clinic*, on the other hand, is usually diagnostic in nature. It attempts to bring participants together to solve problems and identify and resolve issues.

*Retreat.* The retreat differs from other types of meetings in that participants have a sense of withdrawing temporarily from their everyday environments in order to plan for the future, regroup, rethink, and reflect upon personal or organizational goals or both. A retreat may be of short duration or may last a week or more. Many retreats are responsible for rekindling the "spirit" of the leaders and participants involved in it.

*Seminar.* A seminar can be distinguished from other types of meetings in that the participant actively contributes to the discussion or learning process. In a seminar, each person contributes their skills, expertise, and knowledge in order that all may benefit. Seminars are often conducted to plan group or individual goals, to solve problems, to discuss organizational policy or to evaluate an activity, product, or process or a combination of these.

*Institute.* An institute is a short program of instruction that is designed for a particular group. It is primarily concerned with teaching or displaying information. A management institute would specifically focus on topics related to administration, organizational behavior, and so on. An institute can be compared with a school; it offers instruction that is sequential and that progresses from basic concepts to more complex ones.

*Learning Laboratory.* A learning laboratory is usually contained within a specific area and offers "drop in" accessibility for help in solving problems, conflict resolution, and gaining knowledge regarding specific topics. Usually the learning laboratory is very practical in its approach. Participants may be involved in training that requires them to decide how they would respond to "real life" situations and problems. This training is usually provided by staff members within the learning laboratory, and sometimes tapes, computers, and workbooks.

Each of the types of meetings just described has a different purpose and function. As a result, the leader should give careful consideration to the type of meeting used, for some meetings will be more appropriate than others depending upon the needs of the group.

## THE PLANNING PROCESS

The planning and preparation phase for meetings is of critical importance. The actions taken at this time will directly affect the success of the event. A meeting planner might want to use the five *W*'s in the following list for the purpose of outlining and giving direction to the meeting.

*What:* What is the type of meeting or gathering being held?

*Why:* What is the general purpose of the meeting?

*Who:* Who will be the participants at the gathering?

*When:* When is the meeting scheduled? Is it timely? Have the dates been cleared with those persons involved in the event? Is the meeting scheduled at a time that is convenient for the scheduled participants?

*Where:* Where will the meeting occur? What are the travel times and distances involved for most participants? What are the considerations related to expense?

Fundamental to meeting planning is the analysis of the needs of the group being served. It is vital that the leader consider and plan to meet the needs of the participant group for whom the event is being held. The recreation and leisure service leader should obtain as much input as possible from the scheduled participants regarding their perceptions and expectations. If this is done, the cooperation of the participating group will be gained, increasing the likelihood that the meeting will be successful.

### TECHNIQUES USED IN CONDUCTING MEETINGS

There are a number of techniques that can be used in the organization of meetings to facilitate discussion and the transfer and sharing of knowledge and information. The reader will recall the description of some of the specific techniques that can be used to aid small-group discussion presented in Chapter 3. These included the circular discussion method, brainstorming, the buzz group, the huddle method, the case study method, role playing, and experiential exercises. In addition to these methods, there are still other techniques that can be used to shape and structure meetings, such as the lecture, forum, panel discussion, symposium, group interview, colloquy, site visitation, and demonstration. Depending upon the nature and type of meeting, the number of participants attending, and the purpose of the meeting, some of these techniques will be more appropriate than others.

*Lecture.* A lecture can be thought of as an explanatory verbal presentation made by an individual with expertise in a given area. The use of the lecture is common in conferences, workshops, institutes, and clinics. The lecture is usually a one-sided type of presentation with very limited opportunities for involvement by the participants. However, the lecture can be an excellent method for delivery of information if the lecturer is a skilled speaker with the ability to hold and capture the interest of the group.

*Forum.* The forum is similar to the lecture in that it involves an explanatory verbal presentation by an individual of interest or with some expertise. However, the forum format provides opportunities for individuals to ask questions to clarify points made during the presentation. In addition, a forum provides participants with an opportunity to interact with one another after a presentation has been made and to engage in follow up discussion of specific topics or points of view with the presenter.

*Panel Discussion.* A panel discussion is structured so that different points of view regarding a single topic may be presented and discussed. Typically, a panel of several individuals present information on a given topic, one at a time, allowing individuals in the audience to hear different viewpoints. One concern regarding the panel discussion is that the personalities of the panel speakers may affect the way that their presentations are perceived and may overshadow the issues that they are attempting to discuss.

*Symposium.* The symposium format or technique is similar to the panel discussion method. The major difference between them is that presenters at a symposium do not present opposing views. The purpose of the symposium is to allow each speaker to contribute to a common body of information.

*Group Interview.* In the group interview technique, a group of experts respond to questions proposed by an audience. Rather than working from a prepared text, each of the members of the interview panel responds spontaneously to a given question. This approach is often lively, produces interesting responses, and allows for excellent exchange between experts and participants.

*Colloquy.* A colloquy is made up of a panel of individuals who are assisted by a moderator. An interesting aspect of this technique is that half of the panel is made up of representatives selected from the audience. These "audience" panel members pose questions to the other "expert and resource" panel members and interact with them under the guidance of the moderator. The value of this type of format is that it allows for a type of audience participation that otherwise might not be feasible owing to the number of individuals in the audience or other factors that might hinder orderly participation by an entire audience.

*Site Visitations.* Often when a meeting is being conducted, particularly a conference, a meeting can be enhanced by direct visitation to a facility, program, or other area. There are some topics that cannot be adequately covered without the assistance of such site visitations. For example, visiting a new aquatics center can greatly enhance the discussion of the latest techniques in swimming pool design. Generally speaking, this type of technique is well received by participants.

*Demonstrations.* Demonstrations allow individuals actually to observe and perhaps participate, firsthand, in the process being described by the leader. Demonstrating an activity requires careful preparation. The leader using this technique should attempt to get the attention of the group, arouse interest, and then actually demonstrate the activity precisely and in such a way that it can be easily viewed and understood by the audience. Demonstrations tremendously enhance the communication process by providing visual as well as verbal input to participants.

Often meetings, especially conferences, will be described in terms of the type of session being held. For example, a *plenary session* is a meeting in which all of the members of a conference are gathered together at one time. This is also referred to as a general session. Furthermore, conferences often subdivide their activities into *special interest sessions* that focus on topical areas of interest. The same format can also occur in a seminar, where seminar participants may first meet as a group in a plenary session and then subdivide into small discussion groups based upon special interests. Most meetings are concluded with a plenary or general session that attempts to tie the various elements and accomplishments of the conference together and provide a specific ending to the meeting. At conferences, banquets are often the format used for this ending event, at which time speakers may attempt to "sum up" the events and accomplishments that occurred during the conference.

## CHARTING THE PLANNING PROCESS

The most important initial task of the individual attempting to plan a meeting is the organization of human resources into a dynamic and effective planning force. This is often accomplished through the formation of a planning committee. A planning committee can be made up of only a few basic committee chairpeople responsible for decorations, food, entertainment, and so on; or a planning committee can be relatively complex, as when planning for a large convention.

A example of an organization plan for convention committees is found in Table 11.1. For each chairperson and corresponding committee within this type of organizational plan to function efficiently, it is necessary for the conference chairperson with the assistance of the division chairperson to draw up job descriptions for all chairpeople. A sample set of convention planning committee job descriptions is found in Table 11.2.

Committee chairpeople and committee members need to evaluate their planning efforts periodically as they progress. This is

**TABLE 11.1**    Organization Chart for Convention Committees

## STEERING COMMITTEE

Conference Chair
    Program Chair
    Operations Chair
    Finance Chair

| **Program Division** | **Operations Division** | **Finance Division** |
|---|---|---|
| General sessions | Housing | Commercial exhibits |
| Small group sessions | Registration | Educational exhibits |
| Seminar sessions | Hospitality and tours | Budget |
| Banquets | Publicity | |
| Luncheons | Printing | |
| Proceedings | | |

**TABLE 11.2**    Convention Planning Committee Job Descriptions

I. Program Division
  A. Program Division Chairperson
    1. Serve on the convention steering committee.
    2. Appoint program division committee chairpeople in consultation with the convention chairperson.
    3. Prepare tentative objectives, program methods, and time schedule.
    4. Formulate the agenda of the conference program.
    5. Working with committee chairpeople of the division, secure conference speakers, discussion leaders, resource people, and so on.
    6. Prepare and osubmit to the finance chairperson a budget for all committees under his or her direction.
    7. Keep a record of the division's activities and urge each chairperson to do the same.
    8. Maintain liaison with related convention committees (operations, finance).
    9. Inform the public relations chairperson of items of interest that may be used in promotion and publicity.
    10. Confer with the arrangements committee about accommodations for all guests and speakers.
    11. Submit complete program schedule to the public relations chairperson for promotional use and to the printing chairperson for printing the program.
    12. Coordinate program of related program committees such as general sessions, small sessions, interest groups, and so on.
    13. Maintain liaison with housing and arrangements committee for meeting spaces, and so on.
    14. Submit progress and final evaluation reports with recommendations for future chairpeople to the convention chairperson.
  B. General Sessions Chairperson
    1. Serve on the convention program committee.
    2. Plan and administer the program for all general sessions in consultation with the chairperson of the program division, including obtaining speakers.
    3. Obtain personnel to constitute his or her committee in consultation with the program division chairperson.
    4. Prepare and submit a budget for his or her committee to the program division chairperson.
    5. Keep a record and a file of all committee activities.
    6. Inform the public relations chairperson of items judged to have publicity value.
    7. Submit progress and final reports.
  C. Small-Sessions Chairperson
    1. Serve on the convention program committee.
    2. Obtain personnel to constitute his or her committee in consultation with the program division chairperson.
    3. Plan and set up small sessions in consultation with the program chairperson.

**TABLE 11.2**    Continued

   4. Submit a budget for his or her committee to the program division chairperson.
   5. Keep a record and file of committee activities.
   6. Inform the public relations chairperson of items judged to have publicity value.
   7. Submit progress and final reports.
D. Proceedings Chairperson
   1. Serve on convention program committee.
   2. Obtian personnel to constitute his or her committee in consultation with the program division chairperson.
   3. Recruit recorders for each session.
   4. Prepare and submit budgetary needs to the program division chairperson.
   5. Keep a record of committee activities.
   6. Inform the public relations chairperson of items judged to have publicity value.
   7. Obtain, from speakers, copies of prepared material.
   8. Prepare written instructions for recorders.
   9. Conduct instruction sessions for recorders.
  10. Submit progress and final reports.
E. Luncheons and Banquet Chairperson
   1. Serve on the convention program committee.
   2. Obtain personnel to constitute his or her committee in consultation with the program division chairperson.
   3. Submit a budget to the program division chairperson.
   4. Keep a record of all committee activities.
   5. Inform the public relations chairperson of items judged to have publicity value.
   6. Arrange all details for luncheons and banquets, including menu, cost, table decorations, head table seating arrangement, place cards, and so on.
   7. Obtain luncheon and banquet speakers as needed.
   8. Submit a report and evaluation.
II. Operations Division
A. Operations Division Chairperson
   1. Serve on the convention steering committee.
   2. Appoint division committee chairperson in consultation with the general convention chairperson.
   3. Prepare tentative objectives, programs, methods, and time schedules.
   4. Supervise the making of all arrangements for the convention, and coordinate the committees of the division.
   5. Keep a record and file of the division's activities.
   6. Maintain liaison between related convention committees.
   7. Prepare and submit a budget to the finance chairperson.
   8. Submit periodic progress and final evaluative reports with recommendations to the convention chairperson.
B. Arrangements Chairperson
   1. Serve on the operations division committee.
   2. Appoint committee members in consultation with the operations division chairperson.
   3. Arrange for, and assign all rooms for various meetings and groups of whatever kind according to the estimated size of the group.
   4. Work with the hotel to provide blackboards, chalk, erasers, paper, pencils, ink, notebooks, public address system, and so on.
   5. Prepare and submit an estimated budget to the Operations Division Chairperson.
   6. Keep a record of the committee's activities.
   7. Formulate a system for receiving and recording messages in housing registry.
   8. Maintain liaison with the program division chairperson.
   9. Act as liaison between all convention committees and the hotel representatives.
  10. See that provisions are made in the convention hotel for office space for the (1) convention steering committee, (2) exhibitors committee, (3) organization, and (4) staff and officers.

**TABLE 11.2**    Continued

      11.  Submit periodic progress and final evaluative reports with recommendations to the convention chairperson.

  **C.**  Publicity and Promotional Chairperson

      1.  Serve on the operations division committee.

      2.  Appoint committee members in consultation with operations division chairperson.

      3.  Prepare and submit estimated budget to the operations division chairperson.

      4.  Keep a record of committee activities.

      5.  Establish working arrangements for promotion of attendance at the convention.

      6.  Set up a definite time schedule of promotional methods to be used in contacting membership.

      7.  Responsible for establishing policy in relation to all advertisements used anywhere in convention materials and literature, including price, solicitation, collection of fees for same, and approving contents of all advertisements.

      8.  Plan and distribute preconvention publicity to newspapers, magazines, radio, and TV.

      9.  Arrange for radio and TV publicity locally, and provide photographs, and so on, for convention groups and activities.

    10.  Maintain liaison with other appropriate committees to obtain necessary information for carrying on an adequate public relations and promotions program.

    11.  Submit periodic progress and final evaluative reports with recommendations to the convention chairperson.

  **D.**  Hospitality and Entertainment Chairperson

      1.  Serve on operations division committee.

      2.  Appoint committee members in consultation with operations division chairperson.

      3.  Prepare and submit an estimated budget.

      4.  Keep a record of committee activities.

      5.  Inform public relations chairperson of items of interest, which may be used in promotion and publicity.

      6.  Arrange convention's sight-seeing tours.

      7.  Arrange for evening socials following general convention sessions, in cooperation with the program division chairperson.

      8.  Secure data, information, and literature on points of interest that delegates may wish to visit before or following the close of the convention.

      9.  Provide and maintain a hospitality and information desk.

    10.  In cooperation with the chamber of commerce and other civic groups, provide for exhibits of the host city.

    11.  Arrange for the greeting of and accommodations for special program guests in cooperation with arrangements and program chairperson.

    12.  Arrange for a program of fun, fellowship, and relaxation in consultation with program division chairperson.

    13.  Provide hostesses and messenger service at convention headquarters.

    14.  Submit periodic progress and final evaluative reports with recommendations to the convention chairperson.

**III.**  Finance Division

  **A.**  Finance Division Chairperson

      1.  Serve on the convention steering committee.

      2.  Appoint division committee chairpeople in consultation with the convention chairperson.

      3.  Prepare and submit a convention budget to the steering committee for approval.

      4.  Keep a record of the division's activities.

      5.  Submit progress and final evaluative reports with recommendations to the convention chairperson.

      6.  Maintain liaison with related convention committees.

      7.  Arrange a system of receipts for all money received by the various persons authorized to secure funds.

      8.  Select and get steering committee approval of a bank to handle the convention funds, the name of the account, and the method of receiving and depositing funds received.

**TABLE 11.2** Continued

9. In consultation with the steering committee, decide who shall officially be authorized to sign checks drawn on the convention account.
10. Arrange for method of handling all petty cash.
11. Pay all bills by check upon receipt of bills approved for payment.
12. Prepare periodic financial statements as requested and a final statement for audit.

B. Registration Chairperson
1. Serve on the finance division committee.
2. Appoint committee members in consultation with finance division chairperson.
3. Prepare and submit an estimated budget to the finance division chairperson.
4. Keep a record of the committee's activities.
5. Receive and record all registration fees and handle funds according to the instructions of the finance division chairperson.
6. Acknowledge all registrations with a signed receipt.
7. Secure convention badges and session tickets through the printing chairperson.
8. Secure adequate personnel and facilities for efficient handling of registration.
9. Compile and mimeograph an official registration list for distribution to commercial exhibitors and other personnel and officers who should receive such a list.
10. Submit periodic progress and final evaluative reports with recommendations to the convention chairperson.

C. Commercial Exhibits Chairperson
1. Serve on the finance division committee.
2. Appoint committee members in consultation with the chairperson of the finance division.
3. Prepare and submit budgetary needs to the finance division chairperson; recommend exhibitors' fees.
4. Keep an account or "log book" of the committee's activities.
5. Inform the publicity chairperson of items judged to have publicity value.
6. Be responsible for the solicitation and sale of space to exhibiting firms. Assign space to exhibitors.
7. Supply names of exhibitors to program chairpeople for listing in the convention program.
8. Furnish the exhibitors with a complete roster of names and addresses of people attending the convention.
9. Collect and acknowledge receipt of fees from exhibitors, and handle same according to instructions of the finance division chairperson.
10. Maintain liaison with the arrangements committee and the hotel management (especially as regards security).
11. Arrange through the arrangements chairperson for a phone in the exhibits office and a functional system of paging exhibitors receiving phone calls.
12. Submit periodic progress and final evaluative reports with recommendations to the convention chairperson.

D. Educational Exhibits Chairperson
*Note:* This committee might be a subcommittee of the commercial exhibits committee.
1. Serve on the exhibits committee.
2. Appoint subcommittee members in consultation with the chairperson of the finance division.
3. Prepare and submit an estimated budget.
4. Keep a record of committee activities.
5. Submit periodic progress and final evaluative reports with recommendations to the convention chairperson.

E. Printing Chairperson
1. Serve on finance division committee.
2. Ascertain complete printing needs of all committees in all three division.
3. Prepare and submit a tentative budget to the finance division chairperson.
4. Use a "bid" system, selecting a reputable printer doing the best job for the smallest amount.
5. Keep a record of the activities of the committee.
6. Maintain close liaison with committees needing printing.
7. Submit periodic progress and final evaluative reports with recommendations to the convention chairperson.

known as *formative* evaluation. They should make a point of asking themselves questions regarding the comprehensiveness and effectiveness of their planning efforts. They should be able to satisfactorily answer such questions as are presented here.

*Preliminary Questions*

- Type of meeting or function?
- Location?
- Speakers? Exhibits?
- Dates—starting and ending?
- Type and format of meeting or function?
- Theme?
- Participants?
- Key persons to contact?

More specific questions that committee members should ask themselves regarding the planning of meetings are found in Table 11.3. This material is drawn from the pamphlet "How to Conduct Successful Business Meet-

ings" and was developed by Holiday Inns of America. Figure 11.1 on page 230 depicts a flier used to publicize a National Recreation and Park Association regional conference. It illustrates the organization of the convention, including some of the types of sessions held.

**MEETING ROOM ARRANGEMENTS**

Meeting rooms should be structured to accommodate the types of presentations to be given, the number of participants to be involved, and the degree of formality or informality that the leader wants to encourage. Physical arrangements within meeting rooms should complement the type of presentation to be given. The adequacy of physical arrangements can very well determine the success or failure of a meeting. For example, it would be difficult to conduct an effective small-group discussion in an auditorium with row seating. Figure 3.2, presented in Chapter

---

**TABLE 11.3**  Factors to be Considered in Preparing Meetings

---

**MEETING PLANNER'S CHECKLIST FOR A SUCCESSFUL MEETING**

Meeting/Function_____

Location_____

Dates_____

Meeting/Function Begins_____A.M. _____P.M.

Meeting/Function Ends_____A.M. _____P.M.

Sales Contact_____

Address_____

Telephone_____

**Attendance**

1. Total number expected to attend?_____

2. Type of transportation to meeting?_____

3. Transportation to/from airport, bus terminal, etc?_____

**TABLE 11.3**  Continued

## Location

1. Clean and attractive?_____

2. Sleeping clean, adequate?_____

3. Air conditioning?_____

4. Number of rooms needed (single, doubles)?_____

   _____

5. Reservations confirmed?_____

6. Checkout time?_____Extension?_____

7. Adequate public transportation?_____

8. Stores and restaurants nearby?_____

9. Downtown location?_____

10. Suburban location?_____

11. Free parking?_____

## Billing Arrangements

1. Arrangements made?_____

2. Charge arrangements

   a. Do members have written understanding?_____

   b. Do officers have more liberal arrangements?_____

## Guest

1. Invitations to?_____

2. Invitations accepted?_____

3. Transportation arranged?_____

4. Tickets provided?_____

5. Guest speakers forewarned?_____

## Meeting Room Needs

1. Number of rooms needed?_____

**TABLE 11.3**   Continued

2. Types of rooms needed?_____

3. Are they easily accessible?_____

4. Size of rooms (length, width, height)?_____

   Adequate?_____

5. Seating arrangements

   a. Classroom style?_____

   b. Conference style (U-shape table)?_____

   c. Theater style?_____

   d. Head table?_____

   e. Other_____

6. Coffee breaks arranged?_____ Where?_____

7. Registration table arranged?_____ Where?_____

8. Adjoining rooms

   a. How separated?_____

   b. Noise tested?_____

9. When can room be available?_____

   a. Staff to help?_____

   b. Equipment setup?_____

10. Will dining be in same room as meeting?_____

   *Note:* Have table setting done in advance of meeting, to avoid interruption during meeting session.

11. Seating of outside guests arranged?_____

   What is arrangement?_____

12. Diagram of seating provided?_____

13. Miscellaneous items

   a. Ashtrays available?_____

   b. Pencils and paper provided?_____

**TABLE 11.3** Continued

## Audio Visual Requirements

1. Have acoustics been checked for echoes?_____

2. Has all audio equipment been plugged in and checked?

    a. Public address system?_____

    b. Any feedback?_____

    c. Electrical interference or hum?_____

    d. Enough mikes?_____

    e. Mike cords long enough?_____

    f. Mike height okay?_____

    g. Tape recorder working?_____

    h. Recorder tested?_____

    i. Speaker placement adequate?_____

3. Projection Station

    a. Sturdy and rigid?_____

    b. High and wide enough?_____

    c. Distance from screen right?_____

    d. Enough electric power?_____

    e. Circuit breakers of fuses located?_____

    f. Spare fuses or circuits ready?_____

    g. Extension cords or adapters available?_____

    h. Intercom system tested?_____

    i. Signal light or buzzer required?_____

    j. Emergency work light ready?_____

4. Room Lighting

    a. All switches located and identified?_____

    b. Is room dark enough for projection?_____

    c. Are power outlets hot when lights are out?_____

**TABLE 11.3**   Continued

5.  Is door located so that people leaving and entering room will disturb projection?_____ __ ___

6.  Will temperature remain confortable with number of people you expect in room?_____

7.  Location of air conditioning/heating controls working and located?_____

8.  Podium

  a.  Is height comfortable?_____

  b.  Does light work?_____

  c.  Is microphone placement okay?_____

  d.  Is pointer handy?_____

9.  Screen

  a.  Size adequate?_____

  b.  Keystoning eliminated?_____

  c.  Surface appropriate for viewing conditions?_____

  d.  Electrical controls okay?_____

  e.  Curtain controls OK?_____

  f.  Horizontal or square format?_____

10.  Seating

  a.  Front and rear viewing rows adequate?_____

  b.  Picture bright enough for people in side seats?_____

  c.  Do any areas receive a distorted picture?_____

  d.  Right lenses available?_____

  e.  Will people be blocked by others in front?_____

  f.  Spare lamps, belts, fuses, and repair kits?_____

11.  Equipment information_____

  a.  Type of projector?_____

  b.  Type of slide projector?_____

  c.  Filmstrip projector?_____

  d.  Tape recorder?_____

**TABLE 11.3** Continued

    e. Easels, blackboards, chalk, erasers?_____

    f. AC or DC current?_____

    *Note:* Be sure all above equipment is tested and is working properly **before** presentation.

12. Audiovisual material—all correct and in working order?

    a. Films?_____

    b. Slides?_____

    c. Tapes?_____

13. Personnel scheduled

    a. Program chairman okayed schedule?_____

    b. Projectionist, audio man provided scripts?_____

    c. All operators appointed for equipment,

        i. Light switches?_____

        ii. Door guards?_____

        iii. Drapery operators?_____

    d. Presenters checked on mikes?_____

## Food and Beverage Needs

1. Menu selections made?_____

2. Prices set (including tip policy)?_____

3. Number at head table and other tables set?_____

   Specify_____

   Total served?_____

4. Minimum guarantee?_____

5. Place cards arranged?_____

6. Table tents necessary?_____ Arranged?_____

7. Can room be cleared away without disturbance?_____

8. Bar Facilities

    a. Location._____

**TABLE 11.3**    Continued

   b.  Type liquor served?_____

   c.  Purchasing arrangement made? (By drink, by bottle, by person)_____

  9.  Appetizers necessary?_____ Specify_____

_____

10.  Diagram provided for room setup?_____

11.  Times for coffee breaks, meals, reception arranged?_____

12.  Deadline for room setup?_____

## Registration

  1.  Time required?_____

  2.  Cards? (how many? size?)_____

  3.  Name tags required?_____ Arranged?_____

  4.  Personnel arranged?_____

  5.  Number of tables?_____ Chairs?_____

  6.  Equipment

   a.  Ashtrays?_____

   b.  Typewriters (type, number)?_____

   c.  Paper, pencils, pens?_____

   d.  Signs?_____

   e.  Telephones?_____

   f.  Water and glasses?_____

   g.  Lighting?_____

   h.  Bulletin boards (number, size)?_____

## Exhibits

  1.  Number?_____

  2.  Floor plans furnished?_____

  3.  Setup date?_____

  4.  Dismantling date?_____

**TABLE 11.3** Continued

5. Room assignments and daily rentals?_____

6. Name of display company?_____

7. Directional signs?_____

8. Labor charges (electrician, carpenter)?_____

9. Power, steam, gas, water, and waste lines?_____

10. Partitions, backdrops?_____

11. Storage of shipping cases?_____

12. Guard service?_____

## General Conference Items

1. Notices mailed?_____ Date_____

   2. Follow-up

   notice?_____Date

   Kits being used?_____When Ready?_____

4. Agenda made up?_____When Ready?_____

5. Photographer needed?_____Type?_____

6. Special Equipment needed?_____Equipment rental arranged?_____

7. Signs and bulletin boards arranged?_____

8. Information provided to presiding members?_____

   a. Step-by-step agenda?_____

   b. Information for introductions?_____

   c. Head table seating list for introductions?_____

   d. Other table seating lists?_____

## Publicity

1. Advance publicity?_____

2. Advance copies or speeches or presentations necessary?_____

   Specify_____

**TABLE 11.3**  Continued

3. Press conference required for major speaker?_____

   TV?_____ Radio?_____ Paper?_____

4. Coverage of delegates, award winners?_____

                                                a. Local papers?_____

                                                 b. Organization papers?_____

5. Follow-up release necessary?_____

**Evaluation/Follow-up**

1. Critique session?_____

2. Follow-up minutes?_____

3. Follow-up materials?_____

*Source:*  Reprinted with permission of Holiday Inns Inc.

3, depicts meeting room arrangements that can be used for small groups. Figure 11.2, which follows, depicts room arrangements commonly used for large meetings such as conferences.

As this figure indicates, there are eight basic styles that are commonly used when arranging a meeting room for larger groups—conference, *U*- or *E*-shaped tables, reception style, banquet style, classroom style, dinner dance, theater style, and banquet rounds. These arrangements are clearly designed to facilitate different types of participant interaction. For example, the conference arrangement might be best for a discussion group or a buzz group. The theater and classroom arrangement styles would both be effective for a lecture type of meeting. The theater arrangement could accommodate a larger audience, however. The *U*- or *E*-shaped table arrangement might be employed for a panel discussion or might be used if there were many cochairpeople giving leadership to a discussion.

The other room setups depicted—banquet, dinner, and reception—might be used for meetings that were more social in nature in that they allow for ease in circulation and encourage socialization.

### SPECIAL ARRANGEMENTS

***Premeeting Gatherings and Hospitality Suites.***  At many meetings participants are not acquainted with the other persons attending. An excellent ''icebreaker'' for such groups is a social gathering arranged to take place during the premeeting hours or prior to registration for the meeting. This type of gathering can meet several objectives. First, it encourages participants to arrive early for the meeting, ensuring the timely conduct of the meeting. Second, it adds to the cordiality of the event and ''gets the ball rolling'' on the right track. Third, it allows participants to look for other participants that they might know and might expect to attend the meeting or convention.

©1981 "Life Be in it" Company

**1983**
**National Recreation and Park Association**
**Pacific Northwest Regional**
**Recreation & Park Conference**
**Coeur d'Alene, Idaho**
The North Shore Motor Hotel
and Convention Center
**April 23 - 26, 1983**

# "CHANGING TIMES"

### INSTITUTES
Saturday, April 23, 1983
- Boards and Commissions    • Sailing
• Therapeutic Recreation    • Training Volunteer Coaches

AND

### SPECIAL IN-DEPTH SESSIONS
(Sunday through Tuesday)

- Administrative
- Athletics
- Cultural Arts

- Park Practice
- Specialized Recreation
- Students and Employment

PLUS

### OUTSTANDING GENERAL SESSIONS & SPEAKERS
*Thomas Tutko, PhD,* **Sports Pschychologist,**
**San Jose State University**
**Author of "Youth Sports — Winning is Everything,**
**And Other Great American Myths"**

*Dr. Richard Reiselt,* **National Program Director**
**National Youth Sports Coaches Association,**
**West Palm Beach, Florida**

### SPECIAL FEATURES
- Exhibits
- Job Mart

- Spouses Program
- Tours

**Attractive Hotel Rates**
**Special Accommodations for Students**

**Participating States and Provinces**
**Alaska • Alberta • British Columbia • Idaho**
**Oregon • Montana • Saskatchewan • Washington**

*Additional Program Information will be mailed to you. Mark your calendar now and plan to attend the*
*1983 Recreation and Park Conference in Coeur d'Alene, Idaho!*

**FIGURE 11.1**

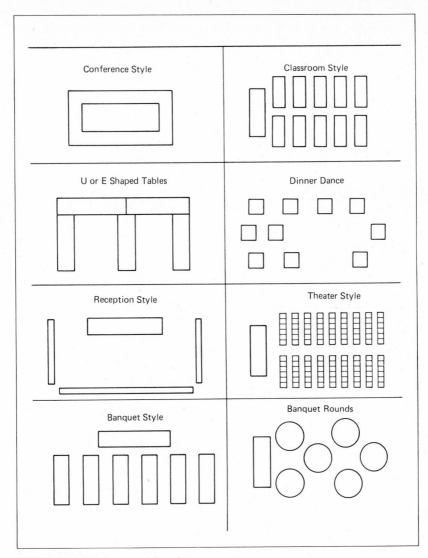

**FIGURE 11.2** Suggested function room setups.

***Spouse and Children's Programs.*** At gatherings where participants are encouraged to bring their families, it is advisable to plan and coordinate a special program for them. The spouse program should not be limited to local tours, socials, and shopping. Educational sessions should also be planned that are stimulating and interesting and that will allow the spouses in attendance to feel that the time that they are investing is well spent. Additionally, it can no longer be assumed that the spouses involved will be female only. The leader planning activities for guests may want to send them a questionnaire prior to the meeting or convention to determine their interests, as in Figure 11.3. The leader can also gain information, brochures and fliers that will help in planning and publicizing guest activities from

Enrich your conference with

# RECREATION AND CULTURAL ACTIVITY

The UO Department of Recreation and Park Management offers a wide choice of leisure activities in the scenic Eugene-Springfield area before, during and after the Summer Education Conferences. The programs are open to conference participants and their spouses for a nominal fee. Enrollment is limited so take a minute right now to indicate your interests below.

- ☐ Whitewater rafting
- ☐ Hult Center for the Performing Arts events
- ☐ Golf, tennis, racquetball
- ☐ Scenic tour of Lane County wineries
- ☐ Rock climbing and rapelling
- ☐ Rainbow and steelhead fishing on the McKenzie River
- ☐ Tour of historic homes
- ☐ Early morning exercise program

To get more information about dates, times and fees mail this form with your name and address to:

Robin McDougall, Department of Recreation and Park Management, 180 Esslinger Hall, University of Oregon, Eugene, Oregon  97403

**FIGURE 11.3**

the hotel at which the meeting is being held and the local convention bureau. Once a program has been planned, the leader should make available to each guest a packet of information regarding the activities planned and other information pertaining to the area. This information may be sent to guests prior to the convention or meeting, or may be distributed to guests as they arrive.

Children's programs may be offered at some larger conventions. Usually these programs have some age limitations. Activities for children tend to be of a "drop-in" nature; that is, parents may drop off their children for short periods of time to participate in supervised play programs that include movies, arts and crafts, and games. Some short trips or tours to local points of interest may also be offered. Convention sites where extensive programming for children is often offered are Anaheim, Orlando, and Las Vegas. Figure 11.4 offers a general list of things that should be considered by the leader planning a guest, family program. The leader will want to determine which of the items on this checklist he or she will make available to guests.

## IMPLEMENTATION OF THE MEETING

If the leader has been conscientious and comprehensive in his or her planning, the implementation of the meeting *should* be smooth and trouble-free. However, this is seldom the case. Often there are unexpected factors that occur, necessitating alterations of the original plan. It is important to remember in the implementation phase that the leader must check and recheck continuously each of the operational aspects of the program in order to ensure that the program progresses in a smooth and professional manner.

The leader should arrive at the meeting site well ahead of the earliest arriving participants, at which time preplanning checklists

**CHECKLIST**

**1. CONVENTION FACILITIES**

- ☐ Meeting rooms
- ☐ Registration
- ☐ Programs
- ☐ Information
- ☐ Hospitality headquarters
- ☐ Gifts
  - Favors
  - Prizes

**2. GENERAL CONVENTION SOCIAL FUNCTIONS**

- ☐ Luncheons
- ☐ Parties
- ☐ Receptions
- ☐ Cocktails
- ☐ Hospitality headquarters

**3. FUNCTIONS**

- ☐ Coffee hours
- ☐ Teas
- ☐ Parties
  - Card
  - Other
- ☐ Luncheons
- ☐ Dinners
- ☐ Receptions

**4. ENTERTAINMENT**

- ☐ Theaters
- ☐ Concerts
- ☐ Museums, art galleries
- ☐ Speakers
- ☐ Spectator sports

**5. SIGHTSEEING**

- ☐ Boat trips, bus trips
- ☐ Shopping
- ☐ Special points of interest
- ☐ Educational
- ☐ Gardens
- ☐ Historic
- ☐ Homes

**6. SPORTS FOR PARTICIPATION**

- ☐ Golf, tennis
- ☐ Swimming

**7. SPECIAL SERVICES**

- ☐ City information
- ☐ Children's programs
- ☐ Day-care programs
- ☐ Other

**FIGURE 11.4**    A checklist for guest and family programs. (*Source:* Adapted from *Western Association Newsletter*, "Convention Planner's Guide: Guest, Family Programs," February 1983.)

should be used to recheck arrangements. In addition, it is advisable to identify, firsthand, key contacts at the site, especially those persons who can be helpful in locating necessary equipment and supplies and who can assist in any last minute "emergency" situations. In conjunction with the preparations that occur immediately prior to the meeting, meeting organizers and support personnel should be provided with up-to-date time schedules that reflect last-minute changes in scheduling, arrangements, food preparations, or program.

Often the meeting leader will find it helpful to perform a "walk through" where he or she "becomes" a participant and tries to view the arrangements from the participants' point of view, one last time.

## EVALUATION AND FOLLOW-UP

As the meeting concludes, the recreation and leisure service leader who has been responsible for its planning and implementation may breathe a sigh of relief. However, the planning process has not been completed until appropriate evaluation procedures and follow-up actions have been completed. A general guideline for evaluation follows, including a debriefing session, written evaluation, and agency report.

*Debriefing Session.* In the debriefing process, those persons who most directly impacted the planning and implementation of the meeting are gathered together for the purpose of evaluative discussion. Ideally, this session should occur at the site of the meeting so that all ideas remain fresh and so that critical problem areas will not have been forgotten. Areas that might be included in the debriefing agenda are noted here.

- Committee impressions and assessment of the meeting (program relevance, logistics, etc.)
- Problem areas
- Participant feedback

Committee members should be encouraged to be frank in their evaluation, but negative comments should be followed with constructive suggestions.

*Written Evaluation.* It is important for both the organizers and the participants involved in a meeting to submit written evaluations. At some meetings, the evaluations of participants occur prior to their departure. At larger meetings or conventions, participants are commonly asked to complete a written evaluation at the end of each general or special session. An evaluation form typically asks questions pertaining to the nature of the presentation, the speaker's effectiveness, room arrangements, and the relevance of the topic presented. An alternative to a written evaluation at the meeting itself or a method that can be used in addition to this evaluation is a comprehensive written evaluation that participants take with them and fill out after they have returned home, mailing their response back to the organizers. Organizers should also

fill out evaluations. Evaluations conducted by organizers are usually more comprehensive than those of participants and include detailed comments regarding committee meetings, physical arrangements, financial arrangements, and so on. The evaluations of both organizers and participants are used in formulating the overall agency report.

*Agency Report.* The recreation and leisure service leader's final responsibility is to provide the sponsoring agency with a written report. The report should be as detailed as possible, providing information regarding all aspects of the meeting. It should include the impressions of the staff involved as well as the information gathered from the responding participants. Details concerning planning arrangements and budget items should be meticulously outlined. The overall goal of the report is to complete the evaluation in a way that would allow another staff member to plan, organize, and implement the meeting in the same manner. A table of contents for a large convention agency report would include the following.

- Organizational chart
- Job descriptions
- Minutes of steering committee meetings
- Reports from all committees, including copies of all correspondence and all printed materials
- Budget
- Speeches
- Proceedings
- Participants (number attending and their evaluation responses)
- Exhibitors
- Evaluation
- Summary statement

## SUMMARY

In this chapter, the authors have identified the steps necessary to plan and implement a meeting. There are several types of meetings in which a recreation and leisure service leader may be involved in terms of planning, organization, and implementation. These include conferences, workshops or clinics, retreats, seminars, institutes, or learning laboratories. There are a variety of techniques that can be used when conducting meetings such as the lecture, forum, panel discussion, symposium, group interview, colloquy, site visitation, and demonstration. The leader involved in the planning and organization of meetings coordinates the efforts of many individuals and groups. A successfully organized meeting can be an enjoyable and worthwhile educational, cultural, or leisure experience or a combination of these.

## DISCUSSION QUESTIONS

1. Identify and define some common types of meetings. What are the purposes and functions of each?

2. What types of techniques can one use in conducting meetings?

3. Contact your state park and recreation association, and determine the structure of their convention program committee.

4. What function does a conference steering committee perform? Program committee? Operations committee? Finance committee?

5. Set up a children's and spouse program for a three-day conference. Assume that you will have groups from 9:00 to 12:00 and 1:30 to 4:00. You may also assume that you have space at the conventional site.

6. Identify guidelines and methods that can be used in evaluating conferences.

7. If you developed an agency report, what specific items might you include?

# 12

# COACHING YOUTH SPORTS PROGRAMS

The leader as a coach can have an important influence on the attitudes, values, and behavior of players.

Many recreation and leisure service organizations are involved in the provision of youth sports programs. Such programs have as leaders either volunteers or paid employees. Paid leaders are usually involved in coaching on a part-time basis, often in conjunction with a playground or community center program. Paid leaders may also work as coaches within highly specialized program areas, such as swimming, gymnastics and ice skating. However, regardless of whether a leader is paid or is a volunteer, knowledge of leadership tech-

niques that can be used in coaching is important to foster a positive, healthy climate that encourages the growth and development of the children participating.

Organized youth sports programs have grown tremendously in the last three decades. Martens sums up the current status of youth sports as follows.

> The growth in children's sports has been phenomenal. The investment in time, energy, and money is huge. Sports themes pervade every cultural level of our society. Presidents and statesmen proclaim the virtues of sports in building a strong nation. Educators and clergy issue edicts heralding the importance of sports in socializing our youngsters. To many, sports are not merely games, they are a religion. Indeed, the baptism of sports has become a significant rite of childhood.[1]

The positive values of organized youth sports programs are many. Through team play, such programs can contribute to the learning of fair play, cooperation, sharing, and democratic principles. Unfortunately, an inappropriate emphasis is often placed on winning . . . sometimes at any cost. The

[1]Rainer Martens, *Joy and Sadness in Children's Sports* (Chicago: Human Kinetics Publishers, 1978), p. 12.

losers in this case are the players, the children for whom the potential outcome of sports participation is the greatest. The recreation and leisure leader can play an influential role in steering the emphasis of youth sports competition from an unhealthy win-at-all cost posture to a more healthy approach, which encourages participation by all, giving of one's best efforts, development of skills, and taking pleasure in the joy that sports of all types have to offer. The purpose of this chapter is to present ideas, concepts, and elementary techniques that can help the recreation and leisure service leader coach organized sports programs for children and youth.

## THE COACHING FUNCTION

The most important figures in the relative success of any sports program are the coaches who assume the responsibility for teams. Regardless of the type of sport involved, the leader who serves as a coach will be the guiding influence of the young people who are participating. The coach, whether male or female, will assume many responsibilities, including some not found in the "job description." Coaches should be able to instruct participants in the sport, demonstrating techniques and teaching the rules of the sport so that even the least athletic of participants can realize success. The coach should motivate each team member to perform to his or her highest capabilities although the disparity of ability among youth of various age ranges is great.

Recreation and leisure service leaders involved in youth sports programs as coaches, as stated, may be paid or may be volunteers recruited from a variety of sources. Parents are a likely source of volunteer coaching personnel, as are college students and other interested community members. Regardless of the source of the coaches who are recruited for service in a program, the following attributes are desirable for those who assume coaching duties.

- Love of children, regardless of size, shape, or physical ability.
- Desire to instill the principles of teamwork, sportsmanship, and fair play in the participants.
- Knowledge of the game being played (teaching knowledge).
- Absolute sense of impartiality and fairness to all.
- Ability to operate from a posture of encouragement rather than discouragement.

The Eugene (Oregon) Sports Program has established a set of guidelines to help coaches understand their roles and responsibilities. These guidelines for coaching leadership are found in Table 12.1.

## LEAGUE PHILOSOPHY AND ORGANIZATION

The leader involved in a youth sports program should attempt to determine the overall purpose of the activity being offered. What are the goals of the sports activity? Is winning the prime motive for participation? Is the teaching of skills the primary focus of the activity, superseding all else? A list follows of some strategies that can be employed by the leader to assist in the organization of a league and the development of its philosophy.

- Prior to the organization of a league or schedule of play, hold an organizational meeting for those whose children intend to participate in the program to discuss its goals and objectives.
- Establish an advisory body through the election of league parent officers.
- Construct a set of bylaws to govern the operation of the league. These bylaws can contain statements that relate to the purposes and goals of the league.
- Consider the incorporation of the league, or seek sanction by the national organization representing the sport being offered.
- After the league is organized, conduct or participate in (or both) leader training sessions to reinforce the league purposes and

**TABLE 12.1**  The Role of the Coach

## THE VOLUNTEER COACH

### Who Are You?

If you are like hundreds of other people in Eugene, you're a person who was in the right place (or wrong place?) at the right time.

The law of averages say you're probably a parent of one of the players; you're an average citizen who, for one reason or another, has agreed to act as a coach. You probably were talked into coaching by a kid, or you may be a person who enjoyed sports and would like to be involved.

### Do You Really Understand Your Job as a Kid's Team Coach?

Many volunteer coaches seem to think that all they have to do is coach a winning team and they've done a good job.

Nothing could be further from the truth because you as a person will have a great influence on the kids of your team. They will notice how you dress, how you talk, whether you know the rules of your sport, whether you have a sense of humor, and a lot of other things will be impressed on their minds. SO YOU SEE, YOU'RE NOT JUST THE AVERAGE PERSON WHO HAS "GRACIOUSLY" AGREED TO VOLUNTEER TIME—YOU'VE GOT A VERY IMPORTANT JOB ON YOUR HANDS.

### Is Being a Volunteer ESP Coach Worth It?

Sure, we could say absolutely! But we want to level with you. Sometimes it will be frustrating, heartbreaking, and discouraging, especially if your team never wins a game. Even if you win, you may be blessed with a group of smart alecks whom you just can't control. Some days everything will go just right, and on other days nothing goes right. That's the bad news.

ESP coaching can be worthwhile if you go into it with the right outlook.

Sure it's great to win, but not everyone can. Teaching kids how to lose on occasion can be one of the greatest opportunities for teaching kids about life.

### If You Think Winning Is the Only Thing that Matters—Maybe You Should Volunteer for Something Else.

In the last few years an attitude that winning is the only thing has crept into youth sports. The purpose of youth sports is to instill those attitudes and characteristics that will help kids become better adjusted adults in the years ahead.

## RESPONSIBILITIES OF AN ESP COACH

### Liability

Many volunteer coaches never stop to think that they are responsible for the welfare of the youngsters they coach. Morally, a volunteer coach is held responsible for the psychological damage he or she may cause youngsters. In a sense, ESP is depending on the volunteer coach to see that proper attitudes are instilled. Volunteer coaches also accept responsibility for the safety of the youngsters they coach. If proved negligent, coaches could be held liable for physical harm incurred by players in their charge.

### Medical Fitness

Prior to starting practice, an ESP coach should meet with parents and find out if any player has any physical problems, illnesses, etc. DON'T TAKE A CHANCE OF SERIOUS INJURY BECAUSE YOU DIDN'T TAKE TIME TO FIND OUT ABOUT A PROBLEM.

### Safe Facilities

Slippery gym floors, inadequate wall padding under a basket, objects and equipment on the gym floor, etc., can result in a multitude of injuries. Look around and ask yourself, "Do things look safe?" If they do, you have no problems.

### Plenty of Liquids

Contrary to what a lot of oldtimers think, water is not only good to drink during practice, it will help prevent heat exhaustion and dehydration. Medical research indicates that during exercise it is necessary to replace water loss.

### How Many Practices and Games Should We Play?

Many coaches get wrapped up in the thrill of coaching and forget what is best for the kids. All ESP teams are limited to four sessions per week. Here are a few reasons why.

1. The physical strain of too many games and practices can affect the overall system of a youngster during adolescence.

**TABLE 12.1**   Continued

    **2.** The psychological strain of winning and losing can take its toll of the emotional growth of a youngster.
    **3.** Kids have home, school and social responsibilities which can be affected by overemphasis.

**Know the Rules**
Agreeing to coach means you also agree to know the rules. Many games are simply lost because a coach did not take the time to learn the game rules, program policies, etc.

**Discipline**
Learning to abide by training, practice, and following rules teaches team discipline. A good rule to follow—be firm, but fair.

**Emotional Control**
Blowups only hamper an individual's success as an athlete and he or she soon learns this. Your example can be very influential in this area.

**Cooperation**
Working together as a team instills in kids the importance of learning to get along with others. Winning teams seem to have this quality—ENCOURAGE COOPERATION whatever the situation.

**Loyalty**
Being faithful to a team, a group, a cause is an important lesson of athletics. A person will not fail himself or herself when he or she has learned the lesson of being true to others.

**Perseverance**
The lesson not to give up is a valuable one learned when the going is tough. Young athletes can learn from slogans like "Quitters never win and winners never quit" and "When the going gets tough, the tough get going."

**Care of Injuries**
ESP coaches should always be prepared to handle minor injuries such as blisters, jammed fingers, scrapes, burns, etc. Every coach is advised to read up on basic first aid techniques. Always have the telephone number of the ambulance service, and always know where the nearest phone is located.

## GETTING THE MOST OUT OF YOUR PLAYERS

Make certain as soon as you have picked your team at the beginning of the season that you let each child know he or she is an integral part of the team. Work players on their individual weaknesses, and make certain they practice their strong points.

    Be sincerely interested in the players' personal problems, and be easy to approach. Have a close personal relationship with team members, but keep their respect.

**Remember These Points Also**

- Maintain discipline without being dictatorial. Be fair and lead rather than drive. Earn players' respect and confidence. Be more concerned with finding the right way than your own way.
- Know the character and respect the individuality of each player, and give each one the treatment that he or she earns and deserves. Do not invade your players' privacy.
- Develop the same sense of responsibility in all team members. Have one team, not regulars and subs, and never refer to any player in a manner that would be embarrassing to him or her.
- Use the "pat on the back" frequently, especially after any criticism. Approval is a great motivator. Make all criticism constructive and avoid sarcasm.
- Consider the team first, but never sacrifice a boy or girl to make an example. It is better to make the mistake of spending too much time with a problem player rather than not enough; however, there must be certain limits.
- Publicly praise your playmakers, rebounders, and defensive men, and privately give credit to your scorers.
- Be quick to give credit and slow to assess blame.
- Organize an offense that tries to equalize scoring opportunities.

*Source:*   1982–1983 Basketball Program: Management Guide for Volunteer Coaches, Eugene (Oregon) Sports Program, pp. 9–12.

goals and to gain knowledge regarding league rules.

In addition, Robert Singer, writing in *Youth Sports Guide for Coaches and Parents,* recommends that coaches for youth sports activities keep the following things in mind when developing an organizational philosophy.

- All children do not learn at the same rate.
- All children do not respond to the same instructional approach in the same way.
- The greater the presence of personal attributes associated with achievements in a particular sport, the greater the potential that will be realized.
- Personal limitations can be compensated for (for example, hustle can overcome certain deficits in size or skill).
- Children have different motives, values, and interests.
- Children come from different types of families and various types of influences and pressures.
- Children have different experiences and dissimilar potential for athletic success.
- Children mature at different rates, thus producing a dissimilar potential for learning and performance.[2]

The leader should recognize the fact that such differences exist between children and avoid a coaching philosophy or posture that will place unrealistic expectations on participants in sports programs. When coaches have unrealistic expectations, there is often unnecessary pressure on the child participating. The Eugene (Oregon) Youth Sports Program has a well-articulated, but simple philosophy that underlies its operation and helps its coaches provide supportive sports programs that enrich the lives of program participants. This unique organization provides programs in the areas of basketball, baseball, softball, football,

and volleyball for both sexes. Table 12.2 presents this philosophy.

### INDIVIDUAL TEAM ORGANIZATION

Following league organization, team organization is the next step in the implementation of a youth sports program. Often, after accepting a job as a team coach, an individual will look about and say, "What next?" Some guidelines follow for successful team organization that should be helpful to any person assuming a coaching responsibility.

- Hold a team coaching meeting to discuss the direction of the team in terms of goals and practice and game strategies. Attempt to define the roles of the coach or coaches and assistant coaches.
- Expect to receive assistance from others (parents) involved with the team.
- Hold a team parents' meeting for the purpose of meeting each parent to establish rapport, to outline schedules and procedures for practicing and participating in games, and to offer parents opportunities to become involved in the sports program.
- Compile and distribute a complete list of team members and coaches, listing their names, addresses, and phone numbers.
- Seek out a volunteer telephone chairperson to organize a system for contacting all team members quickly and efficiently in the event that games or practices are changed or canceled or transportation is needed.
- Provide parents with a league organizational chart, and for larger teams, have a team organizational chart. The team organizational chart should include the coaches and assistant coaches, the roles of parent volunteers, and the team group or groups involved, for example, A team, B team, and C team.

These general guidelines will facilitate the operation of a team, and can be used to motivate parents to become involved in the activities of the team.

[2]Jerry R. Thomas, ed., *Youth Sports Guide for Coaches and Parents* (Manufacturers Life Insurance Co. and National Association for Sport and Physical Education, 1977), p. 54.

**TABLE 12.2**   Philosophy of the Eugene Sports Program

**Role of ESP**
Eugene Sports Program was organized in 1953–1954 to provide sports activities for youngsters living in Eugene and the immediate surrounding area. In 1954, elementary school athletic programs did not exist, and junior high programs were limited to the best 8th and 9th graders. ESP filled the void and continues to do so today.

**Purpose of Programs**
ESP programs are designed to accomplish these goals.

1. Provide a source of fun and recreation that complements existing school and park district programs.
2. Provide a means by which kids can develop a better understanding of sports that will last a lifetime.
3. Give children an opportunity to develop their athletic skills through actual participation.
4. Learn good sportsmanship associated with winning and losing.
5. Learn team values in deference to individual needs.

**Basic Philosophy**
ESP believes participation in sports activities is an important part of every child's learning and growing years. ESP believes children should be given opportunities to experience a multitude of different activities with sports being one of them.

**ESP Strengths**
Eugene Sports Program is unique because the program is designed to meet the needs of the community. What makes ESP special?

**Everyone Plays!**
Any child can register regardless of athletic ability. ESP has no all-star teams. Thirty-five percent of the children enrolled in school play in one or more ESP programs.

**Mandatory Participation!**
ESP has strict rules that guarantee playing time for each child in every game. Each program is designed to provide at least two practice sessions and one game each week for 8 to 10 weeks.

**Modified Game Rules**
Regulation playing rules have been altered and scaled down to a level that physically allows kids to accomplish skills and techniques.

**Neighborhood Teams**
Whenever possible, ESP teams are organized so everyone has a place to play near his or her home.

**Safety First**
Top quality equipment and uniforms are provided.

*Source:*   1982–1983 Basketball Program: Management Guide for Volunteer Coaches, Eugene (Oregon) Sports Program, p. 4.

*Conducting Practice Sessions.*   The leader, as a coach, must be able to conduct effective practice sessions. Many resources are available on the subject of practice sessions for various individual sports. However, a few general guidelines are listed here that can help the leader plan effective practice sessions.

• Start on time; finish on time. Parents want to participate but have family and other obligations to meet that may require strict and timely organization.

• Establish a long-range plan of instruction that includes the definition and explanation of terms, explanation of game elements and rules, development of skills, teaching proper use of equipment, and explanation of the role of officials.

• Establish a plan for each practice session. This plan should specifically detail time for warm-up, review, introduction of new skills, practicing fundamentals, active play, skill drills, theory work, and physical conditioning.

- Break skills into their component parts to be taught. Teach each of these component parts first, and then combine them to form the whole technique or skill to be learned.
- When utilizing parental help in the practice session, ensure that these persons are aware of the expected outcomes of the activity with which they are assisting. In short, make sure they are aware of the correct procedures for ''taking infield'' or ''running sprints.''
- Establish a procedure that can be used in the event of health problems or injuries. (This may be the function of a risk management plan; see Chapter 7.)
- Establish a short period of review at the end of the practice during which all participants are given a ''pat on the back'' and a vote of encouragement.
- Make practice sessions fun! Be creative in your approach while stressing the need for doing one's best.

Tables 12.3 and 12.4 present excellent examples of outlines that can be used in the organization of practice sessions. The reader will note that each plan suggests that practice sessions start with a warm-up activity and finish with an evaluation of the day's activities. Table 12.5 suggests a list of activities and time periods for each activity for a youth sports tackle football program.

**TABLE 12.3**   Outline Useful in Organizing a Practice Session

### SAMPLE PLAN FOR A PRACTICE

Date:
Performance Objectives:
Equipment:
Time Schedule and Parts of Practice:
    4:00–4:10  Warm-up
    4:10–4:30  Practice previously taught skills
    4:30–4:55  Teach and practice new skills
    4:55–5:25  Practice under competitive conditions
    5:25–5:30  Coach's comments
Evaluation of the Practice:

   *Source:*   Reiner Martens, *Coaching Young Athletes* (Champaign, Ill.: Human Kinetics Publishers, 1981).

**TABLE 12.4**

| Planning a Practice Session | | | |
|---|---|---|---|
| Phase of practice | Activities | Organization | Time |
| Warm-up | | | |
| Practice previously taught skills | | | |
| Teach and practice new skills | | | |
| Practice under competitive conditions | | | |
| Fitness training | | | |
| Evaluation | | | |
| | | TOTAL TIME    60 minutes | |

*At the Game.*    The game setting can provide much fun and excitement for players, spectators, and all involved. However, all too often, the game itself creates a fervor, and the result is sometimes behavior that is inconsistent with the goals of the program. A word to players relative to behavioral expectations is wise, and if this is given, their parents will most likely follow suit. The topic of game time demeanor might be discussed at team parent meetings.

The City of Oakland (California) has prepared a list of guidelines that can help the leader, participants, and spectators to act appropriately within the game setting. The use of these guidelines can help officials carry out their jobs more effectively and productively, and, as a consequence, can help to maintain a spirit of friendly and fair competition. An adapted version of these guidelines is presented in Table 12.6.

**TABLE 12.5**

**Youth Tackle Football Lesson Plan**
**Practice Organization**
**(tentative outline of time periods)**

| Offense | Defense |
|---|---|
| 15 min.  Team meeting and chalk talk | 15 min.  Team meeting and chalk talk |
| 15 min.  Prepractice | 10 min.  Running drills |
| 5 min.  Team get off | 5 min.  Team drill (cal's and reaction) |
| 10 min.  Kicking period | 10 min.  Neck and agility drills |
| 25 min.  Fundamental period—basic fund. and techniques | 10 min.  Kicking period |
| 20 min.  Group period | 25 min.  Fundamental period basic fund. and tech. |
|     Tech. related to plays being introduced | 20 min.  Group period (see offense team period) |
|     Drills can be learning or competitive, depending on emphasis | 20 min.  Team period (see offense team period) |
|     Each position should have necessary breakdown drills to master fundamentals required against all defensive possibilities | 5 min.  Winner's period |
|     Half line, outside, dummy, and timing drills | 15 min.  Opportunity period |
| 20 min.  Team period | |
|     Live or full-speed reactions | |
|     Provide game situations for team poise and polish | |

    **1.** 40 yard wind sprints and in
    **2.** 3d situations
    **3.** short ydg.
    **4.** goal line
    **5.** field situation
    **6.** clock situation
    **7.** score situation
    **8.** Tie breaker situation

    Scrimmages

    **1.** all out
    **2.** controlled
    **3.** kicking

5 min.  4th quarter drill (conditioning)
15 min.  Opportunity period

**TABLE 12.6** Guidelines for Behavior at Youth Sports Activities

## THE COACH

Who can do more to build true sportsmanship in a group of youth than the coach? A director or coach, regardless of the type of sport, should adhere to the following guidelines.

- Know the rules.
- Study the rules.
- Teach the rules.
- Officiate to learn the techniques.
- Never argue with an official. (If a director thinks a rule has been violated, he may play under protest.) Remember that an official's judgment is seldom protested.
- Promote good attitudes toward officiating among players and spectators.
- Show complete respect to the officials.
- Control your temper.
- Teach clean.
- Stay off the playing area during a contest.
- Be polite at all times.

## THE PARTICIPANT

Teams and individuals are often judged in sportsmanship and in character by the way in which they play the game and by their reactions toward the officials of the game. The participants' reactions toward the officials will most generally govern the actions of the spectators. If the players' actions are in protest to officials, the spectators' protest will likely follow immediately. Again, the participant can make the job of officiating much more pleasant and successful if he or she follows these simple guides.

- Respect the officials completely.
- Speak to the officials before the game, but do not overdo it.
- Be pleasant even if it hurts.
- Know the rules.
- Play the rules.
- Accept the official's decision even though it may differ from your own.
- Do not let a teammate lose his or her head over an official's decision.
- Play the game—forget the official.
- After the game, do not enter into a discussion of it with officials.
- Be polite at all times.

## THE SPECTATOR

### (Crowd)

For the game to offer more worthwhile experiences to the participants and to ensure greater pleasure for the spectators, the spectators should recognize the following simple guides.

- Know the rules.
- Watch the players, not the officials.
- Cheer, don't jeer.
- Come to enjoy the game, not to criticize it.
- Respect the officials.
- Stay off the court or playing field.
- Be polite at all times.

*Source:* Playground manual, City of Oakland, n.d.

## ENCOURAGING PRODUCTIVE RELATIONSHIPS WITH PARENTS AND OTHERS

A youth sports league will survive only if several conditions are met. These include adequate financial support; good coaching recruiting practices coupled with appropriate support and training; and productive relationships between the league officials, the agency sponsoring the youth sports program, and the parents of the youths participating. As persons become involved in the implementation of the youth sports program, they should be encouraged to assume a small "ownership" in the program itself. The parents and others involved, when given specific tasks to accomplish that will enhance the organization of the league, will be less likely to find fault in the actions of others. They will most likely show a greater degree of willingness to be problem solvers rather than to be the creators of problems. How does the recreation and leisure service leader foster this kind of cooperation? It is actually quite simple, yet requires much forethought and planning with league organizers. Some suggestions for fostering healthy relationships among all of the persons involved in the organization and implementation of leagues and sports programs are as follows.

- Establish a method by which input for change and improvement can be accumulated. Parents feel better knowing that their concerns can be heard!
- Organize a sports program newsletter, indicating rules changes, makeup games, social activities, and meetings of interest to all involved.
- Organize a community sports council that coordinates the scheduling and operation of all of the individual sports programs in the community.
- Offer training sessions for those parents who may be interested in positions of increased responsibility in years to come, including functions as coaches, league officials, and support personnel.

It is also extremely important that the leader and his or her organization communicate effectively with parents of team members. Table 12.7 depicts a form that is given to parents of team members participating in the Eugene (Oregon) Sports Program. It details what the program expects of parents and what parents can expect from the program. It also offers

**TABLE 12.7**

---

### PARENT INFORMATION
### EUGENE (OREGON) SPORTS PROGRAM

#### IMPORTANT INFORMATION—PLEASE READ!

#### Purpose of ESP

The Eugene Sports Program is a nonprofit corporation dedicated to providing year-round sports activities for youngsters. ESP has been in operation since 1954, and programs are set up to accomplish these objectives: (1) Provide children a better understanding of sports; (2) provide a source of recreation; (3) instill values of good sportsmanship associated with winning and losing; (4) develop the values of a team effort; (5) provide an opportunity to learn new skills.

#### Placement on Team

All ESP teams are organized by grade level and by school boundaries. At times it is necessary to combine grades and schools to ensure sufficient numbers to form a team. In many cases, individual schools have enough players to form two and three teams. It is also possible that a school may have enough players for one team but not enough for two, in which case some players may be transferred to another school. Date of registration has no bearing on who is transferred. If you do not want your child transferred, you may apply for a refund.

**TABLE 12.7** Continued

## Notification of First Practice Session

Generally, announcements will be made in the schools as to when and where practice sessions begin. The ESP office does not have this information. When coaches are ready to begin practice, they normally have the school announce practice over the school intercom system or individually telephone players. If your child doesn't hear something at school within a week following the normal starting date, please telephone the ESP office.

## Care and Return of Uniform

All uniforms will be issued to players by the team coach just prior to the team's first game. Uniforms are loaned to players and must be returned to the ESP office or team coach within 30 days following the final game of the season. JERSEYS ISSUED BY ESP MUST BE WORN ONLY DURING GAMES, NOT FOR PRACTICE OR EVERYDAY WEAR.

## Practice Requirements

Coaches have the right to establish reasonable practice attendance rules. Teams are limited to one practice per day and except for tackle football, all practices are limited to 1½ hours (tackle 2 hrs.). A team cannot practice and/or play games involving more than four days per week (tackle 5 days). Practice sessions are scheduled around coaches' availability.

## Mandatory Playing Rules

ESP programs have strict rules that require each child to play in every game. However, a child can be held out of games if he or she misses practice, arrive at games late, or cause problems at practice or games that require the coach to take disciplinary action. A child can never be held out of a game because athletic ability is lacking.

## Games

ESP games are played on weekdays after 5:00 P.M. and on weekends. (All basketball games are played on weekends.) However, no ESP team will be scheduled to play on Sunday more than three times during the regular season (tournaments not included). Most teams will play a season of 8 to 12 games.

## Accident Insurance Coverage

ESP does not provide insurance to cover accidental injury that occurs during participation. Families are responsible for their child's medical and hospital bills resulting from any injury received during ESP play.

## Refund Policy

A full refund of registration fees will be made only when ESP cannot place a player on a team formed within the player's residential area. A partial refund will be made if a player drops from the program prior to the start of the ESP practice owing to illness, injury, moves, or personal reasons. To obtain a refund, a special form must be filed with the ESP office.

---

## PLEASE GIVE TO TEAM COACH AT FIRST PRACTICE

Player's Name_____ ESP Receipt #_____

Home Phone_____ School_____ Grade_____

Emergency Phone_____ Family M.D._____

Please list any medical problems which coach should know about:

_____

Please list child's other activities which may cause conflicts with practice and games, include days and/or approximate times:

_____

I am willing to help my child's team by volunteering to assist the coach in these areas when needed:

_____Transporting players to games

_____Keeping scorebook

_____Operating time clock

_____Help supervise game facility

_____Telephone other parents with important information

parents an opportunity to commit themselves to helping the program in areas such as transportation, telephoning, and score keeping.

## SUMMARY

This chapter has discussed some fundamental purposes of youth sports programming, the coaching function, and some guidelines for establishing good relationships among those involved in youth sports programs. It is especially important to recognize that the virtue of youth sports programs lies in the development of concepts of fair play, sharing, and cooperation, as well as in skill development. With an orientation to these values, recreation and leisure service leaders, as coaches, can contribute to the development of children and youths in positive and meaningful ways. The leader should attempt to encourage a climate of positive reinforcement, encouragement, and genuine interest in the development of children.

## DISCUSSION QUESTIONS

1. What are the positive and negative values of youth sport programs?
2. Identify and discuss some of the functions of coaching.
3. What factors should one consider when developing an organizational or team philosophy?
4. What activities should a coach engage in prior to initial practice sessions?
5. Identify guidelines that can be used in conducting practice sessions.
6. Write out a sample practice plan for a sport of your choice.
7. What is sportsmanship? How does this concept apply to the behavior of participants? Coaches? Spectators?
8. How does one encourage productive relationships with parents and others?

# 13

# OFFICIATING

Recreation and leisure service leaders may be involved in officiating various sports.

The dualistic nature of games is such that each competitive side attempts through offensive and defensive maneuvers to restrict or place the opposition at a disadvantage. This type of conflict occasionally causes rules violations which may be relatively neutralized by compensatory adjustments made in the rules. Games must be officiated to identify these infractions and administer the appropriate equalizing action.[1]

Many recreation and leisure service leaders will likely be asked at some time to officiate sports programs as well as to coordinate the recruitment, selection, and training of other persons charged with officiating responsibilities. The purpose of this chapter is to outline the fundamental precepts of officiating that can be used by the recreation and leisure service leader and the responsibilities pertinent to the successful officiating of recreational sports programs.

## OFFICIATING PHILOSOPHY

The leader or official, whether officiating basketball, baseball, soccer, football, or another sport, should adhere to a basic philosophy that supports and encourages honesty, fair-

In recreation and leisure service organizations, sports programming is one of the most important components. The social outlet created as a function of friendly competition in community leagues is desirable and healthy. By the nature of the activity, however, the action can evolve into highly competitive, and sometimes emotional, play. Thus, it is mandatory that qualified and unbiased leaders serve as officials. Mueller and Reznik identify the purpose of officials in the following way.

[1]Pat Mueller and John W. Reznik, *Intramural-Recreational Sports Programming and Administration*, 5th ed. (New York: John Wiley and Sons, 1979), p. 203.

ness, and integrity. There follows a philosophy statement that can be incorporated into the officiating of any sport.

"It is not who is right, but what is right that is important." Fundamentally true of life and particularly true when concerned with officiating—where judgment and courage are the all-important factors. There is a mistaken belief that the admission and correction of a mistake, whether it be rules or judgment, indicates officiating weakness. On the contrary, it is one of the very strong indicators of officiating strength. Officials who shy away from this precept, undermine the very foundation of officiating.

The official represents the integrity of the game. It is therefore the obligation of all connected with sports to accept and respect the official's decision. However, the official's obligation to the game is even greater. For, by his actions *on and off the court* he must earn—through unquestioned honesty, demonstrated ability, obvious devotion, and full understanding of the game—the confidence and respect of players, coaches, and fans.[2]

Figure 13.1 offers a code of ethics for officials that supports this philosophy.

## OFFICIATING ROLES ASSUMED IN SELECTED SPORTS

Depending upon the sport, there are different roles that the leader, as an official, can assume. Each sport will have specific rules regarding the type and number of officials that must be present at a game. Most sports will have a minimum number of officials required and may increase the number of officials with the level of sophistication of play.

In *football* from two to six individuals may officiate. The chief official is known as the referee. Other officiating roles include the umpire, the head linesman, the field judge, and the back judge. In public recreation and lei-

[2]Adapted from "Referee Guidelines," Willamalane Park and Recreation District, Springfield, Oregon. n.d., p.2.

---

**CODE OF ETHICS FOR OFFICIALS**

1. That I shall always maintain the utmost respect for the game of _____.
2. That I will conduct myself honorably at all times and maintain the dignity of my position.
3. That I shall always honor a contractual obligation.
4. That I will endeavor to attend local meetings and clinics so as best to know the laws of the game and their proper interpretation.
5. That I will always strive to achieve maximum teamwork with my fellow referees and linesmen.
6. That I shall be loyal to my fellow officials and never knowingly promote criticism of them.
7. That I shall be in good physical condition so as to be in the right place at the right time.
8. That I will control the players effectively by being courteous and considerate without sacrificing firmness.
9. That I shall do my utmost to assist my fellow officials to better themselves and their work.
10. That I shall not make statements about any game except to clarify an interpretation of the laws of the game.
11. That I consider it a privilege to be a part of the _____ Referee Association and I will strive to make my actions reflect credit upon that organization and its affiliates.

**FIGURE 13.1**    Code embodying an officiating philosophy. (*Source:* Adapted from the Southern Oregon Soccer Referee Association.)

sure service settings, two officials typically assume all of these duties.

In *soccer* games, there is usually one referee. This individual acts as the timekeeper and enforces the rules. He or she may be assisted by two linesmen who determine which team throws the ball in when it goes out of bounds.

In *basketball*, there can be from one to three officials. The chief official is known as the referee. The other official or officials are known as umpires. When two individuals are officiating, one official customarily stands near the division line, and the other official remains near the basket of the offensive team.

In *baseball* or softball, officials are known as umpires. A game may be officiated by one to six umpires, depending on the level and type of play. However, most baseball or softball games within recreation and leisure settings are officiated by two umpires: the plate umpire and the base umpire. The plate umpire is the most important umpire and is known as the umpire-in-chief. He (or she) primarily calls balls and strikes whereas the base umpire monitors the action within the infield or outfield areas or both.

## CHARACTERISTICS OF A GOOD OFFICIAL

The leader who assumes responsibility for officiating any sport should possess certain characteristics considered to be basic to effective performance. Just ''knowing the rules'' is not sufficient. A list of some of these characteristics follows.

- The official should have firsthand experience in the game.
- The official should possess a thorough knowledge of the rules and regulations for the sport he or she is refereeing. In order to acquire this knowledge, he or she may need to spend considerable time studying the rules, responding to situational exercises, and viewing films and other materials related to the sport. In addition, he or she should remain ''ready to learn.''
- The official should be able to control tense situations in a calm, confident manner without evidence of prejudice, arrogance, indecisiveness, theatrics, or antagonistic behavior.

- The official should be in good physical condition. Officiating can require considerable physical exertion, especially in such sports as basketball and soccer, and the official must have the necessary physical stamina.
- The official's appearance and demeanor should be professional. He or she should be dressed neatly and correctly for the sport being officiated.
- The official should show good judgment, based on common sense, flexibility, and consistency.
- The official should be courteous, prepared to treat all players, coaches, and spectators with respect and fairness. They will most likely respond in the same manner.
- The official should possess honesty and integrity. This should be evident in his or her behavior on and off the court or playing field.
- The official should enjoy his or her role and should have a fondness for the sport at which he or she is officiating. The official should feel a loyalty to the sport itself.
- The official should have the insight and tact necessary to deal with coaches, players, and spectators effectively and positively.
- The official should be willing to ''work hard'' to ensure that he or she is on the spot where the action is as much as possible. In other words, the official should be willing to ''hustle.''
- The leader should be courageous enough to make the ''tough calls.'' Only the weak offical uses such tactics as ''evening up'' to offset a tough call.
- The official should be impartial and fair in his or her dealings with players and coaches. The official should not let feelings carry over from one game to the next. He or she should also be consistent in the assessment of penalties and should not respond defensively to protests of players or spectators.
- The official should be patient, discussing a decision with coofficials if necessary. To de-

lay a decision momentarily is more desirable than issuing a wrong decision that unfairly penalizes a team.

## OFFICIATING DUTIES

Although the duties of an official will vary considerably from sport to sport, there are certain duties for which the official is responsible regardless of what sport is being played. These can be categorized as pregame, game, and postgame duties, as discussed in the following sections.

### PREGAME DUTIES

Before beginning a game, the official should check the area or facility to ensure that it is safe and that no hazardous conditions exist. For example, he or she might check a playing field to ensure that there are no dangerous holes in the ground, check equipment to ensure that it is in good repair, or check the playing area to ensure that there is no equipment or debris lying around that might prove dangerous.

Prior to the game, the official should also meet with the coaches and other officials to confirm the starting time of the game and to offer any other information regarding the rules or conditions of play that is requested by the coaches. In addition, the official should inform coaches of any special ''ground rules'' that should be observed by both teams. The official's conversations with coaches should be friendly, but formal.

The official should, of course, be properly attired and equipped for his or her officiating role. Personal equipment, such as whistles, should be checked, and a spare whistle should be carried. The official's appearance and manner should be professional and poised. He or she should avoid socializing with team members, fans, or coaches, but should cordially offer any assistance requested.

The official should confer with the team members and brief them on how the rules will be interpreted. If the team members are seasoned, the comments should be brief. If, however, the players are unseasoned, the official should inform them as to the hand signals that will be used and other information appropriate to the age group and skill level involved.

Finally, the official, during pregame preparations, should check with scorekeepers and timers. He or she should instruct them and check timing equipment, if appropriate.

### GAME DUTIES

The activities that the official will engage in during the game will most likely be ''game specific.'' Within any sport, however, the official should use crisp, clear signals, make calls that are correct and timely, and avoid unnecessary comments or dramatics. In addition, the official with the best viewpoint should make the call if two or more whistles are blown or flags thrown simultaneously. In the event of injuries, the official should stop play and ensure that further injury is prevented. The official is not responsible for first aid, however. In addition, the official should signal when the official clock is to be started or stopped. Other generalizable suggestions for effective officiating during a game are offered in Figure 13.2, a ''checklist'' for officials.

As mentioned, most of the duties in which the official will engage during the game are ''game specific''; that is, they will reflect the rules and regulations of each type of sport. Although it is not feasible within this chapter to detail specifically the duties of the official for all sports, some general officiating guidelines that pertain to baseball, football, basketball, and soccer will be discussed. The guidelines outlined should in no way substitute for the rules of the sport, but rather should serve as a basis for the general behavior to be exhibited by an official.

*Softball.* The sanctioning organization for softball in the United States is the Amateur Softball Association based in Oklahoma City,

---

**CHECKLIST FOR OFFICIALS**

- Position. Always move for a better position. There is no magic spot. Be flexible.
- Whistle. Sharp, crisp, and meaningful.
- Voice. Strong (not blasting), pleasant, firm, but controlled.
- Signals. Correct, clear, definite. Be dramatic, but not overly dramatic.
- Talk. Keep talk to a minimum.
- Anticipation. Always be ready for changes in movement. Keep up with or ahead of the play.
- The Call. Don't talk with whistle in mouth. Move away from players when making call. Call what you see only; don't guess.
- Concentration. Keep eyes on the play. Don't turn head.
- Manner of Moving. Always look alert. Be on the constant move for a better position.
- Other Officials. Cooperate with other officials. Teamwork is important.
- Judgment. Let the players play. It is easier to blow the whistle than not blow it.
- Courage. Don't be afraid to make the tough calls.
- Appearance. Always look professional. Be friendly, but firm.
- Poise. Maintain your self-control. By your behavior, instill confidence.

**FIGURE 13.2** Officials' checklist. (*Source:* "Referee Guidelines," Willamalane Park and Recreation District, Springfield, Oregon, n.d., pp. 5–6.)

Oklahoma. This organization is the body that provides most of the basis for rules of play of softball in most recreation and leisure service agencies in North America. The following general guidelines are offered for the practicing official by the Amateur Softball Association (ASA) and the Tulsa and Oklahoma City Parks and Recreation Departments.[3]

- Calls should not be made on the run. Correct positioning will help in avoiding this type of problem.

[3]Amateur Softball Association, *ASA Umpiring Manual*, 6th ed. (Oklahoma City: 1980).

- Position yourself as close as possible to each play without causing undue interference.
- If another umpire makes an inaccurate call, stay with him. Avoid the situation where players run from one official to another.
- Do not let the importance of one game outweigh the other. From the standpoint of the official, each game is of the same importance as another.
- Keep your eyes on the ball at all times. The ASA manual suggests following the flight of the ball like a hawk.
- React to all pitched, thrown, or batted balls.
- If you make a bad call during the course of a game, don't let it affect the rest of your performance during the game. It happens to every official at one time or another.
- Arguing with the umpire is almost traditional in baseball and softball; therefore, recognize this and try to view the situation practically. However, determine to what extent theatrics will be allowed, beyond which action will be taken. If an argument occurs, stay as uninvolved as possible. Let the arguing player talk himself or herself out, and then suggest that play continue as soon as possible.
- React quickly and decisively in order to make the many close calls that are apt to occur in baseball and softball.
- Concentrate on the action occurring throughout the game. Since baseball and softball are games with less intense physical action than some other sports, you need to make a special effort to retain your concentration.
- Always use hustle in your actions. The players will respond to your effort with respect if you are obviously involved in the game as exhibited by your demeanor.
- Take extreme care in your appearance at game time. If officiating several games during the course of the day, plan to change clothes, or at least allow time for cleanup between games.

- During the course of the game, make every effort to keep play continuous. Do not allow lulls in play to detract from spectator enjoyment.
- Exhibit a thorough knowledge of the rules. They refer to nearly every ''freak'' play that can occur, so such knowledge is essential. Actively discuss rules with other coaches during the season to clarify and refine your knowledge.
- Prior to making a call on any given play, make sure that the play is completed.
- Stay in tune with your physical condition prior to and during a game. Umpiring can require exceptional physical, mental, and emotional stamina.
- Think ahead of each play for possible outcomes. Try to anticipate correct positioning while being alert to the actual occurrence.

*Basketball.* Few sports can match the excitement and continuous action provided by the sport of basketball. It is, therefore, not surprising that the sport realizes a great deal of popularity in the community recreation and leisure sports program. The art of officiating basketball is just that, an art, and should only be approached by those individuals who are willing to meet the challenges of officiating a sport requiring split-second decisions, absolute concentration, and exceptional physical stamina. The following general guidelines should be useful to the recreation and leisure service leader who is involved in officiating basketball.

- Arrive at the court early enough to dress and inspect the playing surface and the surrounding environment.
- Immediately make contact with the other official and determine the method of switching to be used during the game. Switching refers to the continuous act of positioning on the court and can be used to make the most expeditious use of each official's energy as well as allowing the most

accurate calls to be made from any given position on the floor.
- Determine with the other official who will handle such miscellaneous duties such as ball tossing for jump balls, free-throw ball handling, and sideline activities.
- Determine what type of signal system will be used between officials.
- Check carefully the dress of each player, confirming that the equipment that the players are using is appropriate and that no jewelry is being worn on the court at any time during play.
- During the game, be decisive with signals, and stick by decisions as they are made.
- Constantly monitor the positioning of the other official, and react to his or her position according to the previously defined switching procedure.
- Determine clearly who is the lead official and who is the trail official. This may change periodically during the course of the game depending on the type of league play being officiated and the level of sophistication being exercised in the officiating process.
- Try to appreciate the emotional fervor of the game and the effect it has on players and coaches. Regulate cautiously the issuance of technical fouls, reserving these for the most serious types of violations.
- During the time-outs, officials should confer about problem areas that may have arisen during the course of the game. Strategies should be immediately implemented for rectifying the problems.
- At the end of the game, the officials should confer with the official scorekeepers to affirm the correctness of the score prior to the official entry of a designated winning team.

*Soccer.* Another sport requiring great physical stamina and one which the recreation and leisure service leader may be called upon to officiate is the sport of soccer. Soccer has realized a great surge of popularity probably owing to the fact that persons of all ages, shapes, and sizes can participate. Fundamentally, the requirements for officiating the game of soccer include a complete command of the rules as adopted by the sanctioning agency of the league. Field sizes and number of officials utilized are known to vary from situation to situation; however, the basics of rules interpretation are reasonably standard.

The following are general suggestions for the soccer official. Again, it should be made clear that these suggestions in no way preclude a working knowledge of the rules of the sport.

- Ask coaches to ensure that players and spectators remain on opposite sides of the field in designated areas.
- Discuss with coaches the rules for overtime or substitution or both.
- Advise coaches of the length of game halves and the halftime break.
- Ask players to remove all jewelry and barrettes although barrettes can be taped.
- Inspect the cleats of the players to ensure that cleats are not broken, sharp, or missing.
- Encourage the use of extra ball holders in league play to avoid the lengthy retrieval of the ball with out-of-bound plays.
- The official can use cards, usually yellow and red, to indicate a warning or disqualify players for violations.
- Arrive at least one half hour prior to the designated start of the match to check the field of play, the goals, nets, and field markings.

*Football Officiating.*   Football in its purest form is a combative sport requiring protective equipment for all the players. In the recreation and leisure service setting, the most common form of football play is that of flag football, in which each team member is required to wear a belt to which are attached two flags of a designated color. Special restrictions exist concerning the type of blocking and rushing that can occur. The purpose of these restrictions is to enhance the chance of enjoyment by all participating and to decrease the likelihood of injury on the part of the players. The officials who are charged with the duties of officiating the flag and intramural types of league football can also do much to enhance the enjoyment of the sport. The following guidelines are suggested for the recreation and leisure service leader who is given the responsibility of football league officiating.

- Check to make sure that the down markers and chains are present at the field.
- Confirm that you have your personal equipment in order, including gold flag, whistle (and a spare), watch with a second hand and game card with pencil, if appropriate.
- Inspect the game ball, and instruct the ball person concerning the desired method and timing of the throw in.
- Confirm with other officials the desired positioning during the start of the game and from plays at scrimmage.
- Visually check the appropriateness and safety of the equipment being worn by the members of each team.
- Make calls for penalties clearly and decisively.
- If a disagreement should occur, remove yourself from the surrounding pack of players, and discuss the infraction with the other official or officials. Give full support to the decision rendered.
- Make sure that all officials know the procedures to be used for starting and stopping the clock and that they know which official is charged with the duty of keeping time.
- Make sure that an official supervises any movement of the chains.
- Monitor the continuous flow of communication and information between officials.
- If several officials are being used, deter-

mine, prior to starting the game, who is going to call which types of fouls.

- Make sure that all officials are aware of play that occurs away from the ball.

In any sport, there is no substitute for a complete knowledge of the rules, and the authors recommend membership in a local officials' association for leaders involved in officiating. These types of associations can serve as a great source of training, support, and mutual assistance.

### POSTGAME DUTIES

Following the completion of the game, the official should remain on the premises for at least five to ten minutes. This allows the coaches time to ask questions and advise the official if an appeal is planned. At this time, the official, depending on the sport, may also fill out forms that indicate the official final score, the starting and ending times of the game, the winning team, and the names of the individuals officiating. After the game, the official should fill out reports regarding any flagrant rule violations, to be submitted to the sponsoring organization. An official should not engage in conversations in which he or she attempts to defend a decision following a game. However, questions concerning interpretations of the rules should be answered as completely as possible. Depending on the situation, the official may be responsible for securing the facility on completion of the game and collecting equipment to be returned to the sponsoring agency.

## SUMMARY

Sports are an integral part of many recreation and leisure service organizations. Often these types of organizations will have leaders who serve as officials. Effective officiating is an art. It requires skill and knowledge and an ability to relate to people. It can be learned and, with experience, a leader can become proficient as an official. Officials should always strive to be fair, courteous, and informed. Good officiating may very well determine the success of an individual's leisure experience in sports.

## DISCUSSION QUESTIONS

1. What elements are essential in the establishment of a basic philosophy of officiating?
2. What are the characteristics of a good official?
3. In general, what types of activities should an official concern himself or herself with prior to a game or sporting event?
4. If you are working with another official who makes an inaccurate call, how should it be handled?
5. How does the actual demeanor and behavior of an official affect his or her relationship with players in the game?
6. Should an official always stick by decisions once they have been made, or should calls be reversed?
7. At the conclusion of a game, what should an official do?
8. Organize a one-day training program for officials for a sport of your choice.

# 14

# LEADING COMMUNITY GROUPS

Working with community groups requires knowledge of group dynamics as well as the ability to communicate effectively.

Recreation and leisure service leaders are often called upon to work with community groups. Such groups can include neighborhood associations, youth-serving agencies, as well as other groups of individuals who are interested in organizing, promoting, and implementing their own recreation and leisure service activities, programs, and services. This chapter will discuss the role of the leader working with community groups, the organizing of community groups, and types of community groups and their objectives.

## THE ROLE OF THE LEADER

The role of the direct, face-to-face leader interacting with community groups is different from the more common leadership roles that involve providing instruction, serving as a team leader, or acting as a host or guide. When working with community groups, the recreation and leisure service leader's role can be best described as that of an *enabler*: assisting with group activities, encouraging the development of self-leadership, and helping group members clarify their goals and objectives. In Chapter 6 this type of leadership is defined as *work-oriented leadership*. Whereas the leadership roles involved in providing instruction, serving as a team leader, or acting as a guide require the leader to carry out specific predetermined tasks, the role of the leader working with community groups is concerned with group *processes*; that is, that the leader helps community group members work through the processes of planning, organizing, and implementing programs, services or activities. In contrast to the leader who works with groups that are dependent on him or her for organization, guidance, and direct leadership, the leader working with community groups as an enabler encourages self-help and independence of group members.

A good example of the enabling and facilitating leadership role is the work of the district Boy Scout executive. The responsibilities of this type of leader focus on work with district councils, troop committees, and scout leaders that encourages and enables these individuals to function independently. In contrast to this enabling type of leadership is the work of the scoutmaster, who usually has weekly contact with the boys in his group. The scoutmaster is engaged in *program-oriented* leadership; he has direct, face-to-face contact with the participants on a regular basis. His role is one of teaching the boys skills, supervising their activities, and assisting in the planning and development of weekly programs. The district Boy Scout executive facilitates, coordinates, and acts as a liaison and resource person whereas the scoutmaster is directly responsible for carrying out the program.

Much has been written about the concept of the recreation and leisure service leader as an enabler. Not only can the use of this concept foster participant independence, self-determination, and individual control of opportunities for leisure experiences, but it can be used by an organization to extend, expand, and use its resources more efficiently. The organization of community groups has traditionally provided a method for individuals to meet their needs with the assistance of trained leadership that is process, rather than content, oriented.

## OBJECTIVES OF COMMUNITY GROUPS: WHAT ARE THEY?

Although there are numerous objectives that can be pursued by community groups, in the recreation and leisure service area some common objectives are identified as follows.

- To identify and define problems, issues, and concerns related to the needs, wants, and interests of the group.
- To establish a program of action that meets the needs, wants, and interests of the group.
- To develop a means by which group members can organize and conduct a program of action. This might involve the establishment of policy statements and rules for conducting the group's business, as well as a means of securing resources.
- To establish and maintain networks for sharing and communicating problems, is-

sues, information and programs with other interested parties. Interested parties might include individuals associated with government, business, or other political, economic and social organizations that influence decision-making processes or the allocation of resources.

- To help group members gain new information, acquire new skills, and form new attitudes related to the group's efforts.
- To promote citizenship and democratic action by providing a means for involvement in community concerns.
- To identify individuals within the group capable of leadership and assist in their development.
- To promote community values, norms, and customs or to change such factors in an organized, insightful and creative way.

## TYPES OF COMMUNITY GROUPS

The number and types of community groups that can be assisted by the recreation and leisure service leader are almost limitless. Any group of individuals that has a leisure need or interest could potentially use the support and aid of an enabling leader. Some community groups that are especially likely to benefit from the work of the recreation leader as an enabler are neighborhood associations, clubs and special interest groups, sport associations, youth groups, cultural arts associations, activity or program advisory groups, advocacy associations, and service clubs. Each of these will be briefly described as follows.

*Neighborhood Associations.* A neighborhood association usually consists of a group of individuals who are organized to represent a specific geographic area within a community. These types of groups assess the needs of the area they represent and attempt to capitalize on local resources for improvement projects.

*Clubs and Special Interest Groups.* Clubs and special interest groups, by definition, are those groups of individuals that generate their own leadership. Clubs and special interest groups are often centered around the hobbies of group members, and, as a result, they usually generate a great deal of interest and enthusiasm on the part of participants. In addition, clubs may be comprised of individuals within a certain age grouping; such as clubs for older persons. The recreation and leisure service leader working with these types of groups might assist them by offering to locate a facility for their meetings or might help them locate and acquire more complex community resources. These types of groups are capable of defining their own goals, determining their own programs, and implementing their own activities. Often the role that the leader plays when working with clubs is as a liaison with the parent or sponsoring organization or with other organizations in the community or with both. Clubs and special interest groups are usually very enjoyable for the leader to work with.

*Sport Associations.*    Sport associations are prevalent in many North American communities. These types of organizations are often self-sufficient and may operate extensive direct service programs. There are sport associations that represent nearly every popular sport played in North America. The most common sport association is perhaps the community Little League program. In recent years, sport associations have grown not only to represent youth activities, but also to represent adult sports programs. The leader involved with sport associations may play a minor role, such as assisting in the location of a playing field or facility, or a more extensive role, such as assisting in the planning and organization of an entire sports league.

*Youth Groups.*    Another important type of group with which recreation and leisure service leaders work is the youth group. It is interesting to note that much of the institutionalized work that is done with youth on a professional basis finds the leader in an enabling or facilitating role. Generally speaking,

the recreation and leisure service leader involved with youth groups attempts to train or encourage (or both) either the adult leaders directly serving the youth group or the youths themselves. Leadership development, self-help, and self-reliance are usually encouraged by the leader working with these types of groups.

*Cultural Arts Associations.*    Although they may desire assistance from recreation and leisure service agencies, cultural arts associations usually want to maintain a degree of autonomy in their operations and activities. The type of support given the arts may vary from community to community. The recreation leader may work to help establish exhibits, art shows, and arts and craft fairs. The leader may also help groups in their fund-raising efforts or may act as a liaison between cultural arts groups and other community groups. In addition, the leader and his or her organization may cosponsor cultural events or the leader may help locate needed facilities or resources.

*Activity or Program Advisory Groups.*    Recreation and leisure service leaders may work with a group of individuals who have been organized to provide advice that will assist in the programming of one or more facilities. A school community advisory council is a good example of this type of group. Some of the major functions that a school community advisory council might perform are found in Figure 14.1. As one can see, the work of this type of group may be quite diverse. These types of groups are usually intended to be representative of participants served by the facility or facilities. They attempt to provide information that can be used in the development of activities and services within the facility and in the development of policies that affect the operation of the facility or program. The leader working with these types of groups can gain insight into the needs, wants, and interests of those being served by the organization and the facility or facilities. The interaction that takes place within these types of groups can wed the leader to the participant in such a way that a cooperative, collaborative effort is ensured.

*Advocacy Associations.* Advocacy associations focus specifically on the creation of an awareness of the rights and needs of some type of special population. Although many advocacy associations assume the responsibility for providing direct services, they also are involved in the identification of issues, organization of community resources, and confrontation and negotiation with existing community agencies. The leader working with this type of group often serves as an advocate or perhaps even an activist. For example, leaders within a therapeutic recreation setting might support and work with advocacy groups that strongly champion the rights of individuals with disabilities. A leader in this role might act as a facilitator and enabler of such groups, helping them circulate petitions, organize support groups, and confront appropriate officials or administrators.

*Service Clubs.* Many recreation and leisure service organizations maintain direct ties with service, civic, and fraternal organizations. These types of organizations usually have, as an avowed goal, service to the community. They are a source of great enthusiasm, manpower, and creative ideas. The recreation and leisure service leader often works with these types of groups to help them identify projects in which they would like to become involved and then to help them organize themselves to accomplish such projects. The relationship between the service club and the recreation and leisure service organization can be mutually beneficial.

As one can see, recreation and leisure service leaders can work with diverse types of community groups. And there are still other types of groups that have not been identified here. Working with community groups as a facilitator or enabler usually requires a great deal of time, energy, patience, and skill.

## HOW DOES THE LEADER ENABLE COMMUNITY GROUPS TO ACT?

The term *enabling* suggests that the leader helps others to develop their own abilities and skills, as well as expand their base of knowledge. It suggests that the leader works to give others the means and power to conduct their own affairs to achieve their own goals. The philosophy of enabling is built on the assumption that people can, and do, have the desire to conduct their own affairs and to guide their own destinies. The leader in an enabling role works to achieve this goal.

Enabling community groups can be seen as a method for helping these groups expand their vision and create new conceptual frameworks for dealing with changes in culture, technology, and economics. It also involves helping people to become aware what the existing networks of resources are and how to access them, as well as how to create new resource networks. Resource networks may involve human resources, technological resources, fiscal resources, or physical resources. Enabling, then, is a process that uses resource networks to transform people's ideas, interests, and needs into meaningful actions or outcomes.

Depending upon the goals and objectives of a specific community group, there are many roles that the leader, as an enabler, can assume. Biddle and Biddle have suggested that there are six such roles: encourager or friend, objective observer or analyst, participant in discussion, participant in some action, process expert or adviser, and flexible adjuster to varying needs for prominence.[1] A brief discussion of each of these follows.

[1]William W. Biddle and Loureide J. Biddle, *The Community Development Process* (New York: Holt, Rinehart and Winston, 1965), pp. 71–72.

---

**SOME SCHOOL ADVISORY COUNCIL FUNCTIONS**

The following is a recommended list of some of the major functions that a community school advisory council might perform.

- Communications. The council should concern itself with improving communications within the community. This can best be accomplished by fostering more and better lines of communication between the various governmental units and community residents. The development of a system of continual dialogue should be a major goal in order that community residents are fully involved in the decision-making process on local projects and programs.
- Facility Utilization and Maintenance. The council should concern itself with the manner and extent to which existing public facilities are being used. A major goal should be to ensure that public facilities are being used to the maximum potential for community purposes. The council might also concern itself with investigating the potential to convert existing space within public facilities to more useful and needed purposes. Special consideration might also be given to the possibility of cooperative approaches to building and groups maintenance by officials of many agencies.
- Planning for New Facilities and Renovations of Existing Facilities. The council should be involved in the planning and development of new public facilities in the community. This might include working directly with the school, city and county staffs, and architects to ensure that new facilities reflect the needs and aspirations of the community as well as their maximum utility for community purposes.
- Youth Activities. The council should concern itself with developing an interesting, diversified, and meaningful program of activities and events for the children who reside in the community. It is essential that the council work closely with representatives of the student body and the schools in developing this program.
- Adult Activities. The council should concern itself with developing a diversified, interesting, and meaningful program of activities and events for adult residents of the community. Special emphasis should be given to finding ways to encourage parents to become active in the school and community-sponsored programs, as well as adult programs designed for and by adults. It is recom-

---

*Encourager; Friend.* To encourage people means to give them support, a sense of self-confidence and hope, as well as to help them develop their ideas and actions. The leader in this role acts as a catalyst and sparks interest, enthusiasm, and action. To befriend individuals within groups means, again, serving as a supporter as well as a helper and a companion. The leader, as a friend, is genuinely concerned and interested in the welfare of group members.

*Objective Observer; Analyst.* The leader as an enabler can also work to help individuals carefully examine their past, present, and anticipated future action. Analyzing the work of a community group may involve critical examination of such things as the group's bylaws, organizational structure, promotional methods, program services, or any other factors that might influence the group's effectiveness. To be objective implies that the leader will be unbiased.

*Participant in Discussion.* Often the leader will be involved in the discussions of the community group. The leader will engage in group discussions in order to provide information, establish communication, and help set the tone of the group. Thus, the leader as enabler may become an active participant in such communication with the goal of guiding the group through the various stages of its deliberations. For example, the leader might ask probing questions at strategic moments to help group members clarify their intentions, stay on

mended that a *needs assessment survey* be conducted to determine the needs and desires of the adult community.

- Community Social Concerns. The council should concern itself with gaining a better understanding of the concerns and problems in the community. The council should serve as a "clearinghouse" for such concerns by offering both advice and direct assistance in seeking ultimate solutions. It is anticipated that a council could become involved with such concerns as those related to redevelopment, housing, traffic safety, health, drugs, recreation, unemployment, crime, delinquency, transportation, and so on. To achieve the ultimate goal of eliminating these social ills and improving the quality of life in the community, the council is further advised to relate to and work with the various groups and organizations that operate in the community and utilize the resources of the schools, social service agencies, municipal government, and all the interested parties—making specific referrals and requests when it is deemed desirable and necessary.
- Human Relations. The council should be involved in promoting human relations within the community. Emphasis should be placed on initiating, developing, and implementing programs and activities specifically designed to improve human relations.
- Community Affairs and Activities. The council may encourage the implementation or furtherance of a variety of activities and events designed to stimulate a true feeling of community—involving young children, teenagers, parents, senior citizens, and so on. Appropriate examples of these activities would be fairs, carnivals, dances, dinners, receptions, contests, and so on.
- Coordination of Social Services. The council should be involved in working with the various governmental agencies and nonpublic social service organizations functioning in the community. Efforts should be made to develop coordination and to avoid duplication of services.
- Other Important Considerations.
  * The functions and responsibilities as stated herein are not to be interpreted as all-inclusive.
  * Any resident should feel free to bring any community-related problem to the attention of the council for discussion and potential action.
  * Agency representatives should feel free to bring any related problem or opportunity to the attention of the council for discussion and potential action.

**FIGURE 14.1**   An example of the functions of a community school advisory council.

target, focus on a problem, or steer toward a new direction.

*Participant in Action.* The leader, as an enabler, may also become directly involved in the program of action of a community group. The leader's participation in the action of the group is symbolic of his or her commitment to the ideals of the group. Using our former example, a leader working with a community group championing the rights of individuals with disabilities might picket an inaccessible facility with group members. Or a Boy Scout executive working with a troop committee to establish a new unit might attend their first troop meeting and make a presentation regarding the values and benefits of the Boy Scout

program. In this sense, he would become a participant in the action.

*Process Expert or Adviser.* Enabling is process oriented. This fact is at the heart of the leader's actions as an enabler. Being process oriented means that a leader concentrates on teaching people the means that they can use to achieve the goals that they desire to achieve. A process expert ensures that group members are using a process or course of action that will be effective in meeting their goals. In addition, the leader as a process expert attempts to ensure that group members get the information that they need and that they understand the methods of operation or procedures of the group. As an adviser, the leader might offer his or her opinions regarding the activities of the community group. Whereas the role of the analyst is based on an objective appraisal, the role of the adviser suggests that personal input is given. Personal input or advice can come in the form of encouragement, admonishment, caution, warning, or information.

*Flexible Adjuster to the Varying Needs for Prominence.* The leader must be flexible in the type and degree of help that he or she gives to a community group. The leader working with a community group should be able to assess the needs of the group with which he or she is working to determine the role that should be played by an enabling leader. The leader may want, for example, to engage in one, several, or even all of the roles described earlier in varying degrees of intensity. The leader may want to play a very prominent role within the group, or the leader may want to stay in the background, depending upon the specific needs of the group or the situation. The leader should always bear in mind, however, that his or her ultimate goal is to help the group members succeed on their own.

Much of the work done with community groups is done with small numbers of people. The principles outlined in Chapter 3 for conducting small-group discussions can assist the leader in working with community groups. A review of some of these small-group discussion techniques should be useful here as well. The reader will recall that the leader often works in small groups to identify issues, to develop an appreciation for group needs, to generate interest in new ideas, to supply information, to assist individuals in solving problems, and to help form group opinions and consensus. In addition, a leader might work to help people crystallize their own thinking, move to action, and develop leadership skills. The leader engages in all these activities in order to empower, or enable, group members to move forward to their goals.

## ORGANIZING COMMUNITY GROUPS

The effective organization of community groups is critical to their success. Most community groups coalesce around a need, interest, or concern. Their membership is almost universally voluntary. In general, the initial organization of community groups usually occurs when concerned individuals or the recreation and leisure service leader calls together a group of people to discuss their needs or concerns informally. Group membership, rules, and roles are often loosely defined initially.

Once the group has coalesced around a concern or issue, it begins to define its function, structure, and roles more specifically and to identify potential leaders for the group. This often results in the creation of a set of bylaws that outline the purpose of the organization, its membership requirements, decision-making procedures, roles (officers and their duties), and programs and services. Figure 14.2 presents a set of bylaws for a community council. As the group becomes more specifically defined, the role of the recreation leader may change or evolve. Whereas the leader may be initially quite active, prompting the group's interest and enthusiasm, he or she may shift roles to one outside the focal point of attention as the group members themselves begin to assume responsibility. For example, the leader might distribute a flier designating a meeting place, date, and time; however, the function of advertising future meetings would likely become the responsibility of a group member. The role of the leader might evolve to one of critiquing flier designs and content.

Central to the survival of any community group is the maintenance and revitalization of its membership. Most community groups are open to new members. The group can build its membership by publicizing its existence and efforts by word of mouth or various media sources. In recruiting new members, the group will want to identify the target population from which they want to recruit new members and then direct publicity efforts

**SAMPLE COMMUNITY ADVISORY COUNCIL BYLAWS**

**ARTICLE I: NAME**

The name of this organization shall be the Community Advisory Council.

**ARTICLE II: AREA**

The boundaries of the Community Advisory Council will encompass that property bounded by (insert the boundaries of the community area).

**ARTICLE III: PURPOSE**

The Community Advisory Council is an integral component of the total recreation and leisure service provision in this community. Although the ultimate responsibility for most areas of policy is determined by city ordinance, the Community Advisory Council will play an important role in shaping policies, programs, activities, and functions of the recreation and leisure service agency. The council will also participate in the assessment of leisure needs and the establishment of priorities and will offer advice on the leisure needs of the community.

**ARTICLE IV: MEMBERSHIP**

**Section A.**

The general membership shall be open to residents, property owners, and people employed within the Community Advisory Council boundaries and who are interested in contributing their time and effort to the objectives of this council.

**Section B.**

The membership of the council shall consist of 13 to 17 active members. Membership should include representation from

1. Parents.
2. Educational personnel.
3. Students (elementary, jr. high, and high school).
4. Local business persons.
5. Organized community groups (homeowners' associations).
6. Senior citizens.
7. Churches.
8. Agency liaison (resource person to council, nonvoting member).

**Section C.**

Council members will be either elected, appointed, or otherwise selected by their respective groups.

**Section D.**

A member will serve on the council for two years. The terms of membership for council members will be structured on a ''staggered'' schedule. Thus, some members will serve one-year terms whereas others will serve for two years. This method will ensure that there will not be a complete change in council membership during any given year.

**SAMPLE COMMUNITY ADVISORY COUNCIL BYLAWS**   Continued

**Section E.**

If any member misses three consecutive council meetings, he or she shall be given written notice and replaced at the discretion of the council.

**Section F.**

Resignations from the council will be accepted only upon written notice to the chairperson.

## ARTICLE V: VOTING

**Section A.**

Voting will be restricted to council members.

**Section B.**

A majority vote of those present shall be necessary to act upon any motion or recommendation.

## ARTICLE VI: OFFICERS AND DUTIES

**Section A.**

The officers of the council shall be chairperson, secretary, and executive committee.

**Section B.**

Duties of the chairperson shall be

1. To chair all council meetings.
2. To appoint standing committees and ad hoc task forces.
3. To call special council meetings.
4. To chair all executive committee meetings.
5. To have general charge of the council.

**Section C.**

Duties of the secretary shall be

1. To record minutes during council and executive board meetings.
2. To be responsible for all council correspondence.

**Section D.**

The executive board shall be made up of the council chairperson, secretary, and all standing committee chairpersons. Their duties shall be

1. To develop general council meeting agendas at least two weeks prior to the meeting.
2. To exercise all the functions of the council between general council meetings.

**SAMPLE COMMUNITY ADVISORY COUNCIL BYLAWS**    Continued

3. To make recommendations on council policies, procedures, programs, and activities to the general council.

## ARTICLE VII: ELECTION OF OFFICERS

### Section A.

The candidates for council officers shall be chosen by a nomination committee. This committee will be made up of three people appointed by the council chairperson. There shall be a minimum of two candidates for each office.

### Section B.

Election of officers shall take place at the April general council meeting. Election will be by secret ballot of the general council membership.

### Section C.

Officers will take office in May.

### Section D.

Each officer shall hold office for one year.

## ARTICLE VIII: STANDING COMMITTEES

Standing committees for the Community Advisory Council shall be

### Section A.

Youth Program Committee.

1. This committee will be composed of five to seven members from the community, with at least one member from the general council membership.
2. The duties of this committee shall be
   a. To assess the needs and wants of adults.
   b. To plan and implement ways to meet these identified needs and wants.
   c. To evaluate all programs and activities of the committee .
   d. To keep the general council informed on committee activities.

### Section B.

Adult Program Committee.

1. This committee will be composed of five to seven members from the community, with at least one member from the general council membership.
2. The duties of this committee shall be
   a. To assess the needs and wants of adults.
   b. To plan and implement ways to meet these identified needs and wants.

**SAMPLE COMMUNITY ADVISORY COUNCIL BYLAWS**    Continued

    c. To evaluate all committee activities.
    d. To keep the general council informed on committee activities.

### Section C.

Community Volunteer Recruitment Committee.

1. This committee will be composed of five to seven members from the community, with at least one member from the general council membership.
2. The duties of this committee shall be
    a. To work with the agency liaison, regular professional staff, and youth and adult program committees in order to identify ways community volunteers can be utilized.
    b. To recruit and secure community resources—physical and human—to provide assistance to identified program areas.
    c. To maintain good rapport and communication with community volunteers.
    d. To plan and implement volunteer recognition activities.
    e. To evaluate all committee activities.
    f. To keep the general council informed on committee activities.

## ARTICLE IX: GENERAL COUNCIL MEETINGS

### Section A.

The general council meetings will be held the first Wednesday of September and each alternate month after, with the exception of the months of July and August, when there will be no meetings.

### Section B.

The established meeting time for the Community Advisory Council will be at 7 P.M. at a place designated by the executive committee.

### Section C.

The general council membership is to be notified of the meeting at least one week in advance.

### Section D.

The minutes of the general council meetings will be mailed to all members within ten days after each meeting.

### Section E.

The duration of the general council meetings will not exceed two hours, unless otherwise agreed upon by the assembled body. All unfinished business will be forwarded to the next meeting.

### Section F.

One half of the total general council membership must be present before a meeting can be called to order.

---

**SAMPLE COMMUNITY ADVISORY COUNCIL BYLAWS**   Continued

**ARTICLE X: AMENDMENTS**

These bylaws may be amended or added to at any general council meeting by a majority vote of those attending providing that notice has been given the membership one month in advance of such a meeting.

---

**FIGURE 14.2**   Sample Bylaws

toward this target population. For example in the case of a cub scout troop, the target population would be elementary school age boys of eight and over. Publicity efforts, therefore, could be directed toward children in that category by distributing fliers, making presentations, or setting up displays in elementary schools, community recreation centers, and so on, or by a combination of these. The group may also want to have a membership drive, in which existing members actively recruit new members on a one-on-one basis.

Two factors that often drive people from involvement in community groups are the feelings of being underinvolved or overwhelmed. Thus, to maintain its membership, the group should work to ensure that each member of the group is involved to a degree complementary with his or her level of interest.

## DECISION MAKING IN COMMUNITY GROUPS

Community groups are all involved in decision making, although in varying degrees. The way decisions are made in groups is very important. It can affect group harmony, group cohesiveness, and group effectiveness. Some decision-making processes are very time-consuming whereas others are more efficient and may not require support from all group members. Some decision-making processes will be more effective than others for given groups, depending upon the type of decision to be made, the degree of formality or informality of the group, and, in general, the goals and objectives of the group. Some of the

decision-making processes that can be used by community groups include the following.

- Unanimity—everyone agrees.
- Consensus—general agreement, with possible reservations, at least for a specified time period.
- Majority support—the majority of people agree, often demonstrated by voting.
- Minority support—a minority of people agree, with tacit agreement or lack of open disagreement by the remaining members.
- Handclasp—one or two members actively support and lead group to action.
- Topic jump—the topic shifts before an explicit decision is reached.
- Self-authorization—one person initiates action, with implicit consent or no overt disagreement of other members.
- Plop—one person initiates action, but the group does not respond one way or another; by default, no action is taken.[2]

When working with community groups, one must remember that any of these methods can be used successfully to make decisions. The issues that are explored, the programs that are developed, the means used to organize and conduct activities, as well as other objectives pursued by groups, are determined through one or more of the just discussed decision-making processes. The leader, as an enabler, should help group members understand the importance of decision making and the ways

[2]North West Regional Educational Laboratory, Portland, Oregon, p. 25.

that different decision-making methods can affect the group. For example, unanimity of decision making, although time-consuming, may contribute to greater harmony within the group and greater commitment to the decisions made than decision making by majority support only.

## CONFLICT IN COMMUNITY GROUPS

Whenever two or more people collaborate, there is a possibility of disagreement and conflict. The leader should recognize that conflict is a natural, and possibly necessary, part of working with community groups. Conflict is often thought of as being negative; however, it can be viewed positively as well. For example, conflict can serve to highlight problems, issues, and concerns, as well as the positions of group members. There are a number of ways that people deal with conflict. We can identify these as conflict styles. Six of these conflict styles are detailed in the following list.

*Avoidance* is a style adopted when differences are not considered to be amenable to influence or change. Conflicts that are avoided may never be completely dealt with and may arise repeatedly in a group. Some conflicts, however, will never be resolved and may be best managed by being avoided.

*Accommodation* is similar to avoidance except that a person using the accommodation style focuses on *relationships* as a reason for avoiding conflicts. An "accommodator" sees differences as being detrimental to group relationships and group functioning. A voiced difference is considered a personal rejection. Furthermore, relationships are more important than issues, so conflicts are avoided.

*Coercion* is a quite different style. A person who uses coercion sees all conflict as a win-lose situation and goes to all ends to pursue his or her own interests. For a coercive per-

son there is only one "right" answer or solution.

*Compromise* is used by the individual who realizes that there is no *one* answer in most cases. The common good should govern the resolution of differences, and though everyone should have a voice in decision making, no one should block group progress. A "compromiser" expects the give-and-take of group work to result in everyone's abiding by a majority decision that "splits" any existing differences.

*Collaboration* involves an expectation that some kind of consensus or majority decision will resolve group conflicts; however, the "collaborator," like the accommodator, is *most* concerned about the healthiness of group relationships. The collaborator believes in directly confronting conflict, which is seen as a manifestation of uneasiness in group relationships. A collaborator spends a good deal of conflict-management time in encouraging other group members to assess and deal with group conflicts.

*Negotiation* is the final conflict style. Collective bargaining is a setting in which negotiation as a conflict style predominates. Alternative solutions may not be amenable to compromise; instead, parties in conflict need to be aware of their self-interests, and they need to seek a parity of power with one another.[3]

The leader, as an enabler, should attempt to use conflict in a positive and creative way to further the goals and objectives of the community group or groups with which he or she works. Although conflict may be threatening to some, the leader who understands that conflict can be managed productively will be more effective in leading community groups.

[3]Ibid, p. 26.

## SUMMARY

There are many different types of community groups with which a recreation and leisure service leader may work. They range from neighborhood associations, to program advisory committees to advocacy associations. Working with community groups as a direct, face-to-face leader can be best thought of as an enabling activity. The leader, as an enabler, serves to empower individuals and groups to manage their own affairs and to seek their own goals. The leader empowers groups by helping them attain skills, knowledge, and information related to their purpose and to identify and develop leaders within their ranks. The work of the leader, as an enabler, is complete when the group with which the leader is working is independent and capable of operating successfully with minimal or no assistance.

## DISCUSSION QUESTIONS

1. What are community groups? Identify some groups in your community that a recreation and leisure service leader would work with.
2. What are the objectives of community groups?
3. What roles does the recreation and leisure service leader play in working with community groups?
4. What are the leadership and program implications of the statement ''membership in recreation and leisure service groups is almost universally voluntary''?
5. Identify some of the processes that can be used in decision making in community groups.
6. Identify six ways of dealing with conflict.

# 15

# LEADING VOLUNTEERS

Volunteers are an essential resource of most recreation and leisure service organizations.

Volunteering is one of our North American traditions. It is grounded in our societal values that encourage individuals not only to help themselves, but also to help others. Volunteering offers an opportunity for grass roots participation in local, state, and national organizations and agencies. It provides opportunities for creative action, self-expression, growth, and learning. Volunteer networks also enable individuals to care for themselves, and this, in turn, promotes greater freedom, autonomy, and independence of action.

Without the contributions of volunteers to the operation and maintenance of recreation and leisure service organizations, there would be a tremendous reduction in the quality and quantity of programs and services available. Youth programs (such as sports, outdoor, and citizenship programs), as well as adult and senior programs, greatly utilize volunteers. Consider the management and operation of a cub scout pack or a Camp Fire group. Without mothers, fathers, and other interested parties volunteering their time to plan and implement activities, these programs simply would not exist.

In this chapter, the authors will discuss the processes involved in planning for volunteers as well as the processes that can be used to recruit, select, orient, supervise, and recognize volunteers. Because this book focuses on direct, face-to-face leadership, we will try to discuss these processes from the leader's perspective where possible. However, the role of the leader will vary according to the demands of each situation. In some instances, the leader will be comprehensively involved in the processes related to the selection, recruitment, and placement of volunteers whereas in other situations the leader may have less involvement.

## THE VOLUNTEER

Volunteers come from every segment of our society. Volunteer programs may include individuals from all age groups; they may be children, youths, adults, or older persons. Sometimes volunteers are associated with organizations that provide volunteer community service whereas in other situations the volunteer may act individually. Volunteers may come to leisure service organizations with well-developed and specialized skills, or they may come with just a basic desire to help, without having any special skills or training. The only real criterion for being a volunteer is the willingness to undertake a job and complete it successfully, as indicated by the following.

> Creative and effective organizations are recognizing that only one thing matters in getting the job done—competence. These organizations make sure that they don't lose potential resources because they have outdated criteria for those who can and cannot deliver. They recognize competence as based on life experience, informal education, and personal commitment. They no longer think that an academic degree is the only sign that someone can do a job.[1]

What characteristics are unique to the volunteer? How can the volunteer be distinguished from other members of the recreation and leisure service organization? Generally speaking, the volunteer is someone who gives service to others without expectation of financial reimbursement. The volunteer is willing to give of his or her time, talent, and skills to others without being paid. The volunteer serves to complement and extend the existing human resources of the organization. Thus, a volunteer may be defined as *an individual who, in order to help the organization attain its goals, offers to give service to a recreation and leisure service organization without expectation of reimbursement.*

### WHAT DO VOLUNTEERS DO?

Most commonly we think of the volunteer in a recreation and leisure service organization as a person who assumes or assists in direct, face-to-face leadership. However, there are other forms of important direct and indirect assistance that volunteers can give within a recreation and leisure service organization. For example, the motivated volunteer is often the greatest advocate of the work of the organization and can influence public opinion in a positive manner. Volunteers are also consumers. They often represent the viewpoint of the public being served by an organization and can provide feedback to the leader regarding the work of the organization. In addition, volunteers may assist with fund-raising efforts within an organization. This is especially true in youth-serving organizations. Lastly, volunteers may contribute to the development and formulation of organizational policy. Because of the grass roots nature of volunteerism and the fact that the implementation of direct services often rests with the volunteer, these individuals are often in a position to influence and participate in the policymaking process.

### WHY DO PEOPLE VOLUNTEER?

People volunteer for a myriad of reasons. Individuals may take a great deal of satisfaction in contributing to the lives of others. They may also seek social relationships and a chance to interact with others in a positive environment. In addition, individuals may become involved in volunteer services for the recognition that it provides or to alleviate boredom. Some individuals volunteer in or-

[1]"Volunteers in Your Organization," Ministry of Culture and Recreation, Province of Ontario, n.d., p. 22.

der to learn new skills. For example, an individual might volunteer to work in a fund-raising activity to learn the fund-raising process.

Working as a volunteer may also offer a means to work up to a paid position eventually. Or acting as a volunteer may be a requirement for a school curriculum, youth program, or membership in a service club. For example, many service clubs have as a component of their bylaws and charter that members will volunteer to help with service projects or community activities. Some individuals may have hobbies and special interests that they are excited about and eager to share with others, prompting their volunteerism. For example, a ham radio operator may have a great desire to share his or her interest with others and may volunteer to work with the Boy Scouts as a merit badge counselor in this area.

As one can see, there are many reasons why people may volunteer. The leader working with volunteers should keep this in mind when recruiting, training, and placing volunteers. The leader should not only attempt to meet the needs of the organization when using volunteers, but should also attempt to meet the needs of the volunteers themselves. Knowledge of their motives for volunteering is the first step in doing this.

## PLANNING THE VOLUNTEER EFFORT

The key to using volunteers successfully is the development of an overall plan for their involvement. Good volunteer programs do not appear out of thin air. They require a conscious effort of individuals within the recreation and leisure service organization to determine why volunteers are to be used and how and where they are to be used. The leader who understands the overall picture of volunteer involvement can more successfully employ volunteers in activities, programs, and services. A good way to start planning for the

use of volunteers in an organization is to ask some basic questions regarding the nature and extent of the organization's goals and how they might be accomplished. Some of the questions that might be asked are these.

- What are our organizational (team, department) objectives?
- What activities need to be done to meet these objectives?
- What skills are required for each activity?
- Who has and who can acquire these skills?
- What satisfaction does each activity provide?
- What activities can be grouped together to create a satisfying and effective job?
- What jobs do we have to pay people to do?
- On what criteria do we decide which jobs will be paid for and which will be voluntary? Are these criteria appropriate?
- What are our assumptions about credentials for work? Do we rely on academic qualifications? Do we honor age before experienced youth, status before commitment, male before female?
- Are our assumptions and practices serving us well, or do we need to reevaluate our way of using resources.[2]

Once an agency has addressed these questions, it can proceed to develop a plan to incorporate volunteers into its organization. Generally speaking, the more people within the agency that contribute to the planning process, the greater the likelihood that the volunteer program will be successful. Also, the leader planning to incorporate volunteers into an organization should consider the fact that certain factors can influence the success or failure of the program. Some of the steps that are important in the development of a plan are (1) the establishment of goals and objectives; (2) job design; (3) the development of organizational, administrative, and staff involvement; and (4) the establishment of a

[2]Ibid., p. 21.

plan to encourage the involvement of community members as volunteers.

Such planning often results in the development of a written document or at least the establishment of policies that encourage administrative support of, and staff involvement with, volunteers. However, planning is a dynamic process that must evolve as the needs, wants, and interests of both the organization and its volunteers change and evolve. Consequently, a plan for the utilization of volunteers should be flexible and should continue to evolve, as should the policies and procedures that are associated with it.

## GOALS AND OBJECTIVES

Goals and objectives can be thought of as the ends or the aims of the volunteer program. When a recreation and leisure service organization engages in the establishment of its goals and objectives, it will not only want to consider its own organizational requirements or needs, but also will want to consider the fact that by providing well-designed volunteer opportunities, it is also providing positive leisure time experiences for volunteers. In other words, the organization can often meet the needs of volunteers while at the same time enlisting the aid of volunteers to meet the needs of the organization. Goal statements should reflect this mutually beneficial nature of the volunteer process. Some goal statements may be very general whereas others may be quite specific. General goals that might be found in volunteer programs operated within recreation and leisure service organizations include the following.

- To provide opportunities for volunteers to serve their communities in meaningful ways.
- To extend and enhance the quantity and/or quality of services of an organization by increasing the number of staff without increasing the cost.
- To provide opportunities to volunteers for constructive use of their leisure time.

- To prepare volunteers by establishing orientation and in-service training programs.
- To prepare staff members to acknowledge, accept, and respect volunteers as co-workers.
- To make volunteers, their friends and families, and others in the community aware of the services and activities provided by an organization.
- To initiate and maintain positive liaisons with other agencies in the community that can contribute to, or would like to receive help from, the volunteer group.
- To identify and develop meaningful volunteer opportunities that are consistent with the needs, skills, or capabilities of the volunteers.
- To provide a program of recognition for the efforts of volunteers.

Agencies might desire even more specific goals and objectives depending on the nature and extent of the volunteer program. For example, it might establish short-term goals that define the actual volunteer jobs that need to be done. More specific objectives that might be found in volunteer programs are these.

- To complete a job description for each volunteer in the program.
- To maintain an active list of volunteer opportunities available within the organization.
- To complete a plan for keeping records and making reports.
- To plan and schedule volunteer training programs.
- To outline how often volunteer jobs have to be done and for how long.
- To determine the expected tenure of each volunteer.

The goals of a volunteer program should allow the leader to determine why volunteers are being employed, as well as how and where they will be utilized. Clear goal statements give meaning and direction to the thrust of the volunteer program. As a result, they increase the probability that volunteers will be used in an effective manner and that their experiences will be positive, meaningful, and beneficial to them as individuals.

## JOB DESIGN

Also vital in the planning process is the preparation of a volunteer job design. Meaningful job opportunities for volunteers must be designed and described in order to ensure that the expectations of the organization and the expectations of the volunteer are consistent. A job design also ensures that the volunteer's efforts will be directed toward the goals of the organization. Within a job design is information related to such topics as the type of job to be done, qualifications needed by the volunteer, benefits to the volunteer, training required of the volunteer, and so on. Figure 15.1 presents an example of a volunteer job design for a youth group leader.

## ORGANIZATIONAL, ADMINISTRATIVE AND STAFF INVOLVEMENT

No volunteer program can succeed without adequate *organizational administrative support and staff involvement*. The organization should attempt to create a climate that enables all staff, regular staff and volunteers, to be involved creatively in the planning and implementation of volunteer services. The organization should also structure an active training program for volunteers in which relevant staff within the organization are encouraged to participate. All staff should be encouraged to support, either directly or indirectly, the efforts of the volunteer program. The organization should also have systems for evaluation of the program and for recognition of volunteers for their efforts. Finally, the organization should make known their support of the program by acknowledging it publicly through the media, by supporting it at staff meetings, and by supporting it through the establishment of policies that enable the volunteer effort to accomplish its goals. If the leader is not

comprehensively involved in the overall planning, implementation, and control of the volunteer program, he or she should attempt to ensure that the organization is aware of the need for this type of support. Such support is vital to the success of any volunteer program.

## COMMUNITY INVOLVEMENT

It is absolutely essential that the community be committed to, and involved in, an organization's volunteer program to ensure its success. After all, where do volunteers come from but the community? Enlisting and encouraging the support of the community may entail an active program of public relations. The leader can play an important role in the cultivation of positive public attitudes toward the organization and its programs because the leader is often the primary link between the organization and its constituents. In the development of a volunteer program, it is possible to arouse the interest of community members with media presentations via television, radio, and newspapers; however, it is the one-to-one interaction that occurs between the leader—or other organizational representative—and the potential volunteer that results in commitment to a volunteer effort. This one-to-one interaction also will determine whether a volunteer continues to be interested in, and to participate in, the volunteer program.

It is important that the leader remember that volunteer efforts should be coordinated within the community. Usually, a community will have a volunteer bureau or center that maintains a roster of community volunteer groups and a schedule of their activities. Duplication of effort should be avoided.

## RECRUITMENT, SELECTION, PLACEMENT, ORIENTATION, AND SUPERVISION OF VOLUNTEERS

A recreation leader will often be involved in the recruitment, selection, placement, orientation, and supervision of volunteers. The ex-

**Job Title:** Teen Leader

**Narrative Job Description:** The teen leader works with youth, helping them engage in self-development, problem-solving activities, and leadership development.

## Major Activities

1. Teach problem solving skills.
2. Facilitate group interaction.
3. Lead experiential educational activities.
4. Identify and promote leadership skills.
5. Promote leadership opportunities and involvement.

## Number of Volunteers Working on This Task

2 leaders

## Time Required

Training: 3 hours
Staff meetings: 1 hour per week
Program: 3 hours per week for 15 weeks

## Responsible to

Recreation leader III

## Starting Date

January 15, 1984

## Qualifications

Age: 18 years or older
Sex: Male or Female
Education: Specialized training in leadership desirable
Experience: Previous experience working with youth in leadership development program
Special Skills: Ability to communicate with youth
Interest in leadership and problem solving
Automobile: Not required

## Job Benefits

Experience working with youth
Advanced training in leadership development and problem solving
Advancement possibilities
Recognition
Personal satisfaction
Opportunity to contribute to the community

**FIGURE 15.1**   Volunteer job design.

tent to which the leader is directly involved in these functions will depend on the type and scope of programs organized by the recreation and leisure service organization as well as on the specific needs of the job setting involved. Some volunteer programs are operated very formally in a centralized fashion whereas others are more decentralized and informal. Usually, the leader is more likely to be directly involved in a volunteer program that is decentralized.

## RECRUITMENT OF VOLUNTEERS

From an agency-wide perspective, there are three different approaches that can be employed in the recruitment of volunteers. First, the agency may want to recruit a large pool of volunteers from which to choose individuals for the various tasks that need to be done. Second, the agency may want to attempt to recruit individuals one at a time who have specific skills or knowledge as specific job needs occur. Or, third, the agency may want to use a combination of these two approaches, depending upon the degree of sophistication of the volunteer jobs to be filled. It is important, however, that the agency have jobs for all the volunteers that are recruited. It will create ill will within the community if volunteers are recruited and then are not placed.

The recreation and leisure service leader can be instrumental in the recruitment of volunteers. Often there are participants in programs, parents of participants, or other individuals with whom a volunteer comes in contact who can be recruited into a volunteer effort. Another method that is often used successfully to recruit volunteers within communities is the volunteer fair. This type of program offers an opportunity for agencies within the community to gather together and to advertise and discuss their volunteer opportunities with members of the community. These types of events may be very festive and can serve to promote community pride, build community cohesiveness, and encourage

community commitment. Table 15.1 presents a list of additional settings from which volunteers can be recruited.

## SELECTION AND PLACEMENT OF VOLUNTEERS

Once interest in a volunteer program has been initiated and developed, *selection and placement* of volunteers take place. This process is extremely important in the implementation of the volunteer program. It involves finding the right person for the right job. When this is not accomplished and a good match is not made, both the organization and the volunteer may be dissatisfied. Selection and placement involve two tasks: interviewing and screening.

An *interview* can be thought of as a face-to-face conversation that takes place between a potential volunteer and a representative of the recreation and leisure service agency. Basically, an interview should be structured in such a way that the individual being interviewed is put at ease. It is important that the interviewee feel free to discuss his or her needs, wants, and interests related to the volunteer program. The leader should attempt to gain an understanding of the motivation of the interviewee and to identify his or her experience, skills, and talents. Furthermore, the leader should attempt to determine whether the potential volunteer has latent talents that could be developed with appropriate training. For example, an interviewee might demonstrate a potential for leadership. During the interview process, it is also important that the leader explain the kinds of volunteer opportunities that are available. The leader might even present specific job descriptions of several position options to the interviewee as well as a list of "volunteer rights" and organizational requirements.

*Screening* is a process that takes place after an individual has been interviewed. During the screening process the talents and skills of the individual are matched with the needs of

**TABLE 15.1**   Sources and Strategies That Can Be Used to Recruit Volunteers

| Sources | Strategies |
|---|---|
| • Youth clubs | • Television spots |
| • Volunteer bureaus | • Radio spots |
| • Church groups | • Newspaper advertisements |
| • Neighborhood associations | • A display in a library, school, or large |
| • Special interest groups | business |
| • Other government agencies | • Posters and bulletins, distributed to |
| • Current participants in programs or | grocery stores, businesses, schools, and |
| their friends or relatives | so on. |
| • Professional organizations and societies | • Fliers and brochures, distributed to vari- |
| • High schools | ous community organizations and |
| • Colleges and universities | groups |
| • Schools | • Direct speaking presentations to various |
| • Civic clubs | community groups |
| • Service clubs | • A volunteer fair |
| • Fraternal organizations | |
| • Businesses | |
| • Labor unions | |
| • Political parties | |
| • P.T.A.s | |
| • Senior citizen clubs | |

the organization. The leader involved in the screening process uses the information gained in the individual's initial interview regarding his or her talents, motivation, skills, and knowledge to select a job that will complement these factors.

Once a decision has been made to use a volunteer, the leader should contact the individual. The leader may want to phone or send a letter of welcome. The new volunteer recruit should also receive a letter of understanding or even a contract that describes the responsibilities of the volunteer to the organization and vice versa.

## ORIENTATION AND PROCESSING OF VOLUNTEERS

After the volunteer has been invited to participate in the work of the recreation and leisure service organization, it is essential that an *orientation* program be provided. An orientation program basically provides a brief overview of the goals of the organization, the role of the volunteer within the organization, the organi-

zational structure, and identification of individuals occupying positions within the organization. Volunteers may also be asked to participate in a more extensive *training* program that focuses specifically on skills and talents that might be needed to fulfill their job responsibilities. Orientation and training programs are often carried out in conjunction with one another.

Sometimes the orientation and training of volunteers are not undertaken by supervisory or administrative personnel within the organization in a formalized way. Rather, they may be undertaken by the direct, face-to-face leader, who provides orientation and training on a one-to-one basis. The leader may introduce the new volunteer to co-workers, may define and describe the volunteer's job responsibilities, and may outline the procedures and rules that are employed within the organization. The City of San Jose, California, Parks and Recreation Department has provided a list of suggested activities that recreation leaders should undertake when processing volunteers. These are detailed in the following list.

The recreation leader should

- Welcome the volunteer and establish a friendly cooperative atmosphere.
- Describe the job, its importance, its duration, and how it relates to the total program.
- Acquaint the volunteer with the center and introduce him or her to other people with whom he or she will come in contact.
- Make clear the channels of authority, where and how to get help with daily problems, what resource materials are available, and to whom the volunteer is responsible.
- Work with the volunteer, encouraging his or her suggestions in planning and organizing. Allow him or her full participation in this.
- Assign the volunteer to a job immediately while enthusiasm is high. If possible, try to present two or more jobs he or she might like and that he or she fits.
- Provide assurance that the volunteer will be given sufficient help to accomplish his or her job.
- Make plans for necessary training for the volunteer on a continuing basis.[3]

Many of these suggestions for processing volunteers can be used even though a volunteer has participated in a highly structured training program previously. The leader should make every attempt to make the volunteer feel welcome and needed.

**SUPERVISING THE VOLUNTEER**

The recreation and leisure service leader usually plays a direct role in the supervision and support of volunteers. In fact, the direct, face-to-face leader may be the individual with the

closest contact with volunteers. Consequently, the personal satisfaction experienced by volunteers may be directly related to the amount and quality of communication and direction received from the leader. Some specific guidelines that the recreation and leisure service leader can employ to use volunteers successfully are stated as follows.

In supervising the volunteer, the leader provides

- Guidance and motivation and the teaching of skills necessary for the volunteer to do the job.
- Evaluative information in order to find what the volunteer can do. Start him or her in jobs that he or she already has skills for.
- Instructions the volunteer needs to do the job.
- Stimulus by including the volunteer in planning and organizing and in sharing some of the department's success.
- The authority as well as responsibility for the volunteer to do the job.
- Continuous training so that the volunteer is better prepared to meet problems.
- Opportunity to experiment and do increasingly interesting jobs.
- Recognition by inviting his or her comments and suggestions.[4]

Proper supervision helps the volunteer to enjoy a successful volunteer experience. In addition, it increases the likelihood that volunteers will remain with the agency. A good leader will make volunteers feel a part of the organization and endeavor to use the talents, skills, and abilities of volunteers to the fullest.

The leader supervising volunteers should maintain records and reports documenting the volunteer's contribution. This is essential from several perspectives. First, the volunteer may want to cite his or her experience as a volunteer as a reference for employment elsewhere and, thus, would need agency docu-

[3]"Volunteers: A Handbook for Recreation Leaders," Park and Recreation Department, City of San Jose, California, n.d., p. 6.

[4]Ibid., p. 7.

mentation of his or her efforts. Second, the agency may be funding a volunteer program, based on the premise that a certain number of volunteers are working a certain number of hours. Documentation would be necessary, therefore, to support the provision and continuation of such funds. Last, the maintenance of records and reports is an indication to the volunteer that his or her efforts are of importance.

## EVALUATION AND RECOGNITION

Evaluation and recognition go hand in hand in successful organization and implementation of a volunteer program. *Evaluation* of volunteers ensures not only that they are performing their duties as outlined, but also that the needs of the *volunteers* are being met. Evaluations should not take place intermittently and should not occur only on an annual or semiannual basis. Furthermore, evaluation should not take place only at the conclusion of the volunteer's effort. Rather, evaluation should be an ongoing process carried out on a regular basis. Evaluation may be undertaken through personal observation, comparison of work efforts with performance standards, administration of questionnaires to determine participant satisfaction, and so on. Many individuals would suggest that the evaluation of volunteers should be similar to, or consistent with, the evaluation of full-time employees. Although evaluation is recommended for volunteers, it should be viewed primarily as a means for promoting the growth and development of volunteers. It should attempt to pinpoint ways to make the volunteer experience more satisfying while, at the same time, more productive for the organization.

Individuals who use their leisure to help others in constructive and positive ways deserve the highest accolades and praise that a leader or an organization can bestow. Such recognition can come in the form of verbal compliments, plaques, certificates, and pins. Individuals are very responsive to leaders or organizations who recognize their contributions and provide them with acknowledgment or recognition or both. Just a simple thank-you for a job well done, if it is warm and sincere, can be very meaningful to the volunteer. Recognition is the key to the retention of volunteers. The Scout leader who receives a word of appreciation at the last pack meeting of the year and perhaps a material token of appreciation feels appreciated. Such an individual is more likely to become involved the next year in the activities of the group as a result.

## SUMMARY

In this chapter the process of leading and working with volunteers has been discussed. Volunteers come from all walks of life. They are individuals who give service to an organization without expectation of reimbursement. The recreation and leisure service leader working with volunteers will want to provide encouragement, support, and motivation. Working with volunteers can be an enjoyable and rewarding experience, one that is beneficial both to the individual who gives of his or her time and to the recreation and leisure service organization and its members.

## DISCUSSION QUESTIONS

1. List the recreation and leisure settings where you have found volunteers making major contributions.
2. Define the term *volunteer.*
3. List some of the activities you have seen volunteers engage in in recreation and leisure settings.
4. What are the steps in organizing the voluntary effort?
5. Develop a job description for a volunteer working with (1) youth sports or (2) older persons or (3) an instructional class.

6. Identify some of the sources and strategies that can be used to recruit volunteers in your community.

7. Set up a sample volunteer training program for (1) youth sports or (2) older persons.

8. What are the guidelines that should be followed in supervising volunteers?

9. Why is it important to evaluate volunteers?

10. What are some of the ways that volunteers can be recognized?

# LEADING OLDER PEOPLE

Older individuals engaged in leisure activities and programs can attain personal enjoyment, satisfaction, and a sense of achievement.

gage in physical, social, intellectual, and other types of activity. In this chapter, the authors will discuss common stereotypes applied to older persons, settings in which programs for older persons may occur, and the benefits of participation in leisure programs and activities. The authors have chosen to use the term *older people* or *older persons*, as opposed to terms such as *senior citizens* or *golden agers*. This term is used because it is the authors' belief that this segment of the population is little different from any other age group except that they are older and at a different point in the life cycle.

## BENEFITS OF PARTICIPATION IN RECREATION AND LEISURE PROGRAMS AND ACTIVITIES

For many older persons, work has lent structure to their lives and provided them with a sense of identity and status. Upon retirement, they often face a difficult transition. Participation in recreation and leisure programs and activities can provide older persons with opportunities that can assist them in this transition. Many activities provide structure by encouraging individuals to become involved in them on a regular basis and to become involved in organizational and leadership roles. Other recreation and leisure activities offer older people opportunities for recognition,

Generally speaking, recreation and leisure programs and activities are designed to enhance the quality of life of participants, including older participants. The needs and interests of older persons are the same as for any other age group although the larger amount of leisure time available to older persons may magnify some of these needs. All individuals have a desire to grow and develop, to have friends, to engage in constructive and worthwhile activities, to test themselves, and to en-

status, creativity, a sense of accomplishment, and opportunities to make a contribution to others.

Recreation and leisure programs and activities can also offer older persons opportunities for social interaction with others. The opportunity to form close personal friendships with others can be important to individuals within this age group who may face diminishing contact with family. Such activities can also provide a setting in which friendship can be developed between the sexes for participants who are divorced or widowed.

Finally, leisure activities and programs can offer older persons opportunities to develop themselves physically and mentally. Physical activities can improve circulation and muscle tone, assist in weight loss, assist in tension release, and generally contribute to a feeling of physical well-being. Activities and programs that offer opportunities for participants to expand their knowledge and skills lead to feelings of achievement, interest in further development, and excitement about acquiring new knowledge. Individuals of all ages enjoy and seek out opportunities to learn and grow. A comprehensive table of the potential benefits to older persons of various types of recreation programs and activities can be found in Chapter 4.

## SOME LEADERSHIP OBJECTIVES

Recreation and leisure service organizations that provide services and programs to older persons are concerned with enhancing their quality of life and life satisfaction. Halberg has suggested that the work of the recreation and leisure service leader should be focused on two basic areas. First, leaders should work with older persons to help them develop positive attitudes toward themselves and their leisure experiences. Second, the leader should assist older persons to become involved in the community and in self-help programs. If older persons are encouraged to become in-

volved in their community and to give of themselves to others, feelings of self-worth, dignity, and self-esteem are fostered. Halberg further suggests the following goals for the leader working with older people:

- To serve as a leisure and social resource for older people.
- To encourage and support the pursuit of former, current, and potential interests, abilities and skills.
- To provide opportunities for physical, intellectual, emotional and social challenges.
- To provide opportunities for enjoyment and satisfaction.
- To stimulate social interaction and satisfaction.
- To encourage self-expression and creativity.
- To facilitate and provide experiences which support the development of feelings of self-worth and usefulness.
- To facilitate independence through the development of personal leisure and social skills, positive attitudes, and resources.
- To encourage the development of leadership skills and assumption of leadership roles.[1]

## WHO ARE OLDER PERSONS?

It is important that the leader have knowledge of the demographic characteristics of older people in order to have a greater understanding of this age group. Although older people are similar to other age groups, they have unique demographic characteristics. Perhaps the most important demographic factor that relates to older people is that they are living longer than they ever have before. In 1900 the average life expectancy for an individual was 47.3 years. Now it is 73.3 years. In addition,

[1]Kathleen J. Halberg, "The Role of the Leisure Services Professional," in G. H. Maguire, ed. *Care of the Elderly: A Health Team Approach* (Boston: Little, Brown, in press).

individuals living beyond the age of 65 are expected to live an average of an additional 15.5 years. It is projected that in the year 2000 there will be over 30,000,000 Americans over 65. Although today older persons make up 19 percent of the population, in the year 2000 this figure will be much greater.

Most older people live in urban areas (approximately 75 percent). Forty-one percent live alone and 38 percent live in family units usually composed of a husband and wife. In general, older persons have a lower median income than that of the general population. For example, the median income for the total population in 1975 was $14,678 whereas the median income for individuals 65 years or older was $8,057. This obviously affects their leisure behavior patterns. Most older people are healthy although they usually view themselves as "the exception to the rule."

## THE ROLE OF ATTITUDES AND STEREOTYPES

Perhaps the greatest problems with which older people must deal are related to the negative attitudes and stereotypes that are held about them. For example, when one hears the term "nice little old lady," an immediate image comes to mind: pleasant, caring, talkative, dwells in the past a little too much, lonely, confused at times, and involved in

Most older persons contradict the stereotypes that society has of them.

mostly sedentary activities. Are these perceptions accurate? Consider the following: Ronald Reagan became president of the United States at age 69; Picasso continued to paint productively into his nineties; Cervantes wrote *Don Quixote* after age 60; Artur Rubinstein continued to perform into his sixties; Herman Smith-Johanneson was named Dubonnet "Skier of the Year" at 99 years of age and was named to the Cross-Country Skiing Hall of Fame at age 108! All these examples suggest that older people have the potential to be active and involved and continue to seek challenges throughout their life spans.

Although, indeed, older persons are often faced with health problems, there are many stereotypes and myths that are far more limiting. Stereotypes and myths concerning older persons often affect the ability of a leader to work with this age group effectively. In fact, if the leader's perceptions and attitudes are inaccurate, the activities that he or she offers may be inappropriate and may be limiting to participants. Therefore, it is essential that the leader first examine his or her attitudes, perceptions, values, and stereotypes concerning older persons prior to assuming the leadership of this population. There follows a list of 14 questions to help leaders clarify their perceptions regarding older people.

- Do you "automatically" include games and activities that older people are "supposed to like," such as bingo, card games, and sing-alongs?
- Do you tend to encourage discussion of topics that relate to the past rather than current issues and events?
- Do you avoid activities that require physical exertion?
- Do you plan activities that are basically passive and sedentary in nature?
- Do you find yourself "talking down" to older participants?
- Do you recognize the needs and interests of older people in typical male-female relationships?

- Do you approach older people from the perspective of what they *can't* do rather than what they *can* do?
- Do you assume that older people do not have the capacity or interest to learn new things?
- Do you assume that older people no longer want to be involved in the important activities of the community?
- Do you assume that all people over the age of 65 are the same rather than representative of several age groups?
- Do you assume that all older persons are set in their ways and are uninterested and unwilling to change?
- Do you assume that individuals in their retirement years limit their activities rather than expand them?
- Do you assume that all older people are just a little confused and like to be directed (as opposed to wanting to be self-directed)?
- Do you assume that aging is a process that is uniform for all individuals? That there is a "typical" aging process?

If you have responded affirmatively to any of these questions, you should reevaluate your prejudices, stereotypes, preconceptions, and values regarding older people. Recreation and leisure experiences are probably more limited by the attitudes of society and the leader than by older persons themselves. Obviously, it is an error to generalize about a group of 22 million people (in the United States) or 2.5 million (in Canada), who cover a 30-year span. The range of differences between older persons in matters of health, leisure interests, and personality characteristics is very broad. In fact, a case could be made for the notion that older people are more different from one another than most other segments of the general population owing to their greater variety, depth, and breadth of experience.

It it important that the leader be able to view older persons objectively in order to be able to interact with them appropriately and to "play" to their strengths rather than their weaknesses. Some characteristics of older people include the following.

- Aging is a normal developmental process and is universal.
- While the aging process is normal, aging per se is very individual and variable.
- Illness and handicapping conditions are not universally related to the aging process.
- Older people represent more than one generation, ranging from around 60 to at least 100 years of age.
- Older people can and do change and are capable of adjusting to new circumstances.
- Older people can and do learn new things.
- Older people desire and can remain self-directing.
- Older people want to use their capabilities to contribute to others.
- Older people are not very different from people in other age groups; they happen to be older in years.

These observations provide a more realistic picture of older persons. Based on knowledge and understanding of such information, the leader should be able to interact with older persons in a positive way without the problems associated with our typical stereotypic values, attitudes, and prejudices.

## SETTINGS IN WHICH THE LEADER WORKS WITH OLDER PERSONS

The recreation leader may work in a variety of settings with older persons. However, it is well to remember that 95 percent of people over the age of 65 are found in the *community*. Only 5 percent live in residential institutions of one kind or another at any one time. Consequently, this chapter will focus primarily on community-based programs for older people.

### COMMUNITY-BASED PROGRAMS

Historically, many public recreation and leisure service organizations have operated senior citizens clubs. In the past several decades, these senior citizen clubs have expanded their function and nature. Concerning the transformation of the community senior center from primarily a social club to a multiservice agency, Halberg has written thus.

> The traditional senior center has been concerned with providing leisure and social opportunities for participants: In more recent years this concept has broadened considerably to a more inclusive focus of the multipurpose senior center, which has been defined by the National Council on the Aging as "a community focal point on aging where older persons as individuals or in groups come together for services and activities which enhance their dignity, support their independence, and encourage their involvement in and with the community."[2]

The multipurpose senior center may offer a variety of social, leisure, and health-related programs and services, focused on music, sports, games, outdoor adventure, social activities, service activities, arts and crafts, drama, dance, literature, and educational programs. Table 16.1 lists a number of specific activities in each of these categories that are often found within the recreation component of multipurpose senior citizen centers.

Although specific activities are listed in this table, it is important to recognize that possible leisure activities are as varied as are people. This listing is presented to provide the leader with possible activities initially and should in no way be viewed as all-inclusive.

In addition to the recreation and education programs, centers frequently offer the following services: information, counseling, and referral; health education and services; meals and nutrition education; housing arrangements referral; legal and income counseling; protective services and education; employment referral and training; transportation; outreach programs; and volunteer opportunities.

Are the leadership techniques that an individual would employ dealing with older persons any different from those employed with any other age grouping? Generally speaking, the answer to this question is no. Leadership techniques and methods used in other settings are applicable to work with older people. The reader should refer to the chapter "The Self Directed Program" for more specific information on leading adults, which, of course, includes older people. However, it may be that the recreation and leisure service leader would emphasize certain leadership techniques when working with older persons. As indicated previously, it is important for the leader to keep in mind that older persons span a 30-year range in age. Therefore, although leadership techniques for older people are generally the same as for other age groupings, the leader should use common sense in leading programs and activities for individuals in the upper portion of this 30-year age span, or the relatively small number of older persons who experience health problems of some kind. Some of the techniques and methods that might be used by the leader working with older people in a community-based setting follow.

- The leader working with older people often acts as a facilitator, encouraging *participants* to plan, organize, and implement their *own* activities. The leader is often more assistive, providing information, helping the group identify resources, and suggesting alternative courses of action.
- The leader should attempt to maintain positive productive communication, interacting on an equal level with participants. For some reasons, neophyte leaders (and even some experienced leaders) tend to project their voices, slow down, and articulate carefully when talking to groups of older persons and individuals. The leader should avoid this because it may appear that he or she is "talking down" to them.
- Older persons often like to share their expe-

[2]Halberg, op. cit., p.

**TABLE 16.1**    Some Programs and Services of Senior Citizen Centers

**Music**

| | |
|---|---|
| Music lessons | Music appreciation classes |
| Playing in ensembles | Barbershop quartet contests |
| Choral singing | Attending concerts |

**Active sports**

| | | |
|---|---|---|
| Billiards | Table tennis | Yoga |
| Tennis | Walking | Bowling |
| Badminton | Canoeing | (5 pin, 10 pin |
| Horseshoes | Shuffleboard | and lawn) |
| Swimming | Golf | |

**Table games**

| | | |
|---|---|---|
| Bridge | Bingo | Poker |
| Canasta | Chess | Euchre |
| Cribbage | Checkers | Whist |

**Outdoor**

| | | |
|---|---|---|
| Hiking | Boating | Camping |
| Hunting | Collecting | Photography |
| Fishing | Nature study | Tours |

**Social**

| | | |
|---|---|---|
| Dances | Picnics | Roasts |
| Potlucks | Special events | Other |
| Teas | Theme parties | |

**Service**

| | |
|---|---|
| Gray Ladies | Grandparents |
| Red Cross | Political party volunteers |

**Arts and Crafts**

| | | |
|---|---|---|
| Painting lessons | Cooking classes | Ceramics |
| Woodworking | Pottery | Sketching |
| Quilting | Photography | Candlemaking |
| Embroidery | Stained glass | Sewing |
| Macrame | Art shows | |

**Drama**

| | |
|---|---|
| Attending plays | Costuming |
| Producing plays | Critiquing dramatic events |
| Acting | Movie parties |

**Literature**

| | |
|---|---|
| Book review groups | Book discussions |
| Creative writing groups | Poetry clinics |
| Reading | Library programs |

**Educational**

| | |
|---|---|
| Tours | University and college courses |
| Workshops | Slide shows and films |
| Conferences | Personal development courses |

**Dance**

| | |
|---|---|
| Attending the ballet | Folk dancing |
| Ballroom dancing | Square dance calling |
| Square dancing | Aerobic dancing |

rience and knowledge. The leader may want to attempt to encourage opportunities for participants to be able to engage in this type of contribution. There are some organizations that are designed to facilitate this, for example, SCORE (Senior Core of Retired Executives), Foster Grandparents, RSVP (Retired Senior Volunteer Program), and others.

- Refreshments or meals served in conjunction with recreation and leisure activities should complement any dietary restrictions of participants, such as low sugar or no salt diets.
- Older persons often view themselves, as society views them, incapable of more than sedentary activity, unable to grow and learn. The leader working with these types of participants should attempt to promote individual confidence in ability to perform and participate.
- Since some older people experience hearing loss, it is important to be sensitive to this factor in verbal communications, especially in the group setting, where such losses are magnified by the level of noise. In addition, the leader may want to have large print reading materials available because some older persons may have visual problems.
- It is important to be cognizant and respectful of the differences in values between generations. The values of an older person are based on his or her experiences, and although they may be different, they are not "wrong." Nor are the leader's values, based on different experiences, "right."
- The leader should avoid viewing older persons in terms of the stereotypes of society. We find what we look for. If the leader looks for confirmation of these stereotypes, he or she will find them. If the leader, on the other hand, attempts to view older persons objectively, he or she will find that most participants contradict these stereotypes.
- The leader should be sensitive to any financial limitations that may be experienced by participants. For example, prior to suggesting an expensive excursion for the entire group, the leader might want to evaluate whether anyone might be left out as a result of the cost.
- Leaders should avoid suggesting activities and programs that are below the level of sophistication of participants. Older persons are sometimes encouraged to participate in activities and programs that are almost "childlike." This can adversely affect their feelings of dignity, self-worth, and self-respect.
- The leader should encourage involvement of participants in programs and activities that include a variety of age groups, and not just participation in age-segregated activities. For example, friends and relatives can be invited to attend social functions and trips offered by the sponsoring agency.

### ADULT DAY-CARE CENTERS

Another community-based setting in which older persons are found is the adult day-care center. The purpose of such a center is to provide additional health-related services not available in the senior citizens center, helping older persons to maintain residence in the community. These health-related services might include provision of medication; specific care from a physician, nurse, or other health care professional; or provision of programs that enable family members to work during the day. Although the older participants in such programs are more limited by health-related problems than older persons found at senior citizens centers, they are, for the most part, independent with the assistance of the programs available at the adult day-care center.

The leadership techniques discussed in relationship to senior centers typically apply to participants in adult day-care programs although greater assistance and adaptation may be necessary. Since this population may be somewhat more physically limited, it is especially important that the leader not assume stereotyped perceptions of the participants because they are essentially healthy older people who will find particular benefit in being dealt with as such.

## LONG-TERM CARE FACILITY

Five percent of those over the age of 65 are found in institutions, especially long-term care facilities, that is, nursing homes and homes for the aged. The long-term care facility is a residential institution for those older persons and others who are in need of more complex and sophisticated health care but not at the more costly level available in hospitals. The leader should recognize that some older people do indeed benefit from the programs available in long-term care facilities and return to the community.

In the long-term care facility, the leader will find himself or herself in the position of *activities coordinator*. In this role, the leader assists the resident to maintain his or her lifestyle through motivation and development of opportunities in which he or she can use his or her abilities and continue the daily and more periodic activities that were previously taken for granted. These opportunities may include not only the kinds of recreational activities typically conducted by the leader, but also the less formal spontaneous activities in which each of us engages and takes for granted, for example, being able to continue to read a particular newspaper or magazine that the resident has read throughout his or her life, being able to watch particular television programs, discussion of current events or sporting events, or caring for plants. In other words, the leader encourages the maintenance of lifestyle and life routines.

Although the residents of long-term care facilities are obviously more limited than the older persons discussed earlier and more specialized leadership techniques and methods are frequently necessary, the role of the activities coordinator in providing and facilitating the more typical aspects of living is essential to the well-being and positive self-concept of the resident. The leader who views the resident as a total person with strengths as well as areas of lesser strength and focuses on a familiar and typical part of life has much to do with the quality of life of the resident of the long-term care facility.

## SUMMARY

In this chapter the authors have discussed the role of the recreation leader working with older persons. Although leadership skills and techniques that apply to other populations also apply to work with this age group, the leader should ensure that he or she does not limit his or her perceptions of older people by believing the stereotypes commonly used to describe them. The leader should attempt to remain objective. The authors have offered a number of suggestions for leaders who work with older persons in order to help them interact effectively with this age group.

## DISCUSSION QUESTIONS

1. Why is the term *older people* used rather than senior citizens or golden agers?
2. What goals-objectives are appropriate for leisure programs with older people?
3. What are some of the major demographic characteristics of the older population?
4. Discuss the greatest problem with which older people must deal.
5. List some of the major stereotypes held about older people.
6. What are some of the major characteristics of aging?
7. Describe the program of a multipurpose senior citizens center.
8. Describe the role of the leader in working with older people.
9. Describe the purpose and program of an adult day-care center.
10. Describe the role of the activities coordinator in a long-term care facility.

# WORKING WITH PEOPLE WITH DISABILITIES

Individuals with disabilities have the desire, determination, and ability to participate in recreation and leisure activities.

Society is made up of many individuals with unique characteristics. Recreation and leisure service leaders work with males, females, the young, the old, as well as individuals from all races, religions, ethnic backgrounds, and socioeconomic categories. All these people have circumstances that affect the way that they live their lives. One of these possible circumstances is living with a disability. This chapter will focus on helping the reader understand: (1) the nature of disabling conditions; (2) concepts of mainstreaming-integration; and (3) the role of the general therapeutic recreation and leisure service leader who works with individuals with disabilities, including guidelines and techniques for leadership.

The existence of a disabling condition is not necessarily limiting. Disabling conditions may be viewed as existing on a continuum, depending upon their degree of impact on an individual's life-style. For example, many people have visual impairments, some of which are correctable or partially correctable with glasses or contact lenses, and some of which more severely impact on the individuals' functioning. It is often assumed that the existence of a disabling condition is limiting in and of itself. This is not necessarily the case, the attitudes, behaviors, and values of relatives, neighbors, acquaintances, friends, recreation leaders, and others in society may do more to limit participation than the disabling condition itself. Furthermore, the attitudes and values of the individual with the disability, as learned from the larger society, may also affect his or her self-perception and resulting participation in recreation and leisure service activities. Generally speaking, *a disability can be defined as a condition that has a potential to limit major life activities whereas a handicap is defined as the limiting result of the disability*. Thus, a person may have a disability, but not have a handicap as a result.

## THE RIGHT OF THE INDIVIDUAL WITH DISABILITIES

Although every individual, including people with disabilities, has been guaranteed the right to equal opportunities in the U.S. Constitution, significant legislation, enacted in the 1960s and 1970s, was necessary to mandate equal opportunity for this population specifically. Thus, Public Law 94.142 requires a free appropriate public education in the least restrictive environment. Under the umbrella of this law is included the provision of recreation and leisure services as a related educational service. Further, section 504 of the Rehabilitation Services Act of 1973 states that an individual shall not be discriminated against on the basis of a disabling condition. These two legislative acts have stimulated tremendous growth and have provided new directions for recreation and leisure services for individuals with disabilities.

At this point in time, many community-based recreation and leisure service organizations, voluntary organizations, and other leisure-related organizations have accepted their responsibility for providing services for all citizens within the community, including individuals with disabilities. Though most organizations recognize the need for services, such services are often offered in such a way that they limit participation. Activities may be segregated to include only people with disabilities. These types of services, though well intended and often commendable, in fact encourage the labeling of people and perpetuate the perceived differences between individuals with disabilities and the general public.

## THE LEADER AND MAINSTREAMING-INTEGRATION

Mainstreaming and integration, terms that came into use as a result of legislation and advocacy efforts in the 1960s and 1970s, have as a goal allowing people ''regardless of ability or disability, to interact with each other in settings of individual choice.''[1] A leader in any setting may have the opportunity to work with individuals with disabilities. The leader's goal when working with disabled individuals is to make the experience or experiences as typical as possible. This includes not only working directly with the individual to develop attitudes, skills, and knowledge, but also working with community agencies and other relevant parties that impact upon the individual's leisure experience.

The idea of recreation integration was popularized and further developed by Hutchison and Lord in the book *Recreation Integration* (available from Leisurability Publications, Inc., Box 36, Station A, Islington, Ontario M9A 4X1). Most integration programs, developed in recreation and leisure service settings, involve the use of a process that can be visualized as existing on a continuum. At one end of the continuum, we find individuals with disabilities in segregated activities. A segregated activity can be thought of as one that is separated or isolated, often occurring in hospitals, rehabilitation centers, or other specialized facilities or settings. At the other end of the continuum, we find individuals who have been fully integrated into the regular program offerings of a recreation and leisure service organization. In this situation, the individual with the disability would fully participate regardless of whether or not he or she were ablebodied or disabled.

Although this continuum is most easily depicted according to setting (e.g., segregated, partially integrated, integrated), it is important to recognize that the earlier stages of the continuum tend to focus more on the development of physical, social, and emotional skills of the participant whereas the latter stage tend to focus more on working with agencies,

[1]''Integration Plan,'' Eugene (Oregon) Parks and Recreation Department, p. 2, n.d.

staffs and nondisabled participants. These focuses occur regardless of setting; for example, an individual may be working on skill development in an integrated setting for some activities whereas advocacy with staff may occur in segregated settings, depending on the local situation. The underlying concept of the continuum is that by working concurrently with the participant and the larger community, the community, through its agencies and programs, will increasingly more easily accommodate and accept people with disabilities, and the person with the disability will be increasingly more able to participate in typical leisure opportunities.

The integrated environment is one in which barriers to participation have been successfully removed by both the leader and the individual with the disability. Many recreation and leisure service organizations today are actively involved in providing a full range of programs for the disabled, from segregated ones to fully integrated ones. The process of integration requires not only encouraging individuals with disabilities to upgrade and develop skills, attitudes, and knowledge, but, perhaps more importantly, also requires the leader to work with participants, co-workers, and supervisors in order to eliminate the variety of barriers that can impact on leisure participation. Obviously, one of the biggest barriers to leisure participation by the disabled is architectural barriers. However, even more important may be social and attitudinal barriers that prevent individuals with disabilities and those without from interacting successfully with one another. The larger problem that looms may be changing the attitudes of those individuals without disabilities, including the general public, recreation and leisure professionals, and nondisabled participants.

Specifically, some of the barriers that prevent individuals with disabilities and those without disabilities from successfully participating in activities and programs with one another include the following.

*Architectural Barriers.* Architectural barriers might include the presence of stairs instead of ramps, inaccessible rest rooms, doorways that are too narrow, protruding thresholds, revolving doors, inaccessible drinking fountains and phone booths, and so on.

*Transportation Barriers.* Transportation that is inaccessible can prevent participation in certain leisure activities. For example, lack of public transportation, lack of funds for transportation, the presence of stairs leading to, for example, a bus, train, or plane can all represent transportation barriers.

*Financial Barriers.* Either the disabled individual or the recreation and leisure service agency may experience financial difficulty in providing services for this population. Agencies have frequently cited additional costs associated with the provision of such services as the reason for their inability to provide them. Although additional costs may be incurred by the agency, they typically are not as great as anticipated if leaders and administrators have been oriented or trained to provide these types of services.

*Attitudinal Barriers.* Although the barriers listed earlier do exist, by far the greatest barriers to leisure participation are those related to attitudes and values. Often the leader or the agency can overcome transportation, architectural, and financial barriers if attitudinal barriers are not present as well. Related to overcoming attitudinal barriers is the development of organizational policies and procedures that reflect the organization's commitment to integration-mainstreaming. Though society's awareness and acceptance of individuals with disabilities is growing, attitudes of fear, pity, and guilt accompanied by such behaviors as oversolicitousness, ridicule, rejection, or ignoring are readily apparent. Such attitudes and behaviors come from people's lack of information and knowledge; they tend to have such attitudes when confronted with situations and people who differ from the norm. Particularly important in overcoming attitudinal barriers is adequate and effective communication.

Figure 17.1 offers a model that demonstrates the steps in the mainstreaming/integration process. Phase I typically occurs in clinical settings such as hospitals, institutions, and rehabilitation centers. The role of the recreation leader in these settings, who typically is a therapeutic recreation specialist, is to facilitate the development of skills and attitudes necessary for successful functioning in society. The next phase in the continuum, Phase II, involves the provision of segregated leisure services in the community. Skills and attitudes continue to be developed, and efforts toward transition to Phase III are initiated. During Phase III services become partially integrated in community settings. Here the leader works both with disabled and nondisabled participants to facilitate positive interaction. Services are fully integrated during Phase IV. At this point, the leader provides leisure opportunities to both disabled and nondisabled participants who engage in typical leisure participation. Essentially, this is a theoretical model for moving individuals with disabilities from a segregated institutional setting to a fully integrated program.

Since the vast majority of services today provided for individuals with disabilities are offered by community-based organizations, these types of agencies are also involved in the process of mainstreaming-integration. A good example of a mainstreaming-integration process adopted by a community park and recreation department is that operated by the Eugene (Oregon) Parks and Recreation Department. This agency's "Integration Plan" sets forth a five-step process for individuals with disabilities, moving from segregated community recreation activities to fully integrated activities. The following is the process.

1. Provide specialized recreation programs to a segregated group of disabled individuals in a segregated environment.
2. Provide specialized recreation programs to a segregated group of disabled individuals in an integrated environment.
3. Provide specialized recreation programs to disabled individuals that are also open to nondisabled individuals in an integrated environment.
4. Provide staff support to disabled individuals who wish to integrate into mainstreamed programs or activities.
5. Provide support as requested by participants engaged in community-based leisure activities.[2]

It is important to recall that though the continuum is presented according to specific settings (e.g., segregated, integrated), the process that occurs in relationship to the participant and the community and its agencies is one of increasing skill development on the part of the participant and accommodation by community leisure agencies regardless of setting.

It is also important to recognize that the process of integration occurs not only with the individual with the disability, but also with other participants, parents of participants, professional staff, volunteers, and the community at large. It is important to prepare program participants who are ablebodied and others to be comfortable with themselves when interacting with individuals with disabilities. This preparation may include providing orientation or training or both to program participants and staff members, as well as advocating policy development that is directed toward removing architectural, transportation, fiscal, and attitudinal barriers.

With regard to more specific actions by the

[2]Ibid.

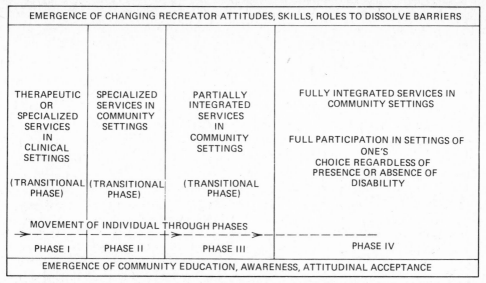

**FIGURE 17.1**   Conceptualization of phases—humanistic mainstreaming continuum. Indicates change in context of community structure and service provision (Roxanne Howe-Murphy, "A Conceptual Basis for Mainstreaming Recreation and Leisure Services: Focus on Humanism," *Therapeutic Recreation Journal*, Vol. 13, No. 4 [1979], pp. 11–18). Used by permission of the author.

leader to facilitate the successful implementation of an integrated recreation activity, the following guidelines may be employed.

- People with disabilities have the desire, determination, and ability to participate with everyone else. All they need is the chance to be included, *and that comes from the leader*.
- Treat the participant as a person just like anyone else in the program.
- Have a positive attitude toward the person. The leader is a model for other program participants.
- The leader may need to spend extra time allowing the person to get things said and done.
- Be sure to address the person directly instead of through another member of the group.
- Try to foresee and eliminate unexpected barriers or conditions that may result in problems.

- Choose activity areas that allow all people to participate and succeed.[3]
- Seek out support from other participants. Encourage them to interact actively in a positive way with individuals with disabilities.
- All participants should be allowed the opportunity to make decisions, some of which may involve a degree of risk or even lead to failure. Failing, with dignity, is a part of the typical learning process for all individuals. We learn from our mistakes, as often as we learn from our successes.
- Provide opportunities for all participants to give the leader feedback regarding the leisure experience. Providing opportunities for feedback may be extended to the

[3]Adapted from Charles C. Bullock, Royal E. Whol, Tracy E. Webneck, and Angela M. Crawford, *Life: Leisure is for Everyone, Resource and Training Manual* (Chapel Hill, N.C.: University of North Carolina, Curriculum in Recreation Administration, 1982), p. 134.

planning, implementation, and evaluation stages of the activity planning process.

- Offer help when it looks as though it might be needed, but do not insist on it if the individual refuses aid.
- Don't "hover." Disabled adults wish to be treated as adults. Children react the same way; they want to be like you and me.
- When a disabled person falls, take it easy. Wait for him or her to give you a cue. If the disabled person can get up by himself or herself, he or she may prefer doing this; if he or she needs a lift, the disabled person will tell you.
- Crutches and wheelchairs are necessary accessories for some people. Don't take them away from a physically disabled person unless the person indicates he or she would like to have them out of the way. It is irritating to have your crutches grabbed quickly as soon as you hit the chair, leaving you stranded.
- Steps can be difficult even for the young and agile. Some disabled people often need help here. Let them tell you how to help. Those who do not need to be helped up the steps usually have methods of their own for making them. Do not pull an arm or push from behind unless such assistance has been requested. Precarious balance can be lost entirely with such tactics.
- Keep your perspective. As Gertrude Stein might say, "An arm is an arm is an arm" and "a leg is a leg is a leg." It is just that. This is not the whole person.
- Relax. No matter what you do, if you are friendly and genuine the disabled person is likely to be comfortable with you.
- Have fun. Talk about the same things you would with another person. A mental or physical disability does not necessarily limit your interest or dampen your sense of humor.
- Be yourself. Don't be sticky sweet. Omit the pious note.

- Let common sense and consideration be your guide, and you will never err seriously. Disabled people are just like you. Their physical differences or mental slowness does not have to mean they feel or think differently from others.
- When in doubt, ask, "May I help you?" and "How can I help?"
- Add "improvise" to your vocabulary, and don't be afraid to do a little of it.[4]

## ORIENTATION TO DISABLING CONDITIONS

When we discuss individuals with disabilities, it is important to reiterate that we are talking about a *person* first, who happens to have been born with or to have acquired a disabling condition. This person has unique needs, interests, preferences, desires, living situation, and economic status and also happens to have a condition that may be limiting to some major life activities although it may not be limiting to other major life activities. Second, although the individual may be limited in some areas because of this condition, he or she also has abilities and strengths. Third, the influence of social and attitudinal variables, especially attitudes, must be considered as they impact on an individual with a disability.

Generally, although attitudes of the general public about individuals with disabilities have become considerably more positive and accepting, negative and limiting attitudes continue to prevail. As individuals with disabilities interact with individuals and agencies within society, they are exposed to these attitudes. More important, individuals may begin to internalize them as they are constantly reinforced. Though this situation does not nec-

[4]*Closing the Gap: An Inservice Training Guide for Mainstreaming Recreation and Leisure Services*, San Jose, CA. Department of Recreation and Leisure Service. San Jose State University, n.d.

essarily always occur, it frequently can have a severe impact on how the person with the disability feels about himself or herself and his or her capabilities. It is hoped that the leader will recognize his or her impact on how the person with the disability feels about himself or herself and also recognize that he or she will be role model for participants.

These points should be kept in mind when the reader reviews Tables 17.1, 17.2, 17.3,

**TABLE 17.1**  Functioning Levels for Physical Disabilities

| Functioning levels | Associated conditions | Implications for recreation |
| --- | --- | --- |
| **Nonambulatory** | | |
| 1. Uses a wheelchair<br>Has upper torso use (para-plegia) | *Note:* Individuals with the associated conditions listed may not always use a wheelchair but may choose to do so for speed and convenience<br><br>Polio<br>Amputation of the legs at a high level<br>Later stages of multiple sclerosis<br>Later stages of progressive muscular dystrophy<br>Small percentage of spinal bifida<br>Severe stroke<br>Spinal cord injury at the low thoracic or lumbar level (lower back)<br>Osteogenesis imperfecta (brittle bones)<br>Cerebral palsy | • Improve manual dexterity and upper torso strength and control in order to prepare for architectural barriers and independent mobility<br>• Build on existing functioning muscles and abilities<br>Possible Modifications:<br>• Playing surface—movement facilitated on smooth surface (concrete, wood—not grass or dirt)<br>• Allow more than one bounce or shorten boundaries<br>• Use lighter equipment to allow more time for person to maneuver chair into place<br>• Other modifications minimal |
| 2. Uses wheelchair<br>Limited upper torso strength (quadriplegia) | Severe stroke<br>Spinal cord injury in mid-high thoracic or cervical region of the vertebrae (middle to upper back)<br>Later stages of progressive muscular dystrophy | • Decubitis ulcer: (breakdown of skin due to prolonged exposure; may need assistance shifting weight at regular intervals).<br>• Resistance to sun is minimal owing to limited ability to perspire. Limit exposure to sun.<br>• Physical activities will require the assistance of adaptive devices or a partner |
| **Respiratory Difficulties** | | |
| | Cystic fibrosis<br>Tuberculosis<br>Bronchial asthma<br>Rheumatic heart disease<br>Muscular dystrophy (progressive) | • Guard against infection of the lungs<br>• Watch for allergic reactions caused by food, air, drugs, nervous tension (particularly for individuals with bronchial asthma)<br>• Avoid activities that are played on or produce high dust levels (sanding)<br>• See modifications for fatigue level also |

**TABLE 17.1** Continued

| Functioning levels | Associated conditions | Implications for recreation |
| --- | --- | --- |
| **Fatigue Level** | | |
| Overwork and fatigue should be avoided. Either fatigues easily or may experience difficulty if pushed to fatigue | Cerebral palsy<br>Muscular dystrophy<br>Arthritis<br>Hypertensive heart disease<br>Stroke<br>Rheumatic heart disease<br>Bronchial asthma<br>Multiple sclerosis<br>Cystic fibrosis<br>Tuberculosis<br>Sickle cell anemia<br>Diabetes | Possible Modifications:<br>• Increase number of rest periods; control stimuli in environment<br>• Provide relaxation exercises (Yoga, self-massage)<br>• Increase number of players<br>• Provide a wide range of creative expressive activities in addition to physical (art, drama . . .)<br>• Activities that require sporadic effort instead of continuous effort (baseball is better than soccer) |
| **Limited Use of Hands** | | |
| Poor fine motor coordination or limited strength in hands | Arthritis<br>Muscular dystrophy<br>Cerebral palsy<br>Multiple sclerosis | Possible Modifications:<br>• Use lighter equipment (plastic bats, whiffle balls)<br>• Slow down moving objects: throw underhand; allow one bounce; roll the ball; decrease weight or air pressure of a ball<br>• Modify the rules: permit additional trials<br>• Reduce size of playing area; increase number of players; decrease height of net or goal<br>• Enlarge size of equipment or alter shape for easier handling (larger cards or card holders) |
| **Limited Ambulatory Mobility** | | |
| Uses braces, crutches, or walkers or a combination | Polio<br>Muscular dystrophy<br>Cerebral palsy<br>Amputation (legs)<br>Scoliosis<br>Stroke | Minimal Modifications:<br>• Be aware of slippery surfaces<br>• Slow moving objects or the pace of the activity<br>• Refer to the sections on wheelchair use |

*Source:  Closing the Gap: An Inservice Training Guide for Mainstreaming Recreation and Leisure Services,* Department of Recreation and Leisure Studies, San Jose State University and the U.S. Office of Special Education, Project No. G007701049, n.d.

17.4, and 17.5 concerning disabling conditions. The reader should note that this discussion does not include all disabling conditions, which are far too numerous to discuss and some of which are found relatively infrequently. Major conditions are grouped into five (5) basic categories. These categories focus on functional level rather than diagnostic category, for this information will be most useful to the leader and, one hopes, will not limit his or her perceptions of people with disabilities.

**TABLE 17.2**   Effects of Hearing Loss for Decibel Levels and Degree of Hearing Loss

| Decibel loss (db)[a] and associated terms | Effects of loss on understanding of language and speech | Program implications and needs |
|---|---|---|
| 26–40 db loss Slight (Hard of hearing) | • May have difficulty hearing faint or distant speech<br>• May experience difficulty with vocabulary and speech articulation | • May benefit from hearing aid as loss approaches 40 db<br>• Proper lighting and close proximity to speaker will help |
| 41–55 db loss Mild | • Understands conversations within 3 to 5 feet if speaker is facing him or her<br>• May exhibit speech defects and limited vocabulary | • Will benefit from hearing aid<br>• Attention to placement of person in relationship to speaker and proper lighting is necessary<br>• Fatigue and extraneous noise will affect person's ability to comprehend speech |
| 56–70 db loss Moderate (Hard of hearing) | • Speech must be loud and distance small for person to comprehend conversation and will have difficulty unless conversation is directed at him or her | • Will need hearing aids<br>• Will need assistance to comprehend new vocabulary, concrete examples and demonstration<br>• Close proximity to speaker and proper lighting is essential with minimum background noise |
| 71–90 db loss Severe (Severely hard of hearing) | • Understands only strongly amplified speech<br>• May hear voices about one foot away | • In addition to the above points, person may have balance problems, depending upon what part of the ear is damaged |
| 71–90 db loss Severe (Severely hard of hearing) (cont.) | • Speech is distorted; may be able to hear vowels, but not all consonants clued into topic and face<br>• Speech and language defects present | • Person will experience more difficulty in a group discussion, will need to be facing the speaker |
| Over 90 db loss Profound (Deaf) | • Maximally amplified speech not understood<br>• May hear loud sounds but is aware of vibrations<br>• Relies on vision rather than hearing as primary communication source | • In addition to the above points, person may need assistance of an interpreter depending on the activity<br>• Demonstration and the use of visual aids is essential<br>• New vocabulary must be taught |

[a]Decibel: A unit used to measure the loudness of sounds. It is based on the smallest change that an acute human ear can hear. A sound of zero decibels is the softest sound. Ordinary conversation is measured at 60–80 decibels. (Chart adapted from Illinois Commission on Children, 1968; and Davis and Silverman, 1970.)

*Source: Closing the Gap: An Inservice Training Guide for Mainstreaming Recreation and Leisure Services*, Department of Recreation and Leisure Studies, San Jose State University and the U.S. Office of Special Education, Project No. G007701049, n.d.

## ROLES AND TECHNIQUES

As stated earlier, the role of the leader in working with people with disabilities has two major facets. First, the leader is working with the person with the disability to develop skills and attitudes that will make integration more comfortable and successful. Second, the leader works with the larger environment of participation of individuals with disabilities through advocacy and training, also to make integration more comfortable and successful. Both facets of the role are essential if true integration is to be accomplished.

When the leader does assume a direct leadership role, most frequently he or she is more

**TABLE 17.3**    Ranges of Visual Impairments (based on optimal visual correction)[a]

| Associated terms or degrees | Functioning levels |
|---|---|
| • Total blindness: complete loss of vision and light perception (very small minority)<br>• No functional vision: can see shadows or shapes but no details, sees shades of gray not black<br>• No peripheral vision, "tunnel vision," sees the world as if looking through a hollow tube; must turn head in line with objects to see them<br>• No central vision; cannot see what is "straight ahead," but can see peripherally<br>• Blurred or cloudy vision; has difficulty focusing on objects, as with cataracts<br>• Limited ability to control the amount of light and accommodate to light changes. As a result, images appear "washed out," few details can be detected | • Will use braille and travel aids (cane, guide dog, or electronic aids or a combination)<br>• Same as above<br>• Can read regular print; independent mobility but may use optical aids for reading street signs. Limited modifications necessary for participation. Has limited depth perception<br>• May use large print books, magnification aids or braille or a combination. Will have difficulty doing close-up work; may use cane<br>• May use braille, large print, or magnification aids or a combination. Can usually travel independently<br>• Wears dark glasses to protect eyes from bright light. May be a print reader with or without magnification aids<br>**Any individual with a visual loss can benefit from talking books, tapes, records, etc. |

[a]Legally Blind: A person whose vision in the better eye, even with ordinary corrective lenses, is no better than 20/200 or whose visual field has a maximum diameter no greater than 20 degrees. This means that a person can see at 20 feet what another individual with normal vision can see at 200 feet or that his or her side vision is severely restricted. Partial Sight: A person whose vision in the better eye, even with ordinary corrective lenses, is no better than 20/70, or whose visual field has a maximum diameter no greater than 20 degrees.

*Source:   Closing the Gap: An Inservice Training Guide for Mainstreaming Recreation and Leisure Services,* Department of Recreation and Leisure Studies, San Jose State University and the U.S. Office of Special Education, Project No. G007701049, n.d.

**TABLE 17.4**    Functional Levels of Mental Retardation

| Associated terms or degrees | Functional abilities for adults (age 21 + ) | % of all people considered retarded |
|---|---|---|
| Mild/Educable | Capable of earning a living and participating fully in community life; may need advice about important decisions and economic matters | 86–89 |
| Moderate/Trainable | Capable of self-maintenance in unskilled jobs, simple, useful, repetitive work task under supervision; can carry on simple conversation and interact with others cooperatively | 6–10 |
| Severe/Custodial or Dependent | Can follow daily routines, perform repetitive tasks, and contribute partially to self-support under complete supervision | 3.5 |
| Profound/Life Support | Some motor and speech development; needs complete care and supervision for self-maintenance; interacts with others in group activities and simple games | 1.5 |

*Source:   Closing the Gap: An Inservice Training Guide for Mainstreaming Recreation and Leisure Services,* Department of Recreation and Leisure Studies, San Jose State University and the U.S. Office of Special Education, Project No. G007701049, n.d.

**TABLE 17.5**  Functional Levels for Emotional or Behavioral Disability

| Functional levels | Associated behaviors | Implications for recreation |
|---|---|---|
| **Emotional Stress Tolerance Level** | | |
| Refers to the person's ability to cope with stress or react to stress caused by changes in the environment or routines, personal interactions with others, or interactions with authority figures. | The degree or severity of the behaviors will vary from one individual to another from situation to situation. | Observe behaviors and try to determine antecedents of behavior. Consistency and acceptance of the person are the keys. Let the person know he or she is accepted but not a particular behavior. Suggestions below apply to *both* aggressive and passive behavior. |
| 1. Aggressive behavior | • Verbal and physical aggression, antisocial in nature<br>• Impulsive, do not consider consequences of their actions<br>• Demanding, attention seeking<br>• Defies authority<br>• Destructive to self, others, or the environment<br>• Quarrelsome, irresponsible | • Establish rules for participant behavior with the group; discuss reasons for the rules and consequences of breaking them. Keep limits clear, concise, and reasonable<br>• Enforce rules consistently; reinforce positive behavior; ignore negative behavior the first time if possible; then give warning and enforce consequences established if behavior continues<br>• Provide cues to expected and appropriate behavior |
| 2. Passive-withdrawn behavior | • Lack of interest, daydreams<br>• Low rate of social interaction<br>• Timid, shy, sensitive, submissive<br>• Feelings of distress, expressed unhappiness<br>• Fears of a general and specific nature<br>• Lack of energy<br>• Low self-esteem (tends to be true for most people with emotional and behavioral problems) | • Don't stress competitive activities; emphasize cooperative experiences, and allow time for solitary activities<br>• Balance program with active and passive activities<br>• Allow release of excess energy through physical activities; provide wind-down and relaxation exercises<br>• Provide opportunities for individual dual and group discussions that point out participants' strengths and common interests and feelings<br>• Provide structure and routine; gradual reintroduction of structure can be introduced as participants can tolerate it<br>• Build on strength and interests<br>• Bring activities to a complete close before moving on to a new one |
| **Awareness of Reality** | | |
| Refers to the degree to which people are aware of their environment, other people, and the task at hand. | • Excessive expression of fantasy<br>• Confused, disoriented, forgetful<br>• Short attention span, excessive daydreaming | • Be honest about your tolerance of participants' behavior<br>• Do not encourage fantasy; ask questions that relate to here and now<br>• Provide opportunities for success and positive attention from peers (important for all people) |

**TABLE 17.5**  Continued

| Functional levels | Associated behaviors | Implications for recreation |
|---|---|---|
| | • Lack of purposeful behavior<br>• Behavior reflects poor judgement in terms of personal safety, anticipated reactions of others<br>• Displacement of feelings onto an object or innocent bystander<br>• Vague, evasive responses | • Be honest in communicating with participants. If you don't understand the person or the behavior, don't pretend to understand. Discuss it with the person<br>• Make sure you have people's attention before giving directions<br>• Give clear, specific directions<br>• Provide clear structure and limits to the activity<br>**Other Points that Apply:**<br>• Some individuals may be on medications. Find out if medications are being taken and how they affect the person<br>• Keep in mind that internal emotional conflicts are very draining of energy. Balance active programs with more passive, relaxing ones |

*Source:    Closing the Gap: An Inservice Training Guide for Mainstreaming Recreation and Leisure Services,* Department of Recreation and Leisure Studies, San Jose State University and the U.S. Office of Special Education, Project No. G007701049, n.d.

of a facilitator, enabler, and advocate working with the person with the disability in a joint effort. A joint effort is essential if the person with the disability is to be truly integrated and function independently in leisure situations. This allows the participant with a disability to have a definite role in skill and attitude development and in attaining his or her optimal level of functioning. Though the typical recreation leader may not be accustomed to this role, it is important to recognize that the leader is completely successful only when the participant is taking part in typical leisure experiences on his or her own, independent of the leader.

Following is a list of techniques that can be used by the leader in order to work more effectively with people with disabilities. However, it should be noted that concepts and discussions of leadership found throughout this book apply to individuals with disabilities as well as the general population. Chapters relating to such topics as motivation, communication, group dynamics, and general leadership theories are applicable. Up until this point in the chapter, the authors have emphasized

functional abilities, instead of diagnostic labels, to encourage the reader to view the person with a disability holistically, or as a total person. However, viewing leadership techniques applicable to various diagnostic categories can also be helpful if the larger perspective of this chapter is kept in mind by the reader. Some of the diagnostic categories that exist, accompanied by leadership techniques that can be applied to these categories, are found in Table 17.6.

## ADAPTING ACTIVITIES

In addition to leadership techniques, it is also possible to modify or adapt an activity to make participation by individuals with disabilities more feasible. Though adaptation is frequently necessary, it is essential that adaptations be kept to a minimum in order to preserve the integrity, essence, and potential benefits of participation in that activity. Even though adaptations are made, the adaptive activity should be kept as close to the original activity in form and content as possible, and only those aspects of the activity that require

**TABLE 17.6**   Hints for Leadership and Programming for Persons with Disabling Conditions

## PHYSICAL DISABILITIES

Ask a disabled member what help is preferred. Assist only as needed. Be courteous, use common sense, and communicate concern.

### Examples of Physical Handicaps

### Blind

- Speak in a normal voice using normal vocabulary words.
- Demonstrate by touch, taste, and smell.
- Describe the surrounding environment—location, shapes, and distances of objects.
- Remove/minimize all hazards in the area.
- Capitalize on all remaining sensory receptors in activities. Add a bell to the ball and play circle dodge ball. Run relays in roped-off lanes. Train for mobility through dance movements or rhythm bands.
- Contact an agency serving the blind. Many games have been adapted in braille and are commercially available.

### Deaf

- Maintain eye contact. $V$ or $U$ shape and semicircles are the best seating formations.
- Speak slowly and distinctly at the person's language level.
- Demonstrate explanations.
- Know about a hearing aid—its operation, care, and wearability.

### Deaf-Blind

- Make your presence known by a simple touch that conveys friendly interest.
- Work out special communication signals between member and leader. Learn and use whatever communication method is known by the member. Be sure to understand each other.
- Encourage use of voice.
- Always orient the member to the surrounding environment.
- Let the member take your arm when walking.
- Swimming is enjoyed most in warm water.

### Amputation

- Functional limitations depend upon amputee.
- Activities should exercise muscles surrounding affected body parts to avoid stiffness.
- Watch for falls as balance is a problem when body weight is not equally distributed.
- Encourage the individual to think of adapted methods.
- Contact a physical therapist or agency serving physically disabled persons. Special adaptive devices are available to help with some skills.

## CRIPPLING AND NEUROLOGICAL DISABILITIES

### Cerebral palsy

- Coordination is a problem. Motor activities such as running, jumping, or throwing are great. Fine motor activities using eye-hand coordination or delicate finger movements can be frustrating.
- Watch for falls—the sense of balance is not even.
- Avoid excessively loud sounds and sudden, unexpected movements. These increase uncontrollable spastic movements.

---

**TABLE 17.6** Continued

---

## MUSCULAR DYSTROPHY

- Watch for signs of fatigue due to muscular weakness and respiratory difficulties.
- Watch for falls due to impaired sense of balance.
- Plan activities involving movement, as these exercise muscles. Activities such as climbing stairs that involve affected muscles, require assistance.
- Participation in activities of all types is desired because youth eventually become wheelchair bound due to the nature of the disease.
- Once wheelchair bound, continue all activities manageable by the individual. Increase mental activities that use the imagination—the brain does not tire, only the muscles!

## SPINA BIFIDA

- Know specifics about the extent of spinal cord injury and paralyzed body parts.
- Watch for signs of fatigue as endurance level is lower.
- Watch for falls since sense of balance is uneven.
- Specialized equipment often helps mobility and functioning—know specifics about use and care.
- Braces enable full participation but may slow movement.
- There is no sensation in injured areas. Watch for injury to the skin from burns (fire, too hot water) or scrapes. Watch for reddened areas resulting from pressure sores. Change sitting-lying position frequently. Watch for swelling and color changes due to circulation problems.
- Wheelchairs will be necessary for some.

### Physical Handling Is an Important Consideration

### Wheelchairs

- Be sure all straps are fastened securely. Sense of balance is not always good.
- Use arms and shoulder muscles when pushing wheelchaired participants up ramps.
- Guide a wheelchair down a ramp backwards.
- Use small foot bars to tilt wheelchairs backwards when going up or down low curbs.
- Change the position of the members in wheelchairs often to prevent sores and make them comfortable.
- Be sure brakes are positioned when member leaves the chair.

### Crutches

- Ask what help is needed.
- Know how to hand crutches to a handicapped member.
- Hold at the waistline when assisting a person on crutches up an incline.

### Braces

- Know when and how the braces are used.
- Know how to maintain the braces.

### Falls

- Catch hold of the hips of a falling handicapped member to help regain lost balance.
- Try to break a fall to prevent much injury.
- Wait for a fallen handicapped member to indicate a need for help; allow a few minutes for rest.
- Check for serious injury and keep your eyes open.

**TABLE 17.6**  Continued

## MENTAL AND EMOTIONAL DISABILITIES

### Mental Retardation

- Full participation in all recreational activities promotes interaction in an increasingly mature manner. Participants can do anything; their limits relate only to slower learning rates.
- Recognize that each individual has a chronological age, a mental age, an emotional age, a social age, and a certain degree of physical ability.
- Plan activities so that everyone has a chance to be good at something and to experience success.
- Be quick to praise.
- Break an activity into parts, and present the most simple feat first.
- Alternate active and quiet games to avoid overstimulation and to compensate for short attention spans.
- Repeat well-liked activities.
- Include only one new activity in a meeting.
- Ease new members into the program gradually . . . have a youth advocate accompany the mentally handicapped youth to the first few meetings. The child feels relaxed and the leader gets first-hand information of the child's special needs.
- Be firm and take a positive leader role.

### Behavior Problems

- Structure activities so that everyone participates in an organized manner.
- Vary the type of activity.
- Plan extra activities to fill a time slot completely.
- Be consistent in what you say and do.
- Focus on the individual and support self-development.

*Source:*  Project INSPIRE Resource Guide, David Austin, Lou Powell (eds.), Department of Recreation and Park Administration, Indiana University, Bloomington, Indiana 47401.

adaptation should be modified. For example, the only major adaptation in wheelchair basketball is that of allowing specified wheelchair movement instead of dribbling the ball, for it would be very difficult to dribble the basketball while moving a wheelchair. Since all other rules and regulations of basketball can be followed in a wheelchair, no other major adaptations are necessary.

The leader should be creative in selecting and adapting activities. It is surprising how, with creative thinking and brainstorming, activities can be selected and adapted for people with disabilities with less effort than one would think. For example, a game that requires recall of a sequence of actions might be selected by the leader for a group that includes both hearing-impaired and ablebodied individuals. Or the leader might adapt a baseball game for visually impaired participants by using a ball with a bell in it to help them locate the ball. Other adaptations of activities include playing on a hard surface when participants are in wheelchairs; decreasing the activity area for people with limited mobility; using larger equipment, for example, large balls or large print for people with visual impairments; using lighter equipment when necessary; increasing or decreasing the number of participants depending on the activity; and increasing or decreasing the number of leaders depending on the activity.

## SUMMARY

In this chapter, the role of the leader working with individuals with disabilities has been presented. Individuals with disabilities are people who have needs, interests, desires, preferences, abilities, and limitations. Additionally, they have been born with or have acquired a disabling condition that may or may not limit functional ability. Increasingly, leaders are called upon to work with individuals who are disabled in programs that have been organized for ablebodied populations. The process of integrating-mainstreaming should underly the leader's efforts working with this population. The leader's role has two facets: (1) working with the individual with the disability to develop his or her skills, attitudes, and knowledge for successful integrated leisure experiences and (2) working with the larger environment of participation of individuals through advocacy and training. The leader's role is that of facilitator, enabler, and advocator, and though specific leadership techniques and activity adaptation have been suggested in the chapter, general principles of leadership, motivation, communication, and group dynamics underlie the work of the leader with this population.

## DISCUSSION QUESTIONS

1. What legislation guarantees the rights of individuals with disabilities?

2. Describe the concept of mainstreaming-integration.

3. Identify barriers that prevent individuals with disabilities from successfully participating in recreation and leisure programs. Which barrier is the most important?

4. Identify some of the more significant actions a leader may take to facilitate an integrated activity.

5. What are some of the roles a leader assumes when working with individuals with disabilities?

6. Select an activity, and discuss the ways it can be adapted.

7. Identify some general guidelines for adapting activities.

8. What does the following statement mean? People with disabilities have the basic right to equal leisure opportunities.

9. In what two areas does the leader work to facilitate integration?

10. What is your role as a general recreation leader with people with disabilities?

# 18

# ORGANIZING FESTIVALS AND PAGEANTS

Community festivals are an excellent way of building community cohesiveness, pride, and spirit.

Festivals and pageants occur in a wide variety of locations. They are held in cities, counties, and states and provinces throughout North America. Events of this type generally have a theme that is historical, religious, geographical, cultural, or one that reflects the unique social makeup of the community or region. Opportunities for recreation and leisure service personnel to give leadership to the organization of festivals and pageants are virtually as unlimited as the themes that might be chosen for such activities.

Festivals and pageants are recreation and leisure events that contribute to community cohesiveness, pride, and spirit and can result in increased revenue for a community. The settings and themes for these types of events can be very diverse. Some of the festivals and pageants that are seen in Canada and the United States are oriented toward such themes as historical sites, dates, personalities, or occurrences; cultural or ethnic heritage; art forms, such as dance, drama, music, art, crafts, film, poetry, and photography; sporting events, agricultural products (for example, the National Peanut Festival in Dothan, Alabama); life-styles (pioneer, farming, and folk); geographic features; time periods (for example, Gay Nineties, Colonial, Civil War); international locations, styles, or events (for example, Scandinavian festivals and Oktoberfests); and seasonal phenomena (for example, a cherry blossom festival).[1] Festivals are also held just for the fun of it, oriented toward novel, unique, or offbeat themes. All festivals and pageants, however, are considered to be an accepted part of our culture in North America.

[1]Robert L. Chapman and Ardath Ann Goldstein, eds., *Arts Festival Planning Guide*, North Carolina Bicentennial, Department of Cultural Resources, State of North Carolina, 1975, pp. 8, 9.

## WHAT ARE FESTIVALS AND PAGEANTS?

Festivals and pageants are celebrations. They are events at which people gather together to celebrate something of significance to them. Although festivals and pageants have many qualities in common, they also have respective qualities that are different from one another. *Festivals* have their roots in primitive societies. Many early civilizations engaged in festivals to ensure continued good fortune and prosperity. These types of events provided opportunities for individuals to express their emotions—joy, fear, and gratitude. From a historical perspective, festivals were often tied to changes in the seasons or religious holidays. As a result, they commonly occurred on a regular basis, usually once a year. Therefore, a festival may be defined as a celebration based upon a significant event that occurs with some regularity, usually annually.

*Pageants* are usually based on legends or history and typically involve elaborate ceremony, exhibition, and display. Participants in pageants often march in procession in colorful costumes. Pageants may also entail elaborate dramatic productions. A pageant, like a festival, is a tremendous source of public entertainment. It celebrates events similar to those of the festival and, in fact, may be a component within a festival celebration.

A pageant is usually planned and executed by a smaller group of people than a festival. A festival commonly involves participation in planning and implementation by an entire community. In addition, a pageant occurs over a short period of time, possibly only a few hours, whereas a festival may occur over an extensive period of time of a few days or a week or more.

## WHAT ARE THE VALUES OF FESTIVALS AND PAGEANTS?

Festivals and pageants have many attributes that are of value to those individuals and communities participating in them. Some of the more important values of these types of events are the following.

*Promotion of Community Spirit.* Festivals and pageants often generate a great deal of enthusiasm, interest, and excitement on the part of community residents. This helps to spark community spirit and pride.

*Promotion of a Community Identity.* Festivals and pageants, especially if they occur annually, can help to focus attention on a given community, region, or area. Ashland, Oregon, for example, draws intensive media attention from its annual Shakespeare Festival. The town's identity has evolved from this festival, for even downtown buildings reflect the nature and character of this event.

*Promotion of Community Cohesiveness and Involvement.* Festivals by virtue of their very magnitude, necessitate the cooperation of a large number of individuals. Often this may entail the cooperation of an entire community. This type of common effort toward a single goal can act to bond individuals together.

*Promotion of Historical Heritage, Cultural Heritage, and Ritual.* Our cultural values and sense of history are learned and reinforced through participation in festival and pageant celebrations. Individuals attending such events learn about, and gain an appreciation for the theme or topic represented (legends, social customs, historical values, artistic endeavors, and so on).

*Promotion of Economic Development.* Successful pageants and festivals can be economically rewarding to communities. Tourists often plan their travel itineraries to attend such events. This can result in increased revenue for a community or the sponsors of the event or for both. A successful event may also serve as an impetus for increased development within the community in terms of new facilities, renovation of existing buildings, or other efforts that occur in conjunction with festival preparations.

Festivals and pageants also provide an excellent opportunity for individuals to enjoy their leisure. They involve people . . . many people. There are individuals who participate in the planning process and in the implementation of the activity. These individuals may spend a large portion of their leisure time in the creation and production of a festival or pageant. On the other hand, there are individuals who participate in the event as consumers. Although their involvement may be less extensive than that of the individuals organizing the event, their participation also represents an important use of their leisure time.

## TYPES OF FESTIVALS AND PAGEANTS

There are numerous types of festivals and pageants. Some of these types of events are based upon ethnic and cultural heritage; sporting activities; geographic areas; and regional, national, and international history. Still others are based upon major holidays such as Christmas, Easter, and Thanksgiving. Some of the most common types of festivals and pageants are described as follows.

*Holiday Celebrations.* The term *holiday* refers to a day or time period of some distinction or significance. A holiday can focus on a secular or nonsecular event of local, regional, national, or international importance. For example, the Fourth of July holiday can serve as an impetus for festival and pageant events.

*Historical Celebrations.* The celebration of historical events and historical individuals is common in many communities in the United States and Canada. Some of the most common historical celebrations are based on political events such as Memorial Day, Washington's Birthday, Lincoln's Birthday, Martin Luther King's Birthday, and, in Canada, Boxing Day, Dominion Day, and Queen Victoria's Birthday.

*Cultural Arts Celebrations.* Cultural arts celebrations are especially popular events. They may focus on the visual arts, performing arts (dance, music, and drama), crafts, and what are termed ''the new arts.'' The new arts are those artistic pursuits that are based on technological innovations such as film, computers, and television. An example of a festival that is based on a cultural arts theme as well as a holiday theme is the 'Harvest Fair and Folk Festival,' sponsored by the Eugene (Oregon) Parks and Recreation Department and the Eugene Folklore Society. Figure 18.1 depicts a promotional poster for this event.

*Ethnic Celebrations.* Our society contains a large number of ethnic groups. These groups are of many national origins and may live within specific geographic regions. Ethnic groups can be an excellent theme source in planning festivals or pageants. Ethnic groups are often eager to share their heritage with others, and the general public can benefit from participation in, and observation of, such events. The Cinco de Mayo Celebration in Dallas, Texas, is an example of a well-run and culturally valuable ethnic celebration.

*Geographical Celebrations.* Geographical festivals and pageants highlight the noteworthy features of a given area. They often are planned in conjunction with some occurrence of local interest, bringing attention to a historical remembrance or culturally unique aspect of the area. In Oregon, for example, the Nehalem River Run Festival is a geographical celebration that focuses attention on the lovely river in that region.

*Religious Celebrations.* Religious festivals and pageants are among the oldest and most significant celebrations in our society. Indi-

**Skinner Butte Park**
**Sunday, September 12,**
**10 a.m.-Dusk**
**Free Admission!!**
**(Washington-Jefferson Park in case of rain)**

**FIGURE 18.1**   Example of a promotional poster for a cultural arts celebration.

viduals of various faiths celebrate prominent religious events. For example, among various faiths, such holidays as Easter, Hanukkah, Flower Day, and Christmas are often celebrated with festivals and pageants. Even though public recreation and leisure service agencies may not become involved in the more serious religious aspects of such holidays, they do, of course, engage in activities associated with major holidays, such as tree trimming, easter egg coloring, caroling, and so on.

*Sports Celebrations.* Many sporting events may serve as the focus for the organization of a festival or pageant. The oldest and most elaborate sports festival and pageant is the Olympic Games. More recently, the Super Bowl in the United States and the Grey Cup in Canada form the nucleus for festivals within the cities in which they are held. These events can spur great economic gain within the communities hosting them and can also provide such communities with recognition and visibility.

*Novelty Celebrations.* Novelty festivals and pageants are based on innovative and unique ideas that are conceived primarily to "have fun." This type of celebration is exemplified by the beauty pageant, the prettiest baby contest, the Texas Chili Cook-Off and Bar-B-Que, and so on. These types of celebrations often attract great interest owing to their unique qualities and the opportunity they provide for participants to have fun and, often, to laugh at themselves.

## THE ROLE OF THE LEADER IN FESTIVALS AND PAGEANTS

There are numerous roles which the recreation and leisure service leader can assume to assist in the planning and implementation of a festival or pageant. In general, the leader is more likely to work as a facilitator or in a face-to-face role with groups of individuals or committees. The leadership role in this type of setting is one of helping to coordinate the work of groups, encouraging individuals, ensuring that deadlines are met, and acting as a liaison between groups, as well as actually contacting individuals to acquire materials, supplies and equipment, facilities, and areas.

When a festival or pageant is actually implemented, the leader may serve as a master of ceremonies, a judge, an official, a contact for emergencies or last-minute needs, a host, or a troubleshooter. The leader involved in an arts festival might engage in such activities as introducing himself or herself to all presenters and offering assistance while they set things up. The leader might also identify himself or herself as someone who could be contacted in the event of any questions or needs. Later the leader might greet participants as they arrive. All these activities involve direct, face-to-face contact with people. Even though some of these tasks may appear to be supervisory, they all involve the provision of service *directly* to people.

### KEY QUESTIONS IN THE PLANNING PROCESS

In organizing a festival or pageant, there are a number of preliminary questions that should be answered that relate to such basic factors as the type of event, dates and times, finances, tourist interest, and so on. A checklist of questions that should be considered by planners of such events is detailed as follows.

- What is the main purpose for staging the event? To celebrate a holiday season or a historical event, to raise funds, to provide a cultural or educational experience, to provide fun and entertainment, or to accomplish some other purpose?
- What type of event would be most in keeping with the community's unique location, history, customs, facilities, and abilities?
- Will the event meet a variety of needs and interests of community residents and perhaps of many visitors as well?
- What time of year should the event be held

to meet best the objectives and purposes for which it was organized? On what dates will the event conflict least with other local programs or those of nearby communities?

- How long should the event last? Hours? One day? Several days? More?
- What basic types of facilities, equipment, and supplies are needed to conduct the event?
- How many people might attend the event?
- How many planners and workers will be needed?
- How much money will be needed to get the event underway?[2]

## CHOOSING A THEME

The theme of a festival or pageant provides the idea around which the planning efforts will revolve. The theme will determine, to a large extent, the direction that the planning will take, the types of activities that will be involved, and so on. The theme will also set the tone of the event. It will determine, for example, whether the celebration is to be serious, humorous, educational, or historical.

When attempting to select a theme, a planning committee may want to consider the history of the community or region within which the celebration is to take place. There may well be historical or cultural attributes of the area that would complement such an event. However, a community that cannot identify such a focus can base a festival or pageant on any theme that they believe would attract participants. The wide diversity of pageants and festivals that exist in Oregon state, for example, are testimony to the creativity and ingenuity of individuals. Festivals in this state range from small novelty festivals to large elaborate pageants. A list of many of the current Oregon festivals and pageants is depicted in Table 18.1.

[2]Robert P. Humke, *Planning Community-Wide Special Events*, Cooperative Extension Service, University of Illinois at Urbana-Champaign, 1976, p. 2.

Once a theme has been selected, the actual name of the festival or pageant should be chosen. An effort should be made to select a name that will have appeal to the participants for whom the event is intended. The theme should also tell participants what to expect if they attend the event. If the festival or pageant is intended to encompass a broad variety of activities, the theme should reflect this and should also be broad. If, on the other hand, a celebration will be narrowly focused on a specific event, the theme should also be specific. In addition, the theme should reflect the nature of the event in terms of the emotions that it is intended to evoke—gaiety, humor, reflection, spiritual awareness, and so on.

Activities within a festival or pageant can be adapted to correspond with the particular theme of the event. For example, a simple marathon run can be adapted to a Thanksgiving festival by calling it a "Turkey Trot." Singing and dancing can also be adapted to various themes. A festival with a Scandinavian theme, for example, might have dances, singing, or even dramatic presentations that relate to this theme.

In addition to choosing the theme of a festival or pageant, the leader should carefully consider the selection of an appropriate date and time. Careful consideration should be given to the date and time in order to avoid conflicts with other community activities and to attract the type and number of participants desired. Furthermore, adequate planning time must be set aside, depending on the nature and complexity of the activity. The planning for a festival or pageant may take an entire year or even longer.

## ORGANIZING FESTIVALS AND PAGEANTS

Although most recreation and leisure service leaders do not assume ultimate responsibility for the organization of festivals and pageants, there are some leaders that will assume this

**TABLE 18.1**   Examples of Current Festivals and Pageants Found in the State of Oregon

| | |
|---|---|
| All-Northwest Barbership Ballad Contest and Gay 90's Festival | Depoe Bay Fleet of Flowers |
| Yachats Arts and Crafts Fair | All-Indian Rodeo and Pow Wow Days |
| Pear Blossom Festival | Guinness Book of World Records Day |
| Miss Rogue Valley Pageant | Timber Carnival |
| Cherry Festival | Daffodil Festival |
| Hood River Valley Blossom Festival | Phil Sheridan Days |
| Loyalty Day Festival | Oregon Shakespearean Festival |
| Curry County Clam Chowder Cook-off Festival | Chief Joseph Days |
| Sawdust Festival | Crooked River Roundup |
| Azalea Festival | Portland Rose Festival |
| Rhododendron Festival | Strawberry Festival |
| Willamette Valley Folk Festival | Peter Britt Music and Arts Festival |
| The Rockhound Pow Wow | Pioneer Day |
| Pi-Ume-Sha Celebration | The National Rooster Crowing Contest |
| Huckleberry Feast | Sandcastle Building Contest |
| Gold Beach Aqua Carnival | The Silver Smelt Fry |
| Obon Festival | Neighborfair |
| Children's Festival | Wood-n-Nickel Days |
| Old-Fashioned Fair | Robin Hood Festival |
| Broiler Festival | Garibaldi Days |
| Applegate Trail Days | Santiam Bean Festival |
| Abbey Bach Festival | Crazee Days |
| Antique Powderland Farm Fair | Western Days Week |
| Nehalem River Run | Thunderegg Days |
| Boone's Ferry Days | Springfield Broiler Festival |
| Poetry Festival | Grande Ronde River Rally and Raft Race |
| Scandinavian Festival | Prospect Jamboree |
| Oktoberfest | Silverton County Festival |
| Pendleton Round-up | Crawfish Festival |
| Illinois Valley Labor Day Festival | Mexican Fiesta |
| Wine Festival | Artquake |
| Melon Festival | Cranberry Festival |
| Alpenfest | Dallas Smilaroo Festival |
| Harvest Festival | Potato Festival |
| Swiss Mid-Winter Festival | Lord's Acre Auction and Bar-B-Que |
| Beachcomber Festival | Sausage and Kraut Festival |
| Rummage Super Bowl | Barnabas' Biennial Christmas Fair |
| | Mini Marathon Run |

role. Further, all leaders can benefit from knowledge regarding such organizational processes. In the organizing of any large-scale event, whether it be a festival, pageant, or other type of large affair, the first step is to identify potential members of a planning, organizing, or steering committee. The function of this type of committee is to give lay-leadership to the organization of the event. The committee may include individuals with special skills in such areas as drama, music, art, finance, or other skills related to the type of festival or pageant being planned. It may be the leader's responsibility to recruit individuals to serve on the steering committee. The leader should attempt to create an atmosphere of enthusiasm and excitement as the planning and organizing process evolves. As the organizing or steering committee takes shape, various subcommittees for planning purposes should be identified. Subcommittees that might be included in the organization of a large festival or pageant are program, physical facilities, publicity, concessions or food, budget, and "troubleshooting" committees. These are discussed individually in the following sections.

*Program.* A program committee is responsible for the selection and development of activities and events that will be included in a festival or pageant. Its duties may include locating entertainment, exhibitors, speakers, and so forth. The program committee will also formulate the structure of the program, as well as the format for activities. They will determine what event is to take place at what time and where. Often a program committee will establish the scope of the event. This is important, for the scope of the event should be consistent with the available resources for the event, the goals of the event, and the number of participants expected. The program committee is often the committee that has "the big picture" of what the form of the event will be, how it will be implemented, and with what resources. As such, it must maintain close contact with the other subcommittees to ensure that plans are carried out in a coordinated and consistent manner.

*Facilities.* The facilities committee serves to identify appropriate physical facilities necessary to hold the event in an efficient and safe manner. This committee must give consideration to the type of program being planned, the safety of persons attending, the props and sound equipment required, the permits needed for concessions and parades, the accessibility of activities and facilities to all participants, the concerns related to transportation and parking and—perhaps most important—the resources necessary for coordinating the setup and teardown of each of the program components being implemented. An additional concern of this committee is whether arrangements should be made for an alternative site in the event of inclement weather. If an alternative site is not planned,

the committee should decide whether or not to schedule an alternative date in the event of inclement weather. The financial ramifications of alternative locations or dates should be determined, as should the safety considerations that might be affected by an alternative location.

*Safety and Security.* Participants should be protected from unsafe conditions from the time they arrive until they depart. The most effective way to ensure this is to formulate a safety and security committee, the purpose of which is the planning for safety prior to the event. The planning of this committee should be coordinated with local fire and police officials. These officials will be able to advise event planners as to how best to circumvent possible problems. In addition, fire and police officials can inform the committee of local regulations regarding licensing, permits, and the like. The physical well-being of those attending the festival or pageant can be enhanced by the provision of rest areas away from the body of festival activities, yet close enough to be easily accessible. In climates that are unusually hot, provisions should be made for a number of drinking stations. Parking is another safety-related concern. Traffic control must be well coordinated with local police for smooth traffic flow to and from the event. If the event includes such activities as auto racing, fireworks, or rodeo activities, special crowd control provisions may be necessary to protect the public.

*Publicity.* The efforts of the publicity committee may well determine the success or failure of the event. The publicity committee must ensure that all possible sources are exhausted in their efforts to promote the festival or pageant. An important part of the promotion process is the identification of the audience or target market for whom the festival or pageant is intended. Once the publicity committee has identified the audience that they want to attract, promotional efforts should be directed toward this select group. For example, if the event is being planned for children, an effective promotional method might be the distribution of colorful fliers to the schools. The publicity committee must decide what media they will attempt to use to publicize the event—radio, television, newspapers, posters, fliers, billboards, or a combination of all of these. Publicity activities can vary greatly in terms of their degree of complexity and scope. Some of the many vehicles that can be used to increase the public's awareness of festivals and pageants are included in Figure 18.2. It should be noted that radio and TV stations are required to provide a certain number of hours of free public service announcements and may be eager to help in promotional efforts.

*Budget.* The budget committee plans the budget for the festival or pageant. It coordinates the budget needs of each of the planning committees and the event as a whole. In addition, such items as ticket pricing and distribution, revenue collection, and banking should be handled by the budget or finance committee. It is vital that the budget committee keep scrupulously accurate records of its transac-

---

**Before the Event**

| | |
|---|---|
| News releases and ads | Radio and television coverage |
| Posters, billboards, and signs | Bumper stickers and buttons |
| Talks to local groups | Fund drives |
| Mayor's proclamation | Printing on shopping bags |
| Parades in neighboring towns | Fliers enclosed with bills |
| Airplane banners | Youth rallies or walkathons |
| Event name or slogan contests | Beard-growing contests |
| Reduced-price ticket sales | Endorsements by local firms |
| Invitations | Newspaper supplements |
| Engraved pens, pencils, etc. | Pennants on vehicles |
| Street banners and marquees | Signs in public transportation |

**During the Event**

| | |
|---|---|
| Appearances of famous persons | Balloon ascensions |
| Newspaper picture stories | Fireworks shows |
| Searchlights | Bumper stickers (I've been to . . .) |
| Cartop announcements | Parades through business district |
| Lettered hats, pennants, etc. | Staging of some activities in other towns |
| Skydiving shows | Guessing contsts (beans in a jar, etc.) |
| Prize drawings for early arrivals, children, senior citizens, etc. | Television and radio coverage |

**After the Event**

| | |
|---|---|
| News releases | Movies or slide shows |
| Speeches to civic groups | Volunteer recognition banquets |
| Postevent parties | Announcement of contest winners |
| Newspaper ads or letters of thanks | Radio and television interviews |

**FIGURE 18.2**   Promotional Methods for Festivals and Pageants. (*Source:* Robert P. Humke, *Planning Community-Wide Special Events*, Cooperative Extension Service, University of Illinois at Urbana-Champaign, 1976, p. 11.)

tions in terms of banking, bills paid, cash received, checks written, and petty cash. Individuals within the committee should be assigned specific responsibilities regarding these functions. An excellent example of a job description for a budget or finance committee chairperson is found in Chapter 10.

***Food or Concessions Operations.*** The provision of food at a festival or pageant can enhance the event tremendously. Food can be theme related, adding to the flair and festivity of the celebration. The planners may desire to take responsibility for food purchasing, preparation, and sales, or they may want to turn this aspect of the operation over to a concessionaire. In either case, it is important that the areas in which food is being served are easily accessible, clean, and logically placed. If a concessionaire is selected, planners should make financial arrangements in advance. There will be local health regulations that pertain to the serving of food. These local regulations should be checked by the food or concessions committee. Often food handlers are required to have a food handlers' permit and proof that certain innoculations are up-to-date, and they must comply with this regulation prior to the event.

Concessions are not confined only to the serving of food, but also can include the sale of products and services. In addition, these may contribute to the theme of the festival or pageant. Such concessions might include souvenirs, arts and crafts, parking concessions, amusement rides, and so on.

It can sometimes be difficult for a food committee to plan how much food they will need to buy for an event. The number of participants that will turn out is almost impossible to predict. The committee can, however, make their "best guess" and buy food from merchants with the understanding that unsold food, still properly packaged, can be returned promptly for a refund. This is not an unusual request to make of local merchants when planning for a large event.

***Troubleshooting.*** Theoretically, the troubleshooting committee examines and scrutinizes the plans and activities of other committees and attempts to identify possible organizational problems and offer solutions to them. Committee members should be independent of the actual planning and decision-making processes, acting in an advisory capacity only. Individuals on this committee also act to solve problems that occur on the day of the event, for example, getting last minute supplies, providing extra parking attendants if needed, answering questions, dealing with emergencies, and so on.

## RECRUITING FOR COMMUNITY INVOLVEMENT

Festivals and pageants often require the mobilization of large numbers of individuals, many with special talents and skills. Therefore, the tapping of community resources is an extremely important part of the organization process of festivals and pageants. Communities have many individuals and groups who are eager to provide their skills, talents, and abilities for a worthwhile cause. The ability of the leader to locate and use such community resources will increase the likelihood that the event will be a success. Figure 18.3 provides a list of groups and organizations that could be tapped to provide talent and workers for festivals or pageants.

A key factor in the use of community resources is pairing the skills and talents of individuals with the tasks that need to be undertaken. For example, an accountant would make a valuable addition to a budget or finance committee. On the other hand, some individuals volunteer their time to work in areas that are unrelated to their vocations. They may view volunteer service as an opportunity to stretch and expand their horizons. This feeling should, of course, be accommodated.

When planning or implementing a festival or pageant, the recreation and leisure service organization might want to align itself with a civic or service club in the sponsorship of the

| | |
|---|---|
| Service clubs | Political parties |
| Civic clubs | Colleges and universities |
| Youth groups | Chamber of commerce |
| Businesses | Board of realtors |
| P.T.A.s | Special interest groups |
| Senior citizen groups | Ethnic groups |
| Historical societies | Arts organizations |
| Religious groups | Craft guilds |
| Media organizations | Governmental agencies |
| | Fraternal organizations |

**FIGURE 18.3**     Resource groups for festivals and pageants.

event. This can provide the recreation and leisure service organization with human resources, finances, and support that might not otherwise be available to conduct the event. The service club, on the other hand, can receive visibility and an opportunity to fulfill its mission of service. This arrangement is not uncommon and, in fact, is often sought by both public agencies and civic and service clubs.

### EVALUATING FESTIVALS AND PAGEANTS

Why evaluate? An evaluation is carried out primarily to provide information that can assist in the planning of similar future events. An evaluation report should impart the knowledge gained through the planning and implementation of the event. For example, included in the evaluation report should be the support groups involved, the media used, the type of committee organization used, the planning schedule, the merchants that might have contributed merchandise or money or may have offered discounts, and the methods and procedures used in all areas of planning and implementation. Theoretically, an evaluation report for a large event should be so complete that another planning group could implement the same event with similar results just by reading it.

Evaluative data (for example, questionnaires and discussion) not only should be gathered at the conclusion of the event, but also throughout the planning and implementation phases of the event. Some of the guidelines that can be used in planning for evaluation are these.

- Planning for evaluation should be included with all other event planning details.
- Information and opinions gathered in the evaluation process should be as objective as possible. It is just as important to record minor failures as it is to record major successes.
- Input into the evaluation process should be made by planning and evaluation committee members and others involved in the event.
- A variety of evaluation methods should be used with the results combined and compared.[3]

Often an evaluation report is concluded with recommendations for similar future programs. Further discussion of evaluation techniques can be found in Chapter 11, Organizing and Leading Meetings.

## SUMMARY

Festivals and pageants provide an exciting format for recreation and leisure activity that captures the interest and enthusiasm of professionals and participants. Themes for festivals and pageants are diverse and can focus on such areas of interest as sports, geography,

[3]Ibid, p. 12.

history, culture, religion, ethnic groups, holidays, and unusual or novel events. A key to the successful implementation of festivals and pageants is the involvement of community members. This type of celebration can be one of the most spectacular of community events.

## DISCUSSION QUESTIONS

1. What is the difference between a pageant and a festival?
2. Identify and discuss some of the values of festivals and pageants.
3. There are a number of different types of festivals and pageants. Identify eight, and provide examples of each in your own state.
4. What role or roles does a leader play in planning and leading festivals and pageants?
5. What are the key questions one must ask when planning a festival or pageant?
6. Choosing the "theme" of a festival or pageant is an important part in the process of planning. How would you select a "theme" for a community festival? Whom would you involve?
7. List some promotional ideas that can be used in festivals and pageants.
8. Community involvement in festivals and pageants is important. Why? What are some of the important sources of community assistance?
9. Identify and discuss guidelines that can be used in evaluating festivals and pageants.
10. We suggest that festivals and pageants are an exciting format capturing the interest and enthusiasm of participants and professionals. Why?

# 19

# SOCIAL RECREATION

People are gregarious by nature; they enjoy social recreation activities, such as parties, picnics, banquets, and other group-oriented activities.

People are gregarious by nature. They like to congregate in small or large groups to socialize—to talk, laugh, observe, or participate. Social recreation, by its simplest definition, is recreation that has socialization as its major motivating factor. This means that many recreational activities may be classified as social recreation even though their forms are dissimilar. Activities that can be classified as social recreation include parties, picnics, banquets, playdays, campfires, conventions, class re-

unions, and many other group-oriented events. Each of these activities often relies on socialization for its success.

Although social recreation activities may appear to have a purpose other than socialization—for example, competition, education or skill development—an activity can be classified as "social recreation" if the social factor is of the greater importance. For example, although some children's parties may include competitive activities, the socializing factor is of greater importance than is the winning factor. This is evidenced by the informality of such competition, where simple skills, a few rules, and improvised equipment are substituted for highly developed skills, exacting rules, and precisely built equipment. Also, prizes may be nominal or nonexistent, and fun for fun's sake takes the place of a concerted effort to win.

Picnics are also forms of social recreation, for socialization is the primary motivator, not hunger. People who plan picnics or who plan to attend picnics really do so because a picnic is an ideal social event, not because they necessarily anticipate hunger. Eating together in an informal setting is fun. It is more work to prepare a picnic and pack everything up to take outdoors than it is to eat at home. Still, judging by the number of picnics held each year, the socialization is worth the extra work. Eating in restaurants and attending banquets are also activities that are motivated more by a desire for socialization than by hunger. A banquet is a lot of work, yet it is an ideal way for a group to celebrate a common cause as a group. A playday, though consisting almost entirely of competitive activities, has as its major purpose having fun together. A convention has educational objectives, yet it is through the socialization of the participants at and between educational sessions that the objectives are often attained.

Social recreation events are of short duration with definite beginnings and endings. The entire event may last one hour, one day, or a few days. Further analysis of social recreation shows that it is a program integrator. In other words, through the social program, the participants are integrated to feel enthusiasm toward a common goal and actually become, for a short while, an integrated unit. Like music, social recreation can transform a "group of individuals" into an "individual group."

Social recreation events can include both horizontal and vertical groups. A horizontal group is a group that is characterized by personal similarities. The cub scouts, a grandmothers' bridge club, or a teen club are examples of horizontal groupings. Vertical groupings are made up of many ages, interests, and abilities. A family reunion is a social event entailing a vertical group. Social recreation is probably the best form of recreation for use with vertical groups.

Social events can be adapted for all people; they require little skill, knowledge, or preparation on the part of participants. Even in a basically competitive playday or field day, there is little highly skilled practice prior to the event. Equipment for social recreation may be simple, improvised, or invented. If a picnic planning group wants to play horseshoes and can't locate any horseshoes, then beanbags, flat rocks, wooden blocks, or even pine cones may be substituted. A balloon may become a volleyball.

The characteristics of social recreation then are socialization; short duration; group integration; horizontal or vertical groupings; little skill, knowledge, or preparation on the part of the participant; and simple equipment.

## PURPOSES AND VALUES OF SOCIAL EVENTS

The *purposes* of social recreation are basically the same for all social events; they get people together to work together, play together, learn together, be together, and have fun together. Depending upon what the event is, parts of this objective will be emphasized or de-emphasized. For example, in order of emphasis, the objectives of a conference are working, learning, and having fun whereas those of a birthday party for 10-year-olds are playing, having fun, and learning.

Each person involved in a social event brings to it his or her own personal objectives and goals. The objectives of the leader, the participant, and the sponsoring organization are usually somewhat different, yet should be compatible. For example, if a YMCA sponsored a one-afternoon camp reunion for boys who attended its summer youth camp, there might be three different objectives. The main purpose of the event, from the perspective of the sponsoring organization, would be to recruit campers for next summer. The objective of the leader organizing the reunion would be to offer opportunities to renew acquaintances, offer safe and wholesome activities, review camp skills and songs, and provide the participants with a good time. The participants' objectives would probably be to have fun and to do things with their camp friends. These objectives, although dissimilar, would also be compatible and logical.

The *values* of social recreation are primarily realized through the group process. Social recreation provides opportunities for all program members to participate on an equal basis. Since skill and competition are of negligible importance, the unskilled can participate on an equal basis with the skilled. The "skills" used in social events are usually those that have not been learned or practiced before and may never be used again.

Another value of social recreation is the fact that group loyalty, solidarity, and a feeling of belonging can be developed through the social process. For example, a community Halloween party, with special activities for all age groups, can contribute to a feeling of community pride, loyalty, friendship, and solidarity. Certain social events can also bring out and encourage the development of latent talents in music, drama, committee organization, and countless other attributes.

Finally, social events can have educational value. The educational value of social recreation can range from the subtle learning regarding cooperation and fairness that takes place at a children's party to the more obvious learning that takes place at a convention. Perhaps one of the finest forms of adult education is the workshop, conference, or convention that is attended voluntarily for social, educational, professional, and personal reasons.

## THE SOCIAL ACTIVITIES PATTERN

Even though social activities vary greatly, all social events can be planned using one format or planning pattern. A planning pattern or outline that can be used to plan any social event is detailed in Table 19.1. Basically, this outline or social activities pattern is relevant whether used for a small social party or for a group of 2000 people. The task is magnified for the larger group, but the organization is the same.

### BACKGROUND MATERIAL

Prior to planning the program for any activity of a social nature, it is imperative that background material be developed, for it is the background material that provides the basis

**TABLE 19.1**    Planning Outline for Social Activities

I. Background Material
   **A.** Type of activity, purpose
   **B.** Participants
   **C.** Date and time
   **D.** Theme
II. Details
   **A.** Operations
      **1.** Facilities
      **2.** Promotion, publicity
      **3.** Decorations
      **4.** Refreshments
   **B.** Program
      **1.** Firstcomers
      **2.** Mixers
      **3.** Active events
      **4.** Quiet events
      **5.** Ending
   **C.** Financial
      **1.** Expense
      **2.** Income
III. Follow-up
   **A.** Cleanup
   **B.** Appreciation
   **C.** Evaluation
   **D.** Report

for planning the program. Background material includes information regarding the type of activity, its purpose, the participants, the date and time of the activity, and the theme. A discussion of these five factors follows.

*Type of Activity.*    There are many types of activities for which a leader might plan a program. The type of activity will determine some of the program's components. A list follows of some of these types of recreation and leisure service activities.

| | |
|---|---|
| banquet | group trip |
| campfire | orientation |
| carnival | party |
| conference | picnic |
| convention | progressive party |
| fair | reunion |
| festival | talent night |
| field trip | workshop |

This list is by no means exhaustive, for other activities may also be classified as social recreation and may follow the same pattern.

*Purpose.*    The purpose of a social event can be simple or complex. The individual or individuals planning a social event should be able to identify what is to be accomplished through the event. The purpose of a banquet might be to recognize a retiring member or to celebrate a victory or to commemorate an anniversary. The purpose of a carnival might be to involve a large number of participants with a wide range of abilities. Or, it might be to coordinate the programs of several playgrounds, to give recognition to youth achievement, or even to raise money for a group. The planning committee should be able to identify the purpose of the event in order to plan effectively to meet the intended goal.

*Participants.*    As in all other phases of recreation, participants and their needs are of paramount importance and, consequently, must be defined and understood before any planning occurs. In social recreation, because of the fact that the participants socialize and often develop a feeling of togetherness and compatibility, it is extremely important that the persons planning the event know as much as possible about the group in advance. Knowing the age *range* of the participants is more important than knowing the age of the majority. A family reunion with members ranging in age from six months to 90 years requires a different program from a class reunion with members ranging in age from 40 to 45.

It is well to keep in mind certain age traits particularly applicable to social events. Young children (ages four to nine) have short attention spans and a great amount of energy. They need more things to do than other age groups and must have things planned *for* them as they cannot plan their own activities. They enjoy surprises and are generally in high spirits. Instructions must be given on their level, and they must be carefully supervised. In events where young children are part of a group of a wide age range, it is necessary to assign leaders to be with the younger children specifically and constantly. At this age, boys and girls will play well together, but all need to receive rewards, recognition, or prizes (if possible). The leader should also plan calm activities to be interspersed among the active ones.

Preteens, in social situations, may be awkward or blasé unless separated from the young children for most of the activities. Boys and girls are better separated for some activities such as games requiring hard physical contact. Other activities lend themselves well to coeducational participation. Teenagers can assume planning responsibilities for many of their own social events. The function of such planning committees is to encourage feelings of belonging as well as to formulate a program of action. With careful supervision teenagers are capable of planning and executing dances, conferences, parties, work projects, and many other social events. In cases where they cannot be involved in much preplanning, they can have responsibilities during the function. They also need an opportunity to be with their peers to socialize.

Adults enjoy conversation more than any other socializer. Certain recreational activities serve as icebreakers and can lead to enjoyable conversations. Any adult social program, be it party, workshop, conference, picnic, or whatever, should balance structured activities with such unstructured activities as conversation. In addition, the activity program should not be crowded, nor should it contain awkward lapses of empty time between activities.

Other factors or variables regarding participants that should be taken into consideration in planning the program are the following.

*Demographic.*    The sex, age, income, marital status, education, and other attributes of participants are all basic factors that should be considered when planning a program. The leader wants to meet the needs of participants. Individuals of low economic status may be able to participate in programs only if they are free or of minimal cost. Young single adults might best be served by a program that emphasizes social interaction and provides a large number of "mixers." Individuals of different age groups will have different physical capabilities that also should be taken into consideration.

*Life-style.*  Life-style variables encompass a broad variety of attributes, ranging from the participants' introversion or extroversion, propensity for risk taking, and liberalism or conservatism. Life-style is also influenced by the norms, customs, and values of the country or the region within which a participant resides. These norms, customs, and values will influence dress, dance, and other aspects of the participants' relationships with others. Life-style variables contribute to the makeup of the personality of the participant, therefore their influence should be considered by the leader involved in program planning.

*Purpose in Attending.*  The reasons that individuals attend social activities vary tremendously. Some individuals have common interests with other members of the group and simply want to share these interests. Other individuals attend a group because of their previous involvement in a leisure opportunity, in order to become involved in a novel experience, or for educational reasons. The reasons that participants seek out a particular program should have an influence on program planning and implementation. If, for example, a participant is attending a program in order to duplicate an earlier positive experience, program planning will be very different from what it will be for a participant who is attending a program in order to experience novel and unique opportunities for leisure.

**Date and Time.**  The length or duration of an activity is an important planning item and should help to determine the program's contents. In turn, the type of group and the purpose of the event should help to determine the length of the event. For example, a Christmas party for children should be about two and a half hours long at the most. A dinner party for adults might last five hours or more. Sometimes the duration of a program is determined by external factors such as cost, availability of a facility, and continuity with other events.

There should be a definite starting and ending time for social events and consideration given to the frequency of occurence of the event. Some social events are scheduled on a weekly or monthly basis whereas others occur annually or biannually or, in the case of something like a golden wedding anniversary, once in a lifetime.

**Theme.**  Regardless of the scope of the program, every social event can be based on a theme, and the use of a theme can enhance the success of the program. World Fairs and International Exhibitions are based on themes, as are national and local conventions. As a matter of fact, themes are used universally whenever a program is designed to develop a feeling of social identity. A theme is a single idea around which a program is planned. A party may be planned around football, hoboes, the circus, or golden days. A conference generally has a more sophisticated theme such as challenge, progress, focus, or relevance.

There are two major functions of program themes. First, they help the participant to identify with a common idea. A theme provides direction to a program and psychologically motivates participants to think along common lines. Through use of the theme, the participants are unified. The second major function of a theme is to help make planning easier. A theme can be the basis for decorations, invitations, and sometimes refreshments. The theme also assists the leader in planning publicity and maintaining continuity within the program. It helps set the stage or the general tone of the program and helps in the coordination of activities.

As mentioned, through proper use of a theme, participants can be encouraged toward a similar frame of mind before the first activity is conducted. A good theme tells the participant in advance what to expect. Too often, when planning parties or programs, social leaders use themes that are too broad and tell too little. A party called Christmas of Holiday Fun or something equally broad tells us nothing. A Christmas program called A Child Is Born connotes a serious religious tone, as does Joy to the World. Christmas Capers connotes an entirely different tone as would Christmas Around the World or a Christmas Carol Carnival. Many activities held at Easter time are religious, yet many are not. A theme such as Easter Celebration could mean a variety of things to a variety of people. On the other hand, themes like Life Eternal, Spring Eternal, Easter Bonnet Parade, or Easter Egg-citement leave little doubt as to what type of Easter program could be expected. Figure 19.1 is an example of a poster from a Valentine's Day party sponsored by the Willamalane Park and Recreation District, Springfield, Oregon. The theme of this program is a ''family'' Valentine's Day.

Examples of other various types of themes that effectively communicate an idea are the following.

| | |
|---|---|
| Hobby Fair | Prophecy Party (January) |
| Pioneer Party | Cupid's Carnival |
| The Year 2000 | (February) |
| Shipwreck | Flanagan's Frolic |
| Rodeo | (St. Patrick's Day) |
| Backward | Fool's Festival (April first) |

### DETAILS

The details component of the social activity pattern depicted in Table 19.1 can be logically divided into three areas: operations, program, and financial. The breakdown of each

of these areas is fundamentally the same for a short party or a long conference, yet because social events can vary widely in duration and complexity, there may be considerable difference between, say, the work of program planning for a two-hour party and for a five-day convention.

*Operations.* Before an actual program is planned, specific operational details should be worked out. Operational details are all those items that must be decided except for the program itself. Generally, they include facilities, promotion, decorations, and refreshments.

*Facilities.* After the group is identified and before one goes further with any but basic planning, the facility where the event will take place should be identified, reserved, and studied. The facility may vary from a room in a private home to a group of hotels or a civic auditorium in a convention city.

Prime considerations in determining facility needs include the following.

- Number of rooms needed for lodging, meetings, meals, exhibits.
- Sizes of rooms needed.
- Utilities and equipment needed and available (electrical outlets, shades for darkening, public address system, projectors, speaker's lecterns, tables, chairs, ventilation, kitchenettes, heat control, soundproofing, exits, water, etc.).
- Rest rooms in proximity to major activities.
- Drinking fountains.
- Parking spaces needed: number, availability, cost.
- The availability of transportation to and from the area, bus, private car, train, plane, taxi.
- Safety and police protection needs.

A facility checklist for special events is found in Table 19.2. This can be used by the leader to ensure that the facility is used safely and effectively.

FIGURE 19.1   A poster from a Valentine's Day party.

**TABLE 19.2**  Facility Checklist for Special Events

| Facility_____ | | |
| Reserved from_____ | | |
| Open when_____ | Keys from_____ | |
| Rest rooms_____ | Open  _____ | |
| Fountains_____ | | |
| Heat_____ | Controls _____ | |
| Lights_____ | Controls _____ | |
| Police_____ | | |
| Fire_____ | | |
| Equipment available_____ | | |
| Cleanup_____ | | |
| Trash_____ | | |
| Parking area_____ | Number | Cost |
| Refreshments: | _____ | _____ |
| store_____ | | |
| heat_____ | | |
| cool_____ | | |
| serve_____ | | |

*Promotion-Publicity.*    Operational concerns include publicity. Publicity for an event may involve a simple invitation or an elaborate series of announcements, articles, and fliers. If invitations are used, they may be in the form of telephone calls, informal notes, catchy theme-oriented cards, or formal engraved notices. Publicity releases contain the same information but are intended to reach a greater number of people living at greater distances from the site of the function.

The purposes of publicity are twofold: educational and motivational. Interest in attending the function must be aroused. Here careful selection of the theme may be a deciding factor. Somehow the social event should be made to sound exciting. If personal invitations are mailed out, the leader should attempt to do something different with paper, color, or cutout shapes, that will be eye-catching. For instance, invitations to a sack social could be written in crayon on very small paper bags. Invitations to a mystery party could be torn into pieces that have to be reassembled to read the message. If the group of people who will be invited to attend a social event are getting together at an earlier date, an impromptu skit or other novel medium could be used to invite them.

*Decorations.*    Decorations may be simple or elaborate. They may consist of flowers, centerpieces, colored lights, banners, costumes, and so on. Decorations are generally in keeping with the theme and are used to create a mood. They show that something special is happening and, like the theme, help participants develop a singular spirit.

*Refreshments.*    Although it it not mandatory to serve refreshments, most social recreation leaders plan for refreshments because they add to the socialization. They are looked forward to, and, in most social events, the serving of refreshments is a good change of pace from other activities. Refreshments may be simple coffee or soft drinks or may be as elaborate as a seven-course dinner. At the party of short duration, they are usually compatible with the theme and may be color coordinated with the decorations as well.

*Program.*    In planning the program for special events, one needs to realize that there is no single program format to follow, for many combinations and arrangements of activities work well. There is, rather than a set format, a curve of action affecting patterns of activity that can be flexible to meet the objectives of a given program. This is known as the social action curve, shown in Figure 19.2.

Since social activities follow a certain pattern or curve, the leader can select and structure activities so that they conform to and support the desired pattern of activity. At a rock concert, for example, the leader may want the excitement of the activity to be highest during the finale. Most parties, however, reach the peak of excitement earlier. The pitch of excitement at a typical children's party is at a natural quiet or low level as participants arrive and start "warming up" to the activities and to each other. Through social events and socialization, the leader should

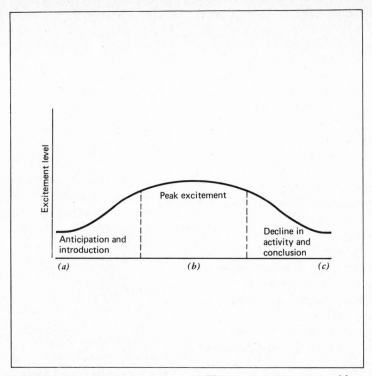

**FIGURE 19.2**    Social action curve. (*a*) The program commences with a low, anticipatory level of excitement. (*b*) At the middle of the program, excitement reaches its peak. (*c*) As the program closes, the pitch of excitement is controlled so that the participants leave in an orderly, calm manner, yet with a warm memory of their participation.

build to the high pitch or greatest excitement of the event approximately midway through the program. Refreshments are generally served about two thirds of the way through the program and can serve as a quieting event. The events after the refreshments should serve to taper off the excitement completely until a definite ending activity, when the party is over on a pleasant note. In the case of a child's party, refreshments are fairly noisy and should be served earlier, just past the middle of the party. They should not be served last at a children's party, for they are not calming. With excitable children, a story told after refreshments will often calm their excitement. The leader wants the group to leave the event calmly and quietly to ensure an orderly and safe return home.

It is important that the leader planning a party try to include activities for the firstcomers, icebreakers, mixers, active events, quiet events, and a definite ending so people will know that the event has ended. Some of these activities are described as follows.

*Firstcomers.*    Firstcomers are, as the word suggests, the people who are first to arrive. Because they arrive before everyone has assembled, they may find themselves at a loss as to what to do. While they wait for the arrival of the others, they should be involved in some type of activity.

A firstcomer activity must be one that can be entered into at anytime by one or more arrivers. It must last until the last person arrives and takes part in it for a short time. It may be competitive or noncompetitive; it may require group work or individual participation. It may be a socializing, mixing activity, or it may be solitary. It probably should have written instructions, and after it has ended, there should be a follow-up that gives recognition to many participants.

A firstcomer activity has a catchy introduction (related to the party theme), clear directions, and a definite ending that is controlled by the leader. In many unstructured social events, the firstcomer activity consists of hanging up the coats, being introduced to other people present, and being offered a cocktail or appetizer. In a structured social event, the firstcomer activity is more of an active event with the participants actually engaging in some type of recreation activity.

An example of a first comer activity for a children's birthday party might be the involvement of guests, as they arrive, in the creation of a "memory scrapbook" for the guest of honor. Each guest could draw a picture representing a memory of the guest of honor and these could be assembled in a scrapbook. Another example of a first comer activity might be the involvement of guests in the "creation" of something related to the party; for example, place cards, name tags, placemats, and so on.

*Icebreakers.*   Many times in social settings people feel inhibited or shy or feel insecure. An icebreaker or defroster activity is designed to break down social barriers through a social activity that causes some mutual amusement or mutual fun. Activities that help people feel at home with others generally involve all people doing something similar. Firstcomer activities that are of the mixer type are also icebreaker activities. As the name suggests, icebreaker activities help to thaw the frigid atmosphere that often permeates a group at the beginning of a party.

One example of an icebreaker is the game "Initial Impression." In this game each guest has attached to his or her back an 8½ × 11 piece of poster board, and all the guests take turns writing on each others cards as to what their initial impesssions are of one another. These impressions could be guesses as to type of work, hobbies, married or unmarried, and so on. After a time limit of 5 minutes or so, the cards are read out loud.

*Mixers.*   A social mixer is designed to encourager participants to move among each other and to socialize. They must converse, question, answer, or communicate with each other somehow. The purpose of the social mixer is to help people to get acquainted informally and to socialize with many others. Some mixers are also firstcomer events.

One of the most common and successful mixers, that can be used for many age groups is the game termed "human bingo." Guests involved in this mixer fill out a slip of paper as they arrive with their name on it and these pieces of paper are collected in a large bowl. Next they are given bingo cards on which there are blank squares. They must mingle among the guests and fill in the blank squares with the names of the others at the party. Following this, the guests play "bingo" with their cards, as the host or hostess draws the names of guests. The winner, of course, would probably win a prize, all of the guests get to know each other's names.

*Active.*   As the name implies, these games are of a physically active nature. Active games are employed more often out of doors, unless there is a sufficiently large indoor area to accommodate them. Some examples of active games are dodgeball, volleyball, baseball or softball, horseshoes, kick the can, and so on. Some active games may be subclassified as stunts. Such activities as pie eating contests, egg throwing contests, or obstacle courses are active games classified as stunts.

*Quiet.*   There are many quiet games that can be enjoyed by a group of guests. Some of these games may be used to begin to tone down the excitement of a party as the end of it approaches. Some examples of quiet games are "concentration" and musical charades.

*Financial.*    Though the finances involved in short-term social events are relatively simple, financing a major convention can be quite complicated and usually entails a finance or budget committee. A discussion regarding finances as they relate to large-scale meetings, conventions, and events is presented Chapter 11. However, the general expenses of a *simple social event budget* can be broken into the following classifications:

Invitations: _____

Decorations: _____

Equipment, prizes, favors: _____

Refreshments: _____

Rentals (if any): _____

Transportation (if needed): _____

Extra personnel (if needed): _____

Total Expenses: _____

Funds for such simple social events are usually obtained from organizational monies earmarked for such activities. However, ticket sales, sales of food and drink, donations of sponsors, or income from raffles or drawings may contribute to the *total income* from small social activities.

## FOLLOW-UP

There are four things that should be accomplished by the leader before the job of administering the social event is over. First, the facility should be cleaned up; the decorations, taken down; the equipment, put away; and the left over refreshments, put away. Second, any persons who helped should be thanked. This should be done for both major social events as well as small parties. A letter of appreciation is always in order to those who were volunteers as well as those who were paid for their services. Third, even a short social event should be evaluated. Fourth, a report should be developed and filed with the agency regarding the social event.

*Evaluation.*    A major event lasting one or more days should be evaluated on three levels: facilities, personnel, and program. A simple check sheet for rating a social event is seen in Figure 19.3. A slightly more comprehensive evaluation work sheet is found in Figure 19.4. The evaluation form in Figure 19.3 requests an evaluation of program only and therefore would not offer enough criteria for the evaluation of a major event. Many events have mediocre or less than desirable programs because of ill-prepared personnel or poor facilities. When these things are evaluated separately, information is obtained that can help in the planning of the next event. Evaluation also allows the leader to assess whether or not his or her program was successful.

*Report.*    Personal parties, picnics, and the like rarely entail reports. However, special events conducted at youth camps, playgrounds, community centers, schools, youth agencies, and so on, should have reports filed to help subsequent leaders in their planning efforts. In addition, the leader of a special event should also keep copies of all reports to help plan future events. These reports can include information such as that reported in the evaluation work sheets, as well as attendance figures, the program's organizational plan, the names and phone numbers of suppliers of equipment and supplies, advice for improvements in the program, and other recommendations. The authors firmly believe, based on past professional experience, that such information improves future programs dramatically both in terms of their overall quality and the ease in preparation.

---

**SOCIAL ACTIVITIES EVALUATION**

Check each item from 1 (low) to 5 (high)

| ITEM | RATING |
|---|---|
| | 5 4 3 2 1 |

I. Planning
1. Was activity organized well?
2. Was equipment readily available?
3. Were there continuity and variety?

Total

II. Program
1. Use of theme
2. Variety
3. Movement from one activity to another
4. Equipment
5. Suitability of activities to group
6. Beginning-firstcomer activities
7. Ending

Total

III. Leadership
1. Enthusiastic and poised
2. Prepared to explain activities
3. Voice clear
4. Position correct
5. Explanations clear and concise
6. Mistakes handled tactfully
7. Responsibilities shared
8. Group control obvious
9. Everyone included in activities
10. Aware of group response

Total
Final Total

**FIGURE 19.3**    Example of a simple check sheet for rating of social events.

## SUMMARY

Social recreation can be defined as any structured or unstructured event where socialization is the primary motivation. There are countless opportunities for persons working in face-to-face leadership positions to be involved in social events. A leader can use the social activities pattern as a basis for program planning, with modifications made when needed. This pattern or format can be used for any type or size of social event.

## DISCUSSION QUESTIONS

1. How does the motivation of participants for social recreation differ from that for other types of recreation?
2. Explain how age differences will affect the planning for the social recreation event.
3. What is the difference between a "horizontal group" and a "vertical group"?
4. In what way may leader objectives and participant objectives be different for a

## PLANNING

1. Is there definite evidence of careful planning?
   a. Was party organized?
   b. Was all equipment readily available?
   c. Were there continuity and variety?
   d. Did the party show unity? Decorations? Activities?
   e. Did the party rise to a peak?
   f. Was there a definite ending?
2. Were the leaders there well in advance of party starting time?
3. Was the party started on time?
4. Was the firstcomer planned for and made welcome?
5. Were activities suited to the group?
6. Did the leaders share responsibilities?
7. Were refreshments a chore, a bore, the peak, or just another part of the evening's fun?

## PROGRAM

1. Was there unity?
2. Did activities follow theme?
3. Was program varied in interest and activity?
4. Did events move smoothly from one event to another?
5. Was there time allowed for ''breathers''?
6. Was there a climax?
7. Did guests know when the party was over?

## LEADERSHIP

1. Was leader friendly and enthusiastic without losing poise?
2. Was he or she thoroughly versed in the activities he or she was explaining?
3. Were explanations clear and concise?
4. Did the leader stand where he or she could be seen and heard?
5. Was control of the group evident?
6. Was the leader aware of group reactions?
7. Were mistakes handled tactfully?
8. Was the leader a sharer?
9. Did he or she give everyone a chance to participate?
10. Was leadership responsibility shared?

Elements Nicely Handled _____

Elements Poorly Handled _____

**FIGURE 19.4**   Evaluation of social recreation events.

social event? In what way may they be similar?

5. What is meant by "theme" in a social event?

6. Explain how a leader might adapt three specific activities to fit a variety of themes.

7. What is covered under "Background Material" in the "Planning Outline for Social Activities"?

8. Explain the three major subsections of the "details" section of the "Planning Outline for Social Activities."

9. What is a "Social Action Curve," and why is it important to consider it when planning a social event?

10. How does evaluation of a lengthy social event differ from evaluation of a social event lasting only a few hours?

# LEADERSHIP OF ARTS AND CRAFTS

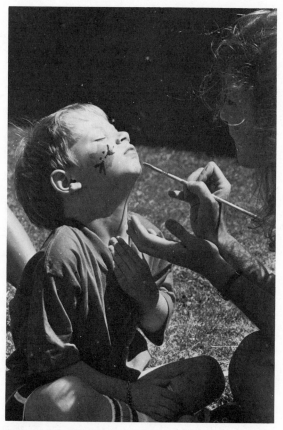

The arts take many forms. Face painting is popular among young participants in the University of Oregon's Family Vacation College.

Art provides a vehicle for creative expression of our ideas, values, feelings, interests, emotions, and fantasies. It is a way of communi-

cating with others. Art not only provides opportunities for individual expression, but also provides a means for collective cultural expression. In this chapter, leadership of arts and crafts, cultural arts, and community arts, including the organization of arts festivals, will be discussed.

## ARTS VERSUS CRAFTS

It is almost impossible to differentiate between arts and crafts so that all artists and all craftspeople will be satisfied. For the purposes of this book, crafts may be viewed as a competent alteration of three-dimensional materials to produce a useful form or product. Generally, whereas crafts have utilitarian value, art is for appreciation. Art objects are usually original creations shown solely for reasons of expression and beauty (real or perceived).

A comparison of activities usually termed "crafts" and those usually called "visual arts" is offered in Figure 20.1. There is never a clear-cut demarcation between the two, however. Much weaving is in the crafts category. Place mats, fabrics, table runners, and so on, are recognized as crafts products. Tapestries, however (particularly those with historic significance), are considered art as is shown by the many on display in well-recognized art museums. Thus, arts and crafts may have some overlaps. The point at which a craft becomes an art can be difficult to deter-

| Crafts | Visual Arts |
|---|---|
| Basketry | Batik |
| Candle making | Etching |
| Ceramics | Glass (stained, ornamental) |
| Drawing, sketching | Painting (oils, watercolor) |
| Framing pictures | Pen and ink drawings |
| Leatherwork | Photography |
| Macrame | Printmaking |
| Nature crafts | Sculpturing (metal, stone, wood) |
| Needlecraft (crocheting, knitting, sewing, etc.) | Sketching |
| Metalcraft | Tapestries |
| Paper craft (papier mâché, origami, etc.) | |
| Weaving | (*Note:* Sometimes art is defined as |
| Woodworking | painting, drawing, and sculpture.) |

**FIGURE 20.1**    Examples of arts versus crafts.

mine. However, we will assume, for the most part, that leaders of crafts activities may have less formal training than leaders of art. For example, crafts leaders may be found among playground leaders, as camp counselors, in community centers, in senior centers, and at Christmas decoration workshops. Leaders of art are usually specialists within their field and may be called artists in residence, art instructors, artists, or designers. They are usually highly trained and well skilled and demand different quality from the participant. As mentioned, the crafts leader is skilled working with objects that have a utilitarian value whereas the art instructor usually works in media for the sake of visual appreciation. In addition, the crafts program usually necessitates a democratic or even laissez-faire style of leadership whereas art instruction may necessitate a formal, more autocratic leadership style, necessary for developing specific skills.

## CRAFTS

There are countless activities that may be included in a crafts program. The depth and breath of the program offerings may depend on the creativity and imagination of the leader. Crafts programs may be established within such settings as senior centers, preschool programs, playgrounds, and day camps for various age groups. Figure 20.2 lists a number of crafts activities, categorized by age, that can be offered by the leader.

### PURPOSES AND VALUES

There are, of course, many purposes of a crafts program. For some individuals, crafts satisfy a desire to be creative, to complete a project, or to experiment with materials. For others, crafts are relaxing and satisfying and bring about a feeling of self-worth. Crafts may appeal to those who are not interested in other programs or who are unable to participate in more active programs because of health, age, or disabling conditions. Furthermore, crafts are flexible and can be modified not only in scope and content, but also may be offered successfully during all seasons of the year.

There may be specific underlying purposes for some crafts. For example, nature crafts are often conducted to teach people about nature, for no one can be involved in collecting

**Preschool**

| | |
|---|---|
| Nature crafts | Papier mâché |
| Clay modeling | Coloring |
| Weaving | Candle making (dipped) |
| Finger painting | Puppet making (bag, stick) |
| Simple paper folding | Collages |

**Lower Elementary Grades**

| | |
|---|---|
| Basketry | Mobiles |
| Tie-dyeing | Papier mâché |
| Simple woodworking | Candle making (dipped) |
| Simple jewelry making | Puppet making |
| Clay modeling | Weaving |

**Upper Elementary Grades**

| | |
|---|---|
| Macrame | Leather craft |
| Model making | Needlework (sewing, knitting, embroidery) |
| Beadwork | |
| Metalcraft | Molded candle making |
| More complex woodworking | Jewelry making |
| Basketry | Tie-dyeing |
| Weaving | Puppet making and marionettes |
| Clay modeling | Decoupage |
| Carving | |
| Linoleum block printing | |

**Junior High Through Adult**

| | |
|---|---|
| Cabinetmaking | Needlework (sewing, knitting, crocheting, embroidery, needlepoint) |
| Pottery | |
| Tole painting | Molded candle making |
| Ceramics | Jewelry making |
| Silk screening | Tie-dyeing |
| Quilting | Weaving |
| Macrame | Beadwork |
| Model making | Metalcraft |
| Carving | Decoupage |
| Leather craft | |

**FIGURE 20.2**  Examples of craft activities for various age groups.

and preparing natural objects without enhancing his or her awareness of the objects themselves. Crafts programs may also be developed or adapted for the mentally or physically disabled. Craft therapy can be used to encourage expression, encourage eye-hand coordination, and enable creative activity unharnessed by many physical disabilities. Finally, crafts programs for older people may be used to help them strengthen their hands, to encourage social interaction, to offer opportunity for self expression, or to create "products" for fund-raising efforts. A list of values attributed to crafts programs follows. Although there may be many others, these are indicative of the wide range of benefits derived from creative crafts activities.

1. Satisfaction of the urge to create.
2. Stimulation of the imagination.
3. Opportunity for each participant to work on his or her own level successfully.
4. Experiencing the joy of accomplishment.
5. Appreciation of the work of others.
6. Involvement in an activity with carry-over value for later enjoyment.

### THE SETTING

Crafts may be conducted both indoors and outdoors equally successfully. Indoors, a crafts room takes little special equipment or space. The room may be large or small, square or rectangular. The furniture should consist of sturdy tables and strong chairs. There should be adequate space for storing tools and materials, with a lockable cabinet mandatory for storing paints and other combustible materials. A sink with running water is always convenient and is usually included whenever a room is built specifically for craftwork; however, one can make do with portable supplies of water for the activity and for cleanup. The most important equipment in a crafts room is enough light without shadows to aid the worker to see the product under construction. Adequate electric outlets are also necessary if power tools or equipment of any kind is used. The outdoors can also offer excellent opportunities for crafts activities, and any outdoor setting may be used. Certainly, sketching landscapes on a warm, sunny summer day is unthinkable inside the four walls of a room!

### MATERIALS AND EQUIPMENT

Crafts materials may consist of hundreds of items, and a wide range of equipment may be used to create crafts. *Materials* for crafts are the substances or components of which they are made; they give them their individuality. For example, crayons, watercolors, and fingerpaints can all be used to create a picture, but each of these pictures will have a very different appearance and character owing to the material used.

Crafts *equipment*, on the other hand, is comprised of the items needed to "equip" participants to use crafts materials. Depending on the type of crafts activity in which the leader is involved, the equipment needed may be inexpensive and simple or more costly and sophisticated. Ceramics, for example, would require molds, special tools, and a kiln whereas weaving would simply require a loom. Basic crafts equipment and materials can consist of such items as the following.

*Equipment.*

| | | |
|---|---|---|
| Molds | Glue | Paintbrushes |
| Scissors | Thread | Loom |
| Wood burner | Needles | Kiln |
| Pins | Stapler | Dowels |

*Materials.*

| | | | |
|---|---|---|---|
| String | Cloth scraps | Leather | Construction paper |
| Tin cans | Wood scraps | Yarn | Ribbons |
| Egg cartons | Crayons | Beads, sequins | Magazines |
| Cardboard | Watercolors | Paraffin | Coat hangers |
| Paper cups | Tempera paints | Felt | Popsicle sticks |
| Clay | Feathers | Paper-towel tubes | |

The leader attempting to conduct a crafts program or activity might note the information provided in Chapter 21, Figure 21.9, which details sources for "scrounged" materials that can be used in some crafts.

## CRAFTS INSTRUCTION

Participants in crafts programs need instruction that is practical, helps them develop skills immediately, and results in a serviceable product. Theory, history, or research regarding the craft is not foremost in the minds of participants, who may return to a second session only if they realize practical progress during the initial lesson.

When one is instructing crafts, it is a good idea to have several finished objects for viewing. If possible, the objects, though utilizing the same techniques, should show creativity, innovation, and considerable difference so that the participant realizes the potential of his or her own imagination. The leader should break the crafts activity down into basic, simple, progressive steps at which every participant will realize some degree of immediate success. Perfecting the skills can come later in subsequent experiences.

Many recreation leaders find themselves assigned some portion of a program related to crafts without having had a formal education program related to crafts or art. Crafts programs for children may be led by those who are not specialists in crafts, although some knowledge of, and training in, crafts is preferable. Many crafts books are readily available, so a beginning crafts teacher should never be at a loss for ideas. There are, however, four basic leadership considerations that are important when conducting crafts activities: safety, quality versus creativity, utility, and demonstration.

*Safety.* The first consideration in leading arts and crafts activities is that of safety. Though many crafts activities are perfectly safe, others require risk management. Some paints can be flammable, and cutting tools, kilns, burning tools, and other crafts tools can cause serious injury to participants if improperly handled. Each craft should be analyzed for potential risk and planned and managed accordingly.

*Quality Versus Creativity.* Surely arts and crafts comprise the medium utilized most to bring out creativity in participants. The creative arts may refer to crafts, music, drama, or literature, but the majority of participants probably express their creativity through crafts activities. A main goal of the crafts leader must be the encouragement of imagination, innovation, creativity, or individual expression. Squelching creativity could be grounds for program failure and certainly is in opposition to recommended leadership principles.

On the other hand, a good crafts leader should be concerned about quality. This means that, regardless of the object made, it should be made well so that it won't fall apart, shrink, or crumble. It takes a careful, analytical leader to decide when to stop creativity in the interest of quality. Certainly, there would be no progress in art if there were no creativity, but crafts that deteriorate in a short time may be a waste of time, money, and materials.

*Utility.* Many crafts activities result in objects intended for some utilitarian purpose, that is, pot holders, bookends, place mats, or knife holders. It will be apparent to the participant that the object *should* be used; however, if the quality is such that the object falls apart or creates an eyesore, it will not be used, and the only result of the crafts program will be hurt feelings. On the other hand, there are some crafts leaders who seem to convince the participant that there is a *need* for some objects with the result that children take home items of no use to anyone there. The leader needs to be sure that the crafts produced have a real utility or that they are purely for visual purposes.

***Demonstration.*** Probably the one technique every crafts leader should use is demonstration. Whether it be painting, sculpting, origami, knitting, building model planes, or cooking, the crafts leader should be able to demonstrate the craft with ease and resulting success. This means thorough understanding of the crafts process from beginning to end including the following.

- Understanding the materials, their source, cost, and structure.
- Knowing the amount of materials needed.
- Knowing the correct use of tools.
- Demonstrating the safe and correct use of tools.
- Demonstrating, by logical progression, step-by-step procedures.
- Stopping at logical places for questions, review, or participant involvement.
- Completing the object.
- Demonstrating how to clean up, maintain, and store tools.

## ARTS

Even though drawing, painting, and sculpture require special instruction and equipment, they should be offered in some form in every community. Art activities should represent an ongoing part of a well-rounded recreation program. The arts can be participated in by both children and adults and can be adapted to meet the needs of special populations. Finally, and of great importance, the arts programs of various organizations, schools, and art groups can coordinate their efforts into arts festivals, workshops, or exhibits. In these latter events, the administration-oriented leader will find ample challenge for his or her talents and interests.

### TEACHING PARTICIPANTS TO OBSERVE

Leadership within the visual arts is a specialty requiring specific skills and knowledge. Yet all leaders can help participants develop basic observational skills that will become integral to their progress in art classes.

Unfortunately, most of us use our eyes to look, but few of us know what it is really to see an object. We all can recognize a rose, but few have seen the rose completely enough to draw it. The same is true with a bowl of fruit, the face of a loved one, or a woodland scene. Even though the leader is not an artist—and perhaps not even an artisan—every leader can help the participant learn to *see*, and that, in turn, will help the participant to sketch, draw, or paint. There are six components of learning to see that can be introduced by every leader.

***Line.*** The first thing a person can see when looking at something is lines. Every object or scene is composed of lines, and the conscious viewer can make out horizontal, vertical, diagonal or intersecting lines or a combination. Lines may be straight, curved, circular, or spiraling. Close observation shows spiral lines in the overlapping scales of a pine cone, the seed placement in a sunflower head, and even the smoke from a chimney on a calm day. Consciously seeing these lines will help the artist draw basic figures.

***Shape.*** A corollary to seeing lines is the recognition of shapes. Whether in nature or in human-shaped objects, one can see squares, rectangles, triangles, circles, pentagons, hexagons, stars, or other shapes. Even though the painter is working in a two-dimensional medium, recognition of three-dimensional shapes is basic to drawing two-dimensional representations.

***Color.*** Many people look at the world and see few colors. The grass is green, the sky is blue, clouds are white, and the sunset is always red. People who paint by number are surprised to find the numbers direct them to put green in the sky—or purple or yellow—and to blend lavender into the white of the snow—or red, orange, or green. When those people look at the world afterwards, they find their own understanding of the simplicity of coloring has become greater and with a view to complexity. We can learn to recognize many colors (hues) throughout items we previously thought were unicolored. In addition to recognizing hue, we can teach people to see the intensity (light or dark) and value (bright or dull) of colors. Thus, a meadow may consist of light bright plants, light dull plants, dark bright plants, and dark dull plants—all in the hue of green. Suddenly the viewer "sees" the meadow as something other than a mass of a single color. Exercises in hue, intensity, and value can expand the world of color manyfold.

*Texture.*  Even though understanding texture is usually done through the tactile sense, texture may also be perceived through sight. Rough, smooth, slippery, fuzzy, soft, hard, sticky, and other descriptions can be used to describe things we see. Thus, the artist can visualize the contrast of rough bark, fuzzy buds, and a smooth rock and try to paint each differently.

*Balance.*  In putting things in perspective, one can analyze to see if they are in balance (symmetrical, even) or unbalanced (asymmetrical, uneven), and it will help in composing the picture or making the object authentic. Many flowers are balanced (equal on left and right sides) whereas others are asymmetrical and cannot be divided in two equally in any direction.

*Space.*  The secret to good composition lies in *spaces*: a single large area, two or three medium areas, and several small areas. Regardless of the subject matter, drawings and paintings should consist of some arrangement of these three sizes of areas. The participant can learn to recognize such spaces in the paintings of others and in composing the content of his or her own work.

Sometimes negative space may be used. In drawing a tree, one may meticulously sketch hundreds of leaves (positive space), or one may look beyond the tree, see the spaces between the leaves, and draw outlines of those negative spaces instead. In that case, the leaves of the tree are not developed; however, the painting shows them as large masses interspersed by small spaces of sky (negative space).

The foregoing six components of learning art can be introduced by any art leader. Certainly, they belong in every child's art program. People can be asked to look at various things each week and see them differently. Pebbles, leaves, buildings, the sky, automobiles, anything. Then, when they are ready to paint or draw, they will have already been introduced to the basic concepts.

The following section has been adapted from material prepared by Charlotte Brainard (*Oil Painting*, 1973) for the Sports and Recreation Branch of the Ministry of Community and Social Services of Ontario, Canada.

## THE ART CLASSROOM

So that each student can have enough room to work comfortably, it is a good idea to choose a studio with plenty of space. Each one should be able to set up an easel and, if possible, a small stand for his or her equipment. If still life arrangments are to be used, one or two should be set up so that everybody will be able to see them at fairly close range.

In a pinch, students can work at large tables either keeping the paintings flat or propping them up at an angle. Easels, however, allow for much greater freedom in working.

Ideally the studio should be equipped with

An easel for each member.

A small table for each student's painting supplies.

Good lighting in all work areas.

Tables or stands for still life arrangements.

Still life objects—bottles, jugs and bowls of various sizes; fruit, flowers, gourds, drapery, and so on.

Sink for washing brushes and hands.

*Supplies.*  Art supply stores are full of exciting and tempting materials. But at first it is a good idea for the student to limit himself or herself to the basic ones, and if interest and budget permit, expand later on.

For a beginning, he or she will need

1. *Paints.* A basic beginning palette is listed below. More white will be used than any other paint, so participants should buy the largest size.

   *Basic palette:*
   titanium white
   cadmium yellow pale
   cadmium yellow medium
   cadmium scarlet
   alizarin crimson
   cobalt blue
   ultramarine blue
   viridian green
   burnt sienna
   burnt umber
   ivory black

2. *Brushes.* Recommended are several varying sizes, plus a two-inch house painting brush useful for applying gesso or latex grounds and for covering large areas with oils or oil washes. The best quality brushes are more satisfactory to use and last longer.

3. *Palette knife.* An ordinary flat palette knife may be used for mixing and painting. Later on if the student wishes to experiment with painting with the knife only, special painting knives may be useful. Each give a different stroke as you would expect from their different shapes.

4. *Palette.* These come in one basic shape with minor variations and size. Medium size is good for general use. It should be light enough to be held easily on the arm and preferably white. Before buying, students should try holding several and choose the one that feels best. Disposable or peel-off palettes of paper are useful if you want to avoid the job of cleaning a permanent palette. But it is difficult to clip on the cups of turpentine or oil, and they spill and ruin the whole pad. If small tables are available for each person, a conventional palette isn't necessary. A slab of plate glass over a piece of white paper makes an excellent, easily cleaned surface. Since it doesn't have to be held in the hand, it can be larger than a regular palette and give more surface for paint mixing.

5. *Clip-on cups.* These hold small amounts of oil, turpentine, or medium and clip over the edge of the palette. A double set is useful since the student may be using two of these liquids at the same time.

6. *Turpentine.* This is the basic solvent used for thinning paint, making washes, and cleaning brushes and palette.

7. *Linseed oil.* This should be bought at the art supply store. It must be refined linseed oil. For most work, very little is needed, so a small size bottle should be bought.

8. *Painting supports.* Masonite or hardboard covered with a couple of coats of good latex interior paint makes a good support.

9. *Newsprint paper.* This will be used for preliminary drawings in charcoal when the class begins working from still life. It is generally available at art supply stores in 18″ × 24″ pads and is about the least expensive paper available. It can also often be obtained from local newspapers inexpensively.

10. *Charcoal.* Several sticks of soft charcoal to use in sketching.

11. *Kneaded dough eraser.* This is a very soft rubber and is best for correcting charcoal drawings. Bits can be pulled off and used for small areas.

12. *Carrying box.* The elegant wooden boxes sold with sets of painting materials are not really necessary although they are useful since the palette, brushes, and so forth can be carried inside. However, a metal tackle box, 6″ × 12″, will hold everything except the palette and is much less expensive.

As the class progresses, they may want to add more colors to the basic palette and to experiment with other types of supports, brushes, and materials. Each student will develop his or her own way of working and should be encouraged to look in the catalogues and art supply stores for equipment that may meet his or her growing needs. Some painters like to experiment with unorthodox equipment, painting with rags, crumpled paper, rubber, or pile rollers and various other materials. Each person will discover through experience which supplies are necessary for his or her own style.[1]

Rather than instruct by the step-by-step method used in some of the training of professional painters, the recreational instructor should encourage experimentation with materials. Participants should be encouraged to explore how to work with colors, shapes, and textures to get the feel of the medium whether it be charcoal, pencil, watercolor, oils, or another. These exercises should be done without any attempt to represent anything.

Some participants may not enjoy such exercises because they may want immediate results and to produce something recognizable; however, once they see what things can be done with the media in terms of color, shape, line, balance, contrasts, and so on, they will enjoy the exercises. Using exercises related to the section entitled "Teaching Participants to See" will naturally lead into sketching and then to the techniques of applying the medium to drawing or painting specific objects. Whereas each person should be encouraged to *see* the components of visual objects, each should also be encouraged to interpret them according to individual desires.

Beyond these initial steps, art leaders should be specialists in their own media. This text does not allow for in-depth discussion of each art medium. There are, however, hundreds of good books on progression in art that can be used by serious art teachers and added to their own libraries.

## THE CULTURAL ARTS

There are probably as many definitions of cultural arts as there are writings on the topic. The definition that seems to apply most to this material is that of Chubb and Chubb in their book *Leisure—One Third of Our Time*, in which they state, "Cultural resources are facilities and programs that provide pleasurable artistic, dramatic, literary, and musical experiences or facilitate enjoyable exploration of our environment, including materials pertaining to the characteristics, achievements, and history of the human race."[2] Referring to this definition, one can understand that there are many forms of cultural arts and the necessity for many types of leaders. We might further divide cultural arts into those related to mass culture, popular culture, and high culture. Mass culture consists of materials such as movies, radio, television, situation comedies, and other forms of communication available to the masses. Popular culture consists of items of music, literature, drama, and art currently popular with many people. Video games are recognized as popular culture. High culture is simply defined as performing and visual arts that have stood "the test of time."

All forms of cultural art—mass, popular, and high—are funded by government or private support or a combination of each. Employed in the production of the cultural arts are directors, conductors, choreographers, historical interpreters, museum staff, gallery guides, play directors, actors, performers, writers, camerapersons, and on and on. All these leaders are specialists with special training for their unique leadership roles. Though their job descriptions, goals, and functions are necessarily quite diverse, their success generally lies in application of the principles attained in the first seven chapters of this text. Regardless of specific techniques for specific

---

[1]Adapted from Charlotte Brainard, *Oil Painting*, Sports and Recreation Branch, Ministry of Community and Social Services, Ontario, Canada, 1973, pp. 6–12.

[2]Michael Chubb and Holly Chubb, *Leisure: One-Third of Our Time* (New York: Wiley, 1981), p. 563.

roles, every leader involved in cultural arts can be a teacher and lead the public toward a higher appreciation of the cultural arts. Whether it be jazz, rock, bluegrass, or the classics; football, tennis, boxing, or ballet; the museum of science, the arboretum, the zoo or a national park; the city newspaper, the evening news on TV, or the morning disc jockey, each involved employee can help the public understand and appreciate the medium presented. Appreciation is usually a learned response. Each medium of the cultural arts is better understood by the listener or viewer if the art is explained.

The participant can absorb knowledge related to cultural arts if the leader presents facts so that they relate to something within the learner's experience. In this way, they can be learned and retained better than unrelated facts. Analogies can be used by the leader to accomplish this. For example, the first four beats of Beethoven's Fifth Symphony have been described as "Knock at the Door." This refers to the fact that Beethoven himself was knocking at the door of his own deafness and realized it when he wrote the symphony. Use of such examples helps people recognize the piece in subsequent hearings. The same use of analogies can be applied to other forms of cultural arts as well. The leader should also offer information in small amounts. Overkill can destroy interest and cause boredom. The secret to helping people develop an appreciation for and understanding of any of the cultural arts is to arouse interest and whet their curiosity. If that is accomplished, the learner will probably seek more information and opportunities in these areas.

## COMMUNITY ARTS

As was mentioned earlier, one function of administration-oriented leaders is that of sponsoring community arts coordinated activities. Community arts activities may be one-day functions, week-long extravaganzas, or year-round events in series. Arts festivals are ex-amples of coordinated community events that can take many forms and relate to a wide variety of people.

Much of the planning for arts festivals is consistent with the principles identified in Chapter 11 on meetings and Chapter 18 on festivals and pageants. However, there are four areas specific to arts festival organization that have been identified by the North Carolina Department of Cultural Resources as the following planning divisions: (1) management and money; (2) forms, patterns, and spaces; (3) art and artists; and (4) media and the public. These are outlined in Figure 20.3.

Prior to the actual planning for an art festival there are preliminary responsibilities that should be met, such as the following.

1. Assemble a steering committee, including community representatives with expertise in the areas under consideration, visionary thinkers, and analysts or organizers who will keep things moving.
2. Appoint a chairperson.
3. Select or hire an overall coordinator. This person implements the ideas and policies of the committee.
4. Choose a theme. Every special event needs a theme to centralize all events and to serve as a main focal point. It may be a seasonal festival, a nature-oriented program, a program for specific media, a festival related to a particular state or event in history (i.e., bicentennial), or countless other ideas. Once the theme is established, the committee can brainstorm about activities to be included—such things as
   • Photography.
   • Movies or rear screen presentations.
   • Live demonstrations.
   • Sale of food, by local groups not otherwise involved.
   • Amateur performances (mime, puppets, instrumentalists).
   • Videotaping visitors in action.
   • Participant involvement (especially in children's arts festivals).

5. Write bylaws (consider incorporating, tax free status). Write the Internal Revenue Service, Washington, D.C., for IRS Publication 557, *How to Apply for Recognition of Exemption for an Organization.* A local arts council may be able to serve as a tax-exempt sponsoring agency if the event is in keeping with the sponsoring agency's purpose as stated in their own articles of incorporation.
6. Involve community groups (schools, PTAs, YMCA, YWCA, museums, civic clubs, youth agencies, churches, and local arts, crafts, music, gardening, and history societies).
7. Organize subcommittees and steering committee liaison.
8. Plan around the four major divisions.

---

**Management and Money**

In general—everything

Applying for grants, finding sponsors, raising funds

Accounting, budget, purchasing

Recruiting volunteer and professional personnel and organizing labor force

Office and staff

Concessions management

Operating on-site headquarters

Event day communications

Accounting for deposits and receipts

Paying bills

Sending ''thank-yous'' to all staff and participants

**Forms, Patterns, and Spaces**

In general—designing, constructing, and maintaining site

Choosing site

Architectural rendering; defining areas and use

Collecting materials

Storage and work area

Tent and other equipment rentals

Health, security, and fire standards

Building permits

Child care facilities

Parking, rest rooms, electric and water facilities

Directional signs

First aid

Insurance

Clean up, knock down

**Art and Artists**

Finding, contacting, and contracting artists, performers, craftspeople

Jurying and selection

Tickets, program information

Ticket sales

Display area and booth assignments

Stage—sound, background lighting

Schedule

Craft sales commissions

Care and feeding of artists, performers, and craftspeople

Collect, tag, display, and return borrowed work

''Thank-yous'' to artists and their hosts

**Media and the Public**

Letterhead, program printing

Press releases, ads, interviews

Fund-raising promotion

Media kit

Care and feeding of visiting media and VIPs

Information booth

''Thank-yous'' to media and VIP hosts

**FIGURE 20.3** Arts festival planning divisions. (*Source:* Robert L. Chapman and Ardath Ann Goldstein, eds., *Arts Festival Planning Guide*, North Carolina Bicentennial, Department of Cultural Resources, State of North Carolina, 1975, pp. 22–23.)

**SAMPLE TRACK FOR A SMALL FESTIVAL**

**Durham Street Art Celebration**

| | Concessions | Media and Public | Art and Artists | Coordination and Money |
|---|---|---|---|---|
| **Aug. 11–17** | Complete firm solicitation | Send fliers, posters to printer | Children's plan meeting | Finalize budget |
| | Recruit and organize volunteers | Arrange TV/radio live coverage | Follow-up list of performing artists | |
| | | Poster distribution plan | Design and draft letter to performing artists | |
| | | Preliminary press release | Invitations to per. artists | |
| **18–24** | Contract sales arranged | Design traffic flow | Technical dir. for artists | Follow-up meeting with member organizations |
| | | | Assign exhibit booths | |
| | | | Finalize children's plan | |
| **25–31** | | Send out radio/TV spots | Assign exhibit booths | |
| | | Arrange paper interviews | | |
| | | Press | | |
| | | Press release (follow-up) | | |
| **Sept. 1-7** | Confirm workers | Press conference | | Develop IDs for staff and exhibitors |
| **8–12** | | Set up parking facilities | | Final steering comm. meeting |
| **13** | EVENT | EVENT—Information Booth | EVENT—Volunteers check booths | EVENT—Management accounts for deposits and receipts |
| **15–19** | Bills/Accounting | | | Return materials Send ''thank-yous'' Pay bills Close books |

**FIGURE 20.4**  Example of a planning track. (*Source:* Robert L. Chapman and Ardath Ann Goldstein, eds., *Arts Festival Planning Guide,* North Carolina Bicentennial, Department of Cultural Resources, State of North Carolina, 1975, p. 27.)

The scope of a community arts festival can be a specific area of the arts, or it can be very broad and encompass many art forms. For example, an arts festival might focus on crafts, visual arts, or one of the performing arts or might include all these together in one large event. Performing arts, as contrasted with the already discussed arts and crafts, include

- Music—instrumental and vocal—classical, electronic, jazz, blues, rock, gospel.
- Drama—classical, contemporary, children's, puppets, mime, pageants, religious, ethnic, experimental.
- Dance—ballet, folk, square, modern, ethnic.
- Film—classical, documentary, nature, children's, ethnic, mixed-media, educational.

Regardless of the medium, the organizational guidelines presented in this section are appropriate for all planning involving community arts. A sample of a planning track for the two final planning months for a small festival is found in Figure 20.4. Naturally, many community arts festivals might necessitate from 12 to 18 months of planning. This brief track, however, will help one to understand and conceptualize the program planning process.

## SUMMARY

In this chapter, the authors have presented techniques that can be used by the leader involved in arts and crafts programs and activities. Although it is difficult to distinguish between arts and crafts, art can be thought of as original creations that are presented for the purpose of expression and beauty. Crafts, on the other hand, are utilitarian in nature. Some of the important factors that should be considered by the leader conducting programs and activities in the area of arts and crafts should be safety, quality and creativity, utility, and demonstrations. Finally, the authors have presented techniques that are useful in organizing cultural arts festivals.

## DISCUSSION QUESTIONS

1. What is the difference between an art and a craft?
2. Identify some of the purposes and values of crafts.
3. Why is the development of a risk management program important when leading a craft activity?
4. What are the six components of learning that can be employed by the leader, providing instruction in the arts?
5. Define cultural arts.
6. What is the difference between mass culture, popular culture, and high culture?
7. What are four areas involved in planning an arts festival?
8. Identify the steps that should be followed in organizing a cultural activity?

# 21

# ORGANIZING AND LEADING DRAMATIC ACTIVITIES

Dramatic activities offer participants many opportunities for creative expression.

Dramatics are as important to a well-rounded recreation program as crafts, games, or sports. However, since few leaders are experienced in dramatics, this area of programming is often overlooked. The opportunity to help individuals participate in dramatic activities can be enjoyable, yet requires meticulous planning and organization on the part of the recreation and leisure service leader. The forms of activity that fall under the category of dramatics are many, including community theater productions, puppetry, skits, storytelling, children's plays, and mime. The purpose of this chapter is to present some of the basic leadership techniques necessary to organize and lead such programs.

## OBJECTIVES OF THE DRAMATICS PROGRAM

At some time in each of our lives we have been called upon to participate in some form of dramatic activity. The reasons for such participation have probably been greatly varied. For some, creative expression might have been the primary reason for engaging in dramatic programs. For others, the social aspects of such activities might have provided motivation. Some objectives that the dramatics leader can help participants achieve are these.

- Learning techniques of creative dramatic expression.
- Learning about and gaining an appreciation for different types of dramatic activities.
- Having an enjoyable experience in terms of social relationships and interaction.
- Enjoying the freedom of expressing movement, actions, and emotions that may be new and different.
- Learning about human values, thought, and concepts through dramatic literature.

## THE ROLE OF THE DRAMATIC ACTIVITIES LEADER

Since dramatic activities are so popular, the leader responsible for organizing a dramatics program or activity should first assess the programs currently existing in the community. Are dramatic programs being conducted elsewhere? Is a little theater already in operation? Are others within the recreation and leisure service agency providing dramatic activities as a part of their programs? Has interest been expressed in certain types of dramatic activities? Such questions should be answered by the leisure service leader prior to selecting, organizing, and implementing specific dramatic activities to avoid duplication of efforts and effectively meet the needs of participants.

The leader involved in dramatic activities may sometimes assume an instructional role, may sometimes act as a facilitator, and may sometimes command the center of attention, as in storytelling. The dramatic activities leader must not only have the skills necessary to deliver related technical information, but must also believe in the value of such programs and must have the ability to bring out the creative talents of others. In discussing the role of the dramatics leader, Kraus and Bates note this.

> [The leader] should be able to view the activity, not just a single event or experience taking place at a given time, but as a part of a continuing series of exposures and involvements in leisure pursuits for participants. . . . [He or she] must regard it as an opportunity for pleasure, for growth, for personal satisfaction, for healthy social involvements, and creative expression . . . [and his or her] leadership style must reflect these values.[1]

The leader of dramatic programs, regardless of which area of activity is involved, is critical to the success or failure of the effort.

## TYPES OF DRAMATIC ACTIVITIES

As mentioned, there are numerous types of dramatic activities ranging from pageants to skits to operettas to creative dramas. A list of

[1]Richard G. Kraus and Barbara J. Bates, *Recreation Leadership and Supervision: Guidelines for Professional Development* (Philadelphia: Saunders, 1975).

various forms of dramatic activity is found in Figure 21.1. Almost all these types of activities can be offered by a recreation and leisure service organization. Some of the more common dramatic activities that the leader may be called upon to instruct, lead, or facilitate are puppetry, skits, mime, storytelling, creative dramatics, and community theater. Each of these will be described in the following sections, and applicable leadership techniques will be discussed.

### PUPPETRY

As a component of the dramatic program, puppetry and puppet play can be very beneficial programmatically. The use of puppets allow persons a training ground, in some cases, for stepping out onto the stage as actors, or actresses themselves. Puppet theaters typically allow the puppeteer to remain behind a screen or curtain while manipulating the puppet and reciting the script or, in some cases, reading the script. Puppet theaters and the production of puppet plays are an ideal way to

| | |
|---|---|
| Blackouts | Monologue |
| Ceremonials | Musical comedy |
| Charades | Observances |
| Children's theater | Operetta |
| Choral speech | Pageants |
| Community theater | Pantomime |
| Creative drama | Peep-box |
| Demonstrations | Plays |
| Dramatic games | Puppetry |
| Dramatizations | Script-in-hand |
| Festivals | Shadow plays |
| Formal drama | Shows |
| Grand opera | Skits |
| Imaginative play | Storyreading |
| Impersonations | Storytelling |
| Light opera | Stunts |
| Marionettes | Symphonic drama |
| Monodrama | Tableaux |
| | Theater in the round |

**FIGURE 21.1** Various forms of dramatic activity. (*Source:* From *The Recreation Program Book* [Chicago: The Athletic Institute, 1963], p. 68.)

involve persons, children, and adults alike in the creativity of dramatics without the anxiety created by appearance on stage for the first time.

Puppets can be as simple as "sock" or "sack" puppets with fabric eyes and painted mouths, or they can be very complex, as are many of the stringed marionettes that require practice for movement control. The participant's initial experience in puppetry might be gained in a "puppet-making" class. The leader might offer such a class with the intention of forming an interest group that would like to progress into the production of puppet plays.

The leader implementing a puppetry program can engage participants in very elaborate construction of puppets or marionettes and sophisticated puppet plays or can conduct a very simple program with puppets that can be made in one sitting and a puppet "theater" made of a cardboard box. However simple or complex the program is, the leader should remember to let the participants do the "acting" and improvising. The leader should allow them to form their own ideas as to how their characters should sound and act. He or she might help them form their opinions, however, by saying, "How would you feel if you were this puppet?" The leader should encourage participants to speak loudly, enunciate so that they can be understood clearly, and avoid trying to deliver their lines over the laughter of the audience.

## SKITS

Skits are a popular form of dramatic activity within all age groups. Skits are simply short plays for which a script can be memorized with appropriate action in a few moments. In addition, they require only simple, "improvised" props, costumes, and sets. They are performed before an audience for amusement and usually have a surprise ending or moral that is pointed out to the audience as the plot unfolds. Skits are tremendously popular in camping activities and are equally appropri-

ate in the community center setting, at dinners and banquets, and at conferences and meetings. A primary value of skits is the fact that participants must work together cooperatively in order to accomplish the intended effect. They also promote social interaction and creative expression.

The recreation and leisure service leader usually has a repertoire of skit ideas that can be shared with participants to bring life and hilarity to any group. Figure 21.2 offers a sampling of skit ideas found in the Palo Alto (California) Recreation Department "Dramatics Manual." As can be seen, the skits are very short. In leading such dramatic activities, the leader should attempt to use some of the following suggestions.

- Change or adapt the skit to suit the present circumstances.
- Let several children try different parts to make the experience more than just a "production."
- Listen for adaptations made by the children.
- Stress the *individual's* expression of the role he or she is taking.
- Skits are not finished or polished performances; the fun is in the spontaneity and creativity.
- Warning—children are sensitive. Select skits that will not embarrass or ridicule.[2]

## MIME

The dramatic program area known as *mime* has realized a surge of popularity during the past few years. Mime refers to the type of performance given by an actor who uses only facial and body action to tell a story. Mimes do not converse with other actors; they simply utilize control over their bodies to portray action, feeling, and expression, and thus they are able to communicate an idea to an audience. In mime, the use of makeup is an im-

[2]Palo Alto (Calif.) Recreation Department Division of Neighborhood Centers and Playgrounds, "Dramatics Manual," n.d., pp. 2, 3.

**SHAKE WELL!**

Two persons are talking; one is shaking all over.

*First.*    What's the matter with you?
*Second.*    I've got to take my medicine as soon as this is over.
*First.*    Well, what's the matter?
*Second.*    You see that bottle?
*First.*    Yeah!
*Second.*    It says, "Shake well before taking!"

**WATER, WATER**

The scene is set by having a narrator describe a desolate desert scene. The only prop is a glass of water, which is to symbolize a beautiful oasis.

The action starts as one individual stumbles onto the set and crawls toward the water, grasping his throat and groaning. He collapses just short of his goal. This action continues with several others until there is an array of bodies surrounding the water. The last person crawls on to the scene, as badly off as the others, but he makes it to the water, reaches in his back pocket, removes his comb, dips it in the water, and proceeds to comb his hair.

**FIGURE 21.2**    Examples of skits. (*Source:* Palo Alto (Calif.) Recreation Department, Division of Neighborhood Centers and Playgrounds, "Dramatics Manual," n.d., pp. 4–5.)

portant factor because the mime typically wishes to assume a hidden identity completely, that is, become unrecognizable as his or her real self. In addition, since there is no speaking, the familiarity of voice patterns is not a distracting factor in the performance of the mime. Mime activities often take the form of creative dramatics, the instructor assigning each class member a part to portray.

The individual leading mime activities can help participants build skills that will enhance their performance. Two specific exercises that can be conducted by the mime leader to assist in skill development are detailed as follows.

- The leader stands in the front of a semicircle or rank-and-file formation and moves various body parts in a flowing but free manner. The class, regardless of the age group being served, follows the motion of the leader, in a free-flowing movement. No words are spoken during the exercise.
- The leader assigns groups of two persons to portray some type of specific action. Each team of two is thereby given the opportu-

nity to rehearse in private, then perform for the group as a whole. The audience or other class members then try to guess the actions of the two mimes after the performance is complete.

In addition, exercises to encourage nonverbal communication, "visual listening," and improvisation will build skills related to success in this dramatic area. The leader can, for example, request participants to practice movements such as "walking through doors," "sitting," "walking or running at various speeds," "taking on other life forms" (i.e., animals or plants), and everyday tasks such as "cooking, cleaning, or eating." Figure 21.3 suggests pantomime material appropriate for various age groups.

**STORYTELLING**

Some persons would believe that the activity of storytelling is a lost art. Storytelling is simply defined as the act of orally delivering the contents of a story or book. Storytelling may sometimes be done from memory, or some-

## PRESCHOOL CHILDREN

Nursery rhymes
The Little Engine That Could
A boy taking castor oil
Stepping into a cold shower

### Hearing

a sudden thundercrack
a dinner bell
a whisper
dance music

### Tasting

hot soup
ice-cream cone on a hot day
bitter medicine
grapes full of seeds

### Situations

a lady trying on a hat
a man stifling a sneeze
four or five people watching an exciting ball game
a woman seeing a mouse
kicking a football
playing tennis
rolling on the grass
pushing each other in swings
being autumn leaves scurrying and dancing among the trees

### Smelling

a burning dinner
a skunk
a Thanksgiving dinner aroma

## CHILDREN 5 to 6

The Hare That Ran Away
The Turkey's Nest
The Three Bears
The Three Little Pigs
The Three Billy Goats Gruff
The Golden Goose

The Lost Apron Pocket
The Runaway Bunny
The Ugly Duckling
The Big Black Engine
Monkey See, Monkey Do
Ferryboats
The Gingerbread Boy

## CHILDREN 7 to 8

The Bremen Town Musicians
 (The Traveling Musicians)
The Elephant's Child
The Adventures of the Little
 Field Mouse
Peter and the Wolf
The King and the Magic Stick
Snow White and Rose Red

The Sleeping Beauty
The Wonderful Pot
The Nutcracker and Sugar Dolly Stories
Jack and the Beanstalk
Peter Pan
The Elves and the Shoemaker

## CHILDREN 7 to 12

The Emperor's New Clothes
And to Think That I Saw It on
 Mulberry Street
The Three Wishes
The Princess on the Glass Hill
King Midas and the Golden Touch

The Little Woman Who Wanted Noise
Pandora
Many Moons
The Tinderbox
Cinderella
Tom Thumb

**FIGURE 21.3** Suggested material for pantomime. (*Source:* Berkeley (Calif.) Recreation and Parks Department, Berkeley, Calif., "Leader Trainee Course," n.d.)

times stories may be read from books. Storytelling demands a special type of leadership. A good storyteller can mesmerize an audience. The person who presents himself or herself as a storyteller must be able to feel the content of the stories he or she tells. He or she must know the material to be presented absolutely, and it must flow smoothly as the storyteller addresses the group.

Various group arrangements are satisfactory for the storytelling activity. The storyteller may wish to position the group in a semicircle *around* him or her, seated on the floor in the room. The storyteller then would feel free to use a variety of free-form body motions to amplify the material being presented. Another method of storytelling might find the audience seated in a semicircle, facing the storyteller. This seating arrangement would be particularly appropriate in storytelling around the campfire. Storytelling is more effective if the group is not too large—having less than 25 to 30 in the group.

The leader conducting a storytelling activity can use various techniques to arouse and hold the interest of participants. If storytelling is a regular activity, the leader may want to do something special to indicate story times, such as wearing a ''magic'' hat. Or he or she may refer to story time in a special way as ''the magic hour.'' When telling stories, the leader may want to use simple props to add interest to his or her presentation. Puppets, magic wands, a crystal ball, or a stuffed animal can heighten the effect of the story being told. Some storytellers use a prop such as a puppet or a doll to help tell the story. The leader should also use dramatic intonations of the voice to hold the attention of the audience and should attempt to talk to each of the participants individually so that everyone feels that the storyteller is talking especially to him or her. Some stories are termed ''audience participation stories.'' They depend on involvement of the group in the story. Each member of the group participates in movements or sounds that help to tell the story. An example of an audience participation story can be found in Figure 21.4.

The leader involved in storytelling should be careful in his or her selection of stories. It is important to take into consideration the age and interests of the participants. It is also important that the leader choose stories with which he or she is very familiar, yet also be able to vary his or her repertoire. To sum up, leadership techniques that can enhance the storytelling activity are these.

- Sit where everyone can see and hear you. (You may want to select a special place that is just for storytelling.)
- Know your story, remember the key events in sequence, and build around them. Project your personality in the way you tell the story. Make use of spontaneous changes that fit into the situation.
- Be aware of the attention span and interest of the children; vary the length to suit the audience.
- Use language suitable for the age listening.
- Maintain eye contact with the children.
- Use facial expressions and gestures. Use different voices for the different characters in the story. Vary the volume of your voice to emphasize the action.
- End the story with the climax; don't let it drag on.[3]

## CREATIVE DRAMATICS

Creative dramatics are *unstructured* forms of dramatic activity in which participants engage in improvisation and other spontaneous creative expression. The philosophy behind creative dramatics can be applied to many dramatic activities, such as skits, mime, puppetry, and informal dramatics. Therefore, any of these activities, if engaged in by participants informally, spontaneously, and using improvisation, can be included within the cat-

[3]''Ibid.,'' p. 18.

**Motions:**

| | |
|---|---|
| Mean old rabbit | Put hands on head to form rabbit ears and a mean look on face. |
| Wide, wide meadow | Extend arms outward. |
| Wavy, wavy grass | Wave hands in a wavy motion. |
| Grab rabbits and pop their heads together | Make motion of grabbing with each hand, and beat fists together. |
| Good fairy | Make halo around head. |
| Goon | Screw up face as you say, ''Goon,'' and curl fingers with both hands. |
| Hare | Form rabbit ears with hands. |

**Story:**

Once upon a time there was a *mean old rabbit*. And this *mean old rabbit* lived in a little hole, in the *wide, wide meadow*, with the *wavy, wavy grass*. Every day this *mean old rabbit* would come out of his little hole in the *wide, wide meadow*, with the *wavy, wavy grass* and grab *a little rabbit* in this hand and a little rabbit in this hand and *pop their heads together*.

All of a sudden the *good fairy* appeared, and she said, ''The next time I catch you, *mean old rabbit*, coming out of your little hole in the *wide, wide meadow* with the *wavy, wavy grass* and *grab a little rabbit* in this hand and a little rabbit in this hand and *pop their heads together*, I'm going to turn you into a *goon*!''

The next day the *mean old rabbit* was sitting by his little hole in the *wide, wide meadow* with the *wavy, wavy grass* watching all the little rabbits running about the meadow, when all of a sudden the *mean old rabbit* jumped up and *grabbed a little rabbit* with this hand and a little rabbit in this hand and *popped their heads together*.

Sure enough the *good fairy* appeared and she said, ''I told you the next time I caught you, *mean old rabbit*, coming out of your little hole in the *wide, wide meadow* with the *wavy, wavy grass* and *grabbing a little rabbit* in this hand and a little rabbit in this hand and *popping their heads together* I was going to turn you into a *goon*.''

So she did, and the moral of this story is . . . . *hare* today and *goon* tomorrow!

**FIGURE 21.4** ''Mean Old Rabbit,'' an example of an audience participation story. (*Source:* Palo Alto (Calif.) Recreation Department Division of Neighborhood Centers and Playgrounds, ''Dramatics Manual,'' n.d., p. 14.)

egory of creative dramatics. Creative dramatics are not formal and do not follow a prepared script. Nor do they require a stage, extensive props, costumes, or lighting. Participants engaged in creative dramatics are encouraged to act out their own feelings, thoughts, and emotions, using their own movements and words that they originate themselves. They use, for props, ''whatever is at hand.'' The leader who engages participants in creative dramatics does so to help them use their imaginations, to help them develop poise in front of a group in a relaxed and informal atmosphere, to allow them to use and develop their emotions, to allow them to participate in social group experiences, and to allow them to learn to use their bodies gracefully.

Creative dramatics may be involved with helping participants act out the role of *an individual or single event,* or it may involve participants in acting out an *entire story.* The leader might help participants learn to portray *an individual or an event* by using any of the various techniques that follow.

- The leader might have participants play games that involve creative dramatics such as charades or the New Games ''Lemonade.''
- The leader might supply participants with various simple props, such as hats, house-

hold items, or objects at hand and ask them to create a scene or character brought to mind by the props.

- The leader might involve participants in "action storytelling," having them act out parts of the story told by the leader (as in Figure 21.4).
- The leader might tell participants a familiar story and then ask them to portray some of its characters. For example, after telling the story of Cinderella, the leader might ask individuals to pretend to be "Cinderella's prancing white horses" or to pretend to be "Cinderella's wicked stepsister trying on the slipper that won't fit."
- The leader might suggest to participants that they act out various scenes from daily life or other specified situations. The leader might say, for example, "pretend you are cooking dinner," "pretend you are playing football," "pretend you are out camping and see a bear," or "pretend you are on the school playground at recess."

Once participants have learned to use their creativity and imagination to portray individuals and single events, the leader may want to involve them in acting out an *entire story*.

Participants acting out an entire story may use mime or may have speaking parts. Speaking parts are usually recommended only for older children. Also, speaking parts, if included, should be completely improvised. Kraus and Bates have outlined a step-by-step process that can be used by the leader to implement a creative dramatics production of an entire story. This outline is detailed here.

1. Select a story. This may be based on a story that the leader tells the children, or it may be one that the children develop independently.
2. The leader tells the story in a relaxed, informal manner, bringing out the humor or suspense in it and using direct dialogue wherever possible. The story should have interesting action and characters but should not have too complicated a plot.

3. The children and the leader discuss the story, analyzing its meaning, the different characters, the most important scenes, and exciting moments.
4. Children should be selected to take different parts. They may volunteer for different roles themselves, or the leader may assign them. If the group is large enough, it may divide into several smaller groups, each of which undertakes to act out the play and assigns roles to its members.
5. The story should be reviewed to develop the basic plot outline, which consists of the most important scenes that will be acted out. Then children begin to act it out. They should be encouraged
   (a) to be natural and to use gestures, movements, or speech that feel comfortable to them
   (b) to pace themselves; to speak slowly, clearly, and with a sense of being the character
   (c) to begin to think of how they "feel" toward the other characters and how the stage action may be laid out so it is most effective.
6. After each of the scenes has been played, children should review the entire experience. They should be helped to analyze both themselves and others in constructive and supportive ways and to make sound suggestions for improvement.
7. If the children wish to, the story may then be played out in its entirety for other children on the playground or for an audience of parents. It is never necessary in informal dramatics to have an audience. However, if children wish to, they may get great satisfaction from performing their work for others.[4]

In addition to the methods and techniques that can be used by the leader to help participants act out entire stories or portray individuals and events, there are some general guide-

---

[4]"Kraus and Bates, op. cit.," p. 196.

lines that the leader can use to facilitate creative dramatics. These are discussed below.

- Try to create and maintain a free and open atmosphere in which participants will feel comfortable expressing themselves and will develop self-confidence.
- Encourage participants to use their imaginations and to use the surrounding environment for "props," and "scenery."
- Praise participants for their creativity and originality.
- If the leader assigns participants roles, the roles should be changed frequently, and the participants should be allowed to act out many varied roles.
- Try to limit the creative dramatics group to from eight to ten participants, for that is usually more effective.
- End the creative dramatic activity while it is still fun, interesting, and productive.

The benefits of creative dramatics activities are many for participants. They not only encourage creativity, imagination, and self-confidence, as mentioned, but they can be enjoyed and engaged in by all participants, not just those who are "talented" in drama. In addition, creative dramatics offer opportunities for physical activity and group participation for individuals who may lack skills in other forms of recreation activity such as sports and games. In other words, "anyone" can be involved in, can be successful at, and can enjoy creative dramatics.

## COMMUNITY THEATERS

In many communities in North America, little theater or community theater is in operation either as a regular function of a recreation and leisure service delivery system or as an independently functioning organization. It can be defined as an "organization, not primarily educational in its purpose, which regularly produces drama on a non-commercial basis and in which participation is open to the

community at large."[5] The participation of individuals in community theater is typically voluntary. They engage in community theater because it offers them opportunities for creative expression, satisfaction, social interaction, theatrical experience, and learning opportunities.

The sophistication of this type of dramatic organization may vary greatly from city to city. In some cities it may be well funded and operate out of an elaborate facility. In other cities community theater is conducted in "make-do" facilities or school auditoriums. However, in either case, community theater is a creative activity in which people participate for the simple pleasure of "doing" and for the social outlet created as a function of such participation. Although the information in this section of the chapter focuses on community theater specifically, the organizational structure and principles discussed can be employed or adapted by the leader to the organization of dramatic efforts at any level, including the production of plays for children and youth.

The most common types of theater presentation will depend, in large part, on the type of physical facility available to the group. For example, a school cafeteria or cafetorium will most typically have a *proscenium* type of stage, possibly elevated, and only allowing audience view from the front. This is an excellent facility to utilize for most productions provided that the entrances and exits can be draped or made usable by the construction of scenery. This type of stage is depicted in Figure 21.5. Another type of stage arrangement that can be easily accommodated in most facilities is *theater-in-the-round*. Depicted in Figure 21.6, this type of stage is actually surrounded by the audience. Actresses and actors enter and exit by aisleways through the audience. The audi-

---

[5]Robert E. Gard and Gertrude S. Bailey, *Community Theatre, Idea and Achievement* (New York: Duell, Sloan, and Pearce, 1959).

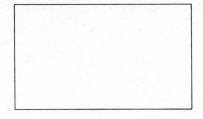

X X X X X X X X X X

X X X X X X X X X X

X X X X X X X X X X

X X X X X X X X X X

**FIGURE 21.5**   Proscenium theater.

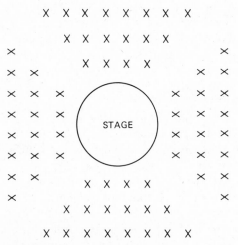

**FIGURE 21.6**   Theater-in-the-round.

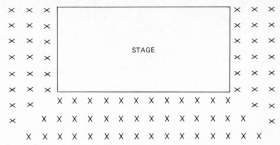

**FIGURE 21.7**   Open or platform stage.

ence in this type of setting gets a true feel for the activity that is occurring. In some communities, *open or platform* stages have been constructed that allow for a dramatic performance to be viewed on three sides by the audience. Open or platform stages may be located in a park setting in the open air, in which case they may be limited to a certain extent by weather conditions. An open or platform stage arrangement is depicted in Figure 21.7.

The leader associated with community theater may be involved in various ways. He or she may act as a facilitator, attempting to help the group locate a facility, solicit operating funds, or "scrounge" for scenery and props; the leader may be more directly involved in some aspects of the play production itself in which he or she may have some expertise; or the leader may simply act as a liaison between a community theater group and a recreation and leisure service agency that sponsors it. As a liaison, the leader might inform the organization as to the needs of the community theater group and conversely inform the community theater group as to the expectations, available resources, and applicable rules and regulations of the recreation and service organization.

The involvement of a recreation and leisure service agency or some other sponsoring agency in community theater is usually prompted by the demonstration of interest by a core group of individuals. Once interest is demonstrated, an organizational meeting may be held with representation from the organization to discuss the feasibility of organizing a community theater and the benefits that could be attained from such an effort. The leader involved in such an organizational meeting or meetings should suggest discussion of topics related to the potential play production, such as the degree of interest and experience of the group organizing the community theater production, the community's needs and resources, and the type of organizational structure to be used. Following is a discussion of these topics.

***Assessing Community Needs and Resources.*** By assessing the experience of the group organizing the community theater production, one can determine the amount of talent already possessed, as well as the degree to which the community theater group will have to recruit others to round out their needs. In addition, the organizational group will want to determine whether or not other similar groups are in operation in the community in order to avoid duplication of efforts.

The group should also assess its human, fiscal, and physical resources. Does the group have access to a facility that can be used for plays? Do they already have a store of props, costumes, or scenery, or will they be starting from scratch? Have other individuals in the community expressed an interest in participating in the community theater program? Do they have any financial resources at their disposal, or will they have to engage in fundraising efforts? The group that may be attempting to put on a production with very limited financial resources may have to "scrounge" for materials. In other words, they need to obtain usable materials for props, scenery, and costumes inexpensively or even free. Figure 21.8 offers information helpful in the acquisition of such materials. A community group that has few resources may be better off producing a modest play well than attempting to stage an elaborate production that looks inadequate because of an insufficient number of experienced actors or inadequate props, costumes, and scenery. Although it should be pointed out that plays can be performed that "suggest" props, scenery, and costumes and this can be very effective if done creatively.

***Play Organization, Selection and Implementation.*** It is impossible for one individual to be responsible for all the duties associated with the production of a play. Some of these responsibilities must be delegated to others, and a system of control must be in effect to ensure that all tasks are completed as scheduled. Commonly a director is employed to "direct" the actors and actresses in their performances, and a producer is employed to coordinate and assume responsibility for all activities other than those of the director. Figures 21.9 and 21.10 detail the chain of command that might exist within a theatrical production and offer brief descriptions of the duties involved in major positions.

Following the initial organizational meetings of the community theater group, in which roles are defined, resources are assessed, and some of the needs of the group are determined, the group should actually collaborate to select the play to be performed. The selection of the play is crucial to the success of the production. The community theater group should assess the type of audience that is likely to come to the play and attempt to put on a production that will meet the expectations of this group. For example, a play organized in a small community may attract a larger audience if it is suitable for, and can be enjoyed by, families than if it is geared to a select adult audience. In play selection, it is also important to assess the human, fiscal, and physical resources that the community theater group is likely to have at its disposal and ensure that the play selected complements these resources. Other considerations that might be made regarding play selection are the length of play desired, the type of facility available and its limitations, and the purpose of the play. The purpose of the play can have a great deal of influence on play selection. Some of the reasons that plays are organized and implemented are these.

- To offer an audience fun and enjoyment.
- To promote values.
- To encourage self-examination and consideration of new thoughts and concepts.
- To involve as many individuals as possible (children's plays often have this as one of their goals).

| Source | Possible Resource | Possible Uses |
|---|---|---|
| Automobile wrecking companies | Steering wheels | Dramatic play; playground apparatus |
| Bottling companies | Wooden soft-drink crates | Substitute for hollow blocks, remove slats and cover with screen for spatter painting |
| | Sturdy fiberboard beer cases | Storage; dramatic play items |
| Camera repair shops, film developers | Old nonrepairable cameras, equipment, and film containers | Dramatic play, sound cylinders, smell bottles, manipulative toys |
| Carpet stores and rug companies | Carpet roll tubes | Constructions |
| | Carpet remnants | Resting mats, mats for library corner, floor covering, bulletin board, wall hanging |
| Construction sites | Felled trees | Climbing trees, stepping blocks, outdoor seating |
| | Excess fill dirt | Earth mounds combined with culvert pipes on playground |
| | Lumber | Woodworking |
| Contractors and building supply companies (many sites have scrap bins or piles) | Lumber, pipes, wire, linoleum, tiles, molding wood, sawdust, wood curls | Constructing, woodworking, investigations |
| Electronics manufacturers | Styrofoam packing | Art projects |
| | Discarded components | Investigation in science |
| Floor companies | Scrap linoleum | Work surface coverings, crafts items |
| Floor covering firms | Tile samples | Color matching, constructions |
| Garage or tire shop | Automobile tires | Swings, climbers, used with boards for balance, series of tires can be a tunnel, artwork |
| Garment factories | Wide variety of materials, yarn, buttons, decorative tape | Art projects, doll clothes, dress-up clothes |
| Ice-cream stores | 3-gallon ice-cream containers | Storage, space helmets, constructions |
| Leather goods manufacturers | Leather and lacing scraps | Art projects, drums or other musical instruments |
| Moving companies, appliance dealers | Large cardboard boxes, smaller boxes | Dramatic play, rocket ship, house, fire station, etc. Art projects, cardboard construction |
| | Styrofoam packing | Easy for initial practice in carpentry, art projects, sculptures |
| Plastic companies | Trimmings, cuttings, tubing, scrap plastic, plexiglas | Sand and water play, constructions |
| Plumbers, plumbing supply companies | Wires, pipes, tile scraps, linoleum | Constructions, experiments |

| Source | Possible Resource | Possible Uses |
|---|---|---|
| Printing shops | Assorted sizes, colors, weights and textures of scrap paper | Art projects, tickets, grocery slips |
| | End rolls of paper | Murals, group art projects, making life-size figures, giant paper sculptures, etc. |
| Salvage companies | Large wire, heavy rope | Climbing |
| | Miscellaneous small parts and machinery | Tinkering with machinery, taking apart and seeing how it works, using parts in mechanical experiments |
| Sewer contractors | Sewer pipes | Tunnels, trains, planters, seats |
| Small-appliance repair shops | Miscellaneous nonrepairable small appliances, such as toasters, blenders, mixers, etc., made safe for children | Good for investigative tinkering, taking apart, then putting together, using parts for other mechanical projects |
| Supermarkets | Boxes in many sizes | Dramatic play items |
| | Cardboard displays | Housekeeping |
| | Fruit crates | Storage |
| Surplus and salvage stores | Furniture | Furnishings for recreation programs |
| | Machinery | Discover what makes it work, playground apparatus |
| | Railroad ties | Sand or earth retainer, playground fort, outdoor stage, short and taller ones for climbing |
| | Large nuts and bolts | Manipulative toys |
| | Used scales, hanging balances | Measurement comparing weights |
| Television repair shops | Older TV cabinets | Take out all parts; use the case for children to put on own TV shows or puppet shows |
| Tile stores | Ceramic tiles | Mosaics, color matching, counting games |
| Utility companies | Excess colored wire | Art and science projects |
| | Telephones and switchboards | Dramatic play and learning how telephones work |
| | Utility poles | Playground apparatus (balance beam, benches, log fort) |
| | Wooden cross arms | Sandbox or retaining wall |
| | Wooden cable spools | Climbing apparatus, tables |
| | Wire | Sculpture, experiments, art projects |

FIGURE 21.8  "Scrounging" for materials that can be used in dramatic and other activities. (*Source:* "Scrounging," United States Department of the Interior, Heritage Conservation and Recreation Service, Washington, D.C., April 1980, p. 6.)

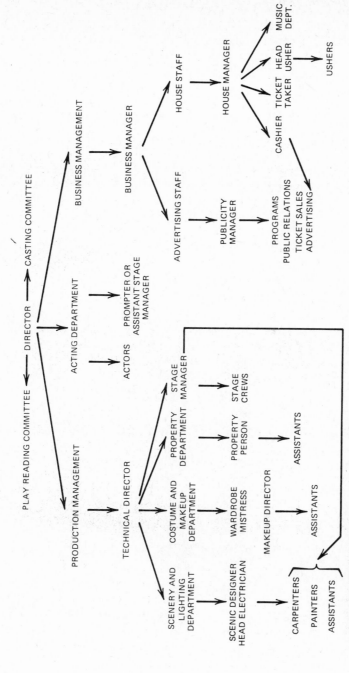

**FIGURE 21.9**  Organizational chart for community theater production. (*Source:* Dan H. Corbin, *Recreation Leadership* [Englewood Cliffs, N.J.: Prentice-Hall, 1959], p. 221.)

### Actors and Actresses

Actors and actresses actually deliver the dialogue of the production on stage. They typically gather for an audition and are selected by the director for particular parts for which they appear to be suited, based on the play content, their manner, body demeanor, voice, and the extent to which, in the judgment of the director, they would be able to interpret the play in the manner intended by the playwright.

### Director

The director is the final authority on artistic matters regarding the play. He or she not only casts the performers, conducts rehearsals, and determines how the play should be interpreted, but also works with individuals in charge of costumes, scenery, lighting, and music to coordinate all the artistic elements of the production. The director must be a leader who has the ability to motivate others to do what he or she wants them to do. It is important that he or she remember that the amateur actor-actress acts only because of enjoyment and that, therefore, directing should be positive and constructive or the director may be without a cast. The director should help performers ''act,'' not show them how to do it. The director should describe the effect that should be achieved and then let the performers do their own acting.

### Technical Director

The technical director works with individuals responsible for *costumes*, *lighting*, *props*, and *scenery* to ensure that all these functions are carried out in a cooperative and complementary manner. In addition, the technical director coordinates all the ''behind the scenes'' activities during performances, supervising the *stage manager*, who directs stage crews, and checking to be sure that all staff members are present and are carrying out their functions as planned and rehearsed.

### Business Manager

The business manager is in charge of the finances for the play production. He or she formulates a budget of expected income and expenditures, disburses funds to pay bills, and is in charge of all *ticket sales*. Usually, the business manager is required to authorize any expenditures by other members of the theater production. In addition, the business manager oversees the efforts of the advertising staff or *publicity manager*. Publicity efforts may involve the use of television, radio, newspapers, posters, fliers, or announcements at meetings. Such efforts should be directed toward the audience that the production hopes to attract, for example, children, adults, families, or young adults.

**FIGURE 21.10**   Key positions in community theater productions.

- To engage the community group in a type of play not previously attempted.
- To expose the audience to different cultures as expressed in dramatic literature.
- To encourage the audience to consider new avenues of thoughts and concepts.
- To uplift the audience spiritually and emotionally.

A play may obviously have more than one of these purposes. For example, a community theater group might simultaneously attempt to expose the audience to the thoughts and concepts of a different culture through a play that is also fun and enjoyable. In addition, the age group to be served will, of course, influence the selection of the play. For example, the purpose of the play production may be "fun and enjoyment," but the type of play selected to fulfill this purpose will vary greatly depending on whether the intended audience consists of children, youths, young adults, older adults, or families.

After selection of the play, the play is cast by the director, and rehearsals commence. The director may want to "block" out the play prior to the first rehearsal. "Blocking" out the play involves planning of the stage set in terms of the placement of furniture, windows, doors, and exits and the movements of actors and actresses within the set. This is often first done with a miniature cardboard model to see if the actors can get on and off stage and can use the props as planned. In other words, the director attempts to make sure that arrangement of props and movement of cast members are physically feasible. The director also attempts to ensure that the set will be balanced in terms of both the props on stage and the positions of the actors. The audience should view a symmetrical arrangement on stage that is pleasing to the eye. The director blocking out the play should also ensure that the central characters in each scene are centrally located on stage and are toward the front of the stage. The characters that are more peripheral to the action on stage should be in less important positions—to the sides and more toward the rear of the stage. After the play has been blocked out in miniature, the actual props (or facsimiles) are placed, and actors and actresses move on stage, basically, according to this plan. A stage is divided up into sections, each of which has a name that refers to its area of location. These parts of the acting stage are depicted in Figure 21.11. The director should refer to these areas by name to avoid confusion by the actors.

As the rehearsals commence, the director "directs" the actors in order to help them achieve a believable and effective performance. Some elementary rules that the director

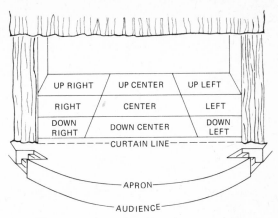

**FIGURE 21.11** Parts of an acting stage. (*Source*: Richard Krause, *Recreation Today: Program Planning and Leadership*, 2d ed. [Santa Monica, Calif.: Goodyear Publishing Co., 1977], p. 441.)

might encourage actors and actresses to follow are these.

- To speak with feeling and emotion and to avoid simply "reading" their lines. They should attempt to "be" the person they are portraying in the play.
- To use body movements and expressions to reflect the emotions being portrayed.
- To be on time to rehearsals and to take rehearsals seriously. The actors and actresses should attempt to make each rehearsal as perfect as they possibly can.
- To face the audience always while speaking.
- To ensure that their positions on stage are accurate at all times.

Following a number of regular rehearsals, the cast will have one or more dress rehearsals in which all costumes, makeup, props, scenery, and dialogue are as they will be during the actual performance. Depending on how well the director and the production staff have done their jobs, the dress rehearsal or rehearsals will go very smoothly, or they will not. Often community theaters will invite an audience to the dress rehearsal to increase the demand upon the actors, actresses, and others for excellence.

The opening night performance itself should be smooth and professional, with conscientious prior preparations. Following the last performance of the play, a cast party is traditional. In addition, the group should help to dismantle the set and should ensure that all props, costumes, and other materials are returned, if borrowed, or stored for later use.

Certainly, there is much effort involved in the production of plays. Such effort can be a pleasure, however, for those who are interested in the theater and believe that many benefits can be derived from this type of program by both the community theater group and the audience. The leader involved in community theater, as either a facilitator or a participant, has a unique opportunity to enhance the lives of others in a very special way.

## SUMMARY

In this chapter the authors have discussed the leadership of dramatic activities. There are numerous and diverse types of dramatic activities in which the recreation and leisure service leader might have a role. This role may be as an instructor, a facilitator, or even a participant. Some of the dramatic activities often associated with recreation and leisure service organizations include, but are not limited to, storytelling, puppetry, mime, creative dramatics, and community theater. Dramatic activities can benefit participants by allowing them opportunities for self-expression, fun, personal growth and development, social interaction with others, and opportunities to learn about themselves and their culture.

## DISCUSSION QUESTIONS

1. Identify and define the objectives of recreation dramatics activities.
2. In your opinion, what are the chief values of a drama program?
3. What is the role of the dramatics activity leader?
4. What role does the recreation and leisure service leader play in creative dramatics? Storytelling? Other types of drama programs?
5. List ten dramatics programs that may be found in your community.
6. How is a community theater program organized?
7. Because financial resources in recreation and leisure service organizations are often limited, drama programs can benefit from ''scrounging for materials.'' What does this term imply? How does one scrounge?

# LEADING SONGS

Leading songs around a campfire is a popular form of leisure activity.

Music is the universal language. People everywhere hum, whistle, sing, tap their feet, and drum their fingers. Without rhythm, our lives would be incomplete. Music is an integral part of such recreation programs as playgrounds, summer camps, senior citizens centers, community centers, and parties. There is no reason why we cannot incorporate music in our recreation programs, for music depends not upon what is *with* us, but what is *within* us.

What qualities does music contain to make it so universally appealing? First of all, for reasons unknown, music is enjoyable. But beyond that, music has certain unique qualities. It is the great unifier for, through music, people become one. All reflect the mood of the song—serious, happy, humorous, gay, appreciative, patriotic. Whatever it is, music unifies our thoughts, our actions, and our moods. Music is an equalizer too. In music all are alike. There are no boundaries of wealth or race or creed. Nor are there newcomers or strangers, as all feel a kinship through a song. Music also provides opportunity for self-expression. One can express happiness, serenity, pathos, and even anger through whistling, humming, or singing. It can be a positive catharsis for any emotion. Beyond these reasons, music has beauty; it is pleasing to the ears; it seems to help satisfy our need for the aesthetic.

The equipment for music may be carried with us. Voices make it possible to carry on a musical program with no additional equipment, although instruments, tape recorders, and phonographs may enhance the program and increase its scope. No special space is needed; music can take place indoors or outdoors on any surface or in any shaped area. No experience is needed; even beginners can find success in musical activities. Anyone and everyone can participate, for music knows no age, size, shape, or sex limitation. The musical program can be varied to fit any situation, any time, any place, any event for anyone.

The scope of music is wide and can be integrated with many other programs. Music can be acted out within action songs, action ballads, or operettas. Music also can be used in games and contests; many games are singing games. Through music we can imagine, remember, believe, and appreciate.

## THE SETTINGS FOR SINGING

The settings in which singing can take place are as diverse as the number of recreation and leisure opportunities that are available. Singing can occur in settings that are formal or informal. It may occur indoors or outdoors, and it is often found in conjunction with other recreation activities and programs. Some of the more informal settings in which singing activities are found are playgrounds, campgrounds, preschool programs, banquets, activities on a bus, cheering of sports teams, on hikes, and caroling at Christmas. Singing that can be thought of as occurring in a more formal sense is usually characterized by considerable preparation and practice on the part of participants. Choral concerts in auditoriums or even at camp, ethnic song celebrations at pageants, children's concerts at community festivals, singing in dramatic presentations—these are all examples of what can be termed more formal settings for singing.

Within all of these settings, both formal and informal, the leader should anticipate the needs of those participating in the singing in terms of such factors as seating arrangements and ability to see the leader. For example, song leading often occurs in dining halls where people are arranged around tables in small groups of 8 to 10 facing each other. Those with backs to the leader should be asked to rise quietly and turn their chairs around or stand and reverse their positions on the benches. If the people at the heads (or feet) of the tables are sitting back to the leader, they are not part of the group and should be asked to turn around. In short, all people should be positioned correctly. When many are seated on a level floor (rather than an inclined auditorium), the leader should be elevated, as described in Chapter 6. In an outdoor setting, a raised amphitheater is desirable. Participants need logs or benches or chairs to sit on, and the leader should be positioned to be seen by all. Just having the participants sitting at random on the ground really leads to discomfort and loss of attention.

## LEADING SONGS

A song *leader* is not the same as a song teacher, for the song leader may assume that the majority of the participants know the song and need someone to lead it. A song *teacher*, on the other hand, may assume that few, if any, participants know the song and that he or she must teach it so all know it.

A belief in music and its value is the first prerequisite for a song leader. Enthusiasm will show through regardless of leadership ability. If the leader demonstrates a belief in the musical activity, lack of experience may not be obvious.

The second prerequisite for successful song leading is, of course, a repertoire of songs. A repertoire is a supply of songs memorized by the leader that can be led without notes or reference to a book, card, or sheet of paper. When the leader uses such props in song leading, contact with the audience is diminished. A leader may have a *repertory* (storehouse) of songs for reference; however, on the job a *repertoire* or ready supply of songs is mandatory.

Leading the song itself is really one of the easiest of all leadership skills. If one can talk, one can sing. If one can lead a game, one can lead a song. Someone once remarked facetiously, "There are three rules for leading a song. One, start when they start. Two, end when they end. And, three, sing the same song they sing." Actually, this is not far from the truth.

The major objective in leading a song *is* really to start the group together, keep them together, and end the song all together. In *leading* a song, one assumes the group already knows the song and merely needs to be reminded what note to start on and how fast to sing. If the leader is not sure of the note, he or she can hum a few bars to himself or herself and try it out before giving the audience the note. Or help may be requested from one of the singers in the audience to volunteer a note. Soliciting the help of participants can enhance group interest.

Starting the group is simple, but keeping them together is often a problem, especially for the neophytes who never seem to know what to do with their hands. Many books tell what to do for $3/4$ time or $2/4$ or $4/4$ or even $6/8$ time, but this seems to frighten the beginner, who probably has no idea what time signatures mean, usually has no reference to find out which time a song was written in, and probably is too unskilled to determine the song's time by listening. There are, however, three different types of hand motion for the unsophisticated song leader that are simple, require no knowledge of music, and are successful.

## BEAT LEADING

Some songs lend themselves naturally to a leading technique called, for the lack of anything more descriptive, the beat technique. Here the leader uses the hand (or hands) to beat the normal cadence of the song. The beat may go from side to side or up and down. If one has trouble determining if the song has a ready ''beat'' or not, tapping a foot or drumming the fingers may bring forth the rhythm automatically. Some songs, especially rounds, are readily led by the beat method. For example, the following songs are naturally accented and can be led by the beat method on the words designated.

The Moŕe We Get Togéther
Rów, Rów, Rów Your Bóat
Thŕee Blínd Míce

## LEVEL LEADING

After beating the music, most leaders find themselves moving automatically into level leading, which is simply using the position of

the hand to indicate whether the note is higher or lower than the one before. The leader indicates each syllable as it is sung by changing the level of the hand in the direction of the tune. As the tune goes up, so does the hand; as the pitch descends, so does the hand. This type of leading is unconsciously automatic with most people. Of course, one cannot use level leading if the group is singing rounds or harmony. Beat leading will work there successfully.

## ACTION LEADING

A third method of song leading, action leading, is used with informal action songs. Action songs are those in which both singers and leaders do something with their hands to act out the words of the song. The leader who may feel uncomfortable beating time or leading by pitch level often finds action songs the answer to the problem of what to do with the hands. Some leaders do not like action songs because they usually require some histrionics; however, others find the dramatic appeal of the action song a logical way to overcome the self-consciousness that accompanies their first attempts to lead. Examples of action songs include the following.

My Hat It Has Three Corners
In a Cottage in a Woods
If You're Happy and You Know It
One Finger, One Thumb
Itsy Bitsy Spider
Lady and the Crocodile

## LEADING AND CONTROL

A good song leader not only leads the singing but also controls the quality of the music. Music is not synonymous with noise; shouting is not singing. Contests wherein groups try to sing louder than other groups at the expense of the music are not quality programs and serve only to downgrade musical experience, not enhance it.

The choice of songs is often up to the leader, who can be discriminating and can choose a musical program of high quality. Some songs do not deserve the efforts of a leader. Many songs are hard to sing because of their unusual melodies and are not suitable or acceptable for group singing. The leader should also use good taste and common sense in selecting songs. Songs and ballads referring to drinking and such are not suitable for children on playgrounds or in camps, nor are they always acceptable to the middle- or senior-aged groups. Many rowdy or risqué songs, which are enjoyed in some settings, should not be selected by a paid leader. People may sing those songs among their own groups, but a leader is hired to maintain or improve quality and to ensure that the program reflects well on the organization for whom he or she works. Therefore, he or she should be discriminating in the selection of songs.

Another thing that leaders can control is the tempo of the song. Too often unperceptive leaders will permit their groups to lead *them* or make already slow songs become dirges or jazz up fast songs beyond the semblance of music. The perceptive leader sets the tempo and permits no song to drag needlessly or race out of control. The leader is also responsible for the pitch of the song. Some songs are often started on a note that seems logical, only to be completely out of the range of most singers on the high notes that follow. "The Star-Spangled Banner" is a prime example of this. The lines "Oh say can you see . . ." must be pitched low, or the singers will never reach the notes of "And the rockets' red glare."

The song leader might want to make note of songs with high notes in the middle in order to remember to start low. Many novices find that once they start a song high, they "think high" and hesitate to restart at a lower note. In case the song is started on the wrong note, the leader should always stop the song and start again.

## TEACHING SONGS

In the teaching of songs, it is important that the singers develop interest in the song and that they are successful in learning at least a part of it the first time they sing it, so that they will look forward to singing it again. The success or failure of a new song very often depends on the way it is presented to the group. The effective leader familiarizes him or herself with the material before introducing it and, as in the introduction of games, arouses interest by a unique introduction. Introducing a song by saying, "We are now going to learn 'Kookaburra,'" violates all principles of introduction. It is authoritarian and arouses little interest among those to whom "Kookaburra" is a meaningless word. Likewise, introducing the same song by saying, "The next song is about a monkey eating gumdrops," is an equally poor introduction, for it is inaccurate. A more factual introduction would be this: "There is an Australian bird that has a song like laughter. It perches in a eucalyptus tree, which the Australians call a gum tree, and it sounds as if it is the merriest bird in the forest (which the Australians call 'bush'). This is a song about this interesting bird." If the leader does not have access to such facts, the song might be introduced as one that the leader used to sing when he or she was a young camper, with elaboration as to the excitement of singing at camp under the trees or the stars.

When one is teaching songs, it is imperative that the leader enunciate clearly, particularly when singing new or uncommon words. A child once asked a camp counselor, after singing "Peace of the River," "Who is Olivia?" The counselor, not having any idea, asked the child where she had heard the name. The youngster answered, "We've been singing 'Peace I Ask of Thee, Olivia.'" More than one child has also sung, "Green Grow the Russians, Ho" instead of "Rushes." How many children have similarly strange ideas of the songs they sing is anyone's guess, but unless the leader takes time to help them understand the meaning of, or to define, a specific word that is not yet in the child's vocabulary, these incidents are bound to be many.

In the actual teaching of the song, it is generally good to start by singing the entire song for the group. This helps them to think of the song as a "whole" and gives a good introduction. Then sing a phrase (or two, if they are not too long), and have the group repeat it after you. In this way, the words and music are learned together, bit by bit. This method is known as "rote teaching" or "lining-out." The Puritans used this method of learning songs, for most of the singers did not possess books. In a song with several verses and a simple chorus, such as "Marching to Pretoria," it is well to teach the chorus first. In this way everyone singing the song is a successful participant immediately, even though he or she doesn't remember all the verses for a while.

If a leader feels ill at ease singing a song through alone, it is possible that some people already know the song and will help. All it takes is the request, "If you know the song, sing it through with me." If only a few know the song and they are spread far apart, have them group together to lend strength and confidence to each other, as well as to you. There are some adults and children who are convinced (unfortunately) that they cannot carry a tune. An excellent song to dispel this fallacy is "Sarasponda." If the accompanying part, which goes, "Boom dah, boom dah, boom dah, boom dah," is taught first, everyone can participate with equal success. Then if the "Sarasponda" part is taught and the two sections sung together, the "nonsinger" suddenly finds the ability to harmonize!

In teaching rounds, have the group sing the song through in unison two or three times; then divide into the number of groups needed. Be sure to announce in advance how many times each group is to sing it through. A good rule of thumb is that the song can be sung through as many times as you have groups. With rounds, as with any other types of songs, though, stop the song while the interest is still high and the group will be eager to sing it the next time.

Use of song sheets for song leading and teaching should be limited. If the time does not allow for review or teaching, song sheets with printed words are justifiable. In a camp, playground, or youth group setting, however, song sheets detract from the program and from the leader. No one can possibly keep eyes on a leader and a printed sheet simultaneously. Because of a fear of singing the wrong words, the singer will keep the eyes on the paper, and the actions and efforts of the leader are wasted. Rustling papers, turning pages, and the tops of heads are all the leader sees when the group uses song sheets.

As with any activity, leading and teaching songs require some practice. No one ever becomes a song leader overnight, and no song leader or teacher became proficient without making mistakes. In recreational singing, one can be forgiven mistakes in method. What is most important in recreational singing is group unification through music that is enthusiastic and of a positive type.

## SUMMARY

Music is an important part of all of our lives. Because of its importance and the fact that it is often associated with recreation and leisure services and programs, the ability to lead musical activities is a valuable skill for the leader to possess. The ability to lead and teach songs enables the leader to draw out a wide range of human emotions. Some songs may be quiet and allow for feelings of reflection and contemplation whereas other songs are energizing and infuse participants with feelings of enthusiasm, excitement, and joy.

## DISCUSSION QUESTIONS

1. Why is music considered the great unifier?
2. Discuss the leisure settings where music may occur.
3. Differentiate between a song leader and a song teacher.
4. Define "beat leading," and give examples of songs easily led by the beat method.
5. When might a leader employ beat leading, and when might action leading be preferable?
6. Discuss the leader's responsibility for controlling the quality of the singing.
7. Why should a song leader be particularly careful in enunciating and explaining the words of songs?
8. How can the self-conscious leader find ease when teaching a new melody to a group?
9. Under what circumstances is it wise to use song sheets? When should they not be used?

# LEADERSHIP IN THE OUTDOORS

Leadership in the out of doors can increase participants' awareness of and interest in the environment.

North Americans by the millions flock to the woods, oceans, mountains, beaches, lakes, and rivers to participate in a myriad of activities that depend on natural resources for their success. Although accustomed to a comfortable life-style of air conditioning, indoor plumbing, and fast food, these individuals select, as sites for pleasure, the outdoors. They do this in spite of the fact that many of these sites are primitive and inconvenient. Their

goals, through participation in such outdoor experiences, are fun, enjoyment, education, and adventure. It is the job of the outdoor leader to help them attain these goals safely.

Outdoor recreation can be defined as *any voluntary leisure activity that involves the use, understanding, or appreciation of natural resources or a combination of these.* The emphasis of this definition is on *natural* resources. Therefore, this chapter will not include discussion of activities conducted outdoors unless their major focus is on the land or water in its natural state. Some activities that *are* included in the category of outdoor recreation are camping, canoeing, walking, backpacking, ice skating, studying nature, horseback riding, hiking, and picnicking.

The recreation and leisure service leader working with participants in the outdoors has a great deal of responsibility. Not only does this type of leader attempt to lead and instruct participants in a way that is meaningful and enjoyable, but he or she must also ensure that participants follow strict safety rules and strict rules for the protection of the natural environment. The outdoor instructional leader must always keep in mind that his or her primary responsibilities are to maintain the quality of natural areas and to ensure the safe return of all participants.

The scope of outdoor activities is so large that thousands of books have been written on

Outdoor activities can satisfy participants' need for adventure.

outdoor related activities ranging from the very simple to complex high-risk activities. The purpose of this chapter is to offer specific techniques that can be applied to most programs in the outdoors.

## OUTDOOR LEADERS' ROLES AND SETTINGS

Although outdoor leaders may be found in any of the roles discussed in Chapter 6 and in other roles as well, there are two major interrelated categories of outdoor leadership. First, there are outdoor leaders whose major functions entail *leading or teaching skills that depend on the natural environment for their performance.* And second, there are outdoor leaders who *teach or lead programs concerned with understanding the environment as it exists in its natural condition.* In addition, within these two major categories, there are smaller categories or subcategories of outdoor leadership.

### LEADERS OF SKILLS IN THE OUTDOORS

Outdoor skill leaders are those individuals who specialize in teaching or leading activities that depend on the natural environment for their success. These activities may be seasonal in nature, may be related to specific land and water forms, or may be a combination of both. Though there are many examples of such activities, the following represent a wide variety of them: downhill or cross-country

skiing, winter (snow) camping, fishing, hunting, orienteering (cross-country racing by map and compass), hiking, backpacking, rock climbing, snow camping, caving, rafting, white water canoeing, sailing, kayaking, and bicycling. The leader of such activities should have knowledge of the physical and psychological needs and characteristics of participants as well as complete familiarity with the skills unique to the activity and a thorough knowledge of the care of the natural resources on which the activity depends.

Outdoor skill leaders may work in a variety of settings with all ages and abilities. The area in which their duties lie is generally labeled as "outdoor recreation." Examples of leadership positions in this area of specialization include the following.

- College outdoor pursuit instructors
- Youth agency trip leaders
- Camp counselors
- Outward Bound, National Outdoors Leadership School, or Wilderness Users Association Instructors
- Yacht club instructors
- Sailing racing coaches
- Commercial guides and outfitters
- Private consultants
- Programmers at resorts
- Ski resort instructors

### LEADERS OF KNOWLEDGE ABOUT THE OUTDOORS

Outdoor knowledge leaders are generally called "outdoor educators" or "environmental interpreters." Their efforts are aimed at increasing the participants' knowledge of natural or historical resources and whetting their curiosity to learn more. The leaders' success depends not on teaching skills, but on provoking interest and instilling facts, attitudes, and concepts through firsthand experiences and real objects. Outdoor educators and environmental interpreters differ in terms of the types of groups they usually work with. The educator usually has a specific class with specific facts to teach whereas the interpreter works among a wide range of people usually organized in informal groups and most of whom are on vacation and are seeking knowledge without effort. Both the educator and the interpreter may be specialists or generalists. A leader who is a specialist may have an expertise in a specific area of knowledge such as ornithology (the study of birds), entomology (the study of insects), geology, botany, zoology, forestry, soils, pond life, marine life, fossils, Native Americans, pioneer history, astronomy, or other areas. Leaders may be generalists in broader categories such as ecological studies, environmental concerns, landscape alteration, or general outdoor awareness. Examples of leadership positions necessitating knowledge of natural or historic resources include the following.

- Outdoor school leader (public school programs)
- Sightseeing trip or tour guide and field trip leader
- Camp nature counselor
- Ranger naturalist (National Park Service)
- Visitor center information specialist (U.S. Forest Service)
- State park trail guide
- Nature center director
- Historic monument guide
- Audubon Society or National Wildlife Federation summer camp instructor
- Interpreter at a living history park
- Arboretum or zoo director

## OUTDOOR LEADERSHIP TECHNIQUES

Regardless of whether the outdoor leader is primarily concerned with skills or with knowledge, there are general leadership techniques that can be used to help the leader effectively involve participants in the study of the natural environment. Some of these are listed as follows.

- It is important to portray a liking for the natural elements and an exuberance that will be infectious among the participants. Regardless of heat, cold, wind, sun, or rain, the outdoor leader should appear comfortable, enthusiastic, and healthy. At the same time, though the outdoor leader may be warmly dressed in the latest wind and rainproof garments, he or she must be cognizant of the fact that participants may not be as appropriately attired and may begin to feel uncomfortable before the leader does.
- Activities should be related to the levels and interests of everyone in the group. This may be more difficult with a larger group. Although there are interpretive programs and tours that serve many participants at the same time, it is difficult for the leader to work with more than 12 people at a time, with the optimal number being 8.
- During the course of the activity, the leader should know how to caution the overly bold and encourage the overly timid.

In addition to these leadership techniques are others adapted from material found in *Principles and Practices of Outdoor/Environmental Education*:[1]

- On a trail (or sidewalk) the leader should be at the head of the line and appoint a "tail," who will bring up the rear. No members of the group should be out of sight of those before and behind them. When the leader comes to an object to be discussed, he or she should go past it a little way, stop, face the group, wait until the entire group is together, and then walk back to the object to be discussed. This way the leader will be in the middle of the group and can give equal attention to each member. The leader should automatically be in a position so

---

[1]Adapted from Phyllis M. Ford, *Principles and Practices of Outdoor/Environment Education* (New York: Wiley, 1982).

that the sun is at the back of the participants—never in their eyes. The participants should be spoken to, not at, and always respond better when addressed by name—correctly pronounced. The voice must carry, yet if the group is close, a whisper can be used for contrast. Since the human voice does not carry above a waterfall, rapidly running water, the surf, or strong wind, there is little point in spending much time talking near these. One can move to a different or sheltered place to discuss the objects pointed to when it was noisy.

- During the discussion of an object, as many participants as possible should be involved by providing them the chance to use their senses, by asking questions, by suggesting activities. The participants will appreciate helping the leader, demonstrating, and sharing. A sense of humor helps, too. A good balance between giving information and asking questions must be maintained.

- There is actually little strenuous physical exercise on most guided walks. If people are cold or when energy runs high, warm them up, calm them down, by the 30-second shake (or the 60-second shake) wherein each stays in the same place and shakes all parts of the body as hard as possible and simultaneously for 30 seconds. Get the participants into different positions; make them take their hands out of their pockets to feel, stoop, see, stretch to touch. With the young and agile, have them lie down and look down, then stretch to touch. If they are dressed in clothes that should stay clean and dry, let each bring a piece of plastic garbage can liner, old shower curtain, or garment bag to use as a "landing pad."

- Participants need time to talk to each other between stops, to be silent, and "to blend in" with the environment. Children who have been to camp and volunteer adult leaders of youth-serving agencies will recognize the hand signal for silence. One open hand upheld, palm forward, by a silent leader means, "Stop talking and stop walking." It is an ancient sign given as a warning to those in a line behind that game, or perhaps an enemy was in sight. No word was spoken; all followers were immediately silent physically and orally.

- On the trail, respect for the environment must be stressed. No picking of specimens. No tearing of branches. The rights of small animals to remain undisturbed must be emphasized.

There are still other guidelines that a leader in the outdoors might heed but that are somewhat more general in nature. Some of these follow.

- Few, if any, people are experts in many areas of environmental understanding. Even experts should be willing to admit they don't know many things and are constantly learning from each other and from the program participants.

- It is more important to look at natural resources as communities (forests, meadows, streams) of many interrelated organisms than to see "things" such as maple trees, granite, lumber, grasses, or any single organism.

- Understanding concepts of ecology (interrelationships) and helping the participant know what is happening are more important than knowing the names of the plants and animals.

- The leisure services profession is ultimately interested in fostering individual growth and development and self-awareness. Through awareness of the world around us, we may be more aware of ourselves.

- Leaders are advised to treat any outdoor pursuits away from urban environments or more than one hour from available emergency aid as high-risk activities. All outdoor leaders are advised to read the material on high risk and prepare carefully for outdoor programs. As the reader will recall, Chapter 13 focuses on the topic of risk management. In that chapter, there is an excellent plan that outlines the preparations necessary to lead a high-risk outdoor recreation activity. It contains recommendations for equipment and clothing; a schedule of activities; and examples of emergency, health, and activity release forms.

## HUMAN NEEDS AND THE OUTDOORS

Unless the participant is physically comfortable, neither too hot nor too cold, neither wet to the skin nor desiccated, there will be little chance of learning new skills or even paying attention to a leader. If the participant is uncomfortable, there is only one thought in mind: "Let's stop!" "Let's get comfortable," or "Let's go home!" In addition, an uncomfortable participant in a natural outdoor setting is more likely to become ill or injured. The participant should also feel "comfortable" psychologically. He or she should be made to feel secure and safe. When working in the outdoors, the leader must recognize these two types of human needs: psychological and physiological. The first relates to how participants feel about themselves, and the second refers to the needs of the human body.

### PSYCHOLOGICAL NEEDS

Basically, every human needs a feeling of security, at-homeness, and belonging. The feelings of security and at-homeness are responsibilities of the leader. Knowing how far they are going, what they should bring, and what they may expect helps to make people feel comfortable. An older person on a loop trail may worry about getting back to the beginning unless he or she is advised at the start that the trip will take no more than 30 minutes. Being caught in a stiff breeze on a picnic may cause people to wish someone had advised bringing jackets, and they may worry about catching cold. Some people feel insecure because they are unfamiliar with the terrain, plants, and animals; they may worry about snakes, bees, thorns, steep trails, or hundreds of unknown elements of nature.

In addition to making participants feel secure and at home, there are several other special psychological considerations to allow for when leading people on trips away from the urban setting.

*Noise.* Leaders should be aware that the noise of one group may disturb another group. A raucous noise from one group may decrease the quality of the experience of another group, for example, when they are watching a rainbow. Late night singing, use of battery-powered radios and televisions, and loud conversations can disturb groups camping in nearby campsites. Leaders can show concern and support for one another by ensuring that their groups are considerate of this factor.

*Visual Disturbance.* In a primitive natural setting used for backpacking, bright, obtrusive shades are disturbing to those who came to "get away from it all." To many, *bright* represents the busy, neon-lit urban environment left behind and is antithetical to the greens and blues and browns of the natural world. When possible, campers today should buy and use tents and tarps in earth tones so as not to disturb others with incongruent colors. In addition, litter, broken branches, and other evidence of disregard for the natural environment can impair the visual harmony of the outdoor setting. The leader should ensure that his or her group leaves the environment as they found it.

*Animal Problems.* Dogs and horses are not loved equally by all. Generally, hiking and packhorse trips do not mix and people understand that. For some unknown reason, it is not as obvious that dogs should not be permitted on trips sponsored by agencies or organizations. Families or private groups make their own policies and may agree to take their pets;

however, groups with paid or appointed leaders should refrain from taking pets. Dogs tend to run ahead and then back to their owners, weaving in and out between the legs of a line of hikers. Several dogs on a trail usually result in a fracas. Leaders should take a firm stand and state, "*No pets.*"

Attention to each of the foregoing points will help the participant to enjoy outdoor situations more fully.

### PHYSICAL NEEDS

Basically, every human body needs shelter from the elements (sun, wind, rain, snow), water, and food. These requirements are necessary for physical comfort and also for psychological security. On a backpacking trip to a remote area, proper preparation for physical needs can literally make the difference between life or death. In a city park, they can make the difference between a pleasant and an unpleasant experience, for meeting the physical needs often helps meet psychological needs. People who are lethargic from riding on a bus may gain instant energy and subsequent renewed interest upon eating a few snacks when they arrive at their destination. People who are cold must be warmed before they can enjoy an activity.

*Shelter.*    Regardless of where an event occurs outdoors, there is always the chance of a change in weather. Shelter from weather may mean a sweater, a rain jacket, a sunshade, a Windbreaker, a tarp, or a building. The type of extra clothing or protection needed varies with the seasons and locale. Leaders in different geographical areas should check with outdoor experts concerning recommended extra clothing and shelter. A few examples follow.

- A day hike in the summer in the forested northern states would necessitate a knapsack containing a hat, sweater, rain jacket, or poncho.
- A cross-country ski trip would necessitate an extra sweater, jacket, Windbreaker, hat, gloves, wind pants, tarp, and, in some areas, rain gear.
- A picnic on a lake side would necessitate extra sweaters and a Windbreaker.
- An interpretive walk through a rose garden in June may necessitate sunglasses or a hat with a brim and a sweater.

In the case of the first two of these scenarios, the leader should also ensure that everyone is equipped to spend the night out. In case of debilitating injury, help may take from 4 to 24 hours to reach a victim, hence the need to be prepared to stay out overnight. The leader must expect the worst weather conditions for the area and time of year and be sure that participants can protect themselves from those adverse conditions. Regardless of the weather report, the leader must anticipate that there might be a change. Regardless of the directions given, the leader must anticipate that some people will not follow them. Even in warm weather, extra sweaters or jackets should be taken along. In the thunderstorm belt, plans should be made so that people are not caught without raincoats while away from shelter. Extra clothes for emergencies and for forgetful individuals should be part of the leader's standard equipment as should a supply of pins, tissues, sunglasses, mittens, and a first aid kit.

*Water.*    The human body can live a few days without water but may suffer serious and permanent damage if forced to go a long time, even a few hours, in a desiccated condition. In any environment—desert, forest, lake, or ice field—the leader should carry extra water to replace that lost through normal perspiration. Eating snow serves to chill the body more than to replenish lost moisture. (There may be only one inch of melted water in one foot of dry powder snow!) Everyone on a hike should carry a pint or more of water. On longer, strenuous hikes in hot weather, two quarts per person may be needed. Gone are the days when people were advised to drink only sips and infrequently. Drinking frequent quantities of water in eight-ounce portions may be *minimum* for some people. The saying "Drink before you are thirsty; eat before you are hungry" is good advice for leaders to give. What is consumed as "liquid" is limited to water, fruit juices, broth, and sometimes tea or coffee. Carbonated and alcoholic beverages are of little or no value in maintaining the physical needs of the participant and may do harm in severe weather conditions.

*Food.*   On all trips, extra food may mean only extra happiness, or it might mean enough energy to last through a night out against the elements. High energy foods— candy, nuts, cheese, or dried fruit—are good to take on trips as well as carbohydrates such as granola. An emergency packet of peanut butter and crackers, cheese, boullion, apricots, date-nut bread, and a candy bar may be adequate to maintain the human body for a few hours of unexpected emergency. A small backpack stove to warm up soup may be a necessity on a cross-country ski trip or even an all-day walk in the woods on a rainy day in October.

To reiterate, the outdoor leader's responsibility for the welfare of participants lies in making them *psychologically* secure and *physically* secure. For participants to be physically secure, the leader should make sure that their body temperature is regulated through shelter and clothing to protect them from the elements, that they have adequate water, and that their energy level is maintained through availability of extra food. To help participants feel psychologically secure, the leader should ensure that they feel safe, comfortable, and "at home"; that they are well informed; and that the harmony of the environment is preserved for their enjoyment.

## CARE OF THE ENVIRONMENT

The concomitant consideration of outdoor leaders is that of developing in the participant an attitude of stewardship for the land accom-panied by behaviors that demonstrate that attitude. Care of the environment is vital, for if the environment is altered perceptively by human-caused problems such as erosion, litter, fire, human waste, vandalism, or others, the quality of the outdoor activity is lessened. Indeed, in some situations, misuse of the environment means elimination of the recreational activity dependent on that environment. People cannot swim in polluted streams or catch fish in polluted water. No one wants to hike or picnic in a burned area. Litter, erosion, and vandalism can turn people away.

Care of the environment means that the leader in all outdoor settings must advise participants against picking plants and cutting across the land instead of using trails, and should ensure that they maintain small, wisely-located campfires. Leaders *in* the outdoors should also be leaders *of* the outdoors. There is no outdoor leader who cannot learn basic ecology and help others to be aware of the world around them. It is incumbent on the outdoor leader to learn about weather, poisonous plants and animals, insect pests, and the common plants of the area. It is further a responsibility of the outdoor leader to know and follow the policies and regulations of the agencies managing the land on which activities and programs occur.

## SUMMARY

All leaders of recreational activities have opportunities to become involved in outdoor activities. Not everyone is expected to be an expert in outdoor leadership; however, every leader involved in programs should understand that safety to the participant and care of the environment are as important as the leadership of the activity itself. Regardless of the activity and how expertly it is led, the ultimate quality of the experience will be diminished without sound environmental practices and recognition of human psychological and physiological needs in natural resource settings.

## DISCUSSION QUESTIONS

1. Explain the two primary responsibilities of leaders in the outdoor setting.
2. Explain the two major categories of outdoor leaders.
3. What behavior might a participant expect to see in a leader of an outdoor activity?
4. Discuss the psychological needs of people in the outdoors.
5. How does meeting physical needs adequately and appropriately affect psychological needs?
6. Defend the wisdom of a leader who insists on taking extra clothes, water, and food on a day trip.
7. What is the responsibility of the leader for stewardship of the land?

# LEADING AQUATIC ACTIVITIES

Aquatic activities are among the most popular leisure pastimes of North Americans. As a result, they are an integral component of most recreation and leisure service organizations. Aquatic activities can involve all age groups, from babies six weeks old to older persons. They contribute not only to the physical well-being of participants, but also provide opportunities for social interaction with others. Furthermore, aquatic programs, when organized and led with the safety of the participants in mind, offer participants activities that are challenging yet enjoyable.

When referring to aquatic activities, we are including activities that occur in and on the water. This can encompass not only swimming, but also scuba diving, waterskiing, water shows and pageants, water polo, canoeing,

sailing, kayaking, and so on. These activities can occur in swimming pools, on lakes, at ocean beaches, and on rivers. Aquatic programs often involve considerable investment financially by public and commercial recreation and leisure service organizations. Because aquatic activities are often so prominent in these types of agencies, it is important that the leader have an understanding and awareness of the roles, purposes, and activities that contribute to the makeup of an aquatic program.

## LEADERSHIP ROLES

To be a leader of aquatic activities entails a great deal of responsibility. Individuals who work with participants in this setting have as their primary and essential responsibility the safety of each participant. The goal of a leader, regardless of the type of aquatic activity involved, should be to provide participants with appropriate knowledge, attitudes, and skills to enable them to participate in, on, and around the water safely. Some of the direct, face-to-face leadership roles that can be assumed in the aquatic setting are the following.

*Lifeguard.* Perhaps one of the most obvious aquatic leadership roles is that of a lifeguard. Lifeguards are found at swimming pools, beaches, and lakes and are responsible for the safety of participants within their jurisdiction. The lifeguard must exercise the greatest care in fulfilling his or her responsibilities. A study reported by the National Swimming Pool Institute has indicated that less than 40 percent of a guard's time is spent surveying swimmers. This study found that guards spent much of their time watching other things. The lifeguard must not only be diligent in watching participants but must also act with confidence and compentence when assisting an individual in distress. A list of guidelines that detail criteria for effective guarding, prepared by the Ferguson, Missouri, Park and Recreation Department, is found in Figure 24.1. Some recreation and leisure service organiza-

---

**EFFECTIVE GUARDING**

1. The pool manager or assistant, while on duty, is in complete charge and is responsible for the safe and efficient management of the facility.
2. The entire staff is responsible for the swimmer's safety. Know and follow safety rules and precautions. Set a good example by complying with them.
3. Ignorance of the pool rules can cause accidents. The staff should correct any infraction—and point out the list of rules posted in the pool area.
4. Every employee must use reasonable care in the performance of duties and act in such a manner as to ensure at *all* times maximum safety to the public, himself or herself, and his or her fellow employees.
5. The personal appearance of the guard is vital to the general atmosphere of the facility.
   (a) All male guards should be clean-shaven while on duty.
   (b) All guards should present a neat, well-groomed appearance.
   (c) Unnecessary ornaments, such as watches, pins, and so on, shall not be worn.
   (d) As much attention should be made to the appearance of the feet as is given to the hands.
6. Lifeguard staff shall wear proper dress while on duty; the uniform's appearance should reflect the guard's pride in his job. No sweat pants, bermuda shorts, and so on.
7. Lifeguards must always be equipped with a whistle.
8. While on duty a guard *shall not*
   (a) Gather with other guards.
   (b) Play musical instruments, smoke, read, or indulge in byplay.
   (c) Teach swimming or diving (unless the pool is specifically restricted for instruction or following clearance with proper authority).
   (d) Swim unless there is a specific relief for this purpose except for rescue purposes.
   (e) Leave his or her post except in cases of emergency or when properly relieved.
   (f) Use the lifeguard stands for checking articles of clothing, radios, and so on.
   (g) Use abusive language or profanity in the execution of his or her duties.
9. The swimming pool water—proper—should be under constant scrutiny at all times while patrons are swimming.
10. Avoid engaging in playful activities that might result in injury to others.
11. The lifeguard in the stand should never overlook the gutter crawlers—corners of the pool—and the deepwater swimmers because the roving guard's attention is concentrated elsewhere.
12. The staff must be consistent in their effort in enforcing the departmental rules against running, horseplay diving in shallow water, glass bottles, drinking, and so on.
13. The experienced employee must be ready to coach the new employee on the fundamentals of good safety practices and make him or her aware of the tremendous liabilities involved through malpractice or laxity on his or her part should the ever-present accident occur.
14. There will be no drinking of intoxicants or being under the influence of same. Violation will result in immediate dismissal.

---

**FIGURE 24.1** Guidelines for effective guiding. (*Source:* City of Ferguson, Missouri Park and Recreation Department, ''Pool Program Handbook,'' n.d., pp. 10–11.)

tions may require all lifeguards to have some type of Red Cross certification.

***Pool Manager.***   A pool manager very often straddles the roles of face-to-face leader and supervisory leader. In his or her face-to-face role, he or she is responsible for greeting the public, ensuring that the swimming area is safe, and resolving problems involving participants. A pool manager will often act in the capacity of a lifeguard, providing rest breaks for staff and filling in for lifeguards who are ill. The pool manager has daily and continuous, direct contact with the public and, therefore, is a type of face-to-face leader. Figure 24.2 presents a job description for a pool manager.

***Waterfront Director.***   A waterfront director is usually associated with a camp resort or other commercial agency providing aquatic services at a lake, beach, or river area. The waterfront director is responsible for training and supervising his or her staff to provide a wide variety of activities, such as swimming, sailing, canoeing, rafting, and so on. The wa-

terfront director, like the pool manager, has daily and continuous direct contact with the public and therefore is a face-to-face leader.

***Instructor.***   Aquatic instructors are individuals who teach, instruct, and lead individuals in and around the water with the distinct purpose of increasing participants' knowledge and capabilities in the area of aquatic activities. The most common type of aquatic instructor is one who teaches individuals the basics of swimming. This particular instructor's role often requires that he or she hold an American Red Cross Water Safety Instructor's Certificate or its equivalent. Aquatic instructors are not, however, limited to just teaching the basics of swimming, but also may provide instruction in the areas of scuba diving, skin diving, boating, sailing, canoeing, kayaking, and other water-related activities. A job description for an aquatics instructor can be found in Figure 24.3. Later in this chapter, some of the teaching techniques that can be used to teach various aquatic activities to different age groups will be discussed.

---

**JOB DESCRIPTION FOR POOL MANAGERS**

A.   The swimming pool manager is directly responsible to the recreation supervisor for the efficient operation of and including all duties pertaining to the management of a swimming pool.

    1.   BRIEF OUTLINE FOR POOL MANAGERS (at least 45 hours per week)

       (a)   Presents a weekly work schedule of entire staff (including assistant manager, instructors, guards, locker room, cashier, and concession personnel) to recreation supervisor before the workweek.

       (b)   Supervises staff relative to performance of duties connected with each position and submits periodic evaluation of personnel to recreation supervisor.

       (c)   Provides periodic in-service training to staff in relation to new methods or techniques.

       (d)   Assigns routine maintenance duties among staff.

       (e)   Requisitions and maintains all equipment and supplies necessary in carrying out the safe and successful operation of the pool during the days and hours it is open.

       (f)   Acts in the capacity of lifeguard-instructor whenever pool load requires additional staffing.

       (g)   Responsible for park's swimming team.

       (h)   Plans and organizes at least one special event every other week.

       (i)   Responsible for completing all records and forms as required and depositing daily receipts as directed by the recreation supervisor.

       (j)   Responsible for maintaining good public relations.

       (k)   *Responsible for all related activities and work assigned by the recreation supervisor.*

B. GENERAL OPERATING PROCEDURES
1. OPENING POOLS
Open the pool and admit patrons at the scheduled time. Ensure that guards and locker room attendants report in adequate time to be in uniform at their station at the scheduled opening time.
2. THINGS TO CHECK BEFORE ADMITTING PATRONS
(a) Guards and attendants are at their stations and ready.
(b) All necessary entrances and exits are open.
(c) Lights and P.A. are turned on.
(d) Bathhouse and pool area are free of litter. There are no slippery areas on floors and decks. Toilets are flushed. Temperature of shower water is correct.
(e) Filter room equipment is functioning properly. (Check air temperature, water temperature, chlorine residue, and pH level at 9:00 A.M.)
3. THINGS TO CHECK DURING SWIMMING HOURS
(a) Air temperature, water temperature, chlorine residual, and pH level are to be checked at 2:00 P.M., 3:30 P.M., and 8:00 P.M. Readings are to be recorded. Chlorine residual must be maintained between .7 and 1 part per million at all times. The pH reading should be between 7.2 and 7.4.
(b) Periodic checks (at least every hour; more often if necessary)
(1) Pool staff are on duty at their stations and have no problems.
(2) Litter on floors, decks, and concession areas does not become excessive.
(3) Toilets are flushed.
(4) Shower water temperature is comfortable, and soap supply is adequate.
(5) Slippery and unsanitary conditions on floors, decks, and concession areas are quickly corrected.
(6) Concession stands are operating properly.
(c) Daily Checks
(1) First aid equipment is complete, and resuscitator is operating.
(2) Lifeguard lockers are neat and clean.
4. CLOSING THE POOL
(a) Inform patrons on P.A. of the pool's closing. Do this 10 minutes before the specified closing time.
(b) Clear pool at specified time.
(c) Do not rush patrons, but do not allow unnecessary loitering in the pool area or bathhouse.
(d) See that guards remain at their stations until the last swimmer is out of the pool area.
(e) Have the guards pick up litter, towels, and anything else left by patrons before they leave the pool area. Have them arrange chairs, tables, and any other movable equipment. (Check to see that concessions are closed and cleaned properly.)
(f) Assign guards to assist the locker attendants in checking lockers, picking up litter, and cleaning floors.
(g) Check time sheets and deliver them to the office.
(h) Check to see that concession inventory is sufficient for next three days.
(i) Turn off lights and the P.A. system. Lock doors and check the filter room.
(j) Closing pools in emergencies
(1) During electrical storms, station a guard at each entrance to prevent dangerous congestion in the showers and dressing rooms.
(2) Do not reopen the pool until you are sure that the disturbance has passed.
(k) All lockers should be opened every night and cleaned once per week.

**FIGURE 24.2** The pool manager. (*Source:* Arlington Heights Park District, Illinois, "Swim Manual," n.d., pp. 11, 12.)

## THE INSTRUCTOR

### Definition

The instructor is to provide instruction for various levels of swimming and serve as lifeguard to prevent loss of life or injury to patrons or visitors in the swim center. The instructor is directly responsible to the pool manager.

### Example of Duties

1. Is responsible for the welfare of all swimmers under his or her care.
2. Conducts swimming or lifesaving classes or both as required.
3. Is to be on duty all the time his or her group is in the pool. He or she is not to leave his or her group for any reason without first clearing with the pool manager.
4. Shall keep all his or her records up-to-date, correct, and complete.
   (a) Daily attendance record.
   (b) Record of tests passed by individuals.
   (c) Be prepared to turn in records to manager periodically for inspection or use in completing manager's records.
5. Shall understand and carry out the lesson plans for each class.
6. Shall be familiar with the program in its entirety so that he or she will be able to answer questions of parents.
7. Before the last class, shall complete as nearly as possible a report on each swimmer. This should be added to, if necessary, at the last class and turned in to the pool manager.
   (a) He or she should urge the child to keep the report card as a permanent record.
   (b) He or she should urge the child to continue lessons through lifesaving.
   (c) He or she should check the swimmer tests sheet to be sure it is completely and correctly filled out for the permanent record file and Red Cross office.
8. It is imperative that the instructor be on time. He or she should be present at least 15 minutes before the scheduled start of the first class.
9. The instructor is to be on the job at specified times. In case of inclement weather, the instructor may be asked to attend staff meetings or planning or group evaluation sessions or to perform other duties at the discretion of the pool manager.
10. Shall help to keep the facilities neat, clean, and so on.
11. Maintains constant vigil over patrons.
12. Sees to the enforcement of rules and regulations.
13. Renders first aid and artificial respiration when necessary.
14. Wears identifying insignia at all times when on duty.
15. Performs any other duties that may be assigned him by the pool manager.

### Qualifications

1. Completion of high school and some experience and training in swim instruction of water safety.
2. Possession of a current Red Cross Water Safety Instructor's Certificate.
3. Age: from 18 to 45 years inclusive at time of appointment.
4. Ability to pass a medical examination administered by a city physician.

**FIGURE 24.3**   Job description of an aquatics instructor. (*Source:* City of Ferguson, Park and Recreation Department, ''Pool Program Handbook,'' n.d., pp. 17, 18.)

*Coach.*    There are many aquatic activities that are competitive in nature and involve the leader as a coach. Types of coaches found in aquatic settings are water polo coaches, swimming coaches, rowing coaches, synchronized swimming coaches, and so on. As indicated in Chapter 6, any team coach is responsible for establishing training programs, teaching new skills, and maintaining team morale. A team coach is also responsible for developing team strategy and maintaining discipline. In addition, this type of coach often fulfills a liaison role with parents of the team members. Parents of team members should be informed of team schedules, goals, and objectives and should also be made to feel a part of the total team effort.

*Activity Leader.*    Often the aquatics leader will be involved in the planning of program activities that complement the aquatic activities. An aquatic leader involved in face-to-face leadership of a canoeing club, for example, may be involved in the planning and implementation of program activities to complement the basic function of the club. The leader might want to organize social gatherings such as picnics or barbecues in conjunction with outings; the leader may want to organize workshops or clinics to enhance the participants' canoeing skills; or the leader may organize trips to areas with special or unique opportunities for canoeing.

The six leadership roles described represent broad categories of aquatic leadership. There are, however, other direct service roles in which the leader may engage that complement and enhance the provision of selected aquatic activities. For example, the leader may act as an official, judge, maintenance worker, concessionaire, and locker room attendant. Any or all of these auxiliary leadership functions might be necessary to conduct successfully certain aquatic activities.

## TECHNIQUES FOR LEADING AQUATIC ACTIVITIES

Although techniques for leading aquatic activities will vary depending on the type of activity involved, its location, the number of participants involved, and the equipment used, there are a number of general leadership techniques that can be applied to various age groups participating in most aquatic activities. First, the leader should attempt to gain *an understanding of the capabilities* of each participant. This will enable the leader to provide a program that will be challenging to each participant without jeopardizing his or her safety. In addition, the aquatic leader should have a firm understanding of the goals that participants should accomplish. In other words, the leader should have a *plan of action* for the activity and should have in mind *the outcomes that should result* from participation in the activity.

There are also several other techniques that should be considered by the leader in terms of their impact on his or her effectiveness. The *positioning of the aquatic leader* in relation to participants, for example, is very important. Participants will not be able to see the leader's demonstrations if the glare of the sun is behind him or her. Also, many aquatic activities, especially swimming, are best taught with the leader in the water. This is especially true with children, for the leader should actually be in the water with the children when demonstrating activities. This can instill confidence in participants and reduce anxiety associated with some water-related activities and instruction. *Effective communication* with participants is also a key to success when instructing aquatic activities. A term often used to describe communication with participants on *their* level is *transference*, a useful technique for leaders teaching aquatic activities. Transference implies that the leader uses words and phrases selectively to communicate effectively with the age group with whom he or she is working. For example, when working with older children, the leader might use a phrase such as "Move your arm as a pitcher does when he or she starts to throw the ball" to describe the motions involved in the backstroke. In other words, the leader transfers technical jargon into terms and words that are relevant and meaningful to the individual or group being instructed.

With these general leadership techniques in mind, following is a discussion of some specific techniques that can be used in working with certain age groups in an aquatic setting, including preschool, elementary, teenage, and adult groups and individuals.

*Preschool Children.*  Perhaps the most important factor that the aquatics leader should keep in mind when working with preschool children is to make the experience enjoyable. The water should be warm, the instructor should attempt to involve the parents, and both the parents and the leader should be patient and relaxed. Often simple games can be used with preschoolers to teach and have fun at the same time. When giving instructions to preschoolers, the leader must bear in mind that children of this age have a short attention span and cannot be given lengthy instructions. Rather, a child of this age will respond best to short directions supported by demonstrations and then by repetition of the directions again. Children this age are often not well coordinated, and this factor also should be kept in mind by the leader. The American Red Cross has provided a number of suggestions for teaching preschool children as follows.

1. The temperature of the water should be comfortable.
2. The children should be healthy, rested, and in a good frame of mind.
3. Never hurry progress or show impatience.

Try to keep the youngster from getting an accidental faceful or noseful of water.
4. Keep the lessons short. Gauge the exact time to coincide with the interest and fun factor.
5. If group instruction is undertaken, a ratio of one aide to each child is recommended. One of the parents might be oriented to be the assisting adult.
6. Parent orientation is important. Help the parents to understand their role in, and responsibility for, supervising the preschool child in all aquatic activities, the limitation of swimming skills that the preschool child can acquire, and the aim and goal of the instructional program.
7. The use of any support should be restricted to periods of instruction and supervised recreation. In recreational periods, if the wearing of artificial supports is allowed, then the nonswimmer should be restricted to the shallow area.[1]

*Elementary-Age Children.*  Aquatic leadership of elementary-age children varies from that of preschool children in that most instruction is carried out within groups rather than on a one-to-one basis. As a result, the leader who is instructing participants within this age group may have to make a special effort to work effectively with group members that progress more quickly or more slowly than the majority of the group. The leader may want to have fast learners engage in extra practice of more difficult skills, for example, so that more time can be spent with slow learners to help them overcome some of their problems. Generally speaking, children between the ages of six and eight will progress more slowly and more unevenly than children who are nine or older. The leader will want to attempt

[1]*Swimming and Water Safety Textbook* (Washington, D.C.: The American National Red Cross, 1968), pp. 37–38.

to make the aquatic activities fun and enjoyable for all, encouraging and rewarding progress. The leader should exhibit assured confidence. If children this age feel that their leader is competent and assured, the children themselves will gain confidence. It is also important that the leader keep children this age busy and active. They are generally a very responsive age group to work with if the activities are presented in an enjoyable way, are demonstrated well, and are presented in a supportive atmosphere, free of ridicule. Some additional guidelines for instructing this age group in aquatic activities are presented as follows.

1. Keep instruction fun. Use of games and stunts will enhance the learning of required skills and keep the experience pleasurable.
2. Use terminology that is not associated with things children fear around the water; instead, liken skills and instructions on performance to things that children know and enjoy. For example, instead of saying, "Put your face under water," the instructor might say, "Hide your face." The substitution of "Float like a log" for "Do a prone float" might give the children a better mental picture of what they are trying to do. Give skills familiar, exciting names; the object is to try to get the class to try to perfect the skills, not to have them know the technical names.
3. Keep the class busy and active. Be ready to change to a new skill or to practice another skill before they become restless and bored.
4. Do not make fun of, ridicule, or threaten the learner.
5. Demonstrate skills slowly and correctly. It may sometimes help to have a class member who is able to do a skill well perform the demonstration.
6. Most important, always provide for overall protection and supervision of the whole class.[2]

***Teenage Children.*** The key to working with teenagers is to create an environment that motivates them. Unlike younger children, teenagers have the mental and physical capabilities to engage in any aquatic activity and excel if properly motivated. Teenagers may be self-conscious, however, if inexperienced, and the leader working with this age group should attempt to be very supportive. It is important that the leader develop a good rapport with the group, not only to gain the confidence of participants, but also for the purpose of control. When instructing teenagers, the leader should avoid talking down to the group and, insofar as is possible, the leader should maintain a mature, adult level of conversation. Perhaps the main points to remember when working with teenagers are to be firm, to be enthusiastically encouraging, to show and expect respect, to share responsibility, and to encourage social interaction between participants. As with other age groups, there is likely to be a range of skills represented within a given group of participants. With this age group, however, the leader may want to have some of the more skilled participants assume an assistive leadership role and aid some of the participants of less skill. This can help to promote the social nature of the experience that, as mentioned, is also desirable when working with this age group.

***Adults.*** Often aquatic leaders make the error of instructing adults in the same manner as they instruct children. Adult learners expect to be treated with respect despite their inexperience and lack of skill. Adults attend instructional classes because they want to; consequently, the leader has a motivated group of participants initially. Whether or not the group continues to be enthused and in-

[2]Ibid., pp. 39–40.

volved in the activity depends on the leader's ability to instill confidence, provide meaningful recognition, create an enjoyable social atmosphere, and provide good, solid information. The adult is very discriminating and will respond poorly to a leader who is not well informed and who is uncomfortable or uninteresting. Many adults who become involved in aquatic activities for the first time, have started late because of a fear of the water. It is important for the leader to assess the needs and possible fears of each adult participant and offer corresponding assistance and encouragement. It is also important for the leader to recognize that adults may become involved in recreation and leisure activities, including aquatic activities, for a variety of reasons. Not only may they want to learn or improve on a specific skill, but they may also want to socialize and make new friends. Often the social aspects of an activity will take primacy over the instructive value of the experience.

Senior adults or senior citizens can benefit from participation in aquatic activities in a number of ways. As indicated in Chapter 4, Table 4.1, aquabics (swimming exercise) can have such benefits for the senior adult as building endurance, helping in weight control, building muscle tone, increasing tolerance to stress, increasing social contact, providing a sense of accomplishment, aiding skill development, and contributing to a healthy appearance.

## AQUATIC SAFETY

The importance of adequate and comprehensive water safety precautions cannot be overemphasized. Thousands of people drown every year in water accidents that are preventable with proper precautions. The leader cannot be too careful when planning a program to ensure the water safety of participants. These programs often involve not only the aquatics staff, but also the participants themselves. The buddy system, for example, is often used in camp settings involving aquatic activities to supplement the use of lifeguards or waterfront directors. With this system, each participant chooses a friend, and the two of them assume responsibility for one another. They make sure that they enter and leave the water together and attempt to keep an eye on each other while in the water. Although aquatic sites may vary from lakes to beaches to pools, the basic rules of safety are very similar for all these sites. Some of the most important rules that a leader should enforce to ensure safety in aquatic areas are detailed as follows.

1. All aquatic leaders must possess a Red Cross or similarly approved Water Safety Instructor's Certificate.
2. Never permit anyone to swim alone. Constant and responsible supervision is a must.
3. Keep basic rescue and lifesaving equipment always available.
4. Post emergency instructions and telephone numbers conspicuously.
5. Have an aquatic first-aid kit available.
6. Enforce commonsense safety rules at all times. At least one responsible person should know how to administer artificial respiration and give intelligent first aid.
7. Clearly mark deep and shallow sections as well as hazardous swimming areas.
8. Prevent dangerous activities inconsistent with the aquatic activity presented (e.g., running).
9. Do not permit glasses, bottles, or other sharp objects in a swimming area.
10. If possible, fence off the swimming areas, and secure with a lock to prevent children from gaining unauthorized entry.[3]

[3]Adapted from *Swimming and Water Safety Textbook* (Washington, D.C.: The American National Red Cross, 1968), pp. 112–113, 115–116.

11. All boaters must wear U.S. Coast Guard approved life jackets, secured completely

The best possible way to ensure aquatic safety is to make sure that each individual has developed swimming competence and is qualified in terms of level of skill to engage in the activities being offered. In addition, each participant should be made aware of, and expected to observe, safety rules. The recreation and leisure service leader should serve as an advocate in the promotion of safety of aquatic activities.

## TYPES OF AQUATIC ACTIVITIES

There is a wide range of aquatic activities that can be planned, organized, and implemented by the recreation and leisure service aquatics leader. The types of aquatic programs that an agency is able to offer will depend on the man-made facilities and geographical resources that are available. Some of the many types of aquatics activities that can be offered by recreation and leisure service organizations are learning to swim programs, drownproofing, lifesaving and water safety instruction, competitive swimming, small-craft programs, skin and scuba diving, recreational or open swimming program, aquatic programs for the disabled, water shows and pageants, swimming fitness activities, and water games, which are described as follows.

*Learning to Swim Programs.* As the name implies, learning to swim programs are involved with teaching individuals to swim. Instructional programs can be held for all age groups and for varying skill levels. The YMCA uses special names to designate the difference between beginning swimming groups and progressively more difficult ones (e.g., pollywog to porpoise). The American Red Cross "Learn to Swim" program uses the titles of "beginner, advanced beginner, intermediate, and swimmer." The beginner program focuses on alleviating participants'

fears and inhibitions and teaching them how to float and swim a short distance. As individuals progress, they learn breath control, turns, a mastery of various swimming strokes, and how to survive in deep water. Programs directed toward the teaching of diving skills would also be included in the "Learn to Swim" category.

*Drownproofing.* Drownproofing is a program that teaches very young children and babies skills that they can use to remain safe in the water. It is based on the notion that a child should be trained to have an automatic reaction when falling into the water that will help him or her survive and that the child should be able to survive without necessarily knowing how to swim. The child is taught not to be afraid of the water and to relax with water covering his or her face. The child is also taught to tread water and to float to support himself or herself, as means of survival.

*Lifesaving and Water Safety Instruction.* Lifesaving and water safety programs are conducted by the American Red Cross. In order to complete the lifesaving program, an individual must pass written and practical tests and demonstrate swimming endurance. Furthermore, individuals who advance to the water safety instructor's program must demonstrate various swimming strokes in proper form as well as learning various instructional procedures.

*Competitive Swimming.* Most communities offer competitive swimming programs. In the United States, swimming competition is sanctioned by several organizations. The National Collegiate Athletic Association and United States Swimming Incorporated conduct programs in the following divisions: 8 years and under, 10 years and under, 11–12 years, 13–14 years, and 15–18 years (senior division).[4] Age group competition is divided by sex—

[4] United States Swimming Incorporated, Procedures Manual, Colorado Springs, Colorado, 1983.

boys competing against boys and girls competing against girls. Events for age group categories include freestyle, backstroke, butterfly, individual medley, and relays. One of the more innovative competitive swimming programs established in the last several decades is the Master's Program. The Master's Program provides opportunities for individuals beyond the senior division to participate in competitive swimming activities, including national championship competition. Individual age classifications in the Master's Program include 25–29, 30–34, 35–39, and continues in five-year increments. Individuals into their eighties participate in the Master's Program. Guidelines for competitive swim programs for all age groups can be found in Figure 24.4.

*Small-Craft Programs.*   The implementation of small-craft programs within recreation and leisure service agencies will depend on the availability of such geographic resources as lakes, rivers, or oceans. Some of the most popular types of small-craft programs include sailing, canoeing, rowing, kayaking, rafting, and windsurfing. Many of these specialized small-craft activities require instructors with a high degree of competence and specialized knowledge. All these types of programs should be conducted with stringent safety considerations in mind. These small-craft programs can vary greatly in the cost to the sponsoring agency and the participant. Perhaps one of the most reasonable small-craft programs is canoeing. This activity can be relatively inexpensive. The recreation and leisure service organization may want to encourage the formation of small-craft clubs, sponsored by the organization but largely operated and administered by participants.

*Skin and Scuba Diving.*   For those persons who wish to explore new and mysterious surroundings, the recreation and leisure service agency may wish to provide opportunities for instruction in skin and scuba diving. Skin div-

ing refers to one who, with the aid of a mask, swimming fins, and a breathing tube or snorkel, swims on or below the surface. Scuba diving, a more sophisticated form of underwater activity, has many applications including lifesaving, fishing and commercial and sport applications. Scuba diving, which involves the use of oxygen tanks, has an extensive body of knowledge related to it. Both of these sports should be classified as high-risk activities and should be treated as such when they are being organized and implemented. Instruction in them should be provided only by a qualified water safety instructor, with experience in skin or scuba diving.

*Recreational or Open-Swim Program.*   Most aquatic facilities provide opportunities for recreational or open-swim activity. This is the case whether the program is located at a swimming pool, lake front, or ocean beach. This type of program basically involves the provision of appropriate leadership to ensure the safety of participants while they are engaging in unstructured swimming. Sometimes the recreational swim program is organized so that different age groups of individuals have access to the pool at different time periods. For example, in a community pool, adult open-swim may occur from 6:00 to 7:00 P.M. whereas children's open or recreational swim program may be from 1:00 to 5:00 P.M.

*Aquatic Programs for the Disabled.*   The leader working with disabled persons is in an excellent position to be able to provide enriching activity via the use of aquatic programming. Aquatic activities often provide a disabled person with a greater degree of freedom of movement and greater opportunities for expression than are possible out of the water. This is especially true in the case of the physically disabled person. Working with the disabled often requires that the leader possesses specialized skills and knowledge although the general techniques for instructing participants in water-related activities are effective guide-

- Clear time and date for each meet. Plan for the entire season and coordinate with other programs.
- Type of meet.
  (a) Competition open to all age groups.
  (b) Competition between agencies.
- Events for meets.
  (a) Novelty swimming events might include such races as egg and spoon race, balloon race, dry towel race, hot dog race, pajama race, and flutterboard race.
  (b) Swimming races might include individual races and several relays of varying lengths to have more campers in the events.

| | |
|---|---|
| freestyle | freestyle relays |
| backstroke | backstroke relays |
| breaststroke | breaststroke relays |
| butterfly stroke | butterfly relays |
| individual medley | medley relays |
| synchronized swimming | fancy diving lowboard (1 meter) |

The events should be varied as to styles of swimming, as to distances, and as to age classifications. In addition, nonswimmers and beginners in an intramural meet should have some competitive experience, such as flutterboard or inner-tube races over shallow water. In other words, not all events should be speed events for swimmers. Clothes changing and towel procedures should be worked out if visiting teams are scheduled, and a responsible person should be assigned to them as a hospitality guide.

- Entry blanks for meet. These should be made out early and submitted to coaches in duplicate in order that they may retain and submit a copy. These blanks should include
  (a) Date and time of meet (or trials).
  (b) Type of meet.
  (c) List or order of events, which will not be altered.
  (d) Awards for meet, if any, and when awards will be presented.
  (e) Point system to be used declaring winners.
  (f) Current records for specific events whenever possible.
- Preparation for meet.
  (a) Publicity should be handled well in advance; and preparation, made to submit results of meet to designated persons.
  (b) Program of events should be duplicated and distributed with names of entries, events, records, and so on.
  (c) Appointed officials should be dressed in appropriate uniforms.
- Meet accessories.
  (a) Stopwatches—three, preferably four.
  (b) Starting revolver and blanks.
  (c) Whistles.
  (d) Score calculation card for diving.
  (e) Diving flash cards.
  (f) Official swimming and diving rule book.
  (g) Awards for presentation ready.
  (h) Running score sheet for meet.
  (i) Team scoreboards.
  (j) Colored place cards for each place winner.
  (k) Lane lines set out (if necessary).
  (l) Numbers on cards (3 by 5) for lane selection by chance method.

(m) Finish rope if needed.

(n) Starting platforms if needed.

(o) Recall rope.

(p) Megaphone or P.A. system or both.

(q) Sufficient towels for competitors.

(r) Seating section reserved.

- Officials for meet.

  (a) Referee (1)—usually acts as the starter and should be most competent.

  (b) Starter (1).

  (c) Five or more finish judges, one as chief judge. Each picks a designated place (i.e., one picks first, two pick second, one picks third, etc.).

  (d) Timers—generally three and an alternate.

  (e) Diving judges—referee is generally designated along with two more.

  (f) Relay touch-off judges, one for each team.

  (g) Recall rope clerks.

  (h) Three diving clerks—one to record score, another to compute, and a third to add.

  (i) Scorer and a runner to obtain results.

  (j) Announcer should be competent, as he can make the meet interesting and attractive. An attempt should be made to instruct as well as to entertain. Such announcements direct attention to personalities, suggest records that may be broken, explain scoring of the meet and the scoring of diving, and so forth.

- The actual meet.

  (a) Have equipment ready before meet time.

  (b) Start on time.

  (c) Use some opening ceremony if feasible.

  (d) Make no changes in order of events.

  (e) Run events that require heats first.

  (f) Announce and introduce important guests.

  (g) Present awards after each event.

  (h) Send results to hometown newspaper.

  (i) Send photos, if possible, with suggested captions.

- Postmeet duties.

  (a) Replace auxiliary equipment in proper storage after drying gear.

  (b) Record and post results on bulletin board.

  (c) Add any new swimming records to record board with names, events, date, and swimming time.

  (d) Check on how meet was conducted, and record procedures that will avoid future mistakes.

  (e) If it is a dual or triangular meet, give a copy of the results to the visiting team or teams. This may be done by having a staff member type results as they occur; a few minutes after the conclusion of the last event, the original and carbon copies will then be available for distribution. This is a service much appreciated by all concerned.

**FIGURE 24.4**    Steps in organizing a swim meet. (*Source:* Adapted from Richard H. Pohndoff *Camp Waterfront Programs and Management*, New York: Association Press, 1960, pp. 106–110.)

lines for working with the disabled. Some activities and techniques will need to be adapted for selected populations, depending on the nature and severity of the disability. As with all recreation and leisure programs, the leader should make an effort to integrate disabled persons into existing aquatic programs. This often means providing training for aquatic instructors who have limited experience in working with the disabled. The attitude of the aquatics leader providing this type of instruction is the key to providing a positive experience for participants.

*Water Shows and Pageants.*   The fun and excitement that can be generated in a community through the production of a water show or pageant can be of great value to the overall aquatic program. Activities of this type provide many opportunities for community involvement and also provide great visibility for the recreation and leisure service organization as a whole. Water shows can be very practical in nature, demonstrating lifesaving techniques, fishing techniques, and small crafts; or they can be very festive, entertaining, and colorful, involving dramatic or musical presentations with elaborate costumes. Some of the shows or pageants designed to provide such entertainment are synchronized swimming, water drama, water ballet, water stunts, and fancy and comedy diving. Competitive swim shows may be presented as well that have as their purpose friendly and informal competition. A recreation and leisure service agency may want to combine all these types of activities—practical demonstrations, dramatic and musical presentations, and informal competition—into an elaborate aquatic pageant that spans several hours or an entire day.

*Swimming Fitness Activities.*   Increasingly, aquatic programs are offered to promote physical fitness. Such programs are often aimed at the adult population. They may range from elaborate aquabics activities to simply reserving time periods during which participants may swim laps at the pool in conjunction with an open-swim or recreational swim program. Swimming fitness activities may focus on certain predetermined goals, for example, cardiovascular improvement.

*Water Games and Activities.*   An aquatics leader may be involved in leading aquatic games, water activities, or auxiliary activities related to aquatic programs. For example, the aquatics leader might organize and teach a water polo team or a synchronized swim team. On another level, the aquatics leader may simply initiate aquatic games that are fun and enjoyable and simple to learn for participants. In community swimming pools, aquatic games may be organized to maintain participant interest and to provide a period of supervised play in which participants are allowed to use game equipment generally not allowed in the pool. In addition, nonaquatic programs that are social in nature may be organized by the aquatics staff to complement aquatic programs. For example, a teenage dance and swim or an adult barbecue and swim might be planned, organized, and led by an aquatics staff. These types of nonaquatic programs can complement aquatic activities and extend the use of aquatic facilities.

*Miscellaneous Aquatic Activities.*   There are several aquatic activities that fall outside of the categories mentioned earlier. Surfing, rafting, and waterskiing are a few of the other aquatic activities that the leader may be called upon to direct in a recreation and leisure setting. As with other types of aquatic activities, the leader should always make a point of researching the safety precautions that should be taken with each type of activity and should then make sure that the participants are also aware of, and observe, safety considerations.

## SUMMARY

This chapter has presented a discussion of leadership roles in aquatic settings, techniques for leading aquatic activities, and various types of aquatic activities found in recreation and leisure service organizations. Some of the direct, face-to-face leadership roles found in aquatic settings are the lifeguard, pool manager, waterfront director, instructor, coach, and activity leader. The techniques used in leading aquatic activities are built on an awareness of the capabilities of participants, the development of a plan of action, and ensuring that effective communication takes place. Some of the types of aquatics activities that can be provided by a recreation and leisure service organization are learning to swim programs, drownproofing, lifesaving and water safety instruction, competitive swimming, small-craft programs, skin and scuba diving, recreational programs or open-swim programs, aquatic programs for the disabled, aquatic shows and pageants, swimming fitness activities, and water games and activities.

## DISCUSSION QUESTIONS

1. Identify some of the leadership roles that can be assumed in an aquatic setting.

2. What general leadership techniques should be used in leading aquatic activities?

3. What specific leadership techniques should be used in working with preschool children? Elementary-age school children? Teenage children? Adults?

4. Note some of the important safety rules one should follow in leading aquatic activities.

5. Identify and describe the various types aquatic activities that a recreation and leisure service organization might offer.

6. Identify in your community the setting in which aquatic programs are offered.

# 25

# CLUBS

Individuals often form or join clubs to pursue their leisure interests. This club is focused on bridge.

Many individuals follow their recreation and leisure interests through participation in clubs. The leader who works with clubs attempts to help participants gather together and organize themselves in such a way that their common interests can be pursued and developed. The club format is a self-sustaining method of organization. Since clubs, by definition, provide their own leadership and usually are responsible for much of their own financing, sponsorship of clubs by recreation and leisure service organizations, in these times of fiscal constraint, can be an effective method of programming. This chapter will identify and discuss types of club organization, club activity ideas, procedures for orga-

nizing clubs, and leadership roles and techniques related to clubs.

## WHAT IS A CLUB, AND WHAT ARE ITS BENEFITS?

Quite simply, a club can be thought of as a group of individuals who share a like or related interest and who organize themselves in such a manner that they can further their knowledge in this area of interest. A key factor in distinguishing a club from another form of organization is that clubs usually provide their own leadership. Clubs have many features that benefit their members. They offer experiences and promote values that are enriching to those who participate in them. A list of some general benefits of club involvement follows.

- Cultivation and development of a leisure interest in a specific area.
- An opportunity to gain an understanding of group dynamics, including decision-making processes, formulation of goals, and conflict resolution.
- Development of social relationships.
- Discovery of new leisure interests and opportunities to develop them.
- An opportunity to develop self-reliance.
- Development of positive values related to increased community involvement, awareness, and participation.

- An opportunity to learn to cooperate with others to pursue common leisure interests.
- Personal character development.
- An opportunity to assume and develop leadership roles.

### WHAT IS THE ROLE OF THE LEADER WORKING WITH CLUBS?

The role of the recreation and leisure service leader, when working with clubs, is usually that of an enabler. As an enabler, the leader assists clubs by helping them organize initially, acquire facilities, develop leadership, and otherwise operate successfully. The leader will know when his or her work with a club has been successful because a successful group will be able to operate independently and self-sufficiently. The role of the leader may fluctuate, depending upon the needs of the club. For example, the club may reach the point of autonomous and independent functioning, but in the event of problems with leadership, finances, or other factors, the leader may become more directly involved in the club's operations in order to help it get back on the "right track."

Another aspect of the role of the leader working with clubs may be the introduction of new ideas or encouraging reevaluation of current ideas and methods of operation. The leader attempting to so guide a club group must be careful to maintain a low profile and to "suggest" ideas rather than to force ideas or suggestions upon the membership. Finally, the leader's role often includes representation of the club to its sponsoring body, for example, a parks and recreation department. The leader, as a liaison between the sponsoring agency and the club, may report on the club's activities, needs, or membership status or a combination of these.

Clubs are fun to work with and also can be very challenging to the leader. Individuals involved in club activities often are keenly interested in their activities. Because of this factor, club members are often dedicated, enthusiastic, loyal, and willing to contribute their energy and talents to ensure that the club succeeds. Club membership often produces an energy that is dynamic. It is important for the leader to recognize that this interest and enthusiasm, if channeled appropriately, can meet the needs, not only of individual members but also of the club group and the community as a whole.

In addition to the leader's assistance to clubs as a contact, resource person, or enabler, a club can be helped in other ways by the recreation and leisure service organization for which the leader works. Specifically, an organization can designate agency resources to the club for operation. Often this type of support includes, but is not limited to, seed funding, budgeting for equipment acquisition, provision of space for club meetings, and assistance in the financial organization of the group. Once organized, clubs are open to the public at large and, as a result, complement, or sometimes even replace, existing direct service programs provided by recreation and leisure service organizations. For example, an art club may offer oil painting classes, relieving the recreation and leisure service organization of this responsibility. Therefore, clubs should be encouraged by the leader and the organization to develop and expand their programs to involve the community as fully as possible.

## TYPES OF CLUBS

The number and types of clubs are almost limitless. As depicted in Table 25.1, clubs can be generally categorized according to the ages of participants, the function or purpose of the club, or the program area that the club focuses on or a combination of these. Every club can be defined and described in terms of these three categories. For example, a puppetry club might be categorized as a children's

**TABLE 25.1**  Categorizing Clubs: Age, Function, and Program Area

**BY AGE**

Children
Youths
Adults
Older Persons

**BY MAJOR FUNCTION**

| | |
|---|---|
| Self-development and improvement (mental or physical) | Creative development and expression |
| Spiritual development | Enjoyment and appreciation |
| Socialization | Communication |
| Exploration | Education |
| Acquisition and collecting | Community service |
| | Political action |

**BY GENERAL PROGRAM AREA**

| | | |
|---|---|---|
| History | Home arts | Social recreation |
| Dance | Environment and ecology | Religion |
| Drama | Graphic and plastic arts | Literature |
| Music | Technological innovations | Games |
| Sports | Outdoor pursuits | |
| Crafts | Horticulture | |
| Cultural arts | Civic affairs | |
| Games | Politics | |

club (by age), devoted to creative expression (by major function), and within the drama category (program area on which the club focuses). A teenage dance club, as another example, might be categorized as a youth club (by age), with a purpose of socialization (major function), and within the dance category (general area of interest). A discussion of these three categories used to define and describe clubs follows.

**AGE**

Club activities can, of course, be found among all age groups. The authors have broken age into four categories: children, youth, adult, and older persons. There are some groups organized exclusively for these age groups whereas other types of clubs may be adapted for various ages. Clubs exclusively associated with children include those sponsored by youth-serving agencies, such as the Cub Scouts, Girl Scouts, Boy Scouts, Camp Fire, and the Y's Indian Guides program. Clubs specifically associated with youth may also include church youth groups, Junior Achievement clubs, and so on. Clubs focusing on adults include the 20–30 Club, the Jaycees, the Welcome Wagon Club, and others. Lastly, clubs organized by and for older persons might include Older American clubs and others. Again, a club within any program area—dance, sports, crafts, and so on—can be organized to focus on, and meet the needs of, a specific age group. In fact, most clubs are adapted so that they are "age appropriate."

**FUNCTION**

Clubs exist for many different purposes or functions. Some of the major reasons why individuals organize and participate in clubs include self-development and improvement, socialization, exploration, spiritual development, acquisition and collecting, creative development and expression, enjoyment and appreciation, financial gain, communication, education, community service, and political action. Many clubs will fulfill more than one of these purposes or functions; however, a club will usually have one *major* function. For example, a teenage club may be organized to focus on educational development; however, the major function of the club may, in fact, be socialization. Junior Achievement clubs for teenagers, as a case in point, are organized to assist youths in understanding the processes involved in the organization and operation of a business. However, possibly the major purpose drawing participants to the club is the opportunity to socialize with other youths the same age and with similar interests.

## GENERAL PROGRAM AREA

The general program area of a club refers to the type of content that the club is centered on. The possibilities for formation of clubs around content areas are numerous. The authors have listed a few of the general program areas that might provide a focus for club organization. Some of these are history, dance, drama, music, sports, crafts, cultural arts, games, home arts, religion, outdoor pursuits, horticulture, and literature. Within these general program areas many specific types of clubs may be organized. For example, within the program area of sports, there might be tennis clubs, raquetball clubs, swimming clubs, rugby clubs, and fishing clubs. As another example, within the program area of technological innovations, there might be photography clubs, film clubs, ham radio clubs, and CB radio clubs. It is interesting to note that as technology advances, there will be still additional clubs organized around new technological products. The personal computer, for example, will serve as the basis for the organization and development of club activities. Table 25.2 lists some specific types of clubs that might be found within the program areas mentioned earlier.

**TABLE 25.2**   Specific Club Ideas

| | | |
|---|---|---|
| Acrobatic | Camping | Creative arts |
| Adult band | Candlemaking | Creative writing |
| Acrylic painting | Canning | Crewel |
| Amateur radio | Canoeing | Cribbage |
| Acting workshop | Car | Crocheting |
| Antique collecting | Card | Cross-country hikes |
| Archaeology | Carpentry | Cross-country skiing |
| Archery | Ceramics | Current affairs |
| Architecture | Cheerleading | Cycling |
| Arts and crafts | Chess | |
| Astronomy | Child and baby care | Dance self-expression |
| Aviation | Children's literature | Diving |
| | China painting | Drama |
| Bagpipe | Chinese cooking | Duplicate bridge |
| Baking | Chinese paper folding | |
| Ballet | Chorus | Electronics |
| Ballroom dancing | Coin collecting | Embroidery |
| Band | Community dramatics | English |
| Banjo | Computer programming | English literature |
| Barbershop harmony | Consumer protection | Entomology |
| Baseball | Conservation | Exercise |
| | Conversational French | |
| Calligraphy | Cooking | Father and son |
| Campers and trailers | | Fencing |
| | | Figure drawing |

**TABLE 25.2**    Continued

| | | |
|---|---|---|
| Filmmaking | Kite making | Sculpturing |
| Fishing | Knitting | Self-development |
| Flag football | Kayaking | Sewing |
| Floral arrangements | | Single-parent club |
| Folk art | Landscaping | Shuffleboard |
| Folk dancing | Leathercraft | Sketching |
| Football (touch and flag) | Local issues | Skiing |
| Foreign cookery | Macrame | Small boats |
| Foreign films | Marching and drill | Soccer |
| Foreign languages | Mexican cooking | Softball |
| Games | Model building | Spanish |
| Gardening | Modern dance | Sports fishing |
| Glassblowing | Mosaics | Square dancing |
| Glee club and chorus | Mother-daughter | Stamp collecting |
| Golf | Motorcycle | Stock market |
| Gourmet cooking | Mountain climbing | Table tennis |
| Great books | Needlepoint | Tailoring |
| Guitar | Nutrition | Teenage club |
| Guns | | Tennis |
| Gymnastics | Oil painting | Toastmasters |
| Handball | Organ | Tole painting |
| Handicraft | Outdoor cooking | Tours and trips |
| Hiking | Photography | Travel film |
| History | Physical fitness | Tumbling |
| Hockey | Pinochle | Ukulele |
| Homemaking | Pistol and rifle | Violin |
| Horsemanship | Pottery making | Volleyball |
| Horseshoes | Puppetry | Water ballet |
| Ice skating | Quilt making | Water polo |
| Indian cooking | Recreational swimming | Waterskiing |
| Indoor gardening | Religions of the world | Weaving |
| Intercultural films | Rocketry | Weight lifting |
| Interior decorating | Rock and gem | Wilderness survival |
| Investments | Roller skating | Wild bird study |
| Japanese cooking | Round dancing | Woodworking |
| Jewelry making | Rug making | World affairs discussion |
| Jogging | Saddle club | Wrestling |
| Judo | Sailing | Yoga |
| Karate | Science club | Your family tree |
| | Scuba and skin diving | |

Viewing clubs in the light of these three categories—age, function, and program area —can be helpful to the leader because the underlying structure of the club is highlighted. This can help the leader focus on the actual purposes of the club. It is important that the leader understand, however, that a club may have several purposes or functions and may be based on more than one program area. A club, for example, might be organized to study art history (representing two program areas) for purposes of self-improvement, education, enjoyment and appreciation, and even socialization. It is also important that the leader understand that the purpose of a club organized around a certain program area may be different for different types of groups (i.e., age groups). For children, a dance club might offer opportunities for creative expression; for teenagers, it might offer opportunities for socialization; for adults, it might be involved in a self-improvement effort; and for older persons, the purpose might be socialization or just enjoyment.

## HOW TO ORGANIZE A CLUB

The recreation and leisure service leader often assists individuals within the community in the formation and organization of clubs of various types. National organizations may support the formation of some types of local groups by providing published materials relating to club organizations or guidelines for operation, or they may have local support staff that are available to help clubs organize and operate. The leader should attempt to locate, acquire, and use such resources if they are available. In addition, the leader may be able to gain help in organizing a club from other similar clubs in the community. Another club may have members who would be willing to act as resource persons, sharing their knowledge to help the club organize and "get on its feet."

### PLANNING AN ORGANIZATIONAL MEETING

After determining the existing resources available to help in the formation and organization of a club, the leader should meet with club organizers to plan organizational meetings. If the club organizers do not have the benefit of national or other resources to help them organize, the following procedures can be used to set up an initial organizational meeting.

Prior to the organizational meeting,

- Set organizational meeting dates. It may be wise to hold two organizational meetings.
- Develop informational fliers that give complete information about the meeting, including date, time, location, and who is eligible to attend.

- Send a public service announcement to the local radio and television station for free publicity. Don't wait until the last minute! It's best to contact the media for exact guidelines for submitting public service announcements.
- Confirm and reconfirm use of the facility in which the meeting is to take place. Make sure the doors will be *unlocked when the organizers arrive*.
- Develop an agenda for the organizational meeting that will encourage discussion of such topics as the club's purpose, goals, rules and regulations, organizational structure, and future meeting dates, times and places.

At the meeting,

- Arrive well in advance of the time of arrival of the first attendees.
- Welcome each person warmly and enthusiastically, but sincerely.
- Serve refreshments (i.e., coffee, tea, punch, etc.) if possible; they are a nice touch.
- Start on time!
- Keep to the agenda, and keep to the agenda timetable.

The second organizational meeting can follow the same basic format as the first meeting although the leader might want to ask newly recruited members to help in the organization of the second meeting or help welcome new attendees to it or both.

### CLUB LEADERSHIP

As the leader assists the club in becoming self-sufficient, he or she will want to encourage the club members to establish a structure that includes leadership roles. This is important because, by definition, a club generates or provides its own leadership. Commonly, clubs are administered by a president, vice-president, secretary, and treasurer. Usually, a club will elect individuals to these positions although it is also possible for leaders to be appointed or achieve their position by acclaim. Brief descriptions of the common duties of club officers follow:

- *President.* It is the responsibility of the club president to oversee the club's operations. In this role, the club president may find it necessary to appoint committees. The president might also attempt to ensure that the club is run according to its bylaws, rules and regulations, and the rules or regulations of its sponsoring agency. The president is the symbol and focal point of the club's activities. He or she will preside over club meetings and, depending upon the formality of the club, may or may not conduct the meeting according to Robert's *Rules of Order.* The president should compile a meeting agenda prior to each club meeting, detailing the topics to be discussed and who is to discuss them.
- *Vice-president.* The vice-president assists the president in his or her duties. This may involve administering certain committees or serving on behalf of the president when he or she is unable to attend meetings. In the event that the president resigns, the vice-president assumes the office of president.
- *Secretary.* The secretary traditionally records the minutes of club meetings, particularly the motions made and whether or not they were carried. The secretary will often prepare a set of the minutes of the previous meetings for each administrative committee member so that he or she can check the minutes for accuracy and approve them. The secretary might also be responsible for membership records or notifying members of the upcoming meetings either by phone or in writing.
- *Treasurer.* The treasurer is responsible for the financial accounting for the club. This may involve receipting income from dues, fund-raising activities, and other sources.

It may also involve disbursement of funds to meet the financial obligations of the group. The treasurer will want to maintain meticulous records of the club's financial transactions and should periodically provide the club with financial reports.

In addition to election or appointment of these officers, a large club might designate certain individuals as committee members to head such committees as fund raising, special projects, publicity, budget, membership, and others.

### THE CLUB MEETING AGENDA

A particular area in which the recreation and leisure service professional can give leadership to those who are involved in the organization of clubs of all types is that of meeting planning and execution. The art of conducting successful meetings is learned easily with adequate education and support. An agenda that could easily be adapted for utilization in most club meetings is detailed here.

- **I.** Call to Order (5–10 minutes)
  - **A.** Welcome and Opening Comments
  - **B.** Introductions
- **II.** Business Meeting (20–30 minutes maximum)
  - **A.** Reading of Minutes of Last Meeting and Approval
  - **B.** Committee Reports (if applicable)
  - **C.** Old or Unfinished Business
  - **D.** New Business
- **III.** Program Presentation (30–40 minutes suggested)
- **IV.** Closing Ceremony and Announcements (10 minutes)
- **V.** Adjournment

### FINANCING CLUB ACTIVITIES

Clubs finance their activities in various ways. One of the most basic methods for raising funds in a club is the assessment of initiation fees or membership dues or both. An *initiation fee* is a payment made for initial entry into a club. Much of the initiation fee is charged to offset the costs of processing the membership papers of the new member. *Membership dues* are moneys that are paid, usually on a regular basis, to a club. They may be paid weekly, monthly, semiannually, or annually. Dues are paid to help defray the club's operating expenses. Club activities are also financed through *fund-raising* activities. A club can use various methods for raising funds, including craft sales, bake sales, car washes, jogathons, pancake feeds, and selling various products. Furthermore, a club may want to organize fund raisers tied to its regular meetings. For example, a square dance club might organize a square dance competition for all clubs in the region and charge an entry fee to raise funds. The club may also solicit financial support from private *businesses* or may attempt to solicit a direct subsidy from a *governmental* organization. Businesses, in particular, often contribute directly to clubs, providing money for entrance fees, travel expenses, and equipment in exchange for advertisement as the club's "sponsor."

Finally, clubs may raise funds through *endowments*. Individuals may leave a substantial sum of money, real estate, or other commodity of value to a club. These can be invested and draw interest to be used in the club's operation. There are also many other creative and innovative ways to finance club activities; however, the methods mentioned are some of the more common ones.

### HELPFUL HINTS

The Cooperative Extension Service of Oregon State University has issued a pamphlet entitled "So You Want to Organize a 4-H Club." Within this pamphlet are some helpful hints for organizing a club, which have been adapted as follows.

- Hold meetings frequently enough to ensure continued member interest.
- Schedule all meetings for the club a year in advance and see that all members receive the schedule.
- Never cancel or postpone a meeting unless absolutely necessary, and then only after notifying all members.
- A business session at each meeting is not necessary.
- Develop an agenda and follow it.
- Club meetings should usually last no more than two hours.
- Involve members in the meeting programs.
- Plan and execute community service projects if appropriate.[1]

These guidelines are valid for the organization of any of the club types outlined previously. If these guidelines are adhered to, particularly when the club is first being organized, the initial interaction between organizers of the club and the membership will be positive and will most likely result in a successful club.

### SUMMARY

Clubs provide a focal point for the organization of individuals who have common interests. The strength gained through the collective efforts of people, in terms of gathering and sharing information and resources, is a powerful statement for the organization of clubs in recreation and leisure service agencies. The leader or facilitator of such groups plays a vital role in their success and perpetuation by offering leadership in the coordination of the organization process, the utilization of facilities, and the acquisition of group resources. The result will enhance the overall recreation and leisure service program.

[1]"So You Want to Organize a 4-H Club," Cooperative Extension Service (Corvallis, Ore.: Oregon State University, 1971), p. 6.

## DISCUSSION QUESTIONS

1. What is a club?
2. What are some of the benefits of a club?
3. What role does the recreation and leisure service leader play when working with clubs?
4. Locate and identify twenty different types of clubs in your community.
5. What are the steps one might take in organizing clubs?
6. What does the following statement imply: "A recreation and leisure service leader should assist clubs to become self-sufficient"?
7. What are some of the ways clubs can be financed?

# ORGANIZING AND LEADING TOUR AND TRAVEL PROGRAMS

The tour leader should be vibrant, enthusiastic, and fun to be with.

Travel is one of our society's favorite pastimes. As discretionary time increases, the public at large seeks opportunities to travel and explore, both at the local level and to far-off lands. Travel and tourism opportunities can range from a trip to Hawaii to a guided whitewater rafting trip to a tour of a bakery. Travel and tourism, although related, are not the same. Travel is simply the physical movement of an individual from one place to another whereas tourism is involved with the amenities that may accompany travel, such as lodging, various types of transportation, food services, entertainment, tours, and the many other types of activities and services that are available to individuals who "travel."

The leader involved in travel and tourism within a nonprofit recreation and leisure service organization may be responsible for organizing and leading tour groups, usually to local points of interest, or he or she may act as a liaison between a recreation and leisure service organization and a travel agency in the organization of more extensive trips outside the local region. This chapter will discuss these two travel and tourism leadership roles, techniques that can be used by the leader engaged in these two roles, motivations for travel, and types of tours.

## WHY DO PEOPLE TRAVEL?

The lure of travel can be addictive for those who have experienced this form of leisure pursuit. The social aspects of travel are important to many people; the travel experience can enable individuals to make and develop new friendships. Others may travel to experience new and unique leisure opportunities. Still others may travel for adventure, excitement, or education. Thomas has outlined the following motivations for participation in travel activities.

*Education and Cultural Motives*

1. To see how people in other countries live, work, and play.
2. To see particular sites.
3. To gain understanding of what goes on in the news.
4. To attend special events.

*Relaxation and Pleasure*

1. To get away from everyday routine.
2. To have a good time.
3. To achieve some sort of sexual or romantic activity.

*Ethnic*

1. To visit the place your family came from.
2. To visit places your family or friends have gone to.

*Other*

1. Weather (to avoid cold).
2. Health (sun, dry climate, etc.).
3. Sports (to swim, ski, fish, or sail).
4. Economy (inexpensive living).
5. Adventure (new areas, people, adventure).
6. One-upmanship (status, relation to one's neighbors and friends).
7. Conformity (keeping up with the Joneses).
8. To participate in history (ancient temples in ruins, current history).
9. Sociological motives (get to know the world).[1]

## TYPES OF TOURS

Tours can be very elaborate and expensive, involving a great deal of planning and effort on the part of the leader, or they can be relatively simple. The degree of complexity of the tour will depend on the destination and the number of participants. Leading a small tour group to a local point of interest will not be very complicated in terms of arrangements; leading a large tour to a destination that is farther away and involves overnight accommodations will be somewhat more complex. There are several types of tours or tour classifications with which the recreation and leisure service leader should be knowledgeable. These are discussed here as adapted from Lundberg.

- *Package Tours.* A package tour is designed to fit the requirements of a particular group of travelers. Some tours cater to special interest groups. Package tours may be either escorted or unescorted. They are advertised in brochures, which contain the cost, terms, and conditions of the offered package.
- *Escorted Tours.* An experienced tour director travels with the group in this type of tour. He or she handles all basic details—hotel reservations, transportation, sight-seeing, baggage, customs, language interpretation when necessary, etc. He or she is responsible for maintaining the overall schedule of the tour. By and large, escorted tours are "all inclusive."
- *Unescorted Package Tours (FIT or DIT).* The more flexible, unescorted package tours enable the traveler to purchase an arranged package with transportation, transfers,

This leader is conducting a "day tour" to the coast of Oregon.

[1] John A. Thomas, "What Makes People Travel," *ASTA Travel News,* 1964.

sight-seeing, hotel accommodations, and usually some meals, but he or she does not travel with a group led by a tour director. Sight-seeing excursions may or may not be arranged. The predetermined cost allows the traveler to budget most of his or her expenses in advance. The basic advantage of a package tour is convenience.

- *Group Tours (GIT)*. A group tour is 15 or more people traveling together who are members of a club, business organization or other affiliated group who have pooled their purchasing power to realize savings, particularly on transportation. Group tours are offered to almost any destination.
- *The Inclusive Tour Charter (ITC)*. By chartering an entire aircraft from one of the supplemental carriers, the cost per traveler is drastically reduced for the longer trip. (It represents little savings for shorter trips, in many cases.) The big advantage to the traveler using this type of charter is that the air fare costs may be up to 50 percent less than the equivalent scheduled fare.[2]

The recreation and leisure service leader working for a municipal recreation and leisure service organization, youth-serving agency, or other nonprofit organization will most commonly be involved in organizing and leading group tours of short duration. Tours of greater complexity or magnitude are typically arranged by a travel agent often with the *assistance* of the leader. A group tour can be either a day tour or an overnight tour. A *day tour* typically has an early departure time with a return scheduled later the same day. An *overnight* group tour occurs when participants travel to a distant location requiring an overnight stay of one or more nights.

There are many simple group tours that can be organized by the leader to local points of interest within any community. These

[2]Adapted from Donald E. Lundberg, *The Tourist Business* (Boston, Massachusettes: CBI Publishing Company, Inc, 1976), pp. 110–111. Third Edition.

tours can be attended by participants of various age groups: children, teenagers, adults, and older people. Such local tours are usually conducted within the span of one day and may or may not involve lunch. Figure 26.1 lists some short local tours that can be given, indicating the wide variety of possibilities. Some of these tours are geared to specific age groups; others, however, would be of interest to all age groups.

## THE ROLE OF THE LEADER

The leader involved in travel and tourism within nonprofit organizations usually functions, as mentioned, in either a comprehensive capacity or as a liaison. The leader who assumes a *comprehensive* role is responsible for the planning, organization, and actual guiding of the tour or travel experience or both. The leader who assumes a *liaison* role works in conjunction with a travel agency to provide tour and travel opportunities for participants. This type of leader does not actually plan, organize, and lead the tour himself or herself, but can assist in one or more of these functions. A discussion of these two leadership roles follows.

### COMPREHENSIVE ROLE

The leader who fills a comprehensive role often is engaged in organizing and leading tours as a part of a larger program. For example, a leader working with a group of older persons, a children's play group, or a teenage center may find that he or she will want to organize and lead tours for these groups in order to broaden and add interest to the program. This type of leader may also plan, organize, and lead "special" tours that are promoted by the recreation and leisure service organization. For example, an organization may advertise tours that will be made available to the general public on certain dates, with the expectation that individuals who are interested will sign up for the tours and attend them.

| | |
|---|---|
| Historical sites | Colleges and universities |
| Sporting events | Wildlife sanctuaries |
| Lumber mills | Museums |
| Banks | Libraries |
| Automobile manufacturers | City halls |
| Parks | Post offices |
| Observation decks and towers | Courthouses |
| Opera houses | Police stations |
| Antique stores | Telephone companies |
| Arenas | Dog and cat hospitals |
| Theaters | Ice-cream companies |
| Canning companies | Outdoor markets |
| Clothing manufacturers | Fish hatcheries |
| Fire stations | Soft-drink bottling companies |
| Weather bureaus | Aquariums |
| Airports | Bakeries |
| Radio and TV stations | Botanical gardens and arboretums |
| Florists | Train stations |
| Grocery warehouses | Farms and dairies |
| Water excursions | Historical homes |
| Light and power companies | Amusement parks |
| Hospitals | Discount outlets |
| Paper manufacturing companies | Nurseries and greenhouses |
| | Zoos |

**FIGURE 26.1**   Selected local group tours.

The individual involved in a comprehensive leadership role is not just a guide or a recreation director. He or she has a responsibility to "manage" the tour so that it runs smoothly and safely. The leader who plans, organizes, and conducts a well-run tour leaves nothing to chance. He or she outlines the route to be taken, the transportation to be used, the costs involved, the weather conditions to be dealt with, the rest stops to be made, and the eating arrangements necessary. The leader should also draw up an itinerary for his or her own information or to share with the group. This itinerary should detail the travel schedule of the group on tour, the transportation to be used, and the stops to be made and at what times. An itinerary can be useful in ensuring that the expectations of the group are consistent with the tour to be given.

The leader conducting a tour must not only make adequate preparations and prepare for contingencies, but must be personable, polite, and considerate as well so that the tour may be enjoyable. He or she should be part "showperson." The leader literally can make or break a tour. If the leader is competent, yet fun to be with, participants will not only enjoy the tour, but will also tell others about their experience. This is good public relations for the sponsoring organization. Other general guidelines that can be used by the "comprehensive" leader conducting group tours follow.

- The leader should adjust his or her tour style to meet the needs of the group attending. For example, the leader may want to "gear" the tour to the age group involved. Children will have a different perspective regarding the information presented in a tour from that of adults. The leader should attempt to make the tour meaningful to the specific age group or type of group he or she is guiding. The leader should also pace the tour to complement the group attending, slowing it down if necessary to accommodate all tour group members.

- The leader should collect any required forms and money in advance of the tour so that travel and other arrangements can be made and paid for in advance if necessary. This can also avoid either last-minute disappointment or loss to the organization if money or forms are forgotten. If children will be attending a tour without their parents, they must turn in a signed permit.

- The leader should ensure that there will be an adequate number of individuals to assist with the tour. When tours are for children, the leader will want to have a certain ratio of adults to children. This ratio is usually suggested by the sponsoring organization.

- The leader should contact individuals at the site to be visited in advance to request the tour, receive special instructions, determine the times that tours are available, and give notification that the tour group will be coming. How far in advance the leader should contact those at the tour destination will vary with the situation. One or two weeks' notice may be sufficient, or the leader may have to make arrangements further in advance.

- When the leader is conducting a tour for children, he or she should have the children use the "buddy system" when engaged in walking portions of the tour.

- The leader should not attempt to include too much within one tour. The tour should be enjoyable, not frantic. A tour that looks as if it might be too much for one trip might be divided into a two-part tour.

- The leader should remain pleasant regardless of the problems that are bound to arise when leading tour groups that include many types of people. The leader must be able to handle such problems firmly but cheerfully.

- The leader should ensure that arrangements are made for meals if necessary. If participants are to bring their own lunches, this should be specified prior to the tour. If the leader will be making other arrangements for lunch, participants should be notified in advance if this will be included in the cost of the tour, or they should bring money to cover the cost of meals. If the group is to eat together at a restaurant, the leader should make arrangements with the establishment in advance so that the group is expected.

- The leader of tours has a great deal of responsibility and should evidence integrity. He or she must follow the rules of the organization or agency being toured, as well as the rules set forth by the sponsoring organization.

- The leader might want to include the price of a snack in the cost of the tour, especially if the tour is for children, and conclude the tour with a "treat" of some kind.

- When the tour group is en route to its tour destination, the leader may want to organize tour members into singing groups or tell them stories or amusing jokes. A bus or car ride or even a long walk can seem much shorter when members of the tour group are engaged in singing and lively conversation. Songs and stories can also be related to the theme of the tour.

- The leader should implement a risk management plan, the complexity of which will depend on the type of tour. In addition, participants should be able to count on the leader to solve any minor or major problems that might occur with calm control. A stalled bus or a delayed tour should be viewed by the leader as an "opportunity" to use his or her leadership skills to the fullest.

- If the leader is conducting a tour for which he or she is to give information, this information should be imparted with ease and familiarity with the subject matter. The leader should rehearse any dialogue to be given and should avoid reading from cards or sheets of paper.

- The leader should attempt to give each of the members of the tour group equal attention. When talking to members of the group, the leader should attempt to talk to "everyone."
- The leader should account for participants at strategic points during the tour. For example, a "head count" should be taken when departing on the tour and when coming back home. This is especially important when leading children's groups.

## LIAISON ROLE

The leader within a nonprofit recreation and leisure service organization may be involved in travel and tourism in various ways. As mentioned, the leader may personally lead tours of individuals to various destinations. Or the leader may act as a *liaison* between a travel agency and a recreation and leisure service organization. The role of the leader who acts as a liaison between the recreation and leisure service organization and a travel agency is depicted in Figure 26.2. As shown, the leader in this role acts as an intermediary between the organization and a travel agency. Typically, this leader might receive a request from participants, for example, within a senior center, to arrange a trip or tour to a certain destination; or his or her organization might advertise tour or travel opportunities for which participants can "sign up." In either case, upon commitment of participants to a particular travel or tour package, usually in the form of a deposit or full payment, the leader would request a travel agency to make appropriate arrangements for accommodations, transportation, sightseeing or touring or a combination of these. Depending on the circumstances, these arrangements might be made by the travel agency in two ways: (1) the agency might make arrangements for accommodations and transportation directly, for example, with hotels and airlines, or (2)

the agency might turn to wholesalers that specialize in domestic independent travel (DIT), foreign independent travel (FIT), or tours (domestic and international) to arrange a tour and travel itinerary and to ensure that reservations are made based on this itinerary. Although the travel agency and its contacts assume the major responsibility for planning and organizing the trip or tour, there are a number of steps that can be taken by the leader, in his or her liaison role, to enhance the quality of the travel or tour experience for participants. Some of these follow.

- *Establish Relationships with Local Travel Agents.* The leader can familiarize himself or herself with local travel agents and ensure that only reputable agencies are allowed to promote and bid on tours within

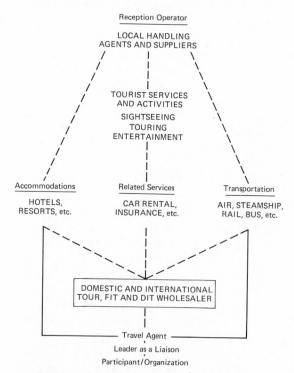

**FIGURE 26.2** The leader as a liaison. (*Source*: Adapted from Armin D. Lehmann, *Travel and Tourism: An Introduction to Travel Agency Operations*, © 1978, The Bobbs-Merrill Company, Inc.)

the organization. Travel agents provide valuable services to the traveling public, typically at no cost to the individuals utilizing such services.

- *Hold Promotional Meetings*. Promotional meetings can be scheduled and held periodically by the leader. This type of activity can serve two functions. First, it can provide an opportunity for individuals wishing to travel to a specific destination to learn more about the area and its recreational amenities. Second, this type of meeting can serve as a recreational program in and of itself.

- *Hold an Organizational Meeting*. The leader may want to hold an organizational meeting for participants who have demonstrated a serious interest in a tour. During this meeting materials can be distributed that give complete information about the tour being offered. If possible, the travel agent responsible for arranging the tour should be present. The travel agent and the leader should make especially clear the method of payment for the tour and the rules regarding reimbursement in the event of cancellation by the participant.

- *Hold Pretrip Meetings*. It is always a good idea to hold pretrip meetings prior to a major excursion. By doing so, the participants can share expectations and excitement and begin to establish a bond, which in turn will enhance the social atmosphere of the tour. Again, if possible, the travel agent should be present in order to give accurate information about the conditions that exist at the destination, travel requirements to particular areas (visas, immunizations, and so on), suggestions for packing, and other helpful insights.

- *Check Departure Procedures*. The leader and the travel agent should ensure that participants are aware of all the departure arrangements. They should know what time they are expected to arrive for departure and where. It may be that the group will be bused to the airport en masse. Participants should also be made aware of baggage limitations and how their baggage is to be handled. The travel agent should be expected to assist the group with many of these details, with the recreation and leisure leader serving as liaison for the group.

- *Establish Contingency Procedures*. The recreation and leisure service leader can do much to enhance the tour by establishing a set of contingency procedures in case problems arise. These procedures may detail suggested action in the event of accident or injury to a participant, loss of funds, or other unanticipated emergencies. The travel agent can assist in contingency planning as well.

- *Travel with the Group*. In some instances, the recreation and leisure service leader might travel with a tour group organized by a travel agency as a representative of his or her organization. The leader, in this role, might help out as needed and act as a contact person for tour group members.

- *Conducting Recollection Seminars*. People often enjoy recalling past travel experiences and sharing them with others. The leader can gather together individuals who have been on a tour and encourage them to share their pictures, slides, stories, and memorabilia with others. This can be enjoyable for both the individuals who participated in the tour as well as interested individuals who may not have an opportunity to travel to the area involved. The leader should encourage individuals making such presentations to focus on the area that was visited and to avoid pictures and slides of a personal nature, showing friends and family.

In addition to these general steps that can be taken by the leader, he or she can use the more specific checklist presented in Figure 26.3 to ensure that participants are prepared for their trip. Many of these items may be handled by the travel agent; however, they

---

- Do all participants know departure time and place?
- Do all participants know clothing recommendations?
- Baggage limits?
- Transfer transportation arranged?
- All tickets and vouchers secured?
- All emergency health information recorded?
- Hotel reservations confirmed and reconfirmed?
- Group baggage handling arranged?
- Sight-seeing trips arranged?
- Are customs procedures understood?
- Information packets distributed?
- All immunizations obtained?
- Shot records and passports with *each* traveler?
- Is a tour plan available to all travelers?
- Is a risk management plan in place?
- Are health records available for each traveler?

---

**FIGURE 26.3**  Travel checklist.

should be double-checked by the leader as a representative of the organization. Use of this checklist, combined with the other suggestions given for the leader operating within a liaison role, and the services of a competent and reliable travel agent should result in a smooth and well-organized travel experience for participants.

## SUMMARY

This chapter has discussed the role of the leader working within nonprofit recreation and leisure service organizations in the program area of travel and tourism. Basically, the leader can be involved in two roles within this program area and setting: a comprehensive role or a liaison role. The leader who engages in a comprehensive role plans, organizes, and leads tours himself or herself. The leader who is involved in a tour and travel program as a liaison engages the services of a travel agent on behalf of the organization's participants interested in a travel opportunity or tour. This type of leader may *assist* the travel agent in the planning, organization, and implementation of a tour-travel program. In either case, the leader is instrumental in ensuring that the tour-travel program is carried out in an effective and organized manner.

## DISCUSSION QUESTIONS

1. Why do people travel?
2. What is the difference between a day tour and an overnight tour?
3. Identify and define four different types of tours.
4. What roles does the recreation and leisure service leader play in the tour organization and implementation process? What is the difference in the role a leader plays in assuming a comprehensive vs. a liaison role?
5. Identify 10 tours in your community that would appeal to youth, teenagers, adults, and older persons.
6. What are the general guidelines that might be followed when managing tours?
7. Organize a sample tour for a community group. List all necessary procedures and methods.
8. Why is it important to develop contingency procedures when organizing tours?

# GAMES AND CONTESTS

New Games are very popular among both children and adults. This group of children is involved in a New Game using an earth ball.

Leaders of games and contests can be found in programs for all ages and abilities, and they may lead games related to physical, mental, dramatic, musical, literary, or dance activities. As will be explained further, some leaders of games and contests are actually performing on a face-to-face level whereas others perform task-oriented functions involved with the administration of many games. Both the program-oriented and the task-oriented recreation and leisure service leader leading games and contests should be thoroughly familiar with the components and leadership techniques of these activities if they are to be successful.

By nature, all games and contests are competitive activities that involve locomotion, ob-

ject handling, or a combination of both. Locomotion in games may be performed by any means imaginable—running, skiing, sliding, crawling, jumping, and so on. Objects may be propelled by throwing, rolling, kicking, hitting, or other methods. In some cases, leaders may modify the original instructions of games and contests to change the forms of locomotion or object handling or both. This may be done in order to make use of an unusual space or to accommodate a special set of participants who may vary in age or ability from those for whom the instructions were originally written.

The difference between games and contests has been discussed in Chapter 6. As a review, we may summarize the differences between the two. Games involve strategy, choice, and interference which impedes the progress of the opponent, whereas a contest is based on individual or group performance with no action impeding the progress of opponents. The following material defines and describes several types of games and contests, discusses techniques for leading games and contests, and presents guidelines for administering events comprised of many games or contests.

## TYPES OF GAMES

Each book on games seems to use a slightly different method for categorizing them. Each has validity. Games can be classified as active or passive or according to age, type of activity, or program area. Furthermore, games may be classified according to their benefits, such as social development, physical development, and so on. The authors have chosen to classify games into nine categories of game types, including (1) low-organized games, (2) lead-up games, (3) team games, (4) table games, (5) mental games, (6) wide games, (7) simulation games, (8) New Games, and (9) initiative games, rope courses, and adventure activities. A description of each of these types of games, including brief examples of them where appropriate, follows.

## LOW-ORGANIZED GAMES

Although usually considered children's activities, low-organized games are played by all ages. They are characterized by having few rules, demanding very simple skills, and requiring little or no cooperation among the players. Another characteristic of low-organized games is that the status of the players (thrower or dodger or runner or chaser) changes frequently, and the games usually can continue until interest wanes or a leader suggests something new. A simple game of dodgeball is an example of a low-organized game.

## LEAD-UP GAMES

Many games requiring highly developed skills, intricate rules, and complex plans for group cooperation are more easily understood by beginners if the leader introduces them through lead-up games. A lead-up game is designed to emphasize one or more facets of a more intricate game and allow participants to become familiar with one aspect of the game before going on to the more complex parts of the activity. A game of keep-away may be used as a lead-up game for basketball as it can emphasize team play, throwing, catching, movement, and feinting. The technical skills and rules come later, and the beginners will already have had a successful experience learning an introductory activity.

## TEAM GAMES

Team games usually bring to mind baseball, basketball, football, and the like, but there may be teams of bridge players, teams for initiative tasks, and so on. Team games may be low-organized games such as crows and cranes, which has one group of players chasing and catching another (See Figure 27.1). This game meets all the prerequisites for a low-organized event; however, it is played by groups of children, of whom one team is the chaser and the other team is the pursued. Team games are characterized by the division of players into groups or teams cooperating together for the good of the group as a whole rather than for each one as an individual. Team games are usually not recommended for the immature or young child who still displays an egocentricity and has not yet developed a team spirit.

The rules of team games are usually quite complex because such games involve many individual players performing a wide variety

---

Establish two goals 60 to 80 feet apart, and line up one team behind each goal. One team is known as crows and the other as cranes. The leader stands in the middle and gives the command, "Forward, march," whereupon the teams march forward. Just after he or she gives the command, the leader calls, "Cr-r-r-rows" or "Cr-r-r-ranes," holding the Cr-r-r sound until the teams are close together. If the call terminates in "crows," the crows dash back to their goal with the cranes in pursuit; if the call is "cranes," the cranes run back. All who are tagged join the other side.

Much of the fun element in the game depends on the cleverness of the leader. The calls should be drawn out as long as possible, thus adding to the suspense and uncertainty of the players. Occasionally, after starting the call, the leader terminates it with either "crackers" or "crawfish," to confuse the players momentarily; he or she then immediately calls the proper word.

**FIGURE 27.1**   Crows and cranes.

of functions according to their roles or positions. For example, baseball, has a pitcher, catcher, people on bases, and fielders, all of whom are defensive players when in the field and offensive players when at bat. Consequently, there are many rules for each player involving catching, throwing, hitting, and running.

Furthermore, team games usually involve advanced and sometimes intricate skills. The lead-up game of keep-away discussed earlier does not resemble the complex game of basketball at all (even though it may be used as an introductory activity). Basketball requires that the participant learn and develop precise and often complicated skills.

### TABLE GAMES

Table games may be low-organized, lead-up, or team games but are played with a table or small flat surface as the game area. Table games may involve boards, as in checkers, Monopoly, Chinese checkers, and so on; or they may involve paper and pencil, as in tic-tac-toe; or they may use cards, dice or chips. A low-organized table game is slapjack or go fish whereas the game farmer and pig (see Figure 27.2) is a table game played as a lead-up activity for checkers.

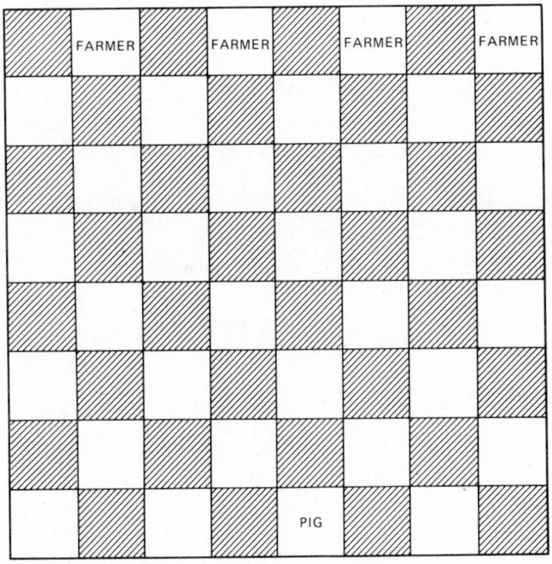

### MENTAL GAMES

Some activities called mental games may be more correctly categorized as contests, for they do not involve interference or impeding strategy. They do, however, involve much choice. Guessing games are mental games as are games designed to "trick" or bluff opponents. The latter would qualify as strategy events. Charades may be considered mental games by some and mental contests by others. A good example of a true mental game is one

**FIGURE 27.2**    Farmers and the pig gameboard.

---

**Title:** Farmers and the Pig

**Type:** Table game

**Participants:** Two to five players

**Age, Sex:** Six years and up, either sex

**Equipment:** Four discs, one disc of a different color (five total)
Game board or chart as for checkers

**Formation:** Place four farmers and a pig in the indicated squares (see chart)

**Object:** The farmers try to pen the pig in so he cannot get by.

*Rules.* Farmers can move forward only on white squares, one space at a time. The pig moves first and then in turn in any direction. All moves must be from space to space and not through the bushes, represented by dark squares. The pig has won the game if he or she can get by all four farmers, as they cannot move backward to go after him or her.

**FIGURE 27.2**    Farmers and the pig.

known as our cook doesn't like peas (Figure 27.3), which is a simple game with many advanced, complex variations.

> One player starts the game by saying, "Our cook doesn't like peas. What can we have for dinner?" He or she points a finger at some player, who must quickly answer with some article of food. To be acceptable, the article must be one that is spelled without the letter *p*. Onions, garlic, cabbage, chocolate, celery, and the like are accepted; but if the player answers with peas, pumpkin pie, parsnips, or some other word having the letter *p*, the leader will say, "I am sorry, but our cook will not prepare that." A player who answers incorrectly may be required to pay a forfeit. Or the game may be played until most of the players get the idea.

**FIGURE 27.3**    Our cook doesn't like peas.

### WIDE GAMES

Called tabloid games by Australians, wide games are actually a series of games or contests for a large group of people in a large (wide) area. In wide games events, participants rotate among several activities made up of individual or small-group skills, contests, quizzes, or manual dexterity races or a combination of these. Wide games activities may consist of knot tying, wood sawing, plant identification, tent pitching, and other similar events. Ten to 15 minutes per event are usually allotted. A group of 200 may be divided into 10 smaller groups, each of which progresses from activity to activity for a total of 20 activities with or without accumulative scores. The activities occur on large fields, in meadows and forests, or in any "wide" area. Suggestions for leading wide games and other such events are found later in the chapter, in the section entitled "Task-oriented Leadership." In wide games, all the activities usually relate to a common theme, such as the Olympics. The events may even be noncompetitive and one of the events in the series may be eating refreshments, thus wide games may be "games" by title only.

### SIMULATION GAMES

Whenever educational events are designed to involve participants in situations simulating real life, the activities are called simulation games. Many times there is no winner although there are considerable strategies, choices, and interference. Simulation games may be designed for children or adults and usually are comprised of role playing, decision making, and necessary trade-offs. We may question the use of the word *game* here, for some simulation games end up as cooperative events. An example of a true game in a simulation model is the freeway planning game seen in Figure 27.4. The freeway planning game was designed for high school students by the California State Department of Education and is reproduced here with their encouragement. This activity was used as a get-acquainted event and icebreaker on the

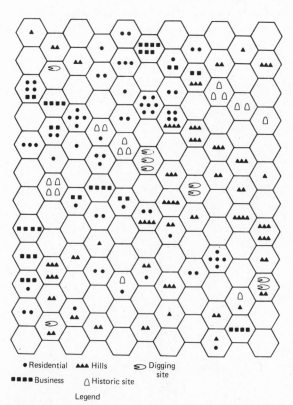

● Residential  ▲▲▲ Hills  ⊃ Digging site
■■■■ Business  ⌂ Historic site

Legend

**FIGURE 27.4**    Simulation game.

opening evening of an adult conservation activity workshop, when it lasted over two hours and resulted in comradeship, points of reference, and illustrations for the remainder of the weekend.

## NEW GAMES

Throughout the world, an interest in New Games has developed as the result of a series of New Games Tournaments, the first of which was held in October 1973 at Gerbode Preserve near San Francisco. The original idea of Stewart Brand, New Games are a concept designed to introduce people to cooperative competition in which the playing is more important than the winning. "Play Hard, Play Fair, Nobody Hurt" soon became the motto of New Games all over the world, and people were reviving and revising old games and inventing new activities, all of which were

---

**Title:** Freeway Planning Game

**Number of Players:** Up to 100, preferably even groups of 6

**Location:** Indoors

**Length:** One hour or more

**Objectives:** To learn about trade-offs in planning.
To understand factors in planning better.

**Materials:** Paper, pencil for each player;
copies of game for each player;
posterboard or blackboard

### Procedure

Divide into groups of six. In each group, participants will assume the roles representing various vested interests—city council, taxpayer, and so on.

Each individual will now plan the freeway that will cost the group he or she represents the least number of penalty points. The freeway must run from the top row of hexagons to the bottom row of hexagons. After all participants have planned their ideal freeway, they should total their penalty points.

The six participants with their assumed interests will now come together as a community and plan the freeway that would be best for the community as a whole. When the community freeway is completed, each participant totals the cost for the group he or she represents. These costs are totaled, and this represents the community cost.

The community with the lowest cost to the total community wins. The penalties to the city council, taxpayers, university, and so on, in the various communities, should also be compared.

Explain scoring very clearly—for example, make sure it is clear that *each space* costs five points, and when houses or hills are on that space, they increase the value of that space. Penalties are in relation to vested interest.

---

**FIGURE 27.4** Simulation game (cont.).

physical and had an emphasis on group fun rather than group winning. Most New Games end up not being true ''games'' as the group competes only against itself, the equipment, or the weather. People pass, planet pass, and the lap sit are three of the most popular New Games (see Figure 27.5).

## INITIATIVE GAMES, ROPES COURSES, AND ADVENTURE ACTIVITIES

Like wide games and New Games, initiative games may be more cooperative than competitive, yet they certainly involve choice and strategy. They do not, however, involve interference by any opponent. The task to be accomplished is interference enough. Many initiative tasks, most ropes course activities,

and most adventure activities require carefully planned and executed high-risk management plans. Two activities that are of medium risk are the all aboard and punctured drum described in Figure 27.6. The most extensive description of these activities is found in *Cowstails and Cobras* by Karl Rohnke of Project Adventure in Massachusetts. These activities are usually conducted outdoors, are physical in nature, and involve decision making to solve problems. The ropes course consists of many configurations of ropes tied to trees, walls, or rocks or a combination of these with sets of climbing, descending, crossing, or swinging stunts. The initiative tasks ask groups to get the team over ropes simulating electric fences without touching them, to move the team

---

**PEOPLE PASS**

Have everyone stand facing the same direction in a double line, as close together as possible. One person at the head of the line leans back and is hoisted up to start a high, overhead, hand-delivered journey on the back over the line, being put down carefully at the end. As soon as one person is passed, another is started, and the activity will be self-perpetuating until the group agrees to pass no more.

**PLANET PASS**

Everyone forms two lines, and all lie down on their backs with heads toward the center of the two lines. Raise hands and pass an earthball down the line (if it slips to the side, tap it with the foot). As soon as the ''planet'' has passed you, get up, run to the end of the line, and lie down again to receive the planet once again. How far can the planet be passed?

**THE LAP GAME**

Everyone available stands in a circle shoulder to shoulder. Turn to the right. Then everyone slowly sit down on the knees of the person behind you. Put your arms out to the side. Hold it for five seconds.

**FIGURE 27.5** Three ''New Games.''

---

**ALL ABOARD**

**Object:** To see how many can get on a platform at once.

**Equipment:** A sturdy stump 3 feet in diameter or a 3-foot by 3-foot square marked on the ground or a 2-foot by 2-foot platform built 18 inches off the ground (any *sturdy* flat surface).

**Rules:** See how many people can get on the platform. Both hands, both feet, and the body must be off the ground. The position must be held for five seconds.

**PUNCTURED DRUM**

**Object:** Use a multipunctured, 55-gallon drum, a one-gallon can or similar container, and a stream or lake. The group must fill the larger drum to overflowing as fast as possible.

**Rules:** Only portions of the participants' anatomy (fingers, toes, noses) may be used to plug the holes.

**FIGURE 27.6** Two initiative tasks.

These children are participating in a game based on group fun, rather than individual or group competition.

across an area that may not be touched by using only pieces of rope and two 14-foot lengths of 4 by 4's or, by using one plank, pole, length of rope, and a stick, retrieve a container placed some distance away across a simulated riverbank.

As mentioned, there are many ways of listing types of games; however, those just described are the types of games generally considered most popular and of greatest current interest.

## TYPES OF CONTESTS

Again, contests are based entirely on individual or group performance with no action that impedes the progress of the opponents. In addition, they follow precise rules concerning the execution of the skill. There are fewer types of contests than types of games although some of the categories are the same. As a matter of fact, many of the events in wide games, New Games, or initiative games may be of a form closer to a contest than a game.

### RELAYS

A true relay is a contest among several teams performing in lines or circles with each indi-

vidual member executing a predesignated action in turn. The winner is the team whose members first complete their assigned functions. There are five basic relay formations: single file, shuttle, square, spoke, and circle. Each form has definite starting, turning, and ending positions as illustrated in Figure 27.7. Relays may involve any form of locomotion or object handling or both, and all can be modified for various ages, abilities, and degrees of skill.

### RACES AND FIELD EVENTS

A simple race, a throwing competition, or a jumping competition fit the description of a contest. Even though certain track events such as long-distance running involve a certain amount of jostling and a carefully planned strategy, some of which actually does impede the opponent's progress, track and field events come under the title of contests. Each person performs a specific skill in an attempt to go faster, higher, or further than other contestants.

### TEAM CONTESTS

A team contest consists of several groups of people working together without contact with the other groups. A bowling team takes turns

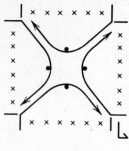

*(a)*

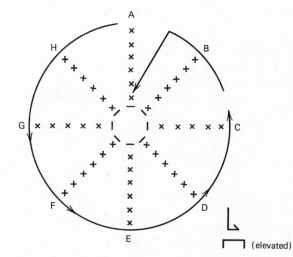

— = Starting line

⌐ = Optional line for file with nonlocomotion

▯ = Turning point for file with locomotion

ᘢ = Leader during explanation

ℒ = Leader during relay

• = Turning point

⤴ = Line of travel

ᘢ = Position of leader

*(c)*

→ = Starting side (when teams cannot
have equal number on each side)

ᘢ = Position of leader

*(b)*

— = Team boundary lines

⤴ = Line of travel of players from team A
(in locomotion — type relay)

ᘢ = Position of leader

*(d)*

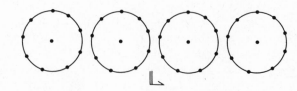

ᘢ = Leader

*(e)*

**FIGURE 27.7** Relay examples.
(a) Single file relay with six teams of six each.
(b) Shuttle relay with four teams of nine each.
(c) Square relay with four teams of six each.
(d) Spoke relay with eight teams of six each.
(e) Circle relay with four teams of ten each.

with each contestant performing individually according to set rules. Another example of a team contest is a puzzle-off, where several teams of four persons each sit at separate tables and compete at assembling identical jigsaw puzzles in the least time. Track and field events are also actually team contests, for individual scores are combined for an aggregate total. In this type of team contest, points are often given for first through fifth place; thus an individual earning one point for a fifth place among many teams may make the difference that creates an overall first place for the team.

### LOW-ORGANIZED CONTESTS

Following the characteristics of low-organized games, low-organized contests involve few rules, simple skills, and little or no cooperation among players. Many low-organized contests involve individual performances in turn; hopscotch, jumping rope, Yo-Yo competitions, and pin the tail on the donkey are just a few examples.

### SELF-TESTING ACTIVITIES

To some extent, self-testing activities are contests. They may be competitive against oneself or against others. Jump-reach, sit-ups, self-timed running, leg lifts and pull-ups are typical self-testing contests.

### MENTAL CONTESTS

Mental puzzles of logic, mathematics, or knowledge solved in less time than an opponent takes are mental contests. They may be listed as self-testing contests, team contests, or just simply contests; but they are mentioned here because all the preceding examples of contests are of a physical nature, yet many contests depend upon mental agility rather than physical ability. Many initiative tasks are successful only because of the innovative solutions worked out from the collective minds of the players.

### GAMES AND CONTESTS TO AVOID

In spite of the availability of hundreds of activities, the prudent leader should be sophisticated enough to scrutinize all activities under consideration to see if they meet the goals of the program. Some activities are not recommended under specific conditions (unusually strenuous events for older persons), and some activities should be modified to fit a theme, season, group, or equipment. Elimination games are those that, as their title suggests, are designed to eliminate players one by one until only one person remains. If the goal of the event is for all people to participate, the elimination activity works to a disadvantage. If the goal is for the unskilled to get much practice, the elimination game defeats the purpose. If, however, the group is already skilled and is competing to identify the best, elimination games are ideal. In these cases, players can be inspired to perform well and may be motivated to enhance their abilities further.

Low-organized elimination games may be modified so that they are played for time, with the game ending as soon as one person has made the "eliminating error" three or four times. Even the old game of musical chairs, which eliminates the one not sitting when the music stops, can be modified. In this activity, there are always fewer chairs than players. Instead of continually taking away chairs with each eliminating round, have those eliminated sit in the chairs, and the remaining players must greet them by name as they pass them. This now becomes a get-acquainted game with the eliminated players serving as a challenge to those left.

Other activities to avoid are relays that cause embarrassment, that are offensive, or that create health problems. For example, passing an orange held between chin and chest to the next player without use of hands or passing a lifesaver from toothpick to toothpick held in the mouth are activities that the leader may want to avoid or modify. A leader who has empathy with the feelings of other individuals can imagine the discomfort caused by shyness when activities involving such close contact are directed. The sensitive leader imagines how people might react and selects activities with great care.

## LEADING GAMES AND CONTESTS

The most successful leaders of games and contests are those who can offer a wide variety of activities—some old, some new, and some modified—so that the participant has a mixture of the security of the familiar, the challenge of the new, and the intrigue of the modified. By classifying the activities to be offered, the leader can determine whether there is variety in the program.

### PROGRAM-ORIENTED LEADERSHIP

In Chapter 6, program-oriented and task- or work-oriented leaders were defined. The program-oriented games and contests leader is the face-to-face director of individuals or teams or both as they participate in each activity. Countless books, pamphlets, brochures, and articles containing descriptions of games and contests are available to the curious leader. As leaders progress, they will collect other activities through participation, conversation, and observation. Unless a concerted effort is made to organize, record, and file activities that the leader has used successfully or would like to use in the future, they will be unused and eventually lost. Besides referring to books with sections devoted to various activities, most games leaders have files of games organized according to type, as well as many cards on which games are recorded. A typical and very useful method of recording games on a four-by-six card is seen in Figure

27.8. The back of the card may contain a diagram of play or formation as well as more directions.

### LEADING ACTIVE GAMES

For low-organized games and games in which players are in a space no larger than one half of a basketball court, leadership techniques are slightly different from those for games in which players are spread out over a large area. In a large area it can be difficult to control interest and gain attention; it is virtually impossible to explain something to a group spread out all over a ball diamond or soccer field. The list of progressive steps on page 417 shows the steps for leading and teaching games in large areas and leading games in smaller areas.

### LEADING TABLE GAMES

When one is leading or teaching table games such as checkers, Monopoly, or others, the best technique is for the leader to sit at the table as a player and demonstrate with a participant as an opponent. Other learners can gather around and look over their shoulders. The leader should introduce the equipment and explain briefly the goal of the activity and simple moves. This should be followed with a demonstration game in which the leader demonstrates the first or opening move and advises the neophyte opponent how to counter. The prepared leader will *set up* situations to the advantage of the opponent so there can be explanations of situations, consequences,

| NAME: | TYPE: |
|---|---|
| No. OF PLAYERS: | SOURCE: |
| FORMATION: | |
| EQUIPMENT: | |
| DIRECTIONS: | |

**FIGURE 27.8**   Format for recording activities on a four-by-six index card.

## STEPS FOR LEADING AND TEACHING GAMES

*Games in Small Area*

1. Examine the activity thoroughly.

2. Get attention.
3. Arouse interest by naming the game or by some other means.
4. Group participants into a formation as close to the game position as possible.
5. Explain and demonstrate (or have someone else demonstrate) the skill.
6. Practice the movement of the skill (throwing, catching, bouncing). Practice *without* equipment if the group is young or unskilled.
7. Practice the skill some more (with equipment).
8. Explain some of the rules.
9. Start play and occasionally add more rules.
10. "Kill it before it dies" (stop before interest wanes).

*Games in Large Area*

1. Same, paying special attention to significant parts.
2. Same.
3. Same.

4. Group participants in a circle or random group close enough to hear the leader.
5. Same.

6. Practice the skills through drills.

7. Explain the positions of the players.

8. Explain some of the rules.
9. Assume positions on the playing field and start play.
10. Add more rules, skills, strategies.

11. "Kill it before it dies" (stop before interest wanes).

strategy, and alternatives. The learners should understand that the leader is showing them *how to play, not trying to win.*

The competitive and inexperienced leader may find it difficult to maneuver into a losing position deliberately; however, it should be done so that attention can be focused on the situations to avoid rather than on the ability of the leader to win. Furthermore, the leader should demonstrate a table game rapidly so that the watchers can see the progression from beginning to end in 10 to 15 minutes (with the neophyte learner being the winner). Any longer demonstration will cause loss of interest. In a second demonstration game, the leader should follow the same practices but ask the watchers for advice. They will probably want to give it anyhow, particularly to their friend, the opponent, with whom they may identify. The leader can ask, "Should I move here?" "What will my opponent do

then?" "What happens if my opponent moves there?" After the second demonstration game, equipment should be given to all who wish to compete. Lead-up games should be used if necessary. Farmer and pig is a lead-up game for checkers, which may, in turn, lead to chess.

## LEADING RELAYS

Although relays appear to be easy to lead, they are actually much more difficult to lead than games because of the need to control actions to eliminate choice and strategy. A list of steps for leading successful relays follows.

*Preliminary Steps*

1. If possible, have an even number of teams.
2. Try to have six to eight players per team. If there are more, consider a shuttle relay so that those waiting in turn will stand idle for a shorter time.

3. Direct at least three consecutive relays. Grouping takes so much time that only one relay is not wise. Also, several successive relays allow the chance of more winners.
4. Maintain the same formation for all the relays. (Going from line to circle and back wastes time.)

*Leading the Relay*

1. Establish specific boundaries: front of line, back of line, and turning points.
2. Prepare equipment with extras on hand in case of breakage.
3. Form teams and place players in position.
4. Give specific directions, including direction of travel, and safety concerns and reiterate the *specifics*. But *be brief*.
5. Explain to participants that, in case of error, the participant recommences from the spot where the error occurred. (*Never* penalize the players by having them return to the beginning.)
6. Explain how to signal the next player. For example, "Go to the end of the line, and pass the ball ahead from person to person until it reaches the front of the line. That person will take the next turn."
7. Demonstrate, or have the first player *on each team* demonstrate.
8. Explain the starting signal.
9. Explain how to signal the leader when you are through, "All sit down at once."
10. Ask for questions.
11. Start the relay.
12. Judge the relay (with help from nonplayers), and recognize the winners. If one or more teams are struggling hopelessly at the very end, ascertain if they want to continue. If not, stop the activity before the bitter end.

## TASK-ORIENTED LEADERSHIP

All games leaders may not be involved on a direct, face-to-face level with participants.

Many are involved in administering events made up of many games or contests or both. Some of these events have been described already in this and other chapters, for example, sports nights, tournaments, wide games, swim meets, water carnivals, New Games, and playground special programs. Other events involving games or contests or both include playdays and the field days. At a playday many teams play each other on a round-robin basis with socialization being more important than competition. The teams may take part in one sport or a number of sports. The field day is much like the playday, but players always rotate among several sports and sometimes even change teams as they rotate.

The duties and functions of the games task-oriented leader planning events made up of many games or contests will vary according to the situation; however, generally, he or she is expected to accomplish the following six tasks.

1. Establish the scope of the event. What are the goals? What types of activities are appropriate? When and how long shall the event take place?
2. Promote the activity through posters, announcements, radio, newspaper, TV, brochures, word of mouth, and so on.
3. Organize the component parts of the event, using participants to share in the planning and implementation.
4. Schedule and examine the facilities, equipment, and supplies.
5. Develop and follow a financial plan (budget).
6. Develop a risk management plan.

Figure 27.9 is a reproduction of a New Games Workshop organized by Professor Effie L. Fairchild of the University of Oregon, using advanced students to help in its planning and organization. Note the goals of the New Games Workshop: "to have fun, to learn to create and adapt New Games, and to participate in a noncompetitive environment." Individuals participating in a New Games

Welcome to the 1983 New Games Workshop. We hope this year's workshop proves to be the best yet!!!

**COURSE OUTLINE**

RPM 408-G, 1 hour credit P/NP only.
Cost: $5.00 facility-supply fee. Proof of payment required at registration. (No refunds.) Registration until 5 P.M., 3-3-83.

**Times:**

Friday, March 4, 2 P.M. to 6 P.M. (Meet in Ger. Sunroom.)
Sat., March 5, 8 A.M. to 2 P.M. (Meet in Ger. Sunroom.)
Sun., March 6, 8 A.M. to 12:30 P.M. (Meet Mac Court.)

**Goals:**

1. To have fun!!
2. To provide games in which everyone can play.
3. To bring people together to learn new games.
4. To be able to apply the new games concept to everyday life.
5. To gain experience in creating new games.
6. To learn how to adapt the new games concept to roller-skating and aquatic settings.
7. To seek out the meaning of true ''fun'' in a positive, noncompetitive environment.

**Requirements:**

1. Attendance and participation at all workshop sessions.
2. Complete an evaluation of the workshop.
3. Write a two-to-three-page (typed) paper on either
   a. The new games you were involved in creating during the workshop.
   b. A new game you have made up yourself incorporating the philosophy of new games (refer to suggested readings).

****Paper due no later than Tuesday, March 8, 5 P.M.
****Turn paper in at RPM office, 180 Esslinger Hall.

**Suggested Readings:** (available at bookstore)

1. *The New Games Book*, edited by Andrew Fluegelman.
2. *More New Games*, edited by Andrew Fluegelman.
3. *Play Fair*, by Matt Weinstein and Joel Goodman.

**Other Readings:**

*Cowstails and Cobras*, by Karl Rohnke. Write: Project Adventure, P.O. Box 157, Hamilton, MA. 01936
*Wide Games*, by Kathleen Houston and Nancy Speakman. Published by Outdoor Adventure Enterprises.
******       ******

**REMEMBER!! NEW GAMES ARE FUN!! THINK SAFETY!!!!**

•• Bring your hat to the workshop everyday!!!
•• Be on time each morning!!!
•• Bring your swimsuit and towel on Sunday!!!
•• Leave your jewelry and sharp objects at home!!!
•• Please do not leave the buildings while the workshop is in session!!!
•• Concessions available!!!

**NEW GAMES DAILY SCHEDULE:**

**Friday:**

| | |
|---|---|
| 2:00–2:45 | Registration |
| 2:45–3:00 | Orientation, Room B-54 |
| 3:00–3:55 | First rotation (game session) |
| 4:00–4:55 | Second rotation (game session) |
| 5:00–5:45 | Third rotation (game session) |
| 5:45–6:00 | Closing, Room B-54 |

**Saturday:**

| | |
|---|---|
| 8:00– 8:20 | Opening, Room B-54 |
| 8:20– 8:30 | Move to game area |
| 8:30– 9:20 | First rotation (game session) |
| 9:20– 9:30 | Move to game area |
| 9:30–10:20 | Second rotation (game session) |
| 10:20–10:30 | Move to game area |
| 10:30–11:20 | Third rotation (game session) |
| 11:20–11:40 | Free time (Please stay in buildings.) |
| 11:40–11:50 | Meet in B-54 |
| 11:50–12:45 | Large group game |
| 12:45– 2:00 | Closing event. Meet in B-54 |

**Sunday:**

| | |
|---|---|
| 7:45 (bright and early) | Group A—Leave Mac Court. |
| 8:30– 9:30 | Roller-skating |
| 9:45----- | Leaving for swimming pool |
| 10:15–11:15 | Swimming games |
| 11:30----- | Return to Mac Court. |

| | |
|---|---|
| 8:00 (bright and early) | Group B—Leave Mac Court. |
| 9:00–10:00 | Swimming games |
| 10:15----- | Leave for skating rink |
| 10:45–11:45 | Roller-skating games |
| 12:00----- | Return to Mac Court. |

**New Games Workshop Staff:**

Kim Winnett* Maureen (Kelly) Howard* Anitra Reaney* Cecilia Holvey* Mark Manfredi* Gerry DuPont* Eileen Welton* Kent Huschke* Jamie Hawley* Mike Watkins* Michael Gray* Wolfgang Savage* Mark

Gardner* Brad Stiltner* Dan Cockburn* Jill O'Connor* Ann Fahland*
Robin Buhler* Sharon Bell* Terry Dobias* Debbie Simpson* Jeff Hagler*
Deval (Dee) Webster* Dave Sargent* Katrina Stacey* Ellen Oare* Alison
Smith* Sandy Berrios* Kurt Krichko* Tricia Kelley* Karen Service*
Doug Creasey* Brad Stevens* Jack Won* Ron Dugdale* Amy Harrison*
Tennise Choruby* Cheri Snell* Julie Johnson* Dennis Clay* Hyung
Won* Mardy Clark*
***Workshop Director: Dr. Effie Fairchild***

**FIGURE 27.9** New games workshop.

Workshop progress from one area to another, at each of which they learn and participate in another New Game or learn strategies for creating and adapting New Games. Since New Games are "games in which everyone can play," they can be used by the leader for all participants, including those who may lack talent in more competitive and structured games.

Actual step-by-step plans for games events will vary with the type of event. However, the following is a list of recommended progressive steps for organizing wide games. A modification of these steps may be implemented for playdays, field days, New Games Workshops and initiative tasks.

1. Set the goals and purpose. For example, to get acquainted, to review new knowledge, to use previously learned skills, to test skills, to practice skills, to try new activities, to socialize, and so on.
2. Plan the organization of the group into smaller units. You want teams of from 4 to 10 members. Do you want to place children among adults and skilled among unskilled to equalize the events? If it is noncompetitive, perhaps children would prefer to be with their peers, or maybe they would enjoy being part of a grown-up team.
3. Examine the area for use, establish boundaries, consider safety, and eliminate or control hazards.
4. Schedule the events. The total time allotted divided by the number of activities yields the number of minutes per event. Or the total time allotted divided by the number of minutes you wish to spend at each activity yields the number of events to plan. Also to be scheduled are the opening and closing remarks, the time it takes to rotate from each event to the next, plus any time it may take to organize people into teams.

Consider the face that from 8 to 10 minutes is ample for each event in many wide games. There should never be more teams than activities, and having more activities than teams is questionable, for some participants will register disappointment at not having been able to participate in some events other people did unless, of course, the leader makes sure there are as many *turns* as there are events.

5. Plan the stations or activities, the equipment, the supervision.
6. Plan how the groups will start, move to the next activity in sequence, report and record scores, and end the wide games.
7. Plan how each event will be scored.
8. Decide how to arrange teams and place participants on them. If the group is very large, break it into two parts, each of which has teams; then double each of the stations. For example, for a group of 300, rather than have 10 teams of 30, make two groups of 150, each of which has 10 teams of 15, and then have 10 events but 2 stations for each event. More people will have longer turns and more success in the activity. Examples of wide game schedules can be found in Figure 27.10.

| TOTAL TIME AVAILABLE | | | |
|---|---|---|---|
| Event | 120 Min. | 120 Min. | 75 Min. |
| Opening | 15 Min. | 15 Min. | 3 Min. |
| Activity | 10 Min. | 20 Min. | 12 Min. |
|   Move to next | 3 Min. | 3 Min. | 1 Min. |
| Activity | 10 Min. | 20 Min. | 12 Min. |
|   Move to next | 3 Min. | 3 Min. | 1 Min. |
| Activity | 10 Min. | 20 Min. | 12 Min. |
|   Move to next | 3 Min. | 3 Min. | 1 Min. |
| Activity | 10 Min. | 20 Min. | 12 Min. |
|   Move to next | 3 Min. | 3 Min. | 1 Min. |
| Activity | 10 Min. | 20 Min. | 12 Min. |
|   Move to next | 3 Min. | 3 Min. | 1 Min. |
| Activity | 10 Min. | 20 Min. | 12 Min. |
|   Move to next | 3 Min. | 3 Min. | 1 Min. |
| Activity | 10 Min. | 20 Min. | 12 Min. |
|   Move to next | 3 Min. | 3 Min. | 1 Min. |
| Closing Ceremony | 15 Min. | 15 Min. | 20 Min. |
| Time elapsed | 121 Min. | 122 Min. | 75 Min. |

**FIGURE 27.10**   Three examples of wide game schedules.

## SUMMARY

In this chapter, the authors have discussed different types of games and contests, as well as leadership techniques associated with these types of activities. A game can be thought of as involving strategy, choice, and interference that impedes the progress of an opponent. Some of the more popular categories of games include low-organized games, lead-up games, team games, table games, mental games, wide games, simulation games, New Games, initiative games, ropes courses, and adventure activities. A contest exists when the performance of an individual or group is not interfered with by an opponent. Some types of contests include relays, races and field events, team contests, low-organized contests, and mental contests. Leadership responsibilities associated with leading games and contests vary from direct, face-to-face interaction with participants to the organization and administration of events made up of many games and contests.

## DISCUSSION QUESTIONS

1. Differentiate between games and contests.
2. The authors discuss nine types of games. Describe five of these.
3. Why are track and field events classified as contests rather than games?
4. What types of games and contests should a leader avoid?
5. How does leading a game in a small space differ from leading a game in a large space?
6. Why is it often difficult for the inexperienced or competitive leader to teach table games?
7. Why are there so many specific steps in leading relays successfully?

8. How may an inexperienced or careless leader change a relay into a game through faulty leadership techniques?

9. In what situations may a leader of games and contests be a program-oriented leader and when might he or she be a task-oriented leader?

10. How may the progressive steps for organizing wide games be modified for a field day?

# 28

# TOURNAMENT ORGANIZATION

Most athletic events involve tournament competition.

Tournaments are merely methods of organizing competitive activities. They can be used for most competitive activities for which several teams or players wish to determine a champion. There are many types of tournaments because there are many reasons for competition, many types of competitive activities, and many types of competitors.

There are fundamentally three categories into which tournaments can be divided: self-perpetuating, round robin, and elimination. There are also some miscellaneous types of tournaments that do not seem to fit any category. Each type of tournament is used for a specific purpose, and each type has its own advantages and disadvantages. Some of the activities that lend themselves to simple tournament organization are softball, bowling, volleyball, basketball, horseshoes, tennis, badminton, checkers, tetherball, marbles, table tennis, and table games for two players or two teams.

## SELF-PERPETUATING TOURNAMENTS

The self-perpetuating or challenge tournament is organized for informal competition. It is a tournament in which participants can compete at different hours throughout the day and which has an undesignated number of games that could, if desired, last from one day to an entire season or longer with little or no supervision. Self-perpetuating or challenge tournaments are less formal and less structured than other types of tournaments. They are often used for young or inexperienced contestants because they give this type of participant more opportunity for practice. They are also used to pick top players for more highly organized tournaments.

## THE LADDER TOURNAMENT

The simplest self-perpetuating tournament is the ladder tournament. For this tournament, players' names are arranged in a vertical column, and any player may challenge either of the two players directly above, as depicted in Figure 28.1. The player challenged must agree to play. In the event of refusal, the name of the person who refuses to accept is moved down to the challenger's position, and the challenger's name is moved up. Usually, a challenged player accepts the challenge, and the two play the number of games designated by the tournament rules, that is, one, three, or five. The winner of the one game or of two out of three or of three out of five has his or her name moved to the higher position of the two names or retains it in that position if it was there before the game. The object of the tournament is to move to the top "rung" of the ladder.

In order to designate which order the names should be placed on the ladder before the first challenge, one of three methods may be used. The leader may arbitrarily place the names on the various rungs, participants' names may be drawn at random, or the participants may be scheduled in the order in which they sign up for the tournament. Probably placement at random is the most acceptable method.

The leader may want to construct a tournament board in order to offer contestants a visual display of their standings. This can be done by using a piece of plywood with a pair of L hooks on which to hang each name tag. A name tag may be made by drilling a hole in each end of a tongue depressor and printing the name of the contestant on it. As standings change, these name tags can easily be moved to reflect the new ranking.

Advantages of the ladder tournament lie in the fact that it is unsupervised and, once organized, it can continue indefinitely. It is best to set a time limit, however, for interest will usually wane after about two weeks. This tournament helps to determine the better players, who may then be selected as participants in a more highly structured tournament. This tournament offers a continual chance for any competitor to practice. Because it never eliminates a player, there is always hope for success. It is also easy to see which players are at the "top," offering opportunities for recognition. In the event that there are large numbers of players with a wide range of skills, it is easy to construct parallel ladders and permit play-

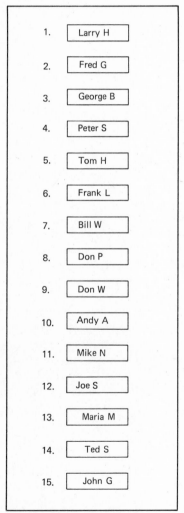

| | |
|---|---|
| 1. | Larry H |
| 2. | Fred G |
| 3. | George B |
| 4. | Peter S |
| 5. | Tom H |
| 6. | Frank L |
| 7. | Bill W |
| 8. | Don P |
| 9. | Don W |
| 10. | Andy A |
| 11. | Mike N |
| 12. | Joe S |
| 13. | Maria M |
| 14. | Ted S |
| 15. | John G |

**FIGURE 28.1**  Ladder tournament.

ers on the top rung of one to challenge one of those on the bottom two rungs of the next ladder to the right with the order of skill level of the ladders ascending from left to right. This type of tournament is excellent for young competitors because it has the elements of choice, hope, and self-involvement.

In spite of its advantages, the ladder tournament has several limitations. First, poor players who remain constantly at the bottom are singled out and may be discouraged. Since this tournament is often used with beginning competitors, identification of the poorest player or players is not always conducive to a desire to compete further. And second, it should be limited to fewer than 25 players, preferably to no more than 12 or 15. It can, however, be divided into several parallel ladders.

## THE PYRAMID TOURNAMENT

The pyramid tournament is like the ladder tournament in that players on a lower level challenge those on a higher one. This tournament, however, has the names arranged in pyramid form. See Figure 28.2. The minimum number of players for a pyramid tournament should probably be 15, for this provides at least five rows to climb.

In the setting up of this type of tournament, the number of rows used will be governed by the number of participants. Figure 28.2 is set up for 15 contestants; however, the addition of one more row would accommodate 21 contestants, the addition of two rows would raise it to 28, and so on.

In operation, the pyramid tournament employs the standard ladder tournament procedure; that is, those on one row challenge those in the row above and, if successful in the challenge, take the place of the contestant challenged in the row above. For example, if a contestant in row 2 were to challenge a contestant in row 3 and emerge victorious, he or she would move to the spot in row 3 where the challenged contestant was. The defeated contestant from row 3 would then move down to the spot on row 2 that was occupied by the challenger.

This tournament, like the standard ladder tournament, may be used as a basis for selecting teams by using the top three or six players to form a team. It is best used for individual competition, but may be used for competition of teams. The pyramid tournament has the advantage over the ladder tournament of being able to accommodate more players efficiently on one chart. A pyramid of 28 is not too unwieldly; furthermore, 2 pyramids of 14 each is a better tournament than 2 ladders of 14 each. At the lower levels, the participant has a much greater choice of persons to challenge. Like the ladder tournament, the pyramid offers a continuous opportunity for practice. Unlike the ladder tournament, the pyramid does not single out one loser. All persons on the bottom row are equals. Psychologically, for younger players, there is a security and feeling of belonging engendered by being a member of a group of equals.

Probably the greatest disadvantage of the pyramid tournament is the fact that its use in selecting top players for further competition or for awarding prizes is limited. Because there are two players on the second tier, there can be no designation of a second-place and a third-place winner.

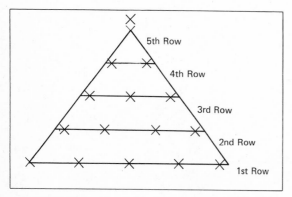

**FIGURE 28.2** Pyramid tournament.

***Variations of the Pyramid Tournament.***
Several variations of the pyramid tournament can be used either to accommodate larger groups or to initiate an element of elimination.

*Funnel Tournament.* The most simple variation of the pyramid tournament is the funnel, which consists of a pyramid with a short ladder projecting from the apex. This enables the top contestants to be ranked hierarchically, in terms of first place, second place, third place, and so on.

*King's Pyramid Tournament.* The king's pyramid tournament is designed to be used with large groups. Depicted in Figure 28.3, the king's pyramid tournament may be set up by placing participants at random on the pyramids or by placing the best players on the top pyramids. It is best, however, if each pyramid is limited to 10 players. Figure 28.3 shows 6 pyramids of 10 contestants per pyramid for a total of 60 players. Each player may challenge someone directly above in the same pyramid until reaching the next-to-the-top row. Here either the top man on that pyramid or 1 of the 4 bottom players on the next pyramid over may be challenged. Of course the top player of the lower pyramids also challenges horizontally. The object of this tournament is to become top person—"king"—and remain there.

*Chinese Ladder Tournament.* The Chinese ladder tournament is devised to accommodate decreasing numbers of players of superior ability, thus leading to a central position, which is that of the champion. Depicted in Figure 28.4, this tournament, sometimes called "the spider web," is generally used on playgrounds where a large number of participants are involved. It is best constructed by using round tags for name tags and hanging them on single hooks. Generally, each internal pyramid is marked with different colored lines, with the center three concentric circles being gold as in an archery target's bull's-eye.

In the spider web or Chinese ladder tournament shown in Figure 28.4, each pyramid has 13 players, and the 8 pyramids join to 4 positions, which, in turn, join to 2 and then to 1. Players may challenge anyone in the row above them in their own pyramid, and they may challenge any player in the same row in an adjacent pyramid.

*The Skyscraper Tournament.* Though the skyscraper tournament is a self-perpetuation challenge tournament set up as a pyramid, it is also a type of elimination tournament. This type of tournament is an excellent tournament for practice as well as for determining high levels of skill. It is best used in situations in which there are not too many players, and it is desirable to spread the playing time over a considerable period. As depicted in Figure

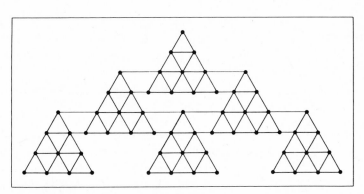

**FIGURE 28.3**  King's pyramid (for large groups).

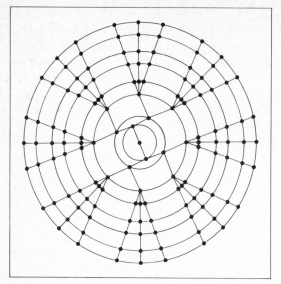

**FIGURE 28.4** Chinese ladder tournament (a variation of the king's tournament).

28.5, from 10 to 15 players make an ideal size group for this type of tournament. It has only as many contestants as there are spaces in the lower row.

The leader using this type of tournament enters each player's name on the lower row of squares, one player to each square. No names are entered on the upper rows until games have been played and winners determined. For a player to advance, he or she may challenge anyone else on the same level. The winner moves up to the next level. Players may

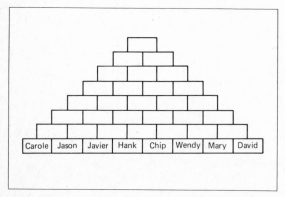

**FIGURE 28.5** Skyscraper tournament.

challenge only those on the same level as themselves. Players are eliminated when they become the last one left on a level. As there is one less square on each level, one player is eliminated on each level.

The number of levels for this tournament will be determined by the number of participants. There will be the same number of levels as there are players. This is an excellent tournament to use when introducing young players to the psychology of elimination tournaments. A player is not eliminated until there is no one left on that level.

## ROUND-ROBIN TOURNAMENTS

Where time and facilities permit, the round-robin tournament is preferable to all other types of tournaments because it operates on the principle of every entry playing every other entry an equal number of times, the winner being the entry with the highest percentage of matches won. In a single round-robin tournament, a single cycle is held, with every entry meeting every other entry once; in a double round-robin tournament, every entry meets every other entry twice; and so on. The round-robin tournament can be an ideal framework for an entire season of play because, with a large number of entries, a single cycle may last an entire season. With a smaller number of entries, a series of cycles may be scheduled to extend over the period desired.

When a round-robin schedule is drawn up, *numbers* should be used instead of names to indicate the various entries because (1) they offer the only quick and sure means of checking a schedule to see that no entry has been omitted and that each entry is slated to play the same number of games, (2) they show at a glance the pattern of the schedule, and (3) they are less cumbersome to work with than names are.

Numbers may be drawn at random for the entries or may be assigned to them. It makes little difference which method is used because all entries play all other entries. However, in the event that there is dissatisfaction on the part of entries over the order in which they may be paired with certain other entries, it might be wise to have participants draw lots for their numbers. Pairings may be indicated by the abbreviation *vs.*, by the symbol *x*, or by a hyphen.

Round-robin schedules should be arranged with the following points in mind.

1. No two entries should meet more than once in any single cycle.
2. No entry should be scheduled to play at more frequent intervals than any other.
3. Whenever possible and practicable, entries should be scheduled to play an equal number of times on the same day of the week and at the same hour (if the schedule is so arranged that each round of play is divided among different days of the week or among different hours of the day) to preclude any entry's blaming defeat on having been assigned all the "bad" days or hours.
4. Whenever more than one playing area is to be used for tournament play, all entries should be scheduled to play, as nearly as possible, the same number of times on each area.

There are some disadvantages to round-robin tournaments. More than one team may complete the tournament with a record of the same number of wins and losses. In such cases, extra matches must be scheduled, or the ties must be allowed to stand. Whether or not extra matches are played, the round-robin tournament is time-consuming. Problems may also arise in round-robin tournaments when teams are often absent or drop out. In the former case, matches may have to be rescheduled, or the "no-shows" may have to forfeit. In the case of one dropout, one team of opponents will find themselves idle each round of the tournament. In case of two dropouts, there will be two idle teams, but they cannot play each other as part of the tourna-

ment because the schedule must be followed. The absences and dropouts cause enough problems so that round-robin tournaments should not be planned unless the director knows enthusiasm and participation will continue throughout the season. Team games are more adaptable to round-robin tournaments than individual-dual games because teams carry substitutes who may play for absent or injured members and only rarely is a game forfeited because of absences.

### SCHEDULING THE ROUND-ROBIN TOURNAMENT

The number of games needed to complete a tournament may be calculated by the formula: $N(N-1) \div 2$, where $N$ equals the number of teams competing. Hence, with 8 teams competing, it would require 28 games to complete a round-robin tournament, as $8(8-1) = 56 \div 2 = 28$. It can be seen that a round-robin tournament of more than 8 teams would mean an extremely large number of games. Ten teams would require 45 games, 12 teams would require 66 games, and 15 teams would require 105 games! Usually, when there are more than 8 teams, the participants are divided into leagues, each of which would play a round-robin tournament. Thus, if there were 15 entrants, 3 leagues of 5 teams each could be formed. Each league would, by the preceding formula, take 10 games. The 3 winning teams could then play a round-robin tournament that would require 3 games. This would make a total of 33 games instead of 105.

When teams are to be scheduled for a round-robin tournament, the pairing must be done carefully to ensure each team's participation at regular intervals and to prevent any two teams from meeting more than once. A popular system for pairing eight teams is shown in Figure 28.6. Team 1 is held in a constant position whereas the other teams move clockwise until each team plays each of the other teams. This rotation continues until one more move would bring each team back

| Round 1 | Round 2 | Round 3 | Round 4 | Round 5 | Round 6 | Round 7 |
|---------|---------|---------|---------|---------|---------|---------|
| 1 vs. 2 | 1 vs. 8 | 1 vs. 7 | 1 vs. 6 | 1 vs. 5 | 1 vs. 4 | 1 vs. 3 |
| 8 vs. 3 | 7 vs. 2 | 6 vs. 8 | 5 vs. 7 | 4 vs. 6 | 3 vs. 5 | 2 vs. 4 |
| 7 vs. 4 | 6 vs. 3 | 5 vs. 2 | 4 vs. 8 | 3 vs. 7 | 2 vs. 6 | 8 vs. 5 |
| 6 vs. 5 | 5 vs. 4 | 4 vs. 3 | 3 vs. 2 | 2 vs. 8 | 8 vs. 7 | 7 vs. 6 |

*Note.* When there is an *even* number of teams, there will be one less number of rounds than the number of teams.

**FIGURE 28.6**   Round-robin schedule for eight teams (28 games).

to its original position. This system may be used for scheduling an *even* number of teams.

For an uneven number of teams, it is necessary to schedule one team with a bye each round. *Bye* is a term used to designate that no match is scheduled. In this case, hold the bye constant, and rotate the positions of all the teams. Each team will eventually receive one bye. See Figure 28.7. The beginning tournament director should practice scheduling tournaments with three, four, five, six, seven, and eight teams, so that this operation becomes simple to execute.

The round-robin schedule for five teams, depicted in Figure 28.7, only covers the pairing of the contestants. To complete the schedule, the leader should either assign numbers to the contestants or replace the numbers with the names of the players or teams. If two rounds of the schedule are to be played, the contestant listed in the first or lefthand column may be designated as the "home" team. If only one round is to be played, then the "home" and "away" parts of scheduling

must be worked out so that each team has, as nearly as possible, the same number of games at home as away. Where there is an uneven number of teams, each will have the same number of games at home as away, but where there is an even number of contestants, half will have one more game at home than away, and half will have one more game away than at home.

**TEAM ROUND-ROBIN TOURNAMENTS**

There are occasions when two teams of several players each wish to compete in a round-robin tournament *between the members of the two teams.* For example, four, five, or six players might make up a tennis, handball, bowling, horseshoes, or shuffleboard team, which might wish to compete against another similar team. In a team round-robin tournament, each player competes against every player of the opposing team. In each of the schedules in Figure 28.8, the numbers represent members from one team whereas the letters represent the members of the second team. There are as many rounds as there are players on one team and as many games as the square of the number of players on one team. In designating the winners, one calculates the total wins and losses of all members of each team. The team with the greatest number of wins among individual players is the winner.

| Round 1 | Round 2 | Round 3 | Round 4 | Round 5 |
|---------|---------|---------|---------|---------|
| Bye - 1 | Bye - 5 | Bye - 4 | Bye - 3 | Bye - 2 |
| 5 vs. 2 | 4 vs. 1 | 3 vs. 5 | 2 vs. 4 | 1 vs. 3 |
| 4 vs. 3 | 3 vs. 2 | 2 vs. 1 | 1 vs. 5 | 5 vs. 4 |

*Note.* When there is an *odd* number of teams, there will be the same number of rounds as the number of teams.

**FIGURE 28.7**   Round-robin schedule for five teams (10 games).

**ELIMINATION TOURNAMENTS**

Elimination tournaments are, as the name suggests, designed to eliminate players who have lost games until there is only one player

## FOUR PERSONS PER TEAM

| Round 1 | Round 2 | Round 3 | Round 4 |
|---------|---------|---------|---------|
| 1–A | 1–B | 1–C | 1–D |
| 2–B | 2–C | 2–D | 2–A |
| 3–C | 3–D | 3–A | 3–B |
| 4–E | 4–A | 4–B | 4–C |

(4 rounds, 16 games)

## FIVE PERSONS PER TEAM

| Round 1 | Round 2 | Round 3 | Round 4 | Round 5 |
|---------|---------|---------|---------|---------|
| 1–A | 1–B | 1–C | 1–D | 1–E |
| 2–B | 2–C | 2–D | 2–E | 2–A |
| 3–C | 3–D | 3–E | 3–A | 3–B |
| 4–D | 4–E | 4–A | 4–B | 4–C |
| 5–E | 5–A | 5–B | 5–C | 5–D |

(5 rounds, 25 games)

**FIGURE 28.8**  Team round-robin tournaments for two teams.

remaining. It is obvious that such a tournament is intended for fairly skilled players and the determination of the most skilled. The major advantage of the elimination tournament is the fact that it is designed to give recognition to excellent playing ability and eliminate mediocrity early in the competition. Other advantages include the relative ease in conducting the simple elimination. A disadvantage is that unless the tournament is set up carefully, good players may be eliminated early, thus negating the major purpose of the tournament. There are several forms of elimination tournaments, each of which is designed to have progressively fewer players at each round.

Elimination tournaments are based upon the perfect powers of 2, that is, 4, 8, 16, 32, 64, 128, 256, and so on. Where the number of entries is not equal to the perfect power of 2, a system of byes is used in the first round in order to bring the number of contestants in the second round to a perfect power of 2.

This type of tournament is best used when a schedule must be completed quickly and there is a large number of teams and contestants. In the straight elimination type, the number of games necessary to complete the play-off will be one less than the number of teams or contestants entered. Where consolation rounds are used in conjunction with the straight elimination tournament, the number of games necessary will be approximately twice the number of contestants. The same will hold true for the double elimination tournament. When this type of tournament is set up, as in other types, the date, time, and place of *all* games on the schedule should be depicted on a tournament chart. The names of the contestants can be filled in as the tournament progresses.

***Seeding.***  Is the process whereby certain individuals or teams are conceded to be the most likely to advance to the final rounds of the tournament and are placed in the schedule in such a way that they will not meet in the early rounds and thus eliminate each other. This method ensures more interesting and closer competition in the final rounds of the tournament. For example, if there were 32 teams or individuals in the tournament and 4 were to be seeded, they would be placed in the first, sixteenth, seventeenth, and thirty-second positions of the first round schedule. If 8 were to be seeded out of 32 entrants, then they would be placed in the first, eighth, ninth, sixteenth, seventeenth, twenty-fourth, twenty-fifth, and thirty-second positions. All unseeded teams or contestants would be placed on the schedule either by a "Luck of the Draw" basis or just spotted in arbitrarily. Where byes are necessary in the first round, the seeded contestants, as a general rule, do not play first-round games. Though it is possible to rate all the entrants in a tournament of this type, it can become a very unwieldy process. Eight contestants are the usual number to be seeded regardless of the size of the entry list. See Figure 28.9. Where only 4 contestants are to be seeded, their names are placed on lines 1, 16, 17, 32. If 8 contestants are to be seeded, their names are placed on the lines 1, 8, 9, 16, 17, 24, 25, and 32.

If the contestants perform according to expectations, 4 seeded teams or players should meet in the semifinal round of the tournament. If 8 seeded players or teams are not defeated by an unseeded team, they will meet in the quarterfinal round. Whenever possible, the name of the most likely winner should be placed on line 1, and the next most likely, on line 32; the next two contestants should go on lines 16 and 17. This spread will give the best possibility of the two best contestants meeting in the final round. The illustration (Figure

28.9) and the preceding numbers apply only to a bracket of 32. If a bracket of 64 were being used, the top 4 seeded contestants would be placed on lines 1, 32, 33, and 64, and the next four lines 16, 17, 48, and 49 to obtain the same desired results. When brackets of 128 and 256 are used, it is best to seed 16 and 32 teams respectively. From Figure 28.9 it can be seen how it is possible for all the seeded teams to meet in the third or quarterfinal round in this 32 entry tournament.

*System of Byes.*    When the number of entries in an elimination tournament is not a perfect power of 2, a play is used that reduces the number to a perfect power of 2 for the second round. *It is possible to find the number of byes necessary by subtracting the number of entries from the next highest perfect power of 2.* For example, if there were 43 entries, the next highest perfect power of 2 is 64, so 43 is subtracted from 64, and the remainder of 21 is the number of byes necessary in the first round. These should be equally divided in the top and bottom halves of the schedules, and where seeding is used, the contestants who are seeded should be included among those who draw first round byes.

### SINGLE-ELIMINATION TOURNAMENT

One distinct advantage of the single-elimination tournament is that there are no restrictions on the number of people who can participate. This type of tournament is also the easiest to administer. A single-elimination tournament can be used for almost any event, but it carries a definite advantage with larger numbers. This kind of tournament is relatively easy to set up. A disadvantage of the single-elimination tournament is the fact that a participant who loses one match is immediately eliminated from the tournament. If the loser is in the first round, there are no further chances to compete. The single-elimination tournament is depicted in Figure 28.10.

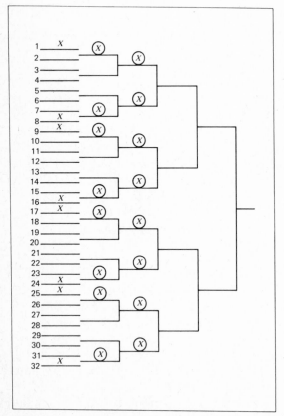

**FIGURE 28.9**   Placing seeded contestants. *Note. X* = a *seeded* contestant; *X = anticipated* position of seeded contestant in second and third rounds.

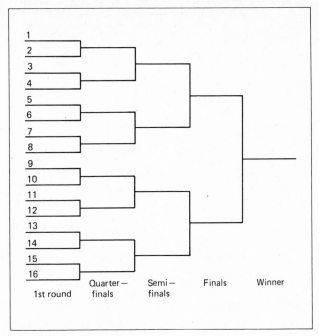

**FIGURE 28.10**   Single elimination tournament.

## STRAIGHT ELIMINATION TOURNAMENT WITH CONSOLATION TOURNAMENT

Figure 28.11 shows how to set up a straight elimination type tournament with a consolation tournament for first-round losers. This is a little better than the straight single-elimination type, for each team plays at least two games before being eliminated.

As in other elimination tournaments, seeding is desirable for the most interest. Further interest may be added by having the winners of the loser's bracket play the winner of the winners' bracket. In Figure 28.11, players A and P progressed to the finals, where P became the winner. B, who was defeated by A in the first round, managed to win all subsequent matches on the consolation side.

## DOUBLE-ELIMINATION TOURNAMENTS

Double-elimination tournaments have become increasingly popular in recent years, particularly in team sports. Double-elimina-tion tournaments are best suited to 4, 8, 16, or 32 teams. In the event that there is an odd number of entries, a team that draws a bye in the first round should not draw another bye after being relegated to the losers' bracket. Teams that have met in the opening round of play should not be paired in the losers' bracket.

Two defeats are necessary to eliminate a player or team. The losers in the first bracket move into the second bracket or losers' bracket. The players or teams that advance the farthest in each bracket meet each other for the championship. Should the winner of the second or losers' bracket defeat the winner of the first or winners' bracket, another game will be necessary because each team or player must be defeated twice for elimination. The champion could be the player or team that was forced to go into the second bracket the first round or thereafter. An eight-team dou-ble-elimination tournament is shown in Fig-ure 28.12. As each team loses its first game, it

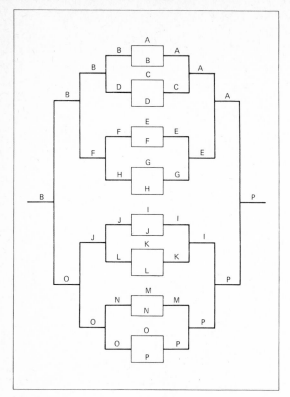

**FIGURE 28.11** Straight elimination tournament with consolation.

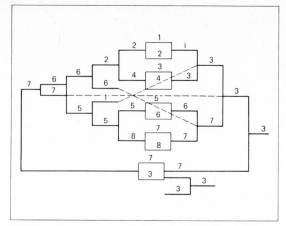

**FIGURE 28.12** Double elimination tournament.

moves into the losers' division for further play. Another loss eliminates it.

### THE SECOND-CHANCE TOURNAMENT

The second-chance elimination tournament gives each defeated team one more opportunity to reenter the play for the championship regardless of the round in which the team was defeated. In other words, until the final rounds, a team must lose two consecutive matches before it is eliminated from the competition. The second-chance tournament thus offers more participation than does the single elimination, but as a result is more time-consuming. The tournament chart for eight teams is shown in Figure 28.13. It should be noted that all teams do not play in every round. Byes are given whenever a team is

awaiting an opponent and thus is not scheduled to play.

## MISCELLANEOUS TOURNAMENTS

There are several tournaments that do not fit into any of the three categories mentioned earlier; however, they are particularly useful in recreational settings such as playgrounds, drop-in hours, summer camps, and playdays.

### BRIDGE TOURNAMENT

The bridge tournament is best used where socialization is an objective of the total program of which this tournament is a part and where the tournament must be concluded in one day or a portion of one day. It is best for activities that are played for points, that is, badminton, volleyball, cribbage, bridge, checkers, and so on. It is an ideal tournament for a playday. It should never be used if the selection of an uncontested winner is a serious object of the play.

All contestants compete simultaneously in a bridge tournament. As a result, the number of teams is based upon the number of playing areas available. The mechanics of the bridge tournament can be seen in Figure 28.14. As-

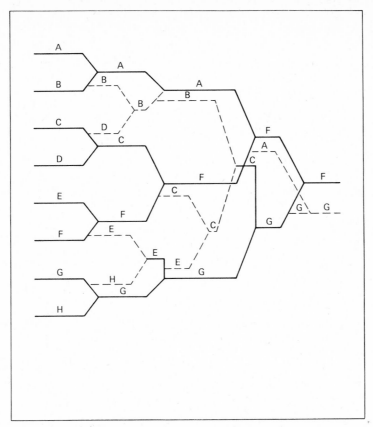

**FIGURE 28.13**   Second-chance tournament.

*Win Loss Results*

A defeated B, defeated B, lost to F, lost to G (eliminated)

B lost to A, defeated D, lost to A, lost to C (eliminated)

C defeated D, lost to F, defeated E, lost to G (3rd place)

D lost to C, lost to B (eliminated)

E lost to F, defeated H, lost to G, lost to C (eliminated)

F defeated E, defeated C, defeated A, defeated G (winner)

G defeated H, defeated E, defeated C, lost to F, defeated A (2nd place)

H lost to G, lost to E (eliminated)

**FIGURE 28.13**   Second chance tournament.

suming that there are 6 courts, 1 hour of playing time, and 12 teams of volleyball players, team 1 would be assigned to play team 2 on court A; teams 3 and 4 would play on court B; and so on. Instead of playing for a given number of points, a bridge tournament is played for time. At the end of a designated period of time, for example 10 minutes, a whistle is blown. The team that is ahead at the time the signal is given is the winner of that round. The winning team moves counterclockwise to the next court; the losers remain in place. At the end of 6 rounds (60 minutes of playing time), play is concluded. At that time the team winning the greatest number of rounds is declared the winner. Or the team that has

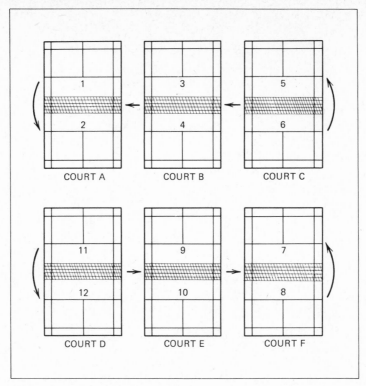

**FIGURE 28.14**   Bridge tournament.

won the greatest number of points may be the winner.

A variation of the procedure is used when teams consist of two players as in tennis doubles or bridge. After the first-round play, the winning team moves to the next court or table. Instead of the winners continuing as partners during the ensuing round, they separate, each one becoming a partner of one of the players still on that court. Winners of round 2 move to the next court and take new partners for the third round. Players thus have new partners during each round. This bridge tournament variation is excellent for socializing purposes and is usually not used for serious competition in recreational settings. The selection of a tournament winner obviously is difficult. This can be accomplished, however, in the following manner. A record of the number of each participant's wins may be re-

corded. This may be done informally by the players themselves. At the end of the playing time, the person with the greatest number of wins is declared the champion. This tournament is popular at social recreation events where whist or bridge are played without serious competition.

**MARKER TOURNAMENT**

A marker tournament is, in one way, a self-perpetuating tournament in that it requires no scheduling or constant supervision. It is a very informal type of tournament and serves as an excellent motivational device for practice. In a marker tournament, the goal is a predesignated score, time, or distance to be reached. When one individual or team achieves this objective, the tournament is terminated. Players may compete as individuals or as teams. When teams compete in activities with individual scores, the scores of all team members are accumulated into a team score. Archery scores, bicycling distance or speed, foul shooting, golf, horseshoes, swimming speed, self-testing skills—all lend themselves to successful marker tournament.

Examples of several types of marker tournaments follow: a group with the highest accumulative score in archery at the end of 16 rounds, shot at 1 round per day, 4 days per week for 4 weeks (a timed marker tournament); a total score of 1000 in bowling—the first bowler to accumulate 1000 points is the winner (this might be scheduled for 1 game per week until the score is reached); swimming an accumulated number of laps of the pool during daily half-hour swims is a distance marker tournament—the first swimmer to accumulate a total of 100 laps during the scheduled hours would win; the first person to shoot 25 consecutive free throws might win another marker tournament; the first person to do 10 consecutive pull-ups might win another. There are innumerable possibilities for marker tournaments.

## RINGER TOURNAMENTS

A variation of the marker tournament is the ringer tournament, which requires that individual or team scores for an activity be recorded one or more times a week over a period of weeks. It can be used for activities such as bowling, archery, golf, riflery, horseshoes, free throws, and so on. One way of determining the winner of a ringer tournament is simply to circle the highest score occurring during the predesignated number of meets. Another way is to circle each person's highest score each week (i.e., if the groups compete three times a week, only the top scores are circled each week) and total them at the end of the predetermined number of weeks. Of course, the person with the highest score would be the winner. This is another tournament that is an excellent motivational device. It is particularly good for beginners playing

two or more games per week, for the poorest games are never included in the final accumulation of points.

## DETOUR TOURNAMENT

One of the best practice tournaments is the detour tournament. It is hard to understand why this is also one of the least used tournaments. This type of tournament exists for the purpose of providing extra practice for the less skillful teams. It is not an elimination type tournament although it is charted in a somewhat similar manner. Each time a team loses a match, it must detour, that is, play a practice game before proceeding to the next round. Since a point is scored against a team for each loss, the winner is the team having accumulated the fewest number of points at the completion of the play. It is particularly useful in a playground situation where a leader is trying to develop a tennis team, for each player has a chance to practice in each round in which he or she is defeated. The detour tournament is suitable only for those numbers of teams that are a multiple of 4 (4, 8, 12, 16, 20, etc.), for the use of byes will destroy the order of play.

The charting of a detour tournament for eight teams is shown in Figure 28.15. The solid lines represent the rounds of the tournament, and the dotted lines represent the intervening practice matches. Losing teams are moved to the right for the practice game, but winners do not compete again until the next round. Teams must be rescheduled for each match because the design of the chart does not move teams automatically into correct positions. In the scheduling of games, teams with no losses are pitted against each other in each successive round until only one undefeated team remains. At that point, the tournament is ended. The round in which this occurs will be followed by the usual practice matches, after which the tournament is concluded. Teams that have suffered defeats may draw or be assigned opponents for each ensuing prac-

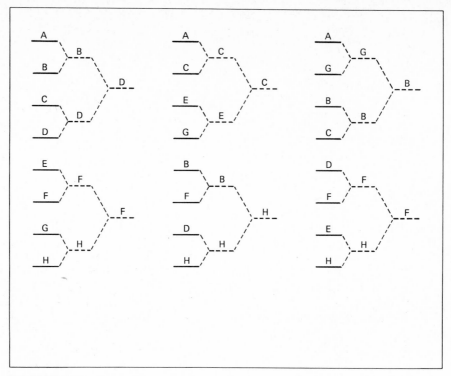

**FIGURE 28.15** Detour tournament.

Score (1 loss = 1 point)

A = 0
B = 4
C = 2
D = 2
E = 1
F = 4
G = 1
H = 4

18 points (18 games)

*Note.* Losers appear above broken lines. Each loss rates 1 point. A, the winner, won each of three games. B lost 4 of 6 games, and so on. The tournament is over because all but one team (A) has been defeated once.

**FIGURE 28.15** Detour tournament.

tice game and round match. The assigning of opponents throughout the tournament has the advantage of preventing the same teams from meeting twice insofar as this is possible.

At the close of round 1, the losers play their practice matches. When these practice games are concluded, the losers' names are moved to the right to facilitate scoring. Round 2 is then scheduled. The winners from round 1, Teams A, C, E, and G, are paired off, and the rest of the teams again either draw or are assigned opponents. Two more practice matches follow for the round 2 losers. The still undefeated teams, A and G, now meet each other in round 3, the final round, and the other teams are paired off as usual. Two losers' detour matches complete the tournament. Since each loss counts one point, team A wins the tourney with no losses and a score of zero. Teams E and G are second with one point each, teams C and D follow with two points each, and teams B, F, and H are last in rank with four points respectively.

## SUMMARY

Knowledge of tournament organization can assist the recreation and leisure service leader in organizing competitive activities. Basically, there are three types of tournaments: self-perpetuating, round robin, and elimination. Self-perpetuating tournaments include ladder tournaments and pyramid tournaments. Round-robin tournaments are used when it is desired that every contestant or entry play every other entry an equal number of times. Elimination tournaments are designed to eliminate competing entries until one winner remains. Miscellaneous tournaments that fall outside these catagories are bridge tournaments, marker tournaments, and ringer tournaments.

## DISCUSSION QUESTIONS

1. What is the main purpose of a tournament?
2. Explain the basic differences between self-perpetuating, round-robin, and elimination tournaments.
3. What are the major advantages and disadvantages of the ladder tournament? Of the pyramid tournament? Of the round-robin tournament?
4. How may pyramid tournaments vary?
5. Schedule a round-robin tournament for six teams. For seven teams.
6. When might one schedule a team round-robin tournament?
7. Why should a leader "seed" players in an elimination tournament?
8. When should a leader utilize a system of "byes"?
9. Differentiate among single-elimination, consolation, double-elimination, and second-chance tournaments.
10. When might a leader utilize bridge, marker, detour, and ringer tournaments?
11. When one is setting up tournaments, which types are usually scheduled for advanced or mature players, and which are generallly utilized for younger or unskilled players?
12. In what situations might a leader recommend that advanced or mature players participate in tournaments usually scheduled for younger or less skilled players?

# INDEX

Ability to work with others, 24
Achievement, 24
Achievement leadership, 38
Acting stage, 359
Active activities, 326
Active listening, 115–117
Activity groups, 258
Activity leader, 380
Adapting activities, 300–302
Addams, J., 23
Adult day care centers, 287
Adults, 210
   guidelines for working with, 211
Advocacy associations, 259
Affective behavior, 195–196
Agon, 160
Alea, 160–161
All Aboard, 414
Amateur Softball Association, 251–252
American Camping Association, 139, 153, 166
American Red Cross, 377, 384
Androgogy, 204–206
Anti-group roles, 65–66
Aquabics, 383
Aquatics, 270–389
   for the disabled, 385
   leadership techniques, 383
   safety, 383
   types of, 384–388
Architectural barriers, 291
Argyris, C., 210
Arlington Heights Park District, 378
Arts, 336
Arousal seeking theory of play, 83
Arts and Crafts, 331–343
   defined, 331
Arts festivals, 340
Assumed similarity between opposites (ASO), 36
Attitudinal barriers, 291
Australian, 364, 409
Authoritarian leadership style, 27
Autocrat, 39–40
Autotelic experience, 83
Avedon, E., 60
Average life expectancy, 282

Baby boom, 203–204
Bailey, G., 352
Barriers, 90
Baseball, 250
Basketball, 250, 253, 409
Bates, B., 351
Benefits, 91
   of participation, 281–282
Benevolent autocrat, 39–40
Berkeley (Calif) Recreation and Parks Department, 348
Berlo, D., 104
Biddle, L., 259
Biddle, W., 259
Blake, Robert, 30, 47
Blanchard, K., 41–42, 47
Boards, 52
Bondi, J., 198
Boxing Day, 307
Boy Scouts, 6, 261, 292
Boys and Girls Clubs, 6
Brainard, C., 337
Brainstorming, 67
Brand, S., 410
Bridge tournament, 434–436
Brightbill, C., 5, 153, 187
Brown, P., 94
Bullock, C., 293
Bureaucrat, 39–40
Buzz group, 67
Byes, 432
By-laws, 263, 266

Coach, 380
Coaching, 236–247
   relationship with parents, 247
Caillois, R., 160
California State Department of Education, 410
Camp fire, 270, 392
Canada, 77, 305, 307, 309
Cannon, E., 109–111
Case study, 68
Carpenter, G., 210
Cervantes, 283
Chapman, R., 305
Charades, 409

Charisma, 8
Check list for guest and family programs, 233
Chili cook-off, 309
Chinese checkers, 409
Chinese ladder tournament, 427–428
Christmas, 307, 322
Chubb, H., 339
Chubb, M., 339
Cinco de Mayo, 307
Circular discussion method, 67
Citizen advisory groups, 52
Civic or community leadership, 14
Civil War, 305
Clinic, 313–314
Clubs, 257, 390–398
  agendas, 396
  benefits, 390–391
  defined, 390
  financing, 396–397
  how to organize, 395
  leadership of, 395
  types of, 391–395
Coercive power, 10
Cognitive behavior, 195
Colby, A., 178, 180–181
Colloquy, 216
Colonial, 305
Committee, 90
Communications, 15, 99–123
  barriers, 121–123
  face-to-face, 117–118
  functions of, 103
  organizational, 100–110
  perception and, 106–112
  process of, 104–106
  styles, 112–115
  techniques of, 117–120
  transactional, 101
  types of, 60, 101–103
Community arts, 340
Community advisory council, 263
Community group conflict, 268
Community groups, 256–269
  decision-making, 267
  objectives, 257
  organizing, 262
  types of, 257–258
Community theaters, 352, 360
  organizational structure, 354, 357
  positions, 358
Comparative analysis, 197
Comparative needs, 75
Competitive groups, 51
Competitive swimming, 384
Compromiser, 39–40
Compton, D., 90

Conference, 197–234
  evaluation of, 233–234
  job descriptions, 217–220
  planning, 217–220
Conflict, 268
Consideration structure, 29
Contests, 407–423
  low organized contests, 413
  mental contests, 413
  races and field events, 412
  relays, 411
  self testing activities, 414
  team contests, 413
Contingency Model of Leadership Effectiveness, 35
Cooperation, 15
Counselor, 132
*Cowstails and Cobras,* 411
Crafts, 432–435
  equipment, 434
  instruction, 435
  materials, 434
  purposes and values, 434
Crandall, R., 82
Created needs, 75
Creative dramatics, 349–352
Crompton, J., 95
Crows and Cranes, 408
Csikszentmihalyi, M., 83, 107
Cub Scouts, 57, 392
Cues, 85–88
  and the physical environment, 85–86
  and the psychological environment, 87–88
  and the social environment, 86–87
Cultural arts, 339
  associations, 258
  celebrations, 307
Cummins, R., 118

Day tour, 401
Decision making, 15, 267
Decisiveness, 24
Democratic leadership style, 27
Demonstrations, 197, 216
Deserter, 39–40
Detour tournament, 437–439
Developer, 39–40
Directed observation, 197
Direct or face-to-face leadership, 13
Directive leadership, 37
Direct program leadership, 126
Disabilities, 289–304
  barriers, 291–292
Disabling conditions, 289, 295–302
  adapting activities, 300–302
  defined, 289
  emotional behavioral, 299–300

hearing, 297
   leadership, 301–303
   mental retardation, 298
   physical, 295–296
   visual impairment, 298
Disability, defined, 289
Discussion, 197
Dominion Day, 307
Don Quixote, 283
Double elimination tournament, 433–434
Dothan, Alabama, 305
Drama, 344–360
   objectives of, 344
   role of the leader, 344
   types of, 345–352
Drill, 197
Drives, 77
   types of, 78–79
Drownproofing, 385
Dumazdier, J., 187

Easter, 307, 309
Edginton, C., 88, 90, 194
Election, 8
Elimination tournament, 430–434
Ellis, M., 83
Emergent leadership, 8
Enabler, 256
Enabling community groups, 259
Environment, care of, 373
Erikson, E., 76–77
Escorted tours, 400
Ethnic celebrations, 307
Eugene Folklore Society, 307
Eugene (Oregon) Parks and Recreation Department,
   290, 292, 307
   integration plan, 292
Eugene (Oregon) Sports Program (ESP), 236, 239–241,
   255
Executive, 39–40
Expectancy, 88
Experiential exercises, 68
Experimentation, 197
Expert power, 11
Expressed needs, 75
Ewert, A., 174

Face-to-face communication, 117–118
Face-to-face leadership, 125–156
   guidelines, 138–139
   types of, 125, 139
Fairchild, E., 418
Farmers and the Pig, 409–410
Felt needs, 75
Ferguson (Missouri) Park and Recreation Department,
   376, 379

Festivals and pageants, 205, 316
   defined, 306
   leading, 309
   organizing, 310–315
   planning, 309–310
   theme, 310
   types of, 307–308
   values, 306
Fiedler, F., 27, 35–37, 47
Field experiences, 197
Field trip, 197
Financial barriers, 291
First comer activities, 325
Flippo, E., 121, 122
Flow, 83
Flower Day, 309
Ford, H., 23
Ford, P., 369
Foster grandparents, 287
Football, 249, 255
Forum, 215
Freeway Planning Game, 412
Funnel tournament, 427

Games, 407–423
   defined, 407
   initiative, 411
   lead up, 408
   low organized, 408
   mental, 409
   new games, 410
   simulation, 410
   table, 409
   team, 408
   wide, 409
Gard, R., 352
Gay nineties, 305
Geographic celebrations, 307
Gerbode Preserve, 410
Gerloff, E., 118
Germany, 204
Girl Scouts, 392
Glenn, J., 23
Goal attainment, 81
Goal-directed activity, 80, 81
Goals, 56
Goals of leisure services, 16–17
Godbey, G., 16
Goldstein, A., 305
Gordon, W., 119
Gray, D., 95–97, 187
Great man theory, 22
Grey Cup, 309
Group(s), 49–72
   communication, 60
   defined, 52

Group(s) (*Continued*)
    types of, 50–52
Group building and maintenance roles, 64–65
Group conflict, 62
Group dynamics, 49–50
Group interview, 215
Group leadership, 59
Group properties, 55
Group roles, 63–66
    anti-group, 65–66
    maintenance, 64–65
    tasks, 63–64
Group size, 61
Group theory of leadership, 25
Group tours, 401
Group work, 197
Gulick, L., 23

Halberg, K., 282, 285
Halloween, 319
Halpin, L., 29
Hanson, C., 90
Hanukkah, 309
Harmin, M., 178, 181–182, 184–187
Harvest Fair and Folk Festival, 307–308
Haun, P., 19
Hawaii, 399
Hayes, G., 194
Hearing loss, 297
Hersey, P., 41–42, 47
Heywood, L., 91–93
Historical celebrations, 307
Hitler, 23
Holiday celebrations, 307
Holmes, R., 121–122
Homans, G., 25
Host-guide, 134–138
Howard, D., 94–96
Howe-Murphy, R., 293
Huddle method, 67
Human needs and the outdoors, 371
Humke, R., 310
Hutchison, P., 290

Ibrahim, H., 82
Icebreakers, 326
Ilinx, 160–161
Inclusive tour charter, 407
Ingalls, J., 205
Initiating structure, 29
Initiative, 24
Institute, 214
Instruction, 50, 93, 131–132, 192–197
    groups, 50
    humanistic approach, 192–193

    leadership, 131–132
    objectives, 197
    strategies, 197
    systems approach, 192–193
Integration, 289–290
Intelligence, 24
Interpersonal communications, 100, 110
Intrinsic motivation, 5

Jay Cees, 392
Jennings, E., 23
Jones, L., 204
Junior Achievement, 392–393

Kanosh, Utah, 110
Kennedy, J.F., 108
King, M.L. Jr., 23, 24, 307
King's Pyramid Tournament, 427
Kirschenbaum, H., 179
Knowles, M., 204, 206
Kookaburra, 364
Krause, R., 160, 350
Kroeger, C., 26
Kusyszyn, I., 82

Laboratory experience, 198
Ladder tournament, 245
Laissez-faire, 27
Lap game, 413
Leader, 6, 12, 19
Leader Behavior Description Questionnaire (LBDQ), 28
Leader participant interaction, 88
Leadership:
    continuum, 32
    defined, 9
    functions and responsibilities, 6
    group theory, 25
    path goal theory, 37
    power, 10–11
    product life cycle, 26
    program oriented, 257
    situational theory, 25, 35
    theory of, 22
    trait theory, 24
    work oriented, 256
Leading songs, 362
Lead-up games, 408
Learning, 191
Learning laboratory, 214
Learn to swim, 384
Least preferred coworker (LPC), 36
Lecture, 198, 215
Lee, J., 23
Legitimate power, 10
Leisure, 3–4

Lesly, P., 153
Levy, J., 82
Lewin, K., 27–28
*Life Be In It*, 99
Lifeguard, 375–376
Lifesaving, 384
Likert's System of Management, 27, 32–33, 47
Lincoln, A., 23
Lincoln's Birthday, 307
Lippitt, R., 27–28
Little League, 258
Long-term care facilities, 288
Lord, J., 290
Low organized contests, 413
Low organized games, 408
Lundberg, D., 400–401
Luthans, F., 78, 108

McCarthy, E., 23
McClelland, D., 78
McDonalds, 103
Mainstreaming-integration, 289–292
Managerial grid, 30–31, 47
Managerial leadership, 13
Manipulative and tactile activity, 198
Marker tournament, 436–437
Martens, R., 236
Maslow, A., 75, 83
Mass communications, 120–121
Master's swimming program, 385
Mather, S., 23
Maturity, 24
Maturity-immaturity continuum, 210–211
Meetings, 213–235
   seating at, 69
   techniques, 215–216
   types of, 213
Memorial Day, 307
Mental games, 409
Mental retardation, 298
Mercer, D., 75
Mereno, J.L., 57
Meyer, A.D., 5
Meyer, H., 153
Mime, 346–347
Mimicry, 160–161
Missionary, 39–40
Mixers, 326
Modeling and imitation, 198
Mondy, R., 121–122
Monopoly, 409
Morrisey, G., 145
Most preferred coworker (MPC), 36
Motivation, 74, 82

Mouton, J., 30, 47
Mueller, P., 248
Muir, J., 23
Murphy, J., 18, 91, 94, 96

National Collegiate Athletic Association, 384
National Council on the Aging, 285
National Peanut Festival, 305
National Recreation and Park Association, 97
National Swimming Pool Institute, 376
Needs, 74–76
Nehalem River Run Festival, 307
Neighborhood associations, 52, 251
Neumayer, M., 187
New games, 350, 410–411, 418–422
New York City, 110
Niepoth, W., 94
Nietzsche, 23
Normative needs, 75
Normative standards, 54
Norms, 56
North America, 258, 270, 305, 367
North Carolina Department of Cultural Resources, 340
Northwest Regional Educational Laboratory, 267
Novelty celebrations, 309

Oakland, California, 243–244
Objectives, 194
Office of Naval Research, 32
Officials, characteristics, 250
Officiating, 248–255
   code of ethics, 249
   duties, 251
   philosophy, 248
Ohio State University leadership studies, 27–29, 47
Oklahoma City, Oklahoma, 251
Oklahoma City (Oklahoma) Parks and Recreation Department, 251
Oktoberfest, 305
Older persons, 281–288
   characteristics of, 284
   living settings, 284–285
   stereotypes, 283–284
Olmstead, F., 23
Olympic Games, 309
Open platform stage, 353
Oregon State University, 397
Organizational communications, 100–110
Outdoor leaders, roles, 368
Outdoor leadership, techniques, 367–374
Outdoor recreation, defined, 367
Outreach worker, 137

Package tour, 400
Palo Alto (Calif.) Recreation Department, 346–347, 350

Panel discussion, 215
Participant motivation, 73
Participant safety, 151–152
Participation benefits, 91–97
Participative leadership, 38
Path-goal theory of leadership, 37
Patton, G., 24
"Peace of the River," 364
Pedagogy, 204
Pelegrino, D., 187
People Pass, 413
Perceived freedom, 4
Perception, 106–112
Perceptual selectivity, 108–109
Peters, T., 139
Physical disabilities, 195–196
Physical need, 372–373
Picasso, P., 283
Planet Pass, 413
Pohndoff, R., 387
Pool manager, 377–378
Position, conducting activities, 142–143
Positive reinforcement, 15
Practice sessions, 241
Primary groups, 53
*Principles and Practices of Outdoor/Environmental Education,* 369
Problem solving, 198
Product life cycle, 26
Professional colleagues, 52
Professional societies and associations, 52
Program instruction, 198
Program oriented groups, 126–129
Program oriented leadership, 257
Proscenium theater, 352–353
Psychological development, stages of, 76
Psychological needs, 371
Psychomotor behavior, 115, 196
PTA's, 341
Public commitment, 54
Public law 94–142, 290
Public relations, 152–154
Publics, 154
Public speaking, 119–120
Punctured drum, 414
Puppetry, 345–346
Puritans, 365
Purpel, D., 177–182, 184, 186–187
Pyramid tournament, 426–428

Queen Victoria's Birthday, 307
Quiet activities, 326

Races and field events, 412
Raths, L., 178, 181
Reading, 198

Reagan, R., 283
Recitation, 198
Recreation, 3–5
*Recreation Integration,* 290
Recreation and leisure service leadership, 5, 13
Recreation swimming, 385
*Recreation Today,* 126
Reddin, W., 27, 38–39, 47
Referent power, 11
Rehabilitation Services Act of 1973, Section 504, 290
Relays, 411, 415
Religious celebrations, 307
Retreat, 214
Reward power, 10
Reznick, J., 248
Ringer tournament, 437
Risk, 15
Risk management, 159–176
    plans, 164–174
River Road Park and Recreation District, 199
Robertson, I., 191
Robert's Rules of Order, 70
Rockefeller, J., 24
Rohnke, K., 411
Role playing, 68, 198
Room set-ups, 231
Rosenfield, L., 102
Round robin tournaments, 428–430
RSVP (Retired Senior Volunteer Program), 287
Rubenstein, A., 283
Ruch, F., 54, 73
Russell, B., 187
Ryon, K., 177–182, 184, 186–187

Sadat, A., 23
Safety, 335
San Francisco, California, 410
Sarasponda, 365
Satisfaction, 90
Scandinavian Festival, 305
Schoenfield, C., 153
Schmidt, W., 27, 33, 47
School advisory council, functions, 206, 261
SCORE (Senior Corps of Retired Executives), 287
Scrounging, 355–356
Seating, tournaments, 431
Secondary groups, 53
Second chance tournaments, 434–435
Self-perpetuating tournaments, 424–428
Seminar, 198, 214
Service clubs, 259
Sessoms, H.D., 5, 12, 23, 153, 202, 212
Shared expectations, 14
Shared participation, 54
Shivers, J., 59
Simon, S., 178, 181–182, 184, 186–187

Singer, R., 240
Single elimination tournament, 432–433
Site visitations, 216
Situational models of leadership, 35
Situational theory of leadership, 25
Skin and scuba diving, 385
Skits, 346
Skyscraper tournaments, 427–428
Small craft programs, 385
Small group communications, 118–119
Small group discussion, 67
Small group techniques, 66
Soccer, 249, 253
Social activities pattern, 319
Social event, 327–328
Social groups, 57
Social recreation, 317–330
    defined, 317
    purposes, 318
    values, 318–319
Social support, 54
Sociometric popularity, 59
Sociometry, 57
Songs, 361–366
    action leading, 363
    beat leading, 363
    level leading, 363
    settings, 362
    teaching, 364–365
Softball, 250–251
Southern Oregon Soccer Referee Association, 249
Sport associations, 258
Sports celebrations, 309
Standard of care, 161
Standards, 19
Star Spangled Banner, 364
State of Victoria, Australia, 97
Status structure, 56
Stereotypes, older persons, 283–284
Stevenson, J., 12, 23
Stone, W., 187
Storytelling, 347–348
Style drift, 39
Style flex, 39
Styles of communication, 112–115
Super Bowl, 309
Supervision, 162
Supervisory leadership, 13
Supportive leadership, 37
Swim instructor, 377, 379
Symposium, 215

Table games, 406
Tannenbaum, R., 27, 33, 47
Tannenbaum and Schmidt Leadership Continuum, 33, 34, 47

Task oriented leadership, 418
Task roles, 63
Team contests, 413
Team leadership, 129–130
Team organization, 240
Team round robin tournaments, 430
Techniques of communication, 117–120
Thanksgiving, 307
Theater-in-the-round, 352–353
*Theory of the Leisure Class*, 203
Thomas, J., 399
3-D Theory of Management Effectiveness, 38
Titzu, 187
Tournaments, 424–439
Tours and travel, 399–407
    defined, 399
    leader roles, 401–406
    types of, 400
Trait theory of leadership, 24
Transactional communication, 101
Transportation barriers, 291
Travel, 399–400
Travel checklist, 406
Tri-dimensional leader effectiveness, 41–42
Trust, 14
Tulsa (OK) Parks and Recreation Department, 252
20-30 Club, 392

Underhill, A., 203
Unescorted package tours, 400
United States, 77, 204, 251, 283, 305, 307, 309, 384
United States Coast Guard, 384
United States Constitution, 290
United States Swimming Incorporated, 384
University of Chicago, 107
University of Michigan, 27, 32, 47

Valentine's Day, 322
Value clarification, 181
Value Clarifying, strategies, 182–183
Value indicators, 183
Values development, 177–189
Values education, 177–180
    direct integrative approach, 180
    direct programmatic approach, 179
    indirect approach, 180
    leadership roles, 179
Veblen, T., 203
Visual impairment, 298
Volunteers, 270–280
    characteristics, 271
    groups, 51
    orientation, 276
    processing, 277
    recognition, 279
    recruitment, 276

Volunteers (*Continued*)
  selection, 276
  supervision, 278
  what they do, 271
  why they volunteer, 271–272

Washington's Birthday, 307
Waterfront director, 377
Watergames, 388
Waterman, R., 139
Water safety, 383–384
Water shows and pageants, 388
Webneck, T., 293
Weiner, A., 29
Welcome Wagon Club, 392
White, R., 27–28
Whol, R., 293
Wide games, 409

Wide games schedule, 422
Wiles, J., 198
Willamalane Park and Recreation District, 249, 252, 322–323
Williams, J., 88, 94
Wofford, J., 118
Work-oriented groups, 126
Work-oriented leadership, 256
Workshop, 213

Y.M.C.A., 6, 10, 318, 341, 384
  Indian Guides, 392
Youth groups, 258
Youth sports, 236
Y.W.C.A., 6

Zimbardo, P., 54, 73